Handbook of Pain and Aging

The Plenum Series in Adult Development and Aging

SERIES EDITOR:
Jack Demick, *Suffolk University, Boston, Massachusetts*

ADULT DEVELOPMENT, THERAPY, AND CULTURE
A Postmodern Synthesis
Gerald Young

THE AMERICAN FATHER
Biocultural and Developmental Aspects
Wade C. Mackey

HANDBOOK OF PAIN AND AGING
Edited by David I. Mostofsky and Jacob Lomranz

PSYCHOLOGICAL TREATMENT OF OLDER ADULTS
An Introductory Text
Edited by Michel Hersen and Vincent B. Van Hasselt

Handbook of Pain and Aging

Edited by

David I. Mostofsky

Boston University
Boston, Massachusetts

and

Jacob Lomranz

Tel Aviv University
Tel Aviv, Israel

Plenum Press • New York and London

Library of Congress Cataloging-in-Publication Data

Handbook of pain and aging / edited by David I. Mostofsky and Jacob Lomranz.
p. cm. -- (The Plenum series in adult development and aging)
Includes bibliographical references and index.
ISBN 0-306-45458-0
1. Pain in old age. I. Mostofsky, David I. II. Lomrants, Yaakov. III. Series.
[DNLM: 1. Pain--in old age. 2. Pain--psychology. 3. Pain--therapy. 4. Aging--physiology. WL 704 H2429 1997]
RB127.H3552 1997
616'.0472'0846--dc21
DNLM/DLC
for Library of Congress 97-16599
CIP

ISBN 0-306-45458-0

A Division of Plenum Publishing Corporation
233 Spring Street, New York, N. Y. 10013

http://www.plenum.com

10 9 8 7 6 5 4 3 2 1

Printed in the United States of America

Contributors

Mark Bradbeer, National Ageing Research Institute and North West Hospital Pain Management Centre, Parkville, Australia 3052

Ralph L. Carasso, Psychopharmacology Laboratory, Department of Psychology, Bar Ilan University, Ramat Gan 02900, Israel, and Department of Neurology, Hillel Yaffe Hospital, Hadera 38100, Israel

Nathan I. Cherny, Department of Medical Oncology, Shaare Zedek Medical Center, Jerusalem, Israel 91031

Nicholas A. Covino, Psychology Division, Beth Israel Hospital, Boston, Massachusetts 02215

Karen Feldt, Ramsey Nursing Home Services, St. Paul, Minnesota 55106

C. Zvi Fuchs, Behavioral Medicine Program, Cambridge Hospital, Department of Psychiatry, School of Medicine, Harvard University, Cambridge, Massachusetts 02139

Lucy Gagliese, Department of Psychology, McGill University, Montreal, Quebec, Canada H3A 1B1

Stephen J. Gibson, National Ageing Research Institute and North West Hospital Pain Management Centre, Parkville, Australia 3052.

Stephen W. Harkins, Department of Gerontology, Medical College of Virginia/ Virginia Commonwealth University, Richmond, Virginia 23298-0228

Marc W. Heft, Claude Denson Pepper Center and Department of Oral and Maxillofacial Surgery, University of Florida, Gainesville, Florida 32610

Robert D. Helme, National Ageing Research Institute and North West Hospital Pain Management Centre, Parkville, Australia 3052

Karen Jacobs, Department of Occupational Therapy, Boston University, Boston, Massachusetts 02215

Merrie Kaas, School of Nursing, University of Minnesota, Minneapolis, Minnesota 55416

Boaz Kahana, Department of Psychology, Cleveland State University, Cleveland, Ohio 44115

Eva Kahana, Department of Sociology, Case Western University, Cleveland, Ohio 44106-7124

Benny Katz, National Ageing Research Institute and North West Hospital Pain Management Centre, Parkville, Australia 3052

Kyle Kercher, Department of Sociology, Case Western University, Cleveland, Ohio 44106-7124

Jacob Lomranz, The Herczeg Institute on Aging, Tel Aviv University, Ramat Aviv, Tel Aviv, 69978 Israel,

Kenneth G. Manton, Duke University, Center for Demographic Studies, Durham, North Carolina 27708-0408

Pamela S. Melding, Department of Psychiatry and Behavioural Science, School of Medicine, University of Auckland, and North Shore Hospital, Waitemata Health, Takapuna, Auckland 10, New Zealand

Ronald Melzack, Department of Psychology, McGill University, Montreal, Quebec, Canada H3A 1B1

Jacob Menczel, Department of Geriatrics, Sarah Herzog Memorial Hospital, Jerusalem, Israel 91351

Barbara E. Millen, School of Public Health, Boston University, Boston, Massachusetts 02118

David I. Mostofsky, Department of Psychology, Boston University, Boston, Massachusetts 02215

Kevan Namazi, Department of Sociology, Case Western University, Cleveland, Ohio 44106-7124

Patricia A. Parmelee, Polish Research Institute, Philadelphia Geriatric Center, Philadelphia, Pennsylvania 19141

Beth Popp, Pain Service, Memorial Sloan Kettering Cancer Center, New York, New York 10021. *Present address*: Director of Palliative Care Service, Department of Oncology, Brooklyn Veterans Affairs, Brooklyn, New York 11205

Charles B. Powers, Psychology Department, University of Massachusetts, Amherst, Massachusetts 01003

Paula A. Quatromoni, School of Public Health, Boston University, Boston, Massachusetts 02118

Jonathan A. Ship, University of Michigan School of Dentistry, Ann Arbor, Michigan 48109-1078

Kurt Stange, Department of Family Medicine, Case Western University, Cleveland, Ohio 44106-7124

Nancy Wells, Department of Nursing Research, Vanderbilt University Medical Center, Nashville, Tennessee 37203

Patricia A. Wisocki, Psychology Department, University of Massachusetts, Amherst, Massachusetts 01003

Shlomo Yehuda, Psychopharmacology Laboratory, Department of Psychology, Bar Ilan University, Ramat Gan 02900, Israel, and Department of Neurology, Hillel Yaffe Hospital, Hadera 38100, Israel

Leonard D. Zaichkowsky, Department of Developmental Studies and Counseling, School of Education, Boston University, Boston, Massachusetts 02215

Preface

From time to time, professional journals and edited volumes devote some of their pages to considerations of pain and aging as they occur among the aged in different cultures and populations. One starts from several reasonable assumptions, among them that aging per se is not a disease process, yet the risk and frequency of disease processes increase with ongoing years. The physical body's functioning and ability to restore all forms of damage and insult slow down, the immune system becomes compromised, and the slow-growing pathologies reach their critical mass in the later years. The psychological body also becomes weaker, with unfulfilled promises and expectations, and with tragedies that visit individuals and families, and the prospect that whatever worlds remain to be conquered will most certainly not be met with success in the rapidly passing days and years that can only culminate in death. Despair and depression coupled with infirmity and sensory and/or motor inefficiency aggravate both the threshold and the tolerance for discomfort and synergistically collaborate to perpetuate a vicious cycle in which the one may mask the other. Although the clinician is armed with the latest advances in medicine and pharmacology, significant improvement continues to elude her or him.

The geriatric specialist, all too familiar with such realities, usually can offer little else than a hortative to "learn to live with it," but the powers and effectiveness of learning itself have declined. Perhaps as a placebo (in its purest purpose of offering help even though such help carries with it no active ingredient for relief), or perhaps in an effort to offer what the state of the art, at its best, is able to provide, a regimen of medications is recommended. The side effects (physical and psychological) of such drug programs—not excluding improper dispensing of too much or too little—are considered part of the inevitable costs in treating older people. Pain is a necessary given; so is aging. But the personal, social, and familial costs to the patient, providers, and the community have been shown to be unacceptable. Personal suffering, health care expenses, and economic loss all begin to reach staggering new heights. With the prospect of an increasing aging population, such conerns can no longer be tolerated or wished away.

The occasional article that draws attention to the relevant issues provides only a fragmented message, so that discipline specialists are usually able to listen only to the voices of their respective teachers, without the benefit of differing perspectives and without access to integrated reviews of research areas appearing in a single source. A major underlying motivation in undertaking the publication of this volume was a desire to rectify this condition. The contributors to this volume are all experts and well-known champions of the positions they represent. The chapters are intended to blend theory with data and experiment with clinical practice. Many fine handbooks and monographs have appeared in the area of aging and others in the area of pain. This attempt to produce a volume that concentrates and focuses on the combined problem areas will doubtless not be the last. The work is not intended to be definitive; it will not provide a complete source of relevant references, nor have all possible leaders in the field been able to participate. But we trust that the concerned audience will benefit from this effort, and that clinicians, theorists, administrators, teachers, and geriatric specialists as well as dolorologists of every persuasion will find this work of use in their professional lives. To them and to the countless aging patients with pain we dedicate this volume.

Contents

Part I. Biobehavioral Issues in Geriatric Pain

Part II. Psychosocial and Psychodynamic Aspects

PART I

Biobehavioral Issues in Geriatric Pain

CHAPTER 1

The Psychology of Pain and Suffering

JACOB LOMRANZ AND DAVID I. MOSTOFSKY

INTRODUCTION

Because pain is at once a universal experience, a response, a stimulus, and a state, it is little wonder that its very existence has been challenged as an unverifiable construct except for the verbal report that validates its presence (Schoenfeld, 1981). Thus, it is claimed, it is perfectly logical to assert that pain does not exist in infrahumans, and that it is at best understood as a private experience rather than as a physical, psychological, or social state. This problem is hardly new, yet the disruptive consequences of pain to the quality of life and often to the very continuance of biological life itself have raised serious concerns for humans and animals since the birth of humankind. While in the main the emphasis has justifiably focused on management and control, the delineation and understanding of the nature of pain as a scientific and phenomenological entity have taken many turns throughout the various stages of inquiry. The more recent discoveries of opiate-binding sites in the brain in 1973, of endorphins in 1975, and the emergence of specialty pain clinics, have contributed to a resurgence of interest by the scientific and medical communities and has inspired much basic research in pain processes, neurobiological substrates, and the development of advanced treatment protocols for the control of pain. Many of these issues are considered in the chapters that follow. Though not popularly identified with biobehavioral and neuroscientific systems, the disciplines that comprise the dynamic and psychoanalytic aspects of human behavior have much to offer pain research in both theoretical development and treatment formulation that too

JACOB LOMRANZ • The Herczeg Institute on Aging, Tel Aviv University, Ramat Aviv, Tel Aviv 69978, Israel.
DAVID I. MOSTOFSKY • Department of Psychology, Boston University, Boston, Massachusetts 02215.

Handbook of Pain and Aging, edited by David I. Mostofsky and Jacob Lomranz. Plenum Press, New York, 1997.

often goes unnoticed. It is with this in mind that we have undertaken to summarize in the current chapter.

The importance of better understanding pain and pain-related phenomena is especially critical for older people, whose advanced age is partly characterized by multidimensional losses and for whom effective and prompt relief of pain is of top priority. The appropriate management of pain requires an understanding not only of the effects of pain itself, including its social, emotional, and psychological results, but also of the psychological determinants and the impact resulting from the style of coping and reactivity of the sufferer and from the medical personnel, as well as the complex character of the interpersonal, social, and cultural environments. The discussion that follows will attempt to complement the conventional writings on the physiological, medical, psychophysical, and experimental aspects of pain and, by adopting a broader perspective, to shed additional light on the more subjective, interpersonal, existential, historical, and cultural perspectives. The overview of the enterprise that is concerned with pain, the elderly, and treatment alternatives can be succinctly (if incompletely) described graphically (Figure 1-1). Ideally, we hope to approach an integration of the biomedical perspective with knowledge that is supplemented by and derived from the individual, including the unique personal and interpersonal characteristics in the context of history and culture. Such an integration can be seen to constitute the basis for psychotherapy as it is related to pain. This is particularly true of many cognitive-behavioral-oriented psychotherapies and, as we shall try to demonstrate, is equally true of dynamic psychotherapy, although it remains an intervention orientation which requires additional refinements and acceptance for effective adjunctive or primary management and treatment of pain. The psychoanalytic and psychodynamic psychotherapies, concerned as they are with the various aspects of intrapsychic dynamics,

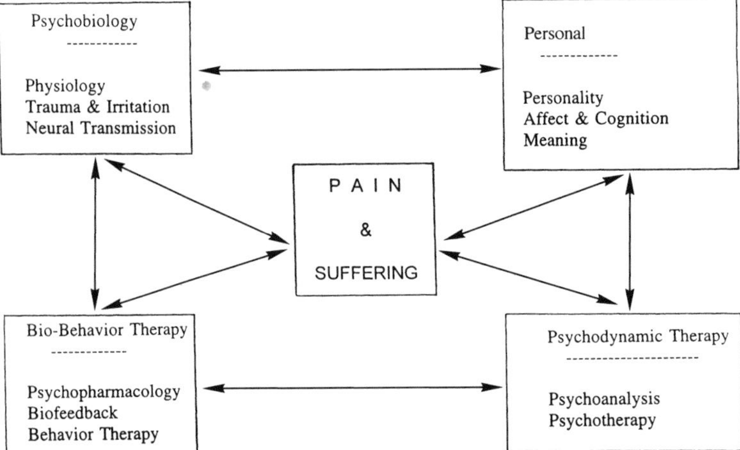

Figure 1-1. A graphic summary of the major theoretical psychological systems and their derived interventions as applied to pain and suffering among the elderly.

affect, meaning, death, and aspects of both the therapist and the client, would appear to be comfortably suited to confronting similar issues as they emerge in chronic pain patients and especially those in the aging population.

THE SEMANTICS OF PAIN AND SUFFERING

The dictionary definition of pain not withstanding ("Suffering, distress of body or mind"—Concise Oxford Dictionary, Clarendon Press, 1956), the investigation of pain has focused mainly on aspects of the body rather than the mind. A more comprehensive appreciation of the intensity and breadth of such distress would urge us to embrace the term *suffering* in that definition. Admittedly, early behaviorists held to a distinction (shared with medicine) between pain and suffering in which pain was to be understood as a sensory impulse communicated within the nervous system, while suffering was formulated as the emotional response to pain. Hence, it could be said of those lobotomized patients who claimed that they could still feel pain but that it no longer "bothered them" that they did not "suffer" (Nemiah, 1962). "Suffering" is harder to express verbally, describe exactly, or pinpoint, then is "pain." In the lexicon of the more technical disciplines, alternative definitions are to be found, such as "Pain is an unpleasant sensory and emotional experience associated with actual or potential tissue damage or described in terms of such damage" (International Association for the Study of Pain—IASP), a definition that does not require the emotional and subjective experience of pain to be connected to actual tissue damage. The professional community regards pain, especially chronic pain and suffering, as an interdependent, inseparable, and multidimensional union of the two elemental human forces that the Greeks called *psyche* ("mind") and *soma* ("body"). The history of the study of pain reflects much evidence of this interdependence (Morris, 1993). Other common definitions include, but are not limited to, formulations such as "Pain is what the patient says it is" (McCaffrey, 1983) or "Pain is a hurt that we feel" (Sternbach, 1968). Modern cognitive-behavioral-experimental theories of pain (e.g., the gate-control theory of Melzack & Wall, 1982; Melzack & Dennis, 1983; Turk, Meichenbaum, and Genest, 1983) have each embraced the behavioral response of verbal report of a sensory quality, while the individual, dynamic, and personality aspects are secondary, even for most psychologists working in the field of dolorology. The suffering dimension has been left mainly to philosophers, historians, and a minority of existential-psychoanalytic-dynamic clinical psychologists, while pain has come under the umbrella of the medical worldview. Too often, physicians attend to the physiological and tissue aspects of pain and do not listen to the "suffering" components (e.g., O'Connor & Goddard, 1994; Kleinman, 1988). To suffer (as defined in the Oxford dictionary) is to "undergo, experience, or be subjected to pain, loss, damage, etc." This definition, while applicable to various types of pains, is the best single descriptor with which to characterize the total and unique experience of the pained individual. Suffering implies a deep and long-seated distress that does not confine its damage to the body alone.

Especially in the elderly population, where there is an interrelatedness of pain and suffering, and where the physical and the psychosocial environments are continuously interacting, the consideration of suffering takes on much importance. The interaction between the older person's loss of physical reserves (e.g., decreased cardiac output, kidney function, and cerebral blood flow) and the attrition older people experience in losing work, family members, and other interpersonal losses—all contribute to a global suffering that may present as psychosomatic illness, pain, and disease (Nowlin & Busse, 1977). If we maintain that we can only *observe* "pain behavior" and cannot actually observe a person's *feeling* of pain, we are required to invoke concepts of personality, emotions, meaning, culture, and psychotherapy; to undertake a delineation of the nature of the suffering; and to permit a rigorous understanding that will generate strategies for treatment and intervention.

There is considerable evidence that prolonged, unresolved emotional distress may ultimately afflict the body, just as chronic pain takes its toll on emotions and psychological well-being. Acute grief does not begin with pain but very quickly produces it. The human sound, utterance, agony, and cry as responses to pain or to suffering are universal. Pain is intrinsic in suffering, as suffering is intrinsically bound up with pain. Neither is fully comprehensible without the other. Pain and suffering emerge at the intersection of body, mind, and culture. Yet, the "myth of two pains" still survives (Krystal, 1981; Morris, 1993), and we seem to continue to promote a dualistic worldview, separating the mind from the body as we persist in discussing physical pain and mental pain as if there are in fact two distinctly different kinds of pain. Despite the accumulating evidence against the myth of two pains, the myth lives on. The rapprochement is to be found less in the technical writings of the scientific literature than in literature and culture and, above all, foremost in the narratives and the important setting of psychotherapy (Kleinman, 1988). It is with our improved familiarity with both pain and suffering as a unitary presenting complaint that we also improve our skills and our programmatic developments for proper treatment and remediation for each individual with his or her unique constellation of history and constitution. The constitutional variable of interest for purposes of the current discussion are largely those of emotion and affect, personality, and sociocultural status.

EMOTIONALITY AND AFFECT

It is of interest to observe that the three components of emotions (i.e., physiological, behavioral, and cognitive) parallel the various models of pain which emphasize the sensory, affective, and evaluative aspects of the pain experience (e.g., Melzack & Dennis, 1983). This of course in a way establishes a congruence between the conceptual domains, but it also directs us to be aware of the confounding nature of pain with other emotions. Affect (including depression, anxiety, hostility, sense of control, and euphoria) influences the personal experience of pain. Guilt, fear, anger, grief, and depression can both reinforce and create pain and a sense of deep suffering. Anxiety, for instance, has been shown to mediate the experience of pain (e.g., Klusman, 1975), and the relationship of anxiety and pain in elderly populations has repeatedly been observed (Oberle, Pau, Wry, & Grace, 1990). Furthermore, while "The experience of pain is not necessarily associated with one particular emotion, such as depression, but may also be accompanied by anxiety, frustration, anger or fear" (Wade, Price, & Hammer, 1990,

p. 304), it has been repeatedly and reliably demonstrated that depression, frustration, and helplessness are able to predict pain behavior (Keefe, Wilkins, & Cook, 1986). In part, this would allow us to confront the realization that the experience of pain exists only as a consequence of our ability to interpret it, a realization that contributes to the notion that pain is a perception rather than a sensation. Beliefs and attitudes will also influence the manner in which pain and suffering are experienced. The Stoics, leading their lives in strict accordance with reason, adopted an uncomplicated strategy for confronting (coping with) pain by regarding it entirely as a phenomenon of the body and, in believing that, by the will, the mind can be victorious over the body. Such convictions allowed them to disregard the bodily aspects of pain. In many ways, biology and science can provide philosophical meaning for pain sufferers, as can faith and religion. These assertions do not by themselves offer us an improved set of guidelines for examining the microstructure of either the pain or the suffering aspects, but they do help us remove any element of surprise when we witness recovery that cannot otherwise be accounted for in the strict and limited context of the physical being.

PERSONALITY AND INTERPERSONAL FACTORS

From a psychodynamic perspective, personality structure and intrapsychic and interpersonal constraints are significant variables that are common to any experience, including that of pain and suffering. Among the more notable assessments that have been examined for their role in pain perception are those of locus of control, sensation seeking, desired and felt control, suggestibility, values and attitudes such as optimism-pessimism, neuroticism, and extroversion-introversion (e.g., Bond & Pearson, 1969). Such variables contribute to the development of "personality styles" and thus may shape the person to adopt a predictable coping profile which, among other things, may lead him or her to be labeled a "pain confronter" or "pain avoider." Specific personality traits have not been inconclusively related to other molar constructs, such as "sensation seekers" or "avoiders," although there appears to be a major research interest in pursuing such objectives (Zuckerman, 1976).

The larger space of social and interpersonal relations is also a partner to the psychobiological and dynamic processes that modulate the perception and consequences of pain and suffering. The well-known British psychiatrist Aubrey Lewis (1967) suggested that being involved in a socially useful occupation may provide a form of inoculation against stress, fears, and pain. To the extent that such an option provides a healthy and effective guard against pain systems, Lewis's assertion bodes ill for the elderly, for whom the world of work may be out of the question. And although Freud claimed that love and work are necessary conditions for happiness, among the elderly—even among those who still have the prospect of a love relationship—there may simply be fewer resources for combating pain and suffering. The hope remains, however, that the availability of love and its associated meaningful relationships, the presence of a "significant other," and an active social support system could all combine to provide a form of inoculation against pain and suffering in old age (Hobfoll, 1988).

THE ROLE OF CULTURE

To acknowledge that pain is "the sum total of past experience and the totality of the present situation in which the individual finds himself" (Vingoe, 1981, p. 130) is to require a comprehensive management approach that will, in its various phases, deal with the psychosocial, historical, and cultural influences which inevitably shape the experience of suffering and pain. Too often neglected is the needed inclusion of historical and cultural considerations as well. The body–mind processes and the derived meaning that they impute to experienced encounters operate within the cultural context which in itself is dynamic and changing. The experiences of pain and suffering are decidedly not immutable or static entities. They are not universal and timeless but are the products of specific periods, social settings, and cultures. The changes arise from many differing sources. Some of the factors that are responsible for change are related to the social agents and forces of gender, social class, religion, and cultural norms and standards, while others can be traced to a much longer history that is rooted in the values and articles of faith of philosophical systems that have become part of a person's life. Just as the Greek Stoics took pride in reason and self-control and thereby found an effective solution to overcoming the effects of suffering and pain, so did medieval Christians transform the meaning of pain into a means of contact with the divine and thereby assigned to pain its own spiritual value. Within Jewish philosophy, the status of pain was, in various formulations, proposed either as a punishment for sin, a test of faith, a possible means of redemption or atonement, and even pure evil. The psychoanalytic theories, based on Freud's *Civilization and Its Discontents*, actually maintained that the price of civilization is such that, to a certain extent, suffering is inevitable. It seems, however, that contemporary Western culture is rapidly losing its understanding of human suffering and has chosen instead to restrict itself to a more clinical and scientific emphasis on pain, as though the present technological age and culture of science advocate avoidance and denial as normative attitudes toward pain. Silence may be one expression of such a form of denial (Morris, 1993). These and similar attitudes are reinforced by reliance on a medical model that promotes an ideal of coping through the use of drugs and surgery and that has exploited the technical efficiency in communication that is provided by the print media, radio, and television.

PAIN AND SUFFERING IN THE OLDER PERSON

The level of suffering and pain in the elderly population has been repeatedly documented and is reviewed in a number of chapters in this volume. Representative summaries of the research and investigations articulate the magnitude of public health concern and the seriousness of the mental health consequences. For instance, an epidemiological analysis of pain among a sample of 3,097 elderly living in rural areas in Iowa revealed that 86% of the those studied reported pain of some type in the year prior to the study and 59% reported multiple pain complaints. That study also concluded that those aged 85 and over were less likely to report pain and that the severity of the pain was constantly increasing (Mobily, Herr, Clark, & Wallace, 1994). Close to 70% of nursing-home residents are assumed to suffer chronic pain (e.g., Sengstaken & King, 1993). The decline in physical function, the intrusion of chronic and acute illnesses, and the resulting suffering and pain conspire to affect the reservoir of the energy level, the will to live, and the quality of life of the elderly person. Epidemiological studies attempting to identify age-related increase in pain have, however, not been consistent, although there is some evidence that older people complain more about pain (Moss, Lawton, & Glicksman, 1991).

Feelings of helplessness, vulnerability, and pain may turn the aging process into a nightmare. Older persons' sense of pride and confidence in their own bodies becomes shaken and may threaten the sense of who they are and an awareness of personal identity (Butler & Lewis, 1986). Physical illness, as well as personal and interpersonal losses, is increasingly prevalent as people age. Pain, its presence, its ravages, and its management may even become a preoccupation of the aged. The elderly are the highest consumers of drugs in the population. For many of the elderly, drugs offer the most consistent source of relief. However, drugs also often produce serious side effects (e.g., dizziness, weakness, nausea, and cognitive disorientation) that can be particularly debilitating and disabling to older people because of the precarious balance of their body economy. Pain and suffering become inseparable and concentrated as part of later life (Moss et al., 1991).

Various chapters in this book focus on the particular brand of pain and suffering that may afflict the elderly, which may include, but are not limited to, the distress of headache, stomach pains, dental pains, joint pains, postoperative pains, pains associated with osteoarthritis and rheumatoid arthritis, pains related to movement and to the wasting of muscles, pain related to angina, and oral or myofascial pains. To these obviously somatic sources of pain must be added those that are depression-related and the sufferings related to grieving and personal loss. Like others, older people deal with the nature and extent of pain according to their lifestyle, personality, interpersonal environment, and cultural background. Older people often fear drugs because of frightening past experiences, and understandably, their preference for maintaining cognitive clarity and strength, combined with a paralyzing fear of losing these abilities, may even be more important than absolute freedom from pain (Butler & Lewis, 1986). Central to an understanding of those who suffer pain in old age is an appreciation of the impact that pain or its cost of removal may have on the aged person's personality. Not infrequently, pain may signify a loss of control and may lead to a loss of autonomy and independence. In the broader context of old age, these considerations of history and loss may contribute to the development of major depression, suicide, and preoccupation with plans for effective euthanasia.

DYNAMIC PSYCHOTHERAPY IN PAIN AND SUFFERING

While the applicability and popularity of behaviorally oriented therapies for pain are well publicized, the traditional camp of dynamic therapies has seemed to maintain a comfortable distance from anything other than frank matters of mental health. This regrettable condition appears to be true in a number of settings in the general areas of behavioral medicine where the potential effective involvement of the dynamic therapies would appear to have much to offer as a treatment modality for numerous non-mental-health disorders. Actually, the use of psychoanalytic and psychodynamic psychotherapy in the treatment of psychosomatic and pain disorders is of long standing and is elaborated in the seminal works of the psychoanalysts, such as Alexander and French (1948). The history of such applications extends to migraine headaches, gastrointestinal disturbances, eczema and other skin disorders, rheumatoid arthritis, and lower back pain.

Psychoanalysis and psychodynamic psychotherapy, including brief dynamic psychotherapy, are being recruited to treat pain in aged patients (Hasenbush, 1977; Bassett, & Pilowsky, 1985). It should also be noted that, in dynamic of psychoanalytic psychotherapy, suffering must be endured by the patient, at least for a time, in contrast to other treatment protocols where the emphasis is on rapid, if not immediate, relief from pain (Strupp, 1978). Because of such constraints, it will not be uncommon for a patient to decline the option of a dynamically oriented treatment program or for psychodynamic therapeutics to be contraindicated for certain pain-suffering clients. For example, anxiety-producing procedures may be harmful with active psychosomatic disorders, and some patients may respond with an exacerbation of their illness (Sifneos, 1974). Yet others will resist or fail to respond to the verbal explorations and to the emphasis on discovering insights which the theoretical principles of such psychodynamic psychotherapy demands. However constraining these considerations may be, they represent only a minor proportion of pain-suffering patients who could otherwise benefit from one of the many variants of nondrug treatments of pain that fall under the psychodynamic psychotherapy label.

Even the option of orthodox psychoanalysis for reliving pain and suffering is beginning to gain acceptance (McDougall, 1991). Indeed, it is a fundamental tenet of psychoanalysis always to recognize the situations in which internal or external circumstances overwhelm the habitual psychological ways of coping and ultimately lead to somatization, psychosomatic illness, and pain and suffering. Psychoanalytic concepts have been applied in the attempt to comprehend the behavior of hospitalized patients (Conran, 1985). It is interesting that the integration of psychoanalysis and psychoanalytic psychotherapy with comprehensive pain management programs is more accepted in Europe (especially France and Germany) than in the United States (Barre, 1983).

The success of such techniques (psychoanalysis) depends in large measure not only on the ability or desire of the patients who elect such a course of therapy to recognize their psychological sufferings; they must also be sufficiently motivated to obtain, confront, and internalize self-knowledge. Although the elderly have been stigmatized unjustifiably as being unable to meet such criteria, psychotherapy with the elderly is now emerging as a constructive choice of treatment (Sadavoy & Leszcz, 1987; Knight, 1993). When properly conducted, the psychotherapy for the pain complaint should provide a means of dealing with the larger issues of "suffering," which do not routinely constitute a primary goal of the medical team (Cassell, 1982). It has been repeatedly confirmed that the intensity of pain experienced by the elderly person is often intertwined with personality structure, accompanying depression, and social relationships, which, for the elderly, are often manifested as social isolation.

Psychodynamic psychotherapy is exquisitely positioned to address the interplay of the emotional and psychological factors that affect the central nervous system and particularly its processing of pain stimuli (Gibson, 1994). The concept of "masking" has been introduced to reflect the suggestion that pain may be a symptom of depression or that it is a serious risk factor that will predictably lead to depression. Similarly, both fear and the tendency to avoid pain have been seen to be determined by the psychosocial context, which itself is influenced by the four factors of "stressful life events, personal pain history, coping strategies and personality characteristics" (Rose, Atkinson, & Slade, 1992, p. 360). Other studies, such as those by Harkins (1988), suggest that personal history, birth cohort (which is especially relevant in the case of elderly), and psychological disposition are all factors which may condition both the experience and the reporting of pain.

From a psychodynamic perspective, pain and suffering serve as indicators that personality change is required in the person. Similar to the mechanism of anxiety, they are signals of threat to the ego (Freud, 1963). Psychoanalytic psychotherapy often traces psychosomatic illness and bodily pains to the preverbal period of infants; since babies cannot yet use words with which to think or to communicate, they necessarily must resort to a somatic response to emotional distress. The theory would also posit that, during this same developmental stage, there is a lack of differentiation or sense of separateness of child from mother, and therein is created an absence of a clear representation of a body image. Such a state of affairs may later be represented unconsciously in the adult patient's mind and may form the basis for the emergence of painful psychosomatic difficulties whenever interpersonal relationships are at stake and bodily boundaries are not adequately demarcated.

Although the distinction between pain threshold and pain tolerance is discussed elsewhere in this volume (Yehuda & Carasso, Chapter 2), other differentiating characteristics are relevant to the present discussion. Both hold importance within psychodynamic thinking, and both are influenced by socialization and interpersonal experience (Krystal, 1987). Dynamic psychotherapy may be expected to induce change in pain tolerance, as well as threshold, and may alter pain behavior. This is a concept whose theoretical origin is to be found in behavioral theory yet is equally crucial for all therapeutic systems to better delineate and address more of the fundamental elements that comprise the patient's pain. The juxtaposition of theoretical constructs in reference to pain (e.g., coping strategies, defense mechanisms, unlearning, "secondary gain," and pain behavior) is commonplace, since all are related and translatable from system to system as the therapeutic program targets the total organism. The separate skills that are demanded by the operationalized constructs will, to be sure, pass hands as the search for expertise requires. Thus, a behavioral observation would conclude that pain behaviors can be understood to set the occasion for obtaining positive reinforcers, while the same observations in a dynamic interpretation would conclude that they function in terms of intrapsychic dynamics and defense mechanisms. The psychodynamic therapist would dwell on intrapsychic defenses and secondary gains or guilt feelings.

With elderly patients, the need to reconcile adult developmental processes is critical (Nemiroff & Colarusso, 1990), as is the impact of reminiscence and the consideration of life review (Butler & Lewis, 1986). The uses of pain for avoidance of internal conflicts has been discussed by others (Coen & Sarno, 1989). An interesting interplay between pain, disease, and defense mechanisms is illustrated in the case in which an adult daughter lost her aged father. When she later developed her own cancer, her preoccupation with its pain represented a defense against guilt and despair. In this way, she saw her cancer as representing a symbolic link to the deceased father, who also died from cancer and whose grief work had been avoided (Hess, 1995). Likewise, "burning-mouth syndrome" has been treated using a psychoanalytic therapeutic framework (Freeman, 1993), and tension and rigid character defenses have been shown to contribute to musculoskeletal pain syndromes (Coen & Sarno, 1989).

A somewhat paradoxical condition, yet a major concern in the psychodynamic tradition, is the treatment of patients who are numb to pain. Weinstein (1968) discussed the issue of symbolic neurology and psychoanalysis where various syndromes of denial are usually described under the rubrics of anognosia. While most of these studies concern hemiparesis and visual deficits, they also include instances of pain after severe burns or operations. Patients may recognize deficits or pain but disclaim personal involvement with them. (Parenthetically, it may be of interest that among the strategic and stylistic variations that are available within "hypnotherapy" for pain are those that attempt to direct the patient's attention away from the locus of the pain or to induce dissociative and reinterpretative states in connection with the offending sensations; (Carasso, Arnon, Yehuda, & Mostofsky, 1988). These patients may deny feeling obviously painful stimuli, even though they may wince and withdraw (pain asymbolia). Neurology may attribute anognosia to a lesion in the parietal-temporal area of the dominant hemisphere which damages the representation of the body image. In a psychoanalytic approach to this problem, Schilder (1951) related the concept of denial to such behaviors and introduced the concept of "organic repression." In a similar fashion, Lifton (1979) dealt with "psychic numbing," which he suggested resembles an interruption of the identification of death-linked images which are known to arise in pain sufferers. Lifton assumed that this response results from an internal dynamic process which gives rise to a symbolic death in order to avoid a permanent physical or psychic death. The extensions and relevance to the world of the ageing do not require detailed elaboration. Perhaps not surprisingly, many elderly patients suffering from psychogenic pain have been shown to be higher in personality traits such as neuroticism and to inhibit aggressiveness (e.g., Valdes, Treserra, Garcia, & de Pablo, 1988). Those among the elderly who are lower in self-esteem tend to report more pain and disability (Hunter, Linn, & Harris, 1982). Psychodynamically oriented psychotherapy is well suited to a focus on issues driven by such traits and allows the therapist an avenue of treatment that is designed to diminish pain intensity by working with patients to obtain a more positive self-image and to increase their sense of control.

INTERPERSONAL DYNAMICS

Freud first based his discussion of pain and suffering on psychological dynamics that portrayed the individual's failure to obtain pleasure and to cling to painful experiences as a form of "repetition compulsion." His theory also maintained that suffering itself can be sensually pleasurable (masochism). In his subsequent writings, he abandoned that position, arguing instead that painful experiences operate "beyond the pleasure principle" and that they have an instinctual character and are derivatives of the death instinct. Most of the object relation theorists, however, rejected the role of instinct and emphasized instead the importance of interpersonal relationships (Greenberg & Mitchell, 1983). The essential striving of the child and the adult, it was claimed, is not for instinctual pleasure but for contact. The other is needed. Even when such contact is harmful (e.g., in the case of a "bad" parent), it is still preferred to an alternative of isolation and noncontact, From this perspective, the treatment of pain and suffering is best designed within the psychodynamic model on the basis of interpersonal functioning and object relationships, as evidenced by the critical role of the spouses of elderly patients with pain and illness (Dar, Beach, Barden, & Cleeland, 1992). It seems valuable to draw from parallel clinical applications with addiction and its resulting pain, where it is now accepted that diagnosis and treatment should represent four distinct dimensions of psychological life: feelings, self-esteem, relationships, and self-care (Khantzian, 1995). In patients with cancer-related pain, the relationship among interpersonal aggression, interpersonal role relationships, sexuality, and elevated pain has been reliably demonstrated (Lance, Vachon, Ghadirian, & Adir, 1994). The applicability of attachment theory (based on the work of J. Bowlby) to the development of and adaptation to chronic pain has also been reported (Mikail, Henderson, & Tasca, 1994). Treatment programs governed by such theoretical guidelines or others, such as self–object and developmental theory (Kohut, 1977) and the object relation approach (Greenberg & Mitchell, 1983), could be formulated with specific reference to the adult and aging populations without sacrifice of any clinical or theoretical rigor (Nemiroff & Colarusso, 1990).

In a classic study entitled "The Pain in Man Wounded in Battle" cited by Beecher (1956), the author ascribes the absence of battlefield pain in wounded soldiers to emotions which have the capacity to block pain. Confirmation of this assertion may be found in studies of postoperative pain, which was shown to be higher among hostile subjects, and of patients suffering from severe headache who realized relief after the removal of psychological inhibitors that block the expression of emotions (Demjen, Bakal, & Dunn, 1990). It has also been repeatedly shown that elderly depressed persons are more likely to have more pain (Parmelee, Katz, & Lawton, 1991) and that depressed affect can be predicted by an increase in pain (Cohen, Mansfield & Marx, 1993). The detrimental impact of negative affect is corroborated by the reciprocal relieving impact of its positive counterpart, as evidenced by the salutary effects of laughter on pain (Adams & McGuire, 1986). The forces of both our culture and our society have too often strengthened an extinction of an otherwise natural and direct affective response which could have offered a valuable coping mechanism for pain. Many elderly unfortunately view pain as a natural part of aging, while many others inhibit the expression or disclosure of experiencing pain. It is here, in working with patients on affect, that psychotherapy may be effective where other programs do not dare to tread. The mandate of the therapeutic plan might well take the form of helping the patient to abandon denial and silence and, rather, to rediscover the natural response of verbally expressing the discomfort of pain in words, cries, or screams. Not infrequently, the therapist may choose to help the older patient develop a creative use for the expression of pain, as has been commonly done for many artists.

THE INTERPRETATION OF PAIN IN DYNAMIC PSYCHOTHERAPY

Pain is always an encounter with meaning, since pain always requires an explanation. David Bakan (1969) noted:

> To attempt to understand the nature of pain, to seek to find its meaning, is already to respond to an imperative of pain itself.... Pain forces the question of its meaning and of its cause.... In those instances in which pain is intense and intractable and in which its causes are obscure, its demand for interpretation is most naked, manifested in the sufferer asking "Why"? (p. 57–58)

Even a cold and distant medical explanation constitutes an explanation, since it helps the patient to make sense of, to give meaning to, the pain. The dynamic emphasis differs from a simple attempt to explain causally the origins of the pain. Rather, the focus is on meaning making when simple answers fail or are not sufficient. Consider, for instance, the Biblical patriarch Job, an Old Testament story being among the most compelling narratives of world literature where people struggle to make sense out of human suffering. Job is covered with boils, agonizingly trying to figure out why God has punished him. What might constitute a straightforward problem in dermatology utterly fails to come to grips with the center of the experience that overtakes the sufferer. Job craves not so much a release from his pain as an acceptable explanation of his punishment. Job's search also indicates that the approach of the Bible finds pain and meaning inseparable, since humans, in their totality, cannot contrast physical and mental suffering. We best understand Job's pain to be his demands to know "why"; he seeks meaning. Lifton (1979) assumed that psychological pain always includes a moral judgment and that such judgments always express psychological conflict and realization. In the great works of religion (e.g., The Book of Job), literature (e.g., Tolstoy's "Death of Ivan Ilych"), and culture, as well as in our accumulated clinical experiences, we encounter narratives of pain which move between the extremes of absolute meaninglessness to full meaning (Klienman, 1988). Psychotherapy has no more fertile territory in which to show its worth.

A similar dynamic approach, that of logotherapy, finds expression in the work of Victor Frankl (1963) and may be profitably employed by clinical psychologists for the treatment of pain. For Frankl, the crucial key to surviving and to dealing with extreme trauma lies in our power to discover or attribute a meaning to our existence and suffering. Such meaning should be expressed not just by contemplation but by action and by the performance of an appropriate task or act. That such a position takes on the features of more behavioral alternatives is interesting but does not affect the special character this psychodynamic orientation. The exercise of will, choice, and human freedom constitutes an existential approach that is used by existential therapists to combat pain and suffering, where the search for meaning constitutes one of the four ultimate concerns that motivate human behavior and that help to explain existence (Yalom, 1980).

A range of other cognitive variables are of legitimate concern to psychotherapeutic analysis, including the status and development of self-control, attitude, and expectations of pain, which influence the experience of pain itself and which contribute to the meaning assigned to that experience, especially if the patient is religious (Arntz, Van-Eck, &

Heijmans, 1990). The appraisal of pain and the meaning ascribed to it have been shown to have a greater impact on the patient than the kind of treatment that is administered for pain attenuation (Barkwell, 1991). Not surprisingly, the style of interpretation that the patient elects in the pain–meaning activity correlates with the coping modes that are used (Arathuzik, 1991). Certainly, of all the basic existential concerns of human beings, the prospect of death is paramount (Becker, 1973). Among many (but not all) elderly, this may be seen as an almost compulsive preoccupation and may even be regarded as fundamental and as being as powerful as the primal Freudian instincts (Yalom, 1980). Suffering and pain lead human cognition, perceptions, and affect to associations with death. "Pain has but one acquaintance ... and that is death", wrote Emily Dickinson (1960). However, Western culture strongly denies death and is ready to do battle with it at any cost (Becker, 1973). The medical resistance to death may seem entirely laudable, since we rightly expect physicians to enhance health and to preserve life. In the course of this battle, however, we risk failing to accept an equally laudable expectation and reality that would have us recognize death as the natural end point on the life continuum and to accept the need to allow it to appear with minimum suffering. The generation of our elders were accustomed to view pneumonia as "the old people's friend," allowing a peaceful termination of biological living, but the vigorous war that medicine wages on the prospect of death often serves only to extend a most demeaning and uncomfortable suffering and existence. This same culture has created a denial of death that has its roots in the impersonal and institutional character of modern death (Kübler-Ross, 1969). Here, too, psychotherapy can help elderly patients "work through" their encounters with death and loss, which are specifically relevant at this period of their life and which may be effectively explored in life-review therapy (Butler & Lewis, 1986). Intervention models have been developed with cancer patients to help them deal with the meaning of their pains and impending death (Ersek & Ferrell, 1994).

The rather common lack of interest in somatic illnesses and pain of many psychoanalysts and psychotherapists may reflect their own fear of dealing with such phenomena as well as with the issues of changes in body image, loss, suffering, finality, and death. As with medical pathologies and disorders that leave the physician and the front-line health team devastated and drained, the treatment of patients with severe pain and related terminal illness—especially the elderly—often leaves the therapist with a strong sense of helplessness. Such a condition carries the cost of inflicting narcissistic hurt, diminished *self*-confidence, and diminished *professional* confidence. Feelings of countertransference of this sort must themselves be given serious attention by the therapist.

EPILOGUE

Prolonged pain and suffering call for a multifaceted and interlaced treatment program in which psychophysiological reactions, physical and psychological status, cognition, emotions, and culture are all viewed as etiological agents and potential sources that will enable relief. A graphic representation of some of the theoretical systems and the interventions they imply appears in Figure 1-1. The comprehensive orientation requires an approach in which individual psychodynamics and psychotherapy are allowed expression in the intervention plan. With special reference to the elderly, substantial evidence indicates the usefulness of dynamic psychotherapy for that group in conditions of pain. Even more dramatic is the evidence that, when psychotherapy is incorporated along with forms of treatment (e.g., biofeedback), the effectiveness for the patient is substantially improved (Olson & Malow, 1987). In combination with the behavioral and cognitive approaches, whose essential strength is the rapid removal of symptoms and daily functioning without reports of sensory distress, the remaining modes of coping that rely on intrapsychic and interpersonal dynamics, culture, and meaning will have much benefit in a judicious integration of traditional forms of psychotherapy into the comprehensive management of pain for the elderly.

REFERENCES

Adams, E., & McGuire, F. (1986). Is laughter the best medicine? A study on the effects of humor on perceived pain and affect. *Activities, Adaptation, and Aging, 8*, 157–175.

Alexander, F., & French, T. (Eds.). (1948). *Studies in psychosomatic medicine*, New York: Ronald Press.

Arathuzik, M. (1991). The appraisal of pain and coping in cancer patients. *Western Journal of Nursing Research, 13*, 714–731.

Arntz, A., Van-Eck, M., & Heijmans, M. (1990). Predictions of dental pain: The fear of any expected evil is worse than the evil itself. *Behavior Research and Therapy, 28*, 29–41.

Bakan, D. (1968). *Disease, pain and sacrifice: Towards a psychology of suffering*. Chicago: University of Chicago Press.

Barkwell, D. (1991). Ascribed meaning: A critical factor in coping and pain attenuation in patients with cancer-related pain. *Journal of Palliative Care, 7*, 5–14.

Barre, C. (1983). De la neurologie à la psychiatrie de secteur ou du palfium ... à la relation. *Perspectives Psychiatriques, 21*, 206–210.

Bassett, D., & Pilowsky, I. (1985). A study of brief psychotherapy for chronic pain. *Journal of Psychosomatic Research, 29*, 259–264.

Becker, E. (1973). *The denial of death*. New York: Free Press.

Beecher, H. (1956). Relationship of significance of wound to the pain experience. *Journal of the American Medical Association, 161*, 1609–1613.

Bond, M., & Pearson, I. (1969). Psychological aspects of pain in women with advanced cancer of the cervix. *Journal of Psychosomatic Research, 13*, 13–18.

Butler, R., & Lewis, M. (1986). *Aging and mental health*, Toronto: Merrill.

Carasso, R. L., Arnon G., Yehuda S., & Mostofsky, D. I. (1988). Hypnotic techniques for the management of pain. *Journal of the Royal Society of Health, 108*, 176–179.

Cassell, E. J. (1982). The nature of suffering and the goals of medicine. *New England Journal of Medicine, 306*, 639–645.

Coen, S., & Sarno, J. (1989). Psychosomatic avoidance of conflict in back pain. *Journal of the Academy of Psychoanalysis, 17*, 359–376.

Cohen-Mansfield, J., & Marx, M. (1993). Pain and depression in the nursing home. *Journal of Gerontology, 48*, 96–97.

Conran, M. (1985). The patient in the hospital. *Psychoanalytic Psychotherapy, 1*, 31–43.

Dar, R., Beach, C., Barden, P., & Cleeland, C. (1992). Cancer pain in the marital system: A study of patients and their spouses. *Journal of Pain and Symptom Management, 7*, 87–93.

Demjen, S., Bakal, D., & Dunn, B. (1990). Cognitive correlates of headache intensity and duration. *Headache, 30*, 423–427.

Dickinson, E. (1960). *The complete poems of Emily Dickinson* (R. Chapman, Ed.) Boston: Little, Brown.

Ersek, M., & Ferrell, B. (1994). Providing relief from cancer pain by assisting in the search for meaning. *Journal of Palliative Care, 10*, 15–22.
Frankl, V. (1963). *Man's search for meaning: An introduction to logotherapy*. New York: Pocket Books.
Freeman, R. (1993). A psychoanalytic case illustrating a psychogenic factor in Burning Mouth Syndrome. *British Journal of Psychotherapy, 10* (2), 220–225.
Freud, S. (1963). *The problem of anxiety*. New York: Norton.
Gibson, H. (Ed.). (1994). *Psychology, pain, and anaesthesia*. London: Chapman & Hall.
Greenberg, J., & Mitchell, S. (1983). *Object relations in psychoanalytic theory*. Cambridge: Harvard University Press
Harkins, S. (1988). Issues in the study of pain and suffering in relation to age. *International Journal of Technology and Aging, 1*, 146–155.
Hasenbush, L. (1977). Successful brief therapy of a retired elderly man with intractable pain. *Journal of Geriatric Psychiatry, 10*, 71–78.
Hess, N. (1995). Cancer as a defense against depressive pain. *Psychoanalytic Psychotherapy, 9*, 175–184.
Hobfoll, S. (1988). *The ecology of stress*. New York: Hemisphere.
Hunter, K., Linn, M., & Harris, R. (1982). Characteristics of high and low self-esteem in the elderly. *International Journal of Aging and Human Development, 14*, 117–126.
Keefe, F., Wilkins, R., & Cook, W. (1986). Depression, pain, and pain behavior. *Journal of Consulting and Clinical Psychology, 54*, 667–669.
Khantzian, E. (1995). Self regulation vulnerabilities in substance abusers: Treatment implications. In S. Dowling (Ed)., *The psychology and treatment of addictive behavior* (pp. 17–41). Workshop Series of the American Psychoanalytic Association. Monograph 8. Madison: International Universities Press.
Kleinman, A. (1988). *The illness narratives: Suffering, healing, and the human condition*. New York: Basic Books
Klusman, L. (1975). Reduction of pain in childbirth by the alleviation of anxiety during pregnancy. *Journal of Consulting and Clinical Psychology, 43*, 162–165.
Knight, B. (1993). Psychotherapy as applied gerontology. *Generations, 17*, 61–64.
Kohut, H. (1977). *The restoration of the self*. New York: International Universities Press.
Krystal, H. (1981). The hedonic element in affectivity. *The Annual of Psychoanalysis, 9*, 93–115.
Krystal, H. (1987). The impact of massive psychic trauma: Later life sequelae. In J. Sadavoy & M. Leszcz (Eds.), *Treating the elderly with psychotherapy*, (pp. 95–156). Madison: International Universities Press.
Kübler-Ross, E. (1969). *On death and dying*. New York: Macmillan.
Lance, W., Vachon, M., Ghadirian, P., & Adir, W. (1994). The impact of pain and impaired role performance on distress in persons with cancer. *Canadian Journal of Psychiatry, 39*, 617–622.
Lewis, A. (1967). *The state of psychiatry: Essays and Addresses*, London: Routledge & Kegan Paul.
Lifton, R. (1979). *The broken connection*. New York: Simon & Schuster.
McCaffrey, M. (1983). *Nursing the patient in pain*. London: Harper & Row.
McDougall, J. (1991). *Theatres of the body: A psychoanalytic approach to psychosomatic illness*. London: Free Association Books.
Melzack, R., & Dennis, S. (1983). Neurophysiological foundations of pain. In R. Sternbach (Ed.), *The psychology of pain* (pp. 1–26). New York: Raven Press.
Melzack, R., & Wall, P. (1982). *The challenge of pain*, New York: Basic Books.
Mikail, S., Henderson, P., & Tasca, G. (1994). An interpersonally based model of chronic pain: An application of attachment theory. *Clinical Psychology Review, 14*, 1–16.
Mobily, P., Herr, K., Clark, M., & Wallace, R. (1994). An epidemiologic analysis of pain in the elderly: The Iowa 65+ rural health study. *Journal of Aging and Health, 6*, 139–154.
Morris, D. (1993). *The culture of pain*. Berkeley: University of California Press.
Moss, M., Lawton, P., & Glicksman, A. (1991). The role of pain in the last year of life of older persons. *Journal of Gerontology, 46*, 51–57.
Nemiah, J. (1962). The effect of leukotomy on pain. *Psychosomatic Medicine, 24*, 75–80.
Nemiroff, R., & Colarusso, C. (1990). *New dimensions in adult development*. New York: Basic Books.
Nowlin, J., & Busse, E. (1977). Psychosomatic problems in the older person. In E. Witkower & H. Warnes (Eds.), *Psychosomatic medicine*. New York: Harper & Row.

Oberle, K., Pau, P., Wry, J., & Grace, M. (1990). Pain, anxiety, and analgesics: A comparative study of elderly and younger surgical patients. *Canadian Journal on Aging. 9*, 13–22.

O'Connor, M., & Goddard, A. (1994). The management of intractable low back pain. In H. Gibson (Ed.), *Psychology, pain, and anaesthesia* (pp. 204–228). London: Chapman & Hall.

Olson, R., & Malow, R. (1987). Effects of biofeedback and psychotherapy on patients with myofascial pain dysfunction who are nonresponsive to conventional treatments. *Rehabilitation Psychology, 32*, 195–204.

Parmelee, P., Katz, I., & Lawton, P. (1991). The relation of pain to depression among institutionalized aged. *Journals of Gerontology, 46*, 15–21.

Rose, M., Atkinson, L., & Slade, P. (1992). An application of the fear avoidance model to three chronic pain problems. *Behavior, Research and Therapy, 30*, 359–365.

Sadavoy, J., & Leszcz, M. (Eds.). (1987). *Treating the elderly with psychotherapy* Madison: International Universities Press.

Schilder, P. (1951). Studies concerning the psychology and symptomatology of general paresis. In D. Rapaport (Ed.), *Organization and pathology of thought* (pp. 519–580). New York: Columbia University Press.

Schoenfeld, W. N. (1981). Pain: a verbal response. *Neuroscience and Biobehavioral Reviews, 5*, 385–389.

Sengstaken, E., & King, S. (1993). The problems of pain and its detection among geriatric nursing home residents. *Journal of the American Geriatric Society, 41*, 541–544.

Sifneos, P. (1974). A reconsideration of psychodynamic mechanisms in psychosomatic symptom formation in view of recent clinical observations. *Psychotherapy and Psychosomatics, 22*, 151–155.

Sternbach, R. (1968). *Pain: A psychophysiological analysis*. New York: Academic Press.

Strupp, H. (1978). Suffering and psychotherapy. *Contemporary Psychoanalysis, 14*, 73–79.

Turk, D., Meichenbaum, D., & Genest, M. (1983). *Pain and behavioral medicine: A cognitive behavioral perspective*. London: Guilford Press.

Valdes, M., Treserra, J., Garcia, L., & de Pablo, J. (1988). Psychogenic pain and psychological variables: A psychometric study. *Psychotherapy and Psychosomatics, 50* (1), 15–21.

Vingoe, F. (1981). *Clinical psychology and medicine: An interdisciplinary approach*. Oxford: Oxford University Press.

Wade, J., Price, D., & Hammer, R. (1990). An emotional component analysis of chronic pain. *Pain, 40*, 303–310.

Weinstein, E. (1968). Symbolic neurology and psychoanalysis. In J. Marmor (Ed.), *Modern psychoanalysis* (pp. 225–250). New York: Basic Books.

Yalom, I. (1980). *Existential psychotherapy*. New York: Basic Books

Zuckerman, M. (1976). Sensation seeking and anxiety traits and states as determinants of behavior in novel situations. In I. Sarason & C. Spielberger (Eds.), *Stress and anxiety*. (pp. 141–170). New York: Plenum Press.

CHAPTER 2

A Brief History of Pain Perception and Pain Tolerance in Aging

SHLOMO YEHUDA AND RALPH L. CARASSO

INTRODUCTION

Both philosophers and scientists of diverse perspectives and theoretical orientations have dealt with the phenomenon of pain. The philosopher conceptualized pain as a reaction to a physical stimulus or as a cognitive action; the religious scholar of ancient times believed pain was the punishment for sins (Turk, Meichenbaum, & Genest, 1983). The logical confusion between pain as a stimulus and pain as a response has even lead to a proposition that pain is little more than a verbal response (Schonfeld, 1981). Only relatively recently have these issues been brought to bear on better understanding the nature, role, and implication of pain for elderly populations. The history of the problem that underlies these concerns is fundamental for an adequate appreciation of that problem.

In the modern era, pain research initially focused on the physiological components which affect the perception of pain. With time, scientists came to realize that pain is a very complex phenomenon which cannot be defined solely in physiological terms. Merskey (1978) reported that patients in general hospitals often reported pain with no organic cause that could be discerned. He assumed the cause of the pain was psychological. Earlier, Merskey (1968) had found that 38% of patients reported pain for which no physiological cause was found. In addition, and not surprisingly, treatments based on medical care alone did not produce satisfactory results. It is also clear that the psychological state of the patient is a significant factor in the efficiency of pain relievers

SHLOMO YEHUDA AND RALPH L. CARASSO, • Psychopharmacology Laboratory, Department of Psychology, Bar Ilan University, Ramat Gan 02900, Israel, and Department of Neurology, Hillel Yaffe Hospital, Hadera 38100, Israel.

Handbook of Pain and Aging, edited by David I. Mostofsky and Jacob Lomranz. Plenum Press, New York, 1997.

(Weisenberg, 1977). These findings led to a general awareness in both the clinical and scientific communities that pharmacological, physiological, and psychological factors all combine to create the perception and experience of pain (Melzack & Wall, 1982).

Two dominant factors drive all discussions about pain: the first is the sensory and neurobiological insult to the tissue that presumably gives rise to the existence of pain, and the second is the behavioral (verbal or nonverbal) expression of pain by which it may be recognized and reported. Only this behavioral element can be measured and observed. In other words, pain is a hypothetical concept which cannot be measured directly, nor can the "objective" sensation it arouses be measured except by indirect and inferential procedures. The "pure" sensation of pain goes through various filters (emotional, cognitive, etc.). Hardy, Wolff, and Goodell (1952) claimed that a person who complains of sensations of pain is defining pain, and that it is not possible to delineate the phenomenon further. Indeed, it seems that the measurement of the behavior of pain is not at all simple. Many researchers claim that self-reports on pain may be exaggerated and inconsistent (Parkhouse & Holmes, 1960) and are affected by emotional (Houde, Wallenstein, & Rogers, 1960) and cultural components (Helson, 1964). In addition, observation of behavior does not objectively reflect the level of pain; rather, it reflects the perception of the observer. This perception, as well, is influenced by many factors. For example, Lenburg, Glass, and Davitz (1970) found a correlation between observers' attribution and their occupation.

The pain research literature reveals a historical process by the research community that began with studying a narrow and specific cause of pain, in which emphasis was placed on the sensation itself, and continued to modern-day investigations that led to the discovery of many other factors (cognitive, emotional, etc.) which were shown to affect the perception of pain. The special considerations that may be unique to pain in the elderly have been only superficially examined and with considerably less investment of resources. While it has long been recognized that the ravages of aging are often accompanied by comorbid chronic diseases that may include pain. The issue of epidemiological status or clinical management for pain among the aging represents a glaring omission in an otherwise aggressive area of research, training, and development.

DEFINING PAIN: A PHYSIOLOGICAL STARTING POINT

About 100 years ago, Goldscheider (1894) proposed that the intensity of the stimulus and its accumulated effect in the central nervous system are an important cause of pain. In his opinion, pain is caused when the general output of the cells exceeds a certain level, as a result of a strong stimulation of the receptors, as might be activated by heat or touch. Sherrington (1989) claimed that pain results from the application of a stimulus whose intensity threatens the integrity of the tissue. According to Beecher (1965), the known receptors are not specific for pain since they lack the ability to identify the painful stimulus. According to Livingston (1943), a forceful stimulation of sensory nerves arouses activity in the nervous mechanisms which are situated in the gray matter in the spinal cord, and that activity is subsequently experienced as pain. Zimmerman

(1979) claimed that there is no single pain center in the brain, and that various areas, such as the thalamus, brain stem, hypothalamus, cerebellum, limbic system, and neocortex, are all involved in the phenomenon. The behavior of pain is a result of an internal interaction of these parts of the brain. For Huskisson (1974), pain is the activation of the receptors sensitive to chemical materials such as bradykinin, which, in small quantities, causes pain. In contrast, Guilband, Bons, and Boesson (1976) claimed that activation of A fibers (in the dorsal horn) by bradykinin does not cause pain. However, activation of C fibers of the spinal column always produces pain. Other materials which cause pain are hydrogen ions, potassium, histamine, salt solution, and acetylcholine. Lindhal (1974) attributed pain to biochemical processes where a rise in the level of hydrogen ions or the level of pH acidity in the nerve may cause pain. There is evidence of types of pain related to acidity, such as ulcers and ischemic pain, but these are preliminary findings only. Walters (1961) claimed that transmission of impulses from the retina to the brain are not different from the impulses within the pain system. The pain sensation system is like any other sensory system. Therefore, we should discuss stimulus rather than the "painful event."

According to Weisenberg (1975), researchers regarded pain as a separate sensation, similar to that of the other senses. The physiological attitude was that pain is a function of the quality and intensity of the sensory-activating stimulus and that the intensity of pain so caused would be relative to the amount of damage to the tissue. This approach was later found to be incorrect. Findings showed that the same painful stimulus administered to different people, or to the same people under different circumstances, or to people from different cultures (Beecher, 1959), does not lead to pain perceived with the same intensity.

Hardy, Wolff, and Goodell (1943) demonstrated that the intensity of pain is subjective and does not necessarily reflect the intensity of the stimulus, the level of damage to the tissue, or the level of danger posed to the organism. It seems that pain perception also involves psychological variables such as stress and past experiences. Indeed, in the early years of the discipline, researchers considered the importance of emotional, motivational, and cognitive factors in experiencing pain (Strong, 1895; Marshall, 1894), but only recently, after accumulated findings on the subject, have these factors begun to be reconsidered. Melzack (1973), followed by Mayer (1975), considered motivational and emotional factors which affect specific pain behavior. They claim these factors are activated by various neurophysiological systems. Gradually, the concept *pain label* (Hardy, Goodell, & Wolff, 1941), which is more general and less focused, was introduced. Beecher (1959) distinguished between primary and secondary components in pain experience. The primary component (original sensation) is the actual pain sensation, while the secondary (psychic processing) relates to the emotional and behavioral response to pain. Beecher's distinction reflects the great confusion in the field that alerted scientists to the realization that there is no direct or simple connection between the physiological damage, its intensity and nature, and the way in which it is perceived.

Melzack and Wall's "gate control theory" (1982) regards pain perception and the response to it as a complex phenomenon, caused by the interaction of sensory, motivational, affective, and cognitive factors. They claimed that the nervous system supports a "gate" which can prevent or enable the penetration of impulses from the peripheral fibers, to the central nervous system. When the amount of information passing through the gate reaches a critical level, pain will be experienced. According to this theory, the gate is situated in the dorsal horn of the spinal cord in the substantia gelatinosa. The impulses reach the gate cell (T cell) via thick, myelinated A (gamma) fibers; thin, nonmyelinated C fibers; and beta fibers that are connected to the autonomic nervous system or to internal organs. The A (gamma) fibers inhibit transmission of the stimulus, and C fibers enable transmission of the stimulus, while beta fibers transmit information but do not affect the gate. The painful stimulus reaching the brain centers is also modulated by psychological factors which are carried by nervous system activity and which in turn affect the opening and closing of the gate. According to Melzack (1983), the motivational, cognitive, and affective factors not only are involved *after* the sensation but also affect the actual sensation. These factors may create a block for the actual pain, a phenomenon dramatically represented by hypnotic treatment procedures. Despite criticism of specific details of this model, most modern pain researchers agree that pain perception is influenced by a combination and interaction of factors (Melzack & Wall, 1982).

PSYCHOLOGICAL AND SOCIAL INFLUENCES ON PAIN PERCEPTION

Sternbach (1976) directed the emphasis of pain perception to personal and subjective experience driven by individual traits and personality. The perception is related to the meaning attributed to the stimulus (duration and nature of the stimulus, and the general array of stimuli to which the person is exposed), the structure of personality, and the level of neuroticism. It was found that there are people who have a general tendency to perceive pain following a relatively low intensity of stimulation, while others tend to perceive pain only in high-intensity conditions (Petrie, Collins, & Solomon, 1960). Among the relevant personality traits, the findings show that people with a high hostility level and paranoidlike thinking perceive medium-level thermal pain as relatively high in intensity (Melzack, 1983). In addition, people with high self-control tend to tolerate a painful stimulus for a longer period than those lower in this trait. According to Sternbach (1967), a person who has an anxiety tendency will have a lower pain threshold than a person who does not have this tendency. In general, he found that anxiety increases sensitivity or responsiveness to pain. Even a cursory consideration of the environmental and psychological circumstances in which geriatric patients find themselves illustrates the aggravation of even moderate or low-level discomforts to a point of pain that would not otherwise be found among younger cohorts. When added to the physical ailments afflicting many in the older age groups (e.g., arthritis), the adverse nature of the psychological variables can be expected to give rise to even greater levels of pain and to feed the cycle of even greater psychological damage to the patient.

In addition to personality factors, cognitive and motivational factors play a major role in pain perception. Beecher (1965) reported on wounded soldiers who consumed relatively small doses of pain relievers, since the wound could well be seen as a savior from death (because of the danger of battle), while civilians with similar wounds consumed larger doses of the medicine, since they regarded the wound as a disaster. In a more dynamic formulation, Szasz (1957) regarded pain as a vehicle for communication. He considered the means of communication important for understanding the response to pain. The response to pain may be interpreted in various ways, such as "Do not touch me," "Help me," and "See, I am being punished."

Under laboratory conditions, various cognitive aspects of pain perception can be better studied and delineated. Zimbardo et al. (1966) found that subjects' responses to electric shocks changed significantly following verbal manipulations. In addition, significant differences were found in pain threshold and pain tolerance between subjects who had control of the intensity of the stimulus and those who did not. When subjects could control the intensity of the stimulus, their pain threshold was higher than in those who could not control the stimulus (Hill & Kornestsky, 1952). These findings were confirmed in later years. According to Notermans (1966), when a subject fears what is expected, there is a tendency to react sooner to pain (lower threshold). Therefore, it is possible to manipulate the level of pain in a simple experimental procedure by providing information that the experiment will include a painful stimulus. For effective pain control, it is important to appreciate the deleterious effect of focusing on the painful stimulus. It was found that when attention is drawn *away* from the painful stimulus, pain tolerance increases (Beecher, 1965). Indeed, drawing attention away from the painful sensation is one of the techniques used in the cognitive treatment of pain. Wynn Parry (1980) reported that people who suffered serious pain after injury were able to reduce the pain by paying less attention to it while focusing on their work. Indeed, we (Carasso, Arnon, Yehuda, & Mostofsky, 1988) have earlier summarized some 17 variations of hypnotic techniques for use in pain management, in which the element of disattention or refocused attention constitutes the central element of the intervention. In recent years, use of cognitive and behavioral therapy has become widespread because of the increased awareness of attitudes (Beecher, 1959; Fordyce, 1976; Lochard, 1978) and other psychological factors and their influence on pain perception.

Yet another important element, so relevant in considerations with elderly and aging populations, is the role played in cultural attitudes in their influence on the pain experience. Beecher (1965) noted two characteristics that can be found in an examination of cultural variables: (1) the perception of pain as inevitable in the situation and (2) the willingness to experience pain. He found that patients of Italian origin were less willing to endure pain than Jewish and Anglo-Saxon patients. The Italian patients frequently reported pain and demanded medication to reduce it before the completion of any medical diagnosis to determine the origin of the pain. The Jewish patients were more likely to demand a diagnosis before receiving medication. The Anglo-Saxon patients did not express their pain verbally. Similarly, in Western cultures, it is customary to regard birth as an event which requires rest; however, Melzack (1973) described a society in which a mother gives birth in the field and immediately continues working while the father remains at home moaning with pain.

Similar findings under laboratory conditions were described by Sternbach (1967), who found that Italian women had a lower pain threshold than Jewish or Irish women. However, Hardy et al. (1952) found that thermal pain was perceived by Jewish and Italian subjects as painful, compared to Anglo-Saxon subjects, who perceived the stimulus as "slightly hot." A similar finding was reported later regarding pain threshold in people born in Nepal, compared to Westerners (Clark & Mehl, 1973). Weisenberg (1975) found differences between Negro, Caucasian, and Puerto Rican subjects with respect to status differences and amount of anxiety related to pain. It is important to emphasize that there are no physiological differences between the cultures. The differences in pain perception as a function of culture have been found in many more studies. It is possible that cultural differences are partially due to modeling processes (Bandura, 1969). People learn to express pain by imitating others who are similar to them. Support for this claim was found in an experiment which showed that a collaborator who was willing to endure high levels of pain also raised the pain threshold of the subjects who observed him (Craig & Weiss, 1972; Craig & Neidermayer, 1974).

The inferences drawn in the this survey of research findings leads us to assert confidently that pain perception necessarily includes the sensory sensation of pain and the feeling evoked by this sensation, each of which is subserved by a host of psychosocial variables. The expressed "feeling" of pain must be understood in the context of an interpretation of the sensation, which is itself influenced by physiological, emotional, cognitive, and social factors. The accepted definition of pain by the International Association for the Study of Pain (IASP) is "Pain is an unpleasant subjective experience related to tissue damage, or described in terms of tissue damage, or related to the two conditions simultaneously." The IASP group emphasizes that pain is always subjective.

THE NATURE OF PAIN

The profile of the expression of pain is often categorized along a periodicity or temporal dimension. The particular form of pain described by a category most often results from the conditions of stimulus or the underlying process or pathology that gives rise to the pain. Though not all-inclusive, the common categories are

1. Acute pain—with a short duration, less than six months. This type of pain is usually related to tissue damage.
2. Periodical chronic pain—pain which occurs occasionally but which, once initiated, may persist for a long period of time (e.g., migraines).
3. Chronic pain—a pain which is felt most of the time, with varying intensities, often in the absence of any biological significance (e.g., back pain or phantom limb pain).
4. Progressive chronic pain—increasing intensity of discomfort with or without enlargement of affected areas (e.g., malignant diseases).
5. Laboratory pain—pain caused by laboratory stimulation rather than as a natural product of a trauma or a disease process (Turk et al., 1983).

Beecher (1965) properly noted that there is a qualitatively important difference between laboratory pain and clinical pain, in that one of the main features in the variables of clinical pain perception concerns the interpretation of pain by the individual, namely, its meaning and predicted consequences. This perception strikingly differentiates labora-

tory from clinical situations. A "cost–benefit" analysis of laboratory pain studies has been sketched by Wolff (1983):
Benefits:

1. It is possible to better control the research and enables more direct measurement of the stimulus–response connection.
2. It is possible to compare the maximal pain (tolerance) and the minimal pain (threshold), and to determine the range between them.

Problems:

1. Pain in the laboratory is more similar to acute pain than to chronic pain, while treatment in pain clinics focuses on chronic pain.
2. Duration of pain is usually short and is controlled by the subject, whereas chronic pain has a longer duration and cannot be stopped by the patient.

Nonetheless, Wolff pointed out that the difference between the two types of pain are not orthogonal. He found that the different parameters for the reactions to laboratory pain in groups of patients were correlated with the different intensities of clinical pain for the same groups. In addition, it can be reliably shown that certain forms of laboratory-induced pain provides a valid model as an analogue of the clinical pain (such as in ischemic pain). By manipulating psychological and social variables in the laboratory, processes similar to clinical pain processes can be created.

AGE AND PAIN PERCEPTION

The proposition that change occurs in sensitivity to pain as a function of age was affirmed by Zoob (1978), who concluded that a decreased sensitivity to pain accompanies increases in age. A contradictory conclusion was arrived at by Fordyce (1976), who noted that older patients complain of pain more than younger ones. The discrepancy was accommodated by Clark and Mehl (1973), who argued that complaints of pain are a function of a tendency to *report* pain and not a function of the sensitivity to its perception. Many other studies investigating the relationship between age and pain have contributed to similar conflicting findings. Among such reports is the work by Chapman (1978), who tested the pain threshold with the thermal method (a heat source located on the subject's forehead). *Stimulus threshold* was defined as "the lowest stimulus level that causes contraction of the outer eye muscles," as defined by observation of the experimenters. The results showed an increase in the pain threshold the older the age of the subject. Later experiments based on these methods showed similar results (Sherman & Robillard, 1964). Schludermann and Zubek (1962) tested pain threshold using the thermal method, with the heat focused on the forehead, arm, thigh, and leg of the subjects. They found that the pain threshold was stable during adolescence and the middle years, but that, starting at age 50, the threshold was significantly elevated. The rise in pain threshold with age was also reported later by Clark and Mehl (1971). These findings may be explained as a result of damage to the central nervous system as well as damage to information-processing common in adults at this age.

It has been proved that there is a deterioration in the ability to receive visual and auditory stimuli, but it is noteworthy that the loss of visual and auditory sensitivity is often related to the change in the functioning of the peripheral receptors, not only damage to central nervous system processes. Furthermore, deterioration of the sensory reception with age is also related to accumulated effects of disease or physical damage over the years. It is therefore not clear whether differences in age groups with regard to pain perception are due to central or peripheral factors or to a combination of the two.

Procacci et al. (1974) also used the thermal method, and found a decrease in sensitivity to pain as age increased. They claimed that this decrease is due to peripheral as opposed to central factors. He recognized the possibility that the threshold rises as a result of changes in the skin of the subjects, a factor not considered in the earlier investigations. According to Procacci, the changes are related to lack of efficiency in receptor functioning and to changes in the skin as age increases.

Changes in sensitivity to pain are not directly linked to the functioning of the central nervous system. Several studies which tested pain threshold with the thermal method did not find any change in the pain threshold as a function of age (Hardy et al., 1943; Schumacher, Goodell, Hardy, & Wolff, 1940; Birren, Shapiro, & Miller, 1959). Mumford (1965) tested the pain threshold with electrical stimulation and found no difference between two age groups. A year later, Notermans (1966) repeated this experiment and found similar results. These results were also replicated in subsequent studies (Harkins & Chapman 1976, 1977b).

Collins and Stone (1966) employed electrical stimulation via electrodes attached to the fingers which enabled them to measure not only pain threshold but also pain tolerance (i.e., the maximum level of pain the subject was able to endure). The resulting increase in sensitivity to pain with increasing age was opposite to the expectations, in that the older individuals showed a lower pain threshold, and their tolerance for pain was also lower than that of the younger subjects. In a later study using mechanical pressure, Woodrow, Friedman, Siegelaub, and Collen (1972) found similar results to the effect that pain tolerance decreases with age.

Hardy et al. (1943) emphasized the importance of attitudes with regard to pain perception and argued that attitudes and judgments must be separated: according to their reports, when the two age groups shared the same attitudes, their response to pain was identical. By applying signal detection theory (Green & Swets, 1966), one is able to distinguish among sensory, cognitive, motivational, and social variables. By this method, Rees and Botwinick (1971) showed a rise in auditory threshold with age resulting from a change in the criterion. Clark and Mehl (1971) found that adults in the middle years tended to set their stimulus criterion for "painful" at a higher intensity. In addition, Harkins and Chapman (1976, 1977a) tested two age groups and demonstrated an interaction between age and attitudes. The interaction affected the estimation of the stimulus: When the stimulus was low, older subjects tended to regard it as less painful than younger subjects. However, at higher stimulus levels, the older subjects reported more pain. Chapman (1978) claimed that older people require more information before reaching a decision, which may contribute to the reported higher pain threshold. It must also be allowed that changes in sensitivity to pain in adults may reflect indicators of changes in social roles with increased age and are not necessarily markers of changes in neural functioning (Weisenberg, 1977).

Clearly, the cumulative force of the inference from the history of the problem leads us to recognize that there is no simple connection between age and pain perception. It is most reasonable to assume that it is the host of intervening variables which affect pain perception and its reports on pain, and it may well be that these very variables which were left uncontrolled in the various experiments are the ones that correlate with age and which influence the direction of the results (Zimbardo, Cohen, Weisenberg, Dworkin, & Firestone, 1966). It would seem profitable to investigate the nature and degree of the influence that these variables exert.

CRITICAL VARIABLES INFLUENCING PAIN PERCEPTION

Personality Types In a study of cardiovascular disorders, the role of personality was shown by Friedman (1988) to account for a substantial portion of the variance in the ability to predict patients with a potential for cardiac crises. According to Friedman (1988), the difference is in *behavior style*, which leads the patients to heart disease. The very same behavior style which may predispose a person to cardiovascular risk may also serve to alter pain perception (or, at least, pain behaviors as evaluated by reports of pain).

What, then, is this pervasive personality style? Jenkins, Zyzanski, and Rosenman (1979) found a connection between heart disease and Type A behavior in various populations worldwide. The behavior was at first described as a constant struggle to achieve goals within as short a time as possible (Friedman, 1989). The struggle not only manifests as pressure for time but is also accompanied by exaggerated aggression, speed, and competitiveness, all of which were described as critical aspects in the definition of Type A. These qualities serve the Type A's need for achievement and provide an aid to overcoming obstacles in the environment. In contrast, Type B is characterized by a calm and peaceful style of behavior with a noticeably slow pace of activity. Friedman and Rosenman (1959) conceptualized Type A not as a personality type but as a style which becomes manifest under certain environmental circumstances (when social rewards are available). However, in later years, they explained the Type A impatience as reflecting basic hostility (Carmelli, Dame, Swan, & Rosenman, 1991a). Suinn (1977) claimed that impatience is a manifestation of stress, and it should be regarded as an acquired personality type and not as a personality trait. He referred to cultural aspects related to this stress: according to him, the Western society is competitive, achievement-oriented, and aggressive, rewarding those who reach social achievements, and he pointed out that there are more women who now fit the Type A description. This finding reflects the social-cultural influences on creating personality types. According to Glass (1977), Type A behavior is an attempt to control the environment, coupled with a feeling of helplessness which increases stress and anxiety. In order to overcome these feelings, the Type A personality continues to cope with the environment while emphasizing high-speed activity, restlessness, and nervousness toward elements standing in its way.

The concluding definition of Type A is a lifestyle characterized by exaggerated competitiveness, a need to achieve, aggression, restlessness, and constant stress. These people are usually very dedicated to their work and tend to neglect other aspects of their life. However, it is important to emphasize that not all the above-mentioned traits are necessary for the definition of a person as Type A. Type A behavior is not identical to behavior characteristic in stressful situations, or to behavior reflecting a response to a disturbing stimulus, a painful event, or discomfort as a result of environmental damage. Type A shows a stable behavioral pattern in both pleasing and displeasing situations.

While focusing on the achievement orientation of Type A, findings show they have higher achievements than Type B. In a study testing college achievements, it was found that Type A students won many more distinctions than students defined as Type B (Glass, 1977). In addition, in an experiment testing short-term visual memory, Type A showed higher achievements than Type B. When Type A people have a difficult physical task to perform, they exert more energy than Type B people and complain less of fatigue. Glass (1977) found a higher pain threshold in Type A personalities than in Type B.

And herein lies the crux of the relevance of Type A to the issue of pain perception: *Type A personalities do not report pain (except for high-intensity stimuli), since they perceive it to be a weakness or failure* (Carmelli et al., 1991b).

The Relation between Previous Painful Experiences and Present Pain Perception

Psychophysical judgments are predicted by Helson's level-of-adaptation theory (1964) to be modified by a previous history of exposure to the test stimuli. In similar fashion, a prior experience with intense pain will cause patients to experience a present painful stimulus as relatively mild. To test the hypothesis that pain perception is related to the frequency with which a person experiences pain, Ryan and Kovacic (1966) designed a three-group experiment composed of (1) athletes of a sport which does not involve physical contact between participants (such as tennis); (2) athletes of a sport which involves physical contact between participants (such as boxing); and (3) nonathletes. The pain induction technique used was thermal, and the results showed a significant difference between the groups with respect to pain tolerance, the second group showing the highest *tolerance* for pain, although no significant differences were found between the groups for pain threshold. In a comparable study, Naliboff, Cohen, and Schandler (1983) compared the pain threshold in a group of chronic-lower-back-pain (CLBP) sufferers with a control group. The investigations by Hazouri and Muller (1950) and Naliboff et al. (1983) both provide support for Helson's adaptation theory. The comparison of pain ratings for patients suffering from temporal mandibular joint (TMJ) pain with a control group indicate a lower pain threshold in the TMJ group, which the authors explained as arising from the overaroused stimulation of the central nervous system (Mallow & Olson, 1981). They offered their results in support of Chapman's theory (1978), which proposes that patients suffering from chronic pain are more sensitive to pain because of their exaggerated focus on the painful stimulus. Naliboff et al. (1983) reexamined this issue and found that CLBP patients' pain yielded a higher threshold. The conflicting results with others (Malow, Grimm, & Olson, 1980; Malow & Olson, 1981) are explained by, among other things, the different techniques are used to produce the painful stimulus. Naliboff used short presentations of different heat intensities, whereas Malow and Olson used the pressure technique, in which the subject feels a steady increase in pain intensity. The dependent variable in the thermal method is the subject's rating of the stimulus intensity, whereas the dependent variable in the pressure method is the time that elapses before pain is felt. Taken together, these studies emphasize the need to control for the type of stimulation that is used in order to better understand the connections among the different variables, as well as their influence on pain perception.

METHODOLOGICAL PROBLEMS

Confounding effects in pain research abound. Naliboff et al. (1983) commented on the type of stimulus as possibly influencing pain threshold and levels of pain tolerance. Indeed, it seems that studies which have investigated the effects of age on pain perception using the thermal method showed a rise in threshold with age, although reports on tolerance were not given (Chapman & Jones, 1944; Schludermann & Zubeck, 1962; Procacci et al., 1974; Clark & Mehl, 1971). These findings contrast with studies in which other methods (electricity, pressure) were employed and where opposite trends were reported, namely, a decrease in pain threshold and pain tolerance with increasing age (Collins & Stone, 1966; Woodrow et al., 1972). Still other findings showed no connection between pain perception and age, whether derived from electrical (Mumford, 1965; Harkins & Chapman, 1976, 1977b) or thermal stimulation procedures (Schumacher et al., 1940; Hardy et al., 1943; Birren et al., 1959).

It appears that significant differences in results can be expected among the various methods. Whereas the thermal method is connected to external skin tissue and thereby creates a focused pain, electricity and pressure create a more diffused pain, more similar to clinical pain (Clark & Mehl, 1971). In addition, it is important to emphasize that, when using thermal stimuli, the added variable of changes that take place in the skin with advancing age must be considered (Procacci et al., 1974). It is possible, therefore, that age does not directly affect pain perception; rather, older subjects may feel the thermal stimulus at a lower intensity because of specific properties and characteristics of their skin structure and composition. Other theoretical formulations consider claims that, with increasing age, the hypothalamic functioning undergoes changes which affect body-temperature thermostatic processes, which result in adult subjects' not noticing the discomfort caused by heat. This further argues the assumption that the specific nature of the thermal stimulus has direct consequences for the subject's response to pain. In the absence of consistency among the various results, it can be assumed that, quite separate from the type of stimulus, other critical variables abound which are likely to influence pain perception and reports on pain, which were not controlled in the studies cited above. As discussed earlier, personality variables and behavior styles must be examined for their influences in the pain problem. Indeed, Glass (1977) found that Type A patients tend to report pain after a greater delay. Melzack and Wall (1982) reported a correlation between age and personality types. The possibility that age groups respond differently to pain because of lack of appropriate control in sampling must be considered. In this case, differences in the variance of personality types may be created within the different age groups. For example, while in general it can safely be stated that prior experience of pain intensifies sensitivity to pain, Chapman (1978) and Naliboff et al. (1983) found that those who suffer from chronic pain estimated an experimental stimulus as being *less* intense than did control subjects, apparently because of the comparison between the present pain sensation and their prior experience with pain.

TYPE OF PAIN AND ITS MEASUREMENT

The very nature of pain, and perhaps the most striking feature of its very existence, is that it is behavioral. Without a verbal response, a grimace, or an exhibited response or report by the subject, pain ceases to be observable. As noted earlier, the objective measurement of pain is a goal that remains unattainable. All reports, by humans or infrahumans, whether verbal or physiological or behavioral, are affected by physiological, social, cognitive, and emotional variables. Above and beyond the variables controlled by the subject, no evaluation or assessment by the observer can be considered truly objective.

Although Green and Swets's signal-detection-theory technique (1966) enables one to differentiate between the sensory response to pain and accompanying emotional or motivational responses, Harkins and Chapman (1976) showed this technique to be inconsistent and to require a large number of trials. Reliance on "unbiased" measures, such as blood pressure, heart rate, sweat, and EEG, can be misleading since they are apt measure more the expectations of pain than the pain itself. Safe methodological guidelines for undertaking the measurements of pain threshold and pain tolerance include (1) the ability to repeat the stimulus both qualitatively and quantitively; (2) a stimulus of sufficient magnitude and/or anatomical placement to create a clear sensation of pain; (3) a stimulus amenable to control and measurement; (4) uncomplicated operations for modifying the parameters of the stimulus; (5) an application of the stimulus that does not cause tissue damage; and (6) electrical or thermal stimuli, when they are used, that meet the minimum safety standards (Hardy et al., 1941; Procacci et al. (1974). The latter is important because the use of thermal methods involves focusing heat on a specified marked spot (usually on the forearm). Time of exposure can be maintained constant while heat intensity is varied, or heat intensity can be maintained, while time of exposure is varied (Hardy et al., 1952). Similarly, using the electricity method involves administering electrical impulses while duration, intensity, and frequency of the stimulus are varied (Mumford, 1965). In all these cases, the measure of pain intensity is the subject's report.

Some important criticisms concerning the laboratory analogues of clinical pain require further elaboration. For example, Chapman (1979) argued that pain created by an electrical stimulus is unlike clinical pain, as opposed to the ischemic stimulus in the laboratory, which is most similar to clinical pain. In this technique, the arm is blocked by a certain pressure, causing a lack of blood supply to the muscle. In addition, some procedures have instituted activation of the muscle during blocking to speed up the process (Beecher, 1959). Levi and Taggart (1984) regarded internal pain mainly as ischemic pain; while Zimmerman (1979) supported the view that the ischemic method yields reliable information regarding subjective reports of pain, causes pain similar to clinical pain, and can be reliably reconstructed, all of which contribute to the consistency of the results.

Our study (unpublished) generally confirms the Harkins conclusion (Harkins, Price, Bush, & Small., 1994) that pain tolerance is lower among elderly than among younger subjects. However, pain threshold was not found to be influenced by the age effect. The same results were found while measuring pain tolerance and pain threshold in young and elderly subjects, by using pressure and thermal stimuli. In addition to following the procedure adopted in the study conducted by Harkins, each of our subjects had been classified as Type A personality or Type B personality. The results showed that extreme Type A personality exhibited even lower pain tolerance, without a change in pain threshold, and offered confirmation of an earlier study conducted by Light et al. (1991). The relationship between pain tolerance and Type A personality has yet not been studied as extensively as has been done on our subjects.

Yet another possibility for accounting for the lower pain tolerance observed in elderly subjects is an examination of the role of opiates in general and morphine and betaendorphin in particular. The role of opiate analgesics differs from the role of nonnarcotic analgesics. While the nonnarcotic "pain killers" act via an increase in pain threshold, the narcotics act via their special properties and ability to exert calming, soothing, and fear-relieving effects. In other words, aspirin increases pain threshold, while opiates increase pain tolerance. During aging, the opiate system changes. The conclusion of many studies (e.g., Bhargava, Matwyshyn, Reddy, & Veeranna, 1994; Messing et al., 1980; 1981; Mikuma, Kumoto, Maruta, & Nitta, 1994; Li, Wong, Hong, & Ingenito, 1992) is that the level of the various endogenous opiates decreases with age. Moreover, the ability of opiates in general and beta-endorphin in particular to stimulate their receptors decreases. Not only does the level decrease, but the number of receptors shrinks and their affinity is lower. We would like to postulate that the lower tolerance observed in elderly subjects correlates with the decline of all aspects of the brain opiate system.

The finding that Type A personality subjects (both young and old; i.e., an effect that goes beyond age) is difficult to explain in terms of brain biochemistry mechanisms. The high level of noradrenaline found among extreme Type A personality subjects (as evidenced by their high blood pressure) may contribute to the low pain tolerance. Above all, a most parsimonious argument would be that psychological variables have much stronger effects than biological factors.

CONCLUSION

This chapter dealt largely with acute pain. Chronic pain constitutes a different, albeit related and complicated, issue. Adding the element of human suffering from chronic pain to the biophysiological substrate of the response to acute pain is considerably complicated, and much beyond the scope of this chapter. An excellent review of these issues can be found in Harkins et al. (1994).

ACKNOWLEDGMENT. This research was supported by the Rose K. Ginsburg Chair for Research in Alzheimer's Disease and the William Farber Center for Alzheimer Research.

REFERENCES

Bandura, A. (1969). *Principles of behavior modification.* New York: Holt Rinehart & Winston.

Beecher, H. K. (1959). *Measurement of subjective responses: quantitative effect of drugs.* New York: Oxford University Press.

Beecher, H. K. (1965). *Quantification of a subjective pain experience: Psychopathology of perception.* New York: Grune & Stratton Inc. *Proceeding of the American Psychopathological Association, 53,* 111–128.

Bhargava, H. N., Matwyshyn, G. A., Reddy, P. L., & Veeranna, E. (1994). Brain and spinal cord kappa opiate receptors and pharmacological response to U-50,488H in rats of differing ages. *Pharmacology, Biochemistry, and Behavior, 48,* 87–91.

Birren, J. E., Shapiro, H. B., & Miller, H. H. (1959). The effect of salicylate upon pain sensitivity. *Journal of Pharmacology and Experimental Therapeutics, 100,* 67–71.

Carasso, R. L., Arnon, G., Yehuda, S., & Mostofsky, D. I. (1988). Hypnotic techniques for the management of pain. *Journal of the Royal Society of Health, 108,* 176–179.

Carmelli, D., Dame A., Swan, G., & Rosenman, R. (1991a). Long-term changes in Type A behavior: A 27-year follow-up of the Western Collaborative Group Study. *Journal of Behavioral Medicine, 14,* 593–606.

Carmelli, D., Halpern, J., Swan, G. E., Dame, A., McElroy, M., Gelb, A. B., & Rosenman, R. H. (1991b). 27-year mortality in the Western Collaborative Group Study: Construction of risk groups by recursive partitioning. *Journal of Clinical Epidemiology, 44,* 1341–1351.

Chapman, C. R. (1978). The perception of noxious events. In R. A. Sternbach (Ed.), *The psychology of pain.* New York: Raven Press.

Chapman, C. R. (1979). Psychologic and behavioral aspects of cancer pain. In J. J. Bonica & V. Ventafridda (Eds.), *Advances in pain research and therapy* (Vol. 2, pp. 45–56). New York: Raven Press.

Chapman, W. P., & Jones, C. M. (1944). Variation in cutaneous and visceral pain sensitivity in normal subjects. *Journal of Clinical Investigation, 23,* 81–91.

Clark, W. C., & Mehl, L. (1971). Thermal pain: A sensory decision theory analysis of the effect of age and sex on d′, various response criteria and 50 percent pain threshold. *Journal of Abnormal Psychology, 78,* 202–212.

Clark, W. C., & Mehl, L. (1973). Signal detection theory procedures are not equivalent when thermal stimuli are judged. *Journal of Experimental Psychology, 97,* 48–53.

Collins, G., & Stone, L. A. (1966). Pain sensitivity, age and activity level in chronic schizophrenics and in normals. *British Journal of Psychiatry, 112,* 33–35.

Craig, K. D., & Neidermayer, H. (1974). Autonomic correlates of pain thresholds influenced by social modeling. *Journal of Personality and Social Psychology, 29,* 246–252.

Craig, K. D., & Weiss, S. M. (1972). Verbal reports of pain without noxious stimulation. *Perceptual and Motor Skills, 34,* 943–948.

Fordyce, W. E. (1976). *Behavioral methods for chronic pain and illness.* St. Louis: Mosby.

Friedman, M. (1988). Type A behavior: A frequently misdiagnosed and rarely treated medical disorder. *American Heart Journal, 115,* 930–936.

Friedman, M. (1989). Type A behavior: Its diagnosis, cardiovascular relation and the effect of its modification on recurrence of coronary artery disease. *American Journal Cardiology, 64,* 12–19.

Friedman, M., and Rosenman, R. H. 1959. Association of specific overt behavior patterns with blood and cardiovascular findings—Blood cholesterol level, blood clotting time, incidence of *arcus senilis,* and clinical coronary artery disease. *Journal of the American Medical Association, 162,* 1286–1296.

Glass, D. C. (1977). *Behavior patterns, stress, and coronary disease.* Hillsdale, NJ: Erlbaum.

Goldscheider, A. (1894). *Ueber den schmerz in physiologischer und klinischer hinsicht.* Berlin: Hirschwald.

Green, D. M., & Swets, J. A. (1966). *Signal detection theory and psychophysics.* New York: Wiley.

Guilband, G., Bons, D., & Boesson, G. B. (1976). Eradykinnin as a tool in neurophysiological studies of pain mechanisms. In J. J. Bonica & D. G. Albe-Fessard (Eds.), *Advances in pain research and therapy* (Vol. 1, p. 67). New York: Raven Press.

Hardy, J. D., Goodell, H., & Wolff, H. G. (1941). Studies on pain. Observation on hyperalgesia associated with referred pain. *American Journal of Psychology, 133,* 316.

Hardy, J. D., Wolff, H. G., & Goodell, H. (1943). The pain threshold in man. *American Journal of Psychiatry, 99*, 744–751.

Hardy, J. D., Wolff, H. G., & Goodell, H. (1952). *Pain sensations and reactions*. Baltimore: Williams & Wilkins.

Harkins, S. W., & Chapman, C. R. (1976). Detection and decision factors in pain perception in young and elderly men. *Pain, 2*, 253–264.

Harkins, S. W., & Chapman, C. R. (1977a). Age and sex differences in pain perception. In B. Andros & B. Mathaws (Eds.), *Pain in trigeminal regions* (pp. 435–441). North Holland, Amsterdam: Elsevier.

Harkins, S. W., & Chapman, C. R. (1977b). The perception of induced dental pain in young and elderly women. *Journal of Gerontology, 32*, 428–435.

Harkins, S. W., Price, D. D., Bush, M. F., & Small, R. E. (1994). Geriatric pain. In R. Melzack (Ed.), *Textbook of pain* (pp. 769–784). Edinburgh: Churchill Livingstone.

Hazouri, J. A., & Muller, A. D. (1950). Pain threshold studies on patients. *Archives of Neurology and Psychiatry, 64*, 607–613.

Helson, H. (1964). *Adaptation level theory: An experimental and systematic approach to behaviors*. New York: Harper & Row.

Hill, H. E., & Kornestsky, C. H. (1952). Studies of anxiety associated with anticipation of pain: Effects of morphine. *Archives of Neurology and Psychiatry, 67*, 612–619.

Houde, R. W., Wallenstein, S. L., & Rogers, A. (1960). Clinical pharmacology of analgesics: Method of assessing analgesic effect. *Clinical Pharmacology and Therapeutics, 1*, 163–174.

Huskisson, E. C. (1974). Pain: Mechanism and measurement. In F. D. Hart (Ed.), *The treatment of chronic pain*. Lancaster: Medical and Technical Publishing.

Jenkins, C. D., Zyzanski, J. S., & Rosenmam, H. R. (1979). *Jenkins activity survey*. Washington, DC: Psychological Corporation.

Lenburg, C. B., Glass, H. P., & Davitz, L. J. (1970). Inferences of physical pain and psychological distress: 2. In relation to the stage of the patients illness and occupation of the perceiver. *Nursing Research, 19*, 392–398.

Levi, L., & Taggart, P. (1984). Stress and strain. *Ciba Review*, Ciba Geigy Limited.

Li, S. J., Wong, S. C., Hong, J. S., & Ingenito, A. J. (1992). Age-related changes in opioid peptide concentrations in brain and pituitary of spontaneously hypertensive rats: Effect of antihypertensive drugs and comparison with deoxycorticosterone acetate and salt hypertension. *Pharmacology, 44*, 245–256.

Light, K. C., Herbst, M. C., Bragdon, E., E., Hinderliter, A. L., Koch, G. G., Davis, M. R., & Sheps, D. S. (1991). Depression and type A behavior pattern in patients with coronary artery disease. *Psychosomatic Medicine, 53*, 669–683.

Lindhal, O. (1974). A general chemical explanation. In J. J. Bonica (Ed.), *Advances in neurology: International symposium on pain* (Vol. 4). New York: Raven Press.

Livingston, W. K. (1943). *Pain mechanisms: A psychologic interpretation of causalgia and its related states*. New York: Macmillan.

Lochard, D. E. (1978). Relationships between pain, anxiety and attitude toward hospitalization in medical patients using a traditional and a non traditional setting. *Dissertation Abstracts International, 38*, 5573.

Malow, R. M., Grimm, L., & Olson R. E. (1980). Difference in pain perception between myofascial pain dysfunction patients and normal subjects: A signal detection analysis. *Journal of Psychosomatic Research, 24*, 303–310.

Malow, R. M., & Olson, R. E. (1981). Changes in pain perception after treatment for chronic pain. *Pain, 11*, 65–72.

Marshall, H. R. (1894). *Pain, pleasure, and aesthetics*. London: Macmillan.

Mayer, D. Y. (1975). Psychotropic drugs and the anti-depressed personality. *British Journal of Medical Psychology, 48*, 349–357.

Melzack, R. (1973). *The puzzle of pain*. New York: Basic Books.

Melzack, R. (1983). *Pain measurement and assessment*. New York: Raven Press.

Melzack, R., & Wall, P. D. (1982). *The challenge of pain*. New York: Basic Books.

Merskey, H. (1968). Psychological aspects of pain. *Postgraduate Medical Journal, 44*, 297–306.

Merskey, H. (1978). Pain and personality. In R. A. Sternbach (Ed.), *Psychology of pain*. New York: Raven Press.

Messing, R. B., Vasquez, B. J., Samaniego, B., Jensen, R. A., Martinez, J. L., Jr., & McGaugh, J. L. (1981). Alterations in dihydromorphine binding in cerebral hemispheres of aged male rats. *Journal of Neurochemistry*, *36*, 784–787.

Messing, R. B., Vasquez, B. J., Spiehler, V. R., Martinez, J. L., Jensen, R. A., Rigter, H., & McGaugh, J. L. (1980). H^3-dihydromophine binding in brain regions of young and aged rats. *Life Sciences*, *26*, 921–927.

Mikuma, N., Kumoto, Y, Maruta, H., & Nitta, T. (1994). The role of the hypothalamic opioidergic system in control of gonadotropin secretion in elderly men. *Andrologia*, *26*, 39–45.

Mumford, H. M. (1965). Pain perception threshold and adaptation of normal human teeth. *Archives of Graduate Biology*, *10*, 957–968.

Naliboff, B. O., Cohen, M. S., & Schandler, S. L. (1983). Signal detection and threshold measures for chronic back pain patients, chronic illness patients, and cohort controls to radiant heat stimuli. *Pain*, *16*, (3), 245–252.

Notermans, S. L. H. (1966). Measurement of the pain threshold determined by electrical stimulation and its clinical application: 1. Methods and factors possibly influencing the pain threshold. *Neurology*, *16*, 1071–1086.

Parkhouse, J., & Holmes, C. M. (1960). Assessing post operative pain relief. *Proceedings of the Royal Society of Medicine*, *56*, 579–604.

Petrie, A., Collins, W., & Solomon P. (1960). The tolerance for pain and for sensory deprivation. *American Journal of Psychology*, *74*, 80–90.

Procacci, P., Della Corte, M., Zoppi, M., Romano, S., Maresca, M., & Voegelin M. (1974). Pain threshold measurement in man. In J. J. Bonica, P. Procacci, & C. Pagoni (Eds.), *Recent advances on pain: Pathophysiology and clinical aspects* (pp. 105–147). Springfield, IL: Charles C. Thomas.

Rees, J., & Botwinick, J. (1971). Detection and decision factors in auditory behavior of the elderly. *Journal of Gerontology*, *26*, 133–147.

Ryan, R. D., & Kovacic, C. R. (1966). Pain tolerance and athletic participation. *Perceptual and Motor Skills*, *22*, 383–390.

Schludermann, E., & Zubek, J. P. (1962). Effect of age on pain sensitivity. *Perceptual and Motor Skills*, *14*, 295–301.

Schonfeld, W. N. (1981). Pain: A verbal response. *Neuroscience and Biobehavioral Reviews*, *5*, 385–389.

Schumacher, G. A., Goodell, H., Hardy, J. D., & Wolff, H. G. (1940). Uniformity of the pain threshold in man. *Science*, *92*, 110–112.

Sherman, E. D., & Robillard, E. (1964). Sensitivity to pain in relationship to age. *Journal ofAmerican Geriatric Society*, *12*, 1037–1044.

Sherrington, C. S. (1989). *Man on his nature*. London: Penguin Books.

Sternbach, R. A. (1967). *Pain, a psychophysiological analysis*. New York: Academic Press.

Sternbach, R. A. (1976). Psychological factors in pain research and therapy. In J. J. Bonica & D. G. Albe-Fessard (Eds.), *Advances in pain research and therapy* (Vol. 1, pp. 293–299). New York: Raven Press.

Strong, G. A. (1895). The psychology of pain. *Psychology Review*, *2*, 329–347.

Suinn, R. M. (1977). Type A behavior pattern. In W. B. Redford & W. D. Gentry (Eds.), *Behavioral approaches to medical treatment* (pp. 55–59). Cambridge, MA: Ballinger.

Szasz, T. A. (1957). *Pain and pleasure: A study of bodily feelings*. New York: Basic Books.

Turk, D. C., Meichenbaum, D., & Genest, M. (1983). *Pain and behavioral medicine: A cognitive-behavioral perspective* (pp. 35–91). New York: Guilford Press.

Walters, A. (1961). Psychogenic regional pain alias hysterical pain. *Brain*, *84*, 1–18.

Weisenberg, M. (1975). *Pain: Clinical and experimental perspectives*. St. Louis: Mosby.

Weisenberg, M. (1977). Pain and pain control. *Psychological Bulletin*, *84*, 1008–1044.

Wolff, B. B. (1983). Laboratory methods of pain measurement. In R. Melzack (Ed.), *Pain measurement and assessment* (pp. 7–13). New York: Raven Press.

Woodrow, K. M., Friedman, G. D., Siegelaub, A. B., & Collen, M. F. (1972). Pain tolerance: Differences according to age, sex, and race. *Psychosomatic Medicine*, *34*, 548–556.

Wynn Parry, C. B. (1980). Pain in invulsion lesions of the brachial plexus. *Pain*, *9*, 41–53.

Zimbardo, P. G., Cohen, A. R., Weisenberg, M., Dworkin, L., & Firestone, I. (1966). Control of pain motivation by cognitive dissonance. *Science*, *151*, 217–219.

Zimmerman, M. (1979). Peripheral and central nervous mechanism of nociception pain and pain therapy: Fact and hypotheses. In J. J. Bonica, J. D. Liebeskind, & D. G. Albe-Fessard (Eds.), *Advances in pain research and therapy* (Vol. 3, pp. 3–32). New York: Raven Press.

Zoob, M. (1978). Differentiating the chest pain. *Geriatrics*, *33*, 95–101.

CHAPTER 3

Chronic Morbidity and Disability in the U.S. Elderly Populations

Recent Trends and Population Implications

KENNETH G. MANTON

INTRODUCTION: HEALTH CHANGES IN THE UNITED STATES

Mortality

In assessing temporal changes in the health and functioning of the elderly U.S. population, and the effects of those changes on the need to manage pain and its potential psychological and physical consequences (e.g., depression, loss of motivation to maintain physical and cognitive functioning, and nutritional maintenance) in the U.S. elderly (65+) and oldest-old (85+) populations, one has to be aware that the United States has been, and will continue to be, in a very dynamic and unique period of history relative to changes in health and mortality at late ages. For example, from 1960 to 1990, the U.S. annual stroke mortality rate (age-adjusted) dropped 65.2% (from 79.7 to 27.0 deaths per 100,000 persons per annum). At ages 85 and over, stroke mortality rates dropped 55.6% from 1960 to 1990—or from 3,680.5 to 1,633.9 deaths per 100,000 persons per annum.

For diseases of the heart, the U.S. decline from 1960 to 1990 was from 286.2 to 152.0 deaths per 100,000 persons per annum (age-adjusted), or 46.9%. For those aged 85 and over, the decline in heart disease mortality rates over the same period was much larger in absolute terms (from 9,317.8 to 6,739.3—or a reduction of 2,578.5 deaths per 100,000

KENNETH G. MANTON • Duke University, Center for Demographic Studies, Durham, North Carolina 27708-0408.

Handbook of Pain and Aging, edited by David I. Mostofsky and Jacob Lomranz. Plenum Press, New York, 1997.

persons per annum), though the relative decline was smaller—27.6%—than for the total U.S. population.

The decline in total mortality for the entire U.S. population 1960 to 1990 (age-adjusted) was 31.7%. For persons aged 85 and over, the relative decline in total mortality rates was less: 22.8%. Though the relative decline in rates for the total U.S. population, and for persons aged 75–84 in particular (31.3%), was larger than for the population aged 85 and over, the absolute decline in mortality rates at ages 85 and over was 4,530.1 deaths per 100,000 persons per year (vs. an absolute decline of 2,738.0 deaths per 100,000 persons per year at ages 75–84)—or a decline 65.4% larger in terms of absolute changes in the mortality rates at ages 75–84 relative to those at ages 85 and above. The standard reported reductions in U.S. mortality rates above age 85 are very likely underestimated over time because the U.S. oldest-old population is, on average, growing ever older (as we will discuss below), and mortality rates reported above age 85 are not typically age-standardized (e.g., National Center for Health Statistics—NCHS, 1992).

Though cause-specific, and total, mortality generally declined from 1960 to 1990, the mortality rates for some important causes of death increased. For example, total U.S. cancer mortality rates increased (age-adjusted) from 149.2 deaths per 100,000 persons per annum in 1960 to 203.2 deaths per 100,000 persons in 1990—or +36.2% (but from a smaller base rate than for heart disease mortality in 1960). Much of the cancer mortality increase was associated with cohort-specific smoking patterns and increases in specific types of cancer (e.g., male lung cancer mortality). At ages 85 and over, the U.S. cancer mortality rate increased from 1,450.0 deaths per 100,000 persons per year in 1960 to 1,752.9 deaths per 100,000 persons per year in 1990—or +20.9%. This increase, on both a relative or an absolute basis, is considerably smaller than the U.S. total, or circulatory-disease, mortality declines above age 85 from 1960 to 1990.

Since cancer is actually a very heterogeneous collection of diseases (e.g., some are of the lymphatic and hematopoietic tissues—leukemias, lymphoma, and multiple myeloma; others are solid tumors—pancreatic cancer, lung cancer, and bladder cancer; others are gender-related and hormonally dependent, such as female breast or male prostate cancer), the overall U.S. cancer mortality trends are thus composed of a wide variety of different trends (some increasing, some decreasing), with the proportional contribution of different tumor types to the total cancer mortality rate for a given year changing over time. U.S. stomach cancer mortality declined on a cohort-specific basis (Manton & Stallard, 1982). While some cancers have peak mortality risks in early (e.g., some leukemias) and middle (Hodgkin's disease) ages (see, e.g., Cook, Fellingham, & Doll 1969), certain types of cancer continue to increase in prevalence to very extreme ages. For males, prostate cancer mortality increases with age to extremely old ages (Manton, Wrigley, Cohen, & Woodbury, 1991b). At those advanced ages (e.g., 85+), the prevalence of prostate cancer as an associated cause of death becomes significant (e.g., about 70% more men over age 85 die with prostate cancer, but of another cause, than die with prostate cancer reported as the underlying cause of death). For females, breast cancer prevalence also increases to very extreme ages (e.g., 85 and over), with over 25% additional female deaths with breast cancer reported at death as an associated cause than with breast cancer reported as the underlying cause of death. Multiple myeloma, in contrast, increases to very advanced ages (e.g., up to ages 95 and over) for both males and females. The risk of multiple myeloma appears to be, in part, related to racial and ethnic factors, with a precursor immunological condition, monoclonal gammopathies of unknown significance (MGUS), reaching a prevalences of 15%–20% in Caucasians above age 90, while MGUS rates are considerably lower in Asian populations of the same age (e.g., Bowden, Crawford, Cohen, & Noyama, 1993; Radl, Sepers, Skvaril, Morrell, & Hijmans, 1975).

Though the increase of the U.S. overall cancer mortality rate (i.e., by 302.9 deaths per 100,000 persons per year) at ages 85 and above from 1950 to 1990 was much smaller than the total mortality decline at that age (i.e., 1,792.1 deaths per 100,000 persons per annum; the cancer increase was only 16.9% the size of the absolute decline in total mortality rates), the cancer trend in particular has important implications for pain management because the terminal stages of many types of cancer are often extremely painful and very difficult to manage. For example, because of the different areas of metastases in many late-stage cancers such as bone versus soft tissue, there may be multiple types of pain to deal with as well as a possibly comorbid clinically depressed state. Consequently, the pain management of late-stage and terminal cancer patients has been, and continues to be, in a rapid state of change and development. In particular, breast and prostate cancer, both being related to hormonal factors, have a propensity to metastasize to bone due to the existence of hormonal receptor sites in bone tissue. Multiple myeloma is itself a neoplasia of bone and bone marrow, so it, too, tends to affect both the bone matrix and the hematopoietic tissue and causes a type of pain difficult to manage with standard pain medications (possibly requiring some of the treatments also potentially useful for Paget's disease and osteoporosis, e.g., the biphosphonates like etidronate; or the newer pamidronate). In addition, as the late-stage survival for some tumor types increases (e.g., from breast cancer, or possibly certain types of ovarian cancer with the use of Taxol), the amount of time that pain has to be controlled for individual cancer patients will tend also to increase.

These large and rapid U.S. total and cause-specific mortality changes 1960 to 1990 (some of which, like stroke, actually started much earlier than 1960) have a number of major public health and therapeutic consequences. First, the very elderly population is rapidly increasing. This is not restricted to just those aged 85 and older. The U.S. centenarian population has been growing at about 7% per year since at least 1980 (Day, 1993; Kestenbaum, 1992) due to declines in total mortality between ages 80 and 100 (Vaupel & Jeune, 1994). Indeed, the problem of dealing with the health and functional problems of persons aged 100 years or more may be a relatively modern phenomenon. The first well-documented individual cases of centenarians occurred in about 1800 (Jeune, 1994; Thoms, 1873; Vaupel & Jeune, 1994). The first well-documented case of a 110-year-old individual did not occur until 1931 (in Britain). The first well-documented cases of a person surviving past age 120 occurred first in Japan in 1987 (a male) and, recently, again in France in 1995 [the latter person, a female, still living (age 122.0 as of February 1997), is perhaps an even better documented case of survival to age 120 than the 1987 report for the Japanese male].

Beyond the small numbers of cases of extremely old persons (e.g., 110+) that can currently be carefully documented, there is a large number of reports of even older persons in the United States, which—in contrast to Sweden, which has had relatively accurate population registration system since 1860 (Vaupel & Jeune, 1994)—simply can't yet be verified because of current U.S. data limitations. There are currently cases recorded in U.S. Social Security files of persons reaching age 126+, most without birth certificate evidence (the U.S. vital registration system was not completed until 1933, when Texas, the final state, entered the system), and there is a recent report of a Mexican-born woman, now living in California, with a birth certificate, claiming to be age 126 (Kautzky, 1995).

Survivors to these very advanced ages will be very difficult to verify in the United States until, with the passage of time, certain of the U.S. national statistical systems (i.e., vital registration, which was completed in 1993; Social Security, which started in 1936–1937; Medicare, which started in 1966–1967) have more fully matured. For example, there appears to be a large improvement in the quality of age reporting in U.S. mortality data beginning with the birth cohorts of 1872–1875—the first cohorts (mostly males because of employment criteria) entitled to Social Security benefits who were required to provide rigorous evidence of their age, and the number of months worked, before qualifying for benefits (Bayo & Faber, 1985; Manton & Stallard, 1997). Questions about U.S. data quality at late ages often arose in the past because analyses of persons aged 110 and over in the mid-1980s necessarily used data from cohorts born before 1870—mortality data where the quality of age reporting has been suspect. By 1995, over 120 years will have passed for persons who are members of the 1872–1875 birth cohorts, so that persons at very advanced ages in the United States (both males, who could be documented in early Social Security data, and females, who had much less work experience in the first eligible cohorts) will be more readily and reliably evaluated in the future.

Morbidity and Disability Changes: Causes and Links to Mortality Trends

A fundamental problem with the rapid growth of the very elderly U.S. population is that the maintenance of health and functioning at very late ages is currently relatively uncharted clinical (e.g., in terms of clinical trial documentation of treatment efficacy) and epidemiological (e.g., few longitudinal studies have significant samples of persons age 95 and over) territory. For example, by 2015, there are projected (in the 1993 U.S. Census Bureau middle series) to be 952 thousand persons aged 95 and over in the United States, with 231,000 persons projected to be over age 100 (Day, 1993). Perls (1994; Perls, Morris, Ooi, & Lipsitz, 1993) suggested that centenarians may be a relatively healthy group (e.g., healthier than those aged 80 on average) because they represent a very highly selected surviving subset of a birth cohort. The issue is how the declines in mortality from ages 80 to 100 that are necessary for larger proportions of a birth cohort to reach advanced ages (i.e., age 100+) will affect the distribution of health and functioning characteristics in the rapidly increasing numbers (and cohort proportions) of very elderly survivors (e.g., Campbell, Busby, & Robertson, 1993).

For example, a major cause of mortality (and disability) at late ages is stroke (i.e., cerebrovascular accidents; ICD, 9th revision, Codes 430–438). Declines in stroke are important in assessing health and functioning at late ages because of their significant effects on the need for institutionalization; the prevalence of (potentially severe) chronic, physical, and cognitive disabilities; and the contribution they may make to late age microinfarct and vascular dementia (Skoog, Nilsson, Palmertz, Andreasson, & Svanborg, 1993). Thus, with the long-term reductions in U.S. stroke mortality rates that have been, and are, occurring comes an increasing proportion of persons surviving stroke events, thereby increasing the size of the population disabled by stroke. Or is stroke being prevented from occurring, possibly due to more effective management of hypertension at younger ages since national hypertension control programs were begun in 1972–1973? What seems, at least in part, to be occurring in the United States is that the average severity of individual stroke events is declining (McGovern et al., 1993), while stroke rehabilitation techniques, likely to be more effective for less severe strokes, are also improving (Kalra, 1994).

A different situation is found in, for example, Japan, the country with the world's currently highest life expectancy at birth (i.e., at birth, male life expectancy was 76.2 years in 1992; 83.0 years for females—about 3 years higher than for both U.S. males and females in 1993). In the immediate postwar period (e.g., 1950), stroke (in particular, hemorrhagic stroke) was a more significant cause of death in Japan than heart disease (Ueda et al., 1988; Ueshimia et al., 1980). This occurred, in part, because of shortages of protein and fats in rural Japanese diets up to at least 1950 (Iso, Jacobs, Wentworth, Neaton, & Cohen, 1989; Ooneda et al., 1978; Tanaka et al., 1982). The type of stroke most manifest in Japan, hemorrhagic stroke, tended to be lethal and to strike in the middle ages (Tanaka et al., 1982). Since 1950, increasing protein and fat intake has helped reduce hemorrhagic stroke mortality at middle age in Japan—though stroke remains a major cause of death among the currently very elderly Japanese cohorts. Japan also has not dealt effectively with the problems of delivering long-term and rehabilitative care for stroke victims (Okamoto, 1992). Consequently, many elderly Japanese stroke patients remain in acute-care hospitals for stays often exceeding six months, rather than receiving specialized therapy and rehabilitation services, and community-based long term care services.

The declines for heart disease mortality are also interesting because they include some components, in particular congestive heart failure (CHF), that, in the United States continued to have increasing mortality rates to at least 1988 (Centers for Disease Control and Prevention, 1994). Ghali, Cooper, & Ford (1990) showed that (age-adjusted) hospitalization rates for CHF in the United States increased roughly 60% between 1973 and 1986. However, more recently, advances in pharmacotherapy (the introduction of ACE-II inhibitors in about 1980; Materson & Preston, 1994) have proved to be cost-effective in reducing hospitalization and disability due to CHF (Paul, Kuntz, Eagle, & Weinstein, 1994; Studies of Left Ventricular Investigators, 1991). As indications for the use of ACE-II inhibitors are changed (and likely to be extended) and they become more extensively used clinically (Materson & Preston, 1994), disability and mortality from CHF may decline—even to fairly advanced ages. This is of special interest in that CHF may be viewed as a "latter" stage in the natural history of coronary heart disease processes, where chronic coronary heart disease, which is either successfully treated when manifested as a heart attack (acute myocardial infarction) at earlier ages (Muhlbaier et al., 1992), or whose progression is slowed by various interventions at late ages (Ko et al., 1992), interacts with age-related physiological declines in cardiac function at advanced age (Kitzman & Edwards, 1990; Lakatta, 1985).

What is most critical in our overall assessment of U.S. health changes is to determine how the changes in the cause-specific and temporal dimensions of U.S. mortality patterns relate to changes in the natural history of those chronic disease processes which have most affected chronic disability prevalence—and what further changes in those diseases are most likely to occur in the future. This means one must be concerned with projecting not only overall U.S. life expectancy, but also the proportion of U.S. life expectancy remaining at a specific age that is expected to be spent in a relatively functionally intact state (so-called active life expectancy; Katz et al., 1983; Robine & Ritchie, 1991; Sullivan, 1971). This involves identifying the various internal and external forces responsible for the age-related changes of mortality, disability and morbidity (Manton & Soldo, 1985). In doing so, it is also important to recognize the greater heterogeneity of the U.S. population relative to most European countries and Japan. For example, while Japan was the country with the highest life expectancy at birth in 1992, there are subpopulations in the United States with far better health profiles (e.g., Asians and Pacific Islanders had, in 1993, a life expectancy at birth of 80.2 years for males and 86.3 years for females—Day, 1993; see Manton, Stallard, & Tolley, 1991a, for discussion of other long-lived U.S. groups) and far worse health profiles (e.g., certain minority groups). The forces forging past, current, and future health and functional changes in the various subgroups of the elderly and oldest-old U.S. population may be roughly divided into five groups for discussion purposes.

Long-Term Nutritional and Hygienic Changes. The first are long-term influences on the health and functioning of the elderly. Many of these changes are likely related to macrolevel nutrition and physical activity. For example, Fogel (1994) assessed the health of Civil War pensioners who had reached aged 65 by 1910 (and who were in the birth cohorts of about 1825–1844). Because of their earlier military service, Civil War pensioners had, at one time presumptively, to be in relatively good physical condition, and to have had their physical and health status assessed and confirmed by U.S. military doctors. When applying for pensions, these individuals had to be reassessed by what was, according to the standards of the time, thorough medical examinations (with errors of diagnostic omission likely to be greater than errors of overdiagnosis for chronic diseases). When the prevalence of chronic conditions in this group of elderly Civil War pensioners was compared to those in World War II veterans aged 65 in 1985–1988 interviewed in the National Health Interview Survey (NHIS), it was found that the prevalence of chronic disease had declined roughly 6% per decade over the 75 intervening years (i.e., 1910–1985). This outcome Fogel (1994) related to changes in early nutrition (i.e., calorie protein malnutrition either in the mother, affecting fetal growth and development, or in children and adolescents at critical phases of growth and development, or malnutrition during periods of exposure to specific infectious diseases) that may have subsequently affected the risk of multiple chronic diseases to relatively late ages.

Of particular interest is the fact that chronic heart problems were 2.9 times more prevalent at age 65 in 1910 than in those World War II veterans aged 65 in the 1985–1988 (NHIS). This suggests that the activity and nutritional factors affecting heart disease have improved over a long period of time—despite the writings of some authors (Dubos, 1965; Omran, 1971) who have suggested that economic development and modern industrial society would likely increase the risks of most chronic diseases. A reason for the failure of chronic disease risk increases to become manifest is possibly related to the second set of health issues discussed below (i.e., the effects of modern society and public health on water quality, food and social hygiene, and food storage). That is, while the first set of factors relate to endogenous energy and nutrient restrictions, and to their effects on the physiological development of the human organism with age, this second set of factors relates to the effects of societal mechanisms on the exposure of individuals to a wide, and possibly evolving, range of viral and bacterial pathogens whose long-term consequences may be manifested in chronic disease.

Viral and Bacteriological Exposures Affecting Chronic Disease. Other studies have identified long-term declines in chronic morbidity that were too early to be attributable to modern chronic disease therapy. Lanska and Mi (1993) examined U.S. stroke mortality trends and found that the declines occurring after 1925 could not be attributed to diagnostic artifact. Mozar, Bal, and Farag (1990) examined the hypothesis that atherosclerosis was a chronic low-grade infectious macroangiopathy aggravated by (i.e., interacting with) other risk factors such as hypercholesterolemia, hypertension, and smoking. The basis for this model of national health changes is that, through contamination of the food chain and water supply, pathogens such as Coxsackie virus B_x (which has been found in human infants with arterial fatty streaks), herpes simplex, and cytomegaly viruses, all of which were found to have the potential to physiologically affect the growth and function of smooth muscle cells in arterial endothelium, cardiovascular disease (CVD) risks were increased. They argued that the increases in CVD risks from 1910 to the mid-1960s were due to the increased consumption of meat (but with relatively small increases in saturated fat and cholesterol intake) which was affected (contaminated) by these pathogens. The recent rapid national declines (e.g., 1968 and beyond) observed in CVD and stroke mortality they attributed to thermal interventions in preparing foodstuffs. Specifically, commercial food processing, which regularly involved heating and canning, increased markedly in the post–World War II period, when economic conditions improved. In addition, regulation and legislation regarding the feeding of livestock (especially swine) were introduced in 1952, 1962, and 1980. As these mandated changes in food handling and production were introduced, it was argued, viral insults from contaminated foodstuffs became less prevalent, leading to the down turn of CVD risks in California in the 1950s (where some of these livestock interventions were introduced earlier) and in the United States as a whole in the late 1960s.

A related problem, not directly discussed by Mozar et al. (1990), is the chronic effects of such viral and bacterial insults on the myocardium. Different viruses can cause various types of cardiomyopathy, and in the past, bacterial agents involved in rheumatic heart disease caused significant damage to the myocardium—often specifically related to cardiac valvular functioning. It has been argued that rheumatic fever, a major problem in the United States in the past and in developing countries today, may reemerge in the U.S. as previously uncommon strains of Group A streptococci with increased virulence (and very likely greater antibiotic resistance) increase in prevalence (e.g., as apparently documented in specific U.S. populations 1984–1988—Kaplan & Keil, 1993). Additionally, it has been argued that there is a linkage of chronic *Chlamydia pneumoniae* infection with chronic heart disease and possibly with acute myocardial infarction, chronic bronchitis, and asthma (Linnanmäki et al., 1993; Thom et al., 1992).

Thus, various social, public health, and possibly early medical interventions that reduced the risks of rheumatic heart fever and other types of chronic viral or bacterial infections could have improved the health of more recent U.S. birth cohorts in terms of reducing the chronic effects of those pathogens—either by reducing their direct tissue involvement or by reducing chronic immunological stimulation by the pathogen, leading to antigen formation (e.g., Epstein-Barr virus can produce immortal clones of B cells) that subsequently damages the target tissue. Indeed, the chronic disease effects of viral and bacterial insults are an area of research just now beginning to be appreciated as new techniques for the study of their effects on DNA (e.g., polymerase chain replication—PCR) are being developed. A reason for the past difficulty in exploring this area is that it is often the autoantibody that is a response to the pathogen that ultimately causes the pathological changes (e.g., in rheumatoid arthritis). Thus, it may be that the pathogen itself is long gone from the organism by the time the disease process is grossly manifest, with only the antigenic product left as indirect evidence of the past infection. For example, carpine lentiviruses may have mutated into an agent capable of human infection 300–400 years ago and may have become the agent involved in rheumatoid arthritis (prior to that period, skeletons in British graveyards only showed osteoarthritic joint degeneration). Making the identification of such disease etiologies even more difficult is that there may have to exist a genetic predisposition in the organism to producing the damaging antigenic response. There is some evidence that it is the lack of these specific genetic predispositions that characterize centenarian populations (Mariotti et al., 1992; Takata, Suzuki, Ishii, Sekiguchi, & Iri, 1987).

We also find such chronic tissue involvement and joint degeneration due to the infectious agent in Lyme disease. Stomach cancer seems to be on the decline in the United States due to reduced exposure to a recently discovered bacterial agent, *Helicobacter pylori* (Forman, 1990). This agent has also been implicated in gastritis, gastric ulcers, and certain lymphomas, so that antibiotic treatment for the *H. pylori* infection frequently cure gastric ulcers (and possibly some early lymphomas; Fennerty, 1994; Hentschel et al., 1993; Hosking, 1994). Recently, a postpolio syndrome has begun to emerge in middle-aged persons (presumably due to late effects of the virus), and viral insults appear to be implicated in both a number of autoimmunological disorders (e.g., multiple sclerosis) and certain types of cancer. For example, Epstein-Barr virus, first implicated with Burkitt's lymphoma, has been associated with an increasing range of tumor types (especially in the nasopharyngeal and respiratory tracts; Niedobitek & Young, 1994).

Health Effects of SES Changes. A third set of factors involve sociopsychological factors and their physiological substrate related to changes in the education and socioeconomic status of elderly cohorts (Adler et al., 1994; Rodin, 1986a,b). Preston (1992) examined the average educational level of persons aged 85–89 from 1980 to 2015. He found that the proportion with less than 8 years of education in that age group declined rapidly from 65%–70% in 1980, to 10%–15% in 2015. A number of health factors and mortality are related to education and SES (Garrison, Gold, Wilson, & Kannel, 1993), with U.S. mortality SES differentials increasing 1960 to 1986 (Pappas, Queen, Hadden, & Fisher, 1993). For example, education was negatively associated with the incidence of Alzheimer's disease (Stern et al., 1994). Education may affect the rapidity with which lifestyle and nutritional changes are accepted by a population (Adler et al., 1994). For example, smoking tended to decline more rapidly in response to public education efforts in better-educated groups in Britain (Townsend, Roderick, & Cooper, 1994). More poorly educated groups tended to respond only to the increased costs of cigarettes and not to efforts at public education. In addition, recent declines in U.S. cholesterol levels have occurred more rapidly in the general U.S. population, and at ages 65–74, than envisioned in the National Cholesterol Education Program of 1988 (Johnson et al., 1993; Sempos et al., 1993).

Not only was compliance with medical therapy and lifestyle changes apparently better for those with higher education, but also early health-care access was likely to be better for more highly educated populations. For example, health insurance for persons under age 65 was held, in the United States, by 91.6% of persons with at least some college education. In contrast, of those with less than 12 years of education, only 79.6% had health insurance (U.S. Bureau of the Census, 1993). Thus, to the degree that health care access is restricted at early ages—and leads to chronic health problems later—there should be declines in chronic health problems for the very old population associated with the major educational changes expected above age 85 from 1980 to 2015 and with the increased coverage of those 65 and older by Medicare starting in 1966–1967.

A less recognized effect of education is perhaps its impact on coping skills at later ages once disability is manifest. For example, in the National Channeling demonstration program, elderly females who had few social and economic resources, but who were better educated, were better able to use the available services to cope with functional disability (Manton, Vertrees, & Clark, 1993c). In addition, it appears that persons who are better educated may also cope better psychologically with the pain and discomfort associated with disability—and to maintain functioning even with similar levels of joint and other physical problems (whether due to osteoarthritis or rheumatoid arthritis; Callahan, Bloch, & Pincus, 1992; Hannan, Anderson, Pincus, & Felson, 1992). Indeed, one of the difficulties in assessing functional impairment is the potential role that depression and "morale" play in the level of impairment accepted, or tolerated, by persons with specific types and intensities of physical functional limitations and pain (Dorevitch et al., 1992; Reuben, Siu, & Kimpau, 1992). Morale is also likely to be affected by the self-perception of the elderly person and the image that he or she has of what constitutes acceptable levels of functioning at a specific age—and his or her expectations about the ability for that pain to be eliminated or controlled by specific behavior changes, or by medical or surgical interventions (e.g., joint replacement surgery). What recent research has suggested, for example, is that resistance weight training and nutritional supplementation can improve mobility functions in even frail, very elderly (up to age 96) populations, where the initiation of the intervention in a previously impaired person may involve a considerable degree of discomfort (e.g., Fiatarone et al., 1990, 1993, 1994). Similar results for maintaining (or very likely regaining) physical activity have been found for cardiac functioning (Kasch, Boyer, VanCamp, Verity, & Wallace, 1993) and acute myocardial infarction (Lakka et al., 1994). A central point is that better-educated persons are more likely to be exposed to this type of information (i.e., on the likely plasticity of aging and on the effects of risk factors, activity, and nutrition on rates of aging) and to change or modify their self-perception of what constitutes an acceptable standard of health and functioning at a specific age. One of the crucial elements in such changes is the perception by a person of a given educational level of the degree to which pain is eliminated or controlled or is viewed as being capable of being eliminated or controlled—and how much that pain control, especially control of chronic pain, relates to the functioning of individuals.

Dysfunction as a Risk Factor. A fourth factor that is currently less well understood, or explicated, is that physical disability is itself a potent and basic risk for chronic disease and mortality (Manton, Stallard, Woodbury, & Dowd, 1994a). This has been less clearly identified in past epidemiological studies. That is, typically, variables such as smoking, high cholesterol, elevated blood glucose, high body mass index, forced expiratory volume, and hypertension have all been viewed as important chronic disease risk factors. However, disability has been found to be a major risk factor for stroke in the elderly—in both the short term (Colantonio, Kasl, & Ostfeld, 1992) and the long term (Shinton & Sagar, 1993). In addition, a number of classical risk factors are related to physical activity and fitness (Lakka et al., 1994). Thus, the exact temporal and age relation of traditional risk factors and functional limitations needs to be further explored to better isolate the causal nexuses (Manton et al., 1994a). For example, cognitive impairment has been linked to heart problems at late ages—possibly due to the degeneration of circulatory efficiency (e.g., due to the loss of tone in voluntary muscle as in the leg, and in overall vascular tone) and possibly the occurrence of small strokes (Aronson et al., 1990). The loss of circulatory and pulmonary efficiency (in addition to lipid and other biochemical changes) could be a direct consequence of reduced physical activity at late ages through a variety of direct and indirect (e.g., hormonal) channels (e.g., Drexler et al., 1992).

In addition, if disability is a major risk factor, there are many nonlethal but chronically disabling medical conditions that have lethal consequences due to the metabolic alterations attendant on reduced physical activity. For example, Alzheimer's disease often leads to death due to hypostatic pneumonia, and due to circulatory events due to general circulatory declines resulting from reductions in physical activity (Burns, Jocoby, Luthert, & Levy, 1990; Kukull et al., 1994). Vision impairment has been found, in both institutional populations (Marx, Werner, Cohen-Mansfield, & Feldman, 1992) and community populations (Salive et al., 1994) to engender a number of activities-of-daily-living (ADL) impairments, which may then lead to general circulatory and pulmonary declines. Degenerative joint diseases (including osteoarthritis) can produce loss of physical functioning that increases stroke and heart disease risks. This is more likely if the disease is associated with significant joint immobility and stiffness. The effects of osteoarthritis may interact with other risk factors, such as smoking (through its effects on circulatory efficiency), to raise mortality risks. Those impairments can lead to more rapid loss of cardiac function (Kasch et al., 1993), increased glucose intolerance, and metabolic declines in skeletal muscle capacity (Drexler et al., 1992). Such impairments have again been found to interact with education (Guralnik et al., 1993).

Another major disease potentially affected by inactivity is osteoporosis. Weight-bearing exercise, along with appropriate nutritional supplementation with calcium and physiologically active isomers of vitamin D [e.g., 1,25$(OH)_2D_3$, which functions as a steroid in modulating cell differentiation and in the production of gene products], may help slow the progression of osteoporosis (especially in osteoporosis Type II, i.e., disease occurring 20+ years after menopause which is strongly related to defects in the vitamin D endocrine system; Eastell et al., 1991) as may new therapies involving such new classes of drugs as salmon calcitonin, parathyroid hormone, or biphosphonates. An important issue specifically for females is whether osteoporosis interacts with atherosclerosis post-menopausally, that is, by increasing serum calcium levels so that existing atherosclerotic plaques become more rapidly calcified (Moon, Bandy, & Davison, 1992). The reduction in estrogen postmenopausally could accelerate this process also by altering blood lipid profiles and enhancing the individual's general risk profile (Beltchetz, 1994; Nabulsi et al., 1993; Stampfer et al., 1991).

Also important is that, as for heart disease, increasing survival has led to changes in the manifest natural history of the disease process (i.e., osteoporosis and derivative fractures) in the very old population. For hip fracture, an important disabling event in osteoporosis, the mean age at presentation increased in Britain from 67 years in 1944 to 79 years between 1989 and 1992—an increase of a quarter year in the man age at presentation per year (Keene, 1993). In addition to the higher mean age of presentation, the nature of the fracture had changed to extracapsular fractures, which have higher costs and morbidity and more extended periods of disability and requirements for pain management. This raises questions about one generally proposed strategy to reduce chronic disease prevalence and associated disability and pain. That is, because chronic disease incidence often increases roughly exponentially with age (so that the prevalence of disease roughly doubles in a fixed number of years, e.g., five years for hip fractures), if the onset of a disease were delayed by a fixed number of years, disease prevalence would be reduced by half (i.e., delaying the age at occurrence of hip fracture by five years on average would reduce its prevalence by half). Such a strategy may not be effective if (1) the nature of a disease changes with age, and (2) if prevention of nonlethal disability disease does, in a more extended natural history, have a significant impact on mortality (i.e., extending the age at onset of these "triggering" conditions would extend the length of life as well).

Another of the important interactions recently documented involving functioning as a risk factor, and nutrition, is that between functional disability and serum albumin levels (Corti, Guralnik, Salvie, & Sorkin, 1994), with relative mortality risks ranging from 7.5 for males to 12.5 for females when both functional ability and albumin are at low levels.

Medical Interventions. Finally, there are many interventions offered by the health care system for the elderly. These can include a wide range of activities such as immunization programs (e.g., pneumococcal and influenza vaccines), treatment programs, and physical therapy. These medical interventions are, in many cases, however, relatively recent developments (e.g., ACE-II inhibitors have been available for 12–15 years; Materson & Preston, 1994), often because of the relatively recent nature of longitudinal, multifactorial studies of the physiological basis of chronic disease and aging. For example, the Framingham Heart Study began in 1949–1950 and took 10–15 years to accumulate enough follow-up to initially identify significant CVD risk factors (with findings continuing to be made from the study population after more than 40 years). The Seven Country Studies began in 1960 (Keys, 1980). Similarly, specialized longitudinal studies of aging changes are relatively recent phenomena; for example, the First Duke Longitudinal Study of Aging began in about 1950 (formally extending to 1970, with mortality followed to 1987), and the second Duke Study started in 1968.

These studies mark the beginning points of such research. It has taken a considerable period of time for the results of those studies to become precisely defined and to suggest specific modes of intervention which are both effective and, especially for chronic diseases requiring chronic therapy, have benign side-effect profiles. For example, while the initial relation of total serum cholesterol to heart disease was found relatively quickly, it took a number of years (1) for the components of cholesterol to become unambiguously identified, with a "good" cholesterol (high-density lipoprotein) and a "bad" cholesterol (low-density lipoprotein) isolated (Gordon et al., 1989), and (2) for the temporal interactions of multiple risk factors to be more precisely defined (Brown, Zhao, Sacco, & Albers, 1993; Feskens, Bowles, & Kromhout, 1991, 1992). In aging studies, it took a while (1) to isolate distinct pathological processes (e.g., Alzheimer's disease and osteoporosis) as potentially treatable conditions from what had initially been viewed as a generalized process of senescence operating at a cellular level (Hayflick, 1965; Hayflick & Moorhead, 1961); (2) to find that those specific processes varied considerably across individuals in their age at manifestation and rates of progression (e.g., Lakatta, 1985); and (3) to discover that the underlying processes were plastic and could be effectively treated—or at least possibly managed—to extreme ages (i.e., beyond ages 75 or 85).

Once risk factors and disease processes can be identified and characterized, it takes time for public health and therapeutic interventions to evolve and then to be disseminated to the general population. The national programs on smoking cessation had their initial impetus in the 1962–1964 Surgeon General's reports (Harris, 1983). National hypertension control efforts began in 1972–1973, and national cholesterol control programs were begun in 1988. With time, the successive introduction of new public-health intervention programs has apparently produced national health impacts more rapidly—both because the scientific basis of recent programs is better defined and because the U.S. population has gradually became more health-conscious and aware of the possibility of health interventions to late ages.

Likewise, some therapies, like any complex technology, simply evolved and improved with time—with fewer side effects. Total mortality was not affected by the first antihypertensive agents (i.e., diuretics and, later, potassium-sparing diuretics) unless they were targeted to high-risk groups. However, there has been an evolution of antihypertensive agents. The second generation of antihypertensives were beta blockers; the third generation were calcium channel blockers (e.g., verapamil). It was not until the fourth generation, the angiotensin-converting enzyme-II inhibitors (e.g., captopril and lisinopril) that very specific physiological mechanisms were targeted that could produce benefits at several levels (Materson & Preston, 1994). For example, ACE-II inhibitors can apparently cause partial remodeling of myocytes in the left ventricle (Pouleur et al., 1993) and may reduce the tendency toward atherosclerotic changes (by influencing smooth muscle cell growth in arterial endothelium) as well as affect glucose tolerance (Pollare, Lithell, & Berne, 1989) and possibly increase beta-receptor density in the myocardium in those with congestive heart failure (CHF) (Gilbert et al., 1993). Such evolution of the applications of specific agents has even occurred for historically well-known drugs. For example, the full benefits and uses of aspirin in preventing thromboses in persons who had a first heart attack were not identified until relatively recently (i.e., in the 1970s and 1980s; Mueller & Scheidt, 1994). Immunization programs (for pneumococcal pneumonia and influenza) are also relatively recent innovations for the elderly—and especially through the Medicare program (e.g., Butler et al., 1993; McBean, Babish, & Prihoda, 1991). Demonstrations have attempted to determine if such immunization programs can be stimulated under Medicare in either a physician or an institutional care setting (Mayer et al., 1994). It has been estimated that immunizations for influenza and pneumococcal and hepatitis B infections could eliminate 50,000–70,000 adults deaths per year in the United States (Fedson, 1994).

One of the possible limitations of immunization programs is whether persons of extreme age (e.g., over age 85) can mount a satisfactory response to an immunological stimulus (Gravenstein et al., 1994). This raises the issue of whether supplemental nutrition (especially supplementation of specific micronutrients) should be viewed as part of the medical intervention at advanced ages. For example, Beregi, Regius, and Rajczy (1991) have shown that mucosal immunity can be improved by the ingestion of specific antioxidant vitamins. Chandra (1992) found that supplementation with antioxidant vitamins could reduce the risk of infections in elderly persons. Some dementias have been associated with low vitamin B_{12} levels (Martin, Francis, Protetch, & Hoff, 1992; Pennypacker et al., 1992) and possibly other antioxidants (Zaman et al., 1992). The role of vitamin D, on the other hand, is complex, both low (osteomalacia) and high (osteoporosis) levels being associated with certain types of degenerative bone diseases and possibly affecting the interaction of osteoporosis and atherosclerosis (Moon et al., 1992). In the latter case, supplementation of foodstuffs with vitamin D may not have been a totally benign intervention. Moon et al. (1992) suggested that increases in CVD up to the mid-1960s may temporally track with U.S. and Canadian efforts to supplement foodstuffs with vitamin D. Vitamin E has been found to have benefits for coronary heart disease and in glucose metabolism (Paolisso, D'Amore, Giugliano, Ceriello, & Varricchio, 1993). Specific isomers (alpha tocopherol succinate) of vitamin E have been found to have better cellular redifferentiating properties than those of retinoic acid (Prasad & Edwards-Prasad, 1992). Recently, the specific genetic mechanisms affected by retinoic acid have been identified (i.e., retinoic acid receptor B; Lotan et al., 1995). Extending beyond the effects of antioxidants, and of cellular redifferentiating agents, are efforts to intervene directly in the genetic basis of specific diseases (e.g., in hypercholesteremia) by using various viral vectors to induce specific genetic changes.

In terms of treatment programs, a number of surgical (Hosking, Warner, Lodbell, Offord, & Melton, 1989; Ko et al., 1992) and medical treatments have been found to be effective at later ages. Of perhaps most importance is the development of specialized geriatric evaluation units (Rubenstein & Josephson, 1989; Wieland, Rubenstein, Hedrick, Reuben, & Buchner, 1994) where specialized diagnostic procedures are used to correct diagnoses and to identify the prevalence of multiple comorbidities often found at advanced ages (McCormick et al., 1994). One of the major areas of advance, discussed elsewhere in this volume, are methods of controlling different types, and consequences, of pain. For example, modalities for handling cancer pain have improved with the efficacy of different agents for different types of pain (e.g., nonsteroidal anti-inflammatory drugs for bone metastases) now being better characterized.

A final area of change in the medical system has to do with recent modifications of the U.S. Medicare program—in particular, declines in acute-care hospital services, large increases in outpatient service use, and extremely large recent increases in the use of the Medicare Home Health and Skilled Nursing Facility benefit. These changes began with the introduction of the Medicare Prospective Payment System, which established case-mix-based reimbursements for acute hospital stays beginning in 1982–1983 and being phased in through 1987. This tended to reduce both the length of hospital stays and the rates of hospitalization—at least relatively early in the program. It was expected that the use of home health agencies (HHAs) and skilled nursing facilities (SNFs) might compensate for the shorter stays for persons with chronic conditions. However, regulation of Medicare payments for home health agencies, after having the limits on the number of home health visits reimbursed eliminated in 1980, were tightened in the period starting in 1982, with HHA reimbursement denial rates peaking in 1986–1987. In 1987, litigation was settled on the definition of intermittent care (i.e., *Duggan v. Bowen*, 1987), which led to the promulgation of new regulations by June 1989. The number of home health agency visits reimbursed by Medicare in 1989 was 42 million; in 1990, it was 70 million (+66.75%); in 1991, it was 98 million (+40%) and has been increasing at about 20% per year since. This pace would cause home health care costs to be about 10% of Medicare reimbursements by the year 2000. In 1988, the Medicare Catastrophic Care Act (MCCA) was passed. Though it was repealed in 1989, it stimulated the nursing-home industry to invest in staff and construction so that 1,624 new Medicare SNFs were licensed, containing about 75,000 new beds—many in underserved areas. Thus, from 1988 to 1989, due to the stimulus of the MCCA, SNF Medicare costs increased almost fivefold, to about $2.8 billion. SNF expenses have also continued to increase. The growth of home health and SNF services could allow for alternate modalities and venues for the delivery of chronic pain management and therapies.

DATA

To explore these recent mortality, morbidity, and disability changes in more specific terms, we will examine the 1982, 1984, and 1989 National Long Term Care Surveys (NLTCSs). These surveys were designed to represent the entire U.S. Medicare-eligible population aged 65 and above—on both a cross-national and a longitudinal basis. In the

NLTCS, a two-stage sampling procedure was used to identify chronically (90 days+) disabled populations who would receive more detailed interviewing and assessment than persons identified as nondisabled in the first, or screening, stage. There were a total of 16,485 responses of chronically disabled community residents to the three surveys, and an additional 5,000 institutional residents were identified in the three years (institutional surveys were done in 1984 and 1989). The samples were drawn from Medicare eligibility rolls, so that all persons in the sample could be continuously tracked for mortality and Medicare Part A and B service use through Medicare data systems over the full 9.5 years of follow-up. Response rates were high in all three years—on the order of 95%. The same base health and functional items were asked in all three years, so there should be relatively few effects on estimates of national changes in disability due to instrument content. In addition, proxy rules and other field procedures use methods (e.g., institutional definitions) that were held constant in all three NLTCSs. The interview intervention, after five years, should have relatively little effect on response behavior—as might shorter (e.g., 1- or 2-year) interview periods. Special longitudinal sample weights were prepared so that the U.S. population over age 65 at each interview time, and its changes between interviews, is appropriately represented.

Though, in the NLTCS instrument, there are only a few direct measures of pain, the medical conditions and functional impairments reported by the U.S. elderly disabled population can be used to describe the distribution of health problems in the U.S. population—specific components of which can be linked to probable problems with different types of pain (e.g., cancer with acute, severe pain and joint disease with different degrees of chronic pain). It is necessary to be aware, in making such condition–pain linkages, that pain often has a subjective dimension which may be highly variable over individuals, and that there are different (and possibly multiple) types of pain that will be manifested. That is, the consequences of certain types of acute pain in cancer patients (e.g., discomfort due to liver ascites) will differ from chronic pain manifested in populations with chronic musculoskeletal problems. One must also differentiate between the direct effects of pain (e.g., limiting physical activity by causing joint immobilization) from indirect effects (e.g., the effects of chronic pain on deep sleep patterns, potentially leading to the expression of depressive symptomatology). The necessary interventions for each of those types of pain may be quite different (e.g., the use of anti-depressants in persons with joint and skeletal pain).

ANALYSIS

Changes 1982–1989 in ADL Functioning

In the first set of analyses, we examined changes in the simple weighted prevalence of chronic disability and institutionalization between 1982 and 1989. National changes in the disability prevalence distribution, specific to intensity level, is shown in Table 3-1 for both activities of daily living (ADLs; Katz & Akpom, 1976) and instrumental activities of daily living (IADLs; Lawton & Brody, 1969). Institutionalization included persons both in nursing homes and in other chronic care institutions providing health services in

Table 3-1. Chronic Disability Prevalence Rates for the Total U.S. Elderly Population, from the 1982 and 1989 NLTCS

Disability level	1980 disability distribution based on 1982 rates applied to 1989 age and sex-specific population	1989 rates and population (in '000's)	1982—1989 change (%)
IADLs only (%)	5.4[a]	4.4	−1.0
N	1,667[b]	1,360	
1–2 ADLS (%)	6.6	6.5	−0.1
N	2,037	1,993	
3–4 ADLS (%)	2.8	3.5	0.7
N	864	1,079	
5–6 ADLS (%)	3.6	2.7	−0.9
N	1,111	833	
Institutional (%)	6.1	5.5	−0.6
N	1,883	1,685	
Disabled (%)	24.5	22.6	−1.9

[a]1982 rate standardized to 1989 age and sex distribution.
[b]1989 population estimated using the 1982 age and sex standardized rates.

all three years. We included institutionalization in the disability distribution so that temporal changes in chronic disability prevalence could not be an artifact of the changing rates (and types) of institutionalization over the study period.

We see that, of the five discrete disability levels presented, only those with 3 to 4 ADLs impaired increased in prevalence from 1982 to 1989 (Manton, Corder, & Stallard, 1993b). Overall, there was a 1.9 percentage-point decrease (age-standardized) in chronic disability and institutionalization prevalence by 1989 (i.e., a relative decline in prevalence of 8.1%). This translates into 612,000 fewer chronically disabled and institutionalized persons 65+ in 1989 than would be expected if the 1982 chronic disability and institutionalization rates had not declined—or over 650,000 fewer disabled persons in 1995 if rates and age structure were held constant. For the severely disabled (i.e., persons with 5 or more ADLs chronically impaired or institutionalized; institutionalized persons in 1984 and 1989 reported an average of 4.8 ADL impairments), who are more likely to have serious problems with pain management, there was a decline in population prevalence from 9.7% to 8.2% in 1989—or a decline of 1.5 percentage points or 476,000 persons—a relative decline of 15.5% in the most severely disabled portion of the elderly population. Declines in chronic disability prevalence were noted at all ages and were relatively higher at late ages (i.e., above age 85). There were strong differences in disability prevalence by education level (Manton & Stallard, 1995), and among persons chronically disabled in 1989, there was more use of special equipment and housing than in 1982 (Manton, Corder, & Stallard, 1993a).

Changes in Morbidity

In Table 3-2, we present the proportion of the U.S. elderly population in 1982 (age and sex standardized to the 1989 population distribution) and 1989 (observed), reporting each of 16 medical conditions or symptoms and the sum of those proportions (Manton et al., 1995).

From 1982 to 1989, the average number of the 16 medical conditions reported by the U.S. noninstitutionalized population 65+ declined 11.2%—from 2.58 to 2.29 conditions. The largest declines were in arthritis and joint problems (a decline of 8%), hypertension (a decline of 6.5%), arteriosclerosis (a decline of 6.5%), and circulatory disease (a decline of 10%). Bronchitis and other heart problems (which contain congestive heart failure as a component) showed the largest increases.

Thus, the condition-specific declines 1982–1989 were generally consistent with the long-term U.S. mortality rate reductions for circulatory disease and stroke. The most prevalent conditions, arthritis and other joint problems, are likely to be highly variable in severity: they are a frequent cause of disability in the community population, with the disabled subpopulation also generally reporting joint problems. In the elderly impaired group, it is a question of interest whether the joint problems are a consequence, or a cause, of functional limitations and other health changes. It also seems likely that, for this group of health problems (i.e., related to muscoskeletal disorders), pain is a major determinant of many the health consequences generated.

Table 3-2. Total U.S. Noninstitutional Elderly Population: Morbidity Prevalence (in Percentages), 1982 and 1989 NLTCS

	1982	1989	
Condition	Age, sex, and disability standardized to the 1989 population distribution (%)	Observed (%)	Difference of 1982 standardized and 1989 observed proportion (%)
1. Arthritis	71.1	63.1	−8.0*
2. Parkinson's	0.8	1.3	0.5*
3. Diabetes	11.4	12.4	1.0
4. Cancer	6.5	5.7	−0.8
5. Arteriosclerosis	21.4	14.9	−6.5*
6. Dementia	2.9	1.7	−1.2*
7. Heart attack	3.8	3.2	−0.7
8. Other heart	20.2	22.9	2.7*
9. Hypertension	46.0	39.5	−6.5*
10. Stroke	3.4	2.6	−0.9*
11. Circulation	42.1	32.1	−10.0*
12. Pneumonia	2.9	4.8	1.8*
13. Bronchitis	9.8	12.1	2.2*
14. Emphysema	8.9	6.4	−2.4*
15. Asthma	6.7	6.3	−0.4
16. Broken hip/fractures	0.5	0.9	0.4*
Average number of conditions	2.58	2.29	−11.2*

*Significant at .05 level.

Definition of Multivariate Status Functional Profiles

One of the problems with using the discrete measures of functional impairment (and morbidity) presented above to measure national changes in disability or morbidity among the very elderly is that they do not reflect the multiplicity of conditions or disabilities affecting a person at a given age—nor their intensity of impairment or illness (e.g., McCormick et al., 1994). This is especially important at late ages (e.g., ages 85+), when most persons can be expected to manifest some degree of impairment—even though they may maintain enough functioning to remain socially autonomous and resident in the community.

To describe this intensity factor, and to isolate specific dimensions of impairment, we took 27 measures of functional impairment reported in the 1982, 1984, and 1989 NLTCSs and subjected them to multivariate analyses in order to analytically identify K multivariate profiles of functional problems. The was done using the grade-of-membership (GoM; Manton, Woodbury, & Tolley, 1994b) analysis, where the probability of 1 of the 27 disabilities' (i.e., for the lth response to the jth trait for persons i; $y_{ijl} = 1.0$) occurring is predicted by two types of coefficients. One describes the likelihood or probability (λ_{kjl}) that a person exactly like one of the basic types or profiles has a given impairment. The second describes the degree (g_{ik}; where $\Sigma\, g_{ik} = 1.0$ and $0.0 \leqslant g_{ik} \leqslant 1.0$) to which a given individual is affected by the problems associated with a given profile. The constraints on the g_{ik} mean that the properties exhibited by each person are additively decomposed by the model's parameters.

The basic relation of parameters to data elements can be expressed as (Manton et al., 1994b; Woodbury, Manton, & Tolley, 1994)

$$\text{Prob}(y_{ijl} = 1.0) = \sum_k g_{ik} \cdot \lambda_{jkl}$$

The λ_{kjl}'s estimated from the 16,485 community responses to the 1982, 1989, and 1989 NLTCSs are described in Table 3-3. In this study population, there were no institutional respondents. Among the 16,485 community respondents there were persons with little impairment or, because they had had impairment (say, in 1982) that improved (e.g., in 1989) currently had no impairments. Of the six types of disabilities found necessary (using a likelihood ratio χ^2 to select the correct value of K) to explain the variation of the 27 items reported by NLTCS community respondents in the three years, Types 1 and 2 are both relatively healthy. Type 2 ("Healthy") had almost no impairments, whereas Type 1 ("Unimpaired") had a few physical impairments (i.e., difficulty climbing stairs or difficulty holding a 10 lb. package, but no ADL or IADL chronic impairments as used to define prevalence in Table 3-1). Type 3 (IADL and physically impaired) manifested 11.57 of 27 impairments on average (42.9%). These had to do with both IADL impairments and significant difficulties in performing specific physical tasks. Type 4 (IADL and cognitively impaired) had slightly more impairment (12.8 of 27.0 impaired, or 47.4%), with more IADL problems, including tasks (money management, taking medication, and phoning) implying early cognitive deficits. This is also suggested by Type 4's having fewer physical problems than Type 3. Type 5 (ADL impaired) had fewer total functions impaired than either Types 3 or 4, but more ADL impairments. The primary physical

Table 3-3. λ_{kjl}'s Describing Six Disability Profiles Necessary to Describe 27 Functional Items for 16,485 Respondents to the 1982, 1984, and 1989 NLTCS

	Frequency	1 Unimpaired	2 Healthy	3 IADL and physically impaired	4 IADL and cognitively impaired	5 ADL impaired	6 Frail
Needs help with:							
Eating	7.0	0.0	0.0	0.0	0.0	0.0	55.2
Getting in/out bed	26.2	0.0	0.0	0.0	0.0	75.4	100.0
Getting about outside	39.9	0.0	0.0	0.0	0.0	100.0	100.0
Dressing	19.4	0.0	0.0	0.0	0.0	0.0	100.0
Bathing	43.1	0.0	0.0	0.0	0.0	100.0	100.0
Using Toilet	21.7	0.0	0.0	0.0	0.0	49.9	100.0
Bed-fast	0.8	0.0	0.0	0.0	0.0	0.0	5.6
No inside activity	1.5	0.0	0.0	0.0	0.0	0.0	10.2
Wheelchair-fast	7.0	0.0	0.0	0.0	0.0	19.9	25.8
Heavy work	71.9	100.0	14.5	100.0	100.0	100.0	100.0
Light work	22.6	0.0	0.0	0.0	35.6	0.0	100.0
Laundry	41.5	0.0	0.0	100.0	100.0	36.4	100.0
Cooking	29.8	0.0	0.0	0.0	100.0	0.0	100.0
Grocery Shopping	56.9	0.0	0.0	100.0	100.0	100.0	100.0
Getting about outside	59.1	0.0	0.0	100.0	61.9	100.0	100.0
Traveling	52.9	0.0	0.0	100.0	100.0	100.0	80.3
Managing money	26.8	0.0	0.0	0.0	100.0	0.0	100.0
Taking medicine	23.5	0.0	0.0	0.0	100.0	0.0	100.0
Telephoning	16.0	0.0	0.0	0.0	87.3	0.0	85.5
Difficulty							
Climbing one flight stairs							
No, some	47.6	33.8	100.0	0.0	88.5	0.0	0.0
Very, cannot	52.4	66.2	0.0	100.0	11.5	100.0	100.0
Bending for socks							
No, some	71.4	100.0	100.0	0.0	100.0	100.0	0.0
Very, cannot	28.6	0.0	0.0	100.0	0.0	0.0	100.0
Holding 10-lb pkg.							
No, some	47.7	38.9	100.0	0.0	58.6	24.9	0.0
Very, cannot	52.3	61.1	0.0	100.0	41.4	75.1	100.0
Reaching over head							
No, some	77.3	100.0	100.0	0.0	100.0	100.0	34.3
Very, cannot	22.7	0.0	0.0	100.0	0.0	0.0	65.7
Combing hair							
No, some	87.6	100.0	100.0	42.8	100.0	100.0	33.7
Very, cannot	12.4	0.0	0.0	57.2	0.0	0.0	66.3
Washing hair							
No, some	70.6	100.0	100.0	0.0	100.0	100.0	0.0
Very, cannot	29.5	0.0	0.0	100.0	0.0	0.0	100.0
Grasping for sm. objects							
No, some	86.3	100.0	100.0	0.0	100.0	100.0	58.9
Very, cannot	13.7	0.0	0.0	100.0	0.0	0.0	41.1
Can't read newspaper	25.7	0.0	0.0	0.0	100.0	0.0	54.6
Number of impairments		2.3	0.2	11.6	12.8	9.6	21.8
Percentage of 27		8.4	0.5	42.9	47.4	35.4	80.8

problems for this group seemed to be mobility limitations. The sixth group ("Frail") was by far the most impaired, with 80.8% of all activities being limited. To help in the discussion below, we developed simple, summary labels for each group that are used in each of the table headings.

Relation of Morbidity to Functional Profiles

To help interpret the six disability profiles defined above for community residents, it is useful to examine their relation to the 29 medical conditions and symptoms that NLTCS respondents reported. The coefficients for the 29 medical conditions or symptoms which relate them to the six profiles of functional limitations are presented in Table 3-4.

In Table 3-4, we underlined those probabilities (λ_{kjl}) that are greater than the marginal frequency for the total community sample. These probabilities were estimated with the coefficients for the functional measures in Table 3-3 held fixed in an ancillary estimation step (Manton et al., 1994b).

There was a greater chance of having fair health in Type 1 and good to excellent health in Type 2 than in the general sample of NLTCS community respondents. Type 1 had a higher-then-expected likelihood of cardiopulmonary problems and symptoms, while Type 2 had lower-than-expected frequencies of almost all conditions. Type 1 tended to be younger (as did Type 2), but with a higher proportion reporting joint problems and some associated stiffness. Thus, though Type 2 may have manifested pain due to their joint problems, they reported few functional limitations resulting from that limitation and the associated discomfort. This might possibly be due to more effective pain management of severe joint problems—or to improved physical therapy for such persons.

Type 3, the IADL and physically impaired, consistent with their physical problems, had a large proportion with arthritis and a higher proportion (50.8%) with permanent stiffness than Type 1 (33.8%). They also had higher risks of cardiopulmonary problems than Type 1—especially of pneumonia, other pulmonary conditions, and heart disease (especially heart attack and other heart problems). Type 4, with average physical health, had a lot of glaucoma (they also had the most trouble reading newspapers) and problems with dementia—as inferred from the three IADL problems involving cognitive impairments in Table 3-3. For example, 26.9% reported dementia problems in Table 3-4. These problems may have been related to the relatively extreme age (mean of 84.6 years) of this subpopulation. Type 5 (with ADLs impaired) was relatively average in terms of health except for having more hip and other fractures—possibly associated with a high proportion of females, osteoporosis, and a relatively advanced mean age. Type 6 (the frail) had, by far, the worst health, including the most cancer (11.0%), dementia (34.1%), and stroke (24.9%).

The morbidity patterns generally correlated with age and sex. The first two types were relatively young. The third type was generally female and also relatively young. The fourth type with moderate dementia, was elderly (84.6 years mean age) and mixed in gender. Types 5 and 6 were elderly (80.2 and 81.2), and Type 5 was more female. Thus,

Table 3-4. λ_{kjl}'s Indicating the Relation of 29 Medical Conditions to Six Disability Profiles for the 16,485 NLTCS Respondents

	Frequency	1 Unimpaired	2 Healthy	3 IADL and physically impaired	4 IADL and cognitively impaired	5 ADL impaired	6 Frail
Subjective healing							
Excellent	13.3	1.1	27.6	0.1	12.4	12.7	3.4
Good	32.2	18.1	49.5	2.3	36.8	41.6	13.3
Fair	33.4	62.7	21.7	40.2	35.3	37.8	20.3
Poor	21.1	18.1	1.2	57.4	15.4	8.0	63.0
Rheumatism arthritis	72.8	97.8	63.0	98.9	44.2	81.6	65.7
Paralysis	8.5	4.8	1.3	6.2	0.0	10.5	34.9
Permanent stiffness	23.4	33.8	11.6	50.8	8.7	25.0	33.6
Multiple sclerosis	0.6	0.6	0.1	0.6	0.0	1.4	1.4
Cerebral palsy	0.4	0.0	0.1	0.8	0.3	0.3	1.0
Epilepsy	0.8	0.3	0.5	1.5	0.8	0.1	2.3
Parkinson's disease	2.8	4.1	0.9	0.8	2.9	1.0	9.4
Glaucoma	9.2	7.6	5.4	5.0	26.2	5.7	12.3
Diabetes	16.3	20.1	9.5	24.3	17.6	16.1	23.1
Cancer	6.0	5.4	5.2	6.2	4.9	4.1	11.0
Constipation	30.8	39.4	16.6	58.9	29.3	25.7	44.4
Insomnia	39.3	61.2	25.8	85.0	26.4	29.4	41.6
Headache	16.6	31.4	7.8	51.1	15.2	4.0	17.8
Obesity	23.6	37.2	24.5	40.9	0.2	29.8	11.8
Arteriosclerosis	27.8	33.4	13.5	38.5	42.3	17.5	48.8
Mental retardation	1.4	0.0	0.0	0.0	5.6	0.1	4.9
Dementia	7.8	0.3	0.5	0.0	26.9	0.5	34.1
Heart attack	5.8	7.7	2.2	16.1	6.3	4.3	7.5
Other heart problem	29.3	48.2	17.3	60.2	26.4	20.0	32.8
Hypertension	45.6	61.6	38.0	72.3	30.3	48.3	40.8
Stroke	6.6	4.5	1.4	3.5	6.6	4.2	24.9
Circulation trouble	50.2	74.1	27.8	88.7	38.5	46.8	66.4
Pneumonia	5.8	7.4	2.6	11.0	5.9	3.6	10.8
Bronchitis	13.6	25.3	9.3	34.7	7.7	5.8	13.3
Flu	17.8	31.1	14.4	32.3	12.6	12.1	15.2
Emphysema	9.7	14.3	6.9	19.5	9.5	5.1	11.2
Asthma	7.3	13.9	5.1	22.1	2.7	3.1	5.5
Broken hip	2.1	0.6	0.3	0.0	0.0	7.4	4.8
Other broken bone	5.2	5.2	3.1	8.8	0.0	8.9	7.8
Mean age		73.5	75.2	75.5	84.6	80.2	81.2
Female	65.5	78.1	51.3	100.0	53.4	81.6	57.8

the linkage of disability profiles with morbidity helps distinguish the health dimensions they are associated with, for example, the extreme differences of the two IADL impaired Type 3 (a group with serious cardiopulmonary problems, but relatively young) and Type 4 (a very elderly group with dementia and vision problems).

Projection of Future Changes in the Chronically Disabled Population

The patterns identified in Tables 3-3 and 3-4 are of interest for their description of the U.S. elderly population and the profiles of disability manifested from 1982 to 1989. However, they are also important in ascertaining what those patterns imply for future changes in health and functioning. We conducted projections using the six types described in Table 3-3 to the year 2045, assuming that the population was of "high" education (i.e., we constructed disability profiles solely for the high-education group, those with eight or more years of schooling). This produces a better population distribution of disability problems, but with more persons surviving to extreme ages. Use of the high-education group in the projections is consistent with, in 2015, only 10%–15% of those aged 85–89 having less than eight years of education. In order to make the projections represent the total U.S. population aged 65 and over, we also added a seventh group to represent the institutionalized population.

A preliminary step in making the projections was to estimate two types of equations from the g_{ik}'s for the roughly 21,500 respondents (16,485 community + 5,000 institutional) and the dates of death of roughly 12,000 persons from Medicare mortality files. The first equation describes how each of the g_{ik}'s change over time and age. The second relates the current values of the g_{ik}'s to the age-dependent risk of death in a selected time interval. From these two sets of equations, we can calculate life table functions that depend on functional status changes by doing iterative computations where (1) first, we use the dynamic coefficients, over a time interval, to describe how the distribution of individual disability profiles change, and then (2) we apply disability- and age-specific mortality coefficients, systematically decrementing the change in the gender- and age-specific distribution of health and functioning in the population for age, gender, and disability-specific mortality selection.

In Table 3-5, we present the proportions projected in each of seven groups for different age categories for the years 1995, 2010, 2025, and 2040. In addition to the six community types, we also present the seventh, institutional, category in the projection. We summed the results for males and females to keep Table 3-5 small.

In the projection, the total U.S. population aged 65 years and older grows from 32.8 to 73.3 million between 1995 and 2040. The population aged 85 and above grows from 3.6 to 15.5 million (i.e., by a factor of 4.3), and the 95+ population grows from 347,000 to 3.2 million (i.e., by a factor of 9.2—or over twice as fast as the 85+ population). The growth of the over-65 population is greater than in the 1989 Census Bureau projections. In the 1993 census projections, the number expected to survive to age 65 and above was actually larger than the projections in Table 3-5. However, there is greater growth of the over-85 population than in the Census Bureau middle series to 2040 (Day, 1993).

As a consequence of the aging of the U.S. population aged 65 and above from 1995 to 2040, the proportion who are healthy should decline, as it does in the projections from 85.9% (i.e., the sum of the first two profiles) in 1995 to 80.9% in 2045. The Census Bureau projections do not utilize information on health or disability. On an age-specific basis, the changes in function are smaller (e.g., for those 95 and over, the two healthy groups decline from 40.1% to 38.6%, reflecting aging of the population even above age 95). The decline in the healthy group at ages 65 and above is 5.8%; at ages 95 and above, it is 3.7%. This is due to the higher mortality for the more disabled profiles (i.e., Types 5 and 6) at late ages. A group that grows significantly over 1995 to 2045 are those in institutions (i.e., over age 65, it grows from 5.7% in 1995 to 9.0% in 2040). The risk of institutionalization (which manifests an average of 4.8 ADLs impaired) varies strongly

Table 3-5. Projections (in '000s) of U.S. Elderly Population Stratified by Functional Types and Age, 1995, 2010, 2025, and 2045

	1	2	3	4	5	6	7	
	Unimpaired	Healthy	IADL and physically impaired	IADL and cognitively impaired	ADL impaired	Frail	Institution-alized	Total age-specific population
				1995				
65+	25,229	2,981	425	422	1,086	803	1,887	32,834
	(76.8%)	(9.1%)	(1.3%)	(1.3%)	(3.3%)	(2.4%)	(5.7%)	
85+	1,636	434	86	112	287	226	857	3,639
	(45.0%)	(11.9%)	(2.4%)	(3.1%)	(7.9%)	(6.2%)	(23.6%)	
95+	111	28	6	9	37	27	129	347
	(32.1%)	(8.0%)	(1.7%)	(2.7%)	(10.7%)	(7.7%)	(37.1%)	
				2010				
65+	31,950	4,043	618	649	1,678	1,268	3,566	43,772
	(73.0%)	(9.2%)	(1.4%)	(1.5%)	(3.8%)	(2.9%)	(8.1%)	
85+	3,612	945	195	258	675	544	2,215	8,444
	(42.8%)	(11.2%)	(2.3%)	(3.0%)	(8.0%)	(6.4%)	(26.2%)	
95+	489	106	27	40	145	114	624	1,545
	(31.6%)	(6.8%)	(1.8%)	(2.6%)	(9.4%)	(7.4%)	(40.4%)	
				2025				
65+	48,074	5,764	856	878	2,296	1,730	4,750	64,347
	(74.7%)	(9.0%)	(1.3%)	(1.4%)	(3.6%)	(2.7%)	(7.4%)	
85+	4,210	1,081	229	304	825	663	2,848	10,161
	(41.4%)	(10.6%)	(2.3%)	(3.0%)	(8.1%)	(6.5%)	(28.0%)	
95+	856	176	47	69	248	191	1,090	2,677
	(32.0%)	(6.6%)	(1.8%)	(2.6%)	(9.3%)	(7.1%)	(40.7%)	
				2045				
65+	52,180	7.099	1,069	1,152	3,006	2,259	6,565	73,330
	(71.2%)	(9.7%)	(1.5%)	(1.6%)	(4.1%)	(3.1%)	(9.0%)	
85+	6,625	1,715	357	471	1,240	997	4,133	15,538
	(42.6%)	(11.0%)	(2.3%)	(3.0%)	(8.0%)	(6.4%)	(26.6%)	
95+	1,014	211	56	82	293	228	1,287	3,170
	(32.0%)	(6.6%)	(1.8%)	(2.6%)	(9.2%)	(7.2%)	(40.6%)	

by gender. The projected growth of those in institutions may be subject to Medicare policy changes on the use of home health and SNF services.

Of interest in anticipating the future demand for pain management is the growth of the impaired Types 3–6, which are disabled community residents reflecting significant medical, as well as functional, problems. The frail, Type 6, grows rapidly (due in part to the aging of the population) from 803,000 to 2,259,000, an increase of 29% in relative terms from 2.4% to 3.1%. The IADL impaired group with cardiopulmonary problems (Type 3) grows from 425,000 to 1,069,000, an increase from 1.3% to 1.5% of the U.S. elderly population. This growth has the most serious problems with musculoskeletal problems and associated stiffness. The IADL and cognitively impaired group shows somewhat greater growth than Type 3 at age 65 (from 422,000 to 1,152,000). The ADL impaired (Type 5) grows from 1,086,000 to 3,006,000, an increase from 3.3% to 4.1%. The proportion of ADL impaired at age 95, in contrast, declines from 10.7% to 9.2%.

The frail group also decreases at ages 95 and above (i.e., from 7.7% in 1995 to 7.2% in 2040) due to the high mortality of this most impaired group. Thus, the projections reflect the dynamic interactions of disability- and age-specific mortality with the age-specific distribution of level of functional impairment. The overall growth of Types 3–6 and the institutionalized, from 1995 to 2040, is quite large above age 65 due both to increases in the number surviving past 65 and to the aging of that population. Thus, the demand for pain management associated with each of those distinct functional types will increase. To the extent that each profile has distinctive health problems requiring specialized pain-management procedures, the growth of the need for specific procedures (e.g., joint replacement for Type 3 and cancer pain management for Type 6) can also be identified.

DISCUSSION

We examined recent changes in U.S. mortality from 1960 to 1990 and national changes in both chronic disability and morbidity from 1982 to 1989. There is evidence that chronic disease and disability risks for individuals are declining (Manton et al., 1993a,b, 1995) and that those declines correlate fairly well with recent cause-specific mortality declines.

To better assess these changes quantitatively, we used a multivariate procedure to translate 27 functional items from the 1982, 1984, and 1989 NLTCSs into six continuous disability scores. The use of the scores to describe changes in functioning have several advantages. First, by averaging over the 27 items, the six scores should be statistically more reliable and less subject to classification error. Being continuously scaled, they reflect the intensity of each type of disability. Because the intensity of disability is described by the scores, the rate of change in scores can be used to describe short-term changes (i.e., for intervals of less than five years; e.g., on monthly basis) in functional status, as well as the interaction of disability changes with age-, gender-, and disability-specific mortality over time.

The calculation of the scores also allowed us to forecast, from 1995 to 2040, changes in the size of the U.S. elderly population and changes in the distribution of disability in that population. Because mortality is also declining for persons with chronic disability, there is some decline in the overall functioning of the population due to its growth overall and, in particular, the growth of its very elderly components. We were also able to assess the likely basic health needs of the population because the functional status profiles are strongly correlated with the manifestation of specific health problems.

The results suggest several important conclusions about the future needs for chronic pain management. First, our qualitative review suggests that the natural history of specific chronic diseases changes with age (and as the population ages with time). Consequently, different types of pain management may be required for the same basic disease processes manifested at more advanced ages (e.g., hip fracture at age 70 vs. age 90). Second, many nonlethal conditions lead to functional impairments. The nonlethal conditions (the most prevalent being osteoarthritis) may lead to functional losses that subsequently raise mortality risks through their effect on comorbid conditions. Thus, the treatment of "nonlethal" conditions may have long-term effects on mortality, increasing the period of exposure to chronic morbidity and mortality. Of interest in this regard is that a recent study of Medicare per capita costs per year of age showed that expenses were much higher at ages 65–70 than for those age 101. This was due to (1) lower costs in the final year at advanced ages and (2) the greater number of years lived from age 65 to 101 were generally without need of high levels of Medicare expenditures (Lubitz, Beebe, & Baker, 1995). Thus, forecasts of the future need for pain management procedures requires a careful evaluation of a number of qualitative factors (e.g., changes in disease natural history) and quantitative factors (e.g., differences in the initial size of the birth cohorts becoming elderly). Failure to do so can lead to potential errors both in policy (e.g., the overly simple model of disease delay for reducing morbidity and disability) and in planning the need for new interventions (i.e., identifying priority areas for research on pain control and management).

ACKNOWLEDGMENTS. Professor Manton's research was supported by grants from the National Institute on Aging.

REFERENCES

Adler, N. E., Boyce, T., Chesney, M. A., Cohen, S., Folkman, S., Kahn, R. L., & Syme, S. L. (1994). Socioeconomic status and health: The challenge of the gradient. *American Psychologist*, *49*, 15–24.

Aronson, M., Ooi, W., Morgenstern, H., Hafner, A., Masur, D., Crystal, H., Frishman, W., Fisher, D., & Katzman, R. (1990). Women, myocardial infarction, and dementia in the very old. *Neurology*, *40*, 1102–1106.

Bayo, F. R., & Faber, J. F. (1985). Mortality rates around age one hundred. *Transactions of the Society of Actuaries*, *35*, 37–59.

Belchetz, P. E. (1994). Hormonal treatment of postmenopausal women. *New England Journal of Medicine*, *330*, 1062–1071.

Beregi, E., Regius, O., & Rajczy, K. (1991). Comparative study of the morphological changes in lymphocytes of elderly individuals and centenarians. *Age and Ageing*, *20*, 55–59.

Bowden, M., Crawford, J., Cohen, H., & Noyama, O. (1993). A comparative study of monoclonal gammopathies and immunoglobulin levels in japanese and United States elderly. *Journal of the American Geriatrics Society*, *41*, 11–14.

Brown, B. G., Zhao, X. Q., Sacco, D. E., & Albers, J. J. (1993). Lipid lowering and plaque disruption and clinical events in coronary disease. *Circulation, 87*, 1781–1791.

Burns, A., Jacoby, R., Luthert, P., & Levy, R. (1990). Cause of death in Alzheimer's disease. *Age and Ageing, 19*, 341–344.

Butler, J., Breiman, R., Campbell, J., Lipman, H., Broome, C., & Facklam, R. (1993). Pneumococcal polysaccharide vaccine efficacy: An evaluation of current recommendations. *Journal of the American Medical Association, 270*, 1826–1831.

Callahan, L. F., Bloch, D. A., & Pincus, T. (1992). Identification of work disability in rheumatoid arthritis: Physical, radiographic and laboratory variables do not add explanatory power to demographic and functional variables. *Journal of Clinical Epidemiology, 45*, 127–1382.

Campbell, A. J., Busby, W. J., & Robertson, C. (1993). Over 80 years and no evidence of coronary heart disease: Characteristics of a survivor group. *Journal of the American Geriatrics Society, 41*, 1333–1338.

Centers for Disease Control and Prevention. (1994). Mortality from congestive heart failure—United States 1980–1990. *Journal of the American Medical Association, 271*, 813–814.

Chandra, R. K. (1992). Effect of vitamin and trace-element supplementation on immune responses and infection in elderly subjects. *The Lancet, 340*, 1124–1127.

Colantonio, A., Kasl, S. V., & Ostfeld, A. M. (1992). Level of function predicts first stroke in the elderly. *Stroke, 23*, 1355–1357.

Cook, N. R., Fellingham, S. A., & Doll, R. (1969). A mathematical model for the age distribution of cancer in man. *International Journal of Cancer, 4*, 93–112.

Corti, M., Guralnik, J., Salive, M., & Sorkin, J. (1994). Serum albumin level and physical disability as predictors of mortality in older persons. *Journal of the American Medical Association, 272*, 1036–1042.

Day, J. C. (1993). Population projections of the United States, by age, sex, race, and Hispanic origin: 1993 to 2050. *Current Population Reports* (Series P25-1104). Washington, DC: USGPO.

Dorevitch, M. I., Cossar, R. M., Bailey, F. J., Bisset, T., & Lewis, S. J. (1992). Then accuracy of self and informant ratings of physical functional capacity in the elderly. *Journal of Clinical Epidemiology, 45*, 791–798.

Drexler, H., Reide, S. U., Munzel, T., Konig, H., Funke, E., & Just, H. (1992). Alterations of skeletal muscle in chronic heart failure. *Circulation, 85*, 1751–1759.

Dubos, R. (1965). *Man adapting*. New Haven and London: Yale University Press.

Eastell, R., Yergey, A. L., Vieira, N. E., Cedel, S. L., Kumaar, R., & Riggs, B. L. (1991). Interrelationship among vitamin D metabolism, true calcium absorption, parathyroid function, and age in women: Evidence of an age-related intestinal reistance to 1,25-dihydroxyvitamin A action. *Journal of Bone Mineral Research, 6*, 125.

Fedson, D. (1994). Adult immunization: Summary of the national vaccine advisory committee report. *Journal of the American Medical Association, 272*, 1133–1137.

Fennerty, M. (1994). Helicobacter pylori. *Archives of Internal Medicine, 154*, 721–727.

Feskens, E., Bowles, C., & Kromhout, D. (1991). Intra- and interindividual variability of glucose tolerance in an elderly population. *Journal of Clinical Epidemology, 44*, 947–953.

Feskens, E., Bowles, C., & Kromhout, D. (1992). A longitudinal study on glucose tolerance and other cardiovascular risk factors: Associations within an elderly population. *Journal of Clinical Epidemiology, 45*, 293–300.

Fiatarone, M., Marks, E., Ryan, N., Merdith, C., Lipsitz, L., & Evans, W. (1990). High-intensity strength training in nonagenarians. *Journal of the American Medical Association, 263*, 3029–3034.

Fiatarone, M., O'Neill, E., Doyle, N., Clements, K., Roberts, S., Kehayias, J., Lipsitz, L., & Evans, W. (1993). The Boston FICSIT study: The effects of resistance training and nutritional supplementation on physical frailty in the oldest old. *Journal of the American Geriatrics Society, 41*, 333–337.

Fiatarone, M., O'Neill, E., Ryan, N., Clements, K., Solares, G., Nelson, M., Roberts, S., Kehayias, J., Lipsitz, L., & Evans, W. (1994). Exercise training and nutritional supplementation for physical frailty in very elderly people. *New England Journal of Medicine, 330*, 1769–1775.

Fogel, R. W. (1994). Economic growth, population theory, and physiology: The bearing of long-term processes on the making of economic policy. *American Economic Review, 84*, 369–395.

Forman, D. (1990). Geographic association of *helicobacter pylori* antibody prevalence and gastric cancer mortality in rural China. *International Journal of Cancer, 46*, 608–611.

Garrison, R. J., Gold, R. S., Wilson, P. W. F., & Kannel, W. B. (1993). Educational attainment and coronary heart disease risk: The Framingham Offspring Study. *Preventive Medicine*, *22*, 54–64.

Ghali, J. K., Cooper, R., & Ford, E. (1990). Trends in hospitalization rates for heart failure in the United States, 1973–1986. *Archives of Internal Medicine*, *150*, 769–776.

Gilbert, E. M., Sandoval, A., Larrabee, P., Renlund, D. G., O'Connell, J. B., & Bristow, M. R. (1993). Lisinopril lowers cardiac adrenergic drive and increases β-receptor density in the failing heart. *Circulation*, *88*, 472–480.

Gordon, D., Pobstfield, J., Garrison, R., Neaton, J., Castelli, W., Knoke, J., Jacobs, D., Bangdiwala, S., & Troyler, H. (1989). High-density lipoprotein cholestrol and cardiovascular disease: Four prospective American studies. *Circulation*, *79*, 8–15.

Gravenstein, S., Drinka, P., Duthie, E., Miller, B., Brown, C., Hensley, M., Circo, R., Langer, E., & Ershler, W. (1994). Efficacy of an influenza hemagglutinin-diphtheria toxoid conjugate vaccine in elderly nursing home subjects during an influenza outbreak. *Journal of the American Geriatrics Society*, *42*, 245–251.

Guralnik, J. M., LaCroix, A. Z., Abbott, R. D., Berkman, L. F., Satterfield, S., Evans, D. A., & Wallace, R. B. (1993). Maintaining mobility in late life: 1. Demographic characteristics and chronic conditions. *American Journal of Epidemiology*, *137*, 845–857.

Hannan, M. T., Anderson, J. J., Pincus, T., & Felson, D. T. (1992). Educational attainment and osteoarthritis: Differential associations with radiographics changes and symptom reporting. *Journal of Clinical Epidemiology*, *45*, 139–147.

Harris, J. E. (1983). Cigarette smoking and successive birth cohorts of men and women in the United States during 1900–80. *Journal of the National Cancer Institute*, *71*, 473–479.

Hayflick, L. (1965). The limited in vitro lifetime of human diploid cell strains. *Experimental Cell Research*, *37*, 614–636.

Hayflick, L., & Moorhead, P. S. (1961). The serial cultivation of human diploid cell strains. *Experimental Cell Research*, *25*, 585–621.

Hentschel, E., Brandstatter, G., Dragosics, B., Hirschi, A., Nemec, H., Schutze, K., Taufer, M., & Wurzer, H. (1993). Effect of ranitidine and amoxicillin plus metronidazole on the eradication of *helicobacter pylori* and the recurrence of duodenal ulcer. *New England Journal of Medicine*, *328*, 308–312.

Hosking, M., Warner, M., Lodbell, C., Offord, K., & Melton, L. (1989). Outcomes of surgery in patients 90 years of age and older. *Journal of the American Medical Association*, *261*, 1909–1915.

Hosking, S., Ling, T., Chung, S., Yung, M., Cheng, A., Sung, J., & Li, A. (1994). Duodenal ulcer healing by eradication of helicobacter pylori without anti-acid treatment: Randomised controlled trial. *The Lancet*, *343*, 508–510.

Iso, H., Jacobs, D., Wentworth, D., Neaton, J., & Cohen, J. (1989). Serum cholesterol levels and six-year mortality from stroke in 350,977 men screened for the multiple risk factor intervention trial. *New England Journal of Medicine*, *320*, 904–910.

Jeune, B. (1994). Hundredarige-hale eller hemmelighed? *Gerontologi og Samfund*, *10*, 4–6.

Johnson, C. L., Rifkind, B. M., Sempos, C. T., Carroll, M. D., Bachorik, P. S., Briefel, R. R., Gordon, D. J., Burt, V. L., Brown, C. D., Lippel, K., & Cleeman, J. I. (1993). Declining serum total cholesterol levels among US adults: The national health and nutrition examination surveys. *Journal of the American Medical Association*, *269*, 3002–3008.

Kalra, L. (1994). The influence of stroke unit rehabilitation on functional recovery from stroke. *Stroke*, *25*, 821–825.

Kaplan, G., & Keil, J. (1993). Socioeconomic factors and cardiovascular disease: A review of the literature. *Circulation*, *88*, 1973–1998.

Kasch, F. W., Boyer, J. L., Van Camp, S. P., Verity, L. S., & Wallace, J. P. (1993). Effect of exercise on cardiovascular ageing. *Age and Ageing*, *22*, 5–10.

Katz, S., & Akpom, C. (1976). A measure of primary sociobiological functions. *International Journal of Health Services*, *6*, 493–508.

Katz, S., Branch, L. G., Branson, M. H., Papsidero, J. A., Beck, J. C., & Greer, D. S. (1983). Active life expectance. *New England Journal of Medicine*, *309*, 1218–1223.

Kautzky, J. E. (1995). Woman of history: At age 126, California Catholic may be oldest living person. *North Carolina Catholic* (Catholic News Service), p. 13, March 12.

Keene, G. S. (1993). Mortality and morbidity after hip fractures. *British Medical Journal*, *307*, 1248–1250.

Kestenbaum, B. (1992). A description of the extreme aged population based on improved Medicare enrollment data. *Demography, 29,* 565–581.

Keys, A. (1980). Seven countries: A multivariate analysis of death and coronary heart disease. Cambridge: Harvard University Press.

Kitzman, D., & Edwards, W. (1990). Minireview: Age-related changes in the anatomy of the normal human heart. *Journal of Gerontology: Medical Sciences, 45,* M33–M39.

Ko, W., Gold, J., Lazzaro, R., Zelano, J., Lang, S., Isom, O., & Kreiger, K. (1992). Survival analysis of octogenarian patients with coronary artery disease managed by elective coronary artery bypass surgery versus conventional medical treatment. *Circulation, 86,* II-191–II-197.

Kukull, W., Brenner, D., Speck, C., Nochlin, D., Bowen, J., McCormick, W., Teri, L., Pfanschmidt, M., & Larson, E. (1994). Causes of death associated with Alzheimer disease: Variation by level of cognitive impairment before death. *Journal of the American Geriatrics Society, 42,* 723–726.

Lakatta, E. (1985). Health, disease, and cardiovascular aging. In *America's aging: Health in an older society* (pp. 73–104). Washington, DC: National Academy Press.

Lakka, T. A., Venalainen, J. M., Rauramaa, R., Salonen, R., Tuomilehto, J., & Salonen, J. (1994). Relation of leisure-time physical activity and cardiorespiratory fitness to the risk of acute myocardial infarction in men. *New England Journal of Medicine, 330,* 1549–1554.

Lanska, D. J., & Mi, X. (1993). Decline in U.S. stroke mortality in the era before antihypertensive therapy. *Stroke, 24,* 1382–1388.

Lawton, M., & Brody, E. (1969). Assessment of older people: Self-maintaining and instrumental activities of daily living. *Gerontology, 9,* 179–186.

Linnanmäki, E., Leinonen, M., Mattila, K., Nieminen, M. S., Valtonen, V., & Saikku, P. (1993). *Chlamydia pneumoniae*-specific circulating immune complexes in patients with chronic coronary heart disease. *Circulation, 87,* 1130–1134.

Lotan, R., Xu, X. C., Lippman, S. M., Ro, J. Y., Lee, J. S., Lee, J. J., & Hong, W. K. (1995). Suppression of retinoic acid receptor-β in premalignant oral lesions and its up-regulation by isotretinoin. *New England Journal of Medicine, 332,* 1405–1410.

Lubitz, J., Beebe, J., & Baker, C. (1995). Longevity and Medicare expenditures. *New England Journal of Medicine, 332,* 999–1003.

Manton, K. G., Corder, L. S., & Stallard, E. (1993a). Estimates of change in chronic disability and institutional incidence and prevalence rates in the U.S. elderly population from the 1982, 1984, and 1989 National Long Term Care Survey. *Journal of Gerontology Social Sciences, 47,* S153–S166.

Manton, K. G., Corder, L. S., & Stallard, E. (1993b). Changes in the use of personal assistance and special equipment 1982 to 1989: Results from the 1982 and 1989 NLTCS. *The Gerontologist, 33,* 168–176.

Manton, K. G., & Soldo, B. J. (1985). Dynamics of health changes in the oldest old: New perspective and evidence. *Milbank Memorial Fund Quarterly, 63,* 206–285.

Manton, K. G., & Stallard, E. (1982). A cohort analysis of U.S. stomach cancer mortality—1950 to 1977. *International Journal of Epidemiology, 11,* 49–61.

Manton, K. G., Stallard, & Corder, L. S. (1995). Changes in morbidity and chronic disability in the U.S. elderly population: Evidence from the 1982, 1984, and 1989 National Long Term Care Surveys. *Journal of Gerontology: Biological Sciences 50B* (4); 5194–5204.

Manton, K. G., Stallard, E. & Tolley, H. D. (1991a). Limits to human life expectancy: Evidence, prospects, and implications. *Population and Development Review, 17* (4), 603–638.

Manton, K. G., Stallard, E., Woodbury, M. A., & Dowd, J. E. (1994a). Time varying covariates in models of human mortality and aging: Multidimensional generalization of the Gompertz. *Journal of Gerontology: Biological Sciences, 49,* B169–B190.

Manton, K. G., Vertrees, J. C., & Clark, R. F. (1993c). A multivariate analysis of disability and health and its change over time in the National Channeling Demonstration data. *The Gerontologist, 33,* 610–618.

Manton, K. G., Woodbury, M. A., & Tolley, H. D. (1994b). *Statistical applications using fuzzy sets.* New York: Wiley.

Manton, K. G., Wrigley, J. M., Cohen, H., & Woodbury, M. A. (1991b). Cancer mortality, aging, and patterns of comorbidity: United States, 1968 to 1986. *Journal of Gerontology, 46,* S225–S234.

Mariotti, S., Sansoni, P., Barbesino, G., Caturegli, P., Monti, D., Cossarizza, A., Giacomelli, T., Passeri, G., Fagiolo, U., Pinchera, A., & Franceschi, C. (1992). Thyroid and other organ-specific autoantibodies in healthy centenarians. *The Lancet, 339,* 1506–1508.

Martin, D., Francis, J., Protetch, J., & Hoff, F. (1992). Time dependency of cognitive recovery with cobalamia replacement: Report of pilot study. *Journal of the American Medical Association, 40,* 168–172.

Marx, M. S., Werner, P., Cohen-Mansfield, J., & Feldman, R. (1992). The relationship between low vision and performance of activities of daily living in nursing home residents. *Journal of the American Geriatrics Society, 40,* 1018–1020.

Materson, B. J., & Preston, R. A. (1994). Angiotensin-converting enzyme inhibitors in hypertension: A dozen years of experience. *Archives of Internal Medicine, 154,* 513–523.

Mayer, J., Jermanovich, A., Wright, B., Elder, J., Drew, J., & Williams, S. (1994). Changes in health behaviors of older adults: The San Diego Medicare preventive health project. *Preventive Medicine, 23,* 127–133.

McBean, A., Babish, D., & Prihoda, R. (1991). The utilization of pneumococcal polysaccharide vaccine among elderly Medicare beneficiaries, 1985 through 1988. *Archives of Internal Medicine, 151,* 2009–2016.

McCormick, W. C., Kukull, W. A., van Belle, G., Bowen, J. D., Teri, L., & Larson, E. B. (1994). Symptom patterns and comorbidity in the early stages of Alzheimer's disease. *Journal of the American Geriatrics Society, 42,* 517–521.

McGovern, P. G., Pankow, J. S., Burke, G. L., Shahar, E., Sprafka, J. M., Folsom, A. R., & Blackburn, H. (1993). Trends in survival of hospitalized strike patients between 1970 and 1985: The Minnesota Heart Survey. *Stroke, 24,* 1640–1648.

Moon, J., Bandy, B., & Davison, A. J. (1992). Hypothesis: Etiology of atherosclerosis and osteoporosis: Are imbalances in the calciferol endocrine system implicated. *Journal of the American College of Nutrition, 11,* 567–583.

Mozar, H. N., Bal, D. G., & Farag, S. A. (1990). The natural history of atherosclerosis: An ecologic perspective. *Atherosclerosis, 82,* 157–164.

Mueller, R., & Scheidt, S. (1994). History of drugs for thrombotic disease: Discovery, development, and directions for the future. *Circulation, 89,* 432–449.

Muhlbaier, L. H., Pryor, D. B., Rankin, S., Smith, L. R., Mark, D. B., Jones, R. H., Glower, D. D., Harrell, F. E., Lee, K. L., Califf, R. M., & Sabiston, D. C. (1992). Observational comparsion of event-free survival with coronary artery disease: 20 years of follow-up. *Circulation Supplement II, 86,* 198–204.

Nabulsi, A. A., Folsom, A. R., White, A., Patsch, W., Heiss, G., Wu, K. K., & Szklo, M. (1993). Association of hormone-replacement therapy with various cardiovascular risk factors in postmenopausal women. *New England Journal of Medicine, 328,* 1069–1075.

National Center for Health Statistics. (1992). *Health, United States, 1992.* U.S. DHHS Pub. No. 92-1232. Hyattsville, MD: Government Printing Office.

Niedobitek, G., & Young, L. (1994). Epstein-Barr virus persistence and virus-associated tumors. *The Lancet, 343,* 333–335.

Okamoto, Y. (1992). Health care for the elderly in Japan: Medicine and welfare in an aging society facing a crisis in long term care. *British Medical Journal, 305,* 403–405.

Omran, A. (1971). The epidemiologic transition: A theory of the epidemiology of population change. *Milbank Memorial Quarterly, 49,* 509–538.

Ooneda, G., Yoshida, Y., Suzuki, K., Shinkai, H., Hori, S., Kobori, K., Takayama, Y., & Sekiguchi, M. (1978). Smooth muscle cells in the development of plasatic arterionecrosis, arteriosclerosis, and arterial contraction. *Blood Vessels, 15,* 148–156.

Paolisso, G., D'Amore, A., Giugliano, D., Ceriello, A., & Varricchio, M. (1993). Pharmacologic doses of Vitamin E improve insulin action in healthy subjects and non-insulin-dependent diabetic patients. *American Journal of Clinical Nutrition, 57,* 650–656.

Pappas, G., Queen, S., Hadden, W., & Fisher, G. (1993). The increasing disparity in mortality between socioeconomic groups in the United states, 1960 and 1986. *New England Journal of Medicine, 329,* 103–109.

Paul, S. D., Kuntz, K. M., Eagle, K. A., & Weinstein, M. C. (1994). Costs and effectiveness of angiotensin converting enzyme inhibition in patients with congestive heart failure. *Archives of Internal Medicine, 154,* 1143–1149.

Pennypacker, L., Allen, R., Kelly, J., Mathews, L., Grigsby, J., Kaye, K., Lindenbaum, J., & Stabler, S. (1992). High prevalence of cobalamin deficiency in elderly outpatients. *Journal of the American Geriatrics Society, 40,* 1197–1204.

Perls, T. (1994). The oldest old. *Scientific American, 274,* 70–75.

Perls, T., Morris, J., Ooi, W., & Lipsitz, L. (1993). The relationship between age, gender and cognitive performance in the very old: The effect of selective survival. *Journal of the American Geriatrics Society, 41*, 1193–1201.

Pollare, T., Lithell, H., & Berne, C. (1989). A comparison of the effects of hydroclorothiazide and captopril on glucose and lipid metabolism in patients with hypertension. *New England Journal of Medicine, 321*, 868–873.

Pouleur, H., Rousseau, M., van Eyll, C., Stoleru, L., Hayashida, W., Udelson, J., Dolan, N., Kinan, D., Gallagher, P., Ahn, S., Benedict, C., Yusuf, S., & Konstam, M. (1993). Effects of long-term enalapril therapy on left ventricular diastolic properties in patients with depressed ejection fraction. *Circulation, 88*, 481–491.

Prasad, K., & Edwards-Prasad, J. (1992). Vitamin E and cancer prevention: Recent advances and future potentials. *Journal of the American College of Nutrition, 11*, 487–500.

Preston, S. H. (1992). Cohort succession and the future of the oldest old. In R. M. Suzman, D. P. Willis, & K. G. Manton (Eds.), *The oldest old* (pp. 50–57). New York: Oxford University Press.

Radl, J., Sepers, J., Skvaril, F., Morell, A., & Hijmans, W. (1975). Immunoglobulin patterns in humans over 95 years of age. *Clinical Experimental Immunology, 22*, 84–90.

Reuben, D., Siu, A., & Kimpau, S. (1992). The predictive validity of self-support and performance-based measures of function and health. *Journal of Gerontology: Medical Sciences, 47*, M106–M110.

Robine, J. M., & Ritchie, K. (1991). Healthy life expectancy: Evaluation of global indicator of change in population health. *British Medical Journal, 302*, 457–460.

Rodin, J. (1986a). Aging and health: Effects of the sense of control. *Science, 233*, 1271–1276.

Rodin, J. (1986b). Health, control, and aging. In M. Baltes & P. Baltes (Eds.) *Aging and control* (pp. 139–165). Hillsdale, NJ: Eribaum.

Rubenstein, L., & Josephson, K. (1989). Hospital based geriatric assessment in the United States: The Sepulveda VA Geriatric Evaluation Unit. *Gerontology: Special Supplement, 7*, 74–79.

Salive, M. E., Guralnik, J., Glynn, R. J., Christen, W., Wallace, R. B., & Ostfeld, A. M. (1994). Association of visual impairment with mobility and physical function. *Journal of the American Geriatrics Society, 42*, 287–292.

Sempos, C. T., Cleeman, J. I., Carroll, M. D., Johnson, C. L, Bachorik, P. S., Gordon, D. J., Burt, V. L., Briefel, R. R., Brown, C. D., Lippel, K., & Rifkind, B. M. (1993). Prevalence of high blood cholesterol among U.S. adults: An updated based on guidelines from the second report of the National Cholesterol Education Program Adult Treatment Panel. *Journal of the American Medical Association, 269*, 3009–3014.

Shinton, R., & Sagar, G. (1993). Lifelong exercise and stroke. *British Medical Journal, 307*, 231–234.

Skoog, I., Nilsson, L., Palmertz, B., Andreasson, L. A., & Svanborg, A. (1993). A population-based study of dementia in 85-year-olds. *New England Journal of Medicine, 328*, 153–158.

Studies of Left Ventricular Dysfunction Investigators. (1991). Effect of Enalapril on survival in patients with reduced left ventricular ejection fractions and congestive heart failure. *New England Journal of Medicine, 325*, 293–302.

Stampfer, M. J., Colditz, G. A., Willett, W. C., Manson, J. E., Rosner, B., Speizer, F. E., & Hennekens, C. H. (1991). Postmenopausal estrogen therapy and cardiovascular disease: Ten-year follow-up from the Nurses' Health Study. *New England Journal of Medicine, 325*, 756–762.

Stern, Y., Gurland, B., Tatemichi, T. K., Tang, M. X., Wilder, D., & Mayeux, R. (1994). Influence of education and occupation on the incidence of Alzheimer's disease. *Journal of the American Medical Association, 271*, 1004–1010.

Sullivan, D. (1971). A single index of mortality and morbidity. *HSMHA Health Reports, 86*, 347–354.

Takata, H., Suzuki, M., Ishii, T., Sekiguchi, S., & Iri, H. (1987). Influence of major histocompatability complex region genes on human longevity among Okinawan-Japanese centenarians and nonagenarians. *The Lancet, 2*, 824–826.

Tanaka, H., Ueda, Y., Hayashi, M., Date, C., Baba, T., Yamashita, H., Shoji, H., Tanaka, Y., Owada, K., & Detels, R. (1982). Risk factor for cerebral hemorrage and cerebral infarction in a Japanese rural community. *Stroke, 13*, 62–83.

Thom, D. H., Grayston, J. T., Siscovick, D. S., Wang, S. P., Weiss, N. S., & Daling, J. R. (1992). Association of prior infection with *Chlamydia pneumoniae* and angiographically demonstrated coronary artery disease. *Journal of the American Medical Association, 268*, 68–72.

Thoms, W. S. (1873). *Human longevity, its facts and its fictions*. London: John Murray.

Townsend, J., Roderick, P., & Cooper, J. (1994). Cigarette smoking by socioeconomic group, sex, and age: Effects of price, income, and health publicity. *British Medical Journal, 309*, 923–927.

Ueda, K., Hasuo, Y., Kihohara, Y., Wada, J., Kawano, H., Kato, I., Fujii, I., Yanai, T., Omae, T., & Fujishima, M. (1988). Intracerebral haemorrage in a Japanese community, Hisye: Incidence, changing patterns during long term follow-up and related factors. *Stroke, 19*, 48–52.

Ueshima, H., Iida, M., Shimamoto, T., Konishi, M., Tsujioka, K., Tanigaki, M., Nakanishi, N., Ozawa, H., Kojima, S., & Komachi, Y. (1980). Multivariate analysis of risk factor for stroke: Eight-year follow-up study of farming villages in Akita, Japan. *Preventive Medicine, 9*, 722–940.

U.S. Bureau of the Census. (1993). *Statistical abstract of the United States, 1993* (113th Ed.). Washington, DC: Government Printing Office.

Vaupel, J. W., & Jeune, B. (1994). *The emergence and proliferation of centenarians.* Aging Research Unit, Odense University, Medical School, Odense, Denmark.

Wieland, D., Rubenstein, L. Z., Hedrick, S. C., Reuben, D. B., & Buchner, D. M. (1994). Inpatient geriatric evaluation and management units (GEMs) in the veterans health system: Diamonds in the rough? *Journal of Gerontology, 49*, M195–M200.

Woodbury, M. A., Manton, K. G., & Tolley, H. D. (1994). A general model for statistical analysis using fuzzy sets: Sufficient conditions for identifiability and statistical properties. *Information Sciences, 1*, 149–180.

Zaman, Z., Roche, S., Fielden, P., Frost, P., Niriella, D., & Cayley, A. (1992). Plasma concentrations of vitamins A and E carotenoids in Alzheimer's disease. *Age and Ageing, 21*, 91–94.

CHAPTER 4

The Assessment of Pain in the Elderly

LUCY GAGLIESE AND RONALD MELZACK

INTRODUCTION

Pain is a multidimensional experience made up of sensory, affective, and cognitive-evaluative components, which interact, and each of which contributes to the determination of the final pain response (Melzack & Casey, 1968). Age may have an effect on each of these dimensions and ultimately on the pain experienced. The assessment of pain in the elderly, therefore, requires a holistic approach with sensitivity to the special concerns of this population.

Most of the research on the assessment of pain in the elderly has focused on the measurement of age differences in reactivity to experimental, acute, and chronic pain. These different types of pain each have their own function, emotional meanings, and perceived consequences, which may make generalizations across them questionable (Melzack & Wall, 1988). For instance, increases in pain threshold during aging do not imply that comparable differences will be seen in the clinical setting. Experimental pain, such as that used to measure threshold, is well controlled, clearly not a sign of illness or a threat to normal functioning, and is associated with only transient emotional reactions (Procacci, Zoppi, & Maresca, 1979). On the other hand, acute or chronic pain may well be associated with a pathological process, long-term impairment, and profound emotional upheaval (Melzack & Wall, 1988). Assessment of such varied experiences requires specific tools and well-defined constructs for each. In this chapter, we will describe the data regarding age differences in the experience of each type of pain. We will also discuss the most frequently used assessment tools. Because pain is a subjective experience, the psychometric instrument used in assessment becomes a critical variable. The tool used

---

LUCY GAGLIESE AND RONALD MELZACK • Department of Psychology, McGill University, Montreal, Quebec, Canada H3A 1B1.

Handbook of Pain and Aging, edited by David I. Mostofsky and Jacob Lomranz. Plenum Press, New York, 1997.

determines what is measured, and caution is necessary when comparing results found using different pain scales.

PSYCHOMETRIC TOOLS

Most pain assessment instruments are either unidimensional measures of pain intensity or multidimensional measures of the pain experience (Melzack & Katz, 1992). A comprehensive pain assessment should include both types of measures, as each samples an important part of the overall experience.

The most widely used unidimensional measure of pain intensity is the visual analogue scale (VAS) (Huskisson, 1974). It usually consists of a 10-centimeter line, either horizontal (Sriwatanakul et al., 1983) or vertical. The ends of the line are anchored with descriptors of the extremes of pain intensity, such as, "no pain" and "worst pain possible." Patients or subjects are asked to indicate which point along the line best represents their current pain. The distance from the anchor "no pain" to the mark made by the patient is the measure of pain intensity. By changing the anchors, the VAS can be used to measure different states, including distress or unpleasantness. There is strong evidence for the validity and reliability of this scale when subjects are given careful instruction and practice (Huskisson, 1983). (For a review of the VAS and other measures of pain intensity, see Jensen & Karoly, 1992.)

It has been suggested that the elderly may have deficits in abstract reasoning which make use of the VAS difficult (Kremer, Atkinson, & Ignelzi, 1981). In fact, increasing age has been associated with a higher frequency of some kinds of incorrect responses to the VAS (Jensen, Karoly, & Braver, 1986). Herr and Mobily (1993) compared several different measures of pain intensity in a sample of elderly patients with leg pain. They found a very low error rate in using the scales. In fact, it was comparable to that reported in the general population by Jensen et al. (1992). Although scores on all of the intensity scales used in this study were highly correlated, the mean scores were significantly different. This difference was due mostly to the horizontal VAS, leading the authors to suggest that a vertical orientation may be more appropriate for this group. Interestingly, 40% of this sample felt that the verbal descriptor scale (VDS), with words such as *mild*, *severe*, and *horrible*, was the easiest to use and described their pain best (see below for a description of this scale). Although the sample in this study was small ($n = 27$), the results suggest that intensity scales, especially the VDS, may be used effectively in the assessment of pain in the elderly.

Unidimensional single-item scales such as the VAS give an indication of only one element of the pain experience: intensity. Multidimensional measures, on the other hand, provide a more comprehensive picture of an individual's pain. The McGill Pain Questionnaire (MPQ) (Melzack, 1975) is the most widely used multidimensional pain inventory (Wilke, Savedra, Holzemer, Tesler & Paul, 1990) (see Figure 4-1). It is made up of 20 sets of adjectives which describe the sensory, affective, evaluative, and miscellaneous components of pain. Subjects are asked to endorse those words which describe their feelings and sensations at that moment. In addition to the adjectives, the MPQ includes line drawings of the body on which patients may indicate the spatial distribution

McGill Pain Questionnaire

Patient's Name ______ Date ______ Time ______ am/pm

PRI: S ______ (1–10) A ______ (11–15) E ______ (16) M ______ (17–20) PRI(T) ______ (1–20) PPI ______

1 FLICKERING, QUIVERING, PULSING, THROBBING, BEATING, POUNDING	11 TIRING, EXHAUSTING
2 JUMPING, FLASHING, SHOOTING	12 SICKENING, SUFFOCATING
3 PRICKING, BORING, DRILLING, STABBING, LANCINATING	13 FEARFUL, FRIGHTFUL, TERRIFYING
4 SHARP, CUTTING, LACERATING	14 PUNISHING, GRUELLING, CRUEL, VICIOUS, KILLING
5 PINCHING, PRESSING, GNAWING, CRAMPING, CRUSHING	15 WRETCHED, BLINDING
6 TUGGING, PULLING, WRENCHING	16 ANNOYING, TROUBLESOME, MISERABLE, INTENSE, UNBEARABLE
7 HOT, BURNING, SCALDING, SEARING	17 SPREADING, RADIATING, PENETRATING, PIERCING
8 TINGLING, ITCHY, SMARTING, STINGING	18 TIGHT, NUMB, DRAWING, SQUEEZING, TEARING
9 DULL, SORE, HURTING, ACHING, HEAVY	19 COOL, COLD, FREEZING
10 TENDER, TAUT, RASPING, SPLITTING	20 NAGGING, NAUSEATING, AGONIZING, DREADFUL, TORTURING
	PPI: 0 NO PAIN, 1 MILD, 2 DISCOMFORTING, 3 DISTRESSING, 4 HORRIBLE, 5 EXCRUCIATING

BRIEF	RHYTHMIC	CONTINUOUS
MOMENTARY	PERIODIC	STEADY
TRANSIENT	INTERMITTENT	CONSTANT

E = EXTERNAL
I = INTERNAL

COMMENTS:

Figure 4-1. McGill Pain Questionnaire. The descriptors fall into four major groups: sensory, 1–10; affective, 11–15; evaluative, 16; and miscellaneous, 17–20. The rank value for each descriptor is based on its position in the word set. The sum of the rank values is the pain rating index (PRI). The present pain intensity (PPI) is based on a scale of 0–5. (Copyright 1975, Ronald Melzack.)

of their pain, words to assess its temporal properties, and a measure of present pain intensity from "no pain" to "excruciating." This measure on its own is often referred to as the Verbal Descriptor Scale (VDS). There is much evidence for the validity, reliability, and discriminative abilities of the MPQ when used with younger adults (for a review of this literature, see Melzack & Katz, 1992).

Herr and Mobily (1991) suggested that the MPQ may be too complex and time-consuming for the elderly. They argued that this group may have difficulty understanding some of the pain descriptors and may be overwhelmed by the large number of choices. These authors did not present data to support this claim. Although reliable use of the MPQ does require basic reading and comprehension abilities, these demands are similar across age groups. In addition, the MPQ has been used reliably with children as young as 12 (Monk, 1980). The concerns of Herr and Mobily may perhaps pertain more directly to issues of educational or reading level than to age.

The short form of the MPQ (SF-MPQ) (Melzack, 1987) is less complicated and may therefore be more appropriate for use with the elderly (Figure 4-2). The SF-MPQ is made up of 15 descriptors drawn from the MPQ. Subjects indicate to what extent, from "none" to "severe," each of the descriptors applies to their pain. Pain intensity is measured on a VAS. There is evidence for the validity and reliability of this version of the MPQ (Melzack, 1987). Helme, Katz, Gibson, and Corran (1989) administered the SF-MPQ, VDS, and VAS to a group of patients seen at a geriatric pain clinic. They found that the sensory and affective scales of the SF-MPQ were significantly correlated with each other, as were scores on the VDS and VAS. These authors concluded that these tools can be used to assess pain in the elderly and that the sensory and emotional components of the pain experience can be separated in this group.

The assessment of pain is complicated by the subjective nature of the experience. We must accept that pain is "whatever the person says it is." Researchers and clinicians, however, strive to quantify the pain experience in order to better understand it. The tools described above appear to be valid and reliable ways to assess different dimensions of that experience. Unfortunately, these tools were designed for use with younger adults, and it is not yet clear that they are valid for use with the elderly. The two studies which have attempted to address this question used small sample sizes, limiting the generalizability of the results. Despite this and the fact that there are no pain assessment tools designed specifically for use with the elderly, those described above have been used in the research which will be discussed in this chapter. The interpretation of this research is therefore limited until we have data which clearly show that these tools may be used with the elderly.

EXPERIMENTAL PAIN

Pain Threshold

Most of the literature on age differences in pain has focused on pain in the laboratory. There are 20 studies of age differences in pain threshold, which is usually defined as "the lowest value at which the person reports that the stimulation feels painful" (Melzack & Wall, 1988, p. 17). The results of these studies have been inconsis-

SHORT-FORM McGILL PAIN QUESTIONNAIRE

RONALD MELZACK

PATIENT'S NAME: ______________________ DATE: ____________

	NONE	MILD	MODERATE	SEVERE
THROBBING	0) ____	1) ____	2) ____	3) ____
SHOOTING	0) ____	1) ____	2) ____	3) ____
STABBING	0) ____	1) ____	2) ____	3) ____
SHARP	0) ____	1) ____	2) ____	3) ____
CRAMPING	0) ____	1) ____	2) ____	3) ____
GNAWING	0) ____	1) ____	2) ____	3) ____
HOT-BURNING	0) ____	1) ____	2) ____	3) ____
ACHING	0) ____	1) ____	2) ____	3) ____
HEAVY	0) ____	1) ____	2) ____	3) ____
TENDER	0) ____	1) ____	2) ____	3) ____
SPLITTING	0) ____	1) ____	2) ____	3) ____
TIRING-EXHAUSTING	0) ____	1) ____	2) ____	3) ____
SICKENING	0) ____	1) ____	2) ____	3) ____
FEARFUL	0) ____	1) ____	2) ____	3) ____
PUNISHING-CRUEL	0) ____	1) ____	2) ____	3) ____

NO PAIN |——————————————————————| WORST POSSIBLE PAIN

PPI

0	NO PAIN	____
1	MILD	____
2	DISCOMFORTING	____
3	DISTRESSING	____
4	HORRIBLE	____
5	EXCRUCIATING	____

Figure 4-2. The short-form McGill Pain Questionnaire (SF-MPQ). Descriptors 1–11 represent the sensory dimension of pain experience and 12–15 represent the affective dimension. Each descriptor is ranked on an intensity sale of 0 = none, 1 = none, 2 = moderate, and 3 = severe. The Present Pain Intensity (PPI) of the standard long-form MPQ and the Visual Analogue Scale are also included to provide overall pain intensity scores. (Copyright 1984, Ronald Melzack.)

tent (see Table 4-1). In fact, several reviewers have drawn vastly different conclusions based on these data. Two have concluded that pain threshold increases with age (Gibson, Katz, Corran, Farrell, & Helme, 1994; Tremblay, 1994), while Harkins and colleagues have concluded in several reviews that threshold does not change with age (Harkins, 1988; Harkins, Kwentus, & Price, 1984, 1994; Harkins, Lagua, Price, & Small, 1995; Harkins & Price, 1992; Harkins & Warner, 1980; Kwentus, Harkins, Lignon, & Silverman, 1985). In addition, two reviewers have found it impossible to draw any firm conclusions (Butler & Gastel, 1980; Ferrell, 1991).

This unfortunate situation may be the result of the weaknesses and diversity of the studies assessing pain threshold. Subject inclusion–exclusion criteria are rarely provided, and the mean age of the groups being compared, the pain induction methods employed, and the psychophysical end points measured are highly variable across studies (Harkins et al., 1994) (see Table 4-1).

The pain induction method deserves careful consideration because the type of pain being studied may influence the results obtained. Cutaneous thermal pain threshold has been the most widely studied, with 7 out of 12 studies reporting an increase in threshold with age. The remaining 5 find no age differences in threshold. Of the 12 studies, 9 employed radiant heat as the noxious stimuli (see Table 4-1). In this technique, the energy produced by a lamp is focused onto the blackened skin of the subject, and the amount of heat energy that produces the first perception of pain is measured (Hardy, Wolff, & Goddell, 1943). Of the 9 studies using this methodology, 5 report an increase in pain threshold with age. The remaining 4 report no age-related changes in threshold. However, 1 of these studies (Clark & Mehl, 1971) did not include an elderly group. Comparisons were made between a young group (age range 18–30 years) and a middle-aged group (age range 28–67). The age range of subjects in the study by Schumacher, Goodell, Hardy, and Wolff (1940) is not reported, making it difficult to interpret this failed replication. Although the remaining studies (Birren, Schapiro, & Miller, 1950; Hardy et al., 1943) included elderly subjects, the sample of one (Birren et al., 1950) was very small, and neither reported threshold data by age group.

Cutaneous thermal pain threshold has also been measured using computer-controlled contact thermodes applied directly to the body. Three studies using this method on the hands and feet are available. Gibson, Gorman, and Helme (1991) found an age-associated increase in threshold of the hand. Kenshalo (1986) found no age differences at either the hands or the feet. Lautenbacher and Strian (1991) replicated this result for the hands, but they reported an age-associated increase in the pain threshold of the feet.

There are seven studies which employ electric current to measure age differences in pain threshold. Although these studies also report inconsistent results, careful examination of the site on the body where the current is applied may help clarify the data. Two of these studies have measured threshold with a constant current to the arm (Neri & Agazzani, 1984; Tucker, Andrew, Ogle, & Davison, 1989) and have found evidence for an increase in threshold with age. In contrast, Collins and Stone (1966), using an electric current applied to the dorsal surface of the fingers of the right hand, found a significant negative correlation between age and pain threshold. However, the subjects in this study ranged in age from only 18 to 53 years (mean age = 27.1 years), and therefore, no conclusions about pain in the elderly can be drawn. Studies using electric current applied to healthy tooth pulp have consistently reported no age-related changes in threshold

Table 4-1. Studies of Age Differences in Pain Threshold

Noxious stimulus	Reference	Subjects (age range and number of subjects)	Site of stimulation	Results
Thermal stimuli				
Radiant heat	Chapman & Jones, 1944	10–85 years $n = 60$	Mid-forehead	Threshold increases with age.
	Hall & Stride, 1954	18–70 years $n = 256$	Mid-forehead	Threshold increases with age.
	Sherman & Robillard, 1960	20–97 years $n = 200$	Mid-forehead	Threshold increases with age.
	Schluderman & Zubek, 1962	12–83 years $n = 171$	Mid-forehead, arms, and legs	Threshold increases with age.
	Procacci et al., 1970	18–70+ years $n = 525$	Forearm	Threshold increases with age.
	Schumacher et al., 1940	No age range reported $n = 150$	Mid-forehead	No age differences.
	Hardy et al., 1943	10–80 years $n = 200$	Mid-forehead	No age differences.
	Birren et al., 1950	19–82 years $n = 16$	Mid-forehead	No age differences.
	Clark & Mehl, 1971	18–67 years $n = 64$	Forearm	No age differences.
Contact heat	Gibson et al., 1991	20–99 years $n = 66$	Hand	Threshold increases with age.
	Lautenbacher & Strian, 1991	17–63 years $n = 64$	Foot	Threshold increases with age.
			Hand	No age differences.
	Kenshalo, 1986	19–84 years $n = 47$	Hand and foot	No age differences.
Electric current				
Cutaneous	Tucker et al., 1989	5–105 years $n = 520$	Upper arm	Threshold increases with age.
	Neri & Agazzani, 1984	20–82 years $n = 100$	Forearm	Threshold increases with age.
	Collins & Stone, 1966	18–53 years $n = 56$	Fingers	Threshold decreases with age.
Tooth pulp	Mumford, 1963	10–73 years n = not reported	Variety of healthy teeth	No age difference.
	Mumford, 1968	18–63 years $n = 111$	Healthy unfilled incisor	No age differences.
	Harkins & Chapman, 1976	21–85 years $n = 20$	Health unfilled incisor	No age differences.
	Harkins & Chapman, 1977	20–81 years $n = 20$	Healthy unfilled incisor	No age differences.
Pin prick	Horch et al., 1992	9–83 years $n = 130$	Fingers	No age differences.

(Harkins & Chapman, 1976; Mumford, 1963, 1965). There may be special characteristics associated with the aging tooth pulp which can explain these results.

One study (Horch, Hardy, Jimenez, & Jabaley, 1992) measured pain threshold using pin-prick stimulation of both hands. There was no evidence of age-related differences in threshold. However, the sample for this study was small, and there were few subjects over 60 years of age.

Based on the evidence presented above, we conclude that there is an increase in pain threshold with age. This conclusion is further supported by data assessing age differences in reactivity to nociceptive stimuli in animals. The tail flick test has been widely used as an experimental model of nociception. In this test, a rat's tail is exposed to noxious thermal stimulation, and the length of time to a withdrawal response (tail flick) is taken as a measure of the latency to the perception of nociceptive inputs. Although there are exceptions in the literature (Crisp et al., 1994; Hamm & Knisely, 1986; Knisely & Hamm, 1989), several investigators (Akunne & Soliman, 1994; Hess, Joseph, & Roth, 1981; Onaivi et al., 1993) have found an age-dependent increase in the latency to respond on this test. Similar results have also been reported with the hot-plate test (Akunne & Soliman, 1994; Hess et al., 1981). In this test, the animal is placed on a heated surface, and the time to paw withdrawal, licking, or an escape attempt is measured. Age differences have also been found in the reactivity to electrical and mechanical tests of nociception using vocalizations and jumps as the behavioral end points (Akunne & Soliman, 1994; Hess et al., 1981; Nicák, 1971). These studies found that a higher intensity of electric shock and mechanical pressure was necessary before older rats would either vocalize or jump. Overall, the evidence suggests that older animals show a decreased sensitivity to nociceptive stimuli similar to that found in human samples.

Pain Tolerance

Pain tolerance refers to the "lowest stimulation level at which the subject withdraws or asks to have the stimulation stopped" (Melzack & Wall, 1988, p. 17). Much less attention has been paid to the effect of age on this variable. Three of the four studies which have addressed this issue report a decrease in pain tolerance with age. This decrease has been shown with several different pain induction methods, including mechanical pressure at the Achilles tendon (Woodrow, Friedman, Siegelaub, & Collen, 1972), cold pressor pain (Walsh, Schoenfeld, Ramamurthy, & Hoffman, 1989), and cutaneous electric current (Collins & Stone, 1966). A possible interactive effect of sex and age on pain tolerance has been investigated but remains unclear. In one study, men showed larger age-related tolerance decreases than women (Woodrow et al., 1972), but in another study (Collins & Stone, 1966), a small age-related increase in pain tolerance in women was reported. However, Neri and Agazzani (1984) found neither age nor sex differences in the tolerance of painful electric current applied to the forearm. It is not clear why this study failed to replicate the other three. Although further research with more directly comparable methodologies is needed, the general conclusion, based on the limited evidence available, is that pain tolerance decreases with age.

Signal Detection Theory

The data reviewed so far indicate that there are age differences in the perception of experimentally induced pain. However, it has been suggested that traditional pain threshold measures are not a pure indication of sensory functioning but also include an attitudinal component (Chapman, Murphy, & Butler, 1973). Thus, it is not clear whether the reported age differences are the result of a sensory deficit, a more cautious attitude, or an interaction of both in the elderly (Harkins & Chapman, 1976). An attempt to separate these components of the pain experience has been made using the principles of signal detection theory (SDT) (Green and Swets, 1966). This psychophysical theory holds that threshold is never absolute and that discrimination between stimuli is probabilistic. The task of the perceiver is to distinguish the signal from the ever-present background noise. In order to decide if a signal is present, the subject sets a criterion for responding. When the intensity of the stimulus is greater than the criterion level, the subject responds that the signal is present, but if the signal falls below the criterion, the subject responds that it is not present. Therefore, the subject's response is determined not only by perceptual sensitivity (d') for a given stimulus but also by the response bias (C) which has been adopted. Each of these factors can be assessed, allowing the separation of sensory variables from motivational and cognitive factors (Green & Swets, 1966).

Three studies have examined age differences in responses to painful stimuli using SDT. Clark and Mehl (1971) presented six intensities of radiant heat to a sample of middle-aged and young subjects who were required to choose the best descriptor of the experience on a 10-point scale ranging from "nothing" to "very painful." These researchers found that the middle-aged subjects, especially the women, were less able than the younger subjects to discriminate among the low-intensity stimuli. At moderate intensities, although they did not differ on d', the middle-aged men were less likely to label stimuli as painful than were younger males and females. Therefore, middle-aged men were as sensitive as the younger subjects but adopted a more conservative response bias and were therefore less likely to label stimuli as painful. The middle-aged women, on the other hand, were less able to discriminate the stimuli and had also adopted a more conservative response bias. The authors conclude that previously reported threshold differences are the result of changes in attitudinal biases with age and do not reflect true differences in sensory-processing abilities. Unfortunately, this study did not include an elderly group, so the conclusions are limited.

Harkins and Chapman (1976, 1977) assessed age differences in the ability to discriminate between two levels of suprathreshold electrical tooth-pulp shocks in young versus elderly men and women. Subjects were required to rate the stimuli on a 6-point scale ranging from "nothing" to "moderate pain." The researchers found no age differences in reaction time or pain threshold. However, the elderly subjects had significantly lower d' than young subjects, reflecting impaired ability to discriminate between the shocks. The elderly were less likely to label faint, vaguely noxious stimuli as painful but, at the higher intensity, were more likely to do so than the younger group. This interaction must be interpreted with caution because only two intensities of shock were employed. These authors concluded that the differences were attitudinal and could be attributed to age-related central deficits in the processing of nociceptive stimuli, since there were no threshold differences.

Although the studies reviewed above find some evidence for changes in pain sensitivity (d') with age, they conclude that previously reported age differences in pain threshold are the result of a conservative attitudinal bias held by the elderly. However, the use of SDT in pain studies has been criticized (Coppola & Gracely, 1983; Rollman, 1977) on both logical and methodological grounds, and the interpretation of the results obtained with this procedure have been questioned. Nonetheless, the conclusions of these studies are widely accepted and have had important implications for the assessment of pain in the clinical setting. It has been assumed that the elderly adopt a conservative attitude toward painful symptoms and therefore are more reluctant to report these symptoms (Tremblay, 1994).

Direct Scaling

In response to the criticisms of the use of SDT in the measurement of pain, several studies have employed direct psychophysical scaling techniques (Marks, 1974). These procedures assess the different dimensions of pain using either visual analogue scaling or magnitude matching. For instance, by changing the anchors of the VAS from descriptors of intensity to ones of perceived unpleasantness, the procedure is said to allow for the dissociation of the sensory and affective qualities of pain. There have been three studies of age differences using this method.

Harkins, Price, and Martelli (1986) compared visual analogue ratings of intensity and unpleasantness in response to six levels of contact heat stimuli in three age groups. They found no age differences in ratings of either dimension, but a significant age-by-temperature interaction. The elderly group rated lower temperatures as less intense and higher temperatures as more intense than the younger groups. This finding closely parallels those of the same group using SDT and suggests an age-related change in the response to noxious stimuli.

Gibson et al. (1991) compared the perceived intensity of radiant heat pulses in four age groups, using a word descriptor scale ranging from "just noticeable" to "strong," and the quality of the pulses, using a list of descriptors such as "tingling, pinching, and burning." They found a significant increase in pain threshold and subjective ratings of threshold with age. The choice of word descriptors was similar at threshold in all the age groups. This finding is much more interesting when one considers the intensity at which the words were chosen. The mean threshold for the youngest group was 1.21 J/cm^2, which was subjectively rated as 16.75 (on a scale of 1–50) and described by the majority of the subjects (65.4%) as "stinging, burning or penetrating." The mean threshold for the oldest group was 2.57 J/cm^2, which was subjectively rated as 20.85 and described by the majority of the subjects (62.2%) as "stinging, burning or penetrating." Therefore, the threshold for the oldest group was more than twice that of the youngest (1.21 vs. 2.57 J/cm^2), and yet, the descriptors of the quality of the stimuli did not differ. It is possible to compare the pain experience of the groups at a similar stimulus intensity. As the oldest group's threshold was twice that of the youngest, it is interesting to compare the ratings by the oldest group at threshold (2.57 J/cm^2) with those made by the youngest at twice threshold (2.42 J/cm^2). At this intensity, the young group's subjective rating was 30.65, while 89.9% of the group now endorsed the most intense descriptors. Therefore, when stimulus intensity was approximately the same (2.42 vs. 2.57 J/cm^2), the subjective ratings by the elderly were lower (30.65 vs 20.85), and they were less likely to choose the most intense descriptors of the experience (89.9% vs. 62.2%). These data clearly indicate that the elderly group had an increased threshold to pain and that this difference was reflected in subjective ratings of both the intensity and the quality of the stimuli.

These results have been replicated by Tremblay (1994), who compared VAS ratings of intensity and unpleasantness in response to thermal stimuli in young versus elderly women. She found that, at the same temperature, the elderly women rated the stimuli as significantly less intense and unpleasant than did the young women.

The data from direct psychophysical scaling techniques appear to suggest that there are age differences in the perception of suprathreshold pain stimuli. These differences are apparent on both the affective and the sensory dimensions of the pain experience.

Proposed Mechanisms

Although not always consistent, the evidence reviewed so far strongly suggests that there are some age differences in the experience of experimental pain. The elderly appear to have an increased pain threshold and decreased tolerance. Although there is some evidence for a more conservative attitude in the elderly groups, this can not account for all of the differences. At suprathreshold levels, the elderly have more difficulty discriminating between stimuli of different intensities. They are less likely than younger groups to label weak stimuli as painful but are more likely to do so with intense stimuli. Compared to younger groups, moreover, the elderly assign lower intensity and unpleasantness ratings to the same stimuli. Mechanisms to account for these differences have been proposed at both the peripheral and central levels of the nervous system.

Procacci, Bozza, Buzzelli, and Della Corte (1970) suggested that age differences in pain thresholds found with thermal stimuli may reflect age-related changes in the periphery. They provided evidence that the skin of the elderly is thinner and that this results in greater rates of heat dispersion. However, age-related histological changes in skin characteristics have not been reported consistently, and there is no general agreement regarding this issue (Kenshalo, 1986). Procacci et al. (1970) also suggested that the changes may be due to an increase in the threshold of "nociceptors." However, there is no direct evidence for changes in free-nerve receptor function, morphology, or density with age (Harkins et al., 1984).

There is some limited evidence for age-related differences in the functioning of C fibers. The integrity of these fibers and the availability of substance P can be assessed with the axon reflex flare (Helme, 1987). This response, which is seen only in innervated skin, consists of a red flush, edema, and an irregular border (Helme & McKernan, 1985). It has been shown that this response decreases with age, the decrease being more pronounced in males than in females (Parkhouse & Le Quesne, 1988; Helme & McKernan, 1985). This suggests that the functioning of C fibers and the availability of substance

P may be compromised in the elderly. Studies of age differences in the functioning of A-delta fibers are lacking, but there is evidence that the amplitude of sensory nerve action potentials decreases with age (Buchthal & Rosenfalck, 1966). Although endogenous endorphins play an important role in the perception of pain, no age differences have been found in the levels of circulating endorphins in humans (Dalayeun, Nores, & Bergal, 1993). The animal literature, however, suggests that there may be decreases in the binding characteristics, affinity, and concentration of opiate receptors in the brain with age (Hess et al., 1981; Messing et al., 1980), as well as decreases in circulating levels of endorphins with age (Dupont, Savard, Merand, Labrie, & Boissier, 1981; Gambert, Garthwaite, Pontzer, & Hagen, 1980) Therefore, there is some limited evidence of peripheral changes associated with aging which may explain, in part, the observed differences in pain threshold. Unfortunately, data are not available which correlate the experience of pain with the activity of nerve fibers or neurotransmitters in different age groups.

An explanation of the age differences which implicates central neural mechanisms may be more promising. Harkins et al. (1984) suggested that there may be an age-related decrease in the capacity or speed of information processing of nociceptive stimuli. There is some evidence to support this view. An age-related decrease in EEG amplitude and a marked increase in response latency to painful stimuli have been reported (Gibson et al., 1991). In addition, there is evidence of reduced cortical activation in the regions associated with pain perception and a change in the topographical distribution of cortical activity with age. While both young and older adults show activation of midline and central cortical regions, older adults also show activation in more frontal and lateral sites (as cited by Gibson et al., 1994). These results suggest a wider recruitment of neurons and slower cognitive processing in response to painful stimuli in the elderly (Gibson et al., 1994).

As is evident from the preceding discussion, the mechanisms responsible for the age-related increase in pain threshold and decrease in tolerance require further elucidation. Undoubtedly, there is an interaction of both peripheral and central changes, including changes in emotional and cognitive factors.

The Relationship of Experimental to Clinical Pain

The age differences described above pertain only to experimentally induced pain. It is not clear if and how these results apply to pain seen in the clinical setting (Procacci et al., 1979). Experimental pain is often an oversimplification of both the acute and the chronic pain experience. The important role that psychological and emotional factors play in pathological pain states can not be replicated in the experimental setting (Procacci et al., 1979). Therefore, the age differences in pain threshold described should not be taken as evidence to support the view that the elderly always experience less discomfort and distress clinically. Unfortunately, this belief is now so pervasive that it has become a stereotype related to aging and may contribute to inadequate assessment and treatment of pain with subsequent declines in the health and overall quality of life of the elderly (Tremblay, 1994).

CLINICAL PAIN

Epidemiological Studies

Epidemiological studies of pain prevalence among individuals living independently in the community have produced inconsistent results. Most have reported that the overall prevalence of pain peaks in middle age and decreases thereafter (Andersson, Ejilertsson, Leden, & Rosenberg, 1993; Brattberg, Thorslund, & Wikman, 1989; Von Korff, Dworkin, La Resche, & Kruger, 1988). However, there have also been reports of an age-related increase in the prevalence of persistent pain (often or usually present and having occurred within the last two weeks) (Crook, Rideout, & Browne, 1984) and of an age-related decrease in the prevalence of pain problems at all sites other than the joints (Sternbach, 1986).

Consideration of various painful conditions suggests that the pattern of age differences may be specific to the location or type of pain. For instance, despite one study which reports a peak at middle-age (Valkenburg, 1988), there is considerable evidence for an age-related increase in the prevalence of joint pain, swelling, and morning stiffness (Badley & Tennant, 1992; Cunningham & Kelsey, 1984; Kelsey, 1982; Lawrence, 1977; Lee, Helewa, Smythe, Bomardier, & Goldsmith, 1985). This may be especially true of the knee, although the overall number of joints affected also increases with age (Badley & Tennant, 1992). Similar data regarding the prevalence of fibromyalgia, a disorder of widespread pain, tenderness, fatigue and psychological distress (Wolfe, 1989) have also been reported (Wolfe, Ross, Anderson, Russell, & Hebert, 1995).

A different pattern is seen with other common disorders. The prevalence of headache peaks in the 40s and decreases thereafter (see review by Lipton, Pfeffer, Newman, & Solomon, 1993). Migraine also decreases after the age of 65 (Cook et al., 1989). In fact, onset of chronic headaches after 55 is strongly suggestive of an organic disorder and calls for careful evaluation (Lipton et al., 1993). A similar pattern of peak prevalence in midlife has also been reported for low back pain (Lavsky-Shulan et al., 1985; Valkenburg, 1988).

Other work has focused on the prevalence of pain complaints within samples of independent, healthy elderly people. Roy and Thomas (1988) found that approximately 70% of those interviewed reported pain problems, although this pain was associated with minimal levels of impairment or distress. In this sample, 78% of the young-old (60–69 years old) reported pain, but only 64% of the old-old (80–89 years old) subjects did. The authors report that the majority of those with pain attributed it to the normal aging process and felt that it was necessary to accept their pain. The interpretation of these data is limited by both the sample and the methodology employed. The subjects were all healthy, active elderly people and therefore may not be representative of the older population. In addition, details are not given regarding the definition of "pain complaint" used by the authors. No measures of pain intensity, location, or duration are provided, which limits the interpretation of the impairment data. Despite these limitations, it is clear that, even within a sample of healthy elderly, the majority report some type of pain complaint.

Studies conducted within nursing homes and chronic care institutions suggest that between 71% and 83% of those interviewed had at least one current pain problem (Ferrell, Ferrell, & Osterweil, 1990; Parmelee, Smith, & Katz, 1993; Roy & Thomas, 1986) which was of an intensity sufficient to interfere with activities of daily living and quality of life (Ferrell et al., 1990). The most frequent problems reported in these studies were back and joint pain.

Pain shortly before death has also been assessed. These studies have attempted to document age differences in the prevalence of pain and the ways in which pain changes during the last year of life. Cartwright, Hockey, and Anderson (1973) reported on the deaths of 785 individuals between 15 and 85+ years of age, the majority of whom were over 65. These deaths were due to a variety of causes and occurred either in the home of the deceased or in an institution. Data were obtained through retrospective interviews with an informant who had been close to the deceased. Pain was the most commonly reported symptom in the year prior to death, the majority of the deceased having experienced pain which was rated as "very distressing." Interestingly, the elderly were less likely to have experienced pain in the last year of life than were the younger groups.

Similar data have been reported regarding cancer deaths in the hospice setting (Morris et al., 1986). This study used a prospective design with direct assessment of pain by both the patients and their primary-care providers. Consistent with observations by Cartwright et al. (1973), patients over 75 years of age were significantly more likely to be free of pain and less likely to be in persistent pain than were younger patients.

However, Moss, Lawton, and Glicksman (1991) recently reported that the frequency and intensity of pain increase over the last year of life and that there is no relationship between age and pain. This study was based on retrospective interviews with the close relatives or friends of 200 deceased elderly people who had not been institutionalized. Death was due to a variety of causes. The apparent inconsistency of these results with those reviewed above may be due to the limited age range of the subjects, all of whom were over 65 years of age.

Despite the many methodological problems associated with these studies (Ross & Crook, 1995), it may be tentatively concluded that, although the overall prevalence and severity of pain may increase in the time shortly prior to death, such increases may be less likely in the elderly. This pattern has been found with death due to a variety of causes, including cancer.

Clearly, studies of age differences in the prevalence of pain give inconsistent results, some suggesting an increase and others a decrease. There may be several reasons. First, decreases in pain prevalence as a function of age in community-dwelling adults may, in fact, be an artifact of higher mortality rates or increased likelihood of institutionalization of the elderly with chronic pain (Harkins, 1988). In addition, the studies reviewed have employed quite different definitions of chronic and/or acute pain, making comparison of the results difficult. Third, these studies assume that there are no age differences in the willingness to report painful symptoms. However, there are data which suggest that the elderly may be more reluctant to do so (Prohaska, Keller, Leventhal, & Leventhal, 1987). Associated with this, the subjects may not define pain in the same way that the researcher does. For instance, Crook et al. (1984) report that some individuals considered recurrent pain problems (e.g., arthritis) temporary and thus did not conform to the definitions used by the researchers. This illustrates the importance of personal schemas or beliefs regarding pain held by individuals, which may influence both the interpretation and the reporting of symptoms (De Good & Shutty, 1992).

Although clear conclusions regarding age differences in the prevalence of pain cannot be drawn, the data reviewed suggest that over 70% (Ferrell et al., 1990; Parmelee, Katz, & Lawton, 1991; Roy & Thomas, 1988) of the elderly, both in the community and in institutions, experience significant pain problems. This is not surprising when one considers that over 80% of this group suffer from at least one chronic ailment (Harkins et al., 1994). The most common pain problems reported are due to arthritis, which afflicts over 80% of the elderly (Davis, 1988), osteoporosis (Harkins et al., 1984), and the neuralgias (Helme et al., 1989).

Acute Pain

The most striking and consistently reported age differences are in the experience of acute pain. This is pain related to specific, brief clinical events which terminates relatively soon after the resolution of the pathological insult (Gibson et al., 1994). In general, the elderly may present with few of the symptoms typically associated with acute clinical syndromes, including pain. The pain which is reported is likely to be referred from the site of origin in an atypical manner. In fact, serious pathological conditions may produce only behavioral changes, such as mental confusion, restlessness, and aggression, or more subtle and nonspecific symptoms such as anorexia and fatigue (Butler & Gastell, 1980).

This pattern of age-related changes in clinical presentation has been well documented in the case of acute cardiac pain. Although the pathophysiology of coronary heart disease is similar in old and young patients, there are clear differences in the major clinical manifestations (acute myocardial infarction, angina pectoris, congestive cardiac failure, arrhythmias, and sudden death) (Gersh, 1986). It has been suggested that the elderly's impaired ability to perceive ischemic pain (Miller et al., 1990) may account, in part, for the dramatic increase in the incidence and prevalence of asymptomatic and atypical myocardial infarction with age (Sigurdsson, Thorgeirsson, Sigvaldason, & Sigfusson, 1995; Bayer, Chadha, & Pathy, 1986). Although relatively uncommon in younger patients, up to 30% of elderly survivors of myocardial infarction do not report any acute symptoms, while another 30% may have an atypical presentation (see review by Ambepitiya, Iyengar, & Roberts, 1993). Often, evidence of myocardial infarction in these patients is detected only through electrocardiographic changes (Kannel & Abbot, 1984). Possible mechanisms to account for this apparent lack of pain are poorly understood (see review by Ambepitiya et al., 1993).

Although not as extensively studied as cardiac pain, there is evidence for similar age differences in the presentation of acute disorders of the gastrointestinal (GI) system. Scapa, Horowitz, Waron, and Eshchar (1989) found that elderly patients with duodenal ulcer were more likely than younger patients to have GI bleeding without abdominal pain as a presenting sign. The older patients were more likely to present with heartburn or bleeding and less often with pain. Studies of acute intra-abdominal infection (Cooper, Shlaes, & Salata, 1994), appendicitis (Albano, Zielinski, & Organ, 1975) and pancreatitis (Gullo, Sipahi, & Pezzilli, 1994) have reported similar data.

To our knowledge, there is only one study which has directly compared the intensity of acute pain reported by younger and older patients. Scapa, Horowitz, Avtalion, Waron, and Eshchar (1992) obtained verbal descriptor scale ratings (from "mild" to "excruciating" pain) from patients diagnosed with either duodenal ulcer or acute myocardial infarction. For both diagnoses, the elderly were more likely to rate their pain in the mild categories than the younger patients, who were more likely to rate their pain as severe. Although more work is needed in the area, it appears that the elderly are less likely to experience pain associated with acute pathology, and when pain is reported, it tends to be less intense than that experienced by younger subjects.

In sum, the assessment of acute pain in the elderly no longer plays the key diagnostic role that it does in younger patients. The elderly are more likely to have an atypical presentation, which may contribute to delayed seeking of treatment, misdiagnosis, and increased mortality (Albano et al., 1975). Therefore, health care providers must rely on other measures to ensure speedy and accurate diagnosis.

Postoperative pain in the elderly has received very little attention, although this group undergoes up to 40% of all surgical procedures (Vowles, 1979). Proper assessment and management of this type of acute pain are critical, as postoperative confusion (Cousins, 1994), suppression of the immune and respiratory systems, and high rates of mortality (Ergina, Gold, & Meakins, 1993) have been associated with inadequate pain control. It has been well documented that older patients receive fewer prescriptions of analgesics and are given a smaller percentage of the prescribed dose than that given to younger patients (Faherty & Grier, 1984). However, older patients do not self-administer fewer analgesics than younger patients (Owen, Szekely, Plummer, Cushnie, & Mather, 1989).

Three studies have directly assessed the relationship of age to postoperative pain levels. Cytryn (1990), in a reanalysis of data originally reported by Melzack, Abbott, Zackon, Mulder, and Davis (1987), found a significant negative correlation between age and MPQ scores. For purposes of the reanalysis, the MPQ was divided into sensory and affective scores using the criteria outlined by Abbott (1986). With this scoring method, there was a significant negative correlation between age and the sensory dimension of the MPQ, but no significant correlation between age and the affective dimension. Analysis of variance between the age groups showed that patients over 75 years of age had significantly lower overall and sensory dimension scores than the three youngest age groups. Once again, there were no significant differences on the affective dimension. There were no significant age differences on the verbal descriptor scale measure of pain intensity (K. Cytryn, personal communication, May 1995).

Similar data were reported by Oberle, Paul, Wry, and Grace (1990), who compared MPQ scores of elderly and younger patients on the second and third postoperative days. Although there were no significant age differences on the VDS on either day, the elderly group had significantly lower MPQ scores than the younger group on the third postoperative day. This difference was due to the elderly subjects' tendency to choose the "less intense" words in each category.

In the final study, Duggleby and Lander (1994) found that age and postoperative pain intensity, as measured on the VAS, were not correlated. These results are not inconsistent with those of Cytryn (1990) and Oberle et al. (1990). In both studies, unidimensional measures of pain intensity failed to discriminate between the age groups. Taken together, the data suggest that there may be a change in the quality rather than in the intensity of postoperative pain with age, and that only measures sensitive to the different dimensions of pain, such as the MPQ, may be able to fully capture this change. A similar age-related dissociation between measures of pain intensity and quality has been reported in the assessment of chronic pain and will be described below.

Chronic Pain

Chronic pain "persists after all possible healing has occurred or, at least, long after pain can serve any useful function" (Melzack & Wall, 1988, p. 36). Although the evidence reviewed above suggests that a significant majority of the elderly may experience chronic pain, this group may be underrepresented in the distribution of patients referred to pain clinics (Harkins, 1988). In fact, some clinics set an upper age limit on the patients they will treat (Sorkin & Turk, 1995). This may be the result of the myth that pain is a normal consequence of aging and therefore not amenable to treatment (Harkins, 1988). Acceptance of this may contribute both to the elderly's reluctance to report symptoms and to a referral bias on the part of health care workers (Harkins, 1988). Another factor which may hinder referral of elderly patients is the misconception that they are less willing to participate in multidisciplinary treatment (Sorkin & Turk, 1995). However, the evidence available regarding elderly patients' attitude towards pain treatment suggests that there are no age differences in treatment expectations (Harkins, 1988), the acceptance of treatment, or the rate of compliance and dropouts (Sorkin, Rudy, Hanlon, Turk, & Stieg, 1990).

Among those pain clinics open to the elderly, Harkins (1988) reports that only 7%–10% of the patients are over the age of 65. This underrepresentation may result, in part, from the costs of the American health care system and therefore may not be representative of Canadian pain clinics. The age distribution of patients referred to the McGill–Montreal General Hospital Pain Centre, located in a large metropolitan area, is presented in Figure 4-3 (Gagliese, 1996). In this Canadian setting, approximately 20% of the patients referred are over the age of 65. The age distribution is consistent with the epidemiological studies which report a peak prevalence of chronic pain in midlife (see above). In addition, comparison with the age distribution of the population of Montreal (Statistics Canada, 1992) suggests that the proportion of elderly patients seen in this centre is not different from that found in the general population ($\chi^2 = 0.94$, $p \leq .8$). Whether these data are representative of other Canadian settings is not clear, and future work should address this.

Appropriate assessment of chronic pain should be sensitive to the multidimensional nature of this experience and thus include measures of the sensory, cognitive, and affective domains. Sensory pain levels are usually assessed with either unidimensional measures of pain intensity or multidimensional measures of the quality of the pain experienced. Data from studies using unidimensional measures have been inconsistent.

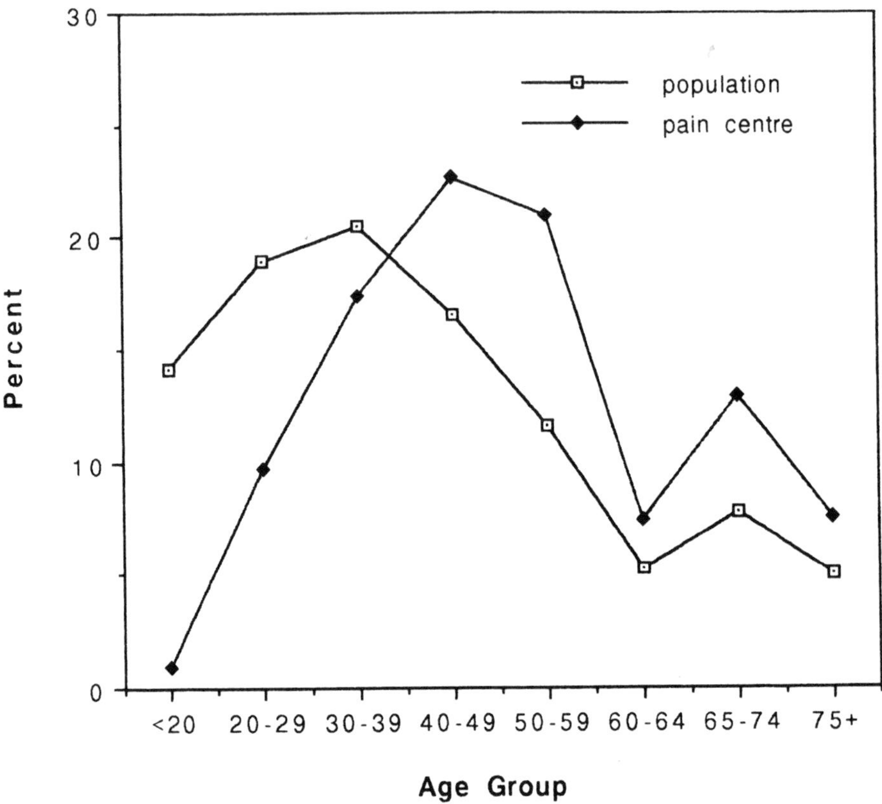

Figure 4-3. The age distribution of patients referred to the McGill–Montreal General Hospital Pain Centre over a five-year period (Gagliese, 1996) versus the age distribution of the population of Montreal (Statistics Canada, 1992).

One study (Puder, 1988), using the verbal descriptor scale (VDS), found that the elderly reported significantly higher pain intensity levels. This result has not been replicated in studies using the VAS, one of which found the opposite pattern (Parker et al., 1988), while two others found no evidence for any age differences (Harkins, 1988; Middaugh, Levin, Kee, Barchiesi, & Roberts, 1988).

Comparisons between age groups using multidimensional measures have been equally inconsistent. Of the two studies using the MPQ, one found no age differences (Corran, Helme, & Gibson, 1993), while the other reported that only the sensory scale of the MPQ was significantly negatively correlated with age (McCracken, Mosley, Plaud, Gross, & Penzien, 1993). Two studies using the West Haven–Yale Multidimensional Pain Inventory (Kerns et al., 1985) reported no age differences (McCracken et al., 1993; Sorkin et al., 1990). Although these results are inconsistent, the data, in general, suggest that there may be no age differences in the sensory domain of chronic pain, whether measured with uni- or multidimensional tools.

However, a different picture emerges when we consider studies in which both types of pain assessment tool are compared in the same subjects. There are two such studies. Gagliese and Melzack (1995) found no age differences in the intensity of pain as measured by several unidimensional scales, including the VAS, the VDS and the Behavioural Rating Scale (Linton & Gotestam, 1983). However, there were significant age differences on the Short-Form McGill Pain Questionnaire. The elderly had significantly lower sensory and affective scores and endorsed fewer words than the younger group. Similar results were reported by McCracken et al. (1993). Although age was not correlated with VAS scores in this sample, it was significantly negatively correlated with sensory SF-MPQ scores.

This dissociation between pain assessment tools is consistent with that reported in postoperative pain levels. One possible explanation of this pattern may be that there are age-related changes in the quality of the pain rather than in the intensity per se. On the other hand, the dissociation may reflect the elderly's reluctance to endorse the "most intense" words on the MPQ (Oberle et al., 1990). However, it may be assumed that this would also cause the elderly to endorse lower levels of pain on the intensity measures, which the data show is not the case. Third, there may be other words of equal or greater intensity, not included in the MPQ, which would more accurately capture the experience of pain in this group. The elderly may not group or rank the adjectives in the same ways as subjects in the original validation studies did (Melzack, 1975), or they may simply fail to comprehend the demands of either or both types of tools (Herr & Mobily, 1991). Our interpretation of this dissociation must await data regarding the validity and reliability of these measures in the geriatric population.

The Cognitive Dimension of Chronic Pain. The assessment of the cognitive dimension of chronic pain often involves measures of coping strategies, the perceived effectiveness of these strategies, and the perceived ability to control one's pain (De Good & Shutty, 1992). Age differences in the use of coping strategies have received some empirical attention. Keefe and Williams (1990) reported no age differences in the frequency of use of various strategies, although there was a trend for the elderly to use more praying and hoping than younger patients. Several other studies (Corran et al., 1993; McCracken et al., 1993; Sorkin et al., 1990) have also suggested that the elderly are more likely to employ externally mediated coping strategies, such as praying and hoping, than younger patients, who rely to a greater extent on internal strategies such as ignoring their pain. A lack of significant age differences in the perceived effectiveness of coping strategies and in the perceived ability to control pain has been consistently reported (Corran et al., 1993; Gagliese & Melzack, 1995; Harkins, 1988; Keefe & Williams, 1990).

The Affective Dimension of Chronic Pain. The affective consequences of chronic pain are most often measured in terms of depression and/or anxiety. Age differences in anxiety have received far less empirical attention than depression. Of the three studies which have addressed this question, two (Corran et al., 1993; McCracken et al., 1993) have reported that elderly chronic-pain patients report lower anxiety levels than younger patients. The third study, which had a much smaller sample than the others, found no age differences in anxiety levels (Middaugh et al., 1988).

Parmelee et al. (1991) assessed the relationship between anxiety and pain in the institutionalized elderly. Among this group, those with higher anxiety levels had more pain complaints and pain of greater intensity than those with lower levels of anxiety. Therefore, there is some limited evidence for age differences in anxiety levels reported by chronic pain patients, and, similar to data reported for younger patients (McCracken & Gross, 1993), anxiety may exacerbate reports of pain in the elderly.

Pain and Depression. The relationship between chronic pain and depression has received extensive empirical attention. It has been well documented that the majority of chronic pain patients have significant depressive symptoms and that depressed individuals are more likely to report painful symptoms than nondepressed individuals (for reviews of this literature see Romano & Turner, 1985; Roy, Thomas, & Matas, 1984). It has been suggested that this relationship may be enhanced in the elderly, as this group may have both an increased prevalence of pain-producing peripheral pathologies and depression (Kwentus et al., 1985). Although there is one exception in the literature (Harkins et al., 1984), there is considerable evidence that there are no age differences in the severity (Gagliese & Melzack, 1995; Herr, Mobily, & Smith, 1993; McCracken et al., 1993; Middaugh et al., 1988; Sorkin et al., 1990) or prevalence (Corran et al., 1993) of depressive symptoms experienced by chronic pain patients. There is also evidence that these two conditions intensify each other. Several studies have reported that elderly people with depression report more intense pain and a greater number of pain complaints than the nondepressed (Casten, Parmelee, Kleban, & Lawton, 1994; Cohen-Mansfield & Marx, 1993; Magni, Schifano, & DeLeo, 1985; Parmelee et al., 1991; Waxman, McCreary, Weinrit, & Carner, 1985). In the community setting, elderly people reporting pain have higher scores on depression scales than those who are pain-free (Roy & Thomas, 1988; Williamson & Schulz, 1992). However, two studies have failed to support this relationship (Ferrell et al., 1990; Harkins & Price, 1992). This may be due to the restricted range of the depression scores obtained in one (Ferrell et al., 1990) and to the small sample size of the other (n = 19; Harkins & Price, 1992).

The evidence reviewed above suggests that there is significant co-morbidity of pain and depression in the elderly. Clinical differentiation of these states may be difficult (Herr & Mobily, 1991). It has been suggested that the patient who presents with early-morning wakening, psychomotor retardation or agitation, anorexia or weight loss, and pain with a puzzling pattern, onset, or distribution may have a significant affective overlay to his or her pain problem, and that thorough evaluation for affective illness is appropriate (Herr & Mobily, 1991). In fact, the elderly may use pain complaints to explain their symptoms of depression (Kwentus et al., 1985). However, the clinician must bear in mind that the elderly are more likely to present with atypical pain (see above) and that the suspicion of depression does not reduce the importance of a comprehensive pain assessment. In fact, all comprehensive pain assessments should include an evaluation of the patient's psychological and social well-being.

There are several well-validated instruments for the assessment of depression in the elderly (Brink et al., 1982). There may be problems, however, in using these scales with the elderly in pain. Many of the items assess the vegetative or somatic symptoms of depression, which may also be part of the pain problem. This would inflate the scores obtained on these scales by chronic pain patients (Bourque, Blanchard, & Saulnier, 1992). It has been suggested that the clinician should use only scales validated for the elderly and that, if feasible, more than one scale should be used (Gibson et al., 1994).

Pain and Dementia. Careful assessment and differential diagnosis between pain and dementia is also necessary in the elderly patient. Pain complaints may be the first signs of dementia (Kisely, Tweddle, & Pugh, 1992) or may be used to explain or hide mild cognitive impairment (Harkins et al., 1984). Also, as we have seen, acute pathologies, which are often associated with pain in younger patients, may manifest only as mental confusion in the elderly (see above).

The assessment of pain in the demented elderly has received little empirical attention. The limited evidence available suggests that the prevalence of painful conditions (Marzinski, 1991), headache (Takeshima, Taniguchi, Kitagawa, & Takahashi, 1990), and localized pain complaints (Parmelee et al., 1993) may decrease as dementia progresses. In addition, the intensity of pain reported by either the patient (Parmelee et al., 1993) or the nursing staff of a chronic care facility (Cohen-Mansfield & Marx, 1993) may also decrease as dementia progresses. However, the results of these studies must be interpreted with great caution. None of the studies based on self-report include evidence that the cognitively impaired subjects understood the demands of the task. For instance, it is not clear that the protocols used also assessed each subject's understanding of the concept of pain or of the method used to quantify intensity. None of the studies used pain tools which were sensitive to the cognitive limitations of the respondents. Harkins and Price (1992) suggested that scales designed for use with children may be appropriate, although the feasibility of using such scales has not been tested. The data from these studies do suggest that further exploration of the relationship between pain and dementia is warranted. The initial challenge appears to be the development of a reliable, quantitative pain-assessment instrument for use with this population.

As dementia progresses, direct assessment of the patient may become impossible. At this point, valuable information may be obtained from significant others or through direct observation of behavior. The clinician should be especially attentive to any abrupt changes in behavior or usual functioning (Marzinski, 1991). However, it is not clear whether consistent pain behaviors are displayed by the elderly and how these might change as a result of dementia.

Facial expressions have been shown to be reliable indicators of painful states (Craig, Prkachin, & Grunau, 1992). However, there is little information regarding the facial expression of pain among the demented elderly. One small study reported on four noncommunicative women with senile dementia of the Alzheimer's type (Asplund, Norberg, Adolfsson, & Waxman, 1991). In this study, facial expressions during pleasant and unpleasant stimuli were compared. Complex facial expressions, which could be taken as indicators of emotion (Collier, 1985), were not seen under either condition. There was an increase in the number of facial movements seen during the unpleasant stimuli, but the responses of each subject were highly variable, and no conclusions regarding which movements were associated with discomfort could be drawn. Much more work is needed to develop systematic guidelines for the assessment of pain in the nonverbal demented elderly.

The Problem of Investigating the Elderly Person

The assessment of pain in the clinical setting should involve a multidimensional and holistic approach regardless of age. However, the elderly patient presents additional challenges. These include, but are not limited to, comorbidity, mental status, functional status, and independence in the performance of daily activities (Harkins & Price, 1992). The assessment of pain in the elderly may be further hindered by sensory impairments such as poor vision and/or hearing. Sensory function must therefore be taken into account and assessment strategies modified to accommodate impairments (Herr & Mobily, 1991). In cases of severe impairment, direct observation of the patient or the report of others may become necessary.

CONCLUSION

In this chapter, we have seen that, although there are exceptions, the majority of the studies suggest that there are age-related differences in experimental, acute, and chronic pain. The most consistent results suggest that increasing age is associated with higher pain threshold, lower tolerance, and impaired ability to discriminate between levels of noxious stimuli. Clinically, the elderly are less likely than younger patients to report pain during acute illnesses such as intra-abdominal infection. Although data regarding age differences in the prevalence of chronic pain are inconsistent, a majority of the elderly report some type of pain complaint. Age differences reported in the experience of chronic pain have also been inconsistent, although some data suggest that there may be a change in the quality, but not the intensity, of chronic pain with age. A similar pattern has been reported for postoperative pain. Each of these conclusions, however, is limited by the pain assessment tools used. None of the measures on which these results are based has been validated for use with the elderly. Future work must address this issue, as well as the development of a set of multidisciplinary assessment guidelines for geriatric pain.

ACKNOWLEDGMENTS. Supported by a Medical Research Council of Canada Studentship Grant to L. G. and Grant A7891 from the Natural Sciences and Engineering Research Council of Canada to R. M.

REFERENCES

Abbott, F. V. (1986). Qualitative differences in effects of opioids in man: Preliminary evidence for multiple mechanisms of analgesic action. *Pharmacology, Biochemistry and Behavior*, *24*, 1247–1251.

Akunne, H. C., & Soliman, K. F. A. (1994). Serotonin modulation of pain responsiveness in the aged rat. *Pharmacology Biochemistry and Behavior*, *48*, 411–416.

Albano, W. A., Zielinski, C. M., & Organ, C. H. (1975). Is appendicitis in the aged really different? *Geriatrics*, *30*, 81–88.

Ambepitiya, G. B., Iyengar, E. N., & Roberts, M. E. (1993). Review: Silent exertional myocardial ischaemia and perception of angina in elderly people. *Age and Ageing*, *22*, 302–307.

Andersson, H. I., Ejilertsson, G., Leden, I., & Rosenberg, C. (1993). Chronic pain in a geographically defined population: Studies of differences in age, gender, social class and pain localization. *Clinical Journal of Pain, 9,* 174–182.

Asplund, K., Norberg, A., Adolfsson, R., & Waxman, H. M. (1991). Facial expressions in severely demented patients: A stimulus-response study of four patients with dementia of the Alzheimer type. *International Journal of Geriatric Psychiatry, 6,* 599–606.

Badley, E. M., & Tennant, A. (1992). Changing profile of joint disorders with age: Findings from a postal survey of the population of Calderdale, West Yorkshire, United Kingdom. *Annals of Rheumatic Disease, 51,* 366–371.

Bayer, A. J., Chadha, J. S., & Pathy, J. (1986). Changing presentation of myocardial infarction with increasing old age. *Journal of the American Geriatrics Society, 34,* 263–266.

Birren, J. E., Schapiro, H. B., & Miller, J. H. (1950). The effect of salicylate upon pain sensitivity. *Journal of Pharmacological and Experimental Therapy, 100,* 67–71.

Bourque, P., Blanchard, L., & Saulnier, J. (1992). L'impact des symptômes somatiques dans l'evaluation de la dépression chez une population gériatrique. *Revue Canadienne des Sciences du Comportement, 24,* 118–128.

Brattberg, G., Thorslund, M., & Wikman, A. (1989). The prevalence of pain in a general population. The results of a postal survey in a county of Sweden. *Pain, 37,* 215–222.

Brink, T. L., Yesavage, J. A., Lum, O., Heersema, P. H., Adey, M., & Rose, T. L. (1982). Screening tests for geriatric depression. *Clinical Gerontologist, 1,* 37–43.

Buchtal, F., & Rosenfalck, A. (1966). Evoked action potentials and conduction velocity in human sensory nerves. *Brain Research, 3,* 1–122.

Butler, R. N., & Gastel, B. (1980). Care of the aged: Perspectives on pain and discomfort. In L. K. Ng & J. Bonica (Eds.), *Pain, discomfort and humanitarian care* (pp. 297–311). New York: Elsevier North Holland.

Cartwright, A., Hockey, L., & Anderson, J. L. (1973). *Life before death.* Boston: Routledge & Kegan Paul.

Casten, R. J., Parmelee, P. A., Kleban, M. H., & Lawton, M. P. (1994, August). *The relationship among pain, anxiety and depression in an institutionalized elderly sample.* Paper presented at the annual meeting of the American Psychological Association, Los Angeles.

Chapman, C. R., Murphy, T. M., & Butler, S. H. (1973). Analgesic strength of 33% nitrous oxide: A signal detection theory evaluation. *Science, 179,* 1246–1248.

Chapman, W. P., & Jones, C. M. (1944). Variations in cutaneous and visceral pain sensitivity in normal subjects. *Journal of Clinical Investigation, 23,* 81–91.

Clark, C. W. M., & Mehl, L. (1971). Thermal pain: A sensory decision theory analysis of the effect of age and sex on d′, various response criteria and 50% pain threshold. *Journal of Abnormal Psychology, 78,* 201–212.

Cohen-Mansfield, J., & Marx, M. S. (1993). Pain and depression in the nursing home: Corroborating results. *Journal of Gerontology: Psychological Sciences, 48,* p96–p97.

Collier, G. (1985). *Emotional expression.* Hillsdale NJ: Erlbaum.

Collins, L. G., & Stone, L. A. (1966). Pain sensitivity, age and activity level in chronic schizophrenics and in normals. *British Journal of Psychiatry, 112,* 33–35.

Cook, N. R., Evans, D. A., Funkenstein, H. H., Scherr, P. A., Ostfeld, A. M., Taylor, J. A., & Hennekens, C. H. (1989). Correlates of headache in a population-based cohort of elderly. *Archives of Neurology, 46,* 1338–1344.

Cooper, G. S., Shlaes, D. M., & Salata, R. A. (1994). Intraabdominal infection: Differences in presentation and outcome between younger patients and the elderly. *Clinical Infectious Diseases, 19,* 146–148.

Coppola, R., & Gracely, R. H. (1983). Where is the noise in SDT pain assessment? *Pain, 17,* 257–266.

Corran, T. M., Helme, R. D., & Gibson, S. J. (1993, August). *Comparison of chronic pain experience in young and elderly patients.* Paper presented at the Seventh World Congress on Pain, Paris.

Cousins, M. (1994). Acute and postoperative pain. In P. D. Wall & R. Melzack (Eds.), *The textbook of pain* (pp. 284–305). Edinburgh: Churchill Livingstone.

Craig, K. D., Prkachin, K. M., & Grunau, R. V. E. (1992). The facial expression of pain. In D. C. Turk & R. Melzack (Eds.), *Handbook of pain assessment* (pp. 257–274). New York: Guilford Press.

Crisp, T., Stafinsky, J. L., Hoskins, D. L., Perni, V. C., Uram, M., & Gordon, T. L. (1994). Age-related changes in the spinal antinociceptive effects of DAGO, DPDPE and β-endorphin in the rat. *Brain Research, 643*, 282–286.

Crook, J., Rideout, E., & Browne, G. (1984). The prevalence of pain complaints in a general population. *Pain, 18*, 299–314.

Cunningham, L. S., & Kelsey, J. L. (1984). Epidemiology of musculoskeletal impairments and associated disability. *American Journal of Public Health, 74*, 574–579.

Cytryn, K. (1990). *Nursing decisions in the administration of analgesic medications and the relation to pain levels reported by patients.* Unpublished master's thesis, McGill University, Montreal.

Dalayeun, J. F., Nores, J. M., & Bergal, S. (1993). Physiology of beta-endorphins. A close-up view and a review of the literature. *Biomedicine and Pharmacotherapy, 47*, 311–320.

Davis, M. A. (1988). Epidemiology of osteoarthritis. *Clinics in Geriatric Medicine, 4*, 241–255.

De Good, D. E., & Shutty, M. S. (1992). Assessment of pain beliefs, coping and self-efficacy. In D. C. Turk & R. Melzack (Eds.), *Handbook of pain assessment* (pp. 214–234). New York: Guilford Press.

Duggleby, W., & Lander, J. (1994). Cognitive status and postoperative pain: Older adults. *Journal of Pain and Symptom Management, 9*, 19–27.

Dupont, A., Savard, P., Merand, Y., Labrie, F., & Boissier, J. R. (1981). Age-related changes in central nervous system enkephalins and substance P. *Life Sciences, 29*, 2317–2322.

Ergina, P. L., Gold, S. L., & Meakins, J. L. (1993). Perioperative care of the elderly patient. *World Journal of Surgery, 17*, 192–198.

Faherty, B. S., & Grier, M. R. (1984). Analgesic medication for elderly people post-surgery. *Nursing Research, 33*, 369–372.

Ferrell, B. A. (1991). Pain management in elderly people. *Journal of the American Geriatrics Society, 39*, 64–73.

Ferrell, B. A., Ferrell, B. R., & Osterweil, D. (1990). Pain in the nursing home. *Journal of the American Geriatrics Society, 38*, 409–414.

Gagliese, L. (1996). *Age distribution of pain centre patients.* Unpublished Ph.D. thesis, McGill University, Montreal.

Gagliese, L. & Melzack, R. (1995, May). *Age differences in the quality but not intensity of chronic pain.* Paper presented at the annual meeting of the Canadian Pain Society, Ottawa, Ontario, Canada.

Gambert, S. R., Garthwaite, T. L., Pontzer, C. H., & Hagen, T. C. (1980). Age-related changes in central nervous system beta-endorphin and ACTH. *Neuroendocrinology, 31*, 252–255.

Gersh, B. J. (1986). Clinical manifestations of coronary heart disease in the elderly. In N. K. Wegner, D. C. Furberg, & E. Pitt (Eds.), *Coronary heart disease in the elderly* (pp. 276–296). New York: Elsevier.

Gibson, S. J., Gorman, M. M., & Helme, R. D. (1991). Assessment of pain in the elderly using event-related cerebral potentials. In M. R. Bond, J. E. Charlton, & C. J. Woolf (Eds.), *Proceedings of the VIth World Congress on Pain* (pp. 527–533). New York: Elsevier.

Gibson, S. J., Katz, B., Corran, T. M., Farrell, M. J., & Helme, R. D. (1994). Pain in older persons. *Disability and Rehabilitation, 16*, 127–139.

Green, D. M., & Swets, J. A. (1966). *Signal detection theory and psychophysics.* New York: Wiley.

Gullo, L., Sipahi, H. M., & Pezzilli, R. (1994). Pancreatitis in the elderly. *Journal of Clinical Gastroenterology, 19*, 64–68.

Hall, K. R. L., & Stride, E. (1954). The varying response to pain in psychiatric disorders: A study in abnormal psychology. *British Journal of Medical Psychology, 27*, 48–60.

Hamm, R. J., & Knisely, J. S. (1986). Environmentally induced analgesia: Age-related decline in a neurally mediated, nonopioid system. *Psychology and Aging, 1*, 195–201.

Hardy, J. D., Wolff, H. G., & Goodell, H. (1943). The pain threshold in man. *American Journal of Psychiatry, 99*, 744–751.

Harkins, S. W. (1988). Pain in the elderly. In R. Dubner, F. G. Gebhart, & M. R. Bond (Eds.), *Proceedings of the 5th World Congress on Pain* (pp. 355–357). Amsterdam Elsevier Science, Biomedical Division.

Harkins, S. W., & Chapman, C. R. (1976). Detection and decision factors in pain perception in young and elderly men. *Pain, 2*, 253–264.

Harkins, S. W. & Chapman, C. R. (1977). The perception of induced dental pain in young and elderly women. *Journal of Gerontology, 32*, 428–435.

Harkins, S. W., Kwentus, J., & Price, D. D. (1984). Pain and the elderly. In C. Benedetti, C. R. Chapman, & G. Morieca (Eds.), *Advances in pain research and therapy* (Vol. 7, pp. 103–121). New York: Raven Press.

Harkins, S. W., Kwentus, J., & Price, D. D. (1994). Pain and suffering in the elderly. In P. D. Wall & R. Melzack (Eds.), *Textbook of pain* (pp. 552–560). Edinburgh: Churchill Livingstone.

Harkins, S. W., Lagua, B. T., Price, D. D., & Small, R. E. (1995). Geriatric pain. In R. Roy (Ed.), *Chronic pain in old age* (pp. 127–159). Toronto: University of Toronto Press.

Harkins, S. W., & Price, D. D. (1992). Assessment of pain in the elderly. In D. C. Turk & R. Melzack (Eds.), *Handbook of pain assessment* (pp. 315–331). New York: Guilford Press.

Harkins, S. W., Price, D. D., & Martelli, M. (1986). Effects of age on pain perception: Thermonociception. *Journal of Gerontology, 41,* 58–63.

Harkins, S. W., & Warner, M. H. (1980). Age and pain. In C. Eisdorfer (Ed.), *Annual review of gerontology and geriatrics* (Vol. 1, pp. 121–131). New York: Springer.

Helme, R. D. (1987). Measurement of flare responses in patients with pain. *Clinical and Experimental Neurology, 24,* 201–205.

Helme, R. D., Katz, B., Gibson, S., & Corran, T. (1989). Can psychometric tools be used to analyse pain in a geriatric population. *Clinical and Experimental Neurology, 26,* 113–117.

Helme, R. D., & McKernan, S. (1985). Neurogenic flare responses following topical application of capsaicin in humans. *Annals of Neurology, 18,* 505–509.

Herr, K. A., & Mobily, P. R. (1991). Complexities of pain assessment in the elderly: Clinical considerations. *Journal of Gerontological Nursing, 17,* 12–19.

Herr, K. A., & Mobily, P. R. (1993). Comparison of selected pain assessment tools for use with the elderly. *Applied Nursing Research, 6,* 39–46.

Herr, K. A., Mobily, P. R., & Smith, C. (1993). Depression and the experience of chronic back pain: A study of related variables and age differences. *Clinical Journal of Pain, 9,* 104–114.

Hess, G. D., Joseph, J. A., & Roth, G. S. (1981). Effect of age on sensitivity to pain and brain opiate receptors. *Neurobiology of Aging, 2,* 49–55.

Horch, K., Hardy, M., Jimenez, S., & Jabaley, M. (1992). An automated tactile tester for evaluation of cutaneous sensibility. *Journal of Hand Surgery, 17A,* 829–837.

Huskisson, E. C. (1974). Measurement of pain. *The Lancet, 2,* 1127–1131.

Huskisson, E. C. (1983). Visual analogue scales. In R. Melzack (Ed.), *Pain measurement and assessment* (pp. 33–37). New York: Raven Press.

Jensen, M. P., & Karoly, P. (1992). Self-report scales and procedures for assessing pain in adults. In D. C. Turk & R. Melzack (Eds.), *Handbook of pain assessment* (pp. 135–151). New York: Guilford Press.

Jensen, M. P., Karoly, P., & Braver, S. (1986). The measurement of clinical pain intensity: A comparison of six methods. *Pain, 27,* 117–126.

Kannel, W. B., & Abbot, R. D. (1984). Incidence and prognosis of unrecognized myocardial infarction: An update on the Framingham study. *New England Journal of Medicine, 311,* 1144–1147.

Keefe, F. J., & Williams, D. A. (1990). A comparison of coping strategies in chronic pain patients in different age groups. *Journal of Gerontology: Psychological Sciences, 45,* p161–p165.

Kelsey, J. L. (1982). *Epidemiology of musculoskeletal disorders.* New York: Oxford University Press.

Kenshalo, D. R. (1986). Somesthetic sensitivity in young and elderly humans. *Journal of Gerontology, 41,* 732–742.

Kerns, R., Turk, D., & Rudy, D. (1985). The West Haven-Yale Multidimensional Pain Inventory (WHYMPI). *Pain, 23,* 345–356.

Kisely, S., Tweddle, D., & Pugh, E. W. (1992). Dementia presenting with sore eyes. *British Journal of Psychiatry, 161,* 120–121.

Knisely, J. S., & Hamm, R. J. (1989). Physostigmine-induced analgesia in young, middle-aged, and senescent rats. *Experimental Aging Research, 15,* 3–11.

Kremer, E., Atkinson, J. H., & Ignelzi, R. J. (1981). Measurement of pain: Patient preference does not confound pain measurement. *Pain, 10,* 241–249.

Kwentus, J. A., Harkins, S. W., Lignon, N., & Silverman, J. J. (1985). Current concepts in geriatric pain and its treatment. *Geriatrics, 40,* 48–57.

Lautenbacher, S., & Strian, F. (1991). Similarities in age differences in heat pain perception and thermal sensitivity. *Functional Neurology, 6,* 129–135.

Lavsky-Shulan, M., Wallace, R. B., Kohout, F. J., Lemke, J. H., Morris, M. C., & Smith, I. M. (1985). Prevalence and functional correlates of low back pain in the elderly: The Iowa 65+ rural health study. *Journal of the American Geriatrics Society, 33*, 23–28.

Lawrence, J. S. (1977). *Rheumatism in populations*. London: Heinemann.

Lee, P., Helewa, A., Smythe, H. A., Bomardier, C., & Goldsmith, C. H. (1985). Epidemiology of musculoskeletal disorders (complaints) and related disability in Canada. *Journal of Rheumatology, 12*, 1169–1173.

Linton, S. J., & Gotestam, K. G. (1983). A clinical comparison of two pain scales: Correlation, remembering chronic pain, and a measure of compliance. *Pain, 17*, 57–65.

Lipton, R. B., Pfeffer, D., Newman, L. C., & Solomon, S. (1993). Headaches in the elderly. *Journal of Pain and Symptom Management, 8*, 87–97.

Magni, G., Schifano, F., & DeLeo, D. (1985). Pain as a symptom in elderly depressed patients: Relationship to diagnostic subgroups. *European Archives of Psychiatry and Neurological Sciences, 235*, 143–145.

Marks, L. E. (1974). *Sensory processes: The new psychophysics*. New York: Academic Press.

Marzinski, L. R. (1991). The tragedy of dementia: Clinically assessing pain in the confused, nonverbal elderly. *Journal of Gerontological Nursing, 17*, 25–28.

McCracken, L. M., & Gross, R. T. (1993). Does anxiety affect coping with chronic pain? *Clinical Journal of Pain, 9*, 253–259.

McCracken, L. M., Mosley, T. H., Plaud, J. J., Gross, R. T., & Penzien, D. B. (1993, August). *Age, chronic pain and impairment: Results from two clinical samples*. Paper presented at the VIIth World Congress on Pain, Paris, France.

Melzack, R. (1975). The McGill Pain Questionnaire: Major properties and scoring methods. *Pain, 1*, 277–299.

Melzack, R. (1987). The short-form McGill Pain Questionnaire. *Pain, 30*, 191–197.

Melzack, R., Abbott, F. V., Zackon, W., Mulder, D. S., & Davis, M. W. L. (1987). Pain on a surgical ward: A survey of the duration and intensity of pain and the effectiveness of medication. *Pain, 29*, 67–72.

Melzack, R., & Casey, K. L. (1968). Sensory, motivational and central control determinants of pain: A new conceptual model. In D. Kenshalo (Ed.), *The skin senses* (pp. 423–439). Springfield, IL: Charles C Thomas.

Melzack, R., & Katz, J. (1992). The McGill Pain Questionnaire: Appraisal and current status. In D. C. Turk & R. Melzack (Eds.), *Handbook of pain assessment* (pp. 152–168). New York: Guilford Press.

Melzack, R., & Wall, P. D. (1988). *The challenge of pain*. London: Penguin Books.

Messing, R. B., Vasquez, B. J., Spiehler, V. R., Martinez, J. L., Jensen, R. A., Rigter, H., & McGaugh, J. (1980). 3H-dihydromorphine binding in the brain regions of young and aged rats. *Life Sciences, 26*, 921–927.

Middaugh, S. J., Levin, R. B., Kee, W. G., Barchiesi, F. D., & Roberts, J. M. (1988). Chronic pain: Its treatment in geriatric and younger patients. *Archives of Physical Medicine and Rehabilitation, 69*, 1021–1025.

Miller, P. F., Sheps, D. S., Bragdon, E. E., Herbst, M. C., Dalton, J. L., Hinderliter, A. L., Koch, G. G., Maixner, W., & Ekelund, L. G. (1990). Aging and pain perception in ischemic heart disease. *American Heart Journal, 120*, 22–30.

Monk, M. (1980). *The nature of pain and responses to pain in adolescent hemophiliacs*. Unpublished master's thesis, McGill University, Montreal.

Morris, J. N., Mor, V., Goldberg, R. J., Sherwood, S., Greer, D. S., & Hiris, J. (1986). The effect of treatment setting and patient characteristics on pain in terminal cancer patients: A report from the national hospice study. *Journal of Chronic Disease, 39*, 27–35.

Moss, M. S., Lawton, M. P., & Glicksman, A. (1991). The role of pain in the last year of life of older persons. *Journal of Gerontology, 46*, 51–57.

Mumford, J. M. (1963). Pain perception in man on electrically stimulating the teeth. In A. Soulairac, J. Cahn, & J. Charpentier (Eds.), *Pain* (pp. 221–229). London: Academic Press.

Mumford, J. M. (1965). Pain perception threshold and adaptation of normal human teeth. *Archives of Oral Biology, 10*, 957–968.

Mumford, J. M. (1968). Pain perception in man on electrically stimulating the teeth. In A. Soulairac, J. Cahn & J. Charpentier (Eds.), *Pain* (pp. 224–229). London: Academic Press.

Neri, M., & Agazzani, E. (1984). Aging and right-left asymmetry in experimental pain measurement. *Pain, 19*, 43–48.

Nicák, A. (1971). Changes of sensitivity to pain in relation to postnatal development in rats. *Experimental Gerontology, 6*, 111–114.

Oberle, K., Paul, P., Wry, J., & Grace, M. (1990). Pain, anxiety and analgesics: A comparative study of elderly and younger surgical patients. *Canadian Journal on Aging*, *9*, 13–22.

Onaivi, E. S., Payne, S., Brock, J. W., Hamdi, A., Faroouqui, S., & Prasad, C. (1993). Chronic nicotine reverses age-associated increases in tail-flick latency and anxiety in rats. *Life Sciences*, *54*, 193–202.

Owen, H., Szekely, J., Plummer, J., Cushnie, J., & Mather, L. (1989). Variations of patient-controlled analgesia: 2. Concurrent infusion. *Anesthesia*, *44*, 11–13.

Parker, J., Frank, R., Beck, N., Finan, M., Walker, S., Hewett, J. E., Broster, C., Smarr, K., Smith, E., & Kay, D. (1988). Pain in rheumatoid arthritis: Relationship to demographic, medical and psychological factors. *Journal of Rheumatology*, *15*, 433–437.

Parkhouse, N., & Le Quesne, P. M. (1988). Quantitative objective assessment of peripheral nociceptive C-fibre function. *Journal of Neurology Neurosurgery and Psychiatry*, *51*, 28–34.

Parmelee, P. A., Katz, I. R., & Lawton, M. P. (1991). The relation of pain to depression among institutionalized aged. *Journal of Gerontology: Psychological Sciences*, *46*, p15–p21.

Parmelee, P. A., Smith, B., & Katz, I. R. (1993). Pain complaints and cognitive status among elderly institution residents. *Journal of the American Geriatrics Society*, *41*, 517–522.

Procacci, P., Bozza, G., Buzzelli, G., & Della Corte, M. (1970). The cutaneous pricking pain threshold in old age. *Gerontological Clinics*, *12*, 213–218.

Procacci, P., Zoppi, M., & Maresca, M. (1979). Experimental pain in man. *Pain*, *6*, 123–140.

Prohaska, T. R., Keller, M. L., Leventhal, E. A., & Leventhal, H. (1987). Impact of symptoms and aging attribution on emotion and coping. *Health Psychology*, *6*, 495–514.

Puder, R. S. (1988). Age analysis of cognitive-behavioral group therapy for chronic pain outpatients. *Psychology and Aging*, *3*, 204–207.

Rollman, G. B. (1977). Signal detection theory measurement of pain: A review and critique. *Pain*, *3*, 187–211.

Romano, J. M., & Turner, J. A. (1985). Chronic pain and depression: Does the evidence support a relationship? *Psychological Bulletin*, *97*, 18–34.

Ross, M. M., & Crook, J. M. (1995). Pain in later life: Present state of knowledge. In R. Roy (Ed.), *Chronic pain in old age* (pp. 3–19). Toronto: University of Toronto Press.

Roy, R., & Thomas, M. (1986). A survey of chronic pain in an elderly population. *Canadian Family Physician*, *32*, 513–516.

Roy, R., & Thomas, M. (1988). Pain, depression and illness behavior in a community sample of active elderly persons: Elderly persons with and without pain, Part 2. *Clinical Journal of Pain*, *3*, 207–211.

Roy, R., & Thomas, M., & Matas, M. (1984). Chronic pain and depression: A review. *Comprehensive Psychiatry*, *25*, 96–105.

Scapa, E., Horowitz, M., Avtalion, J., Waron, M., & Eshchar, J. (1992). Appreciation of pain in the elderly. *Israel Journal of Medical Science*, *28*, 94–96.

Scapa, E., Horowitz, M., Waron, M., & Eshchar, J. (1989). Duodenal ulcer in the elderly. *Journal of Clinical Gastroenterology*, *11*, 502–506.

Schludermann, E., & Zubek, J. P. (1962). Effect of age on pain sensitivity. *Perceptual and Motor Skills*, *14*, 295–301.

Schumacher, G. A., Goodell, H., Hardy, J. D., & Wolff, H. G. (1940). Uniformity of the pain threshold in man. *Science*, *92*, 110–112.

Sherman, E. D., & Robillard, E. (1960). Sensitivity to pain in the aged. *Canadian Medical Association Journal*, *38*, 944–947.

Sigurdsson, E., Thorgeirsson, G., Sigvaldason, H., & Sigfusson, N. (1995). Unrecognized myocardial infarction: Epidemiology, clinical characteristics, and the prognostic role of angina pectoris. *Annals of Internal Medicine*, *122*, 96–102.

Sorkin, B. A., Rudy, T. E., Hanlon, R. B., Turk, D. C., & Stieg, R. L. (1990). Chronic pain in old and young patients: Differences appear less important than similarities. *Journal of Gerontology: Psychological Sciences*, *45*, p64–p68.

Sorkin, B. A. & Turk, D. C. (1995). Pain management in the elderly. In R. Roy (Ed.), *Chronic pain in old age* (pp. 56–80). Toronto: University of Toronto Press.

Sriwatanakul, K., Kelvie, W., Lasagna, L., Calimlin, J. F., Weis, O. F., & Mehta, G. (1983). Studies with different types of visual analog scales for measurement of pain. *Clinical Pharmacology and Therapeutics*, *34*, 234–239.

Statistics Canada. (1992). *Profile of census tracts in Montreal, Part A*. Ottawa: Industry, Science and Technology Canada. 1991 Census of Canada. Catalogue number 95-329.

Sternbach, R. A. (1986). Survey of pain in the United States: The Nuprin pain report. *Clinical Journal of Pain, 2*, 49–53.

Takeshima, T., Taniguchi, R., Kitagawa, T., & Takahashi, K. (1990). Headaches in dementia. *Headache, 30*, 735–738.

Tremblay, N. (1994). Douleurs du vieillard: Revue des connaissances actuelles. In D. J. Roy & C. H. Rapin (Eds.), *Collection Amaryllis: Les Annales de soins palliatifs. Monographie II: Douleur et antalgie* (pp. 99–112). Montreal: Institute de Recherche Clinique de Montreal.

Tucker, M. A., Andrew, M. F., Ogle, S. J., & Davison, J. G. (1989). Age-associated change in pain threshold measured by transcutaneous neuronal electrical stimulation. *Age and Ageing, 18*, 241–246.

Valkenburg, H. A. (1988). Epidemiological considerations of the geriatric population. *Gerontology, 34*, (Suppl. 1), 2–10.

Von Korff, M., Dworkin, S. F., La Resche, L., & Kruger, A. (1988). An epidemiological comparison of pain complaints. *Pain, 32*, 173–183.

Vowles, K. J. D. (1979). *Surgical problems in the aged.* Bristol: John Wright.

Walsh, N. E., Schoenfeld, L., Ramamurthy, S., & Hoffman, J. (1989). Normative model for cold pressor test. *American Journal of Physical Medicine and Rehabilitation, 68*, 6–11.

Waxman, H. M., McCreary, G., Weinrit, R. M., & Carner, E. A. (1985). A comparison of somatic complaints among depressed and nondepressed older persons. *The Gerontologist, 25*, 501–507.

Wilke, D. J., Savedra, M. C., Holzemer, W. L., Tesler, M. D., & Paul, S. M. (1990). Use of the McGill Pain Questionnaire to measure pain: A meta-analysis. *Nursing Research, 39*, 36–41.

Williamson, G. M., & Schulz, R. (1992). Pain, activity restriction and symptoms of depression among community-residing elderly adults. *Journal of Gerontology, 47*, p367–p372.

Wolfe, F. (1989). Fibromyalgia: the clinical syndrome. *Rheumatic Disease Clinics of North America, 15*, 1–18.

Wolfe, Ross, K., Anderson, J., Russell, I. J., & Hebert, L. (1995). The prevalence and characteristics of fibromyalgia in the general population. *Arthritis and Rheumatism, 38*, 19–28.

Woodrow, K. M., Friedman, G. D., Siegelaub, A. B., & Collen, M. F. (1972). Pain tolerance: Differences according to age, sex and race. *Psychosomatic Medicine, 34*, 548–556.

CHAPTER 5

Nutrition, Disability, and Health in the Older Population

PAULA A. QUATROMONI AND BARBARA E. MILLEN

INTRODUCTION

The aging of the U.S. population, where one in eight persons is aged 65 or older, has focused national attention on the development of a continuum of health services which promote healthy aging. While the majority of American elders perceive themselves to be in good to excellent health (Institute of Medicine, 1992; Morley, 1986; *Surgeon General's Workshop on Health Promotion and Aging*, 1988; U.S. Senate Special Committee on Aging et al., 1991), more than four out of five people age 65 and older have at least one chronic disease. Older persons also experience a heavier disease burden. Over half of the older population has two or more coexisting, chronic health problems (U.S. Senate Special Committee on Aging et al., 1991). As well, 7–10 of the years lived after age 65 will include significant disability and major health complaints, including pain and discomfort or reduced function in activities of daily living (*Surgeon General's Workshop on Health Promotion and Aging*, 1988; Institute of Medicine, 1992). Other serious health-related problems, such as malnutrition, dementia, visual and hearing impairments, and incontinence further impact on functional independence and the quality of daily living. Therefore, it is important to recognize and promote preventive health strategies which improve the management of chronic diseases and reduce the accompanying discomfort and disability in older people.

Among the most important strategies for health promotion in the elderly is the assurance that nutrient requirements are met and that appropriate nutritional interventions are incorporated into health services, including managed care. It is now recognized that six of the leading chronic health problems afflicting older persons, including

---

PAULA A. QUATROMONI AND BARBARA E. MILLEN • School of Public Health, Boston University, Boston, Massachusetts 02118.

Handbook of Pain and Aging, edited by David I. Mostofsky and Jacob Lomranz. Plenum Press, New York, 1997.

coronary heart disease, hypertension and stroke, diabetes mellitus, osteoporosis, and kidney disease, are nutrition-related (Morley, 1986). It is also established that, as these diseases progress, their associated disability, pain, anorexia, or psychological manifestations may reduce appetite or inhibit optimal food and nutrient intake. Thus, the prevalent health problems, their painful sequelae, and nutrition are important considerations in promoting healthy aging. Proper nutrition can mitigate existing health problems, improve the management of many chronic diseases, reduce their physical complications, and extend years of healthy living (Posner, Jette, Smigelski, Miller, & Mitchell, 1994). Elders in good nutritional status also have briefer illnesses and shorter and less expensive hospital stays. Thus, health-promotion and disease-prevention strategies and nutrition interventions that enable elders to maintain a high quality of life and functional independence in later years will be increasingly important priorities for the nation's health-system policy agenda.

The purpose of this chapter is to discuss the interrelationships between nutrition, physical functioning, and health with advancing age; to identify the nutrition-related health concerns of the older population; to summarize population-based nutrition recommendations for older Americans; and to describe nutrition programs and services available to improve the health and nutritional status of elders. We will discuss how nutrition interventions can be integrated at various levels of the health care continuum, including home- and community-based long-term care, and will attempt to identify gaps in nutrition services that warrant attention.

NUTRITION, PHYSICAL FUNCTION, AND HEALTH

Optimal nutritional status and physical functioning are essential to the maintenance of health and quality of life with advancing age. Maintenance of nutritional well-being plays a key role in the prevention of chronic diseases and their complications, improved management of acute and chronic illnesses, decreased recovery time from wounds and trauma, delayed onset of medical comorbidity, and reduction in premature mortality (Dwyer, 1991; Posner, Saffel-Schrier, Dwyer, & Franz, 1993b; Posner et al., 1994; Rosenberg & Miller 1992; U.S. Department of Health and Human Services, 1988). Sustained physical functioning with limited pain and suffering is critical to independent living, avoidance of unnecessary institutionalization, and extended years of healthy living (Guccione et al., 1994; Institute of Medicine, 1992; Mor et al., 1989; Rosenberg & Miller, 1992). The importance of these factors increases when the costs associated with treatment and management of chronic diseases in the elderly are considered. The elderly are the heaviest users of health services (U.S. Senate Special Committee on Aging et al., 1991) and account for about 30% of all health care expenditures in the United States (Havlik et al., 1987). Additional costs are incurred when elders become functionally impaired and their ability to live independently is prohibited. Poorly nourished older people become sick more frequently, require longer periods of time to recuperate, and are more likely to have costly complications (Nutrition Screening Initiative, 1994).

Nutritional status and physical functioning are strongly interrelated health paradigms. The major chronic diseases which are related to nutrition, including heart disease, certain cancers, diabetes, hypertension and stroke, and osteoporosis, are associated with losses in physical functioning and decreased independence in the performance of activities of daily living (Barrett-Connor & Wingard, 1991; Guccione et al., 1994; Guralnik & Kaplan, 1989; Harris, Kovar, Suzman, Kleinman, & Feldman, 1989; Jette, Pinsky, Branch, Wolf, & Feinleib, 1988; Kaplan, 1991; Kelly-Hayes et al., 1988; Mor et al., 1989; Nickel & Chirikos, 1990; Pinsky et al., 1985; Pinsky, Jette, Branch, Kannel, & Feinleib, 1990; Satariano et al., 1990). As the number of these coexistent chronic diseases rises and their severity increases, rates of physical disability and associated pain and discomfort rise in the older population (Guralnik, LaCroix, Everett, & Kovar, 1989). Often, this results in the loss of basic functions that ensure the maintenance of nutritional well-being in the elderly, including food shopping, meal preparation, and feeding oneself (Guccione et al., 1994). Thus, older persons, particularly those with multiple chronic conditions and disabling comorbidity, are at increased risk for malnutrition, particularly nutrient deficiencies (Dwyer, 1991; Posner, Saffel-Shrier, Dwyer, & Franz, 1993b; Rosenberg & Miller, 1992; White et al., 1992).

Recent evidence suggests that persons dying at the oldest ages generally have more disability prior to death, but not necessarily more clinical evidence of disease, than those dying at younger ages (Guralnik, LaCroix, Branch, Kasl, & Wallace, 1991). These observations suggest that modification of undesirable health behaviors in midlife and advanced years, including dietary and exercise interventions, can result in "successful aging" (Rowe & Kahn, 1987) and compression of morbidity (Fries, Green, & Levine, 1989). The onset of disease and disability may be delayed or perhaps even prevented.

Unfortunately, there is little available research on the precise strength or direction of the relationships between nutrition, health status, and physical functioning within older populations. The role of positive health behaviors, such as a prudent diet, in increasing life expectancy, extending years of healthy living, or reducing disability, pain, and discomfort with advancing age has not been well investigated (LaCroix, Guralnik, Berkman, Wallace, & Satterfield, 1993; Manton, 1989).

While diet and specific nutritional factors have not been extensively studied as potential predictors or mediators of change over time in functional status with aging, there is abundant scientific evidence to support the association between nutritional well-being and overall health. Nutritional habits are likely to play a central role in both the development and the prevention of disability through its relationships with obesity and a variety of nutrition-related chronic diseases that are prevalent among the elderly (Posner et al., 1993b). Many chronic conditions, particularly when coexisting, are associated with losses in physical functioning and increased pain and disability among the elderly (Guralnik & Kaplan, 1989; Harris et al., 1989; Hubert, Bloch, & Fries, 1993; Lammi et al., 1989; Pinsky et al., 1985). As well, obesity has been repeatedly shown to be a predictor of poor health (Benfante, Reed, & Brody, 1985) and physical functioning (Guralnik & Kaplan, 1989; Harris et al., 1989; Hubert et al., 1993; LaCroix et al., 1993; Pinsky et al., 1985) in aging cohorts.

A number of cross-sectional investigations have demonstrated associations between nutrition and physical functioning or health status. Nutrient intake was compared with self-reported physical functioning in a national probability sample of 2,496 U.S.

elders aged 65–84 (Murphy, Davis, Neuhaus, & Lein, 1990). Three-day food records were used to calculate mean intake levels of nutrients that are often inadequate in the diets of many older Americans (vitamins A, C, B_6 and B_{12}, thiamin, riboflavin, iron, calcium, and magnesium). Dietary adequacy was found to be directly related to self-reported physical functioning. Overall meal quality (based on the quantity and quality of portions consumed from each of four major food groups as reported in a dietary interview) was also found to be inversely related to level of disability (assessed by the 17-item Rapid Disability Scale) among black and white elders over age 65 in Miami (Hunter & Linn, 1979).

There is a rapidly expanding prospective literature which relates diet and nutritional well-being to the development of chronic diseases, but few studies to date have evaluated associations between nutrition, physical functioning, and health outcomes. For example, Posner et al. (1991) demonstrated that baseline dietary levels of total, saturated, and monounsaturated fat were associated with the 16-year onset of coronary heart disease among Framingham males, aged 45–55. These analyses did not include measures of functional capacity or discomfort per se but controlled for self-reported physical activity and other heart disease risk factors, including dyslipidemia, smoking, hypertension, body mass index (BMI), glucose intolerance, and left ventricular hypertrophy.

Obesity was found to be associated with a 20% increased risk of losing physical mobility over four years of follow-up among men in the EPESE (Established Populations for Epidemiologic Studies of the Elderly) cohort and a 40% increased risk among women (LaCroix et al., 1993). Other health behaviors found to be associated with the risk of losing mobility were current smoking, abstinence from alcohol consumption compared with consumption of small to moderate amounts, and low physical activity levels. Three or more weekly sessions of regular physical activity were identified as the health behavior most strongly and consistently associated with maintaining mobility. This research suggests that positive lifestyle behaviors can not only enhance longevity but also reduce the likelihood of losing mobility and functional independence, thus extending active life and curtailing health care costs in later years.

Physical disability among the older National Health and Nutrition Examination Survey (NHANES) I population (50–77 years old at baseline) was directly related to body mass index (BMI) and history of arthritis and was also associated with lower recreational physical activity, less education, and female gender in the NHANES I Epidemiologic Follow-up Study (Hubert et al., 1993). Significantly greater disability was also found among those who were nonwhite, drank less alcohol, had poorer nutritional intake, were taking antihypertensive medication regularly, had lower hemoglobin and serum albumin levels, and had prior diagnoses of a number of different medical conditions, including those affecting the musculoskeletal, cardiovascular, and pulmonary systems. Obesity remained an important predictor of disability even after adjustment for chronic diseases, suggesting that obesity may have an independent effect outside its impact on these chronic conditions.

Recently, Guccione et al. (1994) demonstrated that stroke and heart disease were among the strongest predictors of disability (assessed by measures of function in activities of daily living) in a population of noninstitutionalized Framingham elders. Medical conditions were found to impose major functional limitations on the elderly that were specific to each disease and to each activity. For example, elders with stroke, heart disease, or congestive heart failure were more likely to be dependent on others to perform heavy home chores. Individuals with stroke or diabetes were more likely to be functionally limited in cooking, while those with stroke, heart disease, hip fracture, or depressive symptomatology were more likely to be dependent on others for grocery shopping. Thus, not only may nutritional status contribute to the development of chronic disease, but chronic disease and its associated functional disability, pain, and discomfort may have a negative impact on food intake and nutritional status.

Given the gaps in our current understanding of the relationships between nutrition, chronic disease, and physical functioning, it was recommended that future research focus on the role of nutritional factors in the etiology and prevention of chronic diseases and age-related impairments in organ system function; the development of comprehensive nutrition recommendations relevant to common morbidity patterns among older adults (U.S. Department of Health and Human Services, 1992); the relationships between physical functioning and nutrition; and the determinants of cognitive and functional ability and quality of life in older adults (U.S. Department of Health and Human Services, 1992). It will be important for this research to examine the perceptions of older people concerning the extent to which physical functioning is limited due to pain, discomfort, or other physical and psychological impairments.

NUTRITION-RELATED HEALTH CONCERNS OF THE ELDERLY

The myriad of nutrition problems that affect the elderly span a continuum from nutritional deficiencies to nutrient excesses (Dwyer, 1991, 1993; Dwyer, Coletti, & Campbell, 1991; Goodwin, 1989; Hutchinson & Munro, 1986; Posner & Krachenfels, 1987; Posner & Levine, 1991). The most salient nutrition-related problems afflicting the elderly are chronic diseases that benefit from dietary intervention, such as obesity, coronary heart disease, diabetes mellitus, hypertension, osteoporosis, certain cancers, and gastrointestinal and kidney disorders (American Dietetic Association, 1987; Dwyer, 1991). Studies of diet and health in the free-living older population clearly indicate that, on average, problems of food and nutrient excess are more prevalent than nutrient deficiencies. For instance, estimated mean dietary intake levels of total fat, saturated fat, cholesterol, and sodium are relatively high among American elders and contribute to increased risk for many chronic diseases (U.S. Department of Health and Human Services and U.S. Department of Agriculture, 1986). In a representative sample of free-living New England elders, 70 years and older, mean dietary intake levels of total fat (37% and 35.7% of calories, respectively, in men and women) and saturated fat (12.5% and 11.8%) were far in excess of recommended levels of intake (Posner, Jette, Smith, & Miller, 1993a). Furthermore, as many as 40% of the older population may experience health problems that arise in part from dietary excesses, such as obesity, dyslipidemia, glucose intolerance, and hypertension (Posner, 1979).

While problems of dietary excess are prevalent in older Americans, a relatively small but significant proportion of older people, up to about one in eight persons, may have clinically evident nutrient deficiencies, such as emaciation, protein-calorie malnutrition, or low blood levels of certain vitamins. In national studies of dietary intake, low intake levels of energy, calcium, magnesium, and vitamin B_6 have been reported among certain groups of older persons (Carroll, Abraham, & Dresser, 1983; Food Research and Action Center, 1987; U.S. Department of Health and Human Services, 1988; U.S. Department of Health and Human Services and U.S. Department of Agriculture, 1986). As many as one in four older people may consume diets that are low in fiber, complex carbohydrates, and nutrient-rich fruits and vegetables (American Dietetic Association, 1987; U.S. Department of Health and Human Services, 1988). Recently, marginal to low intake levels of dietary antioxidants (beta-carotene, vitamins C and E, and selenium), fiber, folacin, and calcium have been linked to increased risk of chronic diseases, including heart disease, hypertension, certain cancers, and osteoporosis.

A recent population-based study of elders in New England has identified the major dimensions of health and nutritional risk in free-living older people (Posner et al., 1994). In a representative random sample of 1,156 free-living persons, 1 in 4 older New Englanders perceived themselves to be in fair or poor health, and many reported having significant nutrition-related health problems. Health-related problems were generally more common among the very old (those $\geq$ 80 years) and those in poverty (37.8%), those who lived alone (38.9%), those who were socially isolated (51.9%), and those with mental disorientation (5.2%). Of these New England elders, 16% had a body mass index (BMI) which suggested that they were underweight (< 22 kg/m^2), and 41.5% had a BMI indicative of overweight (> 27 kg/m^2). Some 37.7% had no teeth or had roots only, and 25.2% reported difficulty chewing foods. Slightly more than half (54.8%) had two or more chronic conditions, and 10% reported high levels of alcohol consumption ($\geq$ 5 oz/week).

Important gender differences were noted among these New England elders. Women were more likely than men to be 80 years or older, to have incomes below poverty, to be unmarried, and to live alone. They were also more likely to be underweight, to have limited physical functioning, and to report difficulties chewing food. Women more often had arthritis, osteoporosis, and multiple chronic medical conditions. Older men, on the other hand, were more likely than women to be socially isolated, to smoke or chew tobacco, to have evidence of tooth decay and periodontal disease, and to report high levels of alcohol intake. Men were also more likely to have been hospitalized in the past year and to have a history of heart attack.

Mean intake levels of protein, vitamin A, ascorbic acid, and thiamin met the Recommended Dietary Allowance (RDA) standards, but mean calcium intake fell below RDA guidelines for both men and women in the New England sample (Posner et al., 1994). When examined on an individual basis, a majority (58%) of the sample had estimated intakes below 75% of the RDA for calcium and more than 40% had estimated vitamin A intakes below 75% of the RDA. Finally, 38% had dietary intakes below 75% of the RDA for three or more nutrients. While evidence of dietary inadequacy was present, there was also evidence of nutritional excess among these New England elders. Mean total and saturated fat intakes (36.5% and 12.2% of total calories, respectively) were above published recommendations. Of equal concern, mean carbohydrate intake

(45.3% of total calories) was below suggested intake levels. Mean dietary cholesterol intake (268 mg/day) was within the recommended range.

Factors Related to Nutritional Excess in Older People

We have an increasing, but currently limited, understanding of food purchasing and dietary patterns that result in dietary excesses in the older population. Studies of health and nutrition in older populations have been limited by the relatively low recruitment of older persons (Choi et al., 1990; McIntosh et al., 1990; Posner, Smigelski, & Krachenfels, 1987; Probart et al., 1989; Walker & Beauchene, 1991) and the inclusion of few individuals beyond the seventh decade of life (Choi et al., 1990; Garry et al., 1989; McIntosh et al., 1990; Posner et al., 1987; Probard et al., 1989; U.S. Department of Health and Human Services, 1979; Walker & Beauchene, 1991). In fact, the National Health and Nutrition Examination Survey (NHANES) has not previously examined persons 80 years of age and older (McIntosh et al., 1990). It has been noted (Horwath, 1989) that, of more than 90 studies on the diet and nutritional status of older individuals, the majority were conducted in small, highly selected samples and therefore have limited generalizability.

Often, the consumption patterns reflect habits accumulated over a lifetime. In fact, food-purchasing habits and related nutrient intake are considered extremely complex consumer behaviors (Jacoby, Chestnut, & Fisher, 1978; Rudell, 1979). Consumers make food choices based on past experiences, attitudes, and preferences for foods and attempt to integrate newly acquired information, such as diet-related health claims and new brand-name products, into their food decisions. Their resulting food choices define a pattern of dietary intake over time that is either balanced or leads to excesses, inadequate intakes, or, in some, higher levels of detrimental dietary components but low intakes of others (such as high fat but vitamin-poor diets).

Contributing to food behaviors are numerous sociological, psychological, and demographic factors. Socioeconomic and geodemographic characteristics were shown to influence food consumption patterns in a study of older adults (Akin et al., 1986). For example, living in a southern state was associated with an increased likelihood of having a dietary pattern characterized as "light eaters," and of having higher intakes of sugar (especially among rural dwellers) and legumes (particularly among nonwhites). Frequent consumption of meals outside the home and living in northern states were predictors of higher fat intake. Further research is needed to understand factors related to nutritional excess and to guide clinical interventions and policy development aimed at the older population.

A recent study of New England elders (Posner et al., 1994) demonstrated that advancing age, tobacco use, being male, and living with others were associated with higher dietary intakes of total and saturated fat and cholesterol, as well as both atherogenic dietary profiles and inadequate levels of nutrient intake. These factors suggest ways of targeting nutrition intervention strategies in the community that could improve nutrition so as to reduce chronic disease risk.

Factors Related to Nutritional Inadequacy in Elders

Our understanding of the determinants of low nutrient intake in the older population exceeds that of the contributors to dietary excesses. Major predictors of inadequate food and nutrient intake among the elderly include poverty, homelessness or social isolation, acute and chronic health conditions and the associated reduced functional capacity, low levels of nutrition knowledge, and susceptibility to fraudulent health and nutritional claims (Bailey, 1980; Food Research and Action Center, 1987; Guthrie, Black, & Madden, 1972; House Select Committee on Aging, 1984; Posner et al., 1987; U.S. Department of Health and Human Services, 1972, 1988; Vaughan & Manore, 1988; White House Conference on Aging, 1981). A recent major study of nutrition and health in New England elders (Posner et al., 1994) demonstrated that advancing age, tobacco use, evidence of tooth decay, untreated dental problems, and lower levels of educational attainment were associated with low nutrient intake levels. Lack of monetary resources, eating fewer than two meals per day, and eating few fruits and vegetables were the strongest predictors of inadequate nutrient intake in these elders (Posner et al., 1993a). In addition, older people who comprise ethnic and linguistic minority groups are more likely to need nutritional services, such as congregate and home meals, that promote adequate nutrient intake in older people (Balsam & Rogers, 1988). These factors provide evidence for targeting nutrition interventions to increase dietary levels of essential nutrients and lower risk for related health problems.

Low Income. Numerous studies have reported the relationship between low income and low nutrient intake in the noninstitutionalized elderly population (Allen & Gadson, 1983; Blanciforti, Green, & Lane, 1981; Carroll et al., 1983; Guthrie et al., 1972; Grotkowski & Sims, 1983; U.S. Department of Health and Human Services, 1972; U.S. Department of Health and Human Services and U.S. Department of Agriculture, 1986). In a survey of low-income elders (Food Research and Action Center, 1987), 38.2% reported skipping one or more meals a day, and 17% reported periods of appetite loss at least once a week. Unexplained weight loss appeared in about one-fifth (20.2%) of respondents.

The Surgeon General's report (U.S. Department of Health and Human Services, 1988) acknowledged that poverty is a major problem among older people and that it is often linked to inadequate nutrient intake. Limited financial resources that impair an individual's ability to purchase an adequate diet contribute to insufficient nutrient intake that may result in nutrient deficiencies when patterns of low intake become chronic. In 1986, the U.S. Census report (American Association of Retired Persons and the Administration on Aging, 1987) documented that 12.4% of the noninstitutionalized population over 65 years, or 3.5 million people, had incomes below the poverty level. Another 2.3 million (8%) were classified as "near-poor" (incomes 125% of the poverty level). Poverty is particularly prevalent among minorities; almost one-third of elderly blacks (31%) and one-fourth of elderly Hispanics (23%) are estimated to be poor, in contrast to one of every nine (11%) elderly whites. Among older women, 15% are poor compared with 8% of older men. Also, one-fourth of older people who live alone or with nonrelatives are poor, whereas only 6% of elderly individuals who live with their families are poor (American Association of Retired Persons and the Administration on Aging, 1987).

Social Isolation. Lower nutrient intakes have been documented in adults who are more socially isolated (i.e. those who live alone or who are less likely to be in contact with family members or other people) (Food Research and Action Center, 1987; Lockniskar, 1988; Posner, 1979; Rao, 1973; Roe, 1989). In the general U.S. population, women and those of either gender who live alone are more likely to have poor-quality diets and poorer health (Davis, Murphy, Neuhaus, & Lein, 1990).

Social isolation has been identified as a consistent predictor of morbidity and mortality from chronic disease (House, Landis, & Umberson, 1988) and a measure of reduced functional independence (U.S. Department of Health and Human Services, 1992). Loss of family, friends, and independence can result in loneliness, grief, depression, and other feelings that can affect appetite and compromise food intake. Both the 1986 Census report (American Association of Retired Persons and the Administration on Aging, 1987) and the Supplement on Aging to the National Health Interview Survey (National Center for Health Statistics, 1986) reported that about 8.3 million people over age 65, or one-third of the noninstitutionalized older population, were living alone. This estimate represents a 68% increase in the number of older adults who live alone from the 1970 estimate (American Association of Retired Persons and the Administration on Aging, 1987). Those who live alone tend to be older, widowed, and female, and to have no living children or siblings. Of those over age 65, 14% reported that they had no one to care for them for even a few days if the need arose, while the majority would rely on family (69%) or others (17%) (National Center for Health Statistics, 1986). One study of predominantly low-income elderly people (Food Research and Action Center, 1987) suggested that 28.3% had no one to provide assistance at home if illness confined them to bed. Thus, social support networks are of critical importance in promoting the health and independence of older adults (Institute of Medicine, 1992). Social isolation among the elderly also appears to be inextricably linked with low income.

Acute and Chronic Health Conditions and Loss of Functional Capacity. Poor health and limited functional capacity have repeatedly been found to lower the nutritional well-being of older people (Food Research and Action Center, 1987; Posner, 1979; U.S. Department of Health and Human Services, 1988). The presence of chronic disease may serve as a warning sign of increased nutritional risk. Acute situations, including recent hospitalization, surgery, trauma, infection, and initiation or withdrawal of nutritional therapies, are also indicators of increased nutritional risk among the elderly (Nutrition Screening Initiative, 1994).

Often, nutritional problems are heralded by loss of appetite, prolonged reduction in food intake, and significant weight loss. Loss of appetite may result from chronic illness or confinement to bed, diminished taste and smell sensations, side effects of medications, poor oral health, or neuromuscular or skeletal abnormalities that can make chewing or swallowing difficult.

Functional limitations resulting from acute or chronic illnesses can reduce an elderly person's ability to shop for and prepare foods. Nearly one-fifth (18.3%) of lower-income elders reported an inability to leave home without assistance or to prepare their own food (17.2%). The 1984 Health Interview Survey reported that 10.5% of the noninstitutionalized elderly could not complete their food shopping without assistance, and that 6.2% required assistance with meal preparation (National Center for Health Statistics, 1987).

Poor Nutrition Knowledge. The low level of nutrition knowledge observed among many older people has been identified as a key contributor to poor food choices (Fanelli, 1987; Light, 1976; National Conference on Nutrition Education, 1980; Posner, 1982). The need for nutrition education targeted at older populations has been the subject of national forums, including the 1969 White House Conference on Food, Nutrition, and Health (1970), the 1981 Nutrition Education Conference for Older Americans (Posner, 1982), and *the Surgeon General's Workshop on Health Promotion and Aging* (1988).

Among the most dramatic consequences of inadequate nutrition knowledge among older people is their susceptibility to health and nutrition fraud. Over 30% of health fraud victims in the United States are older people, and it is believed that misconceptions about nutrition are major contributors to their increased susceptibility (House Select Committee on Aging, 1984). Recent reviews suggest that nutritional therapies (including vitamin and mineral supplements) and homeopathic remedies of unproven effectiveness account for substantial unnecessary expenditures by the elderly, in excess of $40 billion for all forms of fraud (American Dietetic Association, 1979; House Select Committee on Aging, 1984). Thus, not only may fraudulent practices pose health and nutritional risk for elders, but they may also compete for precious financial resources that are already limited.

Several studies in older populations indicate significant gaps in their nutrition knowledge (Betts & Vivian, 1985; Caliendo & Smith, 1981; Fanelli & Abernethy, 1986; Fanelli, 1987; Grotkowski & Sims, 1983; Hersey, Glass, & Crocker, 1984). Consistent with earlier research (Fanelli & Abernethy, 1986; Fanelli, 1987), a nutrition knowledge quiz administered to over 300 participants in federally funded nutrition programs for New England elders suggested that, on average, older people could correctly answer only half of the test questions (Levine & Posner, 1989). Significantly lower nutrition knowledge scores were found in those who described their health as poor. The fact that older people may not recognize their need for nutrition education is also of concern. Over 65% of a sample of elders reported that their food intake was "excellent" in terms of providing adequate amounts of nutrients, whereas only 30% actually consumed foods that met 66% to 100% of recommended intake levels (Grotkowski & Sims, 1983).

NUTRITION RECOMMENDATIONS FOR OLDER AMERICANS

Specific objectives to improve the health status of older Americans were recently outlined in the U.S. Department of Health and Human Services report *Healthy People 2000* (1992). Population-based goals identified for the older population targeted the following health-related parameters: reducing morbidity and mortality associated with acute and chronic diseases; increasing years of healthy and independent life; decreasing disability; improving access to and use of supportive social and health care services; decreasing alcohol and tobacco use; and increasing physical activity (U.S. Department of Health and Human Services, 1992). The Year 2000 strategy also emphasized specific nutrition-related objectives for older persons. Primary attention was placed on improvements in dietary intake, particularly reducing total and saturated fat and sodium intakes; ensuring adequate dietary levels of essential micronutrients; reducing the prevalence of obesity; improving access to food and nutrition services (particularly home-delivered meals and congregate feeding); and promoting to the population nutrition assessment, counseling, and education services provided by qualified nutrition professionals (U.S. Department of Health and Human Services, 1992).

In addition to the population-based goals which target nutritional excesses, standards exist to aid in planning diets to ensure their nutritional adequacy. The Recommended Dietary Allowances (RDAs) for energy, macronutrients, and most micronutrients are established for adults and children (National Research Council, 1989b). The RDAs define intake levels of essential nutrients that, on the basis of scientific evidence, are judged to be safe and adequate to meet the known nutritional needs of most healthy individuals. An RDA category is established to meet the needs of all adults over the age of 50. In setting the standards, the Food and Nutrition Board considered subdividing healthy older people into two groups, since increasing age may be associated with changes in lean body mass, physical activity, and intestinal absorption of nutrients that may alter nutritional requirements (National Research Council, 1989b). However, the committee concluded that data are insufficient to establish separate RDAs for people over 70 years of age. While it is important to assess the individualized nutritional requirements of the elderly in the context of their physiological health status, there is no evidence that an increased intake of nutrients above the RDAs is necessary or that higher intakes will prevent the changes associated with aging (National Research Council, 1989b). RDAs for nutrients are amounts intended to be consumed as part of a normal and balanced diet composed of a variety of foods derived from diverse food groups that provide adequate energy. A diet that is adequate with respect to the RDAs is likely to be adequate in all other nutrients as well.

Consistent with the Year 2000 Objectives for the Nation and the RDA, the Surgeon General and others have recognized the importance of targeting public nutrition education at the older population, focusing on dietary means of lowering chronic disease risk, promoting functional independence, and preventing adverse consequences of the use of medications (Institute of Medicine, 1992; U.S. Department of Health and Human Services, 1988). It has been suggested that population-based recommendations for older persons include adopting dietary guidelines to lower total fat and saturated fat; increase complex carbohydrates, fiber, nutrient-rich fruits and vegetables; and lower sodium (Institute of Medicine, 1992; National Research Council, 1989a); and devise strategies for individuals with cognitive and physical impairments to ensure consumption of the recommended levels of essential nutrients (Institute of Medicine, 1992). Thus, population-based dietary guidelines established for the general adult population, including the Food Guide Pyramid (U.S. Department of Agriculture, 1992) and recommendations set forth by the Committee on Diet and Health (National Research Council, 1989a), the National

Cholesterol Education Program (Expert Panel on Detection, Evaluation and Treatment of High Blood Cholesterol in Adults, 1993), and the National Cancer Institute (Havas et al., 1994), are suitable for promoting health and nutritional well-being among the older population as well.

ASSESSING NUTRITIONAL RISK IN THE ELDERLY

Assessment of nutritional risk in the elderly is crucial for identifying those at greatest risk for nutrition-related problems to enable delivery of appropriate interventions. Nutrition screening is one of the first steps that can be taken to address nutrition-related problems among older Americans. It is believed that early professional detection, by way of nutritional screening, and treatment of nutrition-related problems in the elderly should improve the management of chronic conditions and enhance both well-being and quality of life among older persons (Nutrition Screening Initiative, 1991a). While considered important by many medical and public health professionals, nutrition screening has not yet been fully incorporated into our nation's overall strategy for health maintenance and care of older individuals for several reasons (Dwyer, 1991). Barriers to the adoption of a national nutrition screening policy include lack of consensus on basic tools for nutrition screening; limited understanding of the importance of screening; skepticism about its effectiveness; lack of reimbursement for screening, preventive services, and nutritional therapies; and lack of awareness and availability of acceptable, effective interventions to improve or maintain nutritional status (Dwyer, 1991).

The Nutrition Screening Initiative (NSI) is a collaboration of over 25 professional organizations in the United States that are interested in improving the nutrition and health status of the older population. The NSI is committed to increasing public awareness of the nutritional needs of the older population, promoting optimal nutrition in advancing age, and developing strategies for nutritional risk assessment and intervention planning (White, Ham, Lipschitz, Dwyer, & Wellman, 1991). Through a consensus-building process and ongoing research, the NSI has developed strategies for increasing consumer awareness of nutrition problems and detecting nutritional risk among older people (Ham, 1991; Lipschitz, 1991; White, 1991).

The NSI developed a checklist (Figure 5-1) which targets warning signs of poor nutritional status and asks respondents to answer yes or no to a set of 10 questions. It is designed to be a quick self-administered tool that generates a nutritional score and categorizes individuals as being at low, moderate, or high nutritional risk. The checklist is intended to guide high-risk individuals to social service and health care professionals with whom to discuss nutritional concerns, and it refers those at moderate risk to community-based agencies and services for elders. Thus, the checklist provides a foundation for further nutritional assessment and intervention, as appropriate, for persons with identified problems.

The NSI checklist was recently validated against dietary and anthropometric indices of nutritional status. The checklist was administered by telephone interview to a random sample of 749 Medicare beneficiaries, aged 70 years and older, in New England

(Posner et al., 1993a). Elders with higher checklist scores were more likely to have the poorest levels of nutrient intake when compared with the Recommended Dietary Allowances. Elders with higher scores were also found to have increased risk of adverse health events. Twenty-four percent of the Medicare population surveyed was estimated to be at high nutritional risk according to the checklist. Among those in the high-risk group, 56% perceived their health to be "fair" to "poor," and 38% had dietary intakes below 75% of the RDA for three or more nutrients. The NSI checklist was determined to be a brief, easily scored tool that can accurately and reliably identify noninstitutionalized older persons at risk for low nutrient intake and nutrition-related health problems. The checklist may, however, underestimate the extent of nutritional problems related to dietary excess, since the nutritional outcome it examines is nutritional inadequacy. Since this work was conducted in a predominantly Caucasian population, a priority for future research should be to conduct similar studies among minority populations of elders.

In addition to the checklist, Level I and Level II nutrition screens have been developed by the NSI. The Level I Screen (Figure 5-2) is a simple method for identifying those individuals at highest risk who should be referred for further evaluation and possible intervention. Questions on the Level I Screen probe for information regarding body weight, eating habits, living environment, and functional status. The Level II Screen (Figure 5-3) includes more specific diagnostic components, such as anthropometric measurements, physical observations, laboratory data, cognitive and emotional assessments, and more detailed questions to evaluate drug use, eating habits, living environment, and functional status. Use of the Level II Screen helps to identify those individuals with common nutritional problems, such as protein–calorie malnutrition, obesity, or medical conditions, including cognitive impairment or depression, which can have a profound impact on nutritional well-being (Nutrition Screening Initiative, 1994). The NSI has urged clinicians to conduct nutritional screening among free-living and institutionalized elderly in order to develop appropriate treatment strategies. Several recent publications provide guidelines for professionals who are planning nutrition interventions with older individuals (Dwyer, 1991; The Nutrition Screening Initiative, 1991b, 1992, 1994).

NUTRITION INTERVENTIONS

Efforts to promote health and quality of life, improve the management of disease, and contain spiraling health care costs have resulted in an emerging continuum of health care services for older persons provided in institutional, community-based, and home settings (Posner & Krachenfels, 1987). The continuum has begun to offer a spectrum of health care and supportive social services, including home and community-based services, that are tailored to the level of individual need and dependency (American Dietetic Association, 1987; Posner & Krachenfels, 1987; Posner & Levine 1991). Examples of the types of services that may be included in the continuum are preventive health screening and wellness programs implemented in community settings, senior centers, and health clinics; comprehensive care in acute-care hospital settings or rehabilitation facilities; services integrated within nursing facilities for functionally or cognitively impaired

The Warning Signs of poor nutritional health are often overlooked. Use this checklist to find out if you or someone you know is at nutritional risk.

DETERMINE YOUR NUTRITIONAL HEALTH

Read the statements below. Circle the number in the yes column for those that apply to you or someone you know. For each yes answer, score the number in the box. Total your nutritional score.

	YES
I have an illness or condition that made me change the kind and/or amount of food I eat.	2
I eat fewer than 2 meals per day.	3
I eat few fruits or vegetables, or milk products.	2
I have 3 or more drinks of beer, liquor or wine almost every day.	2
I have tooth or mouth problems that make it hard for me to eat.	2
I don't always have enough money to buy the food I need.	4
I eat alone most of the time.	1
I take 3 or more different prescribed or over-the-counter drugs a day.	1
Without wanting to, I have lost or gained 10 pounds in the last 6 months.	2
I am not always physically able to shop, cook and/or feed myself.	2
TOTAL	

Total Your Nutritional Score. If it's—

0-2 **Good!** Recheck your nutritional score in 6 months.

3-5 **You are at moderate nutritional risk.** See what can be done to improve your eating habits and lifestyle. Your office on aging, senior nutrition program, senior citizens center or health department can help. Recheck your nutritional score in 3 months.

6 or more **You are at high nutritional risk.** Bring this checklist the next time you see your doctor, dietitian or other qualified health or social service professional. Talk with them about any problems you may have. Ask for help to improve your nutritional health.

These materials developed and distributed by the Nutrition Screening Initiative, a project of:

AMERICAN ACADEMY OF FAMILY PHYSICIANS

THE AMERICAN DIETETIC ASSOCIATION

NATIONAL COUNCIL ON THE AGING, INC.

Remember that warning signs suggest risk, but do not represent diagnosis of any condition. Please see the Warnings Signs of poor nutritional health.

Figure 5-1. Nutrition Screening Initiative (NSI) checklist.

The Nutrition Checklist is based on the Warning Signs described below. Use the word DETERMINE to remind you of the Warning Signs.

DISEASE

Any disease, illness or chronic condition which causes you to change the way you eat, or makes it hard for you to eat, puts your nutritional health at risk. Four out of five adults have chronic diseases that are affected by diet. Confusion or memory loss that keeps getting worse is estimated to affect one out of five older adults. This can make it hard to remember what, when or if you've eaten. Feeling sad or depressed, which happens to about one in eight older adults, can cause big changes in appetite, digestion, energy level, weight and well-being.

EATING POORLY

Eating too little and eating too much both lead to poor health. Eating the same foods day after day or not eating fruit, vegetables, and milk products daily will also cause poor nutritional health. One in five adults skip meals daily. Only 13% of adults eat the minimum amount of fruit and vegetables needed. One in four older adults drink too much alcohol. Many health problems become worse if you drink more than one or two alcoholic beverages per day.

TOOTH LOSS/MOUTH PAIN

A healthy mouth, teeth and gums are needed to eat. Missing, loose or rotten teeth or dentures which don't fit well or cause mouth sores make it hard to eat.

ECONOMIC HARDSHIP

As many as 40% of older Americans have incomes of less than $6,000 per year. Having less—or choosing to spend less—than $25-30 per week for food makes it very hard to get the foods you need to stay healthy.

REDUCED SOCIAL CONTACT

One-third of all older people live alone. Being with people daily has a positive effect on morale, well-being and eating.

MULTIPLE MEDICINES

Many older Americans must take medicines for health problems. Almost half of older Americans take multiple medicines daily. Growing old may change the way we respond to drugs. The more medicines you take, the greater the chance for side effects such as increased or decreased appetite, change in taste, constipation, weakness, drowsiness, diarrhea, nausea, and others. Vitamins or minerals when taken in large doses act like drugs and can cause harm. Alert your doctor to everything you take.

INVOLUNTARY WEIGHT LOSS/GAIN

Losing or gaining a lot of weight when you are not trying to do so is an important warning sign that must not be ignored. Being overweight or underweight also increases your chance of poor health.

NEEDS ASSISTANCE IN SELF CARE

Although most older people are able to eat, one of every five have trouble walking, shopping, buying and cooking food, especially as they get older.

ELDER YEARS ABOVE AGE 80

Most older people lead full and productive lives. But as age increases, risk of frailty and health problem increases. Checking your nutritional health regularly makes good sense.

Figure 5-1. (*Continued*)

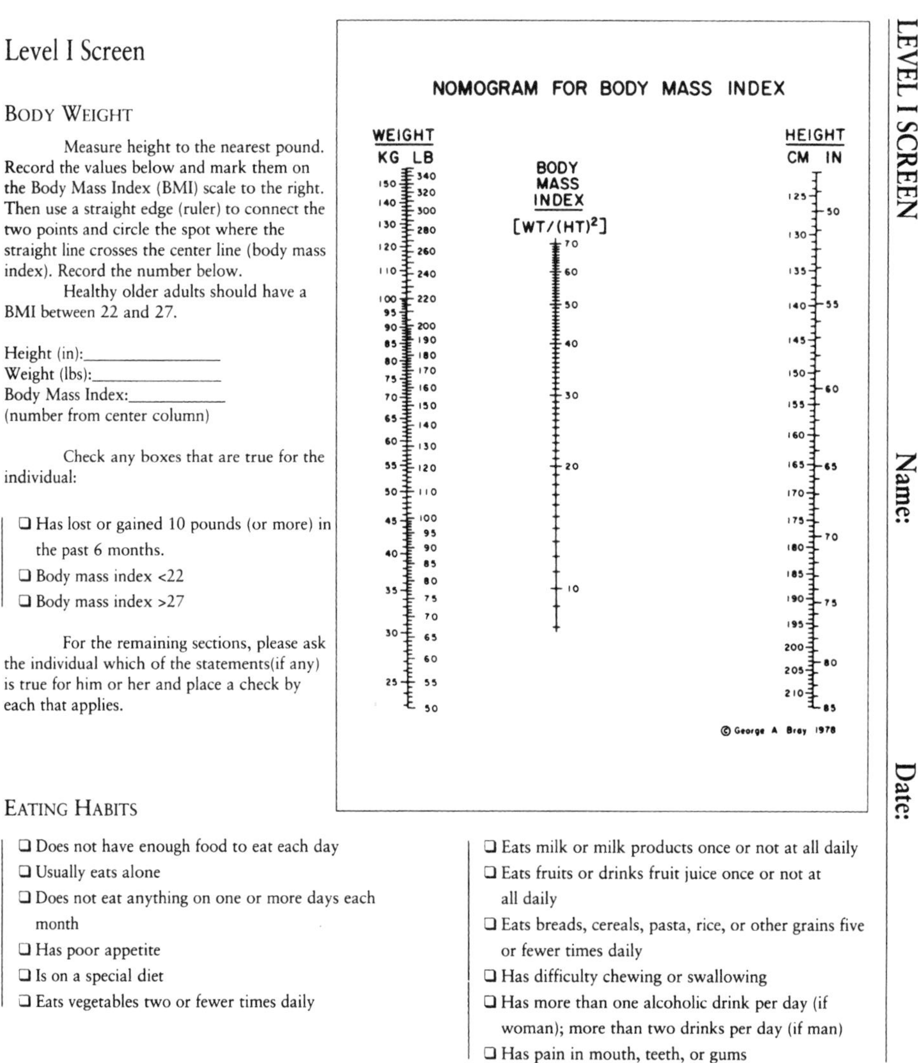

LEVEL I SCREEN Name: Date:

Level I Screen

Body Weight

Measure height to the nearest pound. Record the values below and mark them on the Body Mass Index (BMI) scale to the right. Then use a straight edge (ruler) to connect the two points and circle the spot where the straight line crosses the center line (body mass index). Record the number below.

Healthy older adults should have a BMI between 22 and 27.

Height (in):______________
Weight (lbs):______________
Body Mass Index:___________
(number from center column)

Check any boxes that are true for the individual:

- ❑ Has lost or gained 10 pounds (or more) in the past 6 months.
- ❑ Body mass index <22
- ❑ Body mass index >27

For the remaining sections, please ask the individual which of the statements(if any) is true for him or her and place a check by each that applies.

Eating Habits

- ❑ Does not have enough food to eat each day
- ❑ Usually eats alone
- ❑ Does not eat anything on one or more days each month
- ❑ Has poor appetite
- ❑ Is on a special diet
- ❑ Eats vegetables two or fewer times daily
- ❑ Eats milk or milk products once or not at all daily
- ❑ Eats fruits or drinks fruit juice once or not at all daily
- ❑ Eats breads, cereals, pasta, rice, or other grains five or fewer times daily
- ❑ Has difficulty chewing or swallowing
- ❑ Has more than one alcoholic drink per day (if woman); more than two drinks per day (if man)
- ❑ Has pain in mouth, teeth, or gums

Figure 5-2. NSI Level I Screen.

elders; home care for those who are bedridden or homebound; and hospice care for terminally ill elders (Posner & Krachenfels, 1987).

Because of the well-established role that nutrition plays in the health of older persons, nutrition interventions are crucial at each level of the health care continuum (Posner et al., 1993b). For this reason, the Surgeon General recently recommended that appropriate nutrition services be provided to the elderly in all health and social service settings, with particular reference to nutrition assessment and monitoring activities,

A PHYSICIAN SHOULD BE CONTACTED IF THE INDIVIDUAL HAS GAINED OR LOST 10 POUNDS UNEXPECTEDLY OR WITHOUT INTENDING TO DURING THE PAST 6 MONTHS. A PHYSICIAN SHOULD ALSO BE NOTIFIED IF THE INDIVIDUAL'S BODY MASS INDEX IS ABOVE 27 OR BELOW 22.

LIVING ENVIRONMENT

❑ Lives on an income of less than $6000 per year (per individual in the household)

❑ Lives alone

❑ Is housebound

❑ Is concerned about home security

❑ Lives in a home with inadequate heating or cooling

❑ Does not have a stove and/or refrigerator

❑ Is unable or prefers not to spend money on food (<$25-30 per person spent on food each week)

FUNCTIONAL STATUS

Usually or always needs assistance with (check each that apply):

❑ Bathing

❑ Dressing

❑ Grooming

❑ Toileting

❑ Eating

❑ Walking or moving about

❑ Traveling (outside the home)

❑ Preparing food

❑ Shopping for food or other necessities

If you have checked one or more statements on this screen, the individual you have interviewed may be at risk for poor nutritional status. Please refer this individual to the appropriate health care or social service professional in your area. For example, a dietitian should be contacted for problems with selecting, preparing, or eating a healthy diet, or a dentist if the individual experiences pain or difficulty when chewing or swallowing. Those individuals whose income, lifestyle, or functional status may endanger their nutritional and overall health should be referred to available community services: home-delivered meals, congregate meal programs, transportation services, counseling services (alcohol abuse, depression, bereavement, etc.), home health care agencies, day care programs, etc.

Please repeat this screen at least once each year--sooner if the individual has a major change in his or her health, income, immediate family (e.g., spouse dies), or functional status.

Figure 5-2. (*Continued*)

therapeutic interventions as needed, and nutrition counseling and education (U.S. Department of Health and Human Services, 1988).

Nutrition intervention options include a wide range of preventive and clinical services that can target the many different dietary, medical, socioeconomic, and demographic risk factors and indicators of poor nutritional status (Nutrition Screening Initiative, 1994). While nutrition interventions vary in their effectiveness, many are well documented and efficacious (Dwyer, 1991). Among the best-documented and -tested intervention strategies for older adults are assisted supplemental feeding programs, provision of social support for isolated elders, provision of home-delivered meals to homebound persons, enteral and parenteral nutrition support, weight management programs, referrals for dental care, and appropriate therapeutic dietary management to

LEVEL II SCREEN NAME: DATE:

LEVEL II SCREEN

Complete the following screen by interviewing the patient directly and/or by referring to the patient chart. If you do not routinely perform all of the described tests or ask all of the listed questions, please consider including them but do not be concerned if the entire screen is not completed. Please try to conduct a minimal screen on as many older patients as possible, and please try to collect serial measurements, which are extremely valuable in monitoring nutritional status. Please refer to the manual for additional information.

ANTHROPOMETRICS

Measure height to the nearest inch and weight to the nearest pound. Record the values below and mark them on the Body Mass Index (BMI) scale to the right. Then use a straight edge (paper, ruler) to connect the two points and circle the spot where this straight line crosses the center line (body mass index). Record the number below; healthy older adults should have a BMI between 22 and 27; check the appropriate box to flag an abnormally high or low value.

Height (in):__________________
Weight (lbs):__________________
Body Mass Index
(weight/height²):________________

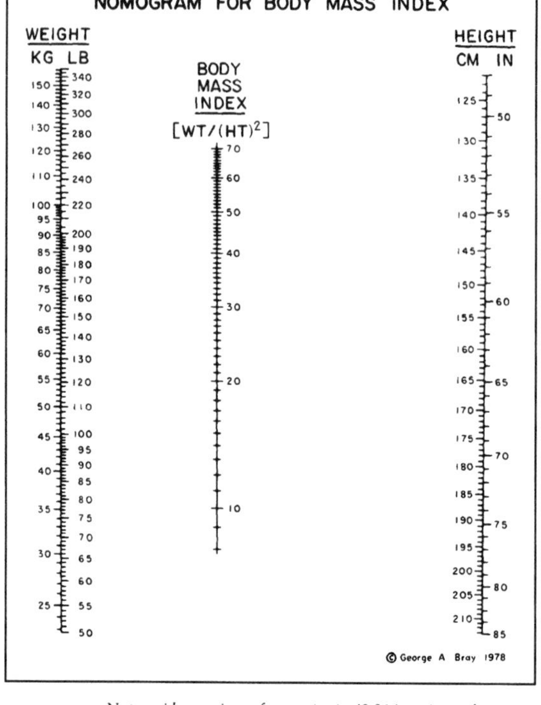

Please place a check by any statement regarding BMI and recent weight loss that is true for the patient.

❑ Body mass index <22

❑ Body mass index >27

❑ Has lost or gained 10 pounds (or more) of body weight in the past 6 months

Record the measurement of mid-arm circumference to the nearest 0.1 centimeter and of triceps skinfold to the nearest 2 millimeters.

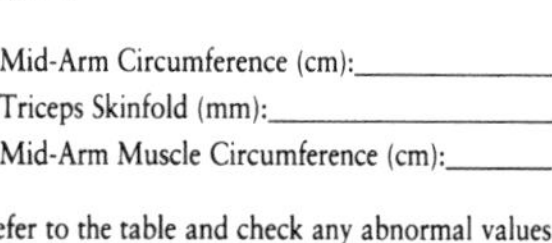

Mid-Arm Circumference (cm):____________
Triceps Skinfold (mm):________________
Mid-Arm Muscle Circumference (cm):_______

Refer to the table and check any abnormal values:

❑ Mid-arm muscle circumference <10th percentile
❑ Triceps skinfold <10th percentile
❑ Triceps skinfold >95th percentile

Note: mid-arm circumference (cm) - {0.314 x triceps skinfold (mm)}= mid-arm muscle circumference (cm)

FOR THE REMAINING SECTIONS, PLEASE PLACE A CHECK BY ANY STATEMENTS THAT ARE TRUE FOR THE PATIENT.

LABORATORY DATA

❑ Serum albumin below 3.5 g/dl

❑ Serum cholesterol below 160 mg/dl

❑ Serum cholesterol above 240 mg/dl

DRUG USE

❑ Three or more prescription drugs, OTC medications, and/or vitamin/mineral supplements daily

Figure 5-3. NSI Level II Screen.

facilitate control of hypertension, diabetes, and dyslipidemia (Dwyer, 1991). The NSI has identified six distinct intervention areas to target specific nutrition-related concerns of older adults: social-service-related, oral health, mental health, medication use, nutrition education and counseling, and nutrition support.

Social-service-related interventions can assist elders in obtaining, preparing, and

CLINICAL FEATURES

Presence of (check each that apply):

❑ Problems with mouth, teeth, or gums
❑ Difficulty chewing
❑ Difficulty swallowing
❑ Angular stomatitis
❑ Glossitis
❑ History of bone pain
❑ History of bone fractures
❑ Skin changes (dry, loose, nonspecific lesions, edema)

Percentile	Men 55-65 y	Men 65-75 y	Women 55-65 y	Women 65-75 y
Arm circumference (cm)				
10th	27.3	26.3	25.7	25.2
50th	31.7	30.7	30.3	29.9
95th	36.9	35.5	38.5	37.3
Arm muscle circumference (cm)				
10th	24.5	23.5	19.6	19.5
50th	27.8	26.8	22.5	22.5
95th	32.0	30.6	28.0	27.9
Triceps skinfold (mm)				
10th	6	6	16	14
50th	11	11	25	24
95th	22	22	38	36

From: Frisancho AR. New norms of upper limb fat and muscle areas for assessment of nutritional status. Am J Clin Nutr 1981; 34:2540-2545.

EATING HABITS

❑ Does not have enough food to eat each day
❑ Usually eats alone
❑ Does not eat anything on one or more days each month
❑ Has poor appetite
❑ Is on a special diet
❑ Eats vegetables two or fewer times daily
❑ Eats milk or milk products once or not at all daily
❑ Eats fruit or drinks fruit juice once or not at all daily
❑ Eats breads, cereals, pasta, rice, or other grains five or fewer times daily
❑ Has more than one alcoholic drink per day (if woman); more than two drinks per day (if man)

LIVING ENVIRONMENT

❑ Lives on an income of less than $6000 per year (per individual in the household)
❑ Lives alone
❑ Is housebound
❑ Is concerned about home security
❑ Lives in a home with inadequate heating or cooling
❑ Does not have a stove and/or refrigerator
❑ Is unable or prefers not to spend money on food (<$25-30 per person spent on food each week)

FUNCTIONAL STATUS

Usually or always needs assistance with (check each that apply):

❑ Bathing
❑ Dressing
❑ Grooming
❑ Toileting
❑ Eating
❑ Walking or moving about
❑ Traveling (outside the home)
❑ Preparing food
❑ Shopping for food or other necessities

MENTAL/COGNITIVE STATUS

❑ Clinical evidence of impairment, e.g. Folstein<26
❑ Clinical evidence of depressive illness, e.g. Beck Depression Inventory>15, Geriatric Depression Scale>5

Patients in whom you have identified one or more major indicator (see pg 2) of poor nutritional status require immediate medical attention; if minor indicators are found, ensure that they are known to a health professional or to the patient's own physician. Patients who display risk factors (see pg 2) of poor nutritional status should be referred to the appropriate health care or social service professional (dietitian, nurse, dentist, case manager, etc.).

Figure 5-3. (*Continued*)

consuming an appropriate diet that meets dietary guidelines and nutrient requirements. This category of interventions includes those that address issues of poverty, functional status, and social isolation (Nutrition Screening Initiative, 1992). Examples of social service interventions are food stamps, congregate nutrition and home-delivered meals, senior centers, adult day care programs, transportation assistance, in-home health aide and personal care services, and respite and caregiver support services (Nutrition Screening Initiative, 1992, 1994). Social service interventions need to be implemented in cooperation with public and private community-based organizations in order to be successful and wide-reaching. Such services are available in most communities nationwide.

Oral health can have a significant impact on nutritional status by affecting chewing and swallowing and subsequently influencing an individual's food intake and dietary quality. In fact, older individuals are at more risk than the general population for nutritional problems resulting from a greater prevalence of oral health problems (Nutrition Screening Initiative, 1994). Common oral problems include tooth loss, untreated caries, gingivitis, periodontitis, temporomandibular joint disorders, changes in salivary gland function, mucositis, alveolar bone loss, diminished sense of taste, candidiasis, and angular cheilitis (Nutrition Screening Initiative, 1994). Since deteriorations in oral health are often the earliest physical signs of malnutrition, early recognition of problems and appropriate referrals for dental care are crucial interventions to help improve nutritional status among the elderly.

Mental health also affects an individual's ability to meet his or her nutritional needs (Nutrition Screening Initiative, 1992). The relationship between mental health and nutritional status appears to be bidirectional, so that changes in mental health affect nutritional status and poor nutritional status influences mental health (Nutrition Screening Initiative, 1992). Unfortunately, mental disorders, which may affect up to 25% of older adults, often go unrecognized (Gatz & Smyer, 1992; George, Blazer, Winfield-Laird, Leaf, & Fishbach, 1988; Rapp, Parisi, Walsh, & Wallace, 1988). Thus, detection of dementia, depression, anxiety disorders, anorexia, alcoholism, and other common mental health problems among older adults is the first step in the intervention process. Nutrition assessment and monitoring, patient and family education, feeding assistance, adjustment of medication regimens, and nutrition support interventions are examples of appropriate strategies for improving the nutritional status of mentally impaired individuals.

Medication use is an important target for intervention activities since it is a prevalent practice among the elderly. The Food and Drug Administration estimates that 80% of adults over the age of 65 have at least one chronic condition requiring long-term medical therapy which commonly includes a drug regimen (Nutrition Screening Initiative, 1994). Among free-living elderly, 85% take medications regularly, and 25% take three or more medications daily (Smith & Bidlack, 1984). Prescription and nonprescription drugs can affect both individual nutrient requirements and physiological responses to nutrients. Side effects and improper medication use can also impair an individual's ability to perform certain nutrition-related functions, like shopping for groceries. Among the common symptoms which limit a person's ability to obtain and prepare meals are susceptibility to falls, fatigue, chest pain, shortness of breath on exertion, incontinence, impaired vision, and mental confusion (Hamdy, 1984). Some medications interfere with a person's ability to eat by causing loss of appetite, mouth dryness, reduced taste and smell sensations, and an overall apathy for food. Because older adults often take large numbers of medications, the NSI recommends that physicians treat patients with alternative therapeutic modalities and/or reduce the dosage and number of medications a patient is taking whenever possible (Nutrition Screening Initiative, 1994).

Nutrition education and counseling are valuable keys to assisting older individuals in modifying their eating habits and other lifestyle behaviors, such as physical activity and alcohol consumption, that are targets of health promotion and wellness programs. Nutrition education activities can help elders adopt and assimilate principles of the Dietary Guidelines (U.S. Department of Agriculture & U.S. Department of Health and Human Services, 1990) and the Food Guide Pyramid (U.S. Department of Agriculture, 1992) to achieve a balanced and varied dietary pattern that meets nutrient requirements. As well, nutrition education programs can assist elders in achieving nutrient intake profiles consistent with preventive nutrition recommendations for lowering chronic-disease risk-factor levels (Expert Panel on Detection, Evaluation and Treatment of High Blood Cholesterol in Adults, 1993; U.S. Department of Health and Human Services, 1992). Nutrition education can address a wide range of problems, including skipping meals, inadequate fruit and vegetable intake, availability of low-fat food choices in the marketplace, and easy methods of meal preparation. Education may also help elders learn how to plan nutritious meals within the constraints of a limited food budget and how to participate in a variety of food assistance programs available in the community. Elders with chronic disease, dietary restrictions, or disabilities are likely to benefit from individualized nutrition counseling and/or nutrition support to help them meet specific nutritional needs. Qualified nutrition professionals and registered dietitians are best suited to provide nutrition counseling and support.

Nutrition support interventions should be considered for individuals with special nutritional needs or for those who are unable to meet nutritional requirements by eating a conventional oral diet. Nutrition support services may increase or decrease nutrients provided by the diet; change the timing, size, or composition of meals; introduce nutritional supplements; modify food textures; and alter the route of administration from oral feeding to tube or intravenous feeding when necessary (Nutrition Screening Initiative, 1992). While it is important to recognize the need for nutrition support and to implement appropriate interventions in a timely manner, it is equally important that patients receiving nutrition support be monitored and evaluated as their needs change over time.

Federally funded nutrition interventions provide the largest existing frameworks for addressing certain nutrition-related risk factors in the elderly, particularly social isolation and inadequate income. The Title IIIc Elder Nutrition Program and its equivalent, Title VI, for Native Americans, are designed to fund a national network of congregate and home meals for older persons and their spouses. The Food Stamp program provides an income subsidy for the purchase of food to reduce the adverse consequences of income insecurity on food purchasing and is available to eligible, low-income elders.

Title III and VI Nutrition Programs for Older Americans

In 1972, the Older Americans Act of 1965 (OAA) was amended to establish a national Nutrition Program for Older Americans (NPOA). This program distributes funding under Title IIIc of the OAA to states and U.S. territories for a national network of programs that provide congregate and home-delivered meals for elderly people. Nutrition programs are required to provide at least one meal a day that meets one-third of the RDA, and to operate five or more days a week (U.S. Department of Health and Human Services, 1985).

In 1992, federal funding for the Title IIIc program was $433 million, and an additional $320 million was available to provide supportive services such as transportation to meal sites, shopping assistance, information and referral, outreach, and, to a limited extent, nutrition counseling and education (Administration on Aging, 1993). Title IIIc nutrition programs request grant funds through their state or area agencies on aging (AAAs). Each state has an office on aging which coordinates community programs for its elderly citizens. In 1992, there were over 15,000 Title IIIc nutrition program sites nationally that served 2.5 million people in congregate settings, and there were an additional 820,000 frail elders who received more than 105 million home-delivered meals (Administration on Aging, 1993).

In its report, *Prevention 86/87*, the U.S. Department of Health and Human Services (DHHS) summarized federal expenditures for health promotion and disease prevention among all age groups and minority groups in the population. The Title IIIc program, included in the Office of Human Development Service budget, accounted for over three-fourths of expenditures by DHHS for health promotion and disease prevention (U.S. Department of Health and Human Services, 1987).

The nutrition programs gain additional spending power from a cash–commodity entitlement program supported by the U.S. Department of Agriculture (USDA) which expands the resources and meals available through the nutrition program. Federal legislation gives states the option to elect to receive food commodities, cash at a fixed amount per meal served to eligible participants per year, or a flexible combination of food and cash. This support from the USDA amounted to $136 million in 1988 (National Association of Nutrition and Aging Services Program, 1988; Administration on Aging, 1990). Other sources of funding are realized from donations by older participants toward meal costs, and from private or public donations for the ongoing provision of services.

Title VI of the OAA establishes a separate grant program to tribal organizations to promote the delivery of social and nutritional services to older American Indians, Native Alaskans, and Native Hawaiians that are comparable to those provided under Title III. In 1992, $14.4 million in Title VI funds were used for nutrition and supportive services, including the provision of approximately 2.4 million meals to nearly 90,000 Native Americans and Native Hawaiians (Ponza, Ohls, & Posner, 1994).

Many evaluations of the impact of the Title III nutrition programs have been conducted (Caliendo, 1980; Kirschner Associates Inc. and Opinion Research Corporation, 1980; Kohrs, O'Hanlon, & Eklund, 1978; Kohrs, 1980; LeClerc & Thornbury, 1983; Nestle, Lee, & Fullarton, 1983; Zandt & Fox, 1986). It appears that this program has been able to attract "high-risk" elders, to improve the nutritional content of their diets, and to provide beneficial socialization and recreation. Balsam and Rogers (1988) found that many NPOA sites had been compelled to become innovative in meeting the nutritional needs of their participants. Beyond the congregate and home meals that are required by law, these researchers found that many nutrition programs across the nation had begun to add provisions for therapeutic diets; food pantries; ethnic meals; luncheon clubs; acceptance of food stamps for meal payments; alternative meal sites; breakfast, weekend, and evening meals; and meals for the homeless older population.

While evaluations of NPOA have demonstrated its impact, it appears that programs often overlook the particularly "needy" segments of the population, including socially isolated, homeless, ethnic and linguistic minority, and extremely functionally impaired, homebound elderly individuals (Balsam & Rogers, 1988). It is also increasingly clear that NPOA and other community programs are being pressured to provide services to larger numbers of frail and homebound elderly. The greater number of those with unmet needs has resulted, in part, from the recent trends toward early discharge of older patients from hospitals before they completely recover and with their more complicated medical conditions. In many areas of the country, requests for nutrition services, particularly Meals-on-Wheels, have increased two- and threefold. These increased demands are likely to persist as cost containment continues to be a major influence on hospital-based care.

The provision of nutrition education within the NPOA programs and the relative impact of these educational efforts has been more dubious than the success of meal delivery. A national evaluation of NPOA suggested that nutrition education was a poorly defined service, highly variable from site to site, and difficult to evaluate (Kirschner Associates Inc. and Opinion Research Corporation, 1980). Selected studies have found little impact of organized nutrition education on the nutrition knowledge of older NPOA participants (Hersey et al., 1984; Kirschner Associates Inc. and Opinion Research Corporation, 1980; LeClerc & Thornbury, 1983). Recognition of this problem led to amendments of the Older Americans Act to support the redesign and development of nutrition education efforts. However, this aspect of the program has not received funding authorization and remains unresolved.

The last nationwide evaluation of the Elderly Nutrition Program was more than 10 years ago. The program has undergone many changes since that time, including increased numbers of home-delivered meals, targeted services for older persons with the greatest economic or social needs, and increased community-based nutrition and social services to prevent premature institutionalization (Ponza et al., 1994). It is clear that a thorough and rigorous new look at the program's impact is warranted. Under the OAA Amendments of 1992, Congress directed the Administration on Aging, in consultation with the Office of the Assistant Secretary for Planning and Evaluation, to evaluate the nutrition services provided under the OAA. The current evaluation is comprehensive and will collect information from all agencies within the administrative hierarchy (state units on aging, area agencies on aging and Indian tribal organizations, nutrition projects, and meal sites), congregate and home-delivered meal program participants in both Title III and Title VI programs, and eligible nonparticipants. The evaluation will include both descriptive assessments and impact analyses. It will describe the characteristics of participants, compare characteristics of congregate and home-delivered program participants, and assess how well the program is reaching elders with special needs, such as low-income and minority elderly (Ponza et al., 1994). The current evaluation will provide estimates of the program's impact on the nutritional and social well-being of participants. It will also include a "process" analysis to describe how the program is administered and operated and the quality and effectiveness of the program's components, along with an analysis of funding issues.

Food Stamps

The USDA Food Stamp Program, which was authorized by the 1964 Food Stamp Act, is the largest federally funded food aid program. It provides an income supplement to low-income households in the form of coupons used to purchase food. About 2 million American households headed by older people, or between 40% and 80% of those within the population who are eligible, currently participate in the Food Stamp Program. Reasons cited for nonparticipation by eligible older people include the "stigma of welfare" associated with the program's income means test, lack of information on program availability, and the perceived complexity of the application process (U.S. Senate Special Committee on Aging, 1987). To encourage participation by those residents aged 65 years and older, Wisconsin and California converted the food stamp benefit to a cash equivalent and added it to the individual's monthly supplemental security income (SSI) check. SSI provides a guaranteed minimal income to the nation's aged (those aged 65 years and older), blind, and disabled people.

Results concerning the impact of food stamps on the nutritional status of participating households have been inconclusive. Butler, Ohls, and Posner (1985) concluded that elderly food stamp participants consumed levels of nutrients that were similar to those of nonparticipants who had otherwise similar characteristics. They suggested that food stamps act more as an income supplement than as a mechanism whereby nutrient intake per se is increased. In contrast, Akin and colleagues (1985) found that food stamp participants consumed higher levels of many nutrients than did members of nonparticipating households with similar incomes. It seems clear, however, that food stamps provide a significant income benefit to the participants and that this may further extend the limited resources of participating households.

Nutrition and Long-Term Care

At present, no comprehensive or coordinated mechanism exists to ensure the availability, accessibility, and provision of appropriate nutrition services to the elderly despite increased recognition of their importance (Posner et al., 1993b). The nutrition services currently offered in the institutional and noninstitutional health care settings are often limited in scope and are typically loosely integrated. For example, congregate and home-delivered meals and income subsidies to purchase food are provided by separate federal and state programs such as the Title IIIc Elderly Nutrition Program and the Food Stamp Program (Posner & Levine, 1991; U.S. Department of Health and Human Services, 1985, 1988). While Medicare, Medicaid, and private health insurance providers may approve third-party reimbursement for nutrition services, coverage varies dramatically, depending on the health and social service setting and funding source (Marketing Sciences Institute, 1982; Posner & Levine, 1991). Within hospital or nursing facilities, clinical nutrition services and nutrition counseling may be reimbursed only if they are considered "medically necessary" (Dwyer, 1991; Posner & Krachenfels, 1987). Typically, reimbursement for home-based nutrition services or those delivered in other settings, such as health maintenance organizations (HMOs), hospices, and respite programs, varies considerably and may be minimal (American Dietetic Association, 1987; Posner & Levine, 1991; U.S. Department of Health and Human Services, 1985, 1988).

In the face of current health-care cost-containment measures that may limit the delivery of nutrition services and minimize their reimbursement, it is imperative that policymakers recognize the benefits of nutrition interventions and services for older Americans. Nutrition services within the continuum of care for the elderly should emphasize promotion of health and functional independence; reduction in the risks and complications associated with nutrition-related chronic diseases; lowering the prevalence of protein-calorie malnutrition; avoidance of nutrient deficiencies; enhanced screening and referral activities; containment of health care costs; improvement and maintenance of physical and cognitive function; and enhancement of the quality of life (Posner et al., 1993b).

CONCLUSION

The promotion of optimal health and nutritional well-being in older adults remains a major concern on the national health care agenda. While significant improvements have been made in this century, large numbers of elderly persons continue to have unmet needs for food and nutritional services. Improper nutrition leads to poor management of chronic diseases, high rates of disease progression and complications, increased pain, discomfort and disability, and reduced quality of life with advancing age.

The most prevalent nutritional problems of people aged 65 and older are associated with overnutrition and the nutrition-related chronic diseases, including heart disease, diabetes, and cancer, which affect the majority of older persons. At the same time, there are distinct groups of elderly people who suffer from undernutrition, notably the socially isolated, the very frail, the disabled, and the economically disadvantaged. A clearer understanding of the factors and personal characteristics that contribute to excessive or inadequate dietary patterns associated with nutritional risk is needed.

Prevention and management of nutritional risk among older persons require screening and intervention activities. Health care professionals need to recognize the clinical signs and symptoms of malnutrition and refer elders for timely and appropriate intervention services. Tools are now available for rapid screening and assessment of nutritional risk in the elderly.

A variety of programs and services are available to help improve the nutritional status of older people, but they are limited in scope and only loosely integrated. No single agency or entity plans, coordinates, or provides nutrition services to older people in home, community, or institutional settings. Third-party reimbursement for nutrition services is highly variable and often restrictive.

It is clear that increased federal attention is needed to develop more explicit guidelines for providing nutrition services to elderly people within the emerging long-term health system. It is crucial that home, community, and institutional services be coordinated so that the nutritional needs of the elderly are met in a comprehensive and integrated way. Through such efforts, progress toward the Year 2000 Health Objectives for the Nation can be achieved, including reduced morbidity and mortality from chronic diseases, increased years of healthy and independent living, and decreased disability.

REFERENCES

Administration on Aging. (1990). *Information Memo AoA-IM-FY-90-5: Title IIIc nutrition program participation in the USDA Cash/Commodity Entitlement Program.* Washington, DC: Administration on Aging, U.S. Department of Health and Human Services.

Administration on Aging. (1993). *National Summary of Program Activities Under Title III and Title VI of the Older Americans Act, Fiscal Year 1992.* Washington, DC: Office of State and Community Programs, Administration on Aging, U.S. Department of Health and Human Services.

Akin, J. S., Guilkey, D. K., Popkin, B. M., and Smith, K. (1985). The impact of federal transfer programs on the nutrient intake of elderly individuals. *Journal of Human Resources, 20,* 382–404.

Akin, J. S., Guilkey, D. K., Popkin, B. M., and Fanelli, M. T. (1986). Cluster analysis of food consumption patterns of older Americans. *Journal of the American Dietetic Association, 86,* 616–624.

Allen, J. E., & Gadson, K. E. (1983). *Nutrient consumption patterns of low-income households.* Technical Bulletin No. 1685. Washington, DC: Economic Research Service, U.S. Dept. of Agriculture.

American Association of Retired Persons and Administration on Aging, U.S. Department of Health and Human Services. (1987). *A profile of older Americans.* Long Beach, CA: American Association of Retired Persons.

American Dietetic Association. (1979). *Costs and benefits of nutrition care: Phase I.* Chicago: American Dietetic Association.

American Dietetic Association. (1987). Position of the American Dietetic Association: Nutrition, aging, and the continuum of health care. *Journal of the American Dietetic Association, 87,* 344–347.

Bailey, L. B. (1980). Vitamin B_{12} status of elderly persons from urban low-income households. *Journal of the American Geriatrics Society, 28,* 276–278.

Balsam, A. L., & Rogers, B. L. (1988). *Service innovations in the elderly nutrition program: Strategies for meeting unmet needs.* Boston: Tufts University School of Nutrition.

Barrett-Connor, E., & Wingard, D. L. (1991). Heart disease risk factors as determinants of dependency and death in an older cohort. *Journal of Aging and Health, 3,* 247–261.

Benfante, R., Reed, D., & Brody, J. (1985). Biological and social predictors of health in an aging cohort. *Journal of Chronic Diseases, 38,* 385–395.

Betts, N., & Vivian, V. (1985). Factors related to the dietary adequacy of noninstitutionalized elderly. *Journal of Nutrition, 4,* 3–13.

Blanciforti, L., Green, R., & Lane, S. (1981). Income and expenditure for relatively more versus relatively less nutritious food over the life cycle. *American Journal of Agricultural Economics,* 63, 225–260.

Butler, J. S., Ohls, J. C., & Posner, B. M. (1985). The effect of the food stamp program on the nutrient intake of the eligible elderly. *Journal of Human Resources, 20,* 405–419.

Caliendo, M. A. (1980). Factors influencing the dietary status of participants in the national nutrition program for the elderly: 1. Population characteristics and nutritional intakes. *Journal of Nutrition for the Elderly, 1,* 23–39.

Caliendo, M. A., & Smith, J. (1981). Factors influencing the nutrition knowledge and dietary intake of participants in the Title III-c meal program. *Journal of Nutrition for the Elderly, 1,* 65–77.

Carroll, M. D., Abraham, S., & Dresser, C. M. (Eds.). (1983). *Dietary intake source data: U.S., 1976–80, NHANES I, II.* Hyattsville, MD: National Center for Health Statistics.

Choi, E. S. K., McGandy, R. B., Dallal, G. E., Russell, R. M., Jacob, R. A., Schaefer, E. J., Sadowski, J. A. (1990). The prevalence of cardiovascular risk factors among Chinese Americans. *Archives of Internal Medicine, 150,* 413–418.

Davis, M. A., Murphy, S. P., Neuhaus, J. M., & Lein, D. (1990). Living arrangements and dietary quality of older US adults. *Journal of the American Dietetic Association, 90*, 1667–1672.

Dwyer, J. T. (1991). *Screening older Americans' nutritional health: Current practices and future possibilities.* Washington, DC: Nutrition Screening Initiative.

Dwyer, J. T. (1993). Nutrition concerns and problems of the aged. In D. Satin (Ed.), *Clinical care of the aged person.* New York: Oxford University Press.

Dwyer, J. T., Coletti, J., & Campbell, D. (1991). Maximizing nutrition in the second fifty. *Clinics in Applied Nutrition, 4*, 19–31.

Expert Panel on Detection, Evaluation and Treatment of High Blood Cholesterol in Adults. (1993). Summary of the Second Report of the National Cholesterol Education Program (NCEP) Expert Panel on Detection, Evaluation and Treatment of High Blood Cholesterol in Adults (Adult Treatment Panel II). *Journal of the American Medical Association, 269*, 3015–3023.

Fanelli, M. (1987). An assessment of the nutrition education needs of congregate meal program participants. *Journal of Nutrition Education, 19*, 131–137.

Fanelli, M., & Abernethy, M. (1986). A nutritional questionnaire for older adults. *The Gerontologist, 26*, 192–197.

Food Research and Action Center. (1987). *A national survey of nutritional risk among the elderly.* Washington, DC: Food Research and Action Center.

Fries, J. F., Green, L. W., & Levine, S. (1989). Health promotion and the compression of morbidity. *Lancet, 1*, 481–483.

Garry, P. J., Rhyne, R. L., Halioua, L., & Nicholson, C. (1989). Changes in dietary patterns over a 6-year period in an elderly population. *Annals of the New York Academy of Sciences, 561*, 104–112.

Gatz, M., & Smyer, M. A. (1992). The mental health system and older adults in the 1990's. *American Psychologist, 47*, 744–751.

George, L. K., Blazer, D. F., Winfield-Laird, I., Leaf, P. J., & Fishbach, R. L. (1988). Psychiatric disorders and mental health service use in later life. In J. Brody & G. Maddox (Eds.), *Epidemiology and aging: An international perspective.* New York: Springer.

Goodwin, J. S. (1989). Social, psychological and physical factors affecting the nutritional status of elderly subjects: Separating cause and effect. *American Journal of Clinical Nutrition, 50*, 1201–1209.

Grotkowski, M., & Sims, L. (1983). Nutrition knowledge, attitudes and dietary practices of the elderly. *Journal of the American Dietetic Association, 47*, 263–268.

Guccione, A. A., Felson, D. T., Anderson, J. J., Anthony, J. M., Yuqing Zhang, M. B., Wilson, P. W., Kelly-Hayes, M., Wolf, P. A., Kreger, B. E., & Kannel, W. B. (1994). The effects of specific medical conditions on the functional limitations of elder in the Framingham Study. *American Journal of Public Health, 84*, 351–358.

Guralnik, J. M., & Kaplan, G. A. (1989). Predictors of healthy aging: Prospective evidence from the Alameda county study. *American Journal of Public Health, 79*, 703–708.

Guralnik, J. M., LaCroix, A. Z., Branch, L. G., Kasl, S. V., & Wallace, R. B. (1991). Morbidity and disability in older persons in the years prior to death. *American Journal of Public Health, 81*, 443–447.

Guralnik, J. M., LaCroix, A. Z., Everett, D. F., & Kovar, M. G. (1989). Aging in the eighties: The prevalence of comorbidity and its association with disability. *Advance Data from Vital & Health Statistics* No. 170, DHHS Publ. No. (PHS) 89-1250.

Guthrie, H. A., Black, K., & Madden, J. P. (1972). Nutritional practices of elderly citizens in rural Pennsylvania. *The Gerontologist, 12*, 330–335.

Ham, P. J. (1991). *Indicators of poor nutritional status in older Americans.* Washington, DC: Nutrition Screening Initiative.

Hamdy, R. C. (1984). *Geriatric medicine: A problem-oriented approach.* London: Balliere Tindall.

Harris, T., Kovar, M. G., Suzman, R., Kleinman, J. C., & Feldman, J. J. (1989). Longitudinal study of physical ability in the oldest-old. *American Journal of Public Health, 79*, 698–702.

Havas, S., Heimendinger, J., Reynolds, K., Baranowski, T., Nicklas, T. A., Bishop, D., Buller, D., Sorensen, G., Beresford, S. A. A., Cowan, A., & Damron, D. (1994). 5 a day for better health: A new research initiative. *Journal of the American Dietetic Association, 94*, 32–36.

Havlik, R. J., Liu, B. M., Kovar, M. C., Suzman, R., Feldman, J. J., Harris, T., & Van Nostrand, J. V. (1987). *Health Statistics on Older Persons, United States, 1986.* Series 3, No. 25. Washington, DC: Government Printing Office; Department of Health and Human Services Publication PHS 87-1409.

Hersey, J., Glass, L., & Crocker, P. (1984). *Aging and health promotion: Market research for public education.* NTIS Accession, No. PB84-211150.

Horwath, C. C. (1989). Dietary intake studies in elderly people. *World Review of Nutrition & Dietetics, 59,* 1–70.

House, J. S., Landis, K. R., & Umberson, D. (1988). Social relationships and health. *Science, 241,* 540–544.

House Select Committee on Aging, Subcommittee on Health and Long-Term Care. (1984). *Quackery: A $10 billion scandal.* Washington, DC: Government Printing Office; Publication No. 98-435.

Hubert, H. B., Bloch, D. A., & Fries, J. F. (1993). Risk factors for physical disability in an aging cohort: The NHANES I Epidemiologic Follow-up Study. *Journal of Rheumatology, 20,* 480–488.

Hunter, K. I., & Linn, M. W. (1979). Cultural and sex differences in dietary patterns of urban elderly. *Journal of the American Geriatrics Society, 27,* 359–363.

Hutchinson, M., & Munro, H. N. (1986). *Nutrition and aging.* New York: Academic Press.

Institute of Medicine, Division of Health Promotion and Disease Prevention. (1992). *The second fifty years: Promoting health and preventing disability* (R. L. Berg & J. S. Cassells, Eds.). Washington: National Academy Press.

Jacoby, J., Chestnut, R., & Fisher, W. A. (1978). A behavioral process approach to information acquisition in nondurable purchasing. *Journal of Market Research, 15,* 532–544.

Jette, A. M., Pinsky, J. L., Branch, L. G., Wolf, P. A., & Feinleib, M. (1988). The Framingham Disability Study: Physical disability among community-dwelling survivors of stroke. *Journal of Clinical Epidemiology, 41,* 719–726.

Kaplan, G. A. (1991). Epidemiologic observations on the compression of morbidity. *Journal of Aging and Health, 3,* 155–171.

Kelly-Hayes, M., Wolf, P. A., Kannel, W. B., Sytkowski, P., D'Agostino, R. B., & Gresham, G. E. (1988). Factors influencing survival and need for institutionalization following stroke: The Framingham Study. *Archives of Physical Medicine and Rehabilitation, 69,* 415–418.

Kirschner Associates Inc. & Opinion Research Corporation. (1980). *Longitudinal evaluation of the national nutrition program for the elderly.* Washington, DC: Administration on Aging; U.S. Department of Health, Education, and Welfare Publ. no. 80-20249.

Kohrs, M. B. (1980). Association of participation in a nutritional program for the elderly with nutritional status. *American Journal of Clinical Nutrition, 33,* 2643–2656.

Kohrs, M. B., O'Hanlon, P., & Eklund, D. (1978). Title VII nutrition program for the elderly: 1. Contribution to one day's dietary intake. *Journal of the American Dietetic Association, 72,* 487–492.

LaCroix, A. Z., Guralnik, J. M., Berkman, L. F. , Wallace, R. B., & Satterfield, S. (1993). Maintaining mobility in late life. *American Journal of Epidemiology, 137,* 858–869.

Lammi, U., Kivela, S., Nissinen, A., Punsar, S., Puska, P., & Karvonen, M. (1989). Predictors of disability in elderly Finnish men—A longitudinal study. *Journal of Clinical Epidemiology, 42,* 1215–1225.

LeClerc, H., & Thornbury, M. E. (1983). Dietary intakes of Title III meal program recipients and nonrecipients. *Journal of the American Dietetic Association, 83,* 573–577.

Levine, E., & Posner, B. (1989). Media use and nutrition knowledge of Title IIIc congregate meal participants in New England. *Journal of the American Dietetic Association, 89*(9 Suppl), A-124.

Light, L. (1976). Cameras help the elderly to improve food patterns. *Journal of Nutrition Education, 8,* 80.

Lipschitz, D. A. (1991). *The development of an approach to nutrition screening for older Americans.* Washington DC: Nutrition Screening Initiative.

Lockniskar, M. (1988). Nutrition and health symposium: University of Texas at Austin, 1988 summary report. *Nutrition Today, 23,* 31–37.

Manton, K. G. (1989). Epidemiological, demographic and social correlates of disability among the elderly. *Milbank Quarterly Fund, 67,* 13–58.

Marketing Sciences Institute. (1982). *Determinants of food consumption in American households, Report No. 82-112.* Cambridge, MA: Marketing Sciences Institute.

McIntosh, W. A., Kubena, K. S., Walker, J., Smith, D., & Landmann, W. A. (1990). The relationship between beliefs about nutrition and dietary practices of the elderly. *Journal of the American Dietetic Association, 90,* 671–676.

Mor, V., Murphy, J., Masterson-Allen, S., Willey, C. Razmpour, A., Jackson, M. E., Green, D., & Katz, S. (1989). Risk of functional decline among well elders. *Journal of Clinical Epidemiology, 42,* 895–904.

Morley, J. E. (1986). Nutritional status of the elderly. *American Journal of Medicine, 81*, 679–695.

Murphy, S. P., Davis, M. A., Neuhaus, J. M., & Lein, D. (1990). Factors influencing the dietary adequacy and energy intake of older americans. *Journal of Nutrition Education, 22*, 284–291.

National Association of Nutrition and Aging Services Programs. (1988). *The aging networks guide to USDA*. Grand Rapids, MI: National Association of Nutrition and Aging.

National Center for Health Statistics. (1986). *Aging in the eighties: Age 65 years and over and living alone, contacts with family, friends, and neighbors. Preliminary Data from the Supplement on Aging to the National Health Interview Survey: United States, January–June, 1984, No. 116*. Hyattsville, MD: U.S. Public Health Service.

National Center for Health Statistics. (1987). *Aging in the eighties: Functional limitations of individuals age 65 years and over. Preliminary Data from the Supplement on Aging to the National Health Interview Survey: United States, No. 133*. Hyattsville, MD: U.S. Public Health Service.

National Conference on Nutrition Education. (1980). Specific recommendations: Low income and elderly populations. *Journal of Nutrition Education, 12*(2 Suppl), 128–130.

National Research Council. (1989a). *Diet and health: Implications for reducing chronic disease risk*. Washington, DC: National Academy Press.

National Research Council. (1989b). *Recommended Dietary Allowances* (10th ed.). Washington, DC: National Academy Press.

Nestle, M., Lee, P. R., & Fullarton, J. E. (1983). *Nutrition and the elderly: A working paper for the Administration on Aging*. Policy Paper No. 2. San Francisco: Aging Health Policy Center, University of California.

Nickel, J. T., & Chirikos, T. N. (1990). Functional disability of elderly patients with long-term coronary heart disease: A sex-stratified analysis. *Journal of Gerontology, 45*, S60–S68.

Nutrition Screening Initiative. (1991a). *Report of nutrition screening 1: Toward a common view*. Washington, DC: Author.

Nutrition Screening Initiative. (1991b). *Nutrition screening manual for professionals caring for older Americans*. Washington, DC: Author.

Nutrition Screening Initiative. (1992). *Nutrition interventions manual for professionals caring for older Americans*. Washington, DC: Greer, Margolis, Mitchell, Grunwald.

Nutrition Screening Initiative. (1994). *Incorporating nutrition screening and interventions into medical practice: A monograph for physicians*. Washington, DC: Author.

Pinsky, J. L., Branch, L. G., Jette, A. M., Haynes, S. G., Feinleib, M., Cornoni-Huntley, J. C., & Bailey, K. R. (1985). Framingham disability study: Relationship of disability to cardiovascular-risk factors among persons free of diagnosed cardiovascular disease. *American Journal of Epidemiology, 122*, 644–656.

Pinsky, J. L., Jette, A. M., Branch, L. G., Kannel, W. B., & Feinleib, M. (1990). The Framingham Disability Study: Relationship of various coronary heart disease manifestations to disability in older persons living in the community. *American Journal of Public Health, 80*, 1363–1368.

Ponza, M., Ohls, J. C., & Posner, B. M. (1994). *Elderly nutrition program evaluation literature review*. Princeton, NJ: MATHEMATICA Policy Research, Inc.

Posner, B. M. (1979). *Nutrition and the elderly*. Lexington, MA: Heath.

Posner, B. M. (1982). Nutrition education for older Americans: National policy recommendations. *Journal of the American Dietetic Association, 80*, 455–458.

Posner, B. M., Cobb, J. L., Belanger, A. J., Cupples, I. A., D'Agostino, R. B., & Stokes, J., III. (1991). Dietary lipid predictors of coronary heart disease in men: The Framingham Study. *Archives of Internal Medicine, 151*, 1181–1187.

Posner, B. M., Jette, A., Smigelski, C., Miller, D., & Mitchell, P. (1994). Nutritional Risk in New England Elders. *Journal of Gerontology: Medical Sciences, 49*, M123–M132.

Posner, B. M., Jette, A. M., Smith, K. W., & Miller, D. R. (1993a). Nutrition and health risks in the elderly: The Nutrition Screening Initiative. *American Journal of Public Health, 83*, 972–978.

Posner, B. M., & Krachenfels, M. M. (1987). Nutrition services in the continuum of care. *Clinics in Geriatric Medicine, 3*, 261–274.

Posner, B. M., & Levine, E. L. (1991). Nutrition services for older Americans. In *Geriatric nutrition: A health professional's handbook*. Gaithersburg, MD: Aspen Publishers.

Posner, B. M., Saffel-Shrier, S., Dwyer, J., & Franz, M. M. (1993b). Position of the American Dietetic

Association: Nutrition, aging, and the continuum of health care. *Journal of the American Dietetic Association, 93*, 80–82.
Posner, B. M., Smigelski, C. G., & Krachenfels, M. M. (1987). Dietary characteristics and nutrient intake in an urban homebound population. *Journal of the American Dietetic Association, 87*, 452–456.
Probart, C. K., Davis, L. G., Hibbard, J. H., & Kime, R. E. (1989). Factors that influence the elderly to use traditional or nontraditional nutrition information sources. *Journal of the American Dietetic Association. 89*, 1758–1762.
Rao, D. B. (1973). Problems of nutrition in the aged. *Journal of the American Geriatrics Society, 21*, 362.
Rapp, S. R., Parisi, S. A., Walsh, D. A., & Wallace, C. E. (1988). Dieting depression in elderly medical inpatients. *Journal of Consulting & Clinical Psychology, 56*, 509–513.
Roe, D. A. (1989). Nutritional surveillance of the elderly: Methods to determine program impact and unmet need. *Nutrition Today, 24*, 24–29.
Rosenberg, I. H., & Miller, J. W. (1992). Nutritional factors in physical and cognitive functions of elderly people. *American Journal of Clinical Nutrition, 55*, 1237S–1243S.
Rowe, J. W., & Kahn, R. L. (1987). Human aging: Usual and successful. *Science, 237*, 143–149.
Rudell, F. (1979). *Consumer food selection and nutrition information.* Westport, CT: Praeger.
Satariano, W. A., Ragheb, N. E., Branch, L. G., & Swanson, G. M. (1990). Difficulties in physical functioning reported by middle-aged and elderly women with breast cancer: A case control comparison. *Journal of Gerontology, 45*, M3–M11.
Smith, C. H., & Bidlack, W. R. (1984). Dietary concerns about the use of medications. *Journal of the American Dietetic Association, 84*, 901–903.
Surgeon General's Workshop on Health Promotion and Aging. (1988). Washington, DC: Government Printing Office; Publication No. 1988-201-875/83669.
U.S. Department of Agriculture. (1992). *The food guide pyramid.* Home and Garden Bulletin No. 252. Hyattsville, MD: Human Nutrition Information Service.
U.S. Department of Agriculture and U.S. Department of Health and Human Services. (1990). *Nutrition and your health: Dietary guidelines for Americans* (3rd ed.). Home and Garden Bulletin No. 232. Hyattsville, MD: Human Nutrition Information Service.
U.S. Department of Health and Human Services. (1972). *Ten-state nutrition survey, V: dietary.* Atlanta, GA: Centers for Disease Control; U.S. Dept. of Health and Human Services Publ. no. HSM 72-8133.
U.S. Department of Health and Human Services. (1979). *Dietary intake source data, United States, 1971–74.* DHEW Publ. No. (PHS) 79-1221. Washington, DC: Government Printing Office.
U.S. Department of Health and Human Services, Office of Human Development Services, Administration on Aging. (1985). *Older American's Act of 1965, as amended.* Washington, DC: Government Printing Office; No. 1985-527-317:30451.
U.S. Department of Health and Human Services, Public Health Service. (1987). *Prevention 86/87, federal programs and progress.* Washington, DC: Public Health Service, OHDS.
U.S. Department of Health and Human Services, Public Health Service. (1988). Aging. In *The Surgeon General's report on nutrition and health.* Washington, DC: Government Printing Office; DHHS (PHS) Publication No. 88-50210.
U.S. Department of Health and Human Services, Public Health Service. (1992). *Healthy People 2000: National health promotion and disease prevention objectives. Full report, with commentary.* Boston: Jones & Bartlett.
U.S. Department of Health and Human Services and U.S. Department of Agriculture. (1986). *Nutrition monitoring in the U.S.: A report from the Joint Nutrition Monitoring Evaluation Committee.* Washington, DC: Government Printing Office; U.S. Public Health Service; USDHHS publ. PHS 86-1255.
U.S. Senate Special Committee on Aging. (1987). *Developments in aging: 1986. A Report of the Special Committee on Aging.* Washington, DC: Government Printing Office ASI No. 25144.3.
U.S. Senate Special Committee on Aging, the American Association of Retired Persons, the Federal Council on the Aging, and the U.S. Administration on Aging. (1991). *Aging America: Trends and projections.* Washington, DC: U.S. Department of Health and Human Services; DHHS Publ. No. (FCoA) 91-28001).
Vaughan, L. A., & Manore, M. M. (1988). Dietary patterns and nutritional status of low income, free-living elderly. *Food & Nutrition News, 60*, 27–30.
Walker, D., & Beauchene, R. (1991). The relationship of loneliness, social isolation, and physical health

to dietary adequacy of independently living elderly. *Journal of the American Dietetics Association, 91*, 300–304.

White, J. V. (1991). *Risk factors associated with poor nutritional status in older Americans.* Washington, DC: Nutrition Screening Initiative.

White, J. V., Dwyer, J. T., Posner, B. M., Ham, R. J., Lipschitz, D. A., Wellman, N. S. (1992). Nutrition Screening Initiative: Development and implementation of the public awareness checklist and screening tools. *Journal of the American Dietetics Association, 92*, 163–167.

White, J. V., Ham, R. J., Lipschitz, D. A., Dwyer, J. T., & Wellman, N. S. (1991). Consensus of the Nutrition Screening Initiative: Risk factors and indicators of poor nutritional status in older Americans. *Journal of the American Dietetics Association, 91*, 783–787.

White House Conference on Aging. (1981). *Final report of the 1981 White House Conference on Aging: A national policy on aging.* Washington, DC: Government Printing Office.

White House Conference on Food, Nutrition and Health: Panel IV-4. (1970). *Popular education and how to reach disadvantaged groups.* Washington, DC: Government Printing Office.

Zandt, S. V., & Fox, H. (1986). Nutritional impact of congregate meals programs. *Journal of Nutrition for the Elderly, 5*, 31–43.

CHAPTER 6

Managing Pain in the Institutionalized Elderly

The Nursing Role

NANCY WELLS, MERRIE KAAS, AND KAREN FELDT

INTRODUCTION

Pain is a common symptom across all age groups but becomes increasingly prevalent in older adults, who experience a variety of chronic diseases that are potentially painful (Ferrell, 1991; Foley, 1993; Harkins, 1988). Attention has recently been focused on the adequate assessment and treatment of pain in the elderly institutionalized population (Ferrell, 1991; Parmelee, Smith, & Katz, 1993; Sengstaken & King, 1993). Although elders residing in the community may not adequately treat pain for a variety of reasons (e.g., personal beliefs and reluctance to take pain medications), institutionalized elders, whether in acute-care or long-term-care settings, rely on nursing staff to appropriately assess pain, administer pain medications as necessary, and evaluate the response to such medications (Carr, 1990; Lavies, Hart, Rounsefell, & Runciman, 1992; Seers, 1987). Nurses wield much of the control over the management of pain in institutional environments.

Two organizations, the American Pain Society (APS) and the Agency for Health Care Policy and Research (AHCPR), have recently developed guidelines to improve pain management (AHCPR, 1992; APS, 1991). These guidelines propose actions to increase health-care-provider and patient awareness of the importance of pain treatment and the available interventions, to improve the use of adequate pharmacological agents, to increase the use of nondrug interventions, and to enhance accountability for pain

NANCY WELLS • Department of Nursing Research, Vanderbilt University Medical Center, Nashville, Tennessee 37203. MERRIE KAAS • School of Nursing, University of Minnesota, Minneapolis, Minnesota 55416. KAREN FELDT • Ramsey Nursing Home Services, St. Paul, Minnesota 55106.

Handbook of Pain and Aging, edited by David I. Mostofsky and Jacob Lomranz. Plenum Press, New York, 1997.

management at a systems level. These guidelines have targeted acute and cancer-related pain, occurring most frequently in acute care hospitals. However, many of the principles and actions can be adapted to long-term-care settings, where many frail elders reside.

This chapter examines the prevalence of pain in the elderly. Emphasis is placed on pain management for elders residing in long-term-care facilities. Barriers to adequate pain management are addressed. Included in the discussion is the issue of pain management for cognitively impaired elders, who comprise an increasing proportion of the patients of long-term-care facilities. Issues of assessment and treatment are addressed with regard to elders' cognitive status. Nursing interventions are identified to improve pain management at both the individual and the system levels. Much of the research reviewed in this chapter was conducted in acute care settings with patients experiencing acute surgical and cancer-related pain, with findings extrapolated to older adults residing in long-term-care facilities.

EXPERIENCE OF PAIN IN THE ELDERLY

Various studies have examined different aspects of pain perception to determine if the physiological experience of pain changes with increasing age. Two components of pain physiology have been studied extensively: pain threshold, which is the least stimulus intensity a subject perceives as pain, and pain tolerance, which is the greatest stimulus intensity a subject is prepared to tolerate (International Association of the Study of Pain, 1979). Laboratory studies have reported conflicting findings with regard to pain threshold in the elderly (Collins & Stone, 1966; Hardy, Wolff, & Goodell, 1943; Harkins & Chapman, 1977; Harkins, Price, & Martelli, 1986; Mumford, 1965; Sherman & Robillard, 1960; Yahuda & Carasso, this volume, Chapter 2). But studies on pain tolerance have concluded that pain tolerance is lower in older subjects (Collins & Stone, 1966; Harkins & Chapman, 1977; Woodrow, Friedman, Siegalaub, & Cohen, 1972; Yahuda & Carasso, this volume, Chapter 2). This means that elders may be less able to cope with the stress of untreated pain than younger adults.

In an attempt to understand the variability of pain threshold and tolerance, pain has been explained as a multidimensional phenomenon (e.g., Melzack & Wall, 1988; Rudy, Kerns, & Turk, 1988). Hall-Lord, Larsson, and Bostrom (1994) proposed a similar model of pain and distress in the elderly. This model includes four interrelated dimensions: sensory, intellectual, emotional, and existential. Although these dimensions may be separate, they interact to explain pain tolerance and perception in the elderly.

Prevalence of Pain in Cognitively Intact Elderly

Various epidemiological studies suggest that a high percentage of community-living elderly experience pain (Chrischilles et al., 1992; Crook, Rideout, & Browne, 1984; Mobily, Herr, Clark, & Wallace, 1994). The data suggest that at least one in four persons over the age of 60 years residing in the community experience persistent pain, and that a minimum of one-third of elders take analgesics to control their pain. Pain is a common experience in hospitalized medical and surgical patients of all ages (Donovan, Dillon, & McGuire, 1987; Gu & Belgrade, 1993; Juhl et al., 1933; Miaskowski, Nichols, Brody, & Synold, 1994; Ward & Gordon, 1994). Although much research has addressed the incidence and treatment of pain in acute care settings, few studies include information about prevalence of pain in older patients in acute care settings. Little research has been conducted on prevalence of pain in long-term-care facilities.

Prevalence of pain in long-term-care facilities ranges between 66% and 79% (Ferrell, Ferrell, & Osterweil, 1990; Parmelee et al., 1993; Sengstaken & King, 1993). In a study of pain experienced during the last year of life, close relatives reported that 37% of a sample of elders experienced pain frequently or all the time in their last year of life, which increased to 66% during their last month (Moss, Lawton, & Glicksman, 1991). Unfortunately, the study excluded persons who were institutionalized for the entire last three months of their lives, so a comparison of the pain experienced by institutionalized and community-residing elders in the last year of life could not be determined.

Prevalence of Pain in Cognitively Impaired Elderly

The prevalence of dementing illnesses increases with increasing age. Epidemiological community-based studies indicate that as many as 47% of elders over the age of 85 have some degree of cognitive impairment (Evans, Funkenstein, & Albert, et al., 1989). Studies suggest that well over half of the elders residing in long-term-care facilities have some degree of cognitive impairment (Chandler & Chandler, 1988; Newman, Griffin, Black, & Page, 1989). Considering the large number of older adults with cognitive impairment, surprisingly little is known about the experience and prevalence of pain in this population.

Anecdotal evidence suggests that, as cognitive capacity is lost, there may be a loss of sensitivity to nociception (Harkins, 1988). The pathophysiological changes for Alzheimer's type dementia involves the destruction of cortical neuronal cells and depletion of cortical chemical neurotransitters; nociceptor response and transmission of pain sensation are not thought to be affected. An "indifference" to pain seen in demented patients may be related to deterioration of cognitive abilities. Anticipation, anxiety, and attention are known to increase pain perception (Melzack & Wall, 1988). Cognitively impaired elders have short attention spans and are easily distracted. They may not remember the painful event or anticipate that pain will be a problem as they proceed with daily activities. Neglect of a painful injury may also be related to poor judgment about whether to seek help, difficulty with decision making because of impaired complex-thinking skills, or a lack of comprehension of the serious nature of the injury.

The anecdotal evidence of reduction of pain report may also be related to a loss of verbal skills rather than loss of sensitivity to nociception. Persons with dementia have a number of changes in language skills that impair their ability to report pain. These include difficulties finding the correct word, paraphasia (i.e., using a word other than the intended word to explain something), anomia (i.e., an inability to name objects or parts), and difficulties acting on what is said or heard. The person with dementia may neglect to report pain because of the inability to adequately conceptualize, express, or explain the perceptions experienced (Parmelee et al., 1993). Attempts to express pain may be misunderstood by health care providers or discounted as unreliable. Frustration with impaired verbal skills or lack of patience on the part of either the patient or the health care provider can thwart efforts to explain pain. In cognitively impaired individuals who maintain some verbal skill, however, pain can be reported as well as it is by cognitively intact elders.

Few studies give any indication of how prevalent pain is in older adults with cognitive impairment. Many researchers routinely eliminate subjects who are thought to be unreliable in their report of pain. However, a community-based study of cognitively intact and impaired elders found no difference in their spontaneous report of pain when discussing physical and mental health symptoms experienced day to day (Brody & Kleban, 1983). In an indirect comparison, Ferrell and colleagues (1990) noted that patients in board-and-care units reported significantly more pain than patients in skilled units, who were more likely to be cognitively impaired. No relationship was found between a mental status examination score and reported pain. In contrast, Parmelee and colleagues (1993) noted that cognitive impairment increased as reports of pain decreased; however, the most disabled, nonverbal, and markedly impaired patients were excluded from this sample. These data provide little evidence that cognitively impaired elders experience less pain than cognitively intact elders; prevalence data of cognitively intact elders indicate that a substantial number experience pain. The difficulty with cognitively impaired elders is that pain complaints may be voiced less frequently or considered unreliable by health care providers. This suggests that the identification and subsequent treatment of pain may be easily overlooked in cognitively impaired elders.

Analgesics are the mainstay of pain management, yet pain is not adequately managed in many health care settings (e.g., Ferrell et al., 1990; Cohen, 1980; Marks & Sachar, 1973). Conditions in long-term-care facilities—for example, fewer licensed staff and altered focus of care—suggest pain may be more poorly managed than in the acute care setting. While no differences by age were found for nurses' estimates of pain in hospitalized patients (Choiniere, Melzack, Girard, Rondeau, & Paquin, 1990; Zalon, 1993), older patients had less pain medication prescribed (Faherty & Grier, 1984) and administered (Faherty & Grier, 1984; Oberle, Paul, Wry, & Grace, 1990). Elderly surgical patients receive approximately 25% of prescribed analgesics (Closs, Fairtlough, Tierney, & Currie, 1993; Short, Burnett, Egbert, & Parks, 1990). Therefore, although providers' assessment of pain does not appear to be influenced by the age of the patient, the administration of analgesics does vary by age of the patient.

FACTORS RELATED TO UNDERTREATMENT OF PAIN

There are many interacting factors influencing pain control. The barriers to adequate pain management identified in patients with cancer-related pain also apply to pain occurring in long-term-care facilities. The barriers can be categorized as patient factors, health care provider factors, and system factors (Cleeland, 1987).

Patient Factors

Patients of all ages have beliefs about pain and the use of opioids, as well as a general lack of knowledge of the available therapeutic options. Many older adults believe that aches and pains are a normal part of life and that some degree of pain must simply be tolerated as they become older (Ferrell et al., 1990). Although research suggests and the AHCPR panel recommends preventing severe pain, over 50% of hospitalized patients would wait until a nurse asked if medication was needed (Carr, 1990; Lavies et al., 1992; Seers, 1987) or wait until pain was severe (Owen, McMillian, & Rogowski, 1990). Clearly, communication about the importance of pain control and the patient's responsibility is lacking (Donovan et al., 1987; Miaskowski et al., 1994), assuming the patient is cognitively aware and able to report the presence of pain.

Patients may hold inaccurate beliefs about opioid medications. They may fear addiction and negative side effects of the use of opioids (Ward et al., 1993). These beliefs contribute to the reluctance of patients to communicate pain, and to take analgesics to relieve pain.

Despite reporting moderate to severe pain during hospitalization, patients generally report a high degree of satisfaction with pain management (Donovan et al., 1987; Lavies et al., 1992; Miaskowski et al., 1994; Ward & Gordon, 1994). The disparity between pain relief reported and satisfaction with pain management may be related to patients' expectations for pain control during hospitalization (Ward & Gordon, 1994). These findings suggest that raising patients' expectations for adequate pain control and informing them of their responsibility to communicate pain are steps that may enhance pain management in institutionalized patients.

Addressing Patient Factors. Patient and family education to increase their knowledge about pain and the options available for pain control is essential for successful pain management (AHCPR, 1992; APS, 1991). Research has demonstrated that patients who have been informed about their pain and the methods of pain control available report less pain (AHCPR, 1992). Dispelling beliefs that pain is "just a part of getting old" and that it must be tolerated is an important aspect of a pain discussion with elderly patients and their family member(s). The rationale for adequately treating pain and an introduction to both pharmacological and nondrug methods of pain management can be addressed during the initial assessment of pain. Because the best indicator of pain is the patient's report, it is important to explain the various intensity measures available to the patient and family (e.g., the visual analogue scale and the verbal descriptor scale), and to allow the patient to select the one that he or she understands the best. For cognitively impaired patients, probing the family for behavioral clues to discomfort and pain will not only provide the nursing staff with baseline assessment information but will also educate the family about pain expression. Educating the family is important in this process. Their involvement in assessing the patient's behavioral cues as well as support in using pain interventions increases the likelihood of success.

When a pain treatment plan has been determined that includes analgesics, information about the administration, desired effects, and common side effects should be discussed with the patient and family. With adequate information, the cognitively intact patient will be able to more accurately report the adequacy of pain relief and side effects, which will help to adjust the interventions used to manage pain. One method to reduce patient reluctance is one-to-one discussion with patients to dispel fears and provide accurate information. Wilder-Smith and Schuler (1992) found that 30 of 40 postoperative patients who initially refused analgesics agreed to take them after a brief discussion with the night nurse about addiction, side effects, and the benefits of pain control after surgery. While this type of intervention may be time-consuming for nurses, it may produce better pain control for elders who are reluctant to take analgesics. Frequent review of information about pain and pain management relevant to the patient will reinforce the importance of reporting pain and pain relief obtained from the various interventions used.

Health Care Provider Factors

Health care provider knowledge deficits about pharmacology (e.g., optimum doses of opioid medications and duration of action) have been well documented (Cohen, 1980; Marks & Sachar, 1973; McCaffery, Ferrell, O'Neil-Page, & Lester, 1990; Vortherms, Ryan, & Ward, 1992). Health care providers consistently overestimate the rate of addiction (Cohen, 1980; Kuhn, Cooke, Collins, Jones, & Mucklow, 1990; Lavies et al., 1992; Marks & Sachar, 1973; McCaffery et al., 1990; Seers, 1987) and respiratory depression (Cohen, 1980). Health care providers may hold the same belief as their patients, that pain is simply a normal part of aging. Fear of harming the patient, either through adverse side effects (e.g., confusion, constipation, and urinary retention) or by promoting addiction, may encourage physicians to underprescribe medications and nurses to underadminister them.

Skepticism about the patient's report of pain can negatively impact health care providers' treatment of pain. The majority of health care providers believe the patient is the expert in determining pain (Cleeland, 1987; Vortherms et al., 1992). However, these studies involved a substantial number of providers who care for cancer patients and tend to have more liberal views of opioid use for pain management. In a general survey of nurses who attended continuing-education programs on pain, McCaffery and Ferrell (1991) describe how nurses reduced the patient's estimate of their pain when behavioral cues were incongruent with pain report. A large number of studies have documented that the relationship between patient report of pain and health care provider estimates is weak to moderate at best (Choiniere et al., 1990; Forrest, Hermann, & Andersen, 1989; Zalon, 1993), with providers underestimating pain in 23% (Bondestam et al., 1987) to 54% (Seers, 1987) of patients.

For patients of long-term-care facilities, other provider issues emerge as problematic. A recent survey of knowledge and attitudes toward pain compared long-term-care and oncology nurses. Findings demonstrate long-term-care facility nurses were more likely to think that patients overreport pain than oncology nurses (Ryan, Vortherms, & Ward, 1994). In long-term-care facilities, there are few licensed nurses available to assess pain and infrequent visits by physicians. Many of the licensed nurses lack previous work experience in acute care, surgery, or oncology units. The majority of hands-on care in nursing homes is provided by nursing assistants, who have no formal training in pain assessment. Even if pain-related behaviors are noted by assistants, these behaviors may not necessarily be reported to nursing staff as pain. Increasing patient demand for pain relief may be ignored by the staff, to suppress this behavior. Crying out or striking out by a cognitively impaired patient during morning care may be viewed as resistive and aggressive behavior; linking this behavior to pain from severe arthritis may not be considered. For example, in a study of patients in long-term care, 5 of 76 vocally disruptive patients were receiving pain medications, compared to 31 of 71 patients who were not vocally disruptive (Cariaga, Burgio, Flynn, & Martin, 1991). Many long-term-care facilities use "trained medication assistants" to pass medications. These are nursing assistants with some basic education about medication, administration of medications, and common side effects. Since pain medications are typically ordered on a *pro re nata* (PRN; "as needed") basis, nursing staff must be aware of the need for pain medication before administering it. If few assessments for pain are conducted, few pain medications will be given.

Addressing Health Care Provider Factors. Education of nursing staff in long-term-care facilities is important in improving pain management. Staff knowledge and attitudes may be barriers to adequate pain assessment and management (Ryan et al., 1994). It is important to determine the education and training of the licensed nursing staff about pain and its treatment in the elderly, in addition to their beliefs about pain expression and relief. Because it is often the nursing assistants who report the patients' expression of pain to the nurse, it is necessary to identify their experiences with pain in their patients and interventions they see as helpful. Management of acute and chronic pain by the nursing staff occurs throughout the day and includes all shifts of nursing personnel. Educational programs, such as in-services and workshops, provide the opportunity to explore beliefs of the staff and to present information about pain expression ad treatment. The APS (1991) recommends easy availability of written materials on pain and pain management for continued use. In most long-term-care facilities, physicians or nurse practitioners manage the patients' medical problems. Because these providers prescribe various methods of pain relief, it is important to understand their perspective so that a pain management plan can be written collaboratively.

System Factors

System factors influencing pain management include the structure of institutions where care is provided and the legal constraints applied to opioids. In an extensive examination of pain management in a variety of hospital settings, Fagerhaugh and Strauss (1977) concluded that lack of accountability was a major deterrent to adequate pain management. This occurs because different providers are responsible for specific aspects of the pain management process. Accountability for pain control is lacking in many health care settings, including long-term-care facilities. Often, the regulation by federal and state laws requiring documentation of medication need and use inhibits adequate pain relief intervention (Zullich, Grasela, Fielder-Kelly, & Gengo, 1992). It is much easier for nursing staff to administer a PRN nonopioid analgesic rather than the more effective, but also more controlled, opioid. The documentation required to prescribe opioids varies, and mechanisms such as the triplicate prescription may make medical providers reluctant to write opioid prescriptions.

Addressing System Factors. Despite education of the nursing staff and medical providers and the involvement of patients and their families in pain management, unless the long-term-care system supports activities to provide adequate pain relief, improvement will be difficult. The AHCPR guideline panel (1992) and the APS (1991) recommend the use of pain standards and a quality assurance program to increase provider accountability. Miaskowski et al. (1994) reported on the use of the APS Quality Assurance Standards in a medium-sized community hospital. Sixty-five percent of patients were told to communicate pain to a health care provider, which is one standard set by the AHCPR guideline (Table 6-1). However, prompt relief of pain once a pain complaint has been made, prompt change in pain control regimen when requested, and adequate relief with analgesics were not met at a 50% level in this institution. Initial monitoring will help to identify areas for improvement (Ferrell, McCaffery, & Ropchan, 1992). Plans to improve pain control can be collaboratively determined, and accountability for pain control should be identified in the process. Intermittent monitoring with timely feedback to the nursing staff will provide ongoing reinforcement for adequate pain management and identify further areas that require improvement (Ferrell et al., 1992). Both guidelines recommend a committee within the organizational structure responsible for review and feedback of quality assurance data.

Putting a quality assurance program into place requires commitment from nursing administration to improve pain management and a commitment to provide the necessary resources (Arndt & Bigelow, 1994; Ferrell et al., 1992). Therefore, assessment of the health care delivery system includes the mechanisms available to implement and monitor a pain management regimen that is usable by the nursing staff. The use of standard assessment forms, for both initial assessment and ongoing evaluation of interventions, provides a system for assessment and documentation activities. A high level of commu-

Table 6-1. Sample Pain Standards

APS standard	Institutional application
Recognize and treat pain promptly.	Assess and document pain regularly: Once a day for patients without pain Every 4 hours for patients with pain 1 hour after analgesic Institute pain control interventions promptly: Within 30 minutes of pain complaint Change intervention or medication promptly when ineffective: Within 1 hour of evaluation
Promise attentive analgesic care.	Discuss importance of pain control and reporting pain promptly with patient and family on admission to facility and after incidents that cause or that may cause pain.

nication and involvement of nursing staff is necessary to come to consensus on institutional standards for pain management (Arndt & Bigelow, 1994; Jacox, Ferrell, Heidrich, Hester, & Miaskowski, 1992). In addition to the nursing staff, physicians and/or nurse practitioners who provide medical care for patients in the long-term-care facilities should be involved in the discussions and decision-making process. Individualized pain management plans and use of both analgesics and nondrug therapies are recommended (AHCPR, 1992).

Before implementing an institutional plan to improve pain management, it is necessary to assess the availability of resources and methods of payment for pain relief interventions. Consulting psychologists, biofeedback equipment, TENS units, exercise equipment, and staff are resources for various pain management interventions, but not all may be reimbursed by health care plans. Some pain management interventions require a quiet, comfortable, and private space, yet that type of space is difficult to find in many long-term-care facilities. Thus, in addition to leadership and organizational policies, resources are needed to successfully make an institutional change in the way pain is managed.

MANAGEMENT OF PAIN

Pain management of long-term-care patients has relied on nonopioid analgesics given on an as-needed (i.e., PRN) basis. Alternative interventions, such as regularly scheduled dosing of analgesics, cutaneous stimulation, relaxation, and exercise, are not generally considered. The changing demographics of the long-term-care population (older patients with more chronic illnesses and patients with more acute illnesses and shorter stays) makes pain management of patients critically important.

Increasing numbers of long-term-care facilities have opened subacute units, where recent surgical and medical patients are admitted temporarily for recovery and rehabilitation. Other subacute units admit elderly cancer patients who are receiving chemotherapy. These patients require acute pain management that is different than that required by patients with chronic pain. Additionally, elderly patients may suffer from both chronic and acute pain. Nursing care of patients with both chronic and acute pain is predicated on a thorough assessment and a multidimensional model of intervention.

Assessment of Pain

Assessment of pain in the elderly, particularly those who are cognitively impaired, presents a challenge to health care providers. Yet assessment is the first step necessary to provide adequate pain control. If health care providers fail to ask about or observe for pain, patients who do not volunteer this information may be unidentified or misdiagnosed (Ferrell, 1993). Complicating the assessment of pain in older adults are the visual impairments and auditory discriminating problems that are common with increasing age. These impairments may frustrate attempts by nurses to assess pain intensity and location.

Cognitively Intact Elders. There are several standardized pain instruments available that could provide a more complete and standard pain assessment format. Unfortunately, most instruments have been validated on younger populations. Instruments such as the McGill Pain Questionnaire (Melzack, 1975, 1987) and the Multidimensional Pain Inventory (Kerns, Turk, & Rudy, 1985) are appealing because they provide information on both intensity and quality of pain; however, the complexity of the instrument may make use with elderly patients more difficult. The Pain Experience Interview (Ferrell, 1993) is a 31-item pain interview schedule adapted for use with the elderly. It provides data on the intensity and sources of pain, and on management strategies used by older persons. This interview consists primarily of yes-no response format items, which reduce the complexity of the instrument for the elderly. Convergent and divergent validity of the Pain Experience Interview were demonstrated in a sample of 92 long-term-care patients (Ferrell, 1993).

Although intensity measures, such as visual analogue scale (VAS) and the verbal descriptor scale (VDS), are unidimensional, they provide a consistent means of evaluating the effect of pain control interventions. Herr and Mobily (1993) tested the use of several intensity instruments in community-residing elders and found that the elders preferred a 7-point VDS. The VDS appeared to be better understood by older persons with lower education levels. Its low failure rate (2%) suggests that the VDS has better reliability in elderly populations than the VAS or numeric rating scales for pain intensity (Gagliese & Melzack, this volume, Chapter 4).

Cognitively Impaired Elders. Assessment of pain in cognitively impaired elders is complicated by the gradual global cognitive losses. A hallmark symptom of Alzheimer's type dementia is a loss of short-term memory. Therefore, instruments that require elders to recall pain over previous weeks may not be reliable when administered to cognitively impaired elders. Persons with dementia may not initiate conversation about pain or seek pain relief because they have forgotten where they are, whom they should tell, or what happened to cause the pain.

Impaired verbal skills further obstruct assessment of pain in this population. Instruments that require the understanding of numerous descriptors of pain or request the older patient to select the one word out of five that best describes pain are far too complex with moderate to severe cognitive impairment. The obvious solution is to attend to behavioral cues indicative of pain, but few instruments exist to measure these nonverbal indicators.

Several instruments are available for measurement of pain behaviors in patients with chronic pain (e.g., University of Alabama Pain Behavior Scale—Richards, Nepomuceno, Riles, & Suer, 1982; Pain Behavior Checklist—Dirks, Wunder, Kinsman, McEhinny, & Jones, 1993). These scales consist of behaviors, such as verbal and vocal expression of pain, facial grimacing, and guarding and bracing postures, thought to reflect the presence of pain. Both of these instruments include items that could lead to inaccurate scores for both cognitively intact and impaired patients. For example, the Pain Behavior Scale includes a category that requires the patient to identify how many minutes are spent in bed during the daytime hours because of pain, an impossible task for severely demented patients. Both instruments assume mobility, which may not apply to nonambulatory elders. Patients are rated as having more pain if they use supportive equipment, such as canes or walkers. These assistive devices are common aids used by the elderly to improve stability and mobility that is not restricted by pain, and they do not necessarily reflect an increased level of pain.

One instrument has been developed to measure discomfort in elders with advanced Alzheimer's type dementia (Hurley, Volicer, Hanrahan, Houde, & Volicer, 1992). Although the authors define discomfort in a slightly different way than pain is defined, the behaviors include behaviors commonly used to indicate pain. The Discomfort Scale consists of nine behaviors (noisy breathing, vocalization, four facial expressions, two kinds of body language, and fidgeting) scored on 100-point scales. Adequate reliability has been demonstrated in a sample of 82 primarily male veterans (Hurley et al., 1992).

Nonverbal cognitively impaired patients may communicate pain through behaviors not included in the scales discussed above. Although the scales include many useful observable behaviors that may signify pain (e.g., vocalization or crying out, facial expressions of grimacing or wincing, wrinkling of the forehead in response to movement, and increased restlessness, rocking, rubbing, or guarding), cognitively impaired patients may also show increased irritability or aggressive behavior, increased resistance to any personal care that requires movement, or social withdrawal (Herr & Mobily, 1991; Marzinski, 1991; Parke, 1992; Ryden & Feldt, 1992; Sengstaken & King, 1993). The possibility that behaviors observed are attributable to factors other than pain in cognitively impaired elders complicates the use of scales developed to measure pain behavior in patients with chronic pain. In addition, the variability of nonverbal pain-related behavior in different patients raises questions about the potential for a standardized behavioral assessment for pain in this patient population. When patients are nonverbal and cognitively impaired, observation of usual behavior(s) and changes in behavior patterns may provide the most useful method of pain assessment (Marzinski, 1991).

Standard Assessment. The most important step in pain management in long-term-care facilities is to develop a comprehensive, standard pain assessment protocol that is understood and used by the nursing staff. This pain assessment protocol needs to be accessible in the nursing record and to be used for both the initial assessment and evaluation of intervention effects. Various authors offer assessment models of pain (Greenlee, 1991; Hall-Lord et al., 1994; McCaffery & Beebe, 1989; Walker, Akinsanya, Davis, & Marcer, 1990). The type of information obtained will depend on the cognitive status of the patient and the presence or absence of family members or close friends (Table 6-2). For cognitively intact patients or the cognitively impaired with family members who can provide a history, description of the pain and the impact of pain on the patient's function are obtained during the admission assessment. Initial assessment of cognitively impaired elders without family occurs over several days through close observation. Individual pain assessment also includes the patient's manner of expressing the pain, which may be particularly useful for cognitively impaired patients. Beliefs about pain and analgesic medications are important as a starting point for a pain treatment plan; they also provide a basis for educating patients and their family members. Because of the strong relationship between depression and pain, especially in elderly patients with chronic pain (Turk, Okifuji, & Scharff, 1995), assessment of depression and

Table 6-2. Components of a Standard Assessment Protocol

Cognitively intact elders	Cognitively impaired elders
Initial assessment	Initial assessment
Source: Patient and family	Source: Family
Pain history and experience	Pain history and experience
Characteristics of pain	Characteristics of pain
Location(s)	Location(s)
Quality	Onset and duration
Intensity	Exacerbating factors
Onset and duration	Palliative measures
Exacerbating factors	Typical manner of expression
Palliative measures	Impact on
Typical manner of expression	Activity and sleep
Impact on	Function
Mood	Observation of patient
Activity and sleep	Verbal/vocalizations
Function	Facial grimacing
Relations with others	Posture and movement
Serial evaluation of intensity	Guarding
Verbal descriptor scale	Bracing
Key behavior(s)	Rubbing
	Resistance to movement
	Change in behavior
	Agitation
	Withdrawal

anxiety is critical (Schuster & Goetz, 1994). Family history of pain and pain management, psychiatric illness, and substance abuse is important information but rarely obtained in long-term-care facilities. Serial pain assessment, using a simple instrument such as the VDS, are essential for patients with pain problems requiring ongoing intervention.

The major treatment goal for acute pain is the prevention of the pain (AHCPR, 1992; APS, 1991; McCaffery & Beebe, 1989). Intervention for chronic pain focuses on the management, rather than the prevention, of pain. Major goals for chronic pain treatment are to increase the sense of control over the pain and decrease the disability and dysfunction (Carlson, Ventrella, & Sturgis, 1987). Unfortunately, long-term-care patients often suffer from both acute and chronic pain and require multiple methods of intervention.

Analgesic Medications

The elderly are at risk for under- and overmedicating because of age-related physiological changes and unclear analgesic dosage parameters. Decreased drug absorption and slower metabolism, distribution, and excretion increase the potential for adverse effects. Few elderly are used as subjects in analgesic drug studies (AHCPR, 1992), and therefore, the use of analgesics for pain control in the elderly has not been adequately tested, and age-normed parameters have not been established. Pain management through medication use must be predicated on a thorough knowledge base of age-related physiological changes, frequent pain assessment using standard measures, and continuous monitoring of both the medication effectiveness and its side effects.

Greenlee (1991) and the AHCPR (1992) offer general approaches to the use of analgesics with elderly patients. First, treat the patient, not the symptom. This includes understanding the patient's history, use of prior pain management techniques, medical problems, individual choice of analgesic and route, and the unique analgesic effect for that patient. Second, the type of drug and its pharmacology need to be understood and used as a basis for administration. Specific drugs should be matched to specific pain. Starting analgesic dosing low and titrating the drug up to the desired effect is recommended (AHCPR, 1992). Analgesics should be administered on a regular basis, not PRN, to prevent pain from reaching intolerable and uncontrollable levels. But the regular dosing of analgesics needs to be balanced with the untoward side effects of those medications in the elderly patient. Third, side effects need to be treated effectively. Because of age-related physiological changes, the elderly are more prone to constipation, urinary retention, sedation, and confusion secondary to analgesic use. Combined analgesic drug use or use of analgesics with the many other types of medications older patients take complicates the side effect picture because of additive effects. Different types of medications can cause the same side effect. For example, tricyclic antidepressants commonly used to treat depression in the elderly, but also used for pain control, have significant anticholinergic effects that can cause or worsen constipation, urinary retention, hypotension, and confusion (Schuster & Goetz, 1994).

Nonopioid Analgesics. Mild to moderate pain can be effectively managed with nonsteroidal anti-inflammatory drugs (NSAIDs) and acetaminophen. Acetaminophen has good analgesic, but not anti-inflammatory, effects, so it is a poor drug for pain related to inflammatory processes. The most common adverse side effect is of acetaminophen is gastrointestinal upset, which can be relieved by taking the medication with food or milk. Acetaminophen should be given every 4 hours to maintain optimum drug level and pain relief. Timing of medication dosing is more important than total daily amount.

There is increased risk of gastric and renal toxicity and cognitive impairment with NSAID use in the elderly (AHCPR, 1992; Greenlee, 1991; Schuster & Goetz, 1994). Baseline mental status examination and appropriate laboratory function tests should be obtained before initiating regular dosing of NSAIDs and should be followed routinely with continuous NSAID use. With aspirin, total daily dose is more important than the amount and time of dose (Greenlee, 1991). Gastrointestinal bleeding is a common side effect of NSAIDs in the elderly that needs to be distinguished from gastric upset. Stool guaiacs can be obtained if there is any indication of rectal bleeding.

Opioid Analgesics. Opioid analgesics have been shown to be effective for acute pain in elderly patients, but there is limited information regarding their use for chronic pain in the elderly (Schuster & Goetz, 1994). Studies indicate that the elderly are more sensitive to the opioid drugs and to the side effects of sedation and respiratory depression because of the physiological changes with aging that reduce drug distribution and excretion (AHCPR, 1992; Greenlee, 1991). Because of additional side effects, such as confusion, urinary retention (especially in males), and hypotension, opioid drug use for pain management mandates thorough assessment and frequent monitoring of the effectiveness balanced with the side effect profile. Nursing staff need to assess daily vital signs and mental status. With cognitively impaired patients taking opioid drugs, it is also important to monitor and document fluid intake, urinary output, and bowel function. Elderly patients maintained on regularly scheduled opioids should have a regular bowel regimen prescribed; prunes (6–10/day) or prune juice in addition to a laxative of choice and judicious use of fluids should be standard care.

Nondrug Interventions

The most often used method of pain relief is medication. Although the literature has suggested the importance and effectiveness of nondrug interventions (Ferrell, Ferrell, Rhiner, & Grant, 1991; Keller & Bzdek, 1986), there is little research that documents the effectiveness of nondrug interventions for pain in the elderly. Unfortunately, most nondrug interventions are used sporadically without consideration of the type of pain and are infrequently evaluated for effect. Consequently, these strategies are abandoned as ineffective (Ferrell et al., 1991). Nondrug interventions are seldom initiated by nursing staff because they are unaware of the intervention benefits or they do not know how to demonstrate various interventions such as relaxation or imagery.

Optimum pain management for the elderly long-term-care patient is best done with a combination of nondrug and drug interventions. Nondrug interventions should be used not as a replacement for analgesics, but as a complement. Analgesics can be used initially to reduce the pain enough for the patient to focus on nondrug interventions, or nondrug interventions can be encouraged first to facilitate the body's ability to use the analgesic more effectively. A comprehensive pain management plan should include the analgesic and nondrug intervention for the specific targeted pain and the patient's personal preference for each. The most common nondrug interventions suggested in the literature for the elderly patient are cutaneous stimulation, relaxation techniques, distraction, and exercise. However, simple nursing interventions, such as positioning, may also produce substantial pain relief.

Positioning. One of the most common and easiest pain relief measures for long-term-care patients is body positioning. Proper body alignment and position increase comfort by decreasing pressure on specific body areas, increasing mobility, and increasing the patient's ability to relax and socialize (Potter & Perry, 1989). Several devices are readily available for the nurse to maintain proper positioning: pillows, footboards, trochanter rolls, sandbags, and handrolls. In a study examining pain management strategies for elderly patients recovering from hip fractures, patients reported that they had the least pain when positioned in bed with their legs supported by pillows (Nelson, Taylor, Adams, & Parker, 1990). They also reported less fear of pain if they were allowed to move at their own pace. Elderly patients who are wheelchair-bound or spend most of the day in bed need to be positioned at least every 2 hours. Proper positioning and body alignment provides a comfortable situation in which the patient can focus on other pain management methods.

Cutaneous Stimulation. Massage, vibration, application of heat and cold, and electrical stimulation do not cure the pain but do offer some comfort as temporary relief measures. The stimulation of large-diameter afferent fibers and convergence in the dorsal horn, hypothesized to diminish pain transmission (Melzack & Wall, 1988), can be applied to the area of pain. When pain occurs in a limb, cutaneous stimulation may be applied to the contralateral limb as well. Massage relaxes muscles, releases toxins and increases blood flow (Saxon, 1991). Different forms of massage have been used, including contact and noncontact therapeutic touch and acupressure.

Massage. Back massage has always been a nursing therapeutic used to promote comfort. In the past, hospitalized and long-term-care patients would receive nightly back rubs to aid in sleeping and bathtime massage to aid in stimulation. Unfortunately, because of time and staffing constraints in our current health care environment, massages have gone the way of the oral mercury thermometer. Fraser and Kerr (1993) studied the psychophysiological effects of back massage on elderly patients. They reported reduced levels of anxiety in those subjects who received back massage compared to those who received no massage. Verbal reports from the patients indicated the back massages were relaxing. Although back massages are the most common massage, other areas of the body can also be massaged for pain relief. Massaging or stroking the scalp, shoulders, arms, hands, legs, and feet can also relax muscles and increase blood flow. Hand and arm massage often reduces agitation in confused patients. Wheelchair-bound patients benefit from back, leg, and foot massage on repositioning.

Therapeutic Touch. Keller and Bzdek (1986) report the reduction of migraine pain using noncontact therapeutic touch with adult subjects. Simington and Laing (1993) used contact therapeutic touch (back rubs) to manage anxiety in institutionalized elderly. Although long-term-care nursing staff have used massage and back rubs as comfort measures, the use of specific therapeutic touch techniques for pain relief has not been reported in the literature. Therapeutic touch is a noninvasive approach to reduce agitation, anxiety, and pain in patients and allows the patient to receive the physical touch that is so often missing in long-term-care facilities.

Vibration. Vibration has also been used to manage pain. Rhiner, Ferrell, Ferrell, and Grant (1993) describe a nondrug intervention program for cancer pain in which five different types of pain methods were used. The most popular was massage or vibration and heat. Electric massagers and vibrators may offer another method of pain relief for long-term-care patients. Vibrators come in varying sizes and speeds and can be placed easily by the patients on specific areas of pain. Special attachments can be used to further localize the vibration to the painful areas. Massage and vibration should not be used for pain associated with infection, acute inflammation, or phlebitis.

Heat. The application of heat or cold is commonly used as a pain relief measure. Additional warm clothing, hot tub baths, electrical heating pads, hotwater bottles, gel packs, and wraps all serve to increase comfort and temporarily reduce pain by dilating blood vessels, increasing blood flow to the area, and increasing tissue metabolism. Because of sensory and skin changes associated with the aging process, caution must be used with local application of heat to prevent burning. Heat should not be directly applied to areas of acute inflammation.

Cold. Application of cold to tissues results in blood vessel constriction, decreased muscle spasm, and some analgesia (Saxon, 1991). Ice packs, cold wraps, and gel packs all serve to reduce pain, especially in areas of inflammation. Because the elderly are more sensitive to cold, this method may not be the first choice for pain relief. Gradual cooling may be better tolerated by older patients than the direct application of ice.

Transcutaneous nerve stimulation. Transcutaneous nerve stimulator (TENS) units have been used for various types of pain. Thorsteinsson (1987) recommends the use of TENS for older patients who experience chronic peripheral neuropathies, cancer pain, some postoperative and fracture pain, periarthritis of the shoulder, and back and neck pain. Often, these units are impractical in long-term-care facilities because they require staff and patient education and can be easily dismantled by the confused patient. TENS units are expensive, and the cost is not always reimbursed by insurance plans or families.

Relaxation. Relaxation is being in a state of relative freedom from muscle tension and anxiety; mind and body are calm (McCaffery & Beebe, 1989). Techniques that have been identified as "relaxation techniques" are controlled breathing, progressive muscle relaxation, and imagery, (Houston, 1993; Saxon, 1991; Schuster & Goetz, 1994). These techniques seek to produce a relaxation response that decreases sympathetic nervous system activity, thereby reducing the pain–anxiety–tension cycle (Houston, 1993). Generally, these techniques are simple to learn and require no special equipment, although they require a quiet environment and a comfortable body position so that relaxation can occur without distraction. The various relaxation techniques do require participation and practice by an elderly patient, who probably has not been accustomed to using these methods and may have varying levels of cognitive and physical functioning. Rhiner et al. (1993) report that it may be easier for an anxious elderly patient with pain to use a physical intervention, such as application of heat, than a cognitive one.

Gaupp, Flinn, and Weddige (1989) caution that, although there is minimal risk, there may be negative reactions to relaxation training. Relaxation may restore some body dysfunction through increased homeostasis previously induced through medication. The elderly patient taking medications to control hypertension, thyroid dysfunction, or diabetes may be at risk for overmedication because of this return to homeostasis. Potential intense emotional reactions (e.g. fear, anger, or grief) may be expressed when physiological tension related to unresolved psychological conflict is reduced. In this case, relaxation should be discontinued and psychotherapy initiated or combined with relaxation training.

Controlled Breathing. Often saying "slow down and breath deeply" is an initial intervention for an anxious person experiencing pain. Attention to the act of breathing and using deep, slow breaths increase oxygenation of the body and increase the sense of relaxation. In controlled breathing, the patient is instructed to fill the chest with air and hold for 4–5 seconds, then exhale slowly. Sometimes, it is helpful to have the patient pretend to blow at a lighted candle and cause it to flicker, not go out. This will facilitate slow exhalation and concentration. Patients are encouraged to relax their bodies while exhaling, blowing out the tension. Controlled breathing can also be combined with imagery. Instructing the patient to imagine the inhaled air as colored (blue or pink), slowly infusing the body, and then slowly exhaled from the body brings a softer, more relaxing image and focuses attention on the movement of air throughout the body.

The controlled breathing should be done intermittently with normal breathing to prevent hyperventilation and to teach the difference between the types of breathing. It may also be helpful to sit close to the patient, touch the arm or place a hand on the chest or back, and breathe with the patient or talk quietly through the breathing exercise. Even those patients with some cognitive impairment can follow simple directions to "breathe in slowly, breathe out slowly." This type of controlled breathing can be done with wandering patients, as the nurse walks beside the patient, holds his or her hand for direction and focus, and talks through the breathing exercise.

Progressive Muscle Relaxation. Another type of relaxation that is often used is the tensing and relaxing of specific muscle groups. In this type of relaxation training, the patient learns how to distinguish between tense and nontense muscles and how to reduce the tension by relaxing specific muscles. Progressive muscle relaxation (PMR) has been shown to increase self-esteem and control in institutionalized elderly (Bensink, Godbey, Marshall, & Yarandi, 1992). Again, this relaxation training takes practice and requires a private, quiet space. There are many PMR sequences and directions, although most begin with the upper body and move to the lower.

PMR audiotapes are frequently used to assist with the instructions and to maximize the relaxation with music. Often, elderly patients have not been exposed to taped messages. One method to reduce unfamiliarity is to have a family member or close friend tape the relaxation script so that the voice is recognizable to the elderly patient. Audiotapes may be difficult to adjust to because of hearing changes and environmental noise. Earphones may be helpful, but many elderly unfamiliar with their use dislike using them. In addition, earphones are not compatible with the use of hearing aids, which are common in this population. Most of the PMR tapes are not expensive, but long-term-care facilities and families may be reluctant to buy them for fear that they will not get used or will get lost.

Guiding the patient through PMR personally is the most effective, but also the most time-consuming, as it takes 20-30 minutes to relax the major muscle groups. Guiding a relaxation group may be more time-efficient; however, group training requires careful selection of patients who can fully participate without disrupting the group. Generally, older patients do better with simple and brief PMR. Caution should be given to the patient not to overtense the muscles when there is pain. Tensing and relaxing should go more slowly and gradually, and patients should be instructed not to hold their breath during muscle tensing to avoid the Valsalva maneuver (Wisocki & Powers, this volume, Chapter 17).

Rocking. Houston (1993) studied the use of rocking chairs as a relaxation technique. Although the results of this research did not establish a significant relationship between active rocking and relaxation in community-living elderly, the study does offer suggestions as to the benefits of active and passive rocking in this age group. The use of motorized rocking chairs can be a relaxation technique that is relatively easy to use for physically and cognitively impaired patients.

Imagery. Imagery is the use of imagination to ease pain through muscle relaxation or distraction. As with PMR, most elderly patients have not used this technique to relieve pain and may have difficulty accepting its usefulness. This technique also requires a nondistracting environment. Nursing staff can assist the patient to visualize what the pain feels like (sharp, stabbing pain as if a knife; knotted rope in the stomach; band of metal or rubber around the head; or metal parts rubbing together). Then, the patient can visualize a way of releasing the pain (e.g., untying the knot) and to feel the positive effects of pain relief. For elders who may have difficulty with imagery, it may be helpful to identify a time or situation when the patient was without pain. In quiet, private surroundings, the nurse can assist the patient to imagine being in that place or situation again. Using colors, smells, sounds, foods, and visual cues to stimulate the imagination is helpful, as it more thoroughly engages the person in the image. This type of visualization can distract the patient from the pain and relax the body with positive images.

Distraction. Other methods of pain management employ various methods of distraction (e.g., music, work, and praying). Depending on the physical and mental capabilities of the elderly long-term-care patient, these methods can be used in conjunction with relaxation methods for pain relief. Listening to audiotapes, videotapes, or television can be beneficial if these are interesting to the patient. Nursing staff can help personalize audiotapes for the patient, using voices of family members, friends, or the patient herself or himself. Easy access at the bedside will increase the likelihood that the tapes will be used.

Some long-term-care facilities have small aviaries, fish tanks, and pets that can offer distraction and comfort to those patients in pain. Research has documented the effectiveness of having pets in the long-term-care facilities and the consequent distraction and decrease in self-absorption.

People with pain often turn to God or religion for consolation (Kodiath, 1991). Using various religious rituals (praying the Rosary, reading the Bible, or singing spiritual music) can be ways of transcending the pain and finding meaning or answers that diminish fears, anxiety, and pain. Often, patients wish to speak to a spiritual adviser to assist them in accepting themselves and their situation. Nursing staff can facilitate the use of spirituality to manage pain by providing access to spiritual practices and professionals.

Exercise. Exercise is vital to optimum physical functioning and mobility. Unfortunately, elderly patients with chronic pain may restrict their levels of exercise, and many long-term-care facilities do not have ongoing exercise programs for even their most active, functioning patients. That means that long-term-care patients have a high risk of losing physical capacity. Exercise programs that increase overall activity level are healthy for all patients. Wood (1993) reported that yoga produced an increase in mental and physical energy more than relaxation or visualization alone. Walking, stretching, and range-of-motion exercises, relaxation exercises, and low-impact calisthenics are beneficial to many patients with chronic pain and are inexpensive to provide in long-term-care facilities. Stationary bicycles and weights require initial expense but could be used by many patients to remain strong and mobile. The exercise equipment is kept in the physical therapy room in most long-term-care facilities. This area is often inconvenient and inaccessible during evenings and weekends. Confused patients are seldom brought to the physical therapy room, yet they may be able to use the exercise equipment to decrease agitation and pain, and to improve mobility. It is suggested that various types of exercise equipment be accessible to all patients, and that simple walking or stretching exercises be used on a regular basis. Volunteers, family members, and other physically active patients could assist the patients in their exercise (Fuchs & Zaichkowsky, this volume, Chapter 16).

Standard Pain Management Plan. The combination of analgesics and nondrug interventions for management of pain in the elderly provides the most likely success for relieving pain. Selection of analgesics requires attention to the intensity of the pain, the patient preferences, and ongoing evaluation and adjustment of dose and drug. Nondrug interventions also require attention to patient preference and ongoing evaluation of effect; level of cognitive function will limit the nondrug interventions applicable to cognitively impaired patients (Table 6-3).

SUMMARY

Adequate pain management for institutionalized elders is an achievable goal. The multiple, interacting factors that may inhibit adequate pain management require changes in attitudes and behaviors of the elderly patients, their family members, and the staff who provide their care. Guidelines are available that may be adapted to long-term-care facilities, with specific recommendations for both individual health care providers and institutions to provide better pain control for older adults who reside in these institutions.

Table 6-3. Standard Pain Management Plan

Pain intensity	Analgesic interventions	Nondrug interventions
Mild to moderate	NSAIDs with regular dosing (e.g., Ibuprofen) NSAID + opioid with regular dosing (e.g., acetaminophen with codeine; Percocet)	Reposition at regular intervals Cutaneous stimulation (e.g., massage, heat, and vibration) every 3–4 hours Simple relaxation techniques (controlled breathing, rocking) every 3–4 hours as needed
Moderate to severe	NSAID + opioid with regular dosing (e.g., oral morphine with Ibuprofen)	Cutaneous stimulation (e.g., heat, cold, TENS) as needed Relaxation techniques (e.g., PMR, imagery) 1–2 times/day Distraction as needed

REFERENCES

Agency for Health Care Policy and Research. (1992). *Acute pain management: Operative or medical procedures and trauma. Clinical practice guideline*. Rockville, MD: AHCPR Pub. No. 92-0032.

American Pain Society, Committee on Quality Assurance Standards. (1991). American Pain Society quality assurance standards for relief of acute pain and cancer pain. In M. R. Bond, J. E. Charlton, & C. J. Woolf (Eds.), *Proceedings of the VIth World Congress on Pain*. Amsterdam: Elsevier Science.

Arndt, M., & Bigelow, B. (1994). The impact of individual and contextual factors on nursing care and the implementation of AHCPR practice guidelines. *Medical Care Review, 61*, 61–82.

Bensink, G. W., Godbey, K. L., Marshall, M. J., & Yarandi, H. J. (1992). Institutionalized elderly relaxation, locus of control, self-esteem. *Journal of Gerontological Nursing, 18* (4), 30–38.

Bondestam, E., Hovgrem, K., Johansson, G., Jern, S., Herlitz, J., & Holmberg, S. (1987). Pain assessment by patients and nurses in the early phase of acute myocardial infarction. *Journal of Advanced Nursing, 12*, 677–682.

Brody, E. M., & Kleban, M. H. (1983). Day-to-day mental and physical health symptoms of older people: A report on health logs. *The Gerontologist, 23*, 75–85.

Cariaga, J., Burgio, L., Flynn, W., & Martin, D. (1991). A controlled study of disruptive vocalizations among geriatric residents in nursing homes. *Journal of the American Geriatrics Society, 39*, 501–507.

Carlson, C. R., Ventrella, M. A., & Sturgis, E. T. (1987). Relaxation training through muscle stretching procedures: A pilot case. *Journal of Behavior Therapy and Experimental Psychiatry, 18*, 121–126.

Carr, E. C. J. (1990). Postoperative pain: Patients' expectations and experiences. *Journal of Advanced Nursing, 15*, 89–100.

Chandler, J., & Chandler, J. (1988). The prevalence of neuropsychiatric disorders in a nursing home population. *Journal of Geriatric Psychiatry and Neurology, 1*, 71–76.

Choiniere, M., Melzack, R., Girard, N., Rondeau, J., & Paquin, M. J. (1990). Comparison between patients' and nurses' assessment of pain and medication efficacy in severe burn injuries. *Pain, 40*, 143–152.

Chrischilles, E. A., Foley, D. J., Wallace, R. B., Lenke, J. H., Hanlon, J. T., Gylnn, R. J., Ostfeld, A. M., & Guralink, J. M. (1992). Use of medications by persons 65 and over: Data from the established populations for epidemologic studies of the elderly. *Journal of Gerontology, 47* (5), M137–M144.

Cleeland, C. (1987). Barriers to the management of cancer pain. *Oncology, 1* (2 Suppl.), 19–26.

Closs, S. J., Fairtlough, H. I., Tierney, A. J., & Currie, C. T. (1992). Pain in elderly orthopaedic patients. *Journal of Clinical Nursing, 2*, 41–45.

Cohen, F. L. (1980). Postsurgical pain relief: Patients' status and nurses' medication choices. *Pain, 9*, 265–274.

Collins, G., & Stone, L. A. (1966). Pain sensitivity, age and activity level in chronic schizophrenics and in normals, *Journal of Psychiatry, 112*, 33–35.

Crook, J., Rideout, E., & Browne, G. (1984). The prevalence of pain complaints in a general population. *Pain, 18*, 299–314.

Dirks, J. F., Wunder, J., Kinsman, R., McEhinny, J., & Jones, N. F. (1993). A pain rating scale and a pain behavior checklist for clinical use: Development, norms, and the consistency score. *Psychotherapy Psychosomatics, 59*, 41–49.

Donovan, M., Dillon, P., & McGuire, L. (1987). Incidence and characteristics of pain in a sample of medical-surgical inpatients. *Pain, 30*, 69–78.

Evans, D., Funkenstein, J., & Albert, M. (1989). Prevalence of Alzeheimer's disease in a community population of older adults. *Journal of the American Medical Association, 262*, 2551–2556.

Fagerhaugh, S. Y., & Strauss, A. (1977). *Politics of pain management: Staff-patient interactions*. Menlo Park, CA: Addison-Wesley.

Faherty, B. S., & Grier, M. R. (1984). Analgesic medication for elderly people post-surgery. *Nursing Research, 33*, 369–372.

Ferrell, B. A. (1991). Pain management in elderly people. *Journal of the American Geriatrics Society, 39*, 64–73.

Ferrell, B. A. (1993). The assessment and control of pain in the nursing home. In L. Z. Rubenstein & D. Weilan (Eds.), *Improving care in the nursing home* (pp. 241–250). London: Sage.

Ferrell, B. A., Ferrell, B. R., & Osterweil, D. (1990). Pain in the nursing home. *Journal of the American Geriatrics Society, 38*, 409–414.

Ferrell, B. R., Ferrell, B. A., Rhiner, M., & Grant, M. M. (1991). Family factors influencing cancer pain. *Postgraduate Medicine Journal, 67*(Suppl. 2), S64–S69.

Ferrell, B. R., McCaffery, M., & Ropchan, R. (1992). Pain management as a clinical challenge for nursing administration. *Nursing Outlook, 40*, 263–268.

Foley, K. M. (1993). Pain management in the elderly. In W. R. Hazzard, E. L. Bierman, J. P. Blass, W. H. Ettinger, & J. B. Halter (Eds.), *Principles of geriatric medicine* (3rd ed.), (pp. 317–331). New York: McGraw-Hill.

Forrest, M., Hermann, G., & Andersen, B. (1989). Assessment of pain: A comparison between patients and doctors. *Acta Anaesthesiology Scandinavia, 33*, 255–256.

Fraser, J., & Kerr, J. R. (1993). Psychophysiological effects of back massage on elderly institutional patients. *Journal of Advanced Nursing, 18* (2), 238–245.

Greenlee, K. K. (1991). Pain and analgesia: Considerations for the elderly in critical care. *AACN Clinical Issues in Critical Care Nursing, 2*, 720–728.

Gu, X., & Belgrade, M. J. (1993). Pain in hospitalized patient with medical illnesses. *Journal of Pain and Symptom Management, 8*, 17–21.

Hall-Lord, M. L., Larsson, G., & Bostrom, I. (1994). Elderly patients' experiences of pain and distress in intensive care: A grounded theory study. *Intensive and Critical Care Nursing, 10*, 133–141.

Hardy, J. D., Wolff, H. G., & Goodell, H. (1943). The pain threshold in man. *American Journal of Psychiatry, 99*, 744–751.

Harkins, S. W., & Chapman, C. R. (1977). Age and sex differences in pain perception. In D. J. Anderson & B. Mathews (Eds.), *Pain in the trigeminal region* (pp. 435–441). Amsterdam: Elsevier.

Harkins, S. W., Price, D., & Martelli, M. (1986). Effects of age on pain perception: Thermoreception. *Journal of Gerontology, 41*, 58–63.

Harkins, W. (1988). Pain in the elderly. In R. Dubner, G. F. Gebhart, & M. R. Bond (Eds.), *Proceedings of the Fifth World Congress on Pain* (pp. 355–367). Amsterdam: Elsevier Science.

Herr, K. A., & Mobily, P. R. (1991). Complexities of pain assessment in the elderly: Clinical considerations. *Journal of Gerontological Nursing, 17* (4), 12–19.

Herr, K. A., & Mobily, P. R. (1993). Comparison of selected pain assessment tools for use with the elderly. *Applied Nursing Research, 6*, 39–46.

Houston, K. (1993). An investigation of rocking as relaxation for the elderly. *Geriatric Nursing, 14* (4), 186–189.

Hurley, A. C., Volicer, B. J., Hanarahan, P. A., Houde, S., & Volicer, L. (1992). Assessment of discomfort in advanced Alzheimer's patients. *Research in Nursing and Health, 15*, 369–377.

International Association for the Study of Pain. (1979). Pain terms: A list with definitions and notes on usage. *Pain, 6*, 247–252.

Jacox, A., Ferrell, B., Heidrich, G., Hester, N., & Miaskowski, C. (1992). A guideline for the nation: Managing acute pain. *American Journal of Nursing, 92* (5), 49–55.

Juhl, I. U., Christensen, B. V., Bulow, H. H., Wilbeck, H., Dreijer, N. C., & Egelund, B. (1993). Post-operative pain relief, from the patients' and nurses' point of view. *Acta Anaesthesiologica Scandinavica, 37*, 404–409.

Keller, E., & Bzdek, V. M. (1986). Effects of therapeutic touch on tension headache pain. *Nursing Research, 35*, 101–106.

Kerns, R. D., Turk, D. C., & Rudy, T. E. (1985). The West Haven-Yale Multidimensional Pain Inventory (WHYMPI). *Pain, 23*, 345–356.

Kodiath, A. (1991). Pain and promise of aging America. *Holistic Nursing Practice, 6* (1), 58–65.

Kuhn, S., Cooke, K., Collins, M., Jones, J. M., & Mucklow, J. C. (1990). Perceptions of pain relief after surgery. *British Medical Journal, 300*, 1687–1690.

Lavies, N., Hart, L., Rounsefell, B., & Runciman, W. (1992). Identification of patient, medical and nursing staff attitudes to postoperative opioid analgesia: Stage 1 of a longitudinal study of postoperative analgesia. *Pain, 48*, 313–320.

Marks, R. M., & Sachar, E. J. (1973). Undertreatment of medical inpatients with narcotic analgesics. *Annals of Internal Medicine, 78*, 173–181.

Marzinski, L. R. (1991). the tragedy of dementia: Clinically assessing pain in the confused, nonverbal elderly. *Journal of Gerontological Nursing, 17* (6), 25–28.

McCaffery, M., & Beebe, R. (1989). *Pain: Clinical manual for nursing practice*. St. Louis: Mosby.

McCaffery, M., & Ferrell, B. (1991). How would you respond to these patients in pain? *Nursing, 21* (6), 34–37.

McCaffery, M., Ferrell, B., O'Neil-Page, E., & Lester, M. (1990). Nurses' knowledge of opioid analgesic drugs and psychological dependence. *Cancer Nursing, 13*, 21–27.

Melzack, R. (1975). The McGill Pain Questionnaire: Major properties and scoring methods. *Pain, 1*, 277–299.

Melzack, R. (1987). The short-form McGill Pain Questionnaire. *Pain, 30*, 191–197.

Melzack, R., & Wall, P. D. (1988). *The challenge of pain* (2nd ed.). London: Penguin Books.

Miaskowski, C., Nichols, R., Brody, R., & Synold, T. (1994). Assessment of patient satisfaction utilizing the American Pain Society quality assurance standards on acute and cancer-related pain. *Journal of Pain and Symptom Management, 9*, 5–11.

Mobily, P. R., Herr, K. A., Clark, M. K., & Wallace, R. B. (1994). An epidemiologic analysis of pain in the elderly. *Journal of Aging and Health, 6* (2), 139–154.

Moss, M. S., Lawton, M. P., & Glicksman, A. (1991). The role of pain in the last year of life of older persons. *Journal of Gerontology, 46*, P51–P57.

Mumford, J. M. (1965). Pain perception threshold and adaptation of normal man teeth. *Archives of Oral Biology, 10*, 957–968.

Nelson, L., Taylor, F., Adams, M., & Parker, D. E. (1990). Improving pain management for hip fractured elderly. *Orthopaedic Nursing, 9* (3), 79–83.

Newman, F., Griffin, B., Black, R., & Page, S. (1989). Linking level of care to level of need: Assessing the need for mental health care for nursing home residents. *American Psychologist, 44*, 1315–1324.

Oberle, K., Paul, P., Wry, J., & Grace, M. (1990). Pain, anxiety and analgesics: A comparative study of elderly and younger surgical patients. *Canadian Journal on Aging, 9* (1), 13–22.

Owen, H., McMillian, V., & Rogowski, D. (1990). Postoperative pain therapy: A survey of patients' expectations and their experiences. *Pain, 41*, 303–307.

Parke, B. (1992). Pain in the cognitively impaired elderly. *Canadian Nurse, 88* (7), 17–20.

Parmelee, P. A., Smith, B., & Katz, I. R. (1993). Pain complaints and cognitive status among elderly institution residents. *Journal of the American Geriatrics Society, 41*, 517–522.

Potter, P. A., & Perry, A. G. (1989). *Fundamentals of Nursing: concepts, process, and practice*. St. Louis: Mosby.

Rhiner, M., Ferrell, B. R., Ferrell, B. A., & Grant, M. M. (1993). A structured nondrug intervention program for cancer pain. *Cancer Practice, 1* (2), 137–143.

Richards, J. S., Nepomuceno, C., Riles, M., & Suer, Z. (1982). Assessing pain behavior: The UAB pain behavior scale. *Pain, 14*, 393–398.

Rudy, T. E., Kerns, R. D., & Turk, D. C. (1988). Chronic pain and depression: Toward a cognitive-behavioral mediation model. *Pain, 35*, 129–140.

Ryan, P., Vortherms, R., & Ward, S. (1994). Cancer pain: Knowledge, attitudes of pharmacological management. *Journal of Gerontological Nursing, 20*, 7–16.

Ryden, M. B., & Feldt, K. S. (1992). Goal-directed care: Caring for aggressive nursing home residents with dementia. *Journal of Gerontological Nursing, 18* (11), 35–41.

Saxon, S. V. (1991). Pain management techniques for older adults. Springfield, IL: Charles C Thomas.

Schuster, J. M., & Goetz, K. L. (1994). Pain. In C. E. Coffey & J. L. Cummings (Eds.), *Textbook of geriatric neuropsychiatry* (pp. 334–350). Washington, DC: American Psychiatric Press.

Seers, K. (1987). Perceptions of pain. *Nursing Times, 83* (48), 37–39.

Sengstaken, E. A., & King, S. A. (1993). The problem of pain and its detection among geriatric nursing home residents. *Journal of the American Geriatrics Society, 41*, 541–544.

Sherman, E. D., & Robillard, E. (1960). Sensitivity to pain in the aged. *Canadian Medical Association Journal, 83*, 944–947.

Short, L. M., Burnett, M. L., Egbert, A. M., & Parks, L. H. (1990). Medicating the postoperative elderly: How do nurses make their decisions? *Journal of Gerontological Nursing, 16* (7), 12–17.

Simington, J. A. & Laing, G. P. (1993). Effects of therapeutic touch on anxiety in the institutionalized elderly. *Clinical Nursing Research, 2* (4), 438–450.

Turk, D. C. Okifuji, A., & Scharff, L. (1995). Chronic pain and depression: Role of perceived impact and perceived control in different age cohorts. *Pain, 61*, 93–101.

Vortherms, R., Ryan, P., & Ward, S. (1992). Knowledge and attitudes regarding pharmacologic management of cancer pain in a statewide random sample of nurses. *Research in Nursing and Health, 15*, 459–466.

Walker, J. M., Akinsanya, J. A., Davis, B. D., & Marcer, D. (1990). The nursing management of elderly patients with pain in the community: Study and recommendations. *Journal of Advanced Nursing, 15* (10), 1154–1161.

Ward, S. E., Goldberg, N., Miller-McCauley, V., Mueller, C., Nolan, A., Pawlik-Plank, D., Robbins, A., Stormoen, D., & Weissman, D. E. (1993). Patient-related barriers to management of cancer pain. *Pain, 52,* 319–324.

Ward, S. E., & Gordon, D. (1994). Application of the American Pain Society quality assurance standards. *Pain, 56,* 299–306.

Wilder-Smith, C. H., & Schuler, L. (1992). Postoperative analgesia: Pain by choice? The influence of patient attitudes and patient education. *Pain, 50,* 257–262.

Wood, C. (1993). Mood change and perceptions of vitality: A comparison of the effects of relaxation, visualization and yoga. *Journal of the Royal Society of America, 86* (5), 254–258.

Woodrow, K. M., Friedman, G. D., Siegalaub, A. B., & Cohen, M. F. (1972). Pain tolerance: Differences according to age, sex, and race. *Psychosomatic Medicine, 34,* 548–556.

Zalon, M. L. (1993). Nurses' assessment of postoperative patients' pain. *Pain, 54,* 329–334.

Zullich, S. G., Grasela, T. H., Fielder-Kelly, J. B., & Gengo, F. M. (1992). Impact of triplicate prescription program on psychotrophic prescribing patterns in long-term care facilities. *Annals of Pharmacotherapy, 26,* 539–546.

PART II

Psychosocial and Psychodynamic Aspects

CHAPTER 7

Rehabilitating the Elderly in Return to Work

KAREN JACOBS

We are all aging. Through economic necessity or preference, many older Americans will remain in or reenter the workforce after the traditional age of retirement (see Figure 7-1). Consider these demographics: In the United States today, 11% of the working population, or 24 million people, have reached or passed the age of 65. In 40 years, this percentage is expected to increase to 18%. By the year 2050, 25% of the U.S. population will be in this age group.

To help keep this working population active, health professionals must become familiar with the aging process and learn to recognize the special needs of the older worker. By becoming familiar with the physiological and functional effects of aging, health professionals will be able to develop better treatment plans and prevention strategies (Coy & Davenport, 1991).

THE AGING BODY

In many cases, aging workers face the same physical demands as their younger counterparts. However, older workers differ greaterly from younger workers in their speed of movement, posture, strength, reaction time, flexibility, and body composition (Coy & Davenport, 1991).

Many factors contribute to an increased risk of injury in the aging population. Connective tissue loses its suppleness as it ages, making ligaments and tendons more prone to injury. Increased pressure on facet joints causes vertebral disk and spine degeneration. In all joints of the body, articular cartilage narrows, and normal lubrication decreases (Coy & Davenport, 1991). Decreased bone density increases the risk of

---

KAREN JACOBS • Department of Occupational Therapy, Boston University, Boston, Massachusetts 02215

Handbook of Pain and Aging, edited by David I. Mostofsky and Jacob Lomranz. Plenum Press, New York, 1997.

Figure 7-1. Older worker continuing to be gainfully employed.

fracture, particularly among postmenopausal women. A reduction in the number and size of muscle fibers causes diminished muscle mass, and strength decreases by approximately 20% by age 65 (Coy & Davenport, 1991). In addition, less oxygen is delivered to older muscles (Isernhagen, 1991). Because endurance fibers do not change, older workers' capacity for endurance is similar to that of younger workers (Isernhagen, 1991).

Many older workers also experience arthritis. Older women in particular experience a significant decrease in their ability to bend at the knees and hips to lift a weight from low level. This stems from a combination of weakness in the quadriceps and osteoarthritis changes in the knees. Commonly, older workers who are unable to bend low injure themselves because they use their backs to lift heavy objects (Isernhagen, 1991).

Reduced lung capacity causes breathlessness in older workers and often limits activity, especially in sedentary workers and those performing duties for which they are not conditioned (Coy & Davenport, 1991; Isernhagen, 1991). At the same time, the progressive decline in maximum heart rate and stroke volume makes many older workers less inclined to engage in extensive physical activity. Slowed reflexes in aging workers result in a diminished protective response. Coordination is also slowed, although there is no decrease in overall accuracy (Coy & Davenport, 1991; Isernhagen, 1991). Older people also experience a loss in balance control, which, combined with slower reaction times, makes older workers less able to prevent injury when they lose their balance (Coy & Davenport, 1991; Jacobs, 1993).

Older workers are less able to tolerate extreme temperature (Porter, 1991). Decreased tolerance of cold can produce hypothermia. In hot conditions, older workers are more severely affected because their physiological responses to heat and exercise are diminished. At the same time, older people with lower pulmonary and heart function experience greater strain in performing physical activity (Porter, 1991).

Finally, changes in both vision and hearing begin to occur around age 40–50 (Coy & Davenport, 1991). Changes in the eye lens cause farsightedness in many older adults, and because their pupils shrink, older people have an increased need for illumination. In terms of hearing, older people have increased difficulty in filtering out background noise and locating the source of sound (Coy & Davenport, 1991; Jacobs, 1993).

ERGONOMICS

All of these factors have an impact on the way older workers perform their work. To some extent, ergonomic changes will help keep aging workers effective. *Ergonomics*, or human factors, refers to the characteristics of people that need to be considered in arranging things that they use so that the people and things will interact most effectively and safely. Ergonomics focuses on humans and their interactions with the environment. It involves interactions with tools, equipment, consumer products, work methods, jobs, instruction books, facilities, and organizations (Rice, 1995, p. 6).

Industry is documenting the effectiveness of incorporating an ergonomic approach into work injury prevention programs (Armstrong, 1986; Bureau of National Affairs, 1988; Buckle & Stuffs, 1989; Jackson, 1991; Joyce, 1988; Lutz & Hansford, 1991; MacLeod et al., 1990; McReynolds, 1991; Moretz, 1989; Pheasant, 1991; Schumacher, 1990). This literature illustrates the effectiveness of ergonomic intervention and describes the benefits in terms of decreased employee sick leave, low injury rates, reduced worker compensation payments, early return to work after injuries, increased worker satisfaction, and overall financial savings (Jacobs, 1993).

The goal of work injury prevention programs is to prevent injuries in the workplace by removing their causes. According to the U.S. Department of Labor, Occupational Safety and Health Administration's (OSHA) *Ergonomics Program Management Guidelines for Meatpacking Plants* (1991).

> The effective management of worker safety and health protection includes all work-related hazards, whether or not they are regulated by specific federal standards. The Occupational Safety and Health Act of 1970 (OSH Act) clearly states that the general duty of all employers is to provide their employees with a workplace free from recognized serious hazards. This included the prevention and control of ergonomic hazards. (p. 1).

Many individuals are involved in workplace injury prevention, such as occupational and physical therapists, occupational health physicians and nurses, insurance representatives, health and safety personnel, managers, and employees. These diverse individuals use various models, methods, and preventive approaches; however, none have proved to be conclusively superior for reducing injuries in all workplaces (Bettencourt, 1995).

Professionals in this field eagerly await the Ergonomics Standard proposed by OSHA, which will provide standards designed to alleviate ergonomic hazards in the workplace. According to the draft summary circulated in June 1994, OSHA seeks a "broad performance oriented rule" designed to prevent occurrence of work-related musculoskeletal disorders; inform employers about such disorders and associated risk factors; promote continuous improvement in workplace ergonomic protection; encourage innovation and technology development; identify design features that prevent exposure; and ensure ongoing and consistent management leadership and employee involvement (Olsen, 1995, p. 118).

Hazard Prevention and Control

Workplace hazards can be placed in two categories. The first is working the body beyond its capabilities. This includes musculoskeletal and sensorimotor, such as abnormal and awkward postures, forceful exertions, repetitive or sustained exertions, contact stress or lack of rest and recovery time; perceptual-motor, as in converting information into motoric reaction; perceptual-cognitive, or the transformation from injury to output; and cognitive, as in the producing and creating of information. Although there is much written about workplace hazards, more empirical laboratory and field studies are needed to verify biomechanical predictions of musculoskeletal stresses (Polakoff, 1995, p. 30).

The second workplace hazard is environmental conditions, such as temperature and humidity, lighting, noise, and vibration.

In addition, certain stressors may not be identified as unusual by themselves but may be hazardous when occurring with other exertions. It is important to identify and quantify potentially synergistic factors in an adverse psychosocial work climate, such as ambiguous work roles, insufficient supervisory support, lack of work autonomy, or job insecurity (Polakoff, 1995, p. 29).

Controls

Four approaches that can be used in concert to control workplace hazards are

1. Applying methods of workplace and job design to provide working situations that capitalize on worker skills.
2. Designing organizational structures that encourage safe working behavior.
3. Training workers in the recognition of hazards and proper work behavior for dealing with these hazards.
4. Improving worker safety behavior through work practice improvement (Gold, 1992, p. 5).

These approaches can be further categorized into engineering, administrative, and work practice controls.

Engineering controls are changes in the workstation, equipment, or tools. It is the preferred method of control since it eliminates hazards at the source. Examples of workstation reconfiguration or redesign are work height or reach adjustments or the relocation of supplies and equipment. Tool and handle design or redesign might include a pistol-grip handle (Aja & Jacobs, 1996).

Administrative controls are decisions made by management intended to reduce the duration, frequency, and severity of exposure to existing hazards. It leaves the hazards at the workplace but attempts to diminish the effects on the worker. Examples of administrative controls include

1. *Job rotation.* The job remains the same, but the worker moves from one job to another.
2. *Job enlargement.* There are two types of job enlargement: Horizontal, or job extention, and vertical, or job enrichment. Horizontal, or job extension, is when job content is increased by giving the worker a greater number of tasks to perform, all with the same level of responsibility. Vertical, or job enrichment, is when the job content includes taking over some responsibilities which were previously assigned to a supervisor.
3. *Work scheduling.* This includes the inclusion of breaks, flexible work hours or job sharing.
4. *Work method.* An example of work method controls is to reduce external pacing, such as providing a "floater" to help reduce pressure or allowing the worker to work ahead of or behind line speed (Aja & Jacobs, 1996).

Work practice controls are a familiar area to therapists and one that we have contributed to greatly in the workplace. These include education and training in safe and proper work techniques (e.g., lifting techniques) and fitness and flexibility exercises (e.g., on-the-job work-related fitness programs).

In all areas of control it is important to take into account designing and programming for the older workers' needs.

Personal protective equipment (PPE) should be provided to accommodate the physical requirements of workers and the job (OSHA, 1991, p. 5). Some examples of PPE include gloves, eye wear, vibration protection, and ear protection. The use of a back belt as PPE has been open to much debate. In 1994, U.S. Department of Health and Human Services, National Institute for Occupational Safety and Health (NIOSH) published a document entitled *Workplace Use of Back Belts: Review and Recommendations*, which states that it does not consider a back belt to be a PPE. The document concludes "that the effectiveness of using back belts to lessen the risk of back injury among uninjured workers remains unproven" (p. 1). In addition,

> There are insufficient data indicating that typical industrial back belts significantly reduce the biomechanical loading of the trunk during manual lifting. There is insufficient scientific evidence to conclude that wearing back belts reduces risk of injury to the back based on changes in intra-abdominal pressure (IAP) and trunk muscle electromyography (EMG). The use of back belts may produce temporary strain on the cardiovascular system. There are insufficient data to demonstrate a relationship between the prevalence of back injury in health workers and the discontinuation of back belt use. (p. 2)

Finally, the NIOSH recommends "that the most effective means of minimizing the likelihood of back injury is to develop and implement a comprehensive ergonomics program" (p. 2).

The procedure for the use of ergonomics in the workplace has three facets:

1. A structured oral interview to identify the worker's perception of hazards and sources of physical discomfort.
2. Screening for impairments and functional limitations—including measures of sensation, strength, and range of motion—to obtain a clearer picture of the nature and severity of the health complaints. The screening is especially helpful when the worker's complaints suggest preclinical stages of disease and when there are still few documented cases of musculoskeletal injuries related to a certain job within a company.
3. An ergonomic work site analysis to determine the relationship between work patterns and musculoskeletal impairment. The objectives of the work site analysis are to recognize, identify, and correct ergonomic hazards (OSHA, 1991, p. 3). Workers' body mechanics, work habits, and any "homemade remedies" for ergonomic problems should be noted. The informal, yet important, educational process should begin at this stage, with the information gleaned from the work site analysis incorporated into refinement of the training and education curriculum through the integration of slides and videotapes taken during these analyses (Aja and Jacobs, 1996; Jacobs, 1993).

The ergonomic work site analyses are confined to three major areas: work methods, workstation design and worker posture, and handle and tool design. Each of these areas will now be described.

Work method analysis is concerned with determining what the worker must do to perform the task successfully. Such a determination requires direct observation or videotaping of the worker, the computing of the number of repetitive movements in a given work cycle, and measuring or estimating the forces required by the job.

In the case of hand and wrist injuries, suspected problem postures are noted and documented. These postures are full extension of the fingers and wrist, full flexion of the wrist with grasp, forceful pinch, or ulnar or radial deviation. The amount of time that the extremity is maintained in a certain stressful posture is important to note because the stress on the structure accumulates. Also considered are the speed, intensity, and pace at which the worker must perform repetitive movements to meet production standards. Analysis of the workstation examines the relationship of the worker and workstation features. Analysis of handle and tool design is important as it is the most common cause of hand and wrist disability. The most common problem is that the handle of the tool is too short for the worker's hand (Habes & Putz-Anderson, 1985; Putz-Anderson, 1988; Tichauer, 1978).

As a general rule, tools or tasks should be designed so that the wrist is maintained in the neutral position (Habes & Putz-Anderson, 1985; Tichauer, 1978). A combination of flexed wrist with significant grip force and repetitive movement requirements is a biomechanical stress commonly associated with cumulative trauma disorders of the hands and wrists (Habes & Putz-Anderson, 1985).

Instructing clients in good body mechanics and ergonomic principles is helpful in managing their symptoms. They can be taught, for example, that decreasing the horizontal distance to lift, enlarging a tool handle so only the distal phalanges of the fingers and thumb overlap, or lowering work surfaces so elbows are not abducted more than 30° from the torso are preventive measures (Heck, 1987).

The American National Standards Institute (ANSI) has established the following general recommendations to reduce work site risk factors:

1. Design the workstation so that the worker can maintain an upright, neutral posture.
2. Minimize contact stress by spreading out the force through tool shape or padding.
3. Arrange the work site to reduce the number of hand–arm directional changes required.
4. Reduce hand–arm vibration by tool selection and appropriate tool grips and/or gloves.

For companies whose workers are required to handle materials, the work site analysis concentrates primarily on lifting tasks using the NIOSH *Work Practices Guide for Manual Lifting* (WPG) to determine if the lifting task places the worker at risk of injury (Habes & Putz-Anderson, 1985; Putz-Anderson, 1988).

With respect to vision, work site improvements can be made to accommodate older eyes. The installation of higher-wattage lamps is a simple and inexpensive solution to vision requirements. Older eyes, susceptible to cataracts, also require a nonglare environment, which can be provided by multisource lighting.

Another simple solution is the use of color cues. Contrasting color cues increase environmental legibility. Research has shown that the eye is most sensitive to yellow. Yellow cues can be easily added to the workplace to compensate for decreased visual abilities.

EXERCISE

In addition to ergonomic and educational considerations, serious attention must be given to promoting exercise programs for older workers. Regular exercise can counteract the physical changes that come with age and that contribute to increased risk of injury (Coy & Davenport, 1991). Fortunately, it is never too late for an individual to begin exercising. Even people who have been sedentary for years can build muscle strength, lower their heart rate, and increase their flexibility (Coy & Davenport, 1991).

Regular activity, especially weight-bearing work or exercise, reduces the loss of bone mass and, in some cases, may recover bone mass already lost. The best exercise for increasing bone mineral content involves weight bearing for the spine, pelvis, and lower extremities, as well as resistive exercise.

Regular activity also helps maintain flexibility and suppleness in connective tissue, thus making an individual less prone to injury involving ligaments and tendons (Coy & Davenport, 1991). Aerobic activity produces beneficial results for individuals with arthritis or with spinal dysfunction (Coy & Davenport, 1991). Because aerobic exercise also helps maintain cardiovascular capacity, its benefits become apparent in the workplace. As workers increase their conditioning level, they also become more productive (Jacobs, 1993).

THE INJURED WORKER

Many of today's medical practitioners favor early return to work and activity because they believe that work-related injuries are best treated by resting the injured part, not the entire body. In designing a rehabilitation program, occupational therapists devise an individualized approach, especially for older workers. For acute care clients, a therapist focuses on controlling pain, relaxing muscles, and remobilizing. Subacute clients can more actively engage in exercise and should be trained in proper body mechanics. Before returning to work, clients must be taught how to perform job tasks without risking reinjury. Any training or education provided to the older worker should be designed using an adult learner model. Knowles (1984, p. 31) has written extensively about the special needs of the adult learner and has outlined several principles that constitute the foundation of adult learning theory:

1. Adults are motivated to learn as they experience needs and interests that learning will satisfy; therefore, these are the appropriate starting points for organizing adult learning activities.
2. Adults' orientation to learning is life-centered; therefore, the appropriate units for organizing adult learning are life situations, not subjects.
3. Experience is the richest resource of adults' learning; therefore, the core methodology of adult education is the analysis of experience.
4. Adults have a deep need to be self-directing; therefore, the role of the teacher is to engage in a process of mutual inquiry with them rather than to transmit his or her knowledge to them and then evaluate his or her conformity to it.
5. Individual differences among people increase with age; therefore, adult education must make optimal provision for difference in style, place, and pace of learning.

These points were further emphasized by Queeney and Smutz (1990, p. 177), who suggested that the following characteristics are important to consider when designing and implementing education programs: frequent interaction among program participants to provide a forum for integrating skills with practice for exchanging alternative approaches and perspectives; guided practice both during and after formal instruction through case studies and client simulations; and small-group activities to facilitate the interactive nature of the instruction (Jacobs, Aja, & Hermenau, 1994).

Various types of intervention are used with clients with the goal of returning to work. The next section focuses on two person-aimed services (work hardening and work conditioning) and on an environmentally aimed service, which views the external environment as the prime target for change (on-site work-return transition programs).

WORK HARDENING

Work hardening is a work-oriented treatment program, the outcome of which is measured in terms of improvement in the client's productivity (Neimeyer & Jacobs, 1989). The ultimate goal is to help the person achieve a level of productivity that is acceptable in the competitive labor market. It is a comprehensive interdisciplinary (e.g., occupational therapist, physical therapist, psychologist, and vocational specialist) approach that uses graded work simulation to address the biomedical and psychosocial problems of the injured worker. The clients who benefit from this type of programming are those who are seriously deconditioned after an impairment caused by an injury or disease and those people who have major discrepancies between their symptoms and objective findings (Matheson, Ogden, Violette, & Schultz, 1985). Improvement in productivity is achieved through graded activity designed to increase work tolerances, improve work rate, master pain, improve work habits, and increase confidence and proficiency with work adaptations or assistive devices. It involves the client in highly structured, simulated work tasks in an environment where expectations for basic worker behaviors, such as timeliness, attendance, and dress, are in keeping with workplace standards. Program duration varies from 2 to 12 weeks, with daily participation ranging from 2–8 hours (Bettencourt, 1991).

Research on the effectiveness of work-hardening programs has been systemically gathered since the mid-1980s. Return-to-work statistics obtained from individual programs range from 50–60% to 85–88% (Neimeyer & Jacobs, 1989). By far, the strongest variable related to return to work in clients entering work-hardening programs was length of disability, whether measured as time since date of injury or since last date worked (Jacobs, 1993; Neimeyer, Jacobs, Reynolds-Lynch, Bettencourt, & Lang, 1994).

WORK CONDITIONING

When a client has an uncomplicated injury but physical limitations preclude return to work, work conditioning may be an appropriate intervention (Darphin, Smith, & Green, 1992). Work conditioning is typically provided as an unidisciplinary or bidisciplinary (occupational and/or physical therapy) half-day program which uses exercise, aerobic conditioning, education, and limited work tasks to restore an individual's systemic and neuromusculoskeletal function (e.g., strength, endurance, movement, flexibility, and motor control), so that the client can return to work, or can become physically reconditioned, so vocational services can commence (Darphin et al., 1992).

Work conditioning may be necessary for older clients who are returning to physically demanding jobs and is appropriate for clinets with a fairly recent injury that has been resolved. Work-conditioning programs build total-body conditioning using strength, endurance, and mobility exercises. In addition, clients practice simulated work tasks and perform work-related exercises (Jacobs, 1993).

ON-SITE WORK-RETURN TRANSITION PROGRAMS

On-site work-return transition programs provide the worker with accommodations and an opportunity to gradually transition back to work through conditioning, education about safe work practices, and work readjustments. Transition work is any job or combination of tasks and functions that may be performed with remuneration. Clinical expertise is brought to the work site to progressively upgrade the level of real work activities to eventual full duty (Jacobs, 1993).

CONCLUSION

Taking an older worker through a full course of rehabilitation can be complex because of the psychological implications injuries have for the elderly. Therapists should encourage management to keep in touch with recovering workers to assure them they are valuable and missed. Research has shown that predictors of an employee's successful rehabilitation include the desire to return to the job and the employer's willingness to accommodate the worker (Porter, 1991).

Finally, older workers have many assets: maturity, good judgment, experience, skills, motivation, a strong work ethic, and decreased absenteeism and turnover rates. All health professionals need to assist this important group to remain contributing members of the workforce.

Finally, this chapter will close with an anonymous quote on aging:

> If you are a man, and you are prejudiced against women, you will never know how a woman feels. If you are white, and you are prejudiced against someone black, you will never know how a black person feels. But if you are young, and prejudiced against the old, you are indeed prejudiced against yourself, because you, too, will have the honor of being old some day.

REFERENCES

Aja, D., & Jacobs, K. (1996). In J. Hammel (Ed.). *Vocational and ergonomic technologies*, (pp. 1–39). Assistive Technology & Occupational Therapy. Bethesda: AOTA.

Armstrong T. (1986). Ergonomics and cumulative trauma disorders. *Hand Clinics, 2*, 553–565.

Bettencourt, C. (1991). Chronic back pain, disability, and rehabilitation of the injured worker. In K. Jacobs (Ed.), *Occupational therapy: Work related programs and assessments*, (pp. 256–273). Boston: Little, Brown.

Bettencourt, C. (1995). Ergonomics and injury prevention programs. In K. Jacobs & C. Bettencourt (Eds), *Ergonomics for therapists*, (pp. 185–204), Newton, MA: Butterworth-Heinemann.

Buckle, P., & Stubbs, D. (1989). The contribution of ergonomics to the rehabilitation of back pain patients. *Journal of the Society of Occupational Medicine, 39*, 56–60.

Bureau of National Affairs. (1988). *Back injuries: Cost, causes, and prevention*. Washington, D.C.: Author.

Coy, J., & Davenport, M. (1991). Age changes in the older worker: Implications for injury prevention. *Work, 2*, 38–46.

Darphin, L., Smith, R., & Green, E. (1992). Work conditioning and work hardening. *Orthopaedic Physical Therapy Clinics, 1*, 105–124.

Gold, M. (1992). Prevention of injury in the workplace. *Work, 2*, 2–7.

Habes, D., & Putz-Anderson, V. (1985). The NIOSH program for evaluating biomechanical hazards in the workplace. *Journal of Safety Research, 16*, 49–60.

Isernhagen, S.J. (1991). An aging challenge for the nineties. *Work, 2*, 10–18.

Jackson, L. (1991). Ergonomics and the occupational health nurse: Instituting a workplace program. *AAOHN Journal, 39*, 119–127.

Jacobs, K. (1993). The aging worker. *Rehabilitation Management, June/July*, 178–179.

Jacobs, K., Aja, D., & Hermenau, D. (1994). Case simulation: A viable means of adult learning. *American Journal of Occupational Therapy, 48*(11), 1089–1092.

Joyce, M. (1988). Ergonomics offers solutions to numerous health complaints. *Occupational Health and Safety*, *58*, 65–66.

Knowles, M. (1984). *The adult learner: A neglected species* (3rd ed.). Houston: Gulf.

Lutz, G., & Hansford, T. (1991). Ethicon, Inc: A success story. *Ergonomics*, *1*, 5–6.

MacLeod, D., Jacobs, P., & Larson, N. (1990). *The ergonomics manual*. Minneapolis: CLMI Ergotech.

McReynolds, M. (1991). Managing the high cost of back injury. *Occupational Health and Safety*, *58*, 62–64.

Moretz, S. (1989). Ergonomics power plant's safety upsurge. *Occupational Hazards*, *March*, 27–29.

Neimeyer, L., & Jacobs, K. (1989). *Work hardening: State of the art*. Thorofare, NJ: SLACK, Inc.

Neimeyer, L., Jacobs, K., Reynolds-Lynch, K., Bettencourt, C., & Lang, S. (1994). Outcome study *American Journal of Occupational Therapy*, *48*, 327–339.

Olsen, G. (1995). New ergonomic standards. *Rehab Management*, 118–119.

Pheasant, S. (1991). *Ergonomics, work and health*. Gaithersburg, MD: Aspen.

Polakoff, P. (1995). Without action on causes and effects, time fails to heal cumulative trauma. *Occupational Health and Safety*, 29–30.

Porter, M.D. (1991). Rehabilitating the older injured worker. *Work*, *2*, 54–60.

Putz-Anderson, V. (Ed.). (1988). *Cumulative trauma disorders: A manual for musculoskeletal diseases of the upper limb*. London: Taylor & Francis.

Queeney, D., & Smutz, W. (1990). Enhancing the performance of professionals: The practice Audit Model. In S. Willis & S. Dubin (Eds.), *Maintaining professional competence: Approaches to career enhancement, vitality, and success throughout a worklife*. San Francisco: Jossey-Bass.

Rice, V. (1995). Ergonomics: An introduction. In K. Jacobs & C. Bettencourt (Eds.), *Ergonomics for therapists* (pp. 3–12). Newton, MA: Butterworth-Heinemann.

Schumacher, A. (1990). Getting a back injury program back on track. *Safety and Health*, *November*, 44–47.

Tichauer, E. (1978). *The biomechanical basis of ergonomics*. New York: Wiley.

U.S. Department of Health and Human Services, National Institute for Occupational Safety and Health (1994). *Workplace use of back belts: Review and recommendations*. Washington, DC: Author.

U.S. Department of Labor, Occupational Safety and Health Administration. (1991). *Ergonomics program management guidelines for meatpacking plants*. Washington, DC: Author.

CHAPTER 8

Coping with Pain in Old Age

PAMELA S. MELDING

Age wins and one must learn to grow old.... I must learn to walk this long unlovely wintry way, looking for spectacles, shunning the cruel looking-glass, laughing at my clumsiness before others mistakenly condole, not expecting gallantry yet disappointed to receive none, apprehending every ache or shaft of pain, alive to blinding flashes of mortality, unarmed, totally vulnerable.
Lady Diana Cooper (1892–1986), British actor, author, *Trumpets from the Steep*

INTRODUCTION

Pain is a common accompaniment of illness in late life and the incidence of disease and illness increases significantly as people age (Marsland, Wood, & Mayo, 1976; Harkins, 1988). For older people, there are many diseases that cause pain, decrease mobility, and reduce ability to engage in active pursuits. Cardiac vessel disease, cerebrovascular disease, stroke, sympathetic dystrophies, peripheral vascular disease, chronic back and neck pain, rheumatoid arthritis, osteoarthritis, and osteoporosis are all much more common in older people and can cause excruciatingly persistent pain. Many of these problems are chronic, the results of age-related organ degeneration, and are not particularly life-threatening. With few treatment available to reverse or cure the underlying disease condition, the individual is left to deal with consequent impairments, deficits, and change in lifestyle. Under these circumstances, factors that influence coping with the problem become major factors in preventing disability and improving quality of life and rehabilitation potential.

Coping is a complex concept. The verb *to cope* comes from the Middle English word *copen*, meaning "to strike" or "to make an active blow against a threat." Folkman and Lazarus (1980) defined coping as "the cognitive and behavioural efforts made to master, tolerate or reduce the specific external and internal demands and conflicts

PAMELA S. MELDING • Department of Psychiatry and Behavioural Science, School of Medicine, University of Auckland, and North Shore Hospital, Waitemata Health, Takapuna, Auckland 10, New Zealand.

Handbook of Pain and Aging, edited by David I. Mostofsky and Jacob Lomranz. Plenum Press, New York, 1997.

between them (page 223). Thus, coping is the evaluating thoughts and the actions taken as a result of those thoughts that are used to reduce a threat or stress and to restore a state of psychological and physical equilibrium. Although coping is essentially a variety of actions and responses, there are a number of biological, personal, cognitive, and psychological factors that impinge on the actual behaviors, influencing a persons' cognitive appraisal of the stressor and ability to manage the stressful episode. These factors are rather like the pieces in a jigsaw puzzle. Each component is important in itself, but assembled together, they are transformed into an observed total picture.

Coping responses have two main functions. The first is to manage or alter the person–environment relationship that is the source of the problem or stress, and the second is to regulate the accompanying emotional response (Folkman & Lazarus, 1980). When coping responses fail to do these two things, subnormal functioning is often the result. Disability is defined as this subnormal functioning as the result of an impairment (Wolcott, 1981). These two functions will now be discussed in more detail.

The Person–Environment Relationship That Is the Source of the Problem or Stress

Personal Variables. Aging does not make a person less sensitive to pain (Harkins, 1988; Harkins, Lagula, Price, & Small, 1995), nor does age induce major changes in the ability to cope with stressful events (Colenda & Dougherty, 1990). However, under normal circumstances, maturity can and does induce refinement and adaptation of problem-solving mechanisms. Most evidence points to normal personalities demonstrating stability in the use of predominant coping strategies throughout the life cycle (Keefe & Williams, 1990; Colenda & Dougherty, 1990; Corran, Gibson, Farrell & Helme, 1994).

Educational level and cognitive ability can make a difference in a person's coping by increasing the repertoire of available responses. As women's life expectancy is greater than men's, they are more likely to develop the chronic painful conditions associated with aging (Roberto, 1994). Apart from this gender disadvantage, gender differences in ability to cope have not been shown to be significant. One small difference was identified by Billings and Moos (1981), who noted that women, presumably because of their increased longevity, experienced more and were more adversely affected by life events. However, they were more likely to access a social support network to assist with adjustment and coping than were their male counterparts.

Aging does bring profound changes in social support networks and in economic resources. Diminishing resources in these areas can increase stress and affect the ability of individuals to solve problems. Social support has been examined as a factor in coping with pain by several authors, as it is thought to have some significance in managing stress. Burke and Flaherty (1993) looked at this factor in arthritis, and Roberto (1992) in women with hip fractures. Seeking social support also has been shown by Turner and Noh (1988) to be a significant activity that assists a person's ability to contend with disability. Most of these authors have examined these social factors in middle-socioeconomic-group elders. Older people who suffer from poverty or social isolation as well as pain may be more at risk for disability in consequence of lack of access to these social resources.

Cognitive Appraisal of the Stressor. A major factor in the person–environment relationship is the view the older person has of the significance of the pain stressor. People can perceive pain simultaneously from several points of view: (1) perception of the nature of the pain; (2) the meaning of the pain and its contextual significance to them; and (3) appraisal of the situation they find themselves in as a result of pain. Folkman and Lazarus (1980) argue that it is the individual's appraisal of the event rather than any objective feature that determines how a person contends with difficulties. The context of a stressor is important for older people. A stressor can represent a loss, a threat, or a challenge (Folkman, cited in McCrae, 1982). Illness, particularly if associated with persistent pain, often signifies a threat to quality of life and mobility, and sometimes, it signifies loss of function, loss of independence, and sometimes loss of life. Not surprisingly, such appraisals determine subsequent responses to the stressor (Bombadier, D'Amico, & Jordan, 1990). However, older people do not necessarily perceive all aches and pains in old age as major stressors or as having deep significance. Normal older subjects are much more likely to ignore milder aches and pains and to put them down to "aging" rather than to attach great significance to them (Colenda & Dougherty, 1990; Lipowski, 1990; Magni, 1987; Leventhal & Prohaska, 1986; Prohaska, Leventhal, Leventhal, & Keller, 1985). The idea that older people have an increased tendency to somatize as they age is a myth and is not borne out by the literature.

Health Status Variables. The normal life span is increasing in all populations, and people are living longer and with generally healthier lives. Morbidity is being compressed into the "old-old" years over 80, years that are distinguished by increased risk of frailty, degenerative disorders, and cognitive decline (Harkins, et al., 1995). In younger adults, health status variables are not as good predictors of outcome for pain patients as are cognitive or coping variables (Keefe & Williams, 1990; Keefe et al., 1987; Rosenthiel & Keefe, 1983), but in elders, they do seem to have much more relevance (Farrell, Gibson, & Helme, 1995; Portenoy & Farkash, 1988). Older people can and often do have more than one physical disorder. For example, an elderly person may have back pain from osteoporosis, complicated by cardiac failure, plus chronic obstructive airways disease, all of which effectively prevent them from doing any physiotherapeutic exercises that might improve their pain. One disorder may tax a frail elderly person's coping abilities, but several can be overwhelming.

Degeneration occurs with aging in all organ systems, including the brain, especially in the population over 80. Approximately 5%–7% of the population over 65 have some degree of organic cognitive impairment, and this increases to over 20% in the over 80s. Cognitively impaired elders also have problems with formal operational thinking. This results in more regressed and juvenile ideas regarding illness and pain (Reisberg, Ferris, & Franssen, 1986) that can lead to miscommunication with health professionals and caregivers concerning the nature and extent of the pain.

Even subtle subclinical decline may make a person forgetful or more vulnerable to the effects of drugs that act on the central nervous system. Drugs that cross the blood–

brain barrier, such as many analgesics, can be a problem for older people with organic cognitive impairment. The aging brain is very vulnerable to these drugs, even in small amounts. Drug metabolism slows in elders, who have reduced numbers of drug-binding sites, altered muscle–fat ratios, and less resilient metabolic systems. These can cause toxicity, electrolyte disturbances, oversedation, and other adverse side effects. Polypharmacy and drug interactions are also common complicating problems. All of these adverse effects can exacerbate the patient's problem; induce detrimental health practices such as noncompliance, poor nutrition, or inactivity; and decrease functioning and the ability to manage the stress of pain (Gurland, Wilder, & Berkman, 1988).

Pain presents great challenges to clinicians assessing older patients. At one end of the spectrum, older people are more likely to ignore and underreport milder aches and pains (Leventhal & Prohaska, 1986; Prohaska et al., 1985). These could go on to more significant problems if left unattended and, if assessed at their onset, might be more remediable than later. The challenge here is to improve education and health-promotional activities for pain in older people so that they do not underreport significant symptoms. At the other end of the spectrum is the "older-old" population, who are likely to have greater morbidity and medical complications. The convolutions of multisystem pathologies can present therapeutic challenges not only to the problem-solving abilities of the individuals but also to those of the treating clinicians!

Mood State. Depression and anxiety are common companions of both physical and emotional stressors. The incidence of depression in older people, with a concurrent physical disorder, ranges, in different surveys, from 5% to 40% (Evans, 1994; Fenton, Cole, Engelsman, & Mansouri, 1994; O'Riordan et al., 1989; Moffic & Paykel, 1975; Schuckit, Miller, & Hahlbohm, 1975). Depression is more common in women, who, in general, live longer than men, and for whom complicating physical illness further increases the risk. The association between the two is also strong when physical illness is the dependent variable. In one epidemiological survey of 890 patients, 70% of the depressed subjects also reported the presence of one or more physical disorders (Lindsay, 1990). The risk of depression markedly increases when physical illness causes restrictions in mobility and activities of daily living, increases dependency, or causes pain (Farrell et al., 1995; Fenton et al., 1994; Lindsay, 1990; Turner & Noh, 1988; Arling 1987; Aneshensel, Frerichs, & Huba, 1984.

Not only does the burden of the physical disorder or its complications compromise coping resources, but the addition of depression makes problem solving more difficult. Suicide may be the outcome of failure to cope adequately (Blazer, Bachar, & Manton 1986; Schulman, 1978). In Catell's (1988) series of elderly people who successfully completed suicide, 21% complained of pain before their deaths. Similar results were found in Hagnell and Rorsman's (1978) prospective Swedish study of 3,000 individuals, where, again, a high incidence of somatic symptoms and pain was found in those who successfully committed suicide. Pain, depression, and physical illness are the three major risk factors for successful suicide, and elderly males are specially at risk.

Depression and anxiety do seem to interact with persistent pain in several ways. Physical illness, persistent pain, and depression all have neurobiological symptoms in common, and they probably share similar neurotransmitter pathways, each of which can curl back and exacerbate the other. No doubt there are biological connections of some sort, but the nature of these has yet to be determined. In one study (Parmelee, Katz, & Lawton, 1991) of 598 institutionalized elders, those who met DSM-IIIR criteria for major depression reported more intense pain than those with minor depression, who in turn reported more pain than those without depression. This finding seems to indicate a close kinship, but other workers are less convinced. Kuch, Cox, Evans, Watson, and Bubela (1993), among others, found in their studies that mood severity did not consistently predict pain intensity and concluded that the relationship between pain and depression is not a linear one. The question remains unresolved and requires further research.

Depression is also an understandable reaction to severe illness and chronic pain, irrespective of any biological connection. Negative mood states profoundly alter people's cognitions concerning their environment. Depression affects the way people think about themselves, their future, and their environment (Beck, 1976), and a person in pain often finds it difficult to view the world in a sanguine way. Individuals may perceive their future to be bleak or nonexistent, the environment as being hostile or uncontrollable, and themselves as being useless or helpless to change events. These depressive cognitions profoundly influence persons' ability to perceive ways in which they might manage the person–environmental problem that is causing the stress" (Kuch et al., 1993; Sullivan & D'Eon, 1990). Depression also affects persons' sense of control, their confidence, their motivation, and their belief in themselves. These concepts are important variables in regulating the emotional response to pain and will be explored in more detail below.

Regulation of the Accompanying Emotional Response and Restoration of Equilibrium

The output side of coping regulates the accompanying emotional response to restore equilibrium. Three major components have been postulated as essential to coping: locus of control, focus for coping, and the strategy employed.

Locus of Control. Locus of control is conceptualized as persons' sense of their ability to control events within their personal environment (Wallston, Wallston, & de Vellis, 1978). This sense of control varies, depending on the event over which persons believe they have control, and most people have a predominant, characteristic sense of control. Locus of control is not a unitary concept, varies according to the situation, and can be situated on a continuum from the wholly external to the wholly internal. Thus, there are control beliefs that events are due to external forces (e.g., fate, luck, and chance) and that no individual can change things; beliefs that control is invested externally in powerful others, such as doctors and nurses, so that the event is believed controllable but only by another person; and beliefs that control is internal to the persons themselves and that individuals are wholly responsible and able to change events.

In a general sense, locus of control does not change with aging, and persons' belief in their locus of control is consistent into late life, but it does seem to become more differentiated with aging in domain-specific areas, probably as a result of maturity and experience (Blanchard-Fields & Irion, 1988). Thus, locus of control for domain-specific areas such as health may be quite different from a person's overall sense of control. Poor health status and depression considerably influence locus of control in this domain-specific area. As many health stressors are indeed out of the person's control, the health locus of control does seem to show a trend toward the external with aging. Consequently, persons may have a strong sense of internality of control for most events in their lives but may have a more external sense of control concerning their health.

In younger adults, beliefs that control is invested in external sources has been shown to be detrimental to outcomes, but this does not seem to be a factor in elders to the same degree. External locus of control due to powerful others is not as predictive of disability or of poor coping in elders. Unlike younger counterparts, older people do not let ideas of external locus of control due to powerful others prevent them from attempting self-control, at least of some aspects of the stressor (Blanchard-Fields & Irion, 1988; Gold et al., 1991). It seems that elders develop a pragmatic acceptance that perhaps, after all, powerful others do control at least some events in people's lives to a greater or lesser extent, but that this shouldn't prevent individuals from attempting to change things for themselves (Blanchard-Fields & Irion, 1988). Instead of the concept of external locus of control (due to powerful others) being detrimental to outcomes, it may assist compliance with treatment and actually be beneficial in older people (Nagy & Wolfe, 1984).

Whereas, in the domain-specific area of health, locus of control invested in powerful others is not as predictive of disability in elders, locus of control invested in chance of fate does seem to be associated with greater depression, worsened pain, and increased disability and predicts the use of more maladaptive coping strategies in both adults and elders (Crisson & Keefe, 1988; Blanchard-Fields & Irion, 1988). Conversely, strong belief in internality of control predicts decreased pain intensity and better psychological adjustment across the age groups (Lipchik, Miles, & Covington, 1993; Rudy, Kerns, & Turk, 1988).

Locus of control is a rather reified concept, and its significance in older people has probably been overemphasized. All the variables previously discussed in this chapter have a bearing on locus of control, and it is impossible either to disengage these from control beliefs or to determine the extent of their influence. Both the literature and clinical observations indicate some inconsistencies in the concept of control with respect to elders, particularly in the area of externality. If the concept of locus of control has any validity as a predictor of psychological adjustment to pain and illness for older people, then the constructs of internal locus versus external locus of control due to chance have more cogency and support from the available literature. However, overall, the evidence regarding health locus of control and health outcomes for elders is not as seductive as it is in younger adults, and the concept of health locus of control as a predictor of outcome in elders should be viewed with caution (Wallhagen, Strawbridge, Kaplan, & Cohen, 1994).

Focus. Coping efforts can focus on the problem or on the emotion that the problem engenders (Billings & Moos, 1981; Folkman & Lazarus, 1980; Lazarus, 1980; Antonovsky, 1979). Problem-focused coping attempts to modify the sources of stress in the person's relationship with the problem environment and directs active attention to changing health status through personal or cognitive variables. Thus, coping may focus on the many practical problems that pain presents for the older person, such as difficulties with normal daily activities (dressing, mobility). Emotion-focused coping concentrates on the management of the emotional consequences of stressors (Billings & Moos, 1981). Emotion is also an inevitable part of the pain experience. Without an associated emotional response, pain is a nocioceptive sensation rather than an unpleasant occurrence. Most people focus on both simultaneously, although one focus pattern or another may predominate. Which focus pattern predominates is often dependent on a person's locus of control beliefs. It does seem that a high sense of internal locus of control predicts the use of more problem-focused active coping; in the domain-specific areas of health, a high sense of external locus of control *due to chance* predicts more emotion-focused passive coping for dealing with health stressors such as pain (Crisson & Keefe, 1988; Felton & Revenson, 1987; Blanchard-Fields & Irion, 1988).

Why should this matter? Is it relevant to the outcome whether problem- or emotion-focused coping strategies are used? The literature certainly implies that emotion-focused coping strategies are maladaptive (McCrae, 1982; Peiffer, 1977) and that they cause increased pain and depression. However, the significant health variables and physical disorders to which older people are more prone are beyond personal control, and indeed are due to fate or chance. If this in turn predicts use of emotion-focused coping, then does this necessarily mean that it is maladaptive for older people and that it will inevitably lead to decreased functioning and distress? This assertion only seems to be true for some styles of coping behaviors that are strongly influenced by an emotional focus and strong beliefs in an external locus of control. It is these that are maladaptive and will be discussed in more detail below.

Coping Behavioral Strategies. The actual behavioral strategy employed makes up the third part of the response triad. For a coping response to have the desired outcome, three criteria have to be met. First, persons must perceive that they have some strategies at their disposal for dealing with the stressor. Second, they must believe that they are capable of performing the required coping responses. Third, they must perceive that the chosen responses will achieve the desired outcome. The aims of coping strategies are not only to solve the problems, but also to cognitively appraise and modify the meaning of the event regarding the individual and to control the stress response.

The determinants behind selection of coping strategies are many and again include all the variables so far discussed. In addition, generational and cohort effects influence styles of coping strongly (Costa & McCrae, 1982). During maturation, people's problem-solving capacities evolve with refinement of effective and the abandonment of ineffective strategies. Older people may have fewer but more practiced strategies at their disposal (Meeks, Carstensen, Tamsky, Wright, & Pellegrini, 1989). Context is also a strong influencing factor, and different contextual stressors are dealt with differently (Folkman, Lazarus, Pimley, & Novacek, 1987; McCrae, 1982). A person may deal with the stress of bereavement in quite a different way to the stress of a painful illness.

*Coping Strategy Styles.*Coping strategies can be divided into active and passive styles. Active strategies for coping include problem solving, cognitive restructuring, seeking support and social networks, help and information seeking, and activity. However, as people age, they tend to become more self-reflective, they place a greater emphasis on life appraisal, and the strategies they choose to deal with problems change from more active to passive (Folkman et al., 1987; Folkman & Lazarus, 1980; Lazarus, 1980; Peiffer, 1977; Vaillant, 1977). Of course, there are exceptions. Whereas, in general, older people do tend toward the more passive styles of coping with age, when dealing with threat stressors such as health, normal older people will initially use more active strategies, such as information finding, active help, and social support seeking (McCrae, 1982).

Several authors, including McCrae (1982), believe that all passive styles of coping are maladaptive, but this assertion is disputed for older people. Some passive styles are the result of maturity and are highly adaptive (Vaillant, 1977). These include acceptance of the situation, humor, sublimation, reappraisal, reflection, distancing, and prayer. These strategies do not change the nature of the pain or the problem but focus on the emotional response. Rather than being maladaptive, when an individual has to contend with an extremely uncontrollable stressor such as a terminal illness or pain associated with severe physical handicap, or when the more active strategies have been employed and have ceased to be effective, these more cognitive, passive styles are highly applicable, and beneficial for controlling associated distress and depression (Fry, 1990; Folkman et al., 1987).

Some passive styles are definitely maladaptive. Ignoring, escape-avoidance, regression, and especially catastrophizing are all significantly associated with increased depression, increased pain and disability, prolonged illness, and poorer psychological adjustment (Keefe & Williams, 1990; Sullivan & D'Eon, 1990; Brown, Nicassio, & Wallston, 1989; Keefe, Brown, Wallston, & Caldwell, 1989; Keefe et al., 1987; Turner & Clancy, 1986; Rosenthiel & Keefe, 1983). These maladaptive passive styles also correlate with strong beliefs in external locus of control, particularly those invested in chance or fate, and have an emotional focus (Blanchard-Fields & Irion, 1988). This combination is also associated with a lowered sense of self-efficacy to perform behavioral intentions.

Self-Efficacy. Self-efficacy (Bandura, 1977) is the confidence in oneself to perform an intentional behavior or coping response. Some older people have great difficulties with self-efficacy and lose confidence very quickly in their ability to perform a coping response and to exercise control over the event. Those older people who previously led an independent and active life and, often for the first time, become ill in late life, have no prior "training" to deal with such illness stressors and may behave like "Humpty Dumpty" (Melding, 1995a,b) with a marked loss of confidence, poor self-efficacy, and increased anxiety. If the painful illness also appears to be out of the person's control, the sense of self-efficacy diminishes even further. In contrast, a strong sense of self-efficacy is predictive of better pain control, an interesting finding that Bandura, O'Leary, Taylor, Gauthier, and Gossard (1987) suggested was possibly due to increased endogenous opioid control.

Security is important to older people and is often the reason older people prefer to retire to places where there is easy access to hospitals, transport, and plenty of doctors and police. A person's belief in their ability to perform a coping response depends not only on their confidence to do so but also on whether they believe that such actions are safe and will not compromise them in any way. For example, if pain or illness affects mobility and activities of daily living, the older person may find it necessary to accept increased dependence rather than to struggle with the difficulty of maintaining self-reliance. Rehabilitation programs for younger adults with pain often emphasize personal autonomy to reduce dependency on drugs and health care systems. This may be inappropriate for older people. Self-efficacy is often a trade-off between a need for security and a desire for personal autonomy. If the autonomous side of self-efficacy is emphasized at the expense of needed security and appropriate dependency, then the result will often be distress, increase in anxiety, and further loss of confidence. If, on the other hand, security is emphasized above autonomy, then the result may be premature dependency and loss of quality of life (Melding, 1995b).

*Outcome Expectancy.*Poor outcome expectancy correlates very closely with a reduced belief in self-efficacy (Kirsch, 1985). However, of itself, outcome expectancy is a less robust concept in coping than self-efficacy. The actual outcome achieved appears to be determined more by persons' appraisal of their ability to perform coping responses (self-efficacy) than by any belief in the likely success of the strategy (outcome expectancy) (Jenson, Turner, & Romano, 1992; Bandura et al., 1987). A depressive affect not only profoundly affects persons' sense of efficacy but can also make them pessimistic about any expected outcome. This can prevent an older person from even trying to perform a coping response. This has practical implications for treatment programs for older adults. Both self-efficacy and outcome expectancy improves when therapists use experiential learning rather than didactic teaching, handouts, or vicarious advice (Bandura, 1977). People do better if shown and taken through the required actions.

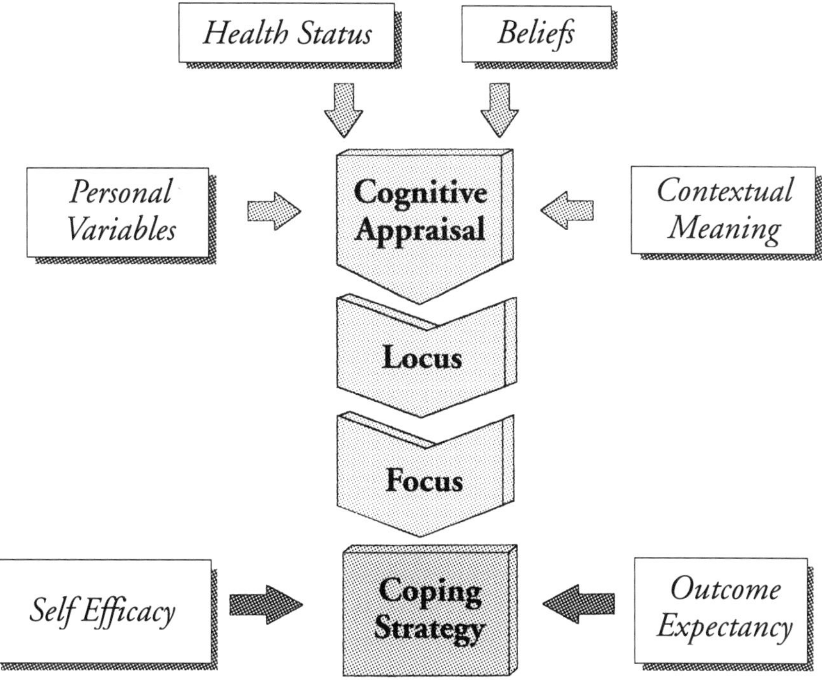

Figure 8-1. A conceptual model of coping.

To summarize the important variables that cause difficulties in coping would appear to be:

- The presence of depression
- Cognitive decline
- Poor social support
- Poor health status
- External locus of control especially if control is attributed to chance or fate (contentious)
- Predominant emotional focus coupled with maladaptive passive strategy, particularly catastrophizing
- Lowered sense of self-efficacy
- Poor outcome expectancy

Inadequate coping leads to decreased functioning and increased risk of disability (see Fig. 8-2). It is therefore important not only to understand how people cope but how they can be helped to handle difficult situations better.

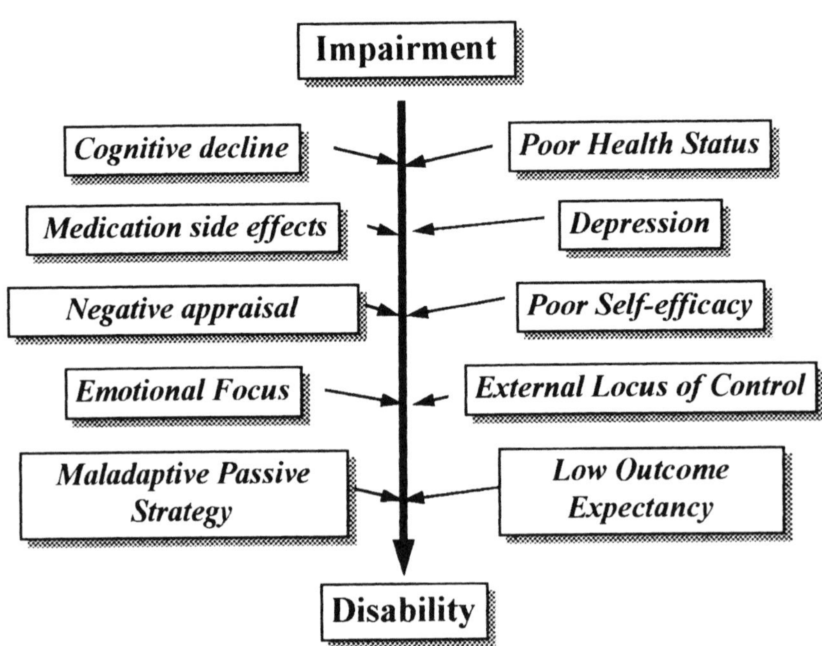

Figure 8-2. Factors that drive impairment toward disability.

STRESS MANAGEMENT AND PROGRAMS FOR HELPING OLDER PEOPLE COPE WITH PAIN

There is no good evidence that shows age to be a disadvantage to outcome in cognitive-behavioral pain and stress management programs (Sorkin, Rudy, Hanlon, Turk, & Steig, 1990; Puder, 1988; Middaugh et al., 1988). Given that older people have reached a developmental stage of life that gives them more time for self-reflection and life appraisal, it should not surprise us that older people can and do adapt to cognitive self-assessment very well and, to a certain extent, are more open to it than younger adults. There are a few reports of pain management programs for older people (Helme et al., 1989; Middaugh et al., 1988). While some are nonspecific, others have controlled for the effect of multiple health status variables by concentrating on discrete problems such as rheumatoid arthritis, osteoarthritis, or pain following hip fracture or knee replacement (Keefe et al., 1990, 1991) and consequently have been able to evaluate individual coping strategies and program outcomes more closely.

Literature reports of pain management programs in old age indicate use of a variety of cognitive, behavioral, educative, and physiotherapeutic techniques (Helme & Katz, 1993; Gold et al., 1993; Helme et al., 1989; Gold, Bales, Lyles, & Drezner, 1989; Middaugh et al., 1988; Puder, 1988; Fry, 1984). These techniques have proven effectiveness in younger adults and have been adapted and refined for the treatment of the older adult.

A Practical Approach to Patient Management Programs

A multidisciplinary approach optimizes management by drawing on the skills of many health professionals, including medical, nursing, clinical psychology, occupational, and physical therapy personnel. Programs that employ a variety of treatment modalities can be developed. The first principle in any management program for pain is to accept that, for the individual, the pain is a real phenomenon, irrespective of cause or degree of complicating cognitive or psychological variables. The second principle is to deal with health status variables as effectively as possible and to stabilize them. Medication should be rationalized, with polypharmacy and any sources of drug interactions eliminated. Pain-relieving techniques, such as transcutaneous nerve stimulation or nerve blocks, together with appropriate analgesia, may be necessary and desirable.

Depression should be treated vigorously. Depression, as already discussed, can reduce quality of life and interfere markedly with confidence, self-efficacy, and motivation. The neurobiological effects of depression negatively influencing sleep, appetite, and circadian rhythms produce fatigue and reduce resilience, and the negative cognitions of depression limit the person's perception of available options. Antidepressants may be indicated, but they should be used with care because of side effects. Tricyclic antidepressants are useful when there is a high degree of anxiety and poor sleep is a complication. However, their anticholinergic and cardiotoxic side effects can contraindicate their use in patients with prostatism, cardiac disease, orthostatic hypotension, and glaucoma. The serotonin reuptake inhibitors have been used relatively safely with good effect in patients with complicating medical illness (Evans, 1993). These newer agents lack the anti-cholinergic disadvantages of the tricyclic antidepressants, but they are not devoid of problem side effects. They may increase anxiety and agitation in some elders, and they have the potential to cause serious and possibly lethal hyponatremia. Nevertheless, they seem to be very useful in depression of old age, in depressed pain patients, and even in some patients with pain without depression. The rules for safely prescribing any antidepressant—and, indeed, any pharmacological agents—for older people are "Start low and go slow," watch carefully for signs of toxicity, and, if possible, monitor blood levels frequently.

Once medical and depressive health status variables are stabilized, the cognitive work to facilitate coping with stress, pain, and illness can begin. For an aged person, access to a clinic or program is a major obstacle, and for those with significant mobility problems, there may be hours of preparation just to attend. As older people have difficulty accessing services, many geriatric units have outreach teams to assess and treat patients at home. While such an arrangement may be ideal for the client, it may not be practical when there are limited resources and personnel.

Therapist and client expectations need to be clarified at the beginning of the program, and some mutual goals should be agreed on. It is useful to measure the level of activity and severity of any physical and emotional symptoms at baseline and at intervals throughout the program, not only for research purposes, but also as a benchmark for the patient to assess personal progress.

It is important to shape programs to match older people's special needs and abilities. Programs may need increased time to achieve their goals. Anecdotally, older people are more concerned with accuracy and "getting it right" than their younger counterparts and often take longer to assimilate ideas. Our experience is that the average program for adults adapted to older adults needs at least 50%–100% extra time to cover the same ground. Information overload is avoided if just one major concept is presented per session, and if there is plenty of time for the client group to discuss and digest. Sessions need to be short; for example, one hour is usually long enough as older people get very tired quickly, particularly if unwell or in pain.

Information should be given plentifully and written down, preferably in big print fonts for persons with failing eyesight. The "take-home" text should be kept simple. Those older persons who want more detail can be given additional reading material. It is important to remember and respect cohort effects and differences. For example, an older woman, never brought up to be assertive, may indeed be suffering from an "unable-to-say-no" syndrome, with suppressed anger, but to confront her, in late life, with the message that more assertion in her younger days might have improved her quality of life will be seen as an ego-dystonic rejection of her life principles. The consequences could be profound intrapersonal feelings of disintegration and despair. It is important to validate older persons' early experience and at the same time to encourage them to move to more adaptive functioning as appropriate for late life. For example, a therapist might say, "This was important to you at that particular time in your life, but now things have changed, and maybe a different response is required."

The current trend is to use a cognitive-behavioral approach. Such an approach has been found to be beneficial to adults (Turk, Meichenbaum, & Genest, 1983). Puder (1988), Sorkin and Turk (1995), Middaugh et al. (1988), Thompson, Gallagher, and Beckenridge (1990), and many others have presented evidence that such programs are effective for older people, exploding the commonly held myth that psychological change cannot occur in old age.

Cognitive-behavioral programs concentrate on enabling clients to understand how their thinking influences their emotions and behavior, as well as on formulating interventions that will change the emotional and behavioral consequences for the individuals. Patients learn to identify maladaptive thoughts and negative "self-talk" that limit their perceptions of alternative behavioral options. Diaries are useful to identify thoughts and perceptions. Once maladaptive thoughts and ways of coping are recognized, patients learn to replace these with more adaptive ways of dealing with the problem or emotional feeling in order to improve their outcome. Problem solving is taught by first identifying potential solutions to the problem in hand and then mapping out the pros, cons, and interesting points about each to establish the person's priority for action. It is important to continually but sensitively feed back to patients the actual and potential consequences of these behavioral choices, so that the cognitions behind maladaptive behaviors can be identified. In addition to changing negative self-talk and learning problem solving, other adaptive behaviors, such as relaxation, self-hypnosis, and graded activity to increase mobility, are established in the behavioral part of the program.

Programs are usually graded to build confidence. Written identified goals are useful tools in building self-efficacy. These larger goals are broken down into smaller achievable steps on a daily and weekly basis. Progress can be monitored with self-report charts plus objective measurements of behaviors, mobility, mood state, pain, and social interaction. We have found that handouts and didactic teaching are insufficient of themselves to build self-efficacy. It is better to guide people experientially through a procedure, giving appropriate encouragement and support.

It is important to identify the individuals' ways of coping with their pain stressor (Fry & Wong, 1991). Instruments such as the Coping Strategies Questionnaire can be useful (Rosenthiel & Keefe, 1983), although this instrument has not yet been validated for use with older people. There is now very good evidence that catastrophic thinking is a major significant factor in inducing depression, poor psychological adjustment, and disability, and stress programs should concentrate on enabling individuals to reduce this cognitive error. However, it has yet to be shown conclusively if specifically reducing catastrophic thinking has a significant effect on outcome. While we await empirical evidence on this specific item, in general, encouraging and enabling patients to use more appropriate active or adaptive, passive strategies for dealing with stress and pain would seem to be a useful activity.

To summarize the principles for programs with elders the following guidelines are offered:

- Accept pain as "real."
- Stabilize health status.
- Use appropriate analgesia as necessary.

- Treat depression vigorously.
- Enlist social and family support, especially if behavior modification is needed.
- Use a cognitive-behavioral approach.
- Build self-efficacy by experiential methods rather than didactic teaching.
- Pace programs at elders' speed.
- Keep sessions short, one major concept at a time.
- Give plentiful information, keep it simple, and use large print fonts.
- Set goals with the individual, monitor progress with charts and instruments, and review frequently.
- Reduce catastrophic thinking.

Not all elderly people with pain can use these programs as delineated above. Those with organic cognitive impairment would find the cognitive and stress management principles difficult to follow because of problems in short-term memory, concept formation, abstract thinking and language difficulties. Nevertheless, the same principles can be adapted for this group, although sometimes "detective work" is required to delineate the symptoms that require intervention, and some creativity may be necessary in designing appropriate interventions. Obviously, the intellectual, cognitive, and educative components of pain programs are limited in usefulness for cognitively impaired patients. Instead, their caregivers often benefit from such information to enable them to understand the problems. It is usually advantageous to emphasize stabilization of health status variables and to provide adequate analgesia and instruction in appropriate physical methods of treatment. Cognitively impaired patients are often unable to identify their symptoms accurately. Bodily symptoms, emotional distress, and pain may be expressed in difficult behaviors rather than in verbal communication. It is important for therapists and caregivers to check for unreported symptoms or drug side effects such as toxicity, constipation, dehydration, and metabolic disturbances. Behavior modification is helpful if the patient somatizes unrecognized emotion into bodily symptoms. Simple relaxation techniques can still be surprisingly effective for the cognitively impaired through the use of modalities such as rocking chairs, massage, and music. These efforts can reduce stress for the patients and their caregivers. Caregiver programs are useful not only in facilitating carers' coping skills but also in providing them with social support, which of itself gives significant assistance in stress management.

SUMMARY AND CONCLUSION

The world is aging as most people are living longer with more healthy lives, and this trend is not just confined to the Western nations, the Third World is fast catching up. The "graying" of world society is changing attitudes about age, as evidenced by more medical interest in technologies that can extend life and media interest showing older people as worthy subjects of everything from documentaries to sitcoms. Recent retirees in the Western nations are among the heaviest purchasers of consumer goods, a fact that has not escaped the advertising industry. Politicians also are taking more interest in policies with which the increasing numbers of elderly voters can identify.

As collective awareness of the needs of older people emerges, it is timely to focus attention on the elderly patient whose quality of life is impaired because of the stress of chronic pain. Chronic pain in any age group has huge financial implications. In the young adult, loss of work has a major fiscal impact. Older people do not usually engage in the paid workforce, and therefore, one assumption is that chronic pain in older people does not have the same economic importance. This assumption is erroneous, as the results of chronic pain are increased dependency and institutionalization, which have major cost implications for governments, for health systems, and for families, not to mention the sufferers themselves.

Programs for elders can and do work. What limits their wider use is health professionals' negative appraisal, nihilism, and poor outcome expectancy of programs without supporting evidence to justify such beliefs. If we are to change these attitudes in elderly people with disability from chronic pain, we must first change them in ourselves. We must accept the idea of pain programs for elders as not only viable but desirable, and we must provide them.

ACKNOWLEDGMENTS. My grateful thanks to my friends and colleagues, Dr. Paul Merrick, Dr. Robert Large, and Ms. Janet Peters for their unfailing support, patience, and constructive advice in the preparation of the manuscript. The development of these concepts and their practical application to older people have been strongly influenced by Paul Merrick and the team at the Kingsley Mortimer Unit of North Shore Hospital, Auckland, New Zealand.

REFERENCES

Aneshensel C. S., Frerichs, R. R., & Huba, G. J. (1984). Depression and physical illness: A multiwave, nonrecursive causal model. *Journal of Health and Social Behaviour, 25*, 350–371.

Antonovsky, A. (1979). *Health, stress, and coping*. San Francisco: Jossey-Bass.

Arling, G. (1987). Strain, social support and distress in old age. *Journal of Gerontology, 42*, 107–113.

Bandura, A. (1977). Towards a unified theory of behavioral change. *Psychological Reviews, 84*, 191–215.

Bandura, A., O'Leary, A., Taylor, C. B., Gauthier, J., & Gossard, D. (1987). Perceived self efficacy and pain control: Opiod and non opoid mechanisms. *Journal of Personality and Social Psychology, 35*, 563–571.

Beck, A. (1976). *Cognitive therapy and the emotional disorders*. New York: International Universities Press.

Billings, A. G., & Moos, R. H. (1981). The role of coping responses and social resources in attentuating the stress of life events. *Journal of Behavioural Medicine, 4*(2), 139–157.

Blanchard-Fields, F., & Irion, J. (1988). The relationship between locus of control and coping in two contexts: Age as a moderator variable. *Psychology and Aging, 3*, 197–203.

Blazer, D. G., Bachar, J. R., & Manton, K. G. (1986). Suicide in late life: Review and commentary. *Journal of American Geriatrics Society, 34*, 519–525.

Bombadier, C., D'Amico, C., & Jordan, J. (1990). The relationship of appraisal and coping to chronic illness adjustment. *Behaviour Research and Therapy, 28*, 297–304.

Brown, G. K., Nicassio, P. M., & Wallston, K. A. (1989). Pain coping strategies in rheumatoid arthritis. *Journal of Consulting and Clinical Psychology, 5*, 652–657.

Burke, M., & Flaherty, M. J. (1993). Coping strategies and health status of elderly arthritic women. *Journal of Advanced Nursing, 18*, 7–13.

Catell, H. R. (1988). Elderly suicide in London: An analysis of coroner's inquests. *International Journal of Geriatric Psychiatry, 3*, 251–261.

Colenda, C. C., & Dougherty, L. M. (1990). Positive ego and coping functions in chronic pain and depressed patients. *Journal of Geriatric Psychiatry and Neurology, 3*, 48–52.

Corran, T. M., Gibson, S. J., Farrell, M. J., & Helme, R. D. (1994). Comparison of chronic pain experience between young and elderly patients. In G. F. Gebhart, D. L. Hammond, & M. P. Jensen (Eds.), *Proceedings of the VIIth World Congress on Pain, Progress in Pain Research and Management* (Vol. 2, pp. 895–906). Seattle: IASP Press.

Costa, P. T., & McCrae, R. R. (1982). An approach to the attribution of aging, period and cohort effects. *Psychological Bulletin, 92*, 238–250.

Crisson, J. E., & Keefe, F. J. (1988). The relationship of locus of control to pain coping strategies and psychological distress in chronic pain patients. *Pain, 35*, 147–154.

Evans, M. E. (1993). Treatment of depression in elderly physically ill in-patients: A twelve month prospective study. *International Clinical Psychopharmacology, 8*(4), 333–336.

Evans, M. E. (1994). Physical illness and depression. In J. R. M. Copeland, M. T. Abou-Saleh, & D. G. Blazer (Eds.), *Principles and practice of geriatric psychiatry* (pp. 525–532). Chichester: Wiley.

Farrell, M. J., Gibson, S. J., & Helme, R. D. (1995). The effect of medical status on the activity level of elderly chronic pain patients. *Journal of the American Geriatrics Society, 43*, 102–107.

Felton, B. J., & Revenson, T. A. (1987). Age differences in coping with chronic illness. *Psychology and Ageing, 2*, 164–170.

Fenton, F. R., Cole, M. G., Engelsmann, F., & Mansouri, I. (1994). Depression in older medical inpatients. *International Journal of Geriatric Psychiatry, 9*, 279–284.

Folkman, S., & Lazarus, R. S. (1980). An analysis of coping in a middle aged sample. *Journal of Health and Social Behaviour, 21*, 219–239.

Folkman, S., Lazarus, R. S., Pimley, S., & Novacek, J. (1987). Age differences in stress and coping processes. *Psychology and Ageing, 2*, 171–184.

Fry, P. S. (1990). A factor analytic investigation of home bound elderly individuals' concerns about death and dying and their coping responses. *Journal of Clinical Psychology, 46*, 737–748.

Fry, P. S. (1984). Cognitive training and cognitive behavioural variables in the treatment of depression in the elderly. *Clinical Gerontology, 3*, 25–45.

Fry, P. S., & Wong, P. T. P. (1991). Pain management training in the elderly: Matching interventions with subjects' coping styles. *Stress Medicine, 7*, 93–98.

Gold, D. T., Bales, C. W., Lyles, K. W., & Drezner, M. K. (1989). Treatment of osteoporosis: The psychological impact of a medical education programme on older patients. *Journal of the American Geriatrics Society, 37*, 417–422.

Gold, D. T., Smith, S. D., Bales, C. W., Lyles, K. W., Westlund, R. E., & Drezner, M. K. (1991). Osteoporosis in late life: Does health locus of control affect psychosocial adaptation? *Journal of the American Geriatrics Society, 39*, 670–675.

Gold, D. T., Stegmaier, K., Bales, C. W., Lyles, K. W., Westlund, R. E., & Drezner, M. K. (1993). Psychological functioning and osteoporosis in late life: Results of a multidisciplinary intervention. *Journal of Women's Health, 2*, 149–155.

Gurland, B. J., Wilder, D. E., & Berkman, C. (1988). Depression and disability in the elderly: Reciprocal relations and changes with age. *International Journal of Geriatric Psychiatry, 3*, 163–179.

Hagnell, O., & Rorsman, B. (1978). Suicide and endogenous depression with somatic symptoms in the Lunby Study. *Neuropsychobiology, 4*, 180–187.

Harkins, S. W. (1988). Pain in the elderly. In R. Dubner, G. F. Gebhart & M. R. Bond (Eds.), *Proceedings of the Vth World Congress on Pain* (pp. 355–367). Amsterdam: Elsevier Science.

Harkins, S. W., Lagula, B. T., Price D. D., & Small, R. E. (1995). Geriatric Pain. In Roy, R. (Ed.), *Chronic Pain in Old Age: An Integrated Biopsychosocial Perspective*. University of Toronto Press, 127–163.

Helme, R. D., & Katz, B. (1993). Management of chronic pain. *Medical Journal of Australia, 158*, 478–481.

Helme, R. D., Katz, B., Neufeld, M., Lachal, J., Herbert, J., & Corran, T. (1989). The establishment of a geriatric pain clinic: A preliminary report of the first 100 patients. *Australian Journal on Aging, 8*(1), 27–30.

Jenson, M. P., Turner, J. A., & Romano, J. M. (1992). Self efficacy and outcome expectancies: Relationship to chronic pain coping strategies and adjustment. *Pain, 44*, 263–269.

Keefe, F. J., Brown, G. K., Wallston, K. A., & Caldwell, D. S. (1989). Coping with rheumatoid arthritis: Catastrophising as a maladaptive strategy. *Pain, 37*, 51–56.

Keefe, F. J., Caldwell, D. S., Martinez, S., Nunley, J., Beckham, J., & Williams, D. A. (1991). Analysing pain in rheumatoid arthritis patients: Pain coping strategies in patients who have had knee replacement surgery. *Pain, 46*, 153–160.

Keefe, F. J., Caldwell, D. S., Queen, K. T., Gil, K. M., Martinez, S., Crisson, J. E., Ogden, W., & Nunley, J. (1987). Pain coping strategies in osteoarthritis patients. *Journal of Consulting and Clinical Psychology, 2*, 208–212.

Keefe, F. J. Caldwell, D. S., Williams, D. A., Gil, K. M., Mitchell, D., Robertson, C., Martinez, S., Nunley, J., Beckham, J. C., & Helms, M. (1990). Pain coping skills training in the management of osteoarthritic knee pain: 2. Follow up results. *Behaviour Therapy, 21*, 435–447.

Keefe, F. J., & Williams, D. A. (1990). A comparison of coping strategies in chronic pain patients in different age groups. *Journal of Gerontology: Psychological Sciences, 45*, 161–165.

Kirsch, L. (1985). Response expectancy as a determinant of experience and behaviour. *American Psychology, 40*, 1189–1202.

Kuch, K., Cox, B., Evans, R. J., Watson, P. C., & Bubela, C. (1993). To what extent do anxiety and depression interact with chronic pain. *Canadian Journal of Psychiatry, 38*, 36–38.

Lazarus, R. S. (1980). The stress and coping paradigm. In C. Eisdorfer, D. Cohen, A. Kleinman, & P. Maxim (Eds.), *Theoretical bases for psychopathology* (pp. 177–214). New York: Spectrum.

Leventhal, E. A., & Prohaska, T. R. (1986). Age, symptom interpretation and health behaviour. *Journal of the American Gerontological Society, 34*, 183–191.

Lindsay, J. (1990). The Guy's Age Concern Survey: Physical health and psychiatric disorder in an urban elderly community. *International Journal of Geriatric Psychiatry, 5*, 171–178.

Lipchik, G. L., Milles, K., & Covington, E. C. (1993). The effects of multidisciplinary pain management treatment on locus of control and pain beliefs in chronic non-terminal pain. *Clinical Journal of Pain, 9*, 49–57.

Lipowski, Z. J. (1990). Somatization and depression. *Psychosomatics, 31*, 13–21.

Magni, G. (1987). On the relationship between chronic pain and depression when there is no organic lesion. *Pain, 31*, 1–21.

Marsland, D. W., Wood, M., & Mayo, F. (1976). *Content of family practice: A statewide study in Virginia with its clinical educational and research implications.* New York: Appleton-Century-Crofts.

McCrae, R. R. (1982). Age differences in the use of coping mechanisms. *Journal of Gerontology, 4*, 454–460.

Meeks, S., Carstensen, L. L., Tamsky, B. F., Wright, T. L., & Pellegrini, D. (1989). Age differences in coping: Does less mean more? *International Journal of Aging and Human Development, 28*, 127–140.

Melding, P. S. (1995a). How do older people respond to chronic pain: A review of coping in elders. *Pain Reviews, 2*, 65–73.

Melding, P. S. (1995b). Psychiatric aspects of chronic pain in the elderly. In R. R. Roy (Ed.), *Chronic pain in old age: An integrated biopsychosocial perspective* (pp. 194–214). Toronto, Buffalo, London: University of Toronto Press.

Middaugh, S. J., Levin, R. B., Kee, W. G., Fiammetta, D., Barchiesi, D., & Roberts, J. M. (1988). Chronic pain: Its treatment in geriatric and younger patients. *Archives of Physical Medicine and Rehabilitation, 69*, 1021–1026.

Moffic, H. S., & Paykel, E. S. (1975). Depression in medical inpatients. *British Journal of Psychiatry, 126*, 346–353.

Nagy, V. T., & Wolfe, G. R. (1984). Cognitive predictors of compliance in chronic disease patients. *Medical Care, 22*, 912–921.

O'Riordan, T. G., Hayes, J. P., Shelley, R., O'Neill, D. Walsh, J. B., & Coakley, D. (1989). The prevalence of depression in an acute geriatric medical assessment unit. *International Journal of Geriatric Psychiatry, 4*, 17–21.

Parmelee, P. A., Katz, I. R., & Lawton, M. P. (1991). The relation of pain to depression among institutionalized aged. *Journal of Gerontology: Psychological Sciences, 46*, 15–21.

Peiffer, E. (1977). Psychopathology and social pathology. In J. L. Birren & K. W. Schaie (Eds.), *Handbook of the psychology of aging* (pp. 658–671). New York: Van Nostrand Reinhold.

Portenoy, R. K., & Farkash, A. (1988). Practical management of non-malignant pain in the elderly. *Geriatrics, 43*, 29–47.

Prohaska, T. R., Leventhal, E. A., Leventhal, H., & Keller, M. L. (1985). Health practices and illness cognition in young, middle aged, and elderly adults. *Journal of Gerontology, 40*, 569–578.

Puder, R. S. (1988). Age analysis of cognitive-behavioural group therapy for chronic pain outpatients. *Psychology and Aging, 3*, 204–207.

Reisberg, B., Ferris, S. H., & Franssen, E. (1986). Functional degenerative stages in dementia of the Alzheimer's type appear to reverse normal human development. In C. Shagass (Ed.), *Biological Psychiatry* (Vol. 7, pp. 1319–1321). New York: Elsevier Science.

Roberto, K. A. (1992). Coping strategies of older women with hip fractures: Resources and outcomes. *Journal of Gerontology: Psychological Sciences, 47*, 21–26.

Roberto, K. A. (1994). The study of chronic pain in later life: Where are the women? In K. A. Roberto (Ed.), *Older women with chronic pain* (pp. 1–7). New York, London, Norwood: Haworth Press.

Rosenthiel, A. K., & Keefe, F. (1983). The use of coping strategies in chronic low back pain patients: Relationship to patient characteristics and current adjustment. *Pain, 17*, 33–44.

Rudy, T. E., Kerns, R. D., & Turk, D. C. (1988). Chronic pain and depression: Towards a cognitive-behavioural mediation model. *Pain, 35*, 129–140.

Schuckit, M. A., Miller, P. I., & Hahlbohm, D. (1975). Unrecognised psychiatric illness in elderly medical-surgical patients. *Journal of Gerontology, 30*, 655–660.

Schulman, K. (1978). Suicide and parasuicide in old age: A review. *Age and Ageing, 7*, 201–209.

Sorkin, B. A., Rudy, T. E., Hanlon, R. B., Turk, D. C., & Steig, R. L. (1990). Chronic pain in old and young patients: Differences appear less important than similarities. *Journal of Gerontology: Psychological Sciences, 45*, 64–68.

Sorkin, B. A., & Turk, D. C. (1995). Pain management in the elderly. In Roy, R. (Ed.), *Chronic pain in old age: An integrated biopsychosocial perspective* (pp. 56–80). Toronto: University of Toronto Press.

Sullivan, M. J. L., & D'Eon, J. L. (1990). Relation between catastrophising and depression in chronic pain patients. *Journal of Abnormal Psychology, 99*, 260–263.

Thompson, L. W., Gallagher, D., & Beckenridge, J. S. (1990). Comparative effectiveness of psychotherapies in depressed elders. *Journal of Consulting and Clinical Psychology, 58*, 371–374.

Turk, D. C., Meichenbaum, D., & Genest, M. (1983). *Pain and behavioural medicine: A cognitive-behavioural perspective*. New York: Guilford Press.

Turk, D. C., & Rudy, T. E. (1987). Towards the comprehensive assessment of chronic pain patients. *Behaviour Research and Therapy, 25*, 237–249.

Turner, J. A., & Clancy, S. (1986). Strategies for coping with chronic low back pain: Relationships to pain and disability. *Pain, 24*, 355–364.

Turner, R. J., & Noh, S. (1988). Physical disability and depression: A longitudinal analysis. *Journal of Health and Social Behavior, 29*, 23–37.

Vaillant, G. E. (1977). *Adaptation of life*. Boston: Little, Brown.

Wallhagen, M. L., Strawbridge, W. J., Kaplan, G. A., & Cohen, R. D. (1994). Impact of internal locus of control on health outcomes for older men and women: A longitudinal perspective. *The Gerontologist, 34*, 299–306.

Wallston, K. A., Wallston, B. S., & de Vellis, R. (1978). Development of the multidimensional health locus of control (MHLOC) scales. *Health Education Monographs, 6*, 160–170.

Wolcott, L. E. (1981). Rehabilitation and the aged. In W. Reichel (Ed.), *Topics in aging and long term care* (pp. 87–110). Baltimore, London: Williams & Wilkins.

CHAPTER 9

The Role of Pain in the Cascade from Chronic Illness to Social Disability and Psychological Distress in Late Life

BOAZ KAHANA, EVA KAHANA, KEVAN NAMAZI, KYLE KERCHER, AND KURT STANGE

Pain has been viewed as an important concomitant of late-life illness that can threaten the quality of life of older adults. In considering linkages between chronic physical illness and psychological distress in late life, the associations between reporting of pain and indices of depression have been extensively studied (Parmelee, 1994; Romano & Turner, 1985). Nevertheless, the role of pain in mediating the effects of ill health on functioning and psychological well-being has seldom been considered in a more comprehensive framework. Such a framework could organize our understanding of the biopsychosocial and ecological context of pain and consider its sequelae for both social and psychological well-being (Kahana & Kahana, 1996).

The goal of this chapter is to consider pain as a key indicator of physical impairment in the framework of the cascade from chronic illness to social and psychological disability (Verbrugge, 1991), which we refer to as the cascade model (see Figure 9-1). Using a biopsychosocial approach (Engle, 1962), we explore the role of pain as a mediator between social dispositions (represented by demographic factors) and chronic

---

BOAZ KAHANA • Department of Psychology, Cleveland State University, Cleveland Ohio 44115. EVA KAHANA, KEVAN NAMAZI, AND KYLE KERCHER • Department of Sociology, Case Western University, Cleveland, Ohio 44106-7124. KURT STANGE • Department of Family Medicine, Case Western University, Cleveland, Ohio 44106-7124.

Handbook of Pain and Aging, edited by David I. Mostofsky and Jacob Lomranz. Plenum Press, New York, 1997.

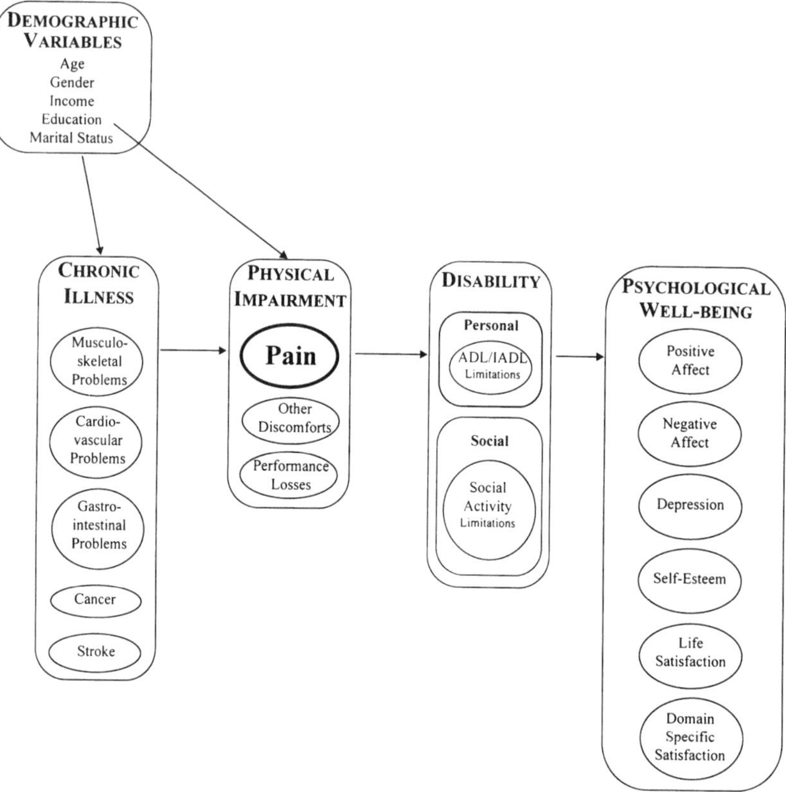

Figure 9-1. The cascade from illness, to impairment, to disability, and quality of life.

illness as antecedent and diminished social functioning and psychological well-being as sequelae.

The negative impact of physical health problems on the quality of life of older adults has been well documented in the gerontological literature. Age-associated increases in chronic illness and negative self-appraisals of health have been found to be accompanied by lower levels of morale and a general absence of psychological well-being (Larson, 1978). Explanations for the decline in psychological well-being among physically frail elders include the hypothesis that physical illness represents a normative late-life stress and as such may overtax adaptive capacities of older adults (Kahana & Kahana, 1996). Other explanations suggest that limitations in the ability to perform valued activities, due to illness, threaten psychological well-being (Verbrugge, 1990). However, relatively little empirical research has investigated the cascade from chronic illness to physical impairments (such as pain) and concomitant social disability, to loss of quality of life among community-dwelling old-old persons.

We recognize that the experience and report of pain are likely to be influenced by illness as well as by social characteristics of older adults. We will explore the nature, social antecedents, and psychological sequelae of pain among a group of 1000 generally healthy community-living old-old persons (i.e., age 75+) residing in three Florida retirement communities. This research is part of a comprehensive study concerned with adaptation to frailty among the old-old (Kahana & Kahana, 1996; Kercher, 1992; Kahana, Kercher, Kahana, & Namazi, 1995; Borowski-Clark, Kinney, & Kahana, 1996). We will first outline our framework for considering pain as part of the chronic illness and psychological disability cascade, and we will then present relevant research background from the literature on pain. This is followed by a report of our empirical study and its research findings.

CONSIDERING PAIN IN THE CONTEXT OF THE CHRONIC ILLNESS–DISABILITY CASCADE

Consideration of pain among the elderly often refers to an isolated symptom that is viewed as a response to biological breakdown of the organism or as a stimulus that elicits adverse psychological reaction in those experiencing pain. As depicted in Figure 9-1, we argue that useful consideration of the role of pain in the quality of life in old age requires that it be viewed in a comprehensive context of the cascade from chronic illness to disability and reduced psychological well-being (Verbrugge, 1990). Contextualizing pain in a broad biopsychosocial framework also helps link objective and subjective dimensions of health. Empirical advances in this area are particularly important because of recent evidence that subjective appraisals of health serve as powerful predictors of both morbidity and mortality, and that subject measures outperform objective indicators in prospective studies (Kasl, 1992). Consideration of subjective experience of pain and other discomforts produced by illness may provide useful clues about the mechanisms which render subjective health such a powerful predictor of long-term morbidity, mortality, and well-being outcomes.

The rapidly growing old-old segment of the U.S. population uses a disproportionate amount of health care resources as it confronts frailty, illness, pain, and disability during the last years of life (Olshansky, Rudberg, Carnes, Cassel, & Brody, 1991). While over 80% of people over the age of 65 have at least one chronic medical condition (Special Committee on Aging, 1985), there is wide variation in activities-of-daily-living (ADL) and instrumental-activities-of-daily-living (IADL) disability within diagnostic categories (Ford et al., 1988). There is a growing consensus in the literature dealing with late-life morbidity that meaningful distinctions exist between organ-level physical impairments and the personal and social disability that develops as a consequence of such impairments (Verbrugge 1990; Nagi, 1990; World Health Organization, 1980). Physical impairments appear to be closely linked to physiological and structural changes in the body, due to the underlying pathology of chronic illness (Fried, Herdman, Kuhn, Rubin, & Turano, 1991). Disabilities, on the other hand, are linked to task demands of daily living and social functioning (Lawton, 1983). The degree of disability exhibited for a given level of impairment will depend on the level of environmental demand and the resources and adaptations of the person experiencing impairment.

Figure 9-1 depicts the causal ordering of the elements of the cascade from chronic illness to impairment, to disability, and the ultimate outcomes of psychological well-being. Our major focus in this cascade concerns the effects of impairment—specifically, pain—on social and personal disability and psychological well-being. These elements of the cascade are best understood in the context of the more comprehensive process by which chronic illness debilitates the elderly and ultimately reduces their ability to perform social and personal activities of daily living and to maintain psychological well-being. This process also includes important social influences on every element of the cascade, which are represented in our model by demographic variables. The health care literature has established sequencing of elements within the cascade model (Nagi, 1990; Verbrugge, 1990). Major advances in clarifying this process, however, await further empirical work to link elements of the cascade. Our goal in this chapter is to link these elements with regard to pain.

We will briefly outline our approach to conceptualizing key components of this cascade. The following definitions of terms will help clarify the concepts relevant to impairment and disability as we have used them in our study. *Impairments* denote deficits in normal functions of organ systems which are manifested in loss of performance (e.g., cannot grasp objects well), or are experienced as discomfort (e.g., pain). *Personal disability* refers to difficulty in independently performing ADLs or IADLs. *Social disability* refers to restriction or limitation in performance of customary and valued social activities. *Psychological well-being* encompasses a broad array of variables which reflect low levels of negative affect and high levels of positive affect and life satisfaction (both global and domain-specific).

ELEMENTS OF THE CASCADE

Elements of the cascade, depicted in Figure 9-1, will be discussed below, with particular attention to causal linkages between pain and other elements of the cascade. The discussion will generally follow the causal sequence shown in Figure 9-1. Demographic antecedents will, however, be presented last, since they can be best understood subsequent to presentation of the other major variables.

Chronic Illness

Medical diagnoses have great utility for decisions about providing medical care for individuals and are useful for predicting mortality. While the elderly are prone to sudden decline and death from cataclysmic health events (Ford et al., 1988), it is primarily the chronic illnesses which result in the long-term physical impairments with which older individuals and health care providers must cope. Attempts to predict levels of disability based on chronic illness have generally met with limited success. Research has shown that there is wide variation in social and psychological functioning even within specific types of chronic illness (Felton & Revenson, 1984; Ford et al., 1988). Such lack of predictability may well be due to the absence of data on degree of impairment in these elderly. Thus, level of impairment, of which pain is a major component in our model, may be viewed as the critical missing link in understanding the impact of chronic illness on social disability. In the present study, specific chronic illnesses reported by respondents were aggregated to yield five major illness groupings (musculoskeletal, heart–lung, cancer, stroke, and gastrointestinal), which may have differential impact on pain. The association of these different illness groups with the reporting of pain was explored.

Physical Impairment

Physical impairments encompass a wide range of organ-level dysfunctions which are reflected in sensory deficits (such as poor vision or hearing), performance deficits (such as inability to bend or reach), and discomforts (such as pain or dizziness).

Pain is a particularly important indicator of system-level impairment, particularly where outcomes of psychological well-being and social functioning are considered. Diverse indicators of impairment are associated with disability in self-care (Reuben & Siu, 1990; Williams, Hadler, & Earp, 1990). A study by Jette, Branch, and Berlin (1990) is one of the first prospective studies to address the linkage between physical impairment and disability. In this 10-year longitudinal study on community-living elderly in Massachusetts, Jette et al. (1990), using Nagi's (1990) conceptual scheme, analyzed impairment as an intervening variable between chronic illness and disability. They measured impairment based on objective ratings of musculoskeletal functioning and self-report data on hearing and visual functioning. Additionally, they measured personal disability as the difficulty in performing ADLs. This research showed that musculoskeletal impairments have a stronger effect than sensory impairment on the development of personal disability. However, Jette et al.'s (1990) pioneering study included only a limited range of impairments. Indications of physical discomfort, and specifically, pain, were not considered.

Although the negative psychological sequelae of pain have been acknowledged, there have been only limited attempts to link pain to both social disability and lack of psychological well-being. A valuable exception is research by Williamson and Schulz (1992), which focused on activity restriction as well as depression among community-dwelling elders.

In the present discussion, our particular focus is on pain as the critical impairment, with important links to personal and social disability. There are divergent definitions of pain, partly because of its multidimensional nature. Pain has been described (Rapin, 1991) as a complex experience which results from sensory stimulations and is modified by the memory, emotions, hopes, and expectations of the individual.

Since our focus in this chapter is on the psychological and social sequelae of pain, we found it helpful to consider pain a global entity which involves diverse sources and types of pain. We believe that it is the total pain experience which shapes the psychological and social sequelae for a community-dwelling (nonclinical) population of elders.

Disability

Disability is conceptualized in our research as comprising limitations in the performance of personal and social activities which are necessarily or customarily engaged in and valued by an individual (Verbrugge, 1990). *Personal disability* has been considered in terms of limitations in activities of daily living (ADLs) and instrumental activities of daily living (IADLs). These day-to-day activities have been referred to as obligatory aspects of functioning which are required for maintenance of independent lifestyles in the community (Verbrugge, 1990). *Social disability* refers to areas of human functioning which connect individuals to role performance and to significant others in society at large. Since the seminal work of Maslow (1970), social scientists have recognized the importance of higher-order functions for adding meaning to human existence and enhancing quality of life. However, researchers interested in pain and its sequelae have seldom examined the relationship of chronic illness and pain to these higher-order social functions. There are few studies of the effects of pain on social participation in organizations, volunteering, or maintaining interactions with friends and family. Verbrugge (1990) has called attention to the need for exploring these neglected aspects, which she calls "the iceberg of disability." In our model of the disability cascade, we attempt to link pain to both personal and social disability.

Psychological Well-Being

Psychological well-being involves a complex set of affective states and cognitive appraisals which, in aggregate, reflect a state of homeostasis and self-appraisals of good quality of life. In terms of affective states, experiencing both positive affect and negative affect is said to reflect the dimension of subjective well-being. Absence of symptoms of psychological distress (e.g., depression and anxiety) and high levels of life satisfaction also reflect important indicators of psychological well-being.

Among psychological concomitants of pain, depressive affect has been most widely studied. The complex relationship between pain and depressive affect has been discussed by Parmelee (1994). There are consistent suggestions that pain which results from chronic physical illness can lead to depressive symptomatology among the aged (Parmelee, Katz, & Lawton, 1989). Similar findings have also emerged from studies of younger age groups (Romano & Turner, 1985). Pain causes discomfort and often signals functional limitations, as in the case of arthritis, where pain induced by motion can limit performance of valued activities. Depression and negative affect are expected concomitants or results of such physical discomfort and limitations.

To the extent that pain can be viewed primarily as a physiological phenomenon, conceptualization of its psychological sequelae would appear to be simple. Thus, distress over chronic pain and attendant social disabilities may readily translate into psychological or affective disturbances. Nevertheless, it should be acknowledged that the experience of pain involves a complex interplay of physiological factors and neurological mechanisms along with psychosocial factors (VonKorff, Dworkin, LeResche, & Kruger, 1988).

Beyond the traditional focus on depression, there has been only limited attention in the literature to other indicators of psychological well-being in relation to pain. Negative affect or mood tone has been associated with high levels of pain in elderly arthritis patients (Dekker, Tola, Aufdemkampe, & Winkers, 1993). Degree of pain has also been found to impact negatively on life satisfaction among adults with orthopedic injuries (Brintnell, Madill, Montgomerie, & Stewin, 1992).

In an extensive Minnesota Multiphasic Personality Inventory (MMPI) study (Fow, Sittig, Dorris & Breisinger, 1994) of 1,766 patients with musculoskeletal pain (ages 17–90), older people were found to demonstrate the lowest MMPI psychopathology scores. (It was not clear to what extent these reflect a generalized age-related trend or a more limited influence of pain on psychological functioning in late life.)

In considering the psychological impact of pain and other impairments during the later years, diverse aspects of psychological well-being must be incorporated. Our study moves beyond consideration of depression as the major indicator of pain-related psychological functioning. Our dependent variables in the cascade model include, in addition to depression, positive and negative affect, cognitive life satisfaction, domain-specific satisfactions, and self-esteem. Some of these outcomes are likely to have components overlapping with depression, but they also expand our understanding of the impact of pain on diverse aspects of psychological well-being.

In considering the pervasive influence of pain on psychological well-being, we anticipated pain to impact not only on general mood tone, but on domain-specific satisfactions as well. We expected that the experience of pain and the resultant absence of positive affect (or presence of negative affect) would result in viewing specific aspects of one's social environment through "dark-colored glasses." Applied to domain-specific satisfactions, those in pain would exhibit reduced satisfaction with social support, which they may view as ineffective in alleviating their discomfort. Pain should also reduce other domain-specific satisfactions such as satisfaction with marriage, paid help, and medical care.

DEMOGRAPHIC ANTECEDENTS OF PAIN

Demographic factors incorporate a broad spectrum of ecological and social-structural influences which are likely to impinge on pain along with other elements of the chronic illness and psychosocial disability cascade. We will next describe results of prior work focusing on demographic and chronic illness antecedents of pain.

Aging and Pain

There are conflicting reports about the relationship between pain and aging, based on studies of health in late life. There is general consensus, based on national data sets, that musculoskeletal pain increases with age (Harkins & Price, 1992). However, older adults report fewer headaches, backaches, and stomachaches than younger adults (VonKorff et al., 1988). Pain is highly prevalent among groups of frail elderly and particularly among older adults residing in nursing homes (Ferrell, Ferrell, & Osterweil, 1990). However, there is also evidence that the intensity of pain diminishes with age. Although the old-old report less pain than the young-old, when health is controlled for, increases in pain have been observed among older adults during their last year of life (Moss, Lawton, & Glicksman, 1991). Reports of reduced pain among older adults may reflect lower sensitivity to pain (Kenshalo, 1977). Alternatively, pain represents an expectable "on-time" phenomenon in late life, and hence may be paid less attention to by older persons (Parmelee, 1994). Recent research findings that old-old individuals (i.e., 75+) report less pain than the young-old (i.e., 65–74) (Thomas & Roy, 1988) may also be due, in part, to differences in expectations regarding pain, and to an acceptance of having to live with chronic pain.

Gender and Pain

The role of gender influences in pain perception has been most extensively studied. Compelling evidence of the role of gender in reporting pain among younger adults comes from a study of 543 dental postoperative patients (age 15–44), which revealed that women report significantly more pain than men across all racial and ethnic groups (Faucett, Gordon, & Levine, 1994). In a study of responses to venipuncture during blood donations, healthy women also reported significantly greater pain than men (France, Adler, France, & Ditto, 1994). Women (age 20–55) have also been found to react more adversely to musculoskeletal pain than men, demonstrating more "catastrophizing" (Jensen, Nygren, Gamberole, & Goldie, 1994). However, there are few studies of gender difference in reporting pain among elderly populations. In research by VonKorff et al. (1988), headache, abdominal pain, and facial pain were found to be more prevalent among women. A recent volume (Roberto, 1994) presents a strong argument for considering female gender as a particularly strong risk factor for chronic pain in late life.

Chronic Illness and Pain

Persistent pain frequently results from musculoskeletal conditions, which are among the most prevalent chronic health conditions in late life (Roberto, 1994). Severe pain has also been found to be a common symptom in advanced cancer (All, 1994). Pain may also accompany other chronic health conditions, although variations in patterns and severity of pain may be associated with different illness profiles.

Income, Education, and Marital Status

Little prior research was found focusing on income, education, and marital status as they may influence or correlate with pain. We nevertheless considered them to be potentially relevant demographic predictors, since they may denote critical social influences relevant to the reporting of pain. Income and education were viewed as providing important resources that may contribute to greater success in pain management. Regarding marital status, the major distinctions in our older sample are between married and widowed respondents. One may anticipate that being married serves a protective role against pain through both affective and instrumental social supports that are found in a care-giving spouse.

RATIONALE FOR DESIGN AND OPERATIONAL APPROACHES OF THE STUDY

The aim of this research was to explore associations between illness-related and social antecedents of pain, on the one hand, and social and psychological sequelae, on the other. Figure 9-1 depicts the components of this cascade model.

Antecedents of Pain

We were primarily interested in exploring demographic characteristics (age, sex, income, education, and marital status) and chronic illnesses (musculoskeletal, heart-lung, stroke, cancer, and gastrointestinal) which may contribute to pain.

Demographics. Based on prior research, older respondents and women were expected to report greater frequency and intensity of pain. In addition, education and income were considered personal resources which may diminish the experience and report of pain, due in part to better use of analgesics and the better medical care of more educated and affluent respondents. Married respondents were expected to report less pain than their unmarried counterparts.

Chronic Illness. We anticipated that respondents reporting a larger number of chronic illnesses and those reporting specific types of illness, such as musculoskeletal conditions, would exhibit more pain than those elderly without such health conditions.

Consequences of Pain

Psychological Well-Being. In considering social and psychological sequelae of pain, our focus was on expanding the traditional emphasis of pain–depression linkages and to consider, instead, a broad array of indicators of psychological distress and well-being. Well-being indicators range from depressive symptoms to positive and negative affect, self-esteem, and cognitive life satisfaction. In addition, we considered the relationship of pain reported to domain-specific satisfaction in the areas of marriage, paid helpers, and medical care. All three of these categories related to key providers of care giving and social support.

Disability. Guided by elements of the physical impairment–disability linkages in the cascade model (Figure 9-1), we can broaden consideration of outcomes associated with pain (representing impairment) to include disability—both social and personal. These links reflect one important component of a model of successful aging developed by the authors (Kahana & Kahana, 1996). This model postulates that outcomes of successful aging, in addition to psychological well-being, include the maintenance of valued social relationships and activities. Successfully aging individuals were expected to maintain both social functioning and psychological well-being even in the face of normative stressors of aging such as chronic illness.

Based on the cascade model (Figure 9-1), we further hypothesize that social and personal disability will serve as *intervening variables* in the effects of pain on psychological well-being. That is, at least part of the reason pain has an effect on psychological, well-being is that pain increases social and personal disability, which, in turn, reduces psychological well-being (Williamson & Schulz, 1992).

Specification of Pain's Relationship with Antecedent and Outcome Variables

In addition to expanding our understanding of pain and psychological well-being by focusing on a broad spectrum of social and psychological outcomes, our research aimed to provide a more differentiated view of pain as an independent variable, with regard to both *types* of pain (intensity vs. frequency) and the *shape* of its relationships (linear vs. nonlinear) with antecedent and outcome variables. Accordingly, we considered the linear relationship (correlation) between psychological well-being and both the intensity and frequency of pain reported by older persons. Our purpose here was to determine whether the two types of pain would show a similar pattern of relationships with antecedent and outcome variables. If so, then we would have support for combining the intensity and frequency measures of pain into a single composite scale. Furthermore, we assessed the linear versus nonlinear shape of the relationship between pain and its antecedents and consequences to discern whether there might be certain levels of pain that were most reactive to antecedent variables or had the strongest effects on outcome variables.

METHODS

Sample

The data derive from the second annual wave of an eight-year longitudinal study that includes face-to-face interviews of an initial, randomly selected sample ($N = 1{,}000$) of elderly individuals living in three retirement communities located in the center of Florida. The environment of the retirement communities studied is oriented toward activity-based living, affording residents many recreational and social opportunities. In order to qualify for the study, respondents had to be 72 years of age or older, in good health, and living in Florida at least nine months of the year. Of those individuals meeting selection criteria, 86.6% agreed to be interviewed at time one. The study sample consisted of 804 respondents participating in the study during wave two.

Age of respondents ranged from 71 to 98 years with a mean age of 80.3. Education of respondents ranged from 1 to 23 years with a mean of 13.4 years. Median income of respondents was in the range of $20,000–$25,000. The majority of the elderly residents had migrated from the midwest. Diverse occupational backgrounds were represented, including teachers, tradespeople, executives, and entrepreneurs. All respondents are Caucasian, with 65.7% female, 47% married, 46.5% widowed, and 82% who rated their health as excellent with only 2% rating their health as poor or very poor.

Measures

The causal ordering of variables in the cascade model (Figure 9-1) relative to pain organizes our description of measures of the model's components. We start with pain (as an index of impairment) and then describe those variables antecedent to pain (demographic measures and chronic illness). Next, we describe measures of pain sequelae that the cascade model proposes as the most immediate outcomes of pain: social and personal disability. Last, we describe measures that the model indicates are the final outcomes of pain: psychological well-being.

Impairment. **Pain** was assessed using two closed-ended questions. The first item inquired about respondents' *frequency of pain* from all sources during the past year (based on a 5-point scale), whereas the second item inquired about *pain intensity* (based on a 10-point scale). A third measure, of *composite pain*, included the sum of the *Z* scores for the frequency and intensity of pain items. These three measures formed the basis of our bivariate analyses, and the composite pain scale was used for the subsequent regression-based path analysis of the cascade model.

Antecedent Variables. Demographic variables and chronic illness comprised the antecedent variables of pain. **Demographic variables** included age, sex, income, education, and marital status. *Age* was coded based on self-reported number of years old. *Income* included interval categories of approximately $10,000 increments. *Marital status* was coded as married (1) and unmarried (0). Gender was coded as female (1) and male (0).

Chronic illness was assessed using the Older American Resources and Services (OARS) inventory (Fillenbaum, 1978), which asked respondents to indicate whether they had been diagnosed as having any one or more of 25 chronic illnesses and disorders. The OARS Chronic Illness Index was selected for inclusion based on its widespread use in the field and documented psychometric properties among elderly respondents (Mangen & Peterson, 1982). Chronic illnesses were categorized into five clusters relevant to prior research on pain and aging. Accordingly, *musculoskeletal conditions* were aggregated, including arthritis, osteoporosis, and orthopedic problems. A second chronic illness cluster was created including *cardiovascular and pulmonary conditions*, such as heart disease, circulatory problems, asthma, and emphysema. A third category included *gastrointestinal problems*, ranging from ulcers to liver disease. In addition, two illnesses (i.e., *cancer* and *stroke*) were analyzed separately because of their overwhelming and catastrophic quality.

Outcome Variables. Disability and psychological well-being comprised the outcome variables of pain. **Disability** included two separate measures. *Personal disability* was assessed by using the ADL and IADL subscales of the OARS inventory (Fillenbaum, 1978). Respondents were asked to indicate how much difficulty they had in performing self-care and home maintenance tasks without assistance from others. Cronbach's alpha for the ADL–IADL scale was .93. *Social disability* was assessed by an index developed by the authors. It is based on the frequency with which the respondents engage in a variety of valued social activities. These activities range from hobbies to social participation and leisure pursuits.

Psychological well-being included five measures: a shortened version of the Center for Epidemiological Studies–Depression Scale (CES-D) shortened versions of the Positive Affect and Negative Affect subscales (PANAS) of Diener's measure of Cognitive Life Satisfaction; a shortened version of the Rosenberg Self-Esteem Scale, and three measures of domain-specific satisfactions, including marital satisfaction, satisfaction with medical care, and satisfaction with paid help.

Our measure of *depression* consisted of 10 of the original 20 items in the CES-D (Radloff, 1977). The 10-item composite measure displayed an alpha reliability in our sample of .83, a mean of 18.5, a standard deviation of 5.4, and a range of 10–43. *Positive affect* (PA) and *negative affect* (NA) each included 5 items (rated on 5-point Likert scales) from the original two 10-item subscales of the PANAS (Watson, Clark, & Tellegen, 1988). In the current study, the PA and NA subscales have respective overall alphas of .78 and .83, means of 15.6 and 8.8, standard deviations of 2.9 and 3.4, and ranges of 5–25 and 5–24, respectively. *Self-esteem* was measured by a four-item index based on Rosenberg's Self-Esteem Scale (1978). This scale had a Cronbach's alpha of .69. *Cognitive life satisfaction* was measured with the Satisfaction with Life Scale (Diener, Emmons, Larsen, & Griffin, 1985), a five-item index. Each item reflects a 5-point Likert scale, wherein respondents endorse statements such as "In most ways my life is close to my ideal." Cronbach's alpha for cognitive life satisfaction was .80. Finally, domain-specific satisfactions were assessed through three single-item, 5-point Likert scales regarding *satisfaction with marriage, satisfaction with paid help*, and *satisfaction with medical care* (primary physician).

RESULTS

Univariate Data

In terms of intensity of pain reported, 49.4% reported experiencing little or no pain, 33.1% reported having some pain, and 17.4% reported experiencing a great deal of pain. In terms of frequency of experiencing pain, 17.5% indicated never or very seldom having pain, 58.9% reported having pain on some occasions, and 22.9% reported being in pain always or most of the time.

In terms of our five chronic illness clusters, musculoskeletal problems were most common, with 55.5% reporting such ailments. These were followed by heart and lung problems reported by 24.9%. Far fewer respondents reported gastrointestinal problems (4.2%), cancer (2.5%), or stroke (0.6%).

Specification of Bivariate Relationships between Pain and Its Antecedents and Consequences

Tables 9-1 and 9-2 provides Pearson correlations between three measures of pain (frequency, intensity, and composite pain) and their antecedents and consequences.

Table 9-1. Specification of Bivariate Correlations between Pain and Its Antecedents

	Pain			
Antecedents	Frequency of pain	Intensity of pain	Composite of pain	Composite of pain with nonlinear (quadratic) relations
Demographics				
Age	−.02	.01	−.01	.01
	(N = 889)	(N = 881)	(N = 881)	(N = 881)
Sex	−.02	−.02	−.02	N/A[a]
	(N = 889)	(N = 881)	(N = 881)	(N = 881)
Income	−.06	−.06	−.06	.07
	(N = 889)	(N = 881)	(N = 881)	(N = 881)
Marital status	.07[b]	.03	.06	N/A
	(N = 889)	(N = 881)	(N = 881)	(N = 881)
Education	−.05	−.06	−.06	.06
	(N = 889)	(N = 881)	(N = 881)	(N = 881)
Chronic illness				
Musculoskeletal	.33[c]	.30[c]	.34[c]	N/A
	(N = 889)	(N = 881)	(N = 881)	(N = 881)
Stroke	−.03	−.05	−.04	N/A
	(N = 889)	(N = 881)	(N = 881)	(N = 881)
Cancer	.02	−.01	.01	N/A
	(N = 889)	(N = 881)	(N = 881)	(N = 881)
Heart–lung	.14[c]	.10[d]	.13[c]	N/A
	(N = 889)	(N = 881)	(N = 881)	(N = 881)
Gastrointestinal	.10[d]	.06	.09[d]	N/A
	(N = 889)	(N = 881)	(N = 881)	(N = 881)

[a]NA, not applicable.
[b]$p < .05$.
[c]$p < .001$.
[d]$p < .01$.

Table 9-2. Specification of Bivariate Correlations between Pain and Its Consequences

Pain	Consequences									
	Disability		Psychological well-being							
	Social disability	Personal disability (ADL/IADL)	Positive affect	Negative affect	Depression	Life satisfaction	Self-esteem	Medical care satisfaction	Marital satisfaction	Paid help satisfaction
Pain measures										
Frequency of pain	.25[a] ($N = 856$)	.15[a] ($N = 888$)	−.15[a] ($N = 889$)	.21[a] ($N = 889$)	.20[a] ($N = 865$)	−.14[a] ($N = 889$)	.11[a] ($N = 889$)	−.09[c] ($N = 889$)	−.07 ($N = 399$)	−.04 ($N = 433$)
Intensity of pain	.19[a] ($N = 856$)	.11[a] ($N = 881$)	−.07[b] ($N = 881$)	.23[a] ($N = 881$)	.19[a] ($N = 857$)	−.10[c] ($N = 881$)	−.09[c] ($N = 881$)	−.10 ($N = 881$)	.05 ($N = 399$)	.02 ($N = 433$)
Composite of pain	.24[a] ($N = 856$)	.13[a] ($N = 881$)	−.10[c] ($N = 881$)	.23[a] ($N = 881$)	.21[a] ($N = 857$)	−.12[c] ($N = 881$)	.10[c] ($N = 881$)	−.10[c] ($N = 881$)	−.06 ($N = 399$)	−.004 ($N = 433$)
Composite of pain with nonlinear (quadratic) relations	.24 ($N = 856$)	.19 ($N = 881$)	.14 ($N = 881$)	.24 ($N = 881$)	.22 ($N = 857$)	−.15 ($N = 881$)	−.11 ($N = 881$)	−.16 ($N = 881$)	−.07 ($N = 399$)	−.06 ($N = 433$)

[a] $p < .001$.
[b] $p < .05$.
[c] $p < .01$.

Here, we wished to assess whether the two measures displayed similar correlates and, thus, whether there was justification for creating a composite scale of pain. Additionally, we assessed whether the composite pain scale formed nonlinear (quadratic) relationships with the other antecedent and outcome variables. Researchers typically assume linear relationships between pain and its correlates. However, assessing potential nonlinear relationships provided us with evidence of whether certain ranges of pain (e.g., from low to medium or, alternatively, from medium to high) were more likely to be influenced by antecedent variables or, conversely, to influence outcome variables.

The results in Tables 9-1 and 9-2 suggest that intensity and frequency of pain have a similar pattern of correlations with antecedent and outcome variables. In other words, the two pain measures behave in a similar fashion in their pattern of relationships with other variables and, thus, appear to be tapping the same underlying, single dimension of pain. A more focused analysis of bivariate results follows below, divided by antecedent variables (demographics and chronic illness) and outcome variables of pain (disability and psychological well-being).

Antecedent Variables. Among the five demographic variables (age, gender, income, education, and marital status), there are generally no statistically significant correlations with the frequency, intensity, and composite pain measures. Marital status shows a weak and barely statistically significant correlation with frequency of pain ($r =$ .07, $p < .05$). However, given that 15 correlations are examined, this single significant finding is likely due to sampling error.

Among the five chronic illness types, only musculoskeletal displays strong correlations with the frequency, intensity, and composite pain measures (r = .3 or greater). Heart-lung and gastrointestinal display statistical significant but weak correlations with pain (.13, $p < .001$ and .09, $p < .01$, respectively). Stroke and cancer show no statistically significant relationships to pain.

Outcome Variables. Correlations of the pain variables generally were found to be stronger with the outcome variables than with the antecedent variables. Social disability shows correlations ranging between $r = .19$ (for intensity of pain) and $r = .25$ (for frequency of pain). Personal disability displays weaker but consistently statistically significant correlations ($p < .05$) ranging from $r = .11$ to $r = .15$.

Among psychological well-being outcomes, depression and negative affect correlate most strongly with the three pain measures, with r's ranging from .19 to .23. Positive affect, cognitive life satisfaction, and self-esteem display somewhat weaker but still statistically significant ($p < .01$) correlations, ranging from $-.07$ (intensity of pain–PA) to $-$ .15 (Frequency of pain–PA). Finally, among the three domain-specific satisfactions, satisfaction with medical care shows consistently significant ($p < .01$) but weak correlations with the three pain measures (r's of .09 to .10). Marital satisfaction and satisfaction with paid help, however, show no statistically significant ($p > .05$) correlations with the pain measure.

Summary of Bivariate Correlations with Pain. Given that the intensity and frequency measures of pain generally show similar patterns of correlations with antecedent and outcomes variables, the results of the present study would support forming a composite scale from the two items. Our results also suggest, however, that the composite pain scale does not display substantially larger correlations with antecedents and consequences of pain than do the two separate indicators of pain.

Additionally, our bivariate results do not provide much support for nonlinear relationships between pain and its antecedents and sequelae. That is, there do not appear to be specific ranges in the level of pain that are likely to have especially strong links to antecedents and consequences. Across 73 comparison, the biggest difference between the linear versus quadratic relationship between composite pain and its correlates occurs for personal disability, with respective *r*'s of .13 (linear relation) and .19 (quadratic relation). Accordingly, our results would appear to support the untested assumption of prior research that pain forms a linear relationship with its correlates.

Examining the Role of Pain in the Cascade Model

Using a path analytic model, we analyzed the role of pain in the context of the cascade model (Figure 9-1), which includes a proposed causal sequence in which antecedent variables of demographic characteristics and chronic illnesses affect pain, and in turn, pain affects sequelae of disability and psychological well-being. Our analysis included a fully "saturated" model in which we included tests for all possible paths between a given variable and any variables antecedent to that variable. Specifically, we initially regressed each dimension of psychological well-being on all variables antecedent to these outcomes. Accordingly, we simultaneously entered the independent variables of social and personal disability, pain, five dimensions of chronic illness, and five demographic variables into separate regression analyses for each of the eight dimensions of psychological well-being. In this manner, we could determine the direct effect of each predictor variable, controlling for all other predictors. We then moved forward in the cascade model to the next most subsequent set of variables (i.e., social and personal disability) and regressed each of these dimensions of disability on all variables antecedent to them. We followed this same sequence of steps to assess predictors of pain, and then predictors of each of the five chronic illnesses.

Figure 9-2 displays the results of our path analysis. Only statistically significant ($p < .05$) paths are displayed. We report results first for antecedents of pain, then for consequences of pain.

Antecedents of Pain

Demographic variables display consistently weak relationships to pain and other variables in the cascade model. What little impact age, sex, and marital status have on pain occurs only indirectly through the intervening variable of musculoskeletal disease. Income has a weak negative direct effect on pain (beta = −.08). Education has no direct or indirect effect on pain. Nor does education have a direct or indirect effect on any other variable in the cascade model. Likewise, the other four demographic variables display few (and always weak) direct and indirect effects on other variables in the cascade in addition to pain.

The five chronic illnesses also display generally weak or nonexistent effects on pain and other variables further down the cascade: all but one beta coefficient for effects of chronic illnesses is below .15. The notable exception to this pattern of results is the substantial direct effect of musculoskeletal disease on pain (beta = .32), a result consistent with our expectations that this specific chronic illness would display the strongest effect on pain. The absence of any direct or indirect effects for stroke (or of any effects of demographics on stroke), however, is very likely an artifact of the very restricted number of persons who have strokes in this healthy aged population.

Outcomes of Pain

Pain has effects on both dimensions of disability: weakly on personal disability (beta = .12) and moderately on social disability (beta = .21). Furthermore, pain has a relatively large number of direct and indirect effects on psychological well-being. Pain's strongest effects occur via a direct path to negative affect (beta = .23) and depression (beta = .19). Additionally, pain displays a weak direct effect on medical care satisfaction (beta = .10) and very weak indirect effects on positive affect and cognitive life satisfaction via the intervening variables of social and personal disability. In sum, the pattern of results suggests that, among the set of variables examined in the cascade model, pain is the most important predictor of the depression and negative affect dimensions of psychological well-being.

Finally, turning to causal linkages among the various outcomes of pain, we see that personal disability, weakly affected by the antecedent variable, has weak or nonexistent effects on all dimensions of psychological well-being. Among only three statistically significant ($p < .05$) direct effects, the betas are $-.07$, $-.07$, and $-.10$ for, respectively, personal disability, cognitive life satisfaction, and satisfaction with paid help. Conversely, social disability does display a substantial direct effect on positive affect (beta $= -.32$). It also has a weak direct effect on cognitive life satisfaction (beta = .15) and self-esteem (beta = $-.07$).

DISCUSSION

Our data provide valuable preliminary evidence about the important role of pain in the proposed cascade from chronic illness to physical impairment, social disability, and psychological distress. Our findings provide strong support for previously noted relationships between pain (as a form of physical impairment) and reduced psychological well-being.

In this community-dwelling population of old-old individuals, musculoskeletal conditions are both the most frequent forms of chronic illness and the ones most strongly associated with reports of pain. Furthermore, our findings underscore the value of expanding the consideration of psychosocial sequelae of pain beyond the traditional

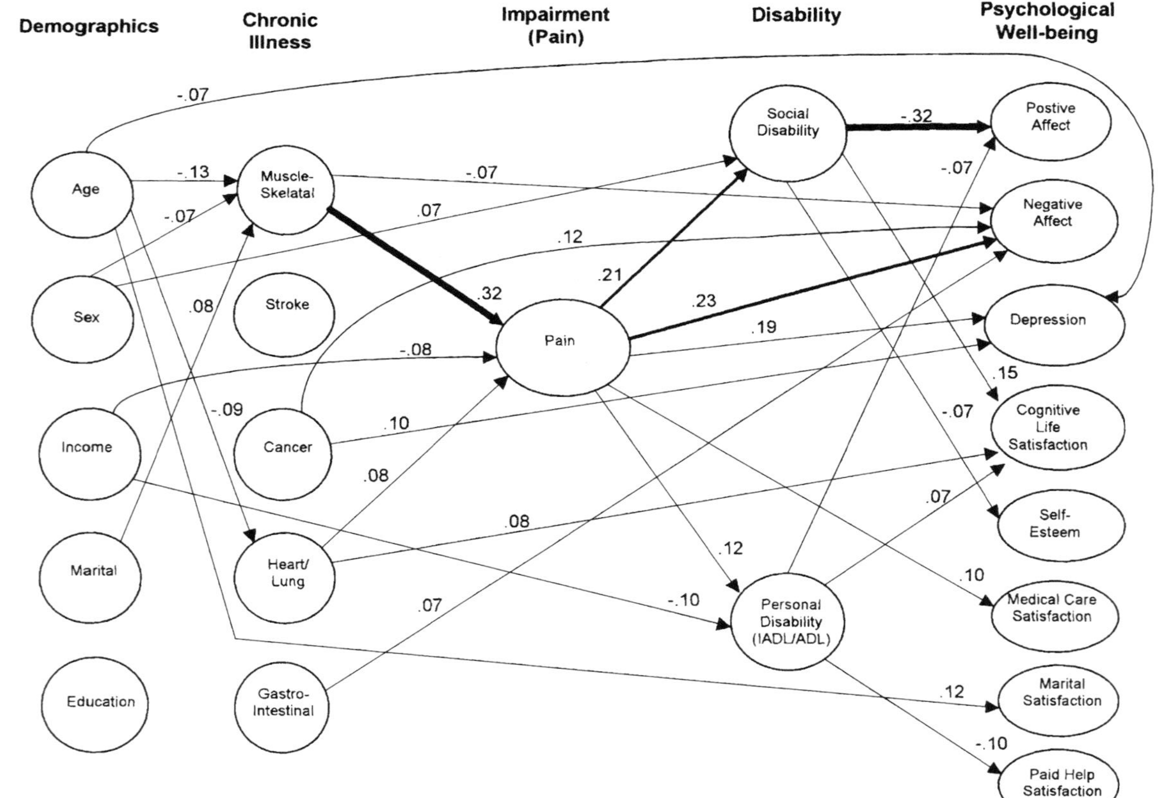

Figure 9-2. Standardized regression coefficients (betas) for the cascade model (path analysis). Only statistically significant paths ($p < .05$) are shown. Thickness of arrows denotes effect sizes, where: → < .15; ➞, paths are > .15 but < .30; ➡, paths are > .30.

focus on depression. Thus, studies of sequelae of pain need to include other dimensions of psychological well-being, as well as outcomes encompassing the ability to perform ADLs and valued social activities. Pain was found to be a moderately strong predictor of social disability and at least a weak predictor of personal disability. Furthermore, pain emerged as a moderately strong predictor of both depression, as measured by the CES-D, and negative affect, as measured by the PANAS. On the other hand, positive affect was only indirectly influenced (via disability) by pain. It is noteworthy that both personal and social disability impacted on positive affect. Thus, pain had a small but consistent indirect influence on expressions of positive affect via restrictions on social activities and limitations on ADLs and IADLs. It is also noteworthy that pain displayed such a distinctive pattern of stronger effects on negative moods (depression and NA), and much weaker effects on positive moods (PA). Our results provide further support for the claim that positive and negative moods are distinctive phenomena with distinct predictors. Consequently, they should not be combined into a single measure of "psychological well-being."

Our research also lends support to the importance of musculoskeletal disease in explaining pain among community-dwelling elderly, thus supporting the work of Hughes, Edelman, Singer, and Chang (1993). It is also noteworthy that other illnesses were found to influence psychological well-being directly, although weakly, without pain as an intervening process. Accordingly, cancer had an impact on both negative affect and depression. This influence, however, was not mediated by pain. Other mechanisms, such as the challenges presented by the life-threatening nature of cancer and its impact on the patient's identity and world outlook may be responsible for its contribution to depression and negative affect (Deimling, Kahana, Schumacher, 1994).

Demographic Antecedents of Pain

In our sample, neither age, gender, income, nor education were found to be significantly associated with pain in our bivariate analyses, despite our large sample size. Income, however, was a significant but weak predictor of pain ($r = .08$, $p < .05$). In considering our multivariate path analysis of the cascade model, which includes controls for other elements in the model, we did find that age, sex, and marital status had weak indirect effects on pain via the intervening variable of musculoskeletal disease. Furthermore, income displayed a small but statistically significant direct negative effect on pain. Particularly noteworthy in our sample is the absence of any bivariate and only very weak multivariate relationships between gender and pain. In interpreting these findings, which are at variance with results of prior research, we should note that the relationship between pain and gender generally has been observed in younger populations and in situations demanding responses to immediate and acute pain. It is possible that older women have developed coping strategies which help them minimize the impact of normative chronic pain, such as pain associated with arthritis and other musculoskeletal conditions of later life.

Much of the research exploring the antecedents and social correlates of pain tends to be descriptive and largely atheoretical in nature. However, there are some promising attempts toward developing a more conceptually meaningful understanding of the complex interactions between biological, psychological, and social factors in both the etiology and the functional consequences of pain. Thus, VonKurff et al. (1988) have developed a dynamic ecological model to inform research on causes and consequences of chronic pain. Their model suggests that physiological, psychological, and social factors may interact in different ways and at different life stages in the expression of pain-related dysfunction. They also suggest that the environmental and ecological context of pain receive greater consideration. Our study has taken an important step toward placing pain in a broader framework of the disability cascade. Confirmation of the linkages between pain and social functioning allows greater understanding of the social and psychological contexts within which pain is embedded during later life.

Limitations and Directions for Future Research

Placing pain in the framework of the disability cascade constitutes a useful step in conceptualizing this critical impairment. Our model stops short of operationalizing the complex interactions which are likely to help further explicate the disability cascade. Accordingly, the progression from chronic illness to impairment and from impairment to social and psychological disability is likely to be buffered by proactive adaptation which activates social and personal resources (Kahana & Kahana, 1996). It is likely that demographic factors, which did not show a prominent influence in our simplified model, exert their major influence by impacting on these social and psychological adaptations. Research currently under way by the authors will address the issue of the role of buffers in the cascade model.

Our model, which has been tested in a cross-sectional design, suggests a parsimonious and logical sequence of causal linkages, which is largely anchored in prior research findings. However, we should note that alternative causal pathways may be proposed in considering some of the key elements of the model. Such reciprocal causal influences (e.g., depression contributing to pain) must await testing in a longitudinal framework.

Demonstration of the relationship of pain-related impairment to other elements of the chronic illness disability cascade makes a useful contribution to our understanding of the ways in which chronic illness impacts on quality of life among community-dwelling old-old persons. Our study also presents a hopeful picture of older adults experiencing pain but nevertheless maintaining independent lifestyles in spite of chronic illness and attendant impairments.

REFERENCES

All, A. C. (1994). Current concepts and management of cancer pain in older women. In K. A. Roberto (Ed.), *Older women with chronic pain*. New York: Harrington Park Press.

Borowski, E., Kinney, J., & Kahana, E. (1996). The meaning of older adults' health appraisals: Congruence with health status and determinant of mortality. *Journal of Gerontology*, *51B*, S157–S170.

Brintnell, E. S., Madill, H. M., Montgomerie, T. C., & Stewin, L. L. (1992). Work and family issues after injury: Do female and male client perspectives differ? *Career Development Quarterly, 41*(2), 145–160.

Deimling, G. T., Kahana, B., & Schumacher, J. (1994). Life-threatening illness and physical and mental health of older adults. *The Gerontologist Program Abstracts, 47th Annual Scientific Meeting, Special Issue, 34*(1), 225.

Dekker, J., Tola, P., Aufdemkampe, G., & Winkers, M. (1993). Negative affect, pain, and disability in osteoarthritis patients: The mediating role of muscle weakness. *Behaviour Research and Therapy, 31*(2), 203–206.

Diener, E., Emmons, R. A., Larsen, R. J., & Griffin, S. (1985). The satisfaction with life scale. *Journal of Personality Assessment, 49*, 71–75.

Engle, G. (1962). *Psychological development in health and disease*. Philadelphia: Saunders.

Faucett, J., Gordon, N., & Levine, J. (1994). Differences in postoperative pain severity among four ethnic groups. *Journal of Pain and Symptom Management, 9*(6), 383–389.

Felton, B. J., & Revenson, T. A. (1984). Age differences in coping with chronic illness. *Psychology in Aging, 2*(2), 164–170.

Ferrell, B. A., Ferrell, B. R., & Osterweil, D. A. (1990). Pain in the nursing home. *Journal of the American Geriatrics Society, 38*, 409–414.

Fillenbaum, G. G. (1978). *Multidimensional functional assessment: The OARS methodology* (2nd ed.). Durham, NC: Duke University Press.

Ford, A. B., Folmar, S. J., Salmon, R. B., Medalie, J. H., Roy, A. W., & Galazka, S. S. (1988). Health and function on the old and the very old. *Journal of the American Geriatrics Society, 36*(3), 187–197.

Fox, N. R., Sittig, M., Dorris, G., & Breisinger, G. (1994). An analysis of the relationship of gender and age to MMPI scores of patients with chronic pain. *Journal of Clinical Psychology, 50*(4), 537–554.

France, C., Adler, P. S., France, J., & Ditto, B. (1994). Family history of hypertension and pain during blood donation. *Psychosomatic Medicine, 56*(1), 52–60.

Fried, L. P., Herdman, S. J., Kuhn, K. E., Rubin, G., & Turano, K. (1991). Preclinical disability: Hypotheses about the bottom of the iceberg. *Journal of Aging and Health, 3*(2), 285–300.

Gold, D. T. (1994). Chronic musculoskeletal pain: Older women and their coping strategies. In K. A. Roberto (Ed.), *Older women with chronic pain*. New York: Harrington Park Press.

Harkins, S. W., & Price, D. D. (1992). Assessment of pain in the elderly. In D. C. Turk & R. Melzack (Eds.), *Handbook of pain assessment* (pp. 315–331). New York: Guilford Press.

Hughes, S., Edelman, P., Singer, R., & Chang, R. (1993). Joint impairment and self-reported disability in elderly persons. *Journal of Gerontology, 48*, s84–s92.

Jensen, I., Nygren, A., Gamberale, F., & Goldie, I. (1994). Coping with long-term musculoskeletal pain and its consequences: Is gender a factor? *Pain, 57*(2), 167–172.

Jette, A. M., Branch, L. G., & Berlin, J. (1990). Musculoskeletal impairments and physical disablement among the aged. *Journal of Gerontology: Medical Sciences, 45*(6), M203–M208.

Kahana, B., Kercher, K., Kahana, E., & Namazi, K. (1995). Mild cognitive impairment and accuracy of survey responses of the old-old. *Proceedings of the AHCPR Methodology Conference*, Denver, August.

Kahana, E., & Kahana, B. (1996). A preventive model of successful aging. In V. Bengtson (Ed.), *Continuities and discontinuities in the life span* (pp. 18–41). New York: Springer.

Kasl, S. (1992). Stress and health among the elderly: Overview of issues. In M. Wykle, E. Kahana, & J. Kowal (Eds.), *Stress and health among the elderly*. New York: Springer.

Kenshalo, D. (1977). Age changes in touch, vibration, temperature, kinesthesis, and pain sensitivity. In J. E. Birren & K. W. Schaie (Eds.), *Handbook of the psychology of aging* (1st ed., pp. 562–610). New York: Van Nostrand Reinhold.

Kercher, K. (1992). Assessing subjective well-being in the old-old. *Research on Aging, 14*(2), 131–168.

Larson, R. (1978). Thirty years of research on the subjective well-being of older Americans. *Journal of Gerontology, 33*, 109–129.

Lawton, M. P. (1983). Environment and other determinants of well-being in older persons. *The Gerontologist, 23*, 349–357.

Maslow, A. (1970). *Motivation and personality* (2nd ed.). New York: Harper & Row.

Moss, M. S., Lawton, M. P., & Glicksman, A. (1991). The role of pain in the last year of life of older persons. *Journal of Gerontology, 46*(2), 51–52.

Nagi, S. Z. (1990). Disability concepts revisited: Implications for prevention. In A. M. Pope & A. R. Tarlov (Eds.), *Disability in America: A national agenda for prevention (Appendix A)*. Washington, DC: National Academy Press.

Olshansky, S. J., Rudberg, M. A., Carnes, B. A., Cassel, C. K., & Brody, J. A. (1991). Trading off longer life for worsening health: The expansion of morbidity hypothesis. *Journal of Aging and Health, 3*(2), 194–216.

Parmelee, P. A. (1994). Assessment of pain in the elderly. In M. P. Lawton & J. A. Teresi (Eds.), *Annual review of gerontology and geriatrics: Focus on assessment techniques* (pp. 281–301). New York: Springer.

Parmelee, P. A., Katz, I. R., & Lawton, M. P. (1989). Depression among institutionalized aged: Assessment and prevalence estimation. *Journals of Gerontology: Medical Sciences, 41*, M22–M29.

Parmelee, P. A., Katz, I. R., & Lawton, M. P. (1991). The relation of pain to depression among institutionalized aged. *Journals of Gerontology, 46*, P15–P21.

Parmelee, P. A., Smith, B. D., & Katz, I. R. (1993). Pain complaints and cognitive status among elderly institution residents. *Journal of the American Geriatrics Society, 41*, 517–522.

Pfeiffer, E. (1975). *Multidimensional functional assessment: The OARS methodology*. Durham, NC: Center for the Study of Aging and Human Development, Duke University.

Radloff, L. (1977). The CES-D scale: A self-report depression scale for research in the general population. *Applied Psychological Measurement, 1*, 385–401.

Rapin, C. H. (1991). The mechanism of pain memory in the elderly patient. *Journal of Palliative Care, 7*(4), 48–50.

Reuben, D. B., Laliberte, L., Hiris, J., & Mor, V. (1990). A hierarchical exercise scale to measure function at the advanced activities of daily living (AADL) level. *Journal of the American Geriatrics Society, 38*, 855–861.

Reuben, D. B., & Siu, A. L. (1990). An objective measure of physical function of elderly outpatients: The physical performance test. *Journal of the American Geriatrics Society, 38*, 1105–1112.

Roberto, K. A. (1994). *Older women with chronic pain*. Binghamton, NY: Harrington Park Press.

Romano, J. M., & Turner, J. A. (1985). Chronic pain and depression: Does the evidence support a relationship? *Psychological Bulletin, 97*, 18–34.

Rosenberg, M., & Pearlin, L. (1978). Social class and self-esteem among children and adults. *American Journal of Sociology, 84*, 53–87.

Special Committee on Aging, U.S. Senate. (1985). *Americans in transition: An aging society* (*1984–85 edition*). Washington, DC: Government Printing Office.

Thomas, M. R., & Roy, R. (1988). Age and pain: A comparative study of the "younger and older" elderly. *Pain Management* (July/August), 174–179.

Trief, P. M., Elliott, D. J., Stein, N., & Frederickson, B. E. (1987). Functional vs. organic pain: A meaningful distinction? *Journal of Clinical Psychology, 43*, 219–226.

Verbrugge, L. M. (1990). The iceberg of disability. In S. Stahl (Ed.), *The legacy of longevity: Health and health care in later life* (pp. 55–75). Newbury Park, CA: Sage.

Verbrugge, L. M. (1991). Survival curves, prevalence rates, and dark matters therein. *Journal of Aging and Health, 3*(2), 217–236.

Von Korff, M., Dworkin, S. F., LeResche, L., & Kruger, A. (1988). An epidemiological comparison of pain complaints. *Pain, 32*, 173–183.

Watson, D., Clark, L., & Tellegen, A. (1988). Development and validation of brief measures of positive and negative affect: The PANAS scales. *Journal of Personality and Social Psychology, 54*(6), 1063–1070.

Williams, M. E., Hadler, N. M., & Earp, J. A. (1990). Timed manual performance in a community elderly population. *Journal of the American Geriatrics Society, 38*, 1120–1126.

Williamson, G. M., & Schulz, R. (1992). Pain, activity restriction, and symptoms of depression among community-residing elderly adults. *Journal of Gerontology, 47*(6), 367–372.

Woodrow, K. M., Friedman, G. D., Siegalaug, A. B., & Collen, M. F. (1972). Pain tolerance: Differences according to age, sex, and race. *Psychosomatic Medicine, 34*, 548–556.

World Health Organization. (1980). *International classification of impairments, disabilities, and handicaps*. Geneva: Author.

Zarit, S., & Zarit, J. M. (1983). Cognitive impairment. In P. Lewishon & L. Teri (Eds.), *Clinical geropsychology*. New York: Pergamon Press.

CHAPTER 10

Pain and Psychological Function in Late Life

Patricia A. Parmelee

Perhaps the most creative of ongoing attempts to resolve the conundrum of objectively defining an internal event is McCaffrey's (1979) often-cited statement that "pain is whatever the experiencing person says it is and exists whenever he says it does" (p. 8). This delightfully obtuse definition is an especially appropriate introduction to this chapter because it telegraphs the inherently phenomenological nature of pain. Psychological processes are inextricable from pain experience across the life span, but they may be especially crucial to understanding pain in late life. Aging almost inevitably brings with it some aches and pains, but the experience and effects of pain vary markedly across individuals. Of course, some sources of this diversity are quite obvious; the most notable is health status. But as we shall soon see, objective factors account for only a small portion of variability in pain and its effects. Psychological factors play an equal and perhaps even greater role in shaping the experience, expression, and effects of pain among older adults.

This chapter offers an overview of the psychological correlates of and the influences on the experience and expression of pain among older adults. To render this admittedly ambitious goal manageable, I shall focus on three major issues. First, to place existing knowledge of late-life pain in psychological context, it will be useful to examine some general social and cognitive processes that may influence older persons' experience and reporting of pain. Second, considerable attention will be given to the association of pain with mood and emotional disorders, specifically, depression and anxiety. Finally, I shall address the critical but thus far shamefully understudied question of pain and cognitive impairment among older persons.

Patricia A. Parmelee • Polish Research Institute, Philadelphia Geriatric Center, Philadelphia, Pennsylvania 19141.

Handbook of Pain and Aging, edited by David I. Mostofsky and Jacob Lomranz. Plenum Press, New York, 1997.

Before delving into these issues, it will be helpful briefly to review a few conceptual points in the nongerontological literature. In particular, general knowledge of the role of physiological versus psychological processes in pain forms a crucial backdrop against which to interpret psychological influences on pain and its expression among older persons.

PAIN AS A PSYCHOLOGICAL PHENOMENON

Our introductory definition notwithstanding, the International Association for the Study of Pain has formally defined pain as "an unpleasant *sensory and emotional experience* associated with actual or potential tissue damage or described in terms of such damage" (Merskey & Bogduk, 1994, p. 210; emphasis added). I have emphasized the phrase *sensory and emotional experience* to highlight once again the fact that pain is inherently a psychological phenomenon. Physiological damage—actual, potential, or imagined—may be the stimulus, but the pain process itself is one of sensation and perception of, motivation to avoid, and affective response to that stimulus.

Indeed, attempts to quantify pain in terms of precisely calibrated stimuli and physiological responses thereto have generally met with limited success. The most basic evidence for this is, of course, laboratory work that has demonstrated tremendous individual differences in thresholds for and tolerance of standard pain stimuli (see review by Wolff, 1983). Physiological measures of pain such as electromyograms similarly correspond only roughly to experienced pain (see review by Flor, Miltner, & Birbaumer, 1992). In a more clinical context, there is no direct correspondence between anatomical state and subjective report of pain among many chronic pain populations. For example, studies of persons with rheumatoid and osteoarthritis (Hagglund, Haley, Reville, & Alarcon, 1989; Hannan, Anderson, Pincus, & Felson, 1992; Keefe et al., 1987) have yielded surprisingly small correlations between pain and objectively assessed indices of disease severity (e.g., serum indicators of inflammatory processes; radiographic evidence of joint inflammation or degeneration). The same is true of cancer pain (Greenwald, Bonica, & Bergner, 1987). In fact, pain can occur in the absence of any observable physical cause. This phenomenon of functional (as opposed to organic) pain is quite well documented; as yet, however, it defies physiological explanation (see Trief, Elliott, Stein, & Frederickson, 1987, for review and discussion). On the other hand, persons may sustain remarkable physical effects of disease or trauma without experiencing any pain at all (see Fernandez & Turk, 1992).

Beyond these gross issues of psychophysiology, other conceptual issues in defining and assessing pain similarly underscore its foundation in basic psychological processes. One needs only to scan the widely used McGill Pain Questionnaire (Melzack, 1975) to appreciate the sensory subtleties of pain experience. The sizable literature on sensory versus affective components of pain (see Fernandez & Turk, 1992) reflects growing interest in how emotional responses shape and are influenced by the experience of painful stimuli. Indeed, there are now several instruments designed specifically to tap affective responses to and components of chronic pain (e.g., Jensen, Karoly & Harris,

1991). Behavioral pain processes, first explicated by Fordyce (1976), have been incorporated into a variety of research foci (e.g., Keefe & Block, 1982) and therapeutic approaches (see, for example, Wisocki & Powers, this volume, Chapter 17).

These basic issues are presented simply to emphasize the point that any discussion of pain and psychological function among older persons necessarily occurs in the presence of considerable conceptual "noise." Pain is patently a psychological process at any age, and many of the phenomena to be examined in this chapter are not unique to aging. On the other hand, physiological and psychosocial aging may color these phenomena, producing different effects in the elderly and younger adults. Unfortunately, the study of pain and psychological function in late life is in a stage of relative infancy compared to the nongerontological literature. As a result, it is difficult at times to determine whether research findings reflect age effects or simply extensions of universal psychological processes. Nonetheless, as we shall see, existing evidence clearly demonstrates the need explicitly to consider life stage when dealing with the psychological concomitants of pain.

PSYCHOSOCIAL INFLUENCES ON THE EXPERIENCE AND EXPRESSION OF PAIN AMONG OLDER ADULTS

A first, very relevant, question is whether aging affects persons' experience and expression of pain. Age differences in basic pain perception have been dealt with elsewhere in this volume (see Yehuda & Carasso, Chapter 2), as have questions of assessment and measurement (Gagliese & Melzack, Chapter 4). The following discussion, therefore, concentrates on social-psychological processes that affect and are affected by pain in late life.

Attitudes toward aging can affect not only persons' interpretations and experience of their own pain, but also other people's responses to pain complaints. Individuals interpret health symptoms of all sorts within the context of age, general health, and social roles (Leventhal & Prohaska, 1986). This can lead older persons to underreport significant pain. Some individuals may dismiss chronic aches and pains as intrinsic in aging and, consequently, not worth health care professionals' attention (Greenlee, 1991). Others, viewing pain as an omen of health decline, increased dependency, and invasive treatment for pain-related disorders, may purposely deny or deemphasize pain (Clinton & Eland, 1990). Severely ill persons may suppress pain complaints in order to avoid upsetting family members (Dar, Beach, Barden, & Cleeland, 1992; Ferrell, Rhiner, Cohen, & Grant, 1991).

Conversely, some older people may exaggerate or overemphasize pain. It has been suggested that pain complaints may be used to "cover" for functional deficits arising from cognitive impairment or other causes (Fordyce, 1978; McIntosh, 1990). In addition, Fordyce's (1976) early analysis of pain behavior suggested that pain complaints may be used to gain others' sympathy or maintain one's "sick role" in interpersonal relationships. More generally, he reasoned that overt behavioral expressions of pain, like any other operant, are susceptible to conditioning. Hence, they are differentially displayed or suppressed depending on their consequences. There is little research on this issue among older people specifically. However, a growing literature on mixed-age chronic pain patients documents a complex role of interpersonal relationships in moderating expressions of pain. Gil, Keefe, Crisson, and Van Dalfsen (1987), in an examination of general social support and pain behavior, found that the number of persons available to provide support was unrelated to observed pain behavior in a laboratory setting. However, persons who perceived their social networks as more supportive displayed higher rates of pain behavior. A number of studies of spouses' responses to pain behavior have directly confirmed the contingency of pain behavior on its interpersonal consequences (e.g., Block, Kremer, & Gaylor, 1980; Kerns, Haythornthwaite, Southwick, & Giller, 1990; Lousberg, Schmidt, & Groenman, 1992). On the other hand, Jamison and Virts's (1990) assessment of general family support indicated a *negative* association of family supportiveness with self-reported pain characteristics, distress, medication use, and a wide variety of lifestyle limitations. Summers, Rapoff, Varghese, Porter, and Palmer (1991) similarly found that pain patients who perceived that a significant other was nonsupportive rated their pain as more intense.

Conflicts among these studies are difficult to resolve because of the broad range of populations, measures, and methods used. However, it seems that divergent findings are due at least in part to assessment of subjective indicators of pain versus overt pain behavior. As Fordyce suggested, behavioral expressions of pain may come to operate at least somewhat independently of pain sensations, depending on interpersonal reinforcement contingencies. Hence, perceived lack of support may well intensify the experience of pain. But whether that translates to behavioral expressions of pain is likely to depend on whether the individual anticipates a rallying of support, lack of response, or even negative reactions from significant others.

As already noted, there has been little exploration of pain behavior and its interpersonal consequences specifically among older persons. However, the argument just set forth takes on added significance in light of existing knowledge of social stereotypes of aging. Evidence reviewed earlier suggests that older persons may self-censor pain complaints because of their own attitudes about aging and its effects. Similar processes may operate on an interpersonal level to shape other persons' reinforcement contingencies for expressions of pain.

Most of us have heard the joke about the elderly man's complaint of knee pain: When his physician responds that pain is to be expected in a knee that is 90 years old, the patients asks why it is, then, that his *other* 90-year-old knee is feeling just fine. Although it has been suggested that ageism may indeed lead health care professionals to dismiss (and hence, undertreat) pain among the elderly (Melding, 1991), there has been precious little empirical research on the issue. There is some evidence that elderly surgical patients receive less pain medication than younger individuals, even when subjective pain intensity and prescribed medications are the same across age groups (Faherty & Grier, 1984; Oberle, Paul, Wry, & Grace, 1990). At this point, however, it is unclear how much of this effect is attributable to health care providers' knowledge of and concerns about age differences in the pharmacodynamics of analgesic medications; to patients' reluctance to ask for pain medication due to factors reviewed earlier; or to ageism on the part of the medical community. Some credence is given the latter possibility by studies demonstrating that physicians do share American society's negative stereotypes of aging and older persons (see review by Coccaro & Miles, 1984). Perhaps, as a result, they also expend less time and fewer diagnostic resources on the elderly than on younger adults (Radecki, Kane, Solomon, Mendenhall, & Beck, 1988a,b).

Of course, it must be borne in mind that all these age-specific interpretations of pain are superimposed on lifelong personality characteristics. The search for a generalized "pain-prone" personality (Blumer & Heilbronn, 1982) has proved relatively fruitless. However, selected personality variables are clearly associated with the experience and effects of pain across the life span. Thus, chronic pain appears to be more intensive, and has more debilitating affective and functional consequences, in persons high in neuroticism (Affleck, Tennen, Urrows, & Higgins, 1992; Harkins, Price, & Braith, 1989) and hypochondriasis (Lichtenberg, Skehan, & Swensen, 1984; Pincus, Callahan, Bradley, Vaughn, & Wolfe, 1986) and those low in perceived control (e.g., Nicassio, Wallston, Callahan, Herbert, & Pincus, 1985). The stability of personality throughout adulthood and old age is clearly established (Costa & McCrae, 1980); hence, personality influences on pain demonstrated in younger adults should generalize straightforwardly to older persons. However, it is likely that those variables interact with the kinds of age-specific concerns outlined earlier to produce unique dynamics. For example, for lifelong hypochondriacs, the aches and pains of normal aging may fan the fires of hypervigilance. Interpersonal processes described earlier may also be affected. It has been demonstrated that patients' emotionality in describing pain markedly affects physicians' attributions of that pain to physical versus psychological causes (Birdwell, Herbers, & Kroenke, 1993. Ageism and older persons' own response biases may well interact with such biases in complex ways.

In summary, in addition to lifelong personality and response patterns, the unique effects of aging on symptom interpretation and communication may affect older persons' expression and experience of pain. Societal and personal processes may similarly influence family members' and health care providers' responses to elders' pain complaints. In addition, aging brings with it increased susceptibility to affective disorders that may strongly affect the experience and expression of pain. We turn now to examining such two such disorders: depression and anxiety.

PAIN AND AFFECT: THE RELATION OF DEPRESSION AND ANXIETY TO PAIN AMONG OLDER ADULTS

Arguably the most intensively studied psychological concomitants of pain at any life stage are mood disorders and negative mood states, particularly depression. A relatively small body of work with older people follows a larger non-age-specific literature in attempting to disentangle the complex associations between the sensory experience of pain and its affective reflection in depressed mood. Much smaller literatures similarly address anxiety. The following sections review the association of pain with depression and anxiety in turn. With respect to each, a brief review of the epidemiology of late-life mood disorders provides a background against which to evaluate their interrelationships with pain.

Pain and Depression Among Older Adults

Epidemiology of Late-Life Depression. From one perspective, the elderly are no more at risk of depression than younger adults. Data from the Epidemiologic Catchment Area (ECA) studies (Blazer, Hughes, & George, 1987; Blazer & Williams, 1988) indicate that the prevalence of major depressive disorder among persons over age 65 is about 3%. This figure is roughly equivalent to that for middle-aged adults, and lower than that for adolescents and post-adolescents. However, those same data reveal strikingly elevated rates of "minor" or "subsyndromal" depressions that do not meet diagnostic criteria for major depression. The term *minor depression* is an unfortunate convention because such syndromes, albeit less debilitating than major depressive disorders, are nonetheless persistent and pervasive and adversely affect quality of life. Blazer and colleagues estimated that the total prevalence of depression, including major and minor syndromes, was about 28% among older community residents.

The high prevalence of depressive syndromes is of itself disturbing, but even these figures do not adequately portray the nature and consequences of late-life depression. A large literature documents the consistent and quite strong association of depression with physical health and functioning among older adults. Rates of both major and minor depression increase dramatically as one moves from general community populations to geriatric medical outpatients (Kukull et al., 1986), acute hospital patients (Fenton, Cole, Engelsmann, & Mansouri, 1994; Koenig, O'Connor, Guarisco, Zabel, & Ford, 1993), and institution residents (Parmelee, Katz, & Lawton, 1989; Rovner et al., 1990). The course of depression, too, is closely linked with physical health. Nondepressed older persons who experience marked declines in health status or functional abilities are at increased risk of incident depression (Murphy, 1983; Kennedy, Kelman, & Thomas, 1990); the trajectory of health declines similarly strongly affects the prognosis of existing depression (Baldwin & Jolley, 1986; Parmelee, Katz, & Lawton, 1992). Recent evidence suggests that the association between depression and ill health may be bidirectional: Just as health declines predispose older persons to depression, depression may also increase the risk of subsequent health decline (Bruce, Seeman, Merrill, & Blazer, 1994).

In some cases, the strong association between health and depression reflects direct effects of disease processes (see Ouslander, 1982, for a review). For example, stroke, Parkinson's disease, and diabetes can precipitate depressive symptoms through neurochemical or anatomical effects of the disease. Yet these and other specific disease dynamics account for only a small proportion of all late-life depressions. Beyond a handful of depressogenic disorders, research has failed to identify specific disease processes that can account for the central role of physical health in late-life depression. Rather, depressive symptoms seem to be linked more strongly with overall number and severity of health problems (Lindesay, 1990; O'Riordan et al., 1989; Stewart et al., 1991). This effect, in turn, appears to be driven primarily by subjectively proximal effects of health status, most notably functional status. Indeed, in some cases, functional disability accounts completely for the association of physical health with depression among older persons (Kennedy, Kelman, & Thomas, 1990; Parmelee et al., 1992).

Pain and Depression in Late Life. The role of subjectively proximal factors such as functional disability in late-life depression beings us logically to pain. Many common physical disorders of late life are inherently painful (e.g., osteoarthritis; diabetic neuropathies) and from 26% to 84% of chronically ill older persons report problems with persistent pain. This broad range of prevalence rates again illustrates the crucial role of health status in late life. Whereas only about one quarter of elderly community residents report problems with pain (Crook, Rideout, & Browne, 1984), as many as four out of five elderly institution residents do so (Ferrell, Ferrell, & Rivera, 1996; Parmelee, 1996; Roy & Thomas, 1986). Thus, like depression, pain in late life appears to be closely linked with physical frailty. Given this convergence, it is not surprising that, in recent years, increasing attention has been devoted to the association between pain and depression. The result is a small but quite consistent body of evidence confirming the strong correlation between pain and depression among diverse samples of older people (Cohen-Mansfield & Marx, 1993; Magni, Schifano, & DeLeo, 1985; Parmelee, Katz, & Lawton, 1991; Williamson & Schulz, 1992, 1995).

As noted earlier, this emerging focus on pain and depression in late life parallels a larger body of non-age-specific work that has developed over a number of years (see Romano & Turner, 1985, for review). That larger literature is instructive regarding not only the general nature and strength of the relationship, but also conceptual and methodological problems in investigating it. A primary concern has been the potential confounding of effects of pain with somatic symptoms and behavioral manifestations of depression. For example, fatigue, sleep difficulties, and withdrawal from previously favored activities are all symptoms of major depressive disorder. However, they may also be based not in affective processes but in disruptive effects of pain and attempts to deal with it (Hnatiuk, 1991; Lichtenberg, Swensen, & Skehan, 1986). Concern about symptom confounding is especially pertinent to gerontological research because even normal aging can affect sleep, appetite, and activity patterns in such a way as to mimic effects of both depression and pain. Furthermore, it has been suggested that the current cohort of older persons may be disinclined to admit to or seek help for emotional problems; instead, they may "mask" depression with complaints of diffuse physical symptoms, including pain (Williamson, 1978).

Although controversy about the confounding of depression, normal aging, and pain continues, converging evidence suggests that it may be less a problem than originally presumed. From a broad standpoint, several recent studies indicate that somatic symptoms do not unduly influence assessments of depression among older persons (Berkman et al., 1986; Davidson, Feldman, & Crawford, 1994; Radloff & Teri, 1986). The particular problem of confounding depression with pain and its effects has received a great deal of attention in non-age-specific research on rheumatoid arthritis and other chronically painful conditions. The bulk of evidence indicates that the correlation of pain with depression remains even when potentially confounding symptoms are controlled methodologically or statistically (Blalock, DeVellis, Brown, & Wallston, 1989; Callahan, Kaplan, & Pincus, 1991; Turk & Okifuji, 1994).

There has been relatively little exploration of the confounding of pain and symptoms of depression among the elderly from a strictly psychometric standpoint. However, our research with an institutional population (Parmelee et al., 1991) and that of Williamson and Schulz with elderly medical outpatients (1992) yielded persistent significant correlations of pain with depression even when health and functional disability were controlled statistically. Williamson and Schulz's path analysis revealed that pain is associated with depression both directly and indirectly through their mutual association with functional disability. A more recent replication with cancer patients (Williamson & Schulz, 1995) indicates that the same pattern of associations among pain, depression, and functional limitations holds across younger and older individuals. Parmelee et al. (1991) specifically addressed the question of masked depression and found little support for that notion. "Functional" pain complaints (i.e., expressed pain in the absence of a plausible physical cause) were no more common among depressed than among nondepressed persons. Rather, depression appeared primarily to exaggerate propensity to report pain for which there was an identifiable underlying health problem.

In sum, existing evidence clearly indicates that, like younger individuals, older persons in pain are often depressed as well. Furthermore, again paralleling nongerontological research, depressed elderly appear to be more sensitive to pain than are their nondepressed age-mates. Hence, depression appears to heighten (or perhaps is a manifestation of) *suffering* due to pain. In light of the previous discussion of social-psychological influences on pain reporting, our findings regarding the exaggeration of pain complaints among depressed elderly institution residents must be interpreted cautiously. Further research may well show that pain complaints among this very frail group are a means of garnering attention or support, or of expressing general emotional distress. However, taken as a whole, existing evidence raises the intriguing implication that pain may well represent a third major aspect of the documented mutual influence of depression and functional disability.

Anxiety, Depression, and Pain Among Older Adults

Epidemiology and Assessment of Anxiety. Late-life anxiety has received far less research attention than has depression both generally and with respect to its association with pain. This is partly because, in contrast to depression, diagnostically pure anxiety disorders are relatively rare among the elderly. Data from the ECA studies indicate that anxiety disorders are evidenced by about 1% of elderly community residents at any given time (Blazer, George, & Hughes, 1990), as compared with about 9% of younger persons (Myers et al., 1984). Note that all these figures represent symptom levels reflecting diagnosable anxiety disorders. When lower-level symptoms of anxiety are included, prevalence estimates are much higher (e.g., Himmelfarb & Murrell, 1984).

As research on late-life anxiety moves forward, it is becoming clear that standard diagnostic approaches may grossly underestimate its prevalence. A primary problem is again confounding, this time in terms of the distinction of depression and anxiety. Standard diagnostic criteria (American Psychiatric Association, 1994) treat depression and anxiety hierarchically, permitting diagnosis of an anxiety disorder only in the absence of a depressive syndrome. Yet depression and anxiety co-occur so often that the basic diagnostic distinction has been questioned even among younger adults (see, e.g., Akiskal, 1985; Kendler, Heath, Martin, & Eaves, 1987). Overlap between the two disorders appears to be even greater among the elderly. Like depression, anxiety is closely associated with physical health and functional disability in a variety of elderly populations (Colenda & Smith, 1993; Parmelee, Katz, & Lawton, 1993). Anxiety is often present as a subsyndrome of late-life major depressive disorder (Alexopoulos, 1991; Blazer, Hughes, & Fowler, 1989). Hence, particularly in medically ill older persons, the two disorders may be virtually indistinguishable (Blazer et al., 1989; Parmelee et al., 1993).

Anxiety and Pain. Given the close association of depression and anxiety across the life span, one might reasonably expect that anxiety, too, is a strong concomitant of pain. Unfortunately, studies of that relationship are both far fewer and less clearly focused than those on pain and depression. There is a sizable and rather complex literature on effects of experimentally induced anxiety on perception of and tolerance for pain (e.g., Cornwall & Donderi, 1988; Weisenberg, Aviram, Wolf, & Raphaeli, 1984). In contrast, the role of anxiety in persistent pain syndromes is not well understood. Early studies of psychiatric outpatients indicated that persons with anxiety disorders reported more problems with pain than did individuals with other psychiatric diagnoses, including depression (Merskey, 1968; Spear, 1967). Unfortunately, these early findings have not been pursued in more recent investigations, which have typically dealt more with anxious symptomatology than with diagnosable disorders. For example, Sofaer and Walker (1994) assessed various mood states of pain clinic patients and found that the predominant negative moods were tension, worry, and irritability, all of which reflect anxiety. Among persons with rheumatoid arthritis and other chronically painful conditions, both state and trait anxiety are correlated with pain ratings, but state anxiety appears to be the stronger independent predictor (Hagglund et al., 1989; Gaskin, Greene, Robinson, & Geisser, 1992; see, however, Moosbrugger & Schermelleh-Engle, 1991). In an elderly sample, Hnatiuk (1991) used experience sampling methods to assess mood and pain over multiple occasions. She found negligible correlations between individuals' average anxiety and pain ratings across occasions. Unfortunately, within-occasion correlations were not reported; thus, it is impossible to judge whether pain and anxiety covaried more closely on a short-term basis.

Given the strong correlation of anxiety and depression across the life span, it is surprising that there has been relatively little research on their respective and combined associations with pain. Strang and Qvarner (1990) found that both anxiety and depression were associated with pain among a mixed-age group of cancer patients. Garron and Leavitt (1979) reported the same finding among a sample of low-back-pain patients. However, after controlling for the intercorrelation of depression and anxiety, only anxiety remained independently associated with pain. A recent analysis documented much the same pattern in a geriatric institutional population (Casten, Parmelee, Kleban, Lawton, & Katz, 1995). Both research-diagnosed anxiety disorders and the anxiety subscale of the Profile of Mood States were significantly associated with pain; the same was true for parallel measures of depression. However, independent associations of the affect measures with pain depended on which measures were being used.

The work of Garron and Leavitt (1979) and Casten and colleagues (1995) offers preliminary evidence that anxiety is more strongly associated with pain than is depression. However, that generalization grossly oversimplifies the situation because it treats all three variables—pain, anxiety, and depression—as unitary syndromes. In particular, there appears to be good reason to extend the long-standing diagnostic distinction of psychic from somatic anxiety to research on pain. DeGood, Buckelew, and Tait (1985) examined anxiety symptoms among (nonelderly) chronic pain patients as compared with pain-free controls. Surprisingly, the pain patients reported markedly *less* anxiety overall; however, they endorsed disproportionately more somatic symptoms. While intriguing, this effect is beclouded by the noncomparability of the pain and nonpain groups. More solid evidence is offered by von Knorring, Perris, Eisemann, Eriksson, and Perris's (1983) comparison of depressed psychiatric inpatients who did and did not complain of pain. Persons with pain reported greater somatic anxiety, but no more psychic anxiety, than pain-free individuals. Krishnan and colleagues (1985) similarly examined the intersection of pain, depression, and anxiety among low-back-pain patients. Somatic anxiety was significantly higher among major depressives than among minor depressives, who in turn exceeded nondepressed individuals. Psychic anxiety showed much weaker effects.

Once again, there is little research addressing this question among older persons. The work of Alexopoulous (1991) with depressed older persons indicates that psychic anxiety is more common than somatic anxiety among late-life depressives and is also more closely tied to a variety of depressive symptoms and syndromes. Together with studies just reviewed, this raises the interesting possibility that symptoms of psychic anxiety are more closely associated with depression, and somatic anxiety with pain. Our recent work (Parmelee, Kleban, & Katz, in press) explored precisely that hypothesis among elderly long-term-care residents. We found that affective symptoms clustered into three basic syndromes: depressed mood, psychic anxiety, and an array of somatic symptoms variously associated with anxiety and depression. The somatic symptoms cluster was far more strongly associated with pain than were either depressed mood or psychic anxiety. This pattern withstood control for health and functional status and appeared to be driven primarily by somatic anxiety. These findings at least tentatively confirm that frail older persons show the same pattern as younger individuals: a relatively stronger association of pain with anxiety than with depression. However, our data parallel those of von Knorring and colleagues (1983) and others in suggesting that it is not simply anxiety per se, but its somatic manifestations that are most closely linked with experienced pain.

PAIN AND COGNITIVE IMPAIRMENT

As noted throughout this chapter, research on pain among older persons is quite sparse in comparison with the general literatures on both pain and aging. Nowhere is this gap more dramatic, nor its implications more ominous, than with respect to pain and cognitive impairment. Converging evidence suggests that a large proportion of older persons are at risk of both pain and intellectual dysfunction, but studies directly examining the association of pain with cognitive status are remarkably few. Thus, much of this section will address pain among cognitively impaired individuals only inferentially, on the basis of indirect evidence. As in previous sections, a brief overview of the epidemiology of cognitive dysfunction among older persons will reveal the potential breadth of the problem and set the stage for review of existing knowledge of the convergence of pain and cognitive impairment. We shall then discuss the problem of assessing pain among older persons with dementia and other cognitive disorders.

The Epidemiology of Cognitive Impairment in Late Life

Alzheimer's disease is by far the most widely publicized of the dementias and has become a synonym for the more general term in many persons' minds. But the cluster of processes described collectively as Alzheimer's disease is only one of a diversity of dementing illnesses. Multi-infarct dementia, caused by insufficient cerebral blood supply, is equally prevalent in the current cohort of older persons; other dementias (e.g., Parkinson's dementia; Pick's disease) are less common but equally debilitating. Thus, *dementia* and *cognitive impairment* are at best catch-all terms. For current purposes, however, they are appropriate, because pain-relevant issues are more closely tied to generalized functional and communication deficits than to underlying disease processes. The following discussion therefore forgoes diagnostic distinctions, instead focusing simply on degree of cognitive impairment.

The majority of epidemiological work on the prevalence of cognitive impairment has focused on relatively marked deficits that indicate presence of a diagnosable dementia. In an early report based on ECA data, Myers and colleagues (1984) defined "severe" cognitive impairment as scores less than 17 on the Mini-Mental State Examination (MMSE) (Folstein, Folstein, & McHugh, 1975). This level of impairment, which almost universally reflects a diagnosable dementia, was observed in just under 5% of persons aged 65 or more. Depending on criteria and populations, other estimates have ranged as low as 1% and as high as 18% (see Jorm, Korten, & Henderson, 1987, for a review). However, the majority of studies report prevalence rates for older persons between 5% and 10% (e.g., Folstein, Anthony, & Parhad, 1985; Sulkava et al., 1985).

Rates of cognitive impairment increase markedly with advanced aged; in fact, the risk of developing a dementing illness doubles every five years past the age of 65 (Jorm et al., 1987). Thus, the prevalence of cognitive deficits may range as high as 47% among persons over 80 (Evans et al., 1989; see also Folstein et al., 1985; Sulkava et al., 1985). This datum takes on particular significance because persons over 85 are the fastest-growing segment of the older population. Thus, as more and more individuals live into their 80s and beyond, the prevalence of dementia is apt to rise accordingly.

This focus on deficits sufficient to infer a diagnosable dementia is somewhat misleading. Many persons experience less severe deficits that, although of ambiguous etiology, clearly compromise daily functioning. For example, Myers and colleagues' (1984) 5% estimate was based on MMSE scores of 17 or less; yet scores as high as 23 are taken as evidence of cognitive dysfunction. When Myers et al. adopted that more inclusive criterion, the prevalence of cognitive impairment among the diverse ECA community samples rose from 5% to 15% (see also Clarke et al., 1991). Note also that many epidemiological studies have excluded institution residents, who display much higher rates of cognitive impairment than community residents. Rovner and colleagues (1990) found that 67% of newly admitted nursing-home patients had diagnosed dementia. Data from the Philadelphia Geriatric Center (PGC) indicated that about 75% of nursing-home residents and 25% of congregate-apartment tenants suffered at least mild cognitive impairment (Parmelee, Katz, & Lawton, 1989).

Prevalence of Pain among Cognitively Impaired Older Persons

I have stressed the prevalence of cognitive dysfunction in nursing homes and other long-term-care facilities not simply because of the high rates of impairment, but also because those are the settings for the few existing empirical studies of pain among cognitively impaired older persons. Early studies dramatically illustrated the extent of pain in such settings but did not deal in any depth with cognitive impairment (e.g., Roy & Thomas, 1986; Ferrell, Ferrell, & Osterweil, 1990). More recent research has explicitly examined the prevalence of pain as a function of cognitive status. Ferrell et al. (1996) examined pain among 217 nursing-home residents with an average MMSE score of 12.1 ($SD = 7.9$), indicating moderate to severe impairment. Of their sample, 62% complained of persistent pain; review of medical charts indicated that musculoskeletal disorders, most notably osteoarthritis, accounted for 70% of pain complaints. Using only medical chart data, Marzinski (1991) found that 43.3% of patients in a special care unit for Alzheimer's disease patients had potentially painful conditions; again, musculoskeletal disorders were the most common pain-related diagnoses. Sengstaken and King (1993) combined self-reports with chart reviews in a sample of 60 cognitively impaired and 40 intact nursing-home residents. Of respondents who were able to self-report, 57% complained of chronic pain; another 9% were identified by chart review. Unfortunately, these authors did not differentiate prevalence of pain as a function of cognitive status.

Research at PGC (Parmelee, 1996) suggests that cognitively impaired long-term-care residents report slightly fewer problems with pain than do their unimpaired coresidents. Given a checklist of 12 common pain complaints (e.g., headache, joint pain, chest pain), 86% of cognitively intact persons endorsed 1 or more persistent pain complaints, as compared with 78% of mildly impaired and only 71% of markedly impaired persons. Similarly, cognitive impairment was negatively associated with total number of pain complaints and reported intensity of pain, even when health status and disability were controlled. However, there were few differences in the types of pain reported: rank orders of specific pain locales were remarkably similar across levels of cognitive impairment. The one exception was headaches, which were more common among cognitively more impaired persons.

Assessment of Pain among Cognitively Impaired Elderly

Our findings suggest that cognitively impaired long-term-care residents experience, or at least report, somewhat fewer problems with pain than do their intellectually intact counterparts. A reasonable question, of course, is whether cognitively impaired individuals are able to provide valid and reliable self-report information about pain. Again, there is little empirical evidence directly examining this issue. However, I have examined internal consistency (Cronbach's alpha) and test–retest reliability of a simple pain-intensity measure across intact, mildly impaired, and markedly impaired groups (Parmelee, 1996). Analyses yielded remarkably similar coefficients, suggesting that pain self-reports are equally psychometrically valid regardless of cognitive status. Parmelee, Smith, and Katz (1993) further assessed validity of localized pain complaints vis-à-vis physicians' identification of a logical physical cause (e.g., cardiac problems in persons complaining of chest pain). Findings again upheld the validity of self-reports even among markedly demented individuals. If anything, cognitively impaired persons were *less* likely than more intact individuals to report pain problems for which physicians identified no plausible cause. Overall, then, insofar as persons are sufficiently cognitively intact to respond meaningfully to questions, their self-reports should be given equal weight as those of unimpaired older persons.

Of course, the findings just reported pertain only to persons who are in fact able to voice responses that have some face validity (i.e., that make sense in context). A more troublesome question is how to assess pain among persons whose cognitive impairments preclude meaningful communication. The confluence of high rates of both cognitive impairment and pain among the extremely old and frail raises a chilling possibility: that severely cognitively impaired persons may be at risk of persistent, untreated pain simply because it is undetected. In fact, profoundly cognitively impaired long term care residents receive fewer pain medications than do cognitively more intact individuals, even when medical diagnoses representing potentially painful conditions are equivalent (Cariaga, Burgio, Flynn, & Martin, 1991; Sengstaken & King, 1993). Indeed, it has been suggested that untreated pain is one likely cause of agitation and other disruptive behavior (Cariaga et al., 1991; Cohen-Mansfield, Billig, Lipson, Rosenthal, & Pawlson, 1990). Thus, it is imperative that care providers be alert to, and able clearly to identify, pain among persons in the latter stages of dementing illness.

Unfortunately, several converging literatures suggest that even when patients *are* able to communicate verbally, second-party informants are at best mediocre judges of their pain. Health care professionals are not particularly adept at estimating the extent of their patients' pain. Although errors occur in both directions, the overall tendency is to underestimate relative to patients' self-reports (e.g., Grossman, Sheidler, Swedeen, Mueenski, & Piantadosi, 1991; Teske, Daut, & Cleeland, 1983). Surprisingly, family members appear little better at estimating pain than are professional care providers, although the nature of their errors is somewhat different (Dar et al., 1992; O'Brien & Francis, 1988). Some of the slippage between self-report and informant ratings may hark back to the kinds of reporting biases discussed earlier. Older persons may wish not to trouble formal or informal caregivers, leaving those individuals to rely on their own very subjective perceptions to estimate the individual's pain. Whatever the cause, it is disturbing to find that, even when communication is clearly possible, interested observers are only very gross judges of pain.

The situation is even more complicated when dementia impairs basic verbal communication, because caregivers are left with only facial expressions and other nonverbal behavior as clues to the presence of pain. There exist a number of validated approaches to identifying pain on the basis of nonverbal cues. These include facial indices (see Craig, Prkachin, & Grunau, 1992, for a review), structured assessments of gross motor behavior (e.g., Keefe & Block, 1982), and methods designed specifically for use in health care settings (e.g., Richards, Nepomuceno, Riles, & Suer, 1982). For most such measures, validation studies have included at least some elderly subjects, but none of these approaches has been widely tested with older individuals. It is therefore quite premature to project how they will generalize to cognitively impaired elders. Research on the facial expression of emotions other than pain suggests that some types of dementia have no effects; others, however, clearly mute facial expressions of emotion (Kasniak, 1995). Nonetheless, one quite interesting study (Asplund, Norberg, Adolfsson, & Waxman, 1991) indicated that at least remnants of facial expressions of pain are present even in profoundly demented, noncommunicative individuals.

More generally, a combination of facial expressions and gross motor behavioral cues has been shown to permit effective identification of general mood states of long-term-care dementia patients (Lawton, van Haitsma, & Klapper (1996). Preliminary work suggests great promise in extending such methods specifically to pain. One scale for assessing discomfort among dementia patients has already been proved effective in discriminating acute disease states (Hurley et al., 1992). In the absence of such structured methods, long-term-care staff appear to use an array of cues, including marked departures from normal behavior patterns, to identify pain among markedly cognitively impaired persons (Marzinski, 1991).

In sum, insofar as older persons with dementia are able verbally to communicate, their expressions of pain should be taken at face value. The task of adequately identifying pain is much more challenging in those with aphasia or other communication deficits. The technology for nonverbal assessment of pain is well developed; it remains to be seen how validly it can be applied to this very difficult population.

SUMMARY AND CONCLUSIONS

This chapter has covered a lot of territory, from basic psychosocial processes that may impede (or facilitate) older persons' expressing pain to the very important problem of identifying pain among those who are unable to communicate in any readily comprehensible way. On the whole, evidence reviewed here indicates that, although the substance of the psychological life space may be somewhat different across the adult life span, its psychological dynamics are much the same. At the same time, though, physical and social aging may converge to color those dynamics in unique ways. Most older persons do have at least a few chronic health problems; as a result, they are at increased risk of depression, anxiety and pain. Each of those phenomena, in turn, places the individual at risk of the others. Social aging, in terms of the roles older persons typically occupy and the stereotypes they encounter, may play a strong role in the experience and expression of pain. Unfortunately, that role appears often to increase the probability that pain will go untreated. Thus, although many pain-relevant processes may be stable throughout the adult years, their content and context change radically as persons advance in age and decline in physical health. Those changes in turn bear strong implications for pain management among older persons.

At this point, perhaps the most central, and certainly the most age-specific, problem in the study of late-life pain is the question of cognitive impairment. We have dealt in some detail with problems of assessment and detection of pain among older persons with cognitive deficits, outlining the need for further research on a number of fronts. Much more remains to be learned about basic nociceptive and pain perceptual processes, in terms of how neurological effects of dementing illnesses affect central, peripheral, and cortical processing of pain stimuli.

Much of this chapter has stressed what gerontological researchers can learn from the more general literature on pain. At this point, we are beginning to see the potential for transfer of knowledge in the opposite direction as well. For example, recent studies of the affective correlates of pain among older persons suggest dynamics that have yet to be documented among younger adults (e.g., Williamson & Schulz, 1995; Parmelee et al., in press). It is to be hoped that future investigations will capitalize on this potential for cross-fertilization, enhancing understanding of the psychological correlates and consequences of pain in persons of all ages.

ACKNOWLEDGMENTS. Preparation of this chapter was supported by National Institute of Mental Health grants R01 MH49846 and R01 MH51800 (P. Parmelee) and P50 MH52129 (I. Katz). The very central contributions of Ira R. Katz and M. Powell Lawton to original research discussed in this chapter are gratefully acknowledged.
Address correspondence to Patricia A. Parmelee, Ph.D., Center for Clinical Epidemiology and Biostatistics, University of Pennsylvania School of Medicine, Philadelphia, PA 19104-6021.

REFERENCES

Affleck, G., Tennen, H., Urrows, S., & Higgins, P. (1992). Neuroticism and the pain-mood relation in rheumatoid arthritis: insights from a rospective daily study. *Journal of Consulting and Clinical Psychology*, *60*, 119–126.

Akiskal, H. S. (1985). Anxiety: Definition, relationship to depression, and proposal for an integrative model. In A. H. Tuma & J. D. Maser (Eds.), *Anxiety and the anxiety disorders* (pp. 787–797). Hillsdale, NJ: Erlbaum.

Alexopoulos, G. S. (1991). Anxiety and depression in the elderly. In C. Salzman & B. D. Lebowitz (Eds.), *Anxiety in the elderly: Treatment and research* (pp. 63–77). New York: Springer.

American Psychiatric Association. (1994). *Diagnostic and statistical manual* (4th ed.). Washington, DC: Author.

Asplund, K. Norberg, A., Adolfsson, R., & Waxman, H. M. (1991). Facial expressions in severely demented patients: A stimulus-response study of four patients with dementia of the Alzheimer type. *International Journal of Geriatric Psychiatry*, *6*, 599–606.

Baldwin, R. C., & Jolley, D. J. (1986). The prognosis of depression in old age. *British Journal of Psychiatry*, *149*, 574–583.

Berkman, L. F., Berkman, C. S., Kasl, S., Freeman, D. H., Leo, L., Ostfield, A. M., Cornoni-Huntley, J., & Brody, J. A. (1986). Depressive symptoms in relation to physical health and functioning in the elderly. *American Journal of Epidemiology* , *124* 372–388.

Birdwell, B. G., Herbers, J. E., & Kroenke, K. (1993). Evaluating chest pain: The patient's presentation style alters the physician's diagnostic approach. *Archives of Internal Medicine, 153*, 1991–1995.

Blalock, S. J., DeVellis, R. F., Brown, G. K., & Wallston, K. A. (1989). Validity of the Center for Epidemiological Studies Depression Scale in arthritis populations. *Arthritis and Rheumatism, 38*, 991–997.

Blazer, D. G., George, L. K., & Hughes, D. (1990). The epidemiology of anxiety disorders: An age comparison. In C. Salzman & B. D. Lebowitz (Eds.), *Anxiety in the elderly: Treatment and research* (pp. 17–30). New York: Springer.

Blazer, D., Hughes, D. C., & Fowler, N. (1989). Anxiety as an outcome symptom of depression in elderly and middle-aged adults. *International Journal of Geriatric Psychiatry, 4*, 273–278.

Blazer, D., Hughes, D. C., & George, L. K. (1987). The epidemiology of depression in an elderly community population. *Gerontologist, 27*, 281–287.

Blazer, D., & Williams, C. D. (1988). Epidemiology of depression and dysphoria in an elderly population. *American Journal of Psychiatry, 137*, 434–443.

Block, A. R., Kremer, E. F., & Gaylor, M. (1980). Behavioral treatment of chronic pain: The spouse as a discriminative cue for pain behavior. *Pain, 9*, 243–252.

Blumer, D., & Heilbronn, M. (1982). Chronic pain as a variant of depressive illness: The pain-prone disorder. *Journal of Nervous and Mental Disease, 170*, 381–406.

Bruce, M. L., Seeman, T. E., Merrill, S. S., & Blazer, D. G. (1994). The impact of depressive symptomatology on physical disability: MacArthur studies of successful aging. *American Journal of Public Health, 84*, 1796–1799.

Callahan, L. F., Kaplan, M. R., & Pincus, T. (1991). The Beck Depression Inventory, Center for Epidemiological Studies Depression Scale, and General Well-Being Schedule Depression Subscale in rheumatoid arthritis. *Arthritis Care and Research, 4*, 3–11.

Cariaga, J., Burgio, L., Flynn, W., & Martin, D. (1991). A controlled study of disruptive vocalizations among geriatric residents in nursing homes. *Journal of the American Geriatrics Society, 39*, 501–507.

Casten, R. J., Parmelee, P. A., Kleban, M. H., Lawton, M. P., & Katz, I. R. (1995). The relationships among anxiety, depression, and pain in a geriatric institutionalized sample. *Pain, 61*, 271–276.

Clarke, M., Jagger, C., Anderson, J., Battcock, T., Kelly, F., & Stern, M. C. (1991). The prevalence of dementia in a total population: A comparison of two screening instruments. *Age and Ageing, 20*, 396–403.

Clinton, P., & Eland, J. (1990). Pain. In M. Maas & K. Buckwalter (Eds.), *Nursing diagnoses and intervention for the elderly* (pp. 348–368). Reading, MA: Addison-Wesley.

Coccaro, E. F., & Miles, A. M. (1984). The attitudinal impact of training in gerontology/geriatrics in medical school: A review of the literature and perspective. *Journal of the American Geriatrics Society, 32*, 762–768.

Cohen-Mansfield, J., Billig, N., Lipson, S., Rosenthal, A. S., & Pawlson, L. G. (1990). Medical correlates of agitation in nursing home residents. *Gerontology, 36*, 150–158.

Cohen-Mansfield, J., & Marx, M. S. (1993). Pain and depression in the nursing home: Corroborating results. *Journal of Gerontology: Psychological Sciences, 48*, P96–P97.

Colenda, C. C., & Smith, S. L. (1993). Multivariate modeling of anxiety and depression in community-dwelling elderly persons. *American Journal of Geriatric Psychiatry, 1*, 327–338.

Cornwall, A., & Donderi, D. C. (1988). The effect of experimentally induced anxiety on the experience of pressure pain. *Pain, 35*, 105–113.

Costa, P. T., Jr., & McCrae, R. R. (1980). Still stable after all these years: Personality as a key to some issues in adulthood and old age. In P. B. Baltes & O. G. Brim, Jr. (Eds.), *Life span edevelopment and behavior* (Vol. 4, pp. 65–102). New York: Academic Press.

Craig, K. D., Prkachin, K. M., & Grunau, R. V. (1992). The facial expression of pain. In D. C. Turk & R. Melzack (Eds.), *Handbook of pain assessment* (pp. 257–274). New York: Guilford Press.

Crook, J., Rideout, E., & Browne, G. (1984). The revalence of pain complaints in a general population. *Pain, 18*, 199–214.

Dar, R., Beach, C. M., Barden, P. L., & Cleeland, C. S. (1992). Cancer pain in the marital system: A study of patients and their spouses. *Journal of Pain and Symptom Management, 7*, 87–93.

Davidson, J., Feldman, P. H., & Crawford, S. (1994). Measuring depressive symptoms in the frail elderly. *Journal of Gerontology: Psychological Sciences, 49*, P159–P164.

DeGood, D. E., Buckelew, S. P., & Tait, R. C. (1985). Cognitive-somatic anxiety response patterning in chronic pain patients and nonpatients. *Journal of Consulting and Clinical Psychology, 53*, 137–138.

Evans, D. A., Funkenstein, H. H., Albert, M. S., Scherr, P. A., Cook, N. R., Chown, M. J., Hebert, L. E., Hennekens, C. H., & Taylor, J. O. (1989). Prevalence of Alzheimer's disease in a community population of older persons: Higher than previously reported. *Journal of the American Medical Association, 262*, 2551–2556.

Faherty, B. S., & Grier, M. R. (1984). Analgesic medication for elderly people postsurgery. *Nursing Research, 33*, 369–372.

Fenton, F. R., Cole, M. G., Engelsmann, F., & Mansouri, I. (1994). Depression in older medical inpatients. *International Journal of Geriatric Psychiatry, 9*, 279–284.

Fernandez, E., & Turk, D. C. (1992). Sensory and affective components of pain: Separation and synthesis. *Psychological Bulletin, 112*, 205–217.

Ferrell, B. A., Ferrell, B. R., & Osterweil, D. A. (1990). Pain in the nursing home. *Journal of the American Geriatrics Society, 38*, 409–414.

Ferrell, B. A., Ferrell, B. R., & Rivera, L. (1996). Pain in cognitively impaired nursing home patients. *Journal of Pain and Symptom Management, 10*, 591–598.

Ferrell, B. R., Rhiner, M., Cohen, M. Z., & Grant, M. (1991). Pain as a metaphor for illness: 1. Impact of cancer pain on family caregivers. *Oncology Nursing Forum, 18*, 1303–1309.

Flor, H., Miltner, W., & Birbaumer, N. (1992). Psychophysiological recording methods. In D. C. Turk & R. Melzack (Eds.), *Handbook of pain assessment* (pp. 169–190). New York: Guilford Press.

Folstein, M., Anthony, J. C., & Parhad, I. (1985). The meaning of cognitive impairment in the elderly. *Journal of the American Geriatrics Society, 33*, 228–235.

Folstein, M. F., Folstein, S. E., & McHugh, P. R. (1975). "Mini-Mental State": A practical method for grading the cognitive status of patients for the clinician. *Journal of Psychiatric Research, 17*, 189–198.

Fordyce, W. E. (1976). *Behavioral methods in chronic pain and illness*. St. Louis: Mosby.

Fordyce, W. E. (1978). Evaluating and managing chronic pain. *Geriatrics, 33*, 59–62.

Garron, D. C., & Leavitt, F. (1979). Demographic and affective covariates of pain. *Psychosomatic Medicine, 41*, 525–534.

Gaskin, M. E., Greene, A. F., Robinson, M. E., & Geisser, M. E. (1992). Negative affect and the experience of chronic pain. *Journal of Psychosomatic Research, 36*, 707–713.

Gil, K. M., Keefe, F. J., Crisson, J. E., & Van Dalfsen, P. J. (1987). Social support and pain behavior. *Pain, 29*, 209–217.

Greenlee, K. K. (1991). Pain and analgesia: Considerations for the elderly in critical care. *AACN Clinical Issues in Critical Care Nursing, 2*, 720–728.

Greenwald, H. B., Bonica, J. J., & Bergner, M. (1987). The prevalence of pain in four cancers. *Cancer, 60*, 2563–2569.

Grossman, S. A., Sheidler, V. R., Swedeen, K., Mucenski, J., & Piantadosi, S. (1991). Correlation of patient and caregiver ratings of cancer pain. *Journal of Pain and Symptom Management, 6*(2), 53–57.

Hagglund, K. J., Haley, W. E., Reville, J. D., & Alarcon, G. S. (1989). Predicting individual differences in pain and functional impairment among patients with rheumatoid arthritis. *Arthritis and Rheumatism, 32*, 851–858.

Hannan, M. T., Anderson, J. J., Pincus, T., & Felson, D. T. (1992). Educational attainment and osteoarthritis: Differential associations with radiographic changes and symptom reporting. *Journal of Clinical Epidemiology, 45*, 139–147.

Harkins, S. W., Price, D. D., & Braith, J. (1989). Effects of extraversion and neuroticism on experimental pain, clinical pain, and illness behavior. *Pain, 36*, 209–218.

Himmelfarb, S., & Murrell, S. A. (1984). The prevalence and correlates of anxiety symptoms in older adults. *Journal of Psychology, 116*, 139–167.

Hnatiuk, S. H. (1991). Experience sampling with elderly persons: An exploration of the method. *International Journal of Aging and Human Development, 33*, 45–64.

Hurley, A. C., Volicer, B. J., Hanrahan, P. A., Houde, S., & Volicer, L. (1992). Assessment of discomfort in advanced Alzheimer patients. *Research in Nursing and Health, 15*, 369–377.

Jamison, R. N., & Virts, K. L. (1990). The influence of family support on chronic pain. *Behavior Research and Therapy, 28*, 283–287.

Jensen, M. P., Karoly, P., & Harris, P. (1991). Assessing the affective component of chronic pain: Development of the Pain Discomfort Scale. *Journal of Psychiatric Research, 35*, 149–154.

Jorm, A. F., Korten, A. E., & Henderson, A. S. (1987). The prevalence of dementia: A quantitative integration of the literature. *Acta Psychiatrica Scandinavica, 76*, 465–479.

Kasniak, A. (1995, August). *Aging and the neuropsychology of emotion: Research and clinical implications.* Presented at the annual meeting of the American Psychological Association, New York.

Keefe, F. J., & Block, A. R. (1982). Development of an observational method for assessing pain behavior in chronic low back pain patients. *Behavior Therapy, 13*, 363–375.

Keefe, F. J., Caldwell, D. S., Queen, K. T., Gil, K. M., Martinez, S., Crisson, J. E., Ogden, W., & Nunley, J. (1987). Pain coping strategies in osteoarthritis patients. *Journal of Consulting and Clinical Psychology, 55*, 208–212.

Kendler, K. S., Heath, A. C., Martin, N. G., & Eaves, L. J. (1987). Symptoms of anxiety and symptoms of depression: Same genes, different environment? *Archives of General Psychiatry, 44*, 451–457.

Kennedy, G. J., Kelman, H. R., & Thomas, C. (1990). The emergence of depressive symptoms in late life: The importance of declining health and increasing disability. *Journal of Community Health, 15*, 93–104.

Kerns, R. D., Haythornthwaite, J., Southwick, S., & Giller, E. L., Jr. (1990). The role of marital interaction in chronic pain and depressive symptom severity. *Journal of Psychiatric Research, 34*, 401–408.

Koenig, H. G., O'Connor, C. M., Guarisco, S. A., Zabel, K. M., & Ford, S. M. (1993). Depressive disorder in older medical inpatients on general medicine and cardiology services at a university teaching hospital. *American Journal of Geriatric Psychiatry, 1*, 197–210.

Krishnan, K. R. R., France, R. D., Pelton, S., McCann, U. D., Davidson, J., & Urban, B. J. (1985). Chronic pain and depression: 1. Classification of depression in chronic low back pain patients. *Pain, 22*, 279–287.

Kukull, W. A., Koepsell, T. C., Inui, T. S., Borson, S., Okimoto, J., Raskind, M. A., & Gale, J. L. (1986). Depression and physical illness among elderly general medical clients. *Journal of Affective Disorders, 10*, 153–162.

Lawton, M. P., Van Haitsma, K., & Klapper, J. (1996). Observed affect in nursing home residents with Alzheimers disease. *Journal of Gerontology: Psychological Sciences, 51*, 3–14.

Leventhal, E. A., & Prohaska, T. R. (1986). Age, symptom interpretation and health behavior. *Journal of the American Geriatrics Society, 34*, 185–191.

Lichtenberg, P. A., Skehan, M. W., & Swensen, C. H. (1984). The role of personality, recent life stress and arthritic severity in predicting pain. *Journal of Psychosomatic Research, 28*, 231–236.

Lichtenberg, P. A., Swensen, C. H., & Skehan, M. W. (1986). Further investigation of the role of personality, lifestyle and arthritic severity in predicting pain. *Journal of Psychosomatic Research, 30*, 327–337.

Lindesay, J. (1990). The Guy's Age Concern Survey: Physical health and psychiatric disorder in an urban elderly community. *International Journal of Geriatric Psychiatry, 5*, 272–278.

Lousberg, R., Schmidt, A. J. M., & Groenman, N. A. (1992). The relationship between spouse solicitousness and pain behavior: Searching for more experimental evidence. *Pain, 51*, 75–79.

Magni, J., Schifano, F., & DeLeo, D. (1985). Pain as a symptom in elderly depressed patients: Relationship to diagnostic subgroups. *European Archives of Psychiatry and Neurological Sciences, 235*, 143–145.

Marzinski, L. R. (1991). The tragedy of dementia: Clinically assessing pain the confused, nonverbal elderly. *Journal of Gerontological Nursing, 17*, 25–28.

McCaffrey, M. (1979). *Nursing management of the patient with pain* (2nd ed.). Philadelphia: Lippincott.

McIntosh, I. B. (1990). Psychological aspects influence the threshold of pain. *Geriatric Medicine, 20*, 37–41.

Melding, P. (1991). Is there such a thing as geriatric pain? *Pain, 46*, 119–121.

Melzack, R. (1975). The McGill Pain Questionnaire: Major properties and scoring methods. *Pain, 1*, 277–299.

Merskey, H., & Bogduk, N. (1994). *Classification of chronic pain: Description of chronic pain syndromes and definition of pain terms* (2nd ed.). Seattle: International Association for the Study of Pain.

Merskey, J. (1968). Psychological aspects of pain. *Postgraduate Medical Journal, 44*, 297–306.

Moosbrugger, H., & Schermelleh-Engel, K. (1991). Determinants of pain experience, perceived competence, trait anxiety, trait depression and moderator effects. *Personality and Individual Differences, 12*, 1261–1266.

Murphy, E. (1983). The prognosis of depression in old age. *British Journal of Psychiatry, 142*, 111–119.

Myers, J. K., Weissman, M. M., Tischler, G. L., Holzer, C. E., III, Leaf, P. J., Orvaschel, H., Anthony, J. C.,

Boyd, J. H., Burke, J. D., Kramer, M., & Stoltzman, R. (1984). Prevalence of psychiatric disorders in three communities. *Archives of General Psychiatry, 41*, 959–967.

Nicassio, P. M., Wallston, K. A., Callahan, L. F., Herbert, M., & Pincus, T. (1985). The measurement of helplessness in rheumatoid arthritis: The development of the Arthritis Helplessness Index. *Journal of Rheumatology, 12*, 462–467.

Oberle, K., Paul, P., Wry, J., & Grace, M. (1990). Pain, anxiety and analgesics: A comparative study of elderly and younger surgical patients. *Canadian Journal on Aging, 9*, 13–22.

O'Brien, J., & Francis, A. (1988). The use of next-of-kin to estimate ain in cancer patients. *Pain, 35*, 171–178.

O'Riordan, T. G., Hayes, J. P., Shelley, R., O'Neill, D., Walsh, J. B., & Coakley, D. (1989). The prevalence of depression in an acute geriatric medical assessment unit. *International Journal of Geriatric Psychiatry, 4*, 17–21.

Ouslander, J. G. (1982). Physical illness and depression in the elderly. *Journal of the American Geriatrics Society, 30*, 593–599.

Parmelee, P. A. (1996). Pain among cognitively impaired older persons. *Clinics in Geriatric Medicine, 12*(3), 473–487.

Parmelee, P. A., Katz, I. R., & Lawton, M. P. (1989). Depression among institutionalized aged: Assessment and prevalence estimation. *Journal of Gerontology: Medical Sciences, 41*, M22–M29.

Parmelee, P. A., Katz, I. R., & Lawton, M. P. (1991). The relation of pain to depression among institutionalized aged. *Journal of Gerontology: Psychological Sciences, 46*, P15–P21.

Parmelee, P. A., Katz, I. R., & Lawton, M. P. (1992). Incidence of depression in long-term care settings. *Journal of Gerontology: Medical Sciences, 46*, M189–M196.

Parmelee, P. A., Katz, I. R., & Lawton, M. P. (1993). Anxiety and its association with depression among institutionalized elderly. *American Journal of Geriatric Psychiatry, 1*, 65–78.

Parmelee, P. A., Kleban, M. H., & Katz, I. R. Pain, anxiety and depression among institutional elderly: The role of somatic symptoms. *Advances in Medical Psychotherapy* (in press).

Parmelee, P. A., Smith, B. D., & Katz, I. R. (1993). Pain complaints and cognitive status among elderly institution residents. *Journal of the American Geriatrics Society, 41*, 517–522.

Pincus, T., Callahan, L. F., Bradley, L. A., Vaughn, W. K., & Wolfe, F. (1986). Elevated MMPI scores for hypochondriasis, depression, and hysteria in patients with rheumatoid arthritis reflect disease rather than psychological status. *Arthritis and Rheumatism, 29*, 1456–1466.

Radecki, S. E., Kane, R. L., Solomon, D. H., Mendenhall, R. C., & Beck, J. C. (1988a). Do physicians spend less time with older patients? *Journal of the American Geriatrics Society, 36*, 713–718.

Radecki, S. E., Kane, R. L., Solomon, D. H., Mendenhall, R. C., & Beck, J. C. (1988b). Are physicians sensitive to the special needs of older patients? *Journal of the American Geriatrics Society, 36*, 719–725.

Radloff, L. S., & Teri, L. (1986). Use of the Center for Epidemiological Studies Depression Scale with older adults. *Clinical Gerontology, 5*, 119–136.

Richards, J. S., Nepomuceno, C., Riles, M., & Suer, Z. (1982). Assessing pain behavior: The UAB Pain Behavior Scale. *Pain, 14*, 393–398.

Romano, J. M., & Turner, J. A. (1985). Chronic pain and depression: Does the evidence support a relationship? *Psychological Bulletin, 97*, 18–34.

Rovner, B. W., German, P. S., Broadhead, J., Morriss, R. K., Brant, L. J., Blaustein, J., & Folstein, M. F. (1990). The prevalence and management of dementia and other psychiatric disorders in nursing homes. *International Psychogeriatrics, 2*, 13–24.

Roy, R., & Thomas, M. R. (1986). A survey of chronic pain in an elderly population. *Canadian Family Physician, 32*, 513–516.

Sengstaken, E. A., & King, S. A. (1993). The problem of pain and its detection among geriatric nursing home residents. *Journal of the American Geriatrics Society, 41*, 541–544.

Sofaer, B., & Walker, J. (1994). Mood assessment in chronic pain patients. *Disability and Rehabilitation, 16*, 35–38.

Spear, F. G. (1967). Pain in psychiatric patients. *Journal of Psychosomatic Research, 11*, 187–193.

Stewart, R. B., Blashfield, R., Hale, W. E., Moore, M. T., May, F. E., & Marks, R. G. (1991). Correlates of Beck Depression Inventory scores in an ambulatory elderly population: Symptoms, diseases, laboratory values, and medications. *Journal of Family Practice, 32*, 497–502.

Strang, P., & Qvarner, H. (1990). Cancer-related pain and its influence on quality of life. *Anticancer Research, 19*, 109–112.

Sulkava, R., Wikstrom, J., Aromaa, A., Raitasalo, R., Lehtinen, V., Lahtela, K., & Palo, J. (1985). Prevalence of severe dementia in Finland. *Neurology, 35*, 1025–1029.

Summers, J. D., Rapoff, M. A., Varghese, G., Porter, K., & Palmer, R. E. (1991). Psychosocial factors in chronic spinal cord injury ain. *Pain, 47*, 183–189.

Teske, K., Daut, R. L., & Cleeland, C. S. (1983). Relationships between nurses' observations and patients' self-reports of pain. *Pain, 16*, 289–296.

Tief, P. M., Elliott, D. J., Stein, N., & Frederickson, B. E. (1987). Functional vs. organic pain: A meaningful distinction? *Journal of Clinical Psychology, 43*, 219–226.

Turk, D. C., & Okifuji, A. (1994). Detecting depression in chronic pain patients: Adequacy of self-reports. *Behavior Research and Therapy, 32*, 9–16.

von Knorring, L., Perris, C., Eisemann, M., Eriksson, U., & Perris, H. (1983). Pain as a symptom in depressive disorders: 2. Relationship to personality traits as assessed by means of KSP. *Pain, 17*, 377–384.

Weisenberg, M., Aviram, O., Wolf, Y., & Raphaeli, N. (1984). Relevant and irrelevant anxiety in the reaction to pain. *Pain, 20*, 371–383.

Williamson, G. M., & Schulz, R. (1992). Pain and depression among community-residing elderly. *Journal of Gerontology: Psychological Sciences, 46*, P367–P372.

Williamson, G. M., & Schulz, R. (1995). Activity restriction mediates the association between pain and depressed affect: A study of younger and older adult cancer patients. *Psychology and Aging, 10*, 369–378.

Williamson, J. (1978). Depression in the elderly. *Age and Aging, 7*(Suppl.), 35–40.

Wolff, B. B. (1983). Laboratory methods of pain measurement. In R. Melzack (Ed.), *Pain measurement and assessment* (pp. 7–13). New York: Raven Press.

CHAPTER 11

Hypnosis and Pain Relief for Older Persons

NICHOLAS A. COVINO

There is a bit of irony in the fact that a technique like hypnosis, which is so dependent on the exercise of "imagination," has so many fantasies attached to its use. These fictions apply both to patients and to practitioners and range from the fanciful to the fearful. By the time that most people reach their senior years, there have been a number of opportunities to witness animated figures with force fields emanating from their eyes issuing commands to somnambulistic respondents. They may also have seen a stage hypnotist invite an embarrassed subject (often a paid accomplice posing as a volunteer) to feel unable to leave the stage to use the bathroom, despite a powerful urge to do so. The more erudite might even have heard the story of Freud's abandonment of hypnosis when a patient allegedly rose from the couch to amorously embrace him. Most patients with chronic pain have doubtless been told that their distress is "all in their head." On the other side, there are alternative medicine enthusiasts who guarantee magical cures from any "mind–body" technique and promise that hypnosis will heal whatever ails a person. If we add to this the popular, though unsubstantiated, idea among clinicians that older persons are not particularly susceptible to hypnosis, it is not surprising that this valuable technique is underemployed in the treatment of pain.

HYPNOSIS DEFINED

Hypnosis is a special form of concentration where suggestions are offered to the motivated patient. These suggestions usually involve ideas for relaxation, perceptual alteration, and behavioral rehearsal. Much as in a daydream, the hypnotist invites the subject to become imaginatively involved in a scene that might facilitate a state of

---

NICHOLAS A. COVINO • Psychology Division, Beth Israel Hospital, Boston, Massachusetts 02215.

Handbook of Pain and Aging, edited by David I. Mostofsky and Jacob Lomranz. Plenum Press, New York, 1997.

relaxation. A parasympathetic "relaxation response" (à la Benson, 1975) is elicited by an invitation to patients to vividly picture a beach, mountain retreat, or other place of leisure "as if they are there at the moment." Patients then use their imagination to become vividly absorbed in the fantasy. Heart and respiratory rates diminish along with muscle tension, arterial blood pressure, and oxygen consumption. The metabolic state that follows is similar to the neurological and physiological activity that customarily occurs with meditation, prayer, yoga, Zen, biofeedback, or any other relaxation technique (Benson, 1989).

Imaginative ability seems to act like an amplifier for the patients' perceptions and often permits them to experience a more profound emotional and physiological reaction. Although the usual approach in hypnosis is to invite a parasympathetic response through (self- or hetero-) hypnosis, it is just as possible to present images that invite sympathetic hyperarousal. It is conceivable that the hypnosis of patients with "active imaginations" will cause or exacerbate some medical and psychiatric disorders by virtue of their ability to intensely imagine events in a negative or threatening fashion (Covino & Frankel, 1993; Covino, Jimmerson, Wolfe, Franko, & Frankel, 1994).

What differentiates hypnosis from the above-mentioned mind–body techniques is the use of *suggestion*. A suggestion is an idea offered to a subject to be considered uncritically. Where the principles of Aristotelian logic might be applied to analyze a particular theory or proposition, responses to suggestions are largely "unreflective" and seem, at times, to be beyond the conscious control of the subject. Suggestions for altered perception are the hallmark of hypnosis, and these can be directed to either the cognitive or the sensory domain. Ideas for changing cognition range from increased motivation to become more involved in a rehabilitation program to an invitation to reinterpret previous pain experiences more neutrally. In the tradition of cognitive psychology (Meichenbaum, 1977; Lazarus & Folkman, 1984), it is expected that patients will have different feelings about something when they "see it" differently. At this level, therapists also work to invite a patient to mentally rehearse more adaptive behaviors. Here, patients are invited to anticipate circumstances in which they are likely to exhibit a maladaptive coping response and, after exploring the threats to a more appropriate response, to picture themselves behaving successfully. In a different fashion, patients are invited to alter sensory input, whether visual, auditory, olfactory, gustatory, or kinesthetic.

Responsivity to these suggestions usually depends on the patient's degree of hypnotizability and willingness to comply with the hypnotist (Bowers & LeBaron, 1986). Empirical research (Hilgard, 1965) leads us to believe that hypnotizability is positively skewed, with about 25% of the population unresponsive to hypnosis and 15% of the population highly responsive. It is unclear what factors influence a person's degree of hypnotizability, but those people who appreciate imaginative pursuits (e.g., art, writing, design, reading) or who have enjoyed self-absorbing activities (e.g., swimming, running, watching movies) that permit a withdrawal of visual scanning, diminished critical analysis, and imaginative involvement seem to do best. The capacity for high levels of self-absorbed fantasy, where the subject seems to be actually unaware of impinging stimuli or ongoing behavior, is seen as dissociation (Lynn & Rhue, 1993). Those who define hypnosis often say that it is a combination of these two characteristics: dissociative ability and responsivity to suggestion.

Like the athletic coach or symphony conductor, even the most talented hypnotist can do little more than to invite the subject to "play along" with the suggestions. These are best presented in a graded fashion that invites the subject to abandon critical judgment and adopt a positive response set. Most research has failed to find any significant personality variables that correlate with hypnotizability or that predict a failure to respond. Those who are overly wary lack sufficient hypnotizability, or are given to expect very little from it are likely to have minimal results from an hypnotic intervention. Those who are responsive to this technique are usually capable of such vivid fantasy that it is difficult for them to adequately distinguish between what is real and what is imagined. Time seems to pass unnoticed, body parts can be dissociated, memories can be altered to conform to new data, and amnesia can be applied to old events or current experiences.

Apart from the lore that has developed among practitioners of hypnosis, there is scant evidence to support the notion that older persons cannot successfully utilize hypnosis when it is properly introduced and applied. Older persons are not a monolithic group! With increasing age, there is increased variability between older subjects (Rowe & Wang, 1988), but age alone provides little information on whether an individual can be successfully hypnotized. However, the presence of certain medical or neurological conditions, such as a dementing illness, might so compromise the patient's ability to concentrate that hypnosis is not possible. A person with a moderate senile dementia of the Alzheimer's type who requires neuroleptics for behavior control may not be able to be hypnotized. Despite some special cases, after a careful review of medications and medical history, little is lost by inviting a patient capable of concentrating and paying attention to instructions, especially one who has demonstrated some previous ability to fantasize, to a trial of hypnosis.

A BRIEF HISTORY OF HYPNOSIS AND PAIN CONTROL

Much of the earliest research in the area of controlling pain by means of hypnosis was undertaken by the anesthesiologist Beecher (1940, 1956, 1968, 1969), and experimental psychologist Ernest Hilgard (1969, 1975) and psychiatrist Josephine Hilgard (1982, 1984). When Beecher was a wartime physician, he noticed that soldiers who had sustained more serious injuries, required less pain medication and often had a more optimistic way of coping with their pain and injuries than he had expected (Beecher, 1940). He surmised that this had something to do with the relief of being taken from the front and being likely to be sent home, as well as the badge of courage that a battle injury symbolized for them. Reminding his colleagues that a boy, bloodied in a fistfight, often saves his tears for later when mother arrives, he posited a two-factor aspect to the pain process (Beecher, 1969). Pain, he said, is a process that involves the initial sensation caused by the injury (physiological) and a later (psychological) reaction that applies meaning to the event. In the same report (Beecher, 1969), he told of a soldier writhing so much in pain that he could not be examined. With only a "small dose of a barbiturate," the man became immediately quiet and almost serene. Beecher concluded that, while a particular injury may be involved in the registration of some pain, the patient's *anxiety* rather than the degree of tissue damage is centrally involved in the patient's suffering.

In a series of postwar investigations, Beecher found that patients who adjusted their attitude could cope more efficiently and effectively with other injuries. When 150 male civilian surgical patients were compared to an equal number of war casualties with similar injuries, for example, Beecher (1956) found that 87% of the former group would respond positively to an offer of morphine for their pain versus only 33% of the latter. After a number of such experiments at Harvard Medical School, he concluded that psychological factors other than the extent of the physical damage due to a wound (i.e., anxiety, personal meaning) are responsible for the patient's "suffering" in pain (Beecher, 1968).

In the research laboratory, Ernest and Josephine Hilgard (1975/1983) found a number of interesting phenomena related to experimentally induced pain. In contrast to the clinical pain of Beecher's patients, the noxious stimuli of the experimental laboratory seemed to be of relatively little psychological significance to subjects. To begin with, the Hilgards and their colleagues ascertained that there was a reliable linear relationship to experimental pain so that subjects would report increased pain with the continued application of a noxious stimulus. When subjects were asked to place their arms and hands in a circulating bath of ice water (cold pressor pain) or to squeeze a ball while a tourniquet was applied to their arm (ischemic pain), not only would they report increased pain with a decrease in temperature (Hilgard, 1969) or an increase in blood pressure (Hilgard, MacDonald, Marshall, & Morgan, 1974), but their heart rates and blood pressure readings would also increase.

When a group of college students were invited to use hypnosis to reduce their experience of cold pressor pain, Hilgard and Morgan (1975) found them significantly able to diminish it. Utilizing suggestions for analgesia, they found not only that the subjects were successful, but that those with increased hypnotic ability had the best results. Of subjects who were found to be in the highly hypnotizable range, 67% reduced their pain by one-third versus only 13% of their low hypnotizable counterparts. A correlation of .50 was found between the subject's level of hypnotizability and success with pain relief.

The Hilgards (1975/1983) cited the work of Greene and Reyher (1972), who assigned highly hypnotizable persons to hypnotic and simulator conditions in an effort to test whether this pain reduction capacity was merely role play or due to something particular in the hypnotic condition. While the simulators were equally able to fool an experienced group of hypnotists, those who were truly experiencing a trance were able to tolerate the pain of an electric shock to a degree much greater than the pretenders. This body of research established another psychological mechanism for the management of pain.

Elaborating on the earlier theory of *dissociation* by Janet (1907), the Hilgards (Hilgard & Hilgard, 1975/1983; E. R. Hilgard, 1977) and their colleagues postulated the involvement of higher cognitive processes of the brain which divide the consciousness of hypnotizable subjects. As in the case of posthypnotic amnesia or when a hypnotist suggests that a subject hallucinate an absent object or ignore a present stimulus, the brain of a hypnotized subject makes information regarding the pain stimuli temporarily unavailable to consciousness. The Hilgards posited a barrier to conscious awareness that is similar to an amnestic barrier which permits an overt experience of pain freedom that includes the absence of grimace and relaxation (Knox, Morgan, & Hilgard, 1974). Covertly, however, the subject may be quite aware of pain and may show it by increased cardiovascular activity and other indicators (e.g., automatic writing). As with suggestions for amnesia, the overt and covert cognition remain segregated, permitting the patient to bear a considerable number of noxious stimuli in comfortable ignorance (see also Lynn & Rhue, 1994).

SOME RECENT LABORATORY AND CLINICAL RESEARCH

Since the experiments of Beecher and the Hilgards and their colleagues, numerous authors have found similar relationships between hypnotic suggestion and the ability to reduce laboratory-induced and clinical pain. Most researchers continue to understand that the efficacy of hypnosis, from a psychological perspective, involves some combination of relaxation, cognitive restructuring, and dissociation. Recent efforts have also endeavored to explore some neurological links between the subjects' response to suggestions for analgesia, relaxation, and dissociation, and a number of physiological phenomena.

Highly hypnotizable subjects who were administered electric shock in the laboratory were better able to tolerate it with the use of hypnosis compared to their baseline, a placebo condition, and their low-hypnotizable counterparts (McGlashan, Evans, & Orne, 1969). A number of laboratory studies (e.g., Karlin, Morgan, & Goldstein, 1980; Spanos, 1984) found results similar to those of Miller and Bowers (1986) who invited 60 undergraduates to immerse their hands and arms in ice water and to keep them there as long as possible. When interventions such as fantasied distraction, stress inoculation, and hypnotic analgesia were compared in high- and low-hypnotizable subjects, the highs reported significantly less pain in all conditions, but they did best ($p < .03$) in the hypnosis condition.

Experimental subjects were also able to tolerate ischemic pain with the use of hypnotically induced suggestions for analgesia (DeBenedittis, Panerai, & Villamira, 1989). The analgesia suggestions had very little impact on the subjects' level of anxiety, leading the authors to present two distinct dimensions of the pain experience: sensory-discriminative and motivational-affective, the former relating to information about the location and intensity of pain, and the latter registering the aversive impact and negative emotional resonance of pain. Suggestions for analgesia are thought to affect the first and those for relaxation the second (Price & Barber, 1987; Malone, Kurtz, & Strube, 1989; Miller, Barabasz, & Barabasz, 1991).

Among the clinical studies, hypnosis has enabled responsive subjects to better tolerate a variety of painful medical procedures. In a study of patients undergoing colonoscopy who were unable to use anaesthesia for pain control (Cadranel et al., 1994), all of the "hypnosis-responsive" patients completed the procedure (vs. 50% of the nonrespondents) and agreed to undertake a follow-up exam under similar conditions

($p < .001$). Hypnosis enabled patients who were undergoing interventional radiographic study (Lang & Hamilton, 1994) and angioplasty (Weinstein & Au, 1991) to tolerate a longer time with the procedure and to do so with significantly less dependence on pain medications. Those who used hypnosis for these procedures had the added benefits of a more technically successful procedure and speedier recovery time. Burn patients who were taught to use hypnosis were much better able to tolerate the pain during wound débridement (Patterson, Everett, Burns, & Marvin, 1992). Children who were required to undergo painful lumbar punctures (LP) and bone marrow transplants were able to manage their pain and anxiety more effectively with the use of hypnosis than with distraction and relaxation techniques alone (Zeltzer & LeBaron, 1982). More specifically, hypnosis was approximately as successful as relaxation training in helping with the anxiety associated with both conditions, but it was significantly better in reducing the pain associated with LP.

While success in managing pain with hypnosis seems to be related to the patient's degree of hypnotizability, cognitive style, motivation to use the technique, expectations, level of cognitive functioning, and "secondary gain" (Evans, 1989; Spira & Spiegel, 1992; Chaves, 1994), clinicians have reported a number of interesting successes among patients with a variety of medical illnesses.

A number of studies with cancer patients have found hypnosis to be more successful than cognitive behavioral treatments alone in controlling both pain and suffering. Spiegel and Bloom (1983) found the combination of group therapy and hypnosis to be most helpful to a selection of patients with breast cancer. The hypnosis group were significantly able to reduce their self-reports of both pain ($p < .02$) and suffering ($p < .03$) in a controlled study. This success was also related to a significant improvement in their mood. These findings were similar to those in a group of Lebanese cancer patients who were randomly assigned to a hypnosis group or a no-treatment control group (Ali, 1990). In a randomized experiment, with 2 initial and 10 follow-up sessions, hypnosis was more successful in helping bone marrow transplant patients to manage their pain than cognitive-behavioral treatment and therapist support (Syrjala, Cummings, & Donaldson, 1992).

As with the cancer studies, clinicians who work with arthritis patients, stroke victims, and those with reflex sympathetic dystrophy and fibromyalgia, among other conditions, have found similar success in teaching their patients to use hypnosis to manage their pain. Suggestions for hypnoanalgesia were successful in permitting a group of arthritic patients to reduce their pain and psychological suffering while demonstrating increases in catecholamine activity (Domangue, Margolis, Lieberman, & Kaji, 1985). A 66-year-old stroke victim was able to use a variety of hypnotic suggestions for motivation and motor movement to speed up her recovery from a stroke (Holroyd & Hill, 1989). At a two-year follow-up, the application of hypnotic strategies for pain relief combined with psychotherapy had been successful in reducing pain in a case of reflex sympathetic dystrophy (Gainer, 1993). Hypnosis was more successful than physical therapy in reducing the pain and suffering of 40 patients with refractory fibromyalgia in a randomized controlled study (Haanen et al., 1991).

Despite more than 50 years of clinical and experimental work on the application of hypnosis to a variety of painful conditions, attempts to identify a particular physiological link between hypnotic suggestion and the relief of pain have proved inadequate. Researchers who have looked beyond explanations such as psychological attention, dissociation, patient compliance, and muscle relaxation have pointed to the potential connection between biogenic amines, the autonomic or opiate endorphin system, and suggestions for analgesia and have found conflicting results (Hilgard & Hilgard, 1983; Domangue et al., 1985; Debenedittis, Panerai, & Villamira, 1989; Gracely, 1995). Studies using cerebral blood flow imaging have found increased brain activity in the somatosensory region when subjects have been offered suggestions for analgesia (Crawford, Gur, Skolnick, Gur, & Benson, 1993). Recently, a group of investigators found a reduction in spinal nociception as measured by the R-III response when a group of 17 hypnotized subjects were asked to reduce their pain and unpleasantness in response to electric shock (Kiernan, Dane, Phillips, & Price, 1995). These authors found a selective difference in the manner and degree that subjects were able to achieve these reductions of pain sensation and unpleasantness. They posited a multidimensional model of pain reduction that includes a reduction in pain sensation by means of suggestions for analgesia processed by the spinal cord antinociceptive mechanism; diminished awareness of the pain sensation if it overcomes the reductions in R-III spinal cord mechanisms and reaches the higher centers of the brain by means of psychological mechanisms; and selective reduction in the affective dimension by distraction and cognitive restructuring techniques. The specificity of suggestions for analgesia is once again asserted, along with a model that obviates some of the methodological problems that have encumbered previous pain studies that have had to rely on questionably valid "subject self-reports" for the objective measurement of changes in pain sensation (Gracely, 1995).

CLINICAL APPLICATIONS

Initial Steps

Clinical and experimental research has opened a number of approaches to the relief of pain with hypnosis. At the start, patients must be invited to participate in a manner that secures their cooperation and trust. This usually requires a discussion of the myths regarding hypnosis that the patients are likely to have learned from the media or elsewhere in the environment. Such discussions usually begin with a description of the elements of hypnosis as well as clear statements about the individual nature of suggestibility. Patients are assured that *they* are in control of what happens during a trance and that nothing will be done to embarrass or frighten them in any way. They are told that they will not comply with any suggestion that seems to be opposed to their value system and are assured that if anything distresses them at all they need only to open their eyes and reorient themselves to the room to terminate the trance. Therapists profitably point to naturally occurring trance experiences in the patients' lives such as daydreaming, reading, highway driving, or relaxing on a porch chair in summer to assure them of the pleasant nature of a trance experience.

Inasmuch as people bring their own personality and a certain amount of learning to a clinical situation, the hypnotist does best both to respond to the patients' questions and to identify other psychological issues that might facilitate compliance or interfere with the suggestions. Bibring and Kahana (1968) stressed the importance of seeing each patient as possessing a different psychological style which must be clearly understood and responded to flexibly by the therapist. For example, the "dependent" patient, they wrote, requires a different approach by the therapist from the "counterdependent" person. If the clinician has the insight and personal flexibility to stress the increased autonomy, control, and personal power that hypnosis will bring to the management of pain, it is likely that the hypnotic suggestions will be more easily received without critical judgment by the counterdependent patient. When there is some meaningful history of developmental, interpersonal, or work issues or some special meaning that the patient attaches to the pain symptom, these must be ascertained and integrated into the hypnotist's approach and work with the patient.

In general, the clinician should answer two questions before undertaking a treatment with hypnosis:

1. Do psychological factors contribute to the variance?
2. How hypnotizable is the patient?

The first question relates to the nature of the presenting complaint and the second to the skills of the person. These days, there are a number of enthusiastic practitioners who laud the virtues of mind–body techniques and universally apply them to medical problems. As we have seen, there do seem to be a number of mechanisms by which trance or suggestion can influence physiological parameters, but it is important to remember that hypnosis is still essentially a psychological technique. When a medical problem is severe or is obviously causing extreme pain, we should assume that there will be little room for a psychological intervention to successfully alleviate it. If a problem is difficult for conventional medicine to treat, the same challenges will be there for the hypnotist. While hypnosis can assist patients with cancer in managing the pain and the unpleasant side effects of treatment, it is most doubtful that this psychological technique can be instrumental in reversing the disease process. Likewise, an evidently bulging disk in the spinal cord is unlikely to represent the same challenge to a hypnotic intervention as the insertion of an intravenous line. When such psychological factors as relaxation, dissociation, attention, memory, suggestion, or symbolization are, or could be, involved in the patient's pain, or when some interaction of cognitive factors with reduction in autonomic nervous system activity adds to the experience of distress, it is sensible to assume that hypnosis can be of benefit. As the scientific techniques for understanding the relationship between cognition and nociception improve, we may be invited to expand this model.

The above having been said, our review of the clinical and experimental literatures points clearly to the ability of those with heightened levels of hypnotizability to modify their experience of pain. More formal testing of hypnotizability might interfere with the patient's compliance with hypnotic treatment, especially if the patient were to fail a number of the more difficult items. When the clinical examination (e.g., history of meditation, interest in imaginative pursuits) leads to the impression that the patient has some special talent for hypnosis, there is good reason to expect a more favorable result.

Some Suggestions for Intervention

In the case of pain, it is best not to promise patients that hypnosis will totally or immediately remove their distress. It is safe to say that this psychological technique can assist the doctor and the patient in their efforts to ameliorate or alleviate pain to some degree. Good suggestions also rarely confront a clinical problem directly but prepare the way by establishing a "positive response set" which can be used by the clinician to graft more challenging suggestions. If the patient is easily able to accomplish initial hypnotic tasks (e.g., following a suggestion to elevate a hand by picturing an inflated balloon attached to the wrist), it is more likely that suggestions for pain relief can be achieved. A selection of suggestions follows:

1. *Distraction.* The idea to be conveyed is that a pain sensation is intermittent and that, while it cannot be easily ignored, it can be put in the background by deliberate concentration and by placing something else more prominently in consciousness. There are many avenues to take with this approach, but the indirect suggestion is "Attention is a very narrow band. You can control noxious sensations by bringing your awareness of neutral or more enjoyable sensory input to the foreground, while disregarding the unpleasant."

At first, the patient is asked to concentrate on the feelings in a pain-free part of the body (e.g., the hand). In the trance, the hypnotist invites the patient to become aware of the way the hand might be touching an article of clothing or another part of the body. Differences in pressure and skin temperature are often present if the back of the hand is exposed and the palm is touching the armrest or clothing. The patient's attention is then directed to another part of the body, such as the neck, where the slight pressure of a shirt collar or necklace is available. As a similar mental exploration is directed to this area, the subject is reminded that it is difficult to be aware of the sensations in the hand "until now." Several parts of the body can be employed to continue with the suggestion.

2. *Memory.* The patient's memory can be used to recall vividly a pain-free time in the past or to forget some unpleasant aspects of the pain situation "as if they never happened." For many people, the experience of pain is highly influenced by past pain experiences, and those who have chronic pain often find it difficult to recall a time of relief.

A subject can be prepared for amnesia by using a trance to call to mind the numerous experiences, facts, and events that are easily forgotten in daily life. From keys, to dates, to telephone numbers, the subject is reminded of the ease with which a person can forget something. Suggestions are offered to let go of the emotions attached to past incidents or to suppress the particulars of the events themselves.

Age regression is a special form of suggestion where the subject is invited to return mentally to a time in the past. By feeling younger and smaller and recalling an emotion, person, or place from an earlier time, the subject is able to temporarily escape the felt experience of pain. Likewise, painful time can pass quickly, as it does when one is absorbed in a good book or a movie.

3. *Selective inattention.* In the manner described by Janet (1907) and the Hilgards

(1975/1983), subjects are encouraged to use the trance to separate or alter their awareness of the body, self, pain, or current time. The trance that follows permits the registration of several events at the same time and allows the patients to minimize, alter, or ignore pain.

As in driving in a car while thinking deeply about something else, subjects can separate their stream of consciousness to have their "mind" attend to other things, while their brain may be registering a painful sensation. Patients can be invited to "place" their pain in another part of their body or to use their imagination to "leave" their body altogether.

Related to these suggestions are guided images (some can be proposed by the patient) that direct the patient's attention away from the body to become sensorially involved in a place he or she has visited or is able to imagine. Subjects are directed to be quite aware of what they might see, hear, feel, smell, taste, and so on, "as if they are right there at the moment." Again, the feelings of relaxation and self-absorption, made more vivid by the patient's imaginings, offer a buffer to noxious stimuli.

4. *Perceptual alteration.* From requests to restructure their thinking about a painful experience, circumstance, or stimulus to the creation of sensory hallucinations, better subjects can use imagination to alter their cognitive and sensory perceptions.

At the cognitive level, a "new outlook" can often motivate patients to expend additional effort toward a goal or to modify their emotions. As with Beecher's war heros, a particular perspective or the reinterpretation of some data can bring about a subjective difference in the pain experience. The patient can be reminded that the purpose of an "alarm" is to alert a person to take remedial action. In the case of chronic pain, since there is nothing to be done in response to the signal, the subject is invited to remain calm and to ignore the warning.

It is sometimes easier for patients to increase their pain by certain imaginings. If a visual analogue scale or number line can be used to indicate a level of pain, a variety of strategies can be offered to the patient to exacerbate it. When the subject indicates that she or he has worsened the pain, a similar effort can reduce it. With success, the exercise teaches the patient about the close connection between mind and body and opens the door for increased pain relief.

In a similar fashion, a burning pain or a chilling sensation can be "traded" for one that is less hurtful. A warm feeling can be cultivated to replace a burning one, and the "hurt can be separated from the pain."

A memory of numbness, such as one receives from the dentist's xylocaine, can be recalled and imagined to occur in the hand. A so-called glove anesthesia is created by adding the sense that the hand is covered by a thick, insulated glove or is immersed in a bucket of water so cold that there is no sensation present. When the subject reports success in achieving this illusion, the numb feeling is applied and "transferred" to an injured part.

SUMMARY

A review of the literature strongly "suggests" that hypnosis, when properly applied, can be of great use to many older persons in their efforts to manage pain. A comprehensive approach that integrates information regarding the patient's presenting complaint, pain history, and manner of conceptualizing pain with an understanding of her or his "psychological style" will be most successful when applied by a clinician who takes the time to properly educate and prepare the patient. Any combination of the above-mentioned techniques will assist patients in the management of pain. As with many clinical interventions, some of the best treatment strategies will be developed in collaboration with the patient.

REFERENCES

Ali, F. F. (1990). The effect of individual hypnosis on stress, anxiety, and intractable pain experienced by Lebanese cancer patients. *Dissertation Abstracts International, 51*, 3111.

Beecher, H. K. (1940). Pain in men wounded in battle. *Annals of Surgery, 123*, 96–105.

Beecher, H. K. (1956). Relationships of significance of wound to pain experienced. *Journal of the American Medical Association, 161*, 1609–1613.

Beecher, H. K. (1968). The measurement of pain in man: A reinspection of the work of the Harvard Group. In A. Soularic, J. Cahn, & J. Carpenter (Eds.), *Pain*. New York: Academic Press.

Beecher, H. K. (1969). Anxiety and pain. *Journal of the American Medical Association, 209*, 1080.

Benson, H. (1975). *The relaxation response*. New York: Morrow.

Benson, H. (1989). Hypnosis and the relaxation response. *Gastroenterology, 96*, 1609–1611.

Bibring, G. L., & Kahana, R. J. (1968). *Lectures in Medical Psychology*. New York: University Press.

Bowers, K. S., & LeBaron, S. (1986). Hypnosis and hypnotizability: Implications for clinical intervention. *Hospital and Community Psychiatry, 37*, 457–467.

Cadranel, J. F., Benhamou, Y., Zylberberg, P., Novello, P., Luciani, F., Valla, D., & Opolon, P. (1994). Hypnotic relaxation: A new sedative tool for colonoscopy? *Journal of Clinical Gastroenterology, 18*, 127–129.

Chaves, J. F. (1994). Recent advances in the application of hypnosis to pain management. *American Journal of Clinical Hypnosis, 37*, 117–129.

Covino, N. A., & Frankel, F. H. (1993). Hypnosis and relaxation in the medically ill. *Psychotherapy and Psychosomatics, 60*, 75–90.

Covino, N. A., Jimmerson, D. C., Wolfe, B. E., Franko, D. L., & Frankel, F. H. (1994). Hypnotizability, dissociation, and bulimia nervosa. *Journal of Abnormal Psychology, 103*, 455–459.

Crawford, H. J., Gur, R. C., Skolnick, B., Gur, R. E., & Benson, D. M. (1993). Effects of hypnosis on regional cerebral blood flow during ischemic pain with and without suggested hypnotic analgesia. *International Journal of Psychophysiology, 15*, 181–195.

DeBenedittis, G., Panerai, A. A., & Villamira, M. A. (1989). Effect of hypnotic analgesia and hypnotizability on experimental ischemic pain. *International Journal of Clinical Hypnosis, 37*, 55–69.

Domangue, B. B., Margolis, C. G., Lieberman, D., & Kaji, H. (1985). Biochemical correlates of hypoanalgesia in arthritic pain patients. *Journal of Clinical Psychiatry, 46*, 235–238.

Evans, F. J. (1989). Hypnosis and chronic pain: Two contrasting case studies. *Clinical Journal of Pain, 5*, 159–176.

Gainer, M. J. (1993). Somatization of dissociated traumatic memories in case of reflex sympathetic dystrophy. *American Journal of Clinical Hypnosis, 36*, 124–131.

Gracely, R. H. (1995). Hypnosis and hierarchial pain control systems. *Pain, 60*, 1–2.

Greene, R. J., & Reyher, J. (1972). Pain tolerance in hypnotic analgesic and imagination states. *Journal of Abnormal Psychology, 79*, 29–38.

Haanen, H. C., Hoenderdos, H. T., van Romunde, L. K., Hop, W. C., Mallee, C., Terwiel, J. P., & Hekster, G. B. (1991). Controlled trail of hypnotherapy in the treatment of refractory fibromyalgia. *Journal of Rheumatology, 18*, 72–75.

Hilgard, E. R. (1965). Hypnosis. *Annual Review of Psychology, 16*, 157–180.

Hilgard, E. R. (1969). Pain as a puzzle for psychology and physiology. *American Psychologist, 24*, 103–113.

Hilgard, E. R. (1977). *Divided consciousness: Multiple controls in human thought and actions.* New York: Wiley.

Hilgard, E. R., & Hilgard, J. R. (1975/1983). *Hypnosis in the relief of pain.* Los Altos, CA: Kaufman.

Hilgard, E. R., MacDonald, H., Marshall, G., & Morgan, A. H. (1974). Anticipation of pain and of pain control under hypnosis: Heart rate and blood pressure responses in the cold pressor test. *Journal of Abnormal Psychology, 83*, 561–568.

Hilgard, E. R., & Morgan, A. H. (1975). Heart rate and blood pressure in the study of laboratory pain in man under normal conditions and as influenced by hypnosis. *Acta Neurobiologiae Experimentalis, 35*, 741–759.

Holroyd, J., & Hill, A. (1989). Pushing the limits of recovery: Hypnotherapy with a stroke patient. *International Journal of Clinical and Experimental Hypnosis, 37*, 120–128.

Janet, P. (1907). *The major symptoms of hysteria.* New York: Macmillan.

Karlin, R., Morgan, D., & Goldstein, L. (1980). Hypnotic analgesia: A preliminary investigation of quantitated hemispheric electroencephalographic and attentional correlates. *Journal of Abnormal Psychology, 89*, 591–594.

Kiernan, D., Dane, J. R., Phillips, L. H., & Price, D. D. (1995). Hypnotic analgesia reduced R-III nociceptive relax: Further evidence concerning multifactorial nature of hypnotic analgesia. *Pain, 60*, 39–47.

Knox, J., Morgan, A. H., & Hilgard, E. R. (1974). Pain and suffering in ischemia: The paradox of hypnotically suggested anesthesia as contradicted by reports from the "hidden observer." *Archives of General Psychiatry, 30*, 840–847.

Lang, E. V., & Hamilton, D. (1994). Anodyne imagery: An alternative to IV sedation in interventional radiology. *AJR Am J Roentgenol., 162*, 1221–1226.

Lazarus, R. S., & Folkman, S. (1984). *Stress appraisal and coping.* New York: Springer.

Lynn, S. J., & Rhue, J. W. (1994). *Dissociation: Clinical and theoretical perspectives.* New York: Guilford Press.

Malone, M. D., Kurtz, R. M., & Strube, M. J. (1989). The effects of hypnotic suggestion on pain report. *American Journal of Clinical Hypnosis, 31*, 221–230.

McGlashan, T. H., Evans, F. J., & Orne, M. T. (1969). The nature of hypnotic analgesia and the process response to experimental pain. *Psychosomatic Medicine, 31*, 227–246.

Meichenbaum, D. (1977). *Cognitive-behavior modification: An integrative approach.* New York: Plenum Press.

Miller, M. F., Barabasz, A. F., & Barabasz, M. (1991). Effects of active alert and relaxation hypnotic induction on cold pressor pain. *Journal of Abnormal Psychology, 100*, 223–226.

Patterson, D. R., Everett, J. J., Burns, G. L., & Marvin, J. A. (1992). Hypnosis for the treatment of burn pain. *Journal of Consulting and Clinical Psychology, 60*, 713–717.

Price, D. D., & Barber, J. (1987). An analysis of factors that contribute to the efficacy of hypnotic analgesia. *Journal of Abnormal Psychology, 96*, 46–51.

Rowe, J. W., & Wang, S. (1988). The biology and physiology of aging. In J. W. Rowe & R. W. Bessie (Eds.), *Geriatric medicine* (pp 1–11). Boston: Little, Brown.

Spiegel, D., & Bloom, J. R. (1983). Group therapy and hypnosis reduce metastatic breast carcinoma pain. *Psychomatic Medicine, 45*, 333–339.

Spira, J. L., & Spiegel, D. (1992). Hypnosis and related techniques in pain management. *Hospital Journal, 8*, 89–119.

Syrjala, K. L., Cummings, C., & Donaldson, G. W. (1992). Hypnosis or cognitive behavioral training for the reduction of pain and nausea during cancer treatment: A controlled clinical trial [see comments]. *Pain, 48*, 137–146.

Weinsten, E. J., & Au, P. K. (1991). Use of hypnosis before and during angioplasty. *American Journal of Clinical Hypnosis, 34*, 29–37.

Zeltzer, L., & LeBaron, S. (1982). Hypnosis and nonhypnotic techniques for reduction of pain and anxiety during painful procedures in children and adolescents with cancer. *Journal of Pediatrics, 101*, 1032–1035.

PART III

Clinical Management and Techniques

CHAPTER 12

Management of Chronic Nonmalignant Pain in the Elderly

Experience in an Outpatient Setting

ROBERT D. HELME, MARK BRADBEER, BENNY KATZ, AND STEPHEN J. GIBSON

INTRODUCTION

A multidisciplinary pain management clinic for older persons was established in Melbourne, Australia, during 1988. Areas of clinical expertise represented in the clinic include medicine (neurology, geriatric medicine), nursing, psychology, physiotherapy, occupational therapy, and pharmacy. In this chapter, we outline the rationale for, and function of, the clinic, describe the characteristics of referred patients, and detail clinical outcomes according to measures of pain, mood, and activity. In general, patients referred to the clinic improve according to these measures. The rationale for pain management clinics specifically for the elderly is discussed, and problems associated with long-term audit of patients in this setting are outlined.

In general, pain resolves spontaneously with the natural history of an injury or illness or following appropriate intervention. There are, however, a minority of individuals who experience persistent pain and suffering, often refractory to standard interventions. Their suffering might be considered to have a "malignant," all-consuming quality in that it affects cognition, mood, behavior, and, indeed, all of life's pleasures. It is these people who may benefit from the intervention of a multidisciplinary pain manage-

ROBERT D. HELME, MARK BRADBEER, BENNY KATZ, AND STEPHEN J. GIBSON • National Ageing Research Institute and North West Hospital Pain Management Centre, Parkville, Australia 3052.

Handbook of Pain and Aging, edited by David I. Mostofsky and Jacob Lomranz. Plenum Press, New York, 1997.

ment clinic. Such clinics have been established worldwide over the past few years, but few have focused exclusively on the special needs of the elderly (Harkins & Price, 1992). Most pain clinics do, however, manage a small number of older people and usually report an even spread of patients across all age groups, at least up to the age of 80 years. This in itself is surprising, as it has been reported that there is an approximate fourfold increase in the prevalence of chronic pain by this age (Crook, Rideout, & Browne, 1984), although studies do differ on the size and cause of this increase (Gibson & Helme, 1995). Geriatricians have also tended to neglect this problem despite a high prevalence of chronic pain reported in nursing-home samples (Ferrell, Ferrell, & Osterweil, 1990). Until recently, most major textbooks on geriatric medicine did not have specific chapters on pain management.

The major clinical issues in aged care such as cognitive disability, immobility, impaired personal care, and incontinence often result in social isolation and respond to multidisciplinary care. Hence, there is a common emphasis on multidisciplinary care in geriatric medicine and in pain management clinics, an approach which we have adopted in establishing the clinic described here. Indeed, it is surprising that pain has not been more conspicuous among the disabilities reported by geriatric services, as it is common in and expected by the majority of older people (Helme, Corran, & Gibson, 1992). In this chapter, we outline the function of a pain clinic for older people; describe the demographic, medical, and social characteristics of the referred patient group; detail clinical outcomes according to measures of pain, mood, and activity; and briefly discuss issues pertinent to this patient population.

THE CLINIC

In 1988, a clinic specifically for the management of chronic pain in older patients was established at North West Hospital, a comprehensive aged-care and rehabilitation facility in Melbourne, Australia. This was an extension of our brief previous experience elsewhere in the city (Helme et al., 1989). The clinic has been staffed by a neurologist, geriatrician, a clinical psychologist, two physiotherapists, one or two nurses, an occupational therapist, a pharmacist, and a secretary-receptionist. Referrals predominantly originate from medical practitioners in the municipalities in close proximity to the hospital, but there is no restriction in this regard. Patients are accepted for assessment if they are over 55 years of age, although on occasion this age criterion is waived if the referred patient has multiple disabilities. The clinic operates on one morning each week. Although it is structured as an outpatient clinic, facilities are also readily available for a short course of inpatient pain management. Initial contact with the patient is made at the patient's home by a nurse or through an information kit delivered by post if the patient lives too far from the clinic to allow a home visit. An initial battery of psychometric tests (see section on evaluation below) are included for completion by the patient. The completed assessments are reviewed on the patient's first attendance at the clinic. These instruments are not applicable if the patient has a cognitive or severe physical disability, or if English is not his or her first language. Such patients, when entered into a management program, are monitored using only the most basic process measures of attendance and subjective team view of progress.

New patients attend the clinic for a one-hour medical consultation. Further psychometric evaluation is undertaken during this visit by a research nurse. At the next appointment, the patient undergoes assessment by the clinical psychologist and a physiotherapist. Close relatives are included in the assessment process when indicated. Following these assessments, the clinical problem is discussed at a team meeting. The aim of this conference is to assign the patient to a diagnostic category on the basis of a consensus decision. If there is potential to rectify the condition causing the pain, this is offered in preference to symptom management. If cure is not feasible, then pain management is discussed. A decision is made as to the best pain management modalities for that individual, and whether such treatment can be offered in the clinic or whether the patient should be referred elsewhere.

Programs in the clinic usually take the form of individual reviews with a physician and a physiotherapist, and of a formal group therapy program supervised by the occupational therapist for one hour over six consecutive weeks. Individual appointments may be offered with the clinical psychologist or the pharmacist as appropriate. Progress is monitored at team meetings which follow the clinic, and other interventions, such as communication with community-based aged-care providers, are discussed and implemented as appropriate. Referring physicians are kept informed of assessments, management, and progress, as it is intended that the general practitioner will continue the program after the patient has been discharged from the clinic. Most individual programs require 10–12 attendances at the clinic.

A standard medical assessment forms the basis of the initial medical consultation with a full history and physical examination. Data are recorded on a computer database regarding demographic details, past therapists and treatments for pain, social and community support systems, and a complete current medication regime. The physical examination is more detailed when it comes to the origin of the pain, with emphasis on accurately recorded pain complaint and musculoskeletal and neurological examinations. For example, the presence of hyperalgesia, hyperpathia, and allodynia is carefully evaluated, and the relative contribution of nociceptor, neuropathic, and psychological elements of the pain syndrome is ascertained.

Once a patient has been accepted into a program, the physician has an overall role monitoring progress, particularly analgesic use, reinforcing the principles being discussed by each therapist with the patient, and ensuring the patient understands the basic mechanisms contributing to her or his pain experience. There is usually more emphasis on counseling than on pharmacological therapies. Intercurrent medical problems not directly related to the pain are referred back to the family practitioner for management or are referred elsewhere following consultation with that practitioner.

Pharmacological management of pain in older patients requires detailed attention to relevant pharmacokinetic and pharmacodynamic factors, and to the potential of associated diseases to alter drug action and interaction. This is a major function of the physicians in the clinic. Standard texts should be consulted for these details, and we and others have recently discussed them in detail (Ackerman, Diede, & Racz, 1994; Foley, 1994; Gibson, Katz, Corran, Farrell, & Helme, 1994; Helme & Katz, 1993, 1995).

In brief, analgesics may be divided into those which are most useful in nociceptor and neuropathic pain syndromes. Simple analgesics, including acetaminophen (paracetamol), aspirin, and nonsteroidal anti-inflammatory drugs (NSAIDs) are mostly used for nociceptor pain, such as subacute postinjury syndromes and arthritides, where pain derives from stimulation of somatic and visceral nociceptors. Combination medications, such as acetaminophen (paracetamol) or aspirin with codeine or dextropropoxyphene, may provide an adequate level of analgesia with fewer side effects than a simple analgesic given alone at a higher dose. Combinations of NSAIDs do not confer greater analgesia but, instead, increase risks of adverse reactions. Opioids are not usually indicated in nonmalignant pain syndromes but can be justified if quality-of-life issues predominate. However, particular care is required in the elderly because of an increased sensitivity to these drugs combined with reduced metabolism (Kaiko, Wallenstein, Rogers, Grabinski, & Houde, 1982).

Neuropathic pain resulting from damage to peripheral or central nociceptive conducting pathways (e.g., trigeminal neuralgia, postherpetic neuralgia, painful peripheral neuropathy, poststroke pain) is relatively insensitive to the analgesic effects of simple or semisynthetic opioids. Certain medications, referred to as *adjuvant analgesics* (that is, agents without intrinsic analgesic properties), may be effective in reducing pain in these specific conditions. They include antidepressant medications and anticonvulsants. Amitriptyline appears to be the most effective tricyclic adjuvant analgesic (Onghena & Van Houdenhove, 1992), particularly when the neuropathic pain has a burning or dysesthetic quality. Amitriptyline may be replaced by another tricyclic agent if it is not tolerated because of its anticholinergic or sedative properties. Anticonvulsants may be effective when the pain has a shooting or stabbing quality. Carbamazepine is often the first drug in this group tried, but like the tricyclics, failure to respond to one medication is not predictive of the response to another medication within the same class. For example, sodium valproate is often used in this situation because of its relatively limited side-effect profile in the elderly. Tricyclics and anticonvulsants may be cautiously used in conjunction, but this requires special care in older patients because of the potential for additive side effects.

Some authors advocate the use of antipsychotic agents for the management of neuropathic pain. However, in our experience, the rare favorable response is outweighed by the significant side-effect profile of this class of medication. Local anesthetics are also used as adjuvant medication, whether as topical preparations, as local peripheral nerve blocks, or for more central actions, by the epidural or intravenous route. If these medications are not useful, narcotics, often in higher doses than are used for nociceptor pain, may be considered. Thus, the principles of "the ladder and the clock" emphasized by the World Health Organization for cancer pain (Foley, 1985) also apply to nonmalignant pain.

Insomnia and anxiety states associated with painful conditions may be treated with anxiolytic drugs such as the benzodiazepines. However, they are associated with an increased propensity for adverse reactions in the elderly, such as daytime sedation, confusion, and falls. They are more appropriate for short-term therapy while the underlying cause is being investigated.

A number of topical agents are also available. The most common are those containing capsaicin, local anesthetics, and the rubefacients methylsalicylate and nicotinate. Although individual trials of these preparations are occasionally undertaken, the patient rarely persists with the product over the longer term.

Neuropathic pain syndromes are rarely completely controlled by analgesics or adjuvant agents, and care must be taken not to induce toxicity with medications which may at best be only partially effective. In most neuropathic pain syndromes, multidisciplinary approaches should be invoked early, with neurostimulation techniques and cognitive strategies.

Medication taken on a regular schedule rather than "as required" often results in better analgesia, less anxiety, and a lower total analgesic intake. This is in keeping with our cognitive-behavioral approach, discouraging a focus on the level of pain as a means of determining when the next dose of medication is due. In general, it is appropriate to begin therapy with a low dose (usually half the normal adult dose) and adjust upward as necessary, although standard adult doses of simple analgesics such as acetaminophen (paracetamol) can be used with safety. Medications with long half-lives should generally be avoided as they have a higher likelihood of toxicity. Nonsteroidal anti-inflammatory medications are considered problematic in the elderly because of their side-effect profile, particularly gastrointestinal hemorrhage and fluid retention, and should be used only when there is clear evidence of an active inflammatory process. The physician must be alert to the potential for drug toxicity, as medications with different proprietary names may be obtained from multiple sources (other doctors, pharmacies, relatives, friends, supermarkets, etc.) and patients may not realize they often contain the same active principle. Continuous and meticulous review of analgesic intake, including over-the-counter preparations, is imperative.

Conversely, fear of adverse side effects from medication may result in the older patient being undermedicated for a condition which is quite amenable to therapy. It is therefore appropriate to have a detailed understanding of the pharmacological properties of a small number of medications, rather than a superficial understanding of many. It is not only the prescribers who may be reticent in using appropriate medications at appropriate doses, and careful explanation to patients and their relatives or other carers regarding the use of medications is required.

A basic principle espoused in most behaviorally based treatment programs is to eliminate the use of reinforcements to pain behaviors by encouraging the use of regular analgesia rather than use on an "as-needed" basis. Thus, where there is concern regarding medication compliance or inappropriate medication use, we frequently dispense a "pain mixture," which is a bland-colored and -flavored base to which various pharmacological agents may be added. The patient remains blinded to the active ingredients of the pain mixture. Patients who do not comply with prescribed analgesic regimens often find the pain mixture novel and demonstrate better compliance when taking it. This allows an evaluation of the effects of time-contingent medication, and of the response to different combinations and dosages of medications on the individual's self-reporting of pain. This approach with the pain mixture, in which control over the drug use is taken away from the patient, may appear to contradict the philosophy of the clinic, which encourages self-empowerment. However, it is usually only a short-term strategy until the optimal medication regimen is determined, and it is instructive in demonstrating the value of regular analgesia in chronic pain states. The patient is transferred to the tablet equivalent once the intention of therapy has been achieved.

A final point to be made regarding the use of medication in older people is the potential for multiple drug interactions because of the many treated conditions from which they may suffer. Continuous meticulous detail in the recording of all medications, with regular review by a pharmacist, has proved most valuable.

The initial physiotherapy assessment is focused on the pain complaint, with appropriate recording of the relevant details, together with a physical examination. This often provides a useful aid to diagnosis, particularly in regard to the role of musculoskeletal structures. There is also an emphasis on forming a profile of the patients' activities of daily living, their actual physical exertion, and how pain affects these functions. The program devised for each individual at the team meeting is heavily dependent on this initial assessment. Although a wide range of standard physical therapies are available through the clinic, the three most heavily utilized are graded exercise programs, attention to posture, and transcutaneous electrical nerve stimulation (TENS).

The physical benefits of exercise for the elderly are well established, and even those of extreme age can achieve a training effect (Fiatarone et al., 1990). The level of exercise to achieve these results need not be strenuous. In younger nonclinical subjects, exercise may raise pain thresholds and tolerance through a number of neurophysiological mechanisms (Janal, Colt, Clark, & Glusman, 1984). However, these effects have yet to be demonstrated in the elderly. Similarly, the positive effects of exercise shown for young adult patients have not yet been clearly established in the elderly with chronic pain. Nevertheless, the use of exercise to increase power and reduce disability is a widely held dictum of geriatric medical practice. Exercise has also been proposed as a modulator of mood state across the age spectrum, but again, this has not been clearly established among the elderly. Hydrotherapy is one treatment modality which attempts to provide the benefits of gently graded exercise while preserving full joint range of movement.

Correction of poor posture and range of movement is an important management strategy in patients with degenerative disease of the vertebral column and large joints. In some instances, however, such as with pain from vertebral canal stenosis, adoption of a flexed posture while walking may improve walking distance. Back braces and other orthoses may be prescribed in individual circumstances.

Most electrotherapy modalities produce only transient pain relief and are consequently of dubious benefit to the chronic pain sufferer. TENS is an exception to this rule. It is inexpensive, portable, and safe and can be administered by the patient. Although clinical trials of TENS often appear in the literature, they often suffer from the lack of a suitable placebo. Most trials resort to dead-battery TENS, which, at best, allows for only single-blinded studies. The weight of evidence would, however, suggest that this modality warrants a trial in most pain conditions irrespective of age, as it is safe, and some individuals benefit greatly, particularly those with postherpetic neuralgia and pain following subacute injury (Johnson, Ashton, & Thompson, 1991; Thorsteinsson, 1987). Cure is not a goal of this therapy. Absolute indications for particular stimulation characteristics do not exist, and patients should be encouraged to experiment with these parameters before rejecting TENS altogether, as this not only ensures that all options have been considered but also encourages empowerment and self-reliance. A suitable trial would use TENS for up to six hours per day over two weeks (see Woolf & Thompson, 1994).

The clinical psychologist undertakes an initial assessment which focuses on broader issues which may influence the pain experience, such as early life events, relationships with family, and degree of psychological insight. The psychologist takes responsibility for the overall supervision of psychological treatment strategies without necessarily personally administering them.

Many patients with chronic pain have a condition where cure is not possible and an alternative approach to symptom management is needed. An eclectic treatment program targeted at maintaining appropriate levels of activity and coping strategies can often assist these patients. However, it has also been established that a significant number of patients attending multidisciplinary pain clinics experience a concomitant emotional disturbance with their chronic pain condition. There is now evidence (Klapow et al., 1993) that a distinction can be made between patients described as experiencing a chronic pain syndrome and those with chronic pain without significant emotional disturbance. For patients with a chronic pain syndrome, psychological interventions are critical in order to decrease their affective symptoms and other psychopathology.

As emotional disturbance plays a significant role in the chronic pain syndrome, attempts to manage patients by using medications and physical modalities of treatment, without addressing psychological factors, often fail. Common symptoms observed in such patients include depressed mood, sleep disturbance, somatic preoccupation, fatigue, and reductions in appetite, activity, and libido. Two major psychological models have been applied to the treatment of those patients identified as having a chronic pain syndrome: (1) a behavioral operant conditioning approach and (2) cognitive therapy which seeks to alter belief structures, attitudes, and thoughts of the patient in order to modify the experience of pain and suffering. Aspects of each model have been combined into an integrated cognitive-behavioral approach which has gradually evolved into the mainstay of psychological treatment for chronic pain.

In brief, pain behaviors such as grimacing, limping, rubbing or holding the affected area, verbal complaint, inactivity, and medication usage can be respondent or operant in nature. Respondent behavior is behavior elicited by antecedent noxious stimulation, while operant behavior is behavior that becomes reinforced by subsequent environmental, social, and interpersonal influences. Thus, due to the effects of positive reinforcement of abnormal illness behavior and lack of reinforcement of normal healthy behavior, previously respondent behavior may persist as invalidism and chronic pain behavior even in the absence of continuing noxious stimulation. These considerations are thought to be particularly relevant in the elderly, whose expressions of pain are likely to elicit attention from carers and perhaps provide a source of social contact which would otherwise be unavailable (Kwentus, Harkins, Lignon, & Silverman, 1985).

A full description of treatment protocols using behavior modification techniques can be found in a review article by Fordyce and colleagues (1973). Briefly, an explicit treatment contract is made with the patient, incorporating specific and realistic goals for increased healthy behaviors (e.g., exercise) and a reduction in inappropriate medication use and other pain behaviors. Medications are normally administered in accordance with a time-contingent schedule (e.g., every four hours) rather than on the conventional "as-needed" basis, which is more appropriate for intermittent pain due to known precipitants. In cooperation with the patient's family, positive reinforcement (praise) is provided for behavior unrelated to pain and for successful attainment of goals, while all pain behaviors, such as moaning, limping, and grimacing, are ignored (extinction). There are few studies on the effectiveness of these methods for elderly adults, although Fordyce maintains that such procedures are applicable to all chronic pain patients, regardless of age (Fordyce, 1978).

The second approach involves the use of various cognitive strategies that attempt to modify pain behaviors. A principle which is fundamental to all types of cognitive therapy is the notion that one's beliefs, appraisals, and thoughts relating to a situation will in large part determine the emotional and behavioral responses to it. It is argued that many patients with chronic pain exhibit maladaptive, distorted, or dysfunctional beliefs which contribute to greater subjective levels of pain and suffering (Turk & Meichenbaum, 1994). The basic aims of cognitive treatment are to educate patients on the strong interrelationships between thoughts, emotions, and consequent levels of pain and maladaptive behaviors; to assist with reconceptualizing such thoughts; and to provide alternative and effective coping strategies. The patient is encouraged to take an active role in this process and accept responsibility for the pain rather than being regarded as a passive victim. Typically, a multidimensional model of pain is presented and contrasted with the unidimensional sensory-physiological model held by many patients. This leads to better understanding of the importance of psychological states such as anxiety, fear, and helplessness in exacerbating the subjective experience of pain, and it helps demonstrate to patients that they have the ability to modify the cognitive and affective dimensions of the pain experience even if the sensory-physiological dimension remains unaltered. Upon identifying negative pain-engendering thoughts (e.g., catastrophizing), patients can be instructed in the use of more adaptive cognitive processes such as positive self-statements of coping and the ignoring of pain sensations (Turner & Romano, 1990; Corran, Gibson, Farrell, & Helme, 1994). It should be noted that cognitive therapy is rarely used in isolation. Relaxation training (with or without biofeedback), guided imagery, and various behavioral modifications such as goal setting, increasing behavioral activity, and appropriate medication usage are frequently incorporated into an overall cognitive-behavioral approach to pain management.

Cognitive therapy (Fernandez & Turk, 1989; Malone & Strube, 1988) and cognitive-behavioral approaches to pain management (Malone & Strube, 1988; Turk & Meichenbaum, 1984) have been shown to be very effective in young and middle-aged adults. There have been some suggestions that the elderly may be less responsive to psychological treatment strategies (Portenoy & Farkash, 1988), and it is true that physical impairment such as general frailty and hearing, memory, and communication difficulties, all of which are more common in older adults, may prevent participation in certain elements of psychologically focused treatment programs. Despite these considerations, several studies have reported that cognitive-behavioral programs within a multidisciplinary treatment setting are of benefit to elderly patients suffering from chronic pain (Puder, 1988); the benefits are maintained at 10-month follow-up (Hornsby, Katz, Helme, Gibson, & Corran, 1991).

In the pain clinic, the bulk of this program is provided within the group therapy program. Patients, in groups of up to six, meet weekly for one hour with the occupational therapist. The framework emphasizes coping strategies for pain and develops those suited to each individual. There is discussion and recording of activities, as well as encouragement to use them as coping strategies. Patients are provided with relaxation tapes and are asked to use them at least twice daily. Some individuals who do not obtain initial benefit from relaxation techniques may obtain benefit from prolonged use as self-control improves.

The clinical psychologist is responsible for the implementation of other strategies and programs when necessary. These include hypnosis, psychotherapy, supportive counseling, stress inoculation techniques, and marital therapy. A small number of patients identified as having a major affective disorder are referred to a psychiatrist for the elderly (psychogeriatrician). A supportive environment is also created in the clinic waiting room, where nursing staff encourage informal communication between peers.

EVALUATION

Over several years, a number of instruments have been used to assess patient status and progress. These can be divided into the broad categories of outcome and mediating variables similar to the methodology suggested by Klapow and colleagues (1993). Current outcome variables used are measures from the long-form McGill Pain Questionnaire (MPQ—Melzack, 1975), the Geriatric Depression Scale (GDS—Yesavage, Brink, Rose, & Adey, 1983), and the Spielberger State Anxiety Inventory (SAY—Spielberger, 1983), which have been used to assess pain and mood state. The Human Activity Profile (HAP—Fix & Daughton, 1988) and the Rapid Disability Rating Scale, Number 2 (RDR-2–Linn & Linn, 1982) are used to assess activity, and the Sickness Impact Profile (SIP—Riley, Ahern, & Follick, 1988) is used as a measure of both psychosocial and physical impairment due to pain. Mediating variables are represented by the Pain Coping Strategies Questionnaire (Rosenthiel & Keefe, 1983), the Multidimensional Health Locus of Control (Wallston, Wallston, & Develli, 1978), and the Eysenck Personality Questionnaire (Eysenck & Eysenck, 1975). The information collected is transferred to a database and held for later audit and analysis. The justification for use of these and other psychometric instruments in our clinic has been argued at length by the clinic team. The arguments have primarily concerned utility and validation, particularly among older people. A battery which lasts more than one hour cannot be justified with this population. Indeed, because of ongoing studies of validation incorporating tests other than those listed here (Corran, Helme, & Gibson, 1991), we divide the psychometric assessment into two parts. Other tests we use include a variety of visual analogue and word descriptor scales for pain, pain interference, and mood. The Profile of Mood States (McNair, Lorr, & Droppleman, 1981), although validated by us within an elderly pain clinic population, has recently been deleted, as has the short form McGill Pain Questionnaire (Melzack, 1987), because of the wider coverage offered by the other mood measures.

Over approximately seven years since commencing in mid-1988, 510 patients have been evaluated in the clinic. The gender, age, and duration of pain for the patients is shown in Table 12-1. Approximately 3% of patients were less than 50 years of age, mostly younger disabled nursing-home residents and a few patients judged to be suitable for the expertise of the clinic after brief review of referral information.

Over 80% reported having chronic pain of more than six months' duration. The majority of the remaining 20% had "subacute" pain of between one and six months' duration. The mean age was 72 years, with a female predominance of 70%, which exceeds that expected for the Australian population, which is 63% at this age. At the team meeting, patients are assigned a diagnostic category (Table 12-2), and their suitability for a program is considered. Arthritides, postherpetic neuralgia, and psychological conditions have been the most prevalent diagnoses. During this time the psychological diagnosis was based on the classification provided by the DSM-III-R of the American Psychiatric Association, which has now been superseded by DSM-IV. Cancer, although common in this age group, was rarely seen and illustrates clearly the referral bias relevant to this and all other chronic pain management facilities. Nevertheless, the remaining causes reflect the general experience of physicians engaged in geriatric medical practice. The most common central nervous system disease was predominantly stroke, although diseases such as tumor, syringomyelia, and multiple sclerosis occasionally occurred. Single examples of a wide range of other pathologies are also seen at the clinic. A classification of "uncertain predominance" is applied when the team cannot clearly differentiate between two or more elements as the major cause of presentation. The most common examples are in patients with concurrent organic and psychological problems. Some patients, especially if severely demented or aphasic, are difficult to assess reliably, and some remain a mystery even after being assessed by multiple experts both inside and outside the clinic.

Table 12-1. Profile of Patients Referred to the Pain Management Centre over Six Years

Gender		
Total	Male	Female
510	154 (30.2%)	356 (69.8%)

Age (years)						
Mean (*SD*)	<50	50–59	60–69	70–79	80–89	>89
72.38 (10.2) Min 30, max 95	16 (3.1%)	36 (7.1%)	118 (23.4%)	212 (41.6%)	115 (22.7%)	13 (2.5%)

Pain duration (months)			
6 or less	7–12	13–24	more than 24
88 (17.3%)	64 (12.5%)	93 (18.2%)	265 (52.0%)

Table 12-2. Diagnostic Category for Predominant Pain Problem ($N = 510$)

Musculoskeletal disease	Number of patients	Percentage of total group
Arthritides	150	(29.4%)
Osteoporotic features	29	(5.7%)
Nervous system disease		
Peripheral		
Post herpetic neuralgia	77	(15.1%)
Neuropathy/trauma	23	(4.5%)
Central	43	(8.4%)
Psychiatric diagnosis[a]		
Somatoform pain disorder	39	(8.9%)
Depression	16	(3.7%)
Other	2	(0.5%)
Other categories		
Cancer	9	(1.8%)
Other specific diagnoses	49	(9.5%)
Uncertain predominance	29	(5.7%)
Unassessable	5	(1.0%)
Unknown diagnosis	32	(6.3%)

[a]Classified according to DSM-III-R criteria.

Patients offered a management program are then able to accept or reject it at review with their clinic physician. The number of patients in each of these categories is shown in Table 12-3. Twenty-five percent of patients failed to complete their program, which is clearly a problem for overall evaluation of the clinic. Most, however, were discharged from the clinic and, for those who were able, completed a psychometric battery at exit. Of the 279 patients who completed the program, 58% were able to complete the psychometric evaluation.

Table 12-3. Patients' Progress from Assessment to Discharge and Their Psychometric Evaluation

Patient progression	Clinic status	Psychometric evaluation
Completed clinical assessment (510)	36 not offered program 36 declined program 438 entered program	347 completed initial tests
Entered program (438)	41 continued program 118 failed to complete program or died 279 discharged	310 completed initial tests
Discharged from program (279)	—	163 completed initial and discharge tests

Table 12-4. Social Profile of Patients ($N = 200$)

Marital status					
Single	Married	Widowed	Divorced	Separated	Other
15 (7.5%)	95 (47.5%)	70 (35.0%)	14 (7.0%)	3 (1.5%)	3 (1.5%)
Usual living arrangements					
Home with spouse	Home alone	Home of carer	Hostel	Nusing home	Other
79 (39.5%)	67 (33.5%)	34 (17.0%)	14 (7.0%)	5 (2.5%)	1 (0.5%)
Social support systems					
Spouse	Relative	Friends	Other		
90 (45.0%)	114 (57.0%)	80 (40.0%)	41 (20.5%)		
Community services					
Home help	Delivered meals	Community nurse	Physical therapies	Social interaction	
68 (34%)	33 (16.5%)	26 (13.0%)	26 (13.0%)	19 (9.5%)	

A demographic and social profile was obtained consecutively on 200 of the 510 assessed patients. A summary of these data is shown in Table 12-4. As expected, most females were living alone, and most males were married and living at home with their spouse. Almost half the patients depended on social and community supports, illustrating the rather high level of functional disability of the referred population. In general, these 200 patients had engaged in a number of pain treatment strategies before attending the clinic and often expressed anger at their experience with the medical community. These treatments are summarized in Table 12-5. As expected, most had been managed by their local doctor, although a small minority of doctors had chosen to refer their patients directly to the clinic for care of a rare pain problem. Very few of these patients had received psychologically based treatments, which is not surprising, as third-party payment for this facility is rare in Australia outside accident and employment insurance programs. Involvement in litigation is extremely rare in this population.

Of course, even if a specific therapy has been used in the past, it has not necessarily been used appropriately for that patient's condition. For example, TENS used twice for half an hour may not have been effective, whereas a longer period, such as two hours twice daily with different electrode placement, may be effective. Similar comments are also pertinent to medications. On many occasions, approaches which had previously

Table 12-5. Previous Pain Treatment Strategies ($N = 200$)

Personnel	Number of cases	Percent of cases	Specific treatments	Number of cases	Percent of cases
Local doctor	195	(97.3%)	Simple analgesics	183	(91.5%)
Specialist	127	(63.5%)	Semisynthetic		
Hospital inpatient	97	(48.5%)	narcotics[a]	122	(61.0%)
Physiotherapist	97	(48.5%)	Antidepressants	100	(50.0%)
Alternative therapist	45	(22.5%)	NSAIDs[b]	80	(40.0%)
Day hospital/clinic	42	(21.0%)	TENS[c]	59	(29.5%)
Pain clinic	31	(15.5%)	Anticonvulsants	51	(25.5%)
Chiropractor	26	(13.0%)	Narcotics	41	(20.5%)
Psychologist	17	(8.5%)	Surgery	29	(14.5%)
			Corticosteroids	26	(13.0%)
			Nerve block	22	(11.0%)
			Antipsychotic drugs	11	(5.5%)

[a]Codeine, dextropropoxyphene.
[b]NSAIDs—nonsteroidal anti-inflammatory drugs.
[c]TENS—transcutaneous electrical nerve stimulation.

been tried unsuccessfully were able to be used effectively in our hands when meticulous attention was paid to detail so as to ensure correct usage and compliance.

Details of comorbidity for this cohort are shown in Table 12-6. The severity of this pathology and its impact on function were also recorded. These data are in striking contrast to those usually cited in publications which contain detailed descriptions of patients' demographic and clinical characteristics. Older people have multiple disabilities from comorbidities which influence management and the usefulness of outcome measures. Shortness of breath and fatigue from cardiac failure, for example, affect mood state, exercise potential, and drug selection, and any benefits in terms of quality of life might just as easily derive from improvement in cardiac status rather than pain alleviation. Patients may also be unclear in ascribing benefits to pain relief or improved cardiac function when completing their psychometric assessments.

A summary of a complete data set obtained from 114 of the 510 patients who completed psychometrics at the time of their original assessment is given in Tables 12-7 through 12-9. Patients ascribed pain to sensory and affective domains as well as to cognitive and miscellaneous domains. The MPQ (long form) contains a number of word descriptors for each of the sensory and affective domains; the maximum score for sensory descriptors is 42, and that for affective descriptors is 14. The present pain intensity of the MPQ has six levels ranging from 0 (no pain) to 5 (excruciating). A visual analogue scale is a horizontal 10-cm line with "no pain" at one end and "pain as severe as it could possibly be" at the other. A mark placed by the patient is measured in centimeters and recorded as his or her pain experience. All these measures are for pain "right now," which is often minimal in arthritic patients who are sitting in order to complete this test. There was no statistical difference in pain description according to diagnosis for all these types of measures, although the psychiatric group tended to report

Table 12-6. Comorbidity Requiring Maintenance Therapy or Causing Symptoms or Disability (N = 200)

Comorbidity	Number of patients	Percent
Cardiovascular	90	(45.0%)
Gastrointestinal	51	(25.1%)
Psychiatric	40	(20.0%)
Neurological	37	(16.5%)
Endocrine-metabolic	33	(16.5%)
Respiratory	32	(16.0%)
Musculoskeletal	32	(16.0%)
Urological-reproductive	19	(9.5%)
Malignancy	13	(6.5%)
Dementia	12	(6.0%)
EENT[a]	9	(4.5%)
Hematological	7	(3.5%)
Dermatological	1	(0.5%)

[a]EENT—eye, ear, nose, throat.

greater severity of symptoms on most measures. These results are concordant with other reports suggesting little variation in pain report between different diagnostic categories of chronic pain. Duration of pain complaint was shorter in patients with pain from nervous system injury than in patients with a predominantly psychological cause for pain, perhaps reflecting the discomfort of physicians in managing unusual persistent pain syndromes.

Table 12-7. Pain Scores[a]

Diagnostic category (N)	Duration of pain (months)	Sensory scale (MPQ-L)[b]	Affective scale (MPQ-L)	Present intensity (MPQ)	Word descriptor[c]	Visual analogue scale
Total (114)	53.3	12.2	3.14	2.23	4.01	6.71
	(62.4)	(8.85)	(3.08)	(1.34)	(1.68)	(2.60)
Musculoskeletal (37)	46.0	12.5	3.05	2.35	4.14	7.24
	(46.7)	(8.56)	(2.48)	(1.36)	(1.49)	(1.93)
Nervous system (36)	43.1	11.9	3.03	2.39	4.19	6.45
	(50.7)	(9.12)	(3.22)	(1.29)	(1.74)	(2.91)
Psychiatric (10)	64.9	15.4	4.20	2.50	4.50	6.95
	(67.5)	(13.2)	(3.77)	(1.43)	(1.78)	(2.91)
Other (31)	70.2	11.2	3.03	1.81	3.48	6.30
	(84.6)	(7.30)	(3.40)	(1.30)	(1.75)	(2.83)

[a]Values reported as means with standard deviations in parentheses; no significant differences between categories by MANOVA.
[b]MPQ-L—McGill Pain Questionaire—(long-form).
[c]Word descriptor range of severity 0–8.

Table 12-8. Mood Scores[a]

Diagnostic category (*N*)	Depression (GDS)[b]	Anxiety (SAY)[c]
Total (114)	11.9	43.4
	(6.7)	(13.7)
Musculoskeletal (37)	10.4	43.6
	(5.1)	(12.0)
Nervous system (36)	11.8	41.6
	(6.9)	(14.0)
Psychiatric (10)	15.0	43.2
	(9.1)	(16.2)
Other (31)	12.6	45.4
	(7.1)	(14.7)

[a]Values reported as means with standard deviations in parentheses; no significant differences between categories by MANOVA.
[b]GDS—Geriatric Depression Scale.
[c]SAY—Spielberger State Anxiety Inventory.

Many patients reported depressive symptoms according to the GDS (Table 12-8), with 30% ranked above 16, which is an arbitrary cut-off used by us to describe a group with a very high likelihood of clinical depression needing intervention. Patients with a predominantly psychological cause for pain showed evidence of greater depression, although this did not reach statistical significance. Activity by the HAP measure did not vary according to diagnostic category, although this does become evident with more

Table 12-9. Activity Scores[a]

Diagnostic category (*N*)	Total impact (SIP)[b]	Physical impact (SIP)	Psychosocial impact (SIP)	Maximum activity score (HAP)[c]	Adjusted activity score (HAP)	Disability (RDR-2)[d]
Total (114)	17.4	20.4	14.6	52.4	35.6	5.08
	(10.7)	(14.4)	(12.7)	(16.7)	(17.3)	(5.58)
Musculoskeletal (37)	16.6	22.9	9.91	50.7	32.6	4.57
	(7.7)	(12.1)	(7.10)	(12.5)	(14.1)	(4.17)
Nervous system (36)	15.6	16.5	15.3	50.8	36.6	5.50
	(10.2)	(15.0)	(11.6)	(21.1)	(20.4)	(6.73)
Psychiatric (10)	26.1[e]	28.4	27.1[e]	51.1	32.7	7.00
	(15.7)	(15.1)	(22.9)	(12.0)	(13.2)	(5.42)
Other (31)	17.6	19.4	15.5	56.7	38.9	4.58
	(11.5)	(15.05)	(12.2)	(16.4)	(17.9)	(5.58)

[a]Values reported as mean with standard deviations in parentheses.
[b]SIP—Sickness Impact Profile.
[c]HAP—Human Activity Profile.
[d]RDR—Rapid Disability Rating.
[e]Significant differences between categories by MANOVA ($p < .05$) and related specifically to indicated group (determined by posthoc Student Newman-Keuls procedure).

detailed breakdown by pathological diagnosis as opposed to the nociceptor, neuropathic, psychological classification shown here (Farrell, Gibson, & Helme, 1995). Disability was rated highly by patients with psychological causes for pain according to the SIP. Change in psychometric measures of pain, mood, and activity in three cohorts of patients who completed the program at approximately two-year intervals is summarized in Table 12-10. An improvement in pain and mood is shown for the first cohort, and following the introduction of the SIP to record the impact of pain on activity, scores were also observed to decrease using this measure for the second cohort at discharge from the clinic. For the third cohort, the long-form MPQ was substituted for the short form. The change in the psychosocial dimension of the SIP was not as obvious coming from a lower base, but the changes in pain and mood were marked.

Table 12-10. Pain, Mood, and Activity at Clinic Entry and Discharge[a]

	Entry	Discharge	Significance ($p =$)
Cohort 1 $N = 34$			
Pain (MPQ-S)[b]			
Sensory	11.8 (7.6)	5.97 (4.4)	.000
Affective	3.74 (3.4)	2.62 (3.39)	.068
Mood (POMS)[c]			
Depression	49.1 (8.1)	44.8 (8.2)	.001
Anxiety	49.4 (7.7)	44.4 (9.0)	.000
Cohort 2 $N = 41$			
Pain (MPQ-S)			
Sensory	10.1 (5.8)	4.63 (4.37)	.000
Affective	4.34 (3.0)	2.00 (2.34)	.000
Mood (GDS and SAY)[d,e]			
Depression	12.8 (7.5)	8.71 (6.06)	.000
Anxiety	38.5 (13.1)	36.0 (9.17)	.113
Activity (SIP)[f]			
Physical	20.2 (12.8)	16.00 (13.8)	.032
Psychosocial	19.7 (16.3)	13.00 (13.2)	.009
Cohort 3 $N = 52$			
Pain (MPQ-L)			
Sensory	10.4 (7.08)	6.87 (6.38)	.001
Affective	2.40 (2.67)	1.25 (1.82)	.002
Mood (GDS and SAY)			
Depression	9.79 (6.27)	7.33 (5.02)	.000
Anxiety	40.4 (13.3)	32.0 (10.7)	.000
Activity (SIP)			
Physical	20.4 (14.1)	16.8 (14.7)	.015
Psychosocial	12.7 (9.10)	10.0 (9.63)	.062

[a]Values reported as means with standard deviations in parentheses; analysis by repeated-measures MANOVA followed by posthoc univariate analysis.
[b]MPQ—McGill Pain Questionnaire: S—short form; L—long form.
[c]POMS—Profile of Mood States.
[d]GDS—Geriatric Depression Scale.
[e]SAY—Spielberger State Anxiety Inventory.
[f]SIP—Sickness Impact Profile.

GENERAL DISCUSSION

Nonmalignant Pain in the Elderly

Advances in technology and pharmacology have increased the range of therapeutic options and efficacy of treatment for those suffering chronic pain, although improvements in management of chronic nonmalignant pain have not been as impressive as those in the management of acute pain and cancer pain. Despite these limitations it is underrecognition of pain in the elderly and ageist attitudes which probably deny most elderly patients the opportunity to have their suffering minimized. Doctors are not solely to blame for these ageist attitudes; it is often the elderly themselves who consider pain a normal part of aging and fail to report it.

Chronic pain is not just acute pain which has persisted. It is often associated with psychosocial sequelae and adverse economic impacts. When chronic pain cannot be eradicated, especially when there is associated psychosocial dysfunction, referral to a multidisciplinary pain management clinic may be helpful. However, the number of patients who might benefit from referral for specific pain management in any one doctor's practice of, for example, 6,500 annual patient visits, may be as few as 2 per year. These patients are easily forgotten among the many, especially if they follow a pattern of dissatisfaction with their care, which often leads to doctor shopping and hence a relatively brief if uncomfortable acquaintance with the busy practitioner. Alternatively, chronic pain patients may become dejected, failing to insist on referral because of negative attitudes toward their prognosis.

Apart from isolated reviews (see Harkins, Kwentus, & Price, 1984), there has been almost complete inertia in the field of pain management for older people up to the last few years, when a few articles have begun to appear in the literature on this topic (Ackerman et al., 1994; Foley, 1994; Gibson et al., 1994). Much of the impetus for raising the profile of pain and its management has come from the International Association for the Study of Pain (IASP) through its journal *Pain* and the IASP triennial congresses on pain. It is worth noting that a special interest group for the study of pain in older persons has now been formed within the IASP and that pain in older persons will be featured in the program of the international congress into the foreseeable future.

What is important for the clinician to realize is that symptom relief with appropriate careful management does occur in older people. Perhaps this is less frequent than in young adults, although even this view can be disputed. Many patients may be treated with modest improvement in order to make substantive gains with only a few. On the other hand, minimal functional improvement, despite a continuing complaint of pain, may lead to relatively large gains in quality of life. If mood and mobility can be slightly improved, this may mean the difference between living at home and requiring institutional care.

The management strategies which are emphasized in this chapter are those which revolve around psychological constructs and interventions. We and others (Foley, 1994; Helme & Katz, 1995) have written about the details of pharmacological interventions, and these should be consulted as necessary. Other approaches to nonmalignant pain in the elderly are equally valid, especially when one considers individual pain syndromes, and relevant but not age-related literature abounds on these clinical problems. Finally, anesthetic (Ackerman et al., 1994) and neurosurgical interventions should also be considered.

A Specialized Clinic for Older People with Pain

A general description of pain treatment facilities was outlined by Loeser (1991) at the Sixth International Meeting of IASP in Adelaide in 1991. He refers to the multidisciplinary pain center, the multidisciplinary pain clinic, the pain clinic, and the modality-oriented clinic. His task force was strongly committed to the idea of a multidisciplinary approach to diagnosis and treatment. The preference is for a facility with interdisciplinary assessment and management with at least three health-care professional groups being represented. The multidisciplinary pain center differs from the clinic only in that research and teaching are undertaken in the former. The multidisciplinary clinic should have the facility for regular communication between health care professionals regarding programs and individual management, clear lines of process and management, and have records suitable for the evaluation of individual treatments and program effectiveness. The program described in this chapter fulfills the description of a pain management center according to these criteria. Its teaching role has not been described here, but is undertaken at undergraduate and graduate levels in medicine, nursing, and physiotherapy. A wider range of educational activities is planned for the future. Research is undertaken at a number of levels, as reflected in the growing publication record of the center, which works intimately with research facilities in the National Ageing Research Institute (Australia), where refinements of psychometric assessments are being made, and where other psychophysical and physiological research programs focused on the problem of pain in older people are being undertaken.

The question remains whether a facility for managing pain in older people should exist at all, and if it does, whether it should be on an inpatient, outpatient, or mixed basis. The first part of this question is controversial. Some would argue that the multidisciplinary pain clinic manages older people as well as the young, and therefore, there is no need for specialized facilities. Indeed, specialized facilities for older people can easily lead to unfair discrimination in terms of the allocation of resources (increased or decreased) and health care professional skills, as well as providing an artificial division between young and old which is not present in the real world. On the other hand, it is not always clear from reports in the literature whether the (often) minority of older people in the clinic are indeed managed as well as the young. The numbers are small, the psychometric instruments used are not necessarily valid in that population, and the things that matter to older people are not necessarily measured. Such things include cognitive status, functional measures, and issues relating to comorbidity, polypharmacy, and socioeconomic circumstances.

Thus, there are several specific considerations which may justify the provision of a multidisciplinary pain management service specifically for older persons. First, this type of clinic is able to provide expertise in chronic pain conditions which are common to older individuals. Osteoarthritis, postherpetic neuralgia, and poststroke pain syndrome comprise almost 60% of the total patient intake in our clinic, yet these conditions are relatively rare in younger adults. While the general principles of multidisciplinary pain management apply regardless of diagnosis, knowledge about the presenting features of these conditions and familiarity with specific management approaches for these conditions can be of advantage.

Second, the desired treatment outcome and the treatment focus of the program may vary somewhat as a function of age. Occupational rehabilitation is likely to be a major consideration for young-adult chronic-pain patients, whereas the maintenance of functional independence within a community setting is one of the important priorities for elderly patients.

Third, a group with shared life experiences, with similar aspirations, and facing similar problems is likely to become a more cohesive and effective forum for a group cognitive-behavioral management program. In fact, continued social contact and informal support networks have often developed spontaneously after the group program has been completed. We believe this is an important aspect of the multidisciplinary treatment package, yet an older person may feel somewhat alienated from this process if attending a general pain clinic where the vast majority of patients are from a younger age cohort.

Finally, increased frailty among the elderly can decrease their tolerance for pharmacological management and undermine the more physical activities that divert attention from pain. The older person is more likely to be socially isolated due to physical and social handicaps such as death of friends and family and may have different coping strategies (Corran et al., 1994). These factors can all affect the pain experience for older people. These issues are important and justify a research-oriented pain management center for older people where these questions can be explored. Whether outcomes are sufficiently different to justify multidisciplinary pain-management clinics for older people remains to be proved, although the demographic change toward an older population in most countries makes the question worthy of serious consideration.

Should such a facility be only outpatient-based? The clinic described in this chapter is focused on outpatient management. It must be stated, however, that it operates in the context of a regional geriatric service that has access to many levels of care which can be matched to the level of need of its client group. This is a fundamental tenet of geriatric medicine, whereby the team has access to acute teaching hospital beds, as well as beds for assessment, rehabilitation, and restorative care; day hospital, day center, and community-based facilities for meals; home maintenance; and so on. The team can access "hostel" care for those people capable of an intermediate level of self-support, and nursing-home care for those needing a high level of skilled nursing care. Although each country has its own preferred model for delivery of care to older people (indeed, some countries have many models often intertwined in the same geographic territory), the system essentially operates according to these principles, or there is no recognizable practice of geriatrics. The pain center described here operates within a well-developed regional geriatric service serving a total population of 500,000, 12% being over 65 years, and is also offered as a resource within a statewide health care system for 4 million people.

The focus of the clinic is to maintain older people in their own homes, and so community-dwelling patients dominate the referral pattern. This does not preclude referral, assessment, and treatment of patients from institutionalized settings. Nor does it stop the pain clinic team from using all the resources available to it through the regional geriatric service. For example, patients are occasionally considered by the team to be more appropriate for an individualized inpatient program of management. This is designed to be implemented over two weeks in a specified acute assessment ward where staff have been trained to observe and implement management programs set out by the pain clinic team. Such programs might be undertaken as the initial program in situations of dangerous patterns of medication use, or they may be used after an outpatient program has been judged unsuccessful yet the team is still hopeful of progress, especially if environmental influences are seen to be the major impediment to progress. Such patients need special consideration, as relapse on reintroduction to the environment is highly likely unless these external factors can be addressed while the patient is in the highly protected and artificial inpatient environment.

The composition of the management team also needs some comment, as successful outcomes for individuals are inevitably going to be biased by the expertise of the staff. If a clinic has no anesthetist, it will not do well with patients who need anesthetic procedures such as those with acute herpes zoster, acute osteoporotic crush fractures, and a variety of cancer-related symptoms. Referrers learn quickly, and appropriately, not to refer these patients to the pain clinic. After a while, unless one is careful, there is a tendency to promote the service as being comprehensive when it is, in fact, biased to a particular set of patient characteristics.

The clinic described here has internal medicine expertise at its core and thus is unlike many other multidisciplinary pain management clinics, where the anesthetist and the psychiatrist predominate. With a geriatrician who is a general physician (internist) by training, the expected expertise is in the effects of comorbidity on the pain problem. This is especially important to any pain clinic treating older people. A neurologist is useful in this context because much of the comorbidity is neurological in nature, and the pain problem has a high likelihood of having a neurological basis, as found in our clinic with its relatively high prevalence of postherpetic neuralgia and cauda equina syndromes from degenerative spine disease and stroke. We have also utilized the skills of at least one physiotherapist who is trained in geriatrics, where multiskilling is realized as being essential to the craft. It could be argued that a psychogeriatrician might be a useful addition to the team, but we have managed by referring on a consulting basis as required. The clinical psychologist perhaps also brings skills that a psychogeriatrician would not, such as expertise in marital therapy, drug abuse, sexual abuse, and the implementation of nonpharmaceutical treatments such as biofeedback and hypnotherapy. Because most older people who attend our clinic have never had the benefit of psychological assessment and treatment, there is often a reluctance to meet with the clinical psychologist which must be overcome early in the assessment process. The other health care professionals in the clinic represent necessary expertise that is widely utilized in such settings, including secretarial, pharmacy, nursing, and group work. In our clinic, this last area of expertise is provided by an occupational therapist who also provides skills in functional assessment. A community nurse, by making observations in the patient's home, contributes to this overall functional assessment while building an initial trust between patient and clinic.

Comorbidity

Something needs to be said on the matter of management of comorbidity. We judge that it is not the role of the pain clinic team to manage any but the most minor comorbidity unless it directly reflects on the pain problem. This does not sit easily with the holistic approach to management which sits at the core of geriatric medicine. The team is, of course, ever vigilant to identify comorbidity which is a part of that geriatric medical approach. Management of comorbidity, however, is usually triaged back to the local doctor or to other parts of the regional geriatric service, where there is expertise in the mainstream clinical issues of geriatrics such as cognitive impairment, immobility and falls, and incontinence, as well as expertise in a range of other subdisciplines of internal medicine.

Of particular importance in the evaluation of older people with pain is the issue of dementia. Pain, as opposed to nociception, is a construct with sensory, emotional, and cognitive components. Dementia has the potential to impact on all facets of the pain experience. There is little written about the interaction of these two common syndromes in older people, yet the association is common in the institutionalized elderly (Parmelee, Smith, & Katz, 1993). Here we merely describe some of the factors which need to be borne in mind when managing such patients. First, dementia is not always readily apparent at interview. We regularly use a screening psychometric measure in the clinic such as the Abbreviated Mental Test Score (Hodkinson, 1972). Second, measurement of pain using standard psychometric instruments is probably unreliable in patients with severe dementia. Indeed, nonspecific behavioral observations are often the only clinical methods available for these patients. Simple measurement tools, however, can still be reliably used in less affected individuals. Because behavioral disturbance is often due to other morbidities in the demented patient, pain, which is often easily treated, is overlooked. Memory for pain may also be grossly inaccurate in the demented patient, which makes objective observation and recording of complaint and behavior mandatory. Finally, management is limited, by the very nature of the cognitive impairment, to medication (bearing in mind the risk of side-effects exacerbating cognitive disability) or simple physical maneuvers executed by carers. There is no place for cognitive approaches to cope with the pain in those patients with more advanced cognitive impairment. The demented patient needs meticulous clinical assessment and judiciously chosen pertinent investigations to ensure accurate diagnosis.

Measurement Issues

In practice, apart from mediating variables, there are two dimensions to measurement of clinic activities: process and outcome. We use the term *process issues* here to refer to matters such as referral procedures, appointment numbers, times and duration, and correspondence with referrers. We have not reported these matters in this chapter and, like others, find it difficult to justify the resources to maintain a continuous audit of this type. It is clear, however, from Table 12-3 that issues such as cognitive impairment and inability to speak English precluding full psychometric evaluation, as well as dropout from management programs, are important to the assessment of overall outcomes and need to be monitored continuously. We have produced a procedure manual for the clinic which is regarded as a dynamic document subject to regular intermittent review of clinic processes and which is made available to our many visitors.

Outcome measures may also seem to be easily chosen and interpreted, but this is a much more complex matter than appears at first sight. There is a substantial literature on this subject, and only a few issues pertinent to our clinic are raised here. First, what should be measured? It is obvious to pain clinic staff that the patient group is clearly different from patients described in other clinics. But how does one document these differences? Apart from age, gender, and pain-related disease state, we believe there is a need to record comorbidity (including frailty and *all* medications), socioeconomic status, and functional status, using validated measuring instruments. Some of this is difficult (e.g., frailty and social support systems) because of a lack of widely used instruments that allow comparison across cultures and countries.

Measurement does not get any easier for major outcomes such as pain, mood, and activity. Although validated measures are available for young adults, these are not necessarily appropriate for older patients. For example, we have generally found that older people report pain and mood states in a similar way to young adults, but mean levels for aged control samples are generally 1 standard deviation underreported compared to young adult controls. On the other hand, activity is usually overestimated by older people. These difficulties in measurement also apply to constructs underlying the meaning and connectivity between pain, mood, and activity, such as coping and locus of control. Nevertheless, we have been able to show improvements in our major outcome criteria between entry into and discharge from the clinic. This does not reflect efficacy in terms of duration of improvement, which we have shown for at least one subgroup 10 months after discharge (Hornsby et al., 1991).

There are other measures which could be undertaken to assess the effectiveness of the clinic. Turk and Rudy (1990, 1991; Turk, Rudy, & Sorkin, 1993) refer to referral patterns, failure to enter treatment, attrition, relapse, noncompliance, and adherence enhancement as important issues often ignored in the literature. Another issue, of more relevance in geriatric medicine, is the importance of economic benefit, which is always a difficult problem when considering health-related interventions in this age group. We have briefly reported on the economic evaluation of our clinic elsewhere (Segal, Helme, Corran, & Gibson, 1993).

Research

A pain management center is, by definition, involved in research and teaching. What are some of the research issues, apart from those explored above, which should be on the agenda of a geriatric pain center. There are two major areas of activity that we find interesting, apart from the validation of psychometric instruments. These are, first, the interrelationships between the variables measured, the direction of those relationships, and the constructs that best explain them. We have reported some of these findings recently (Corran et al., 1994) in relation to differences in coping strategies between young and old referred to pain clinics in Melbourne. Second, we are interested in the effectiveness of various components of therapy in relation to each other and the whole. It is remarkably difficult, in the clinical setting, to control for the effects of pain clinic milieu, social interventions in the community, medication adjustment, relaxation and coping strategies, exercise programs, TENS, and all the other many factors that impact on the patient. Yet, if we are to continue to improve treatment programs, and we cannot claim to help all the patients referred to us, we need to identify how each modality affects a particular individual, so that we can target our strategies and, hopefully, develop new ones that impact even more on the quality of life of our patients.

CONCLUSION

In conclusion, what are the clinical lessons we have learned from the clinic? (See Table 12-11.) First, meticulous attention to the detail of diagnosis and selection of therapy is mandatory when treating pain in older patients. Then, it must be remembered that the presence of abnormal findings on investigation do not necessarily indicate causality. Judgments are based on the known facts in the case under review and clinical experience. Second, following selection of the appropriate treatment schedule, meticulous attention must be paid to ensuring compliance with therapy. Patients have often failed to respond

Table 12-11. Pain in the Elderly: Important Clinical Lessons

1. The initial evaluation must be meticulous.
   Pay attention to
   - Diagnosis by yourself and others.
   - Past therapies; they may require independent confirmation.
   - Previous investigations; all radiology needs to be inspected.
   - Cognitive state; do your own evaluation.
   - Environmental factors; a home visit is often helpful.
2. Abnormal pathology results do not necessarily indicate the cause of pain.
3. Consider the pathophysiological basis for the pain in selecting therapy.
4. Involve patients in their management.
5. Define the intention of treatment.
   Pain cure versus symptom management.
   What are the patient's goals if pain is diminished?
6. Medications need constant attention.
   Review medications from all sources, including over the counter.
   Use medications by the clock, not as required according to pain level.
   Side effects may occur at lower doses in the elderly.
7. Monitor all treatments.
   Failure to respond may indicate added or alternative diagnoses, or worsening mood state.
8. Multidisciplinary pain clinics
   Should be considered for patients who
   - Fail to respond to conventional therapy.
   - Have significant psychosocial distress.
   - Have major physical disability associated with their pain syndrome.

to the correct therapy in the past because of noncompliance, inadequate dose or duration of therapy, or a lack of understanding of and involvement in their treatment program. On the other hand, vigilance is required to recognize the first early signs of drug toxicity such as imbalance, dizziness, and confusion. Third, when progress appears unduly limited or slow, one must reconsider the possible contribution of other diagnoses or altered mood state to the pain syndrome which has been underreported by the patient.

It must be always remembered that the goal of therapy in chronic pain must be clearly delineated; the target is more often pain management than it is pain cure. Excessively aggressive therapy aimed at pain eradication in the elderly often results in intolerable side effects of the treatment. Finally, empowerment is a key factor in ensuring satisfying and long-lasting outcomes; the patient must be an active participant in the therapy at all times.

ACKNOWLEDGMENTS. The authors have been supported by the Victorian Health Promotion Foundation and the National Health and Medical Research Council of Australia. The contribution of the multidisciplinary team is gratefully acknowledged.

REFERENCES

Ackerman, W. E., Diede, J., & Racz, G. B. (1994).Chronic pain treatment in the elderly patient. *Pain Digest, 4*, 195–203.

Corran, T. M., Helme, R. D., & Gibson, S. J. (1991). An assessment of psychometric instruments used in a geriatric outpatient pain clinic. *Australian Psychologist, 26*, 128–131.

Corran, T. M., Gibson, S. G., Farrell, M. J., & Helme, R. D. (1994). Comparison of chronic pain experience in young and elderly patients. In G. F. Gebhart, D. L. Hammond, & T. S. Jenson (Eds.), *Proceedings of the VIIth World Congress on Pain, Progress in Pain Research and Management* (pp. 895–906) Seattle: IASP Press.

Crook, J., Rideout, E., & Browne, G. (1984). The prevalence of pain complaints in a general population. *Pain, 18*, 299–314.

Eysenck, H. J., & Eysenck, S. B. G. (1975). *Manual of the Eysenck Personality Questionnaire (Junior and Adult).* Kent: Hodder & Stoughton.

Farrell, M. J., Gibson, S. J., & Helme, R. D. (1995). The effect of medical status on the activity of elderly pain clinic patients. *Journal of the American Geriatrics Society, 43*, 102–107.

Fernandez, E., & Turk, D. C. (1989). The utility of cognitive coping strategies for altering pain perception: A meta-analysis. *Pain, 38*, 123–135.

Ferrell, B. A., Ferrell, B. R., & Osterweil, D. (1990). Pain in the nursing home. *Journal of the American Geriatrics Society, 38*, 409–414.

Fiatarone, M. A., Marks, E. C., Ryan, N. D., Meredith, C. N., Lipsitz, L. A., & Evans, W. J. (1990). High-intensity strength training in nonagenerians. *Journal of the American Medical Association, 263*, 3029–3034.

Fix, A. J., & Daughton, D. M. (1988). *Human Activity Profile: Professional manual.* Gainesville, FL: Psychological Assessment Resources.

Foley, K. M. (1985). The treatment of cancer pain. *New England Journal of Medicine, 313*, 85–95.

Foley, K. M. (1994). Pain management in the elderly. In W. R. Hazzard, E. L. Bierman, J. P. Blass, W. H. Ettinger, & J. B. Halter (Eds.), *Principles of geriatric medicine and gerontology* (pp 317–331). New York: McGraw-Hill.

Fordyce, W. E. (1978). Evaluating and managing chronic pain. *Geriatrics, 33*, 59–62.

Fordyce, W. E. (1986). Learning processes in pain. In R. A. Steinbach (Ed.), *The psychology of pain* (2nd ed., pp. 49–65). New York: Raven Press.

Fordyce, W. E., Fowler, R., Lehmann, J., DeLateur, B., & Trieschmann, R. (1973). Operant conditioning in the treatment of chronic pain. *Archives of Physical Medicine, 54*, 399–408.

Gibson, S. J., & Helme, R. D. (1995). Age differences in pain perception and report. *Pain Reviews, 2*, 111–137.

Gibson, S. J., Katz, B., Corran, T. M., Farrell, M. J., & Helme, R. D. (1994). Pain in older persons. *Disability and Rehabilitation, 16*, 127–139.

Harkins, S. W., Kwentus, J., & Price, D. D. (1984). Pain and the elderly. In C. Benedetti, C. R. Chapman, & G. Moricca (Eds.), *Advances in pain research and therapy* (pp. 103–121). New York: Raven Press.

Harkins, S. W., & Price, D. D. (1992). Assessment of pain in the elderly. In R. Melzack & D. C. Turk (Eds.), *Handbook of pain assessment* (pp. 315–331). New York: Guilford.

Helme, R. D., Corran, T. M., & Gibson, S. J. (1992). Pain in the elderly. *Proceedings of the Australian Association of Gerontology, 27*, 26–30.

Helme, R. D., & Katz, B. (1993). Management of chronic pain. *Medical Journal of Australia, 158*, 478–481.

Helme, R. D., & Katz, B. (1995). Pain management. In C. George, K. Woodhouse, & W. J. MacLennan (Eds.), *Drug therapy in old age*. Chichester: Wiley.

Helme, R. D., Katz, B., Neufeld, M., Lachal, S., Herbert, T., & Corran, T. M. (1989). The establishment of a geriatric pain clinic: A preliminary report of the first 100 patients. *Australian Journal on Ageing, 8*, 27–30.

Hodkinson, H. M. (1972). Mental Test Score. *Age and Aging, 1*, 233–238.

Hornsby, L., Katz, B., Helme, R. D., Gibson, S. J., & Corran, T. M. (1991). Outcome following discharge from a pain clinic. *Australian and New Zealand Journal of Medicine, 21*, 582.

Janal, M. N., Colt, E. W. D., Clark, W. C., & Glusman, M. (1984). Pain sensitivity, mood and plasma endocrine levels in man following long distance running: Effects of naloxone. *Pain, 19*, 13–25.

Johnson, M. I., Ahston, C. H., & Thompson, J. W. (1991). An indepth study of long-term users of transcutaneous electrical nerve stimulation (TENS): Implications for clinical use of TENS. *Pain, 44*, 221–229.

Kaiko, R. F., Wallenstein, S. L., Rogers, A. G., Grabinski, P. Y., & Houde, R. W. (1982). Narcotics in the elderly. *Medical Clinics of North America, 66*, 1079–1089.

Klapow, J. C., Slater, M. A., Patterson, T. G., Doctor, J. N., Atkinson, J. H., & Garfin, S. R. (1993). An empirical evaluation of multidimensional clinical outcome in chronic low back pain patients. *Pain, 55*, 107–118.

Kwentus, J. A., Harkins, S. W., Lignon, N., & Silverman, J. J. (1985). Current concepts of geriatric pain and its treatment. *Geriatrics, 40*, 48–54.

Linn, M. W., & Linn, B. S. (1982). The rapid disability rating scale, scale 2. *Journal of the American Geriatrics Society, 30*, 378–382.

Loeser, J. D. (1991). Desirable characteristics for pain treatment facilities: Report of the IASP Taskforce. In M. R. Bond, J. E. Charlton, & C. J. Woolf (Eds.). *Proceedings of the VIth World Congress on Pain*, pp. 411–415. Amsterdam: Elsevier.

Malone, M. D., & Strube, M. J. (1988). Meta-analysis of non-medical treatments for chronic pain. *Pain, 34*, 231–244.

McNair, D. M., Lorr, M., & Droppleman, L. F. (1981). *Manual for the profile of mood states*. San Diego: Educational and Industrial Testing Service.

Melzack, R. (1975). The McGill Pain Questionnaire: major properties and scoring methods. *Pain, 1*, 277–299.

Melzack, R. (1987). The short-form McGill pain questionnaire. *Pain, 30*, 191–197.

Onghena, P., & Van Houdenhove, B. (1992). Antidepressant-induced analgesia in chronic nonmalignant pain: A meta-analysis of 39 placebo-controlled studies. *Pain, 49*, 205–220.

Parmelee, P. A., Smith, B., & Katz, I. R. (1993). Pain complaints and cognitive status among elderly institution residents. *Journal of the American Geriatrics Society, 41*, 517–522.

Pathy, M. S. J. (Ed.). (1985). *Principles and practice of geriatric medicine*. Chichester: Wiley.

Portenoy, R. K., & Farkash, A. (1988). Practical management of non-malignant pain in the elderly. *Geriatrics, 5*, 29–47.

Puder, R. S. (1988). Age analysis of cognitive-behavioral group therapy for chronic pain outpatients. *Psychology and Aging, 3*, 204–207.

Riley, J. R., Ahern, D. K., & Follick, M. J. (1988). Chronic pain and functional impairment: Assessing beliefs about their relationships. *Archives of Physical Medicine and Rehabilitation, 69*, 579–582.

Rosentheil, A. K., & Keefe, F. J. (1983). The use of coping strategies in chronic low back pain patients: Relationship to patient characteristics and current adjustment. *Pain, 17*, 33–34.

Segal, L., Helme, R. D., Corran, T. M., & Gibson, S. (1993). Economic evaluation of a multidisciplinary pain clinic for the elderly: A qualitative approach. *7th World Congress on Pain*, Paris, France, Abstracts, p. 602.

Spielberger, C. D. (1983). *Manual for the state-trait anxiety inventory*. Palo Alto, CA: Consulting Psychologists Press.

Thorsteinsson, G. (1987). Chronic pain: Use of TENS in the elderly. *Geriatrics, 42*, 75–82.

Turk, D. C., & Meichenbaum, D. (1994). A cognitive-behavioral approach to pain management. In P. D. Wall & R. Melzack (Eds.), *Textbook of pain* (pp. 1337–1348). Edinburgh: Churchill Livingstone.

Turk, D. C., & Rudy, T. E. (1990). Neglected factors in chronic pain treatment outcome studies—Referral patterns, failure to enter treatment, and attrition. *Pain, 43*, 7–25.

Turk, D. C., & Rudy, T. E. (1991). Neglected topics in the treatment of chronic pain patients—Relapse, noncompliance, and adherence enhancement. *Pain, 44*, 5–28.

Turk, D. C., Rudy, T. E., & Sorkin, B. A. (1993). Neglected topics in chronic pain treatment outcome studies: Determination of success. *Pain, 53*, 3–16.

Turner, J. A., & Romano, J. M. (1990). Cognitive-behavioral therapy. In J. J. Bonica (Ed.), *The management of pain* (Vol. 2, pp. 1711–1722). Philadelphia: Lea & Febiger.

Wallston, K. A., Wallston, B. S., & Develli, R. (1978). Development of the multidimensional health locus of control scale. *Health Education Monographs, 6*, 160–170.

Woolf, C. J., and Thompson, J. W. (1994). Stimulation fibre-induced analgesia: transcutaneous electrical nerve stimulation (TENS) and vibration. In P. D. Wall and R. Melzack (Eds.). *Textbook of Pain*, pp. 1191–1208. Edinburgh: Churchill Livingstone.

Yesavage, J. A., Brink, T. G., Rose, R. L., & Adey, M. (1983). The geriatric depression rating scale: Comparison with other self-report and psychiatric rating scales. *Journal of Psychological Research, 17*, 37–49.

CHAPTER 13

Cancer Pain in the Elderly

NATHAN I. CHERNY AND BETH POPP

Management of cancer pain in older patients presents a variety of challenges to the practicing physician, whether that physician is an oncologist, a gerontologist, or a physician who specializes the provision of primary care. The elderly experience more pain, both chronic and acute, than their younger counterparts (Closs, 1994). Furthermore, the balance between beneficial and adverse effects of pharmacotherapy and nondrug therapy is often more tenuous in the older patient, due to age-related physiological changes and the interaction between analgesics, concurrent illness, and pharmacotherapy for concurrent illness.

There are limited data on the prevalence of pain in the elderly, and often, we must extrapolate from data derived from studies of younger patients. We do know that cancer is a major problem in the geriatric population, and that cancer pain is common (Ferrell, Ferrell, Ahn, & Tran, 1994). Fifty percent of all cancers occur in the population over the age of 65. Age-specific cancer incidence rises progressively through life (Crawford & Cohen, 1987). In a projection study based on Bureau of the Census population projections and age-specific cancer incidence rates for 1985 to 1989 from the National Cancer Institute's Surveillance, Epidemiology and End Results program, the number of incident cancers diagnosed annually in the United States among persons aged 65 and over is projected to reach 1.5 million by the year 2030, or 2.4 times the number estimated for 1990 (Polednak, 1994).

One-third of cancer patients in active therapy and two-thirds of patients with advanced disease have significant pain (Bonica, Ventafridda, & Twycross, 1990b; Foley, 1985). Older patients are also more likely to have concurrent illness with resultant noncancer pain superimposed on their cancer pain (Closs, 1994; Scapa, Horowitz, Avtalion, Waron, & Eshchar, 1992).

NATHAN I. CHERNY • Department of Medical Oncology, Shaare Zedek Medical Center, Jerusalem, Israel 91031. BETH POPP • Pain Service, Memorial Sloan Kettering Cancer Center, New York, New York 10021. *Present address*: Director of Palliative Care Service, Department of Oncology, Brooklyn Veterans Affairs, Brooklyn, New York 11205.

Handbook of Pain and Aging, edited by David I. Mostofsky and Jacob Lomranz. Plenum Press, New York, 1997.

Despite the widespread acceptance of a highly effective therapeutic strategy for the management of cancer pain (Figure 13-1), surveys suggest that more than 40%–50% of patients in routine practice settings fail to achieve adequate relief (Bonica, Ventafridda, & Twycross, 1990b; Brescia et al., 1990; Cleeland, 1991; Portenoy et al., 1992; Twycross & Fairfield, 1982; Von Roenn, Cleeland, Gonin, Hatfield, & Pandya, 1993). There are numerous barriers to effective pain management: clinicians are frequently ill equipped to treat pain (Cleeland, 1984, 1988; Cleeland, Cleeland, Dar, & Rinehardt, 1986; Portenoy, 1993b; Ward et al., 1993), patients who complain of severe pain may not be believed (Grossman, Sheidler, Swedeen, Mucenski, & Piantadosi, 1991), assessment is often inadequate (Cleeland, 1984, 1988, 1989; Cleeland et al., 1986; Von Roenn et al., 1993; Weissman, Gutmann, & Dahl, 1991), and knowledge of pain management approaches is often rudimentary (Von Roenn et al., 1993; Weissman et al., 1991). Improved patient outcome requires substantial improvement in the prevailing levels of knowledge and practice.

CLINICAL ASSESSMENT OF CANCER PAIN IN OLDER PATIENTS

Pain Characteristics and Identification of Pain Syndromes

Cancer pain syndromes are defined by the association of particular pain characteristics and physical signs with specific consequences of the underlying disease or its treatment. Syndromes are associated with distinct etiologies and pathophysiologies and have important prognostic and therapeutic implications. Pain syndromes associated with cancer can be either acute (Table 13-1) or chronic (Table 13-2). Whereas acute pains experienced by cancer patients are usually related to diagnostic and therapeutic interventions, chronic pains are most commonly caused by direct tumor infiltration. Adverse consequences of cancer therapy, including surgery, chemotherapy, and radiation therapy, account for 15%–25% of chronic cancer pain problems, and a small proportion of the chronic pains experienced by cancer patients are caused by pathology unrelated to either the cancer or the cancer therapy (Banning, Sjogren, & Henriksen, 1991; Foley, 1982; Twycross & Fairfield, 1982; Twycross & Lack, 1984).

The evaluation of pain characteristics provides some of the data essential for syndrome identification. These characteristics include intensity, quality, distribution, and temporal relationships.

Pain Intensity. The evaluation of pain intensity is pivotal to therapeutic decision making (World Health Organization, 1990). It indicates the urgency with which relief is needed and influences the selection of analgesic drug, route of administration, and rate of dose titration. Furthermore, the assessment of pain intensity may help characterize the pain mechanism and underlying syndrome. For example, the pain associated with radiation-induced nerve injury is rarely severe; the occurrence of severe pain in a previously irradiated region therefore suggests the existence of a recurrent neoplasm or a radiation-induced second neoplasm.

Pain Quality. The quality of the pain often suggests its pathophysiology. Somatic nociceptive pains are usually well localized and described as sharp, aching, throbbing, or

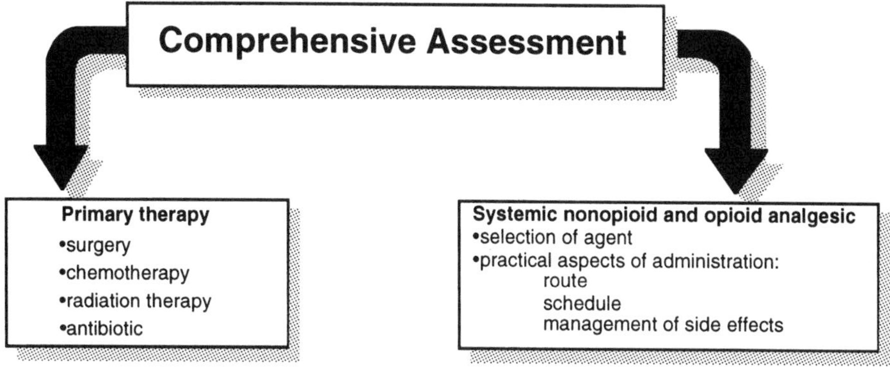

If balance between pain relief and side effects is suboptimal, consider.....

Non-invasive strategies to improve balance between analgesia and side effects

Reduce opioid requirement:

- appropriate primary therapy
- addition of nonopioid analgesic
- addition of an adjuvant analgesic
- use of cognitive or behavioral techniques
- use of an orthotic device or other physical medicine approach

Switch to another opioid

If balance between pain relief and side effects is suboptimal, consider.....

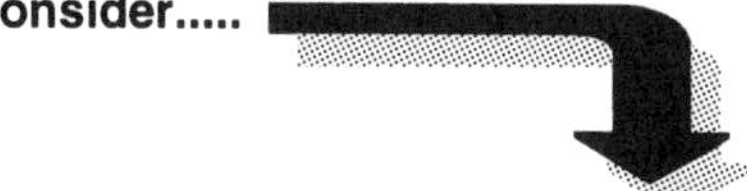

Invasive strategies to improve balance between analgesia and side effects

- Regional analgesic techniques (spinal or intraventricular opioids)
- Neural blockade
- Neuroablative techniques

If balance between pain relief and side effects is suboptimal, consider.....

Role of sedating pharmacotherapy

Figure 13-1. A strategy for the management of chronic pain.

Table 13-1. Acute Cancer Pain Syndromes[a]

- Acute pain associated with diagnostic and therapeutic interventions
  - Acute pain associated with diagnostic interventions, e.g.,
    - Lumbar puncture headache
    - Arterial or venous blood sampling
    - Bone marrow biopsy
    - Lumbar puncture
  - Acute postoperative pain
  - Acute pain caused by other therapeutic interventions, e.g.,
    - Pleurodesis
    - Tumor embolization
  - Acute pain associated with analgesic techniques, e.g.,
    - Injection pain
    - Spinal opioid hyperalgesia syndrome
    - Epidural injection pain
- Acute pain associated with anticancer therapies
  - Acute pain associated with chemotherapy infusion techniques
    - Intravenous infusion pain
      - Venous spasm
      - Chemical phlebitis
      - Vesicant extravasation
      - Anthracycline-associated flare reaction
    - Hepatic artery infusion pain
    - Intraperitoneal chemotherapy abdominal pain
  - Acute pain associated with chemotherapy toxicity, e.g.,
    - Mucositis
    - Corticosteroid-induced perineal discomfort
    - Painful peripheral neuropathy
    - Diffuse bone pain from transretinoic acid or colony-stimulating factors
  - Acute pain associated with hormonal therapy
    - Luteinizing-hormone-releasing-factor (LHRF) tumor flare in prostate cancer
    - Hormone-induced pain flare in breast cancer
  - Acute pain associated with immunotherapy
    - Interferon (IFN)-induced acute pain
  - Acute pain associated with radiotherapy, e.g.,
    - Incident pains
    - Oropharyngeal mucositis
    - Acute radiation enteritis and proctocolitis
- Acute pain associated with infection
  - Acute herpetic neuralgia

[a]Adapted from N.I. Cherny and R.K. Portenoy (1994). Cancer Pain: Principles of assessment and syndromes. In P.D. Wall and R. Melzack (Eds.), *Textbook of Pain*. (3rd ed.). New York: Churchill Livingstone, pp. 787–823.

pressurelike. Visceral nociceptive pains are generally diffuse and may be gnawing or crampy, when due to obstruction of a hollow viscus, or aching, sharp or throbbing, when due to involvement of organ capsules or mesentery. Neuropathic pains may be described as burning, tingling, electric, or shocklike (lancinating).

Pain Distribution. Patients with cancer pain commonly experience pain at more than one site (Portenoy et al., 1992). The distinction between focal, multifocal, and generalized pain may be important in the selection of therapy, such as nerve blocks, radiotherapy, or surgical approaches. The term *focal pain*, which is used to denote a single site, has also been used to depict pain that is experienced in the region of the underlying lesion. Focal pains can be distinguished from those that are referred, that is, experienced in a site remote from the lesion. Familiarity with pain referral patterns is essential to target appropriate diagnostic and therapeutic maneuvers (Table 13-3) (Kellgren, 1939; Ness & Gebhart, 1990; Torebjork, Ochoa, & Schady, 1984).

Temporal Relationships. Cancer-related pain may be acute or chronic. Acute pain is defined by a recent onset and a natural history characterized by transience. The pain is often associated with overt pain behaviors (such as moaning, grimacing, and splinting), anxiety, or signs of generalized sympathetic hyperactivity, including diaphoresis, hypertension, and tachycardia.

Chronic pain has been defined by persistence for three months or more beyond the usual course of an acute illness or injury, by a pattern of recurrence at intervals over months or years, or by association with a chronic pathological process (Bonica et al., 1990b). Chronic tumor-related pain is usually insidious in onset, often increases progressively with tumor growth, and may regress with tumor shrinkage. Overt pain behaviors and sympathetic hyperactivity are often absent, and the pain may be associated with affective disturbances (anxiety and/or depression) and vegetative symptoms, such as asthenia, anorexia, and sleep disturbance (Coyle, Adelhardt, Foley, & Portenoy, 1990; McCaffery & Thorpe, 1989; Reuben, Mor, & Hiris, 1988; Ventafridda, Ripamonti, De Conno, Tamburini, & Cassileth, 1990b).

Transitory exacerbations of severe pain over a baseline of moderate pain or less may be described as *breakthrough pain* (Portenoy & Hagen, 1990). Breakthrough pains are common in both acute and chronic pain states. These exacerbations may be precipitated by volitional actions of the patient (so-called incident pains), such as movement, micturition, cough, or defecation, or by nonvolitional events, such as bowel distention. Spontaneous fluctuations in pain intensity can also occur without an identifiable precipitant.

Inferred Pathophysiology

Inferences about the mechanisms that may be responsible for the pain are valuable in the assessment and management of cancer pain. The assessment process provides the data necessary to infer a predominant pathophysiology.

Nociceptive pain is pain that is believed to be commensurate with the tissue damage associated with an identifiable somatic or visceral lesion. Nociceptive pains (particularly somatic pains) usually respond to opioid drugs (Arner & Meyerson, 1988; Cherny et al., 1994) or to interventions that ameliorate or denervate the peripheral lesion.

Neuropathic pain is pain that is due to injury to, or disease of, the peripheral or central neural structures or that is perceived to be sustained by aberrant somatosensory processing at these sites (Devor et al., 1991; Portenoy, 1991). Neuropathic pain is most strongly suggested when a dysesthesia occurs in a region of motor, sensory, or autonomic dysfunction that is attributable to a discrete neurological lesion. Although neuropathic

Table 13-2. Chronic Cancer Pain Syndromes

- Tumor-related pain syndromes
  - Bone pain
    - Multifocal or generalized bone pain
      - Multiple bony metastases
      - Marrow expansion
    - Vertebral syndromes
      - Atlantoaxial destruction and odontoid fratures
      - C7–T1 syndrome
      - T12–L1 syndrome
      - Sacral syndrome
    - Back pain and epidural compression
    - Pain syndromes of the bony pelvis and hip
  - Headache and facial pain
    - Intracerebral tumor
    - Leptomeningeal metastases
    - Base of skull metastases
    - Painful cranial neuralgias
  - Tumor involvement of the peripheral nervous system
    - Tumor-related radiculopathy
      - Postherpetic neuralgia
    - Cerivcal plexopathy
    - Brachial plexopathy
    - Malignant lumbosacral plexopathy
    - Tumor-related mononeuropathy
    - Paraneoplastic painful peripheral neuropathy
  - Pain syndromes of the viscera and miscellaneous tumor-related syndromes
    - Hepatic distention syndrome
    - Midline retroperitoneal syndrome
    - Chronic intestinal obstruction
    - Peritoneal carcinomatosis
    - Malignant perineal pain
    - Ureteric obstruction
  - Paraneoplastic nociceptive pain syndromes
    - Tumor-related gynecomastia
- Chronic pain syndromes associated with cancer therapy
  - Postchemotherapy pain syndromes
    - Chronic painful peripheral neuropathy
    - Avascular necrosis of femoral or humeral head
    - Plexopathy associated with intra-arterial infusion
  - Chronic pain associated with hormonal therapy
    - Gynecomastia with hormonal therapy for prostate cancer
  - Chronic postsurgical pain syndromes
    - Postmastectomy pain syndrome
    - Post-radical-neck-dissection pain
    - Post-thoracotomy pain
    - Postoperative frozen shoulder
    - Phantom pain syndromes
    - Stump pain
    - Postsurgical pelvic floor myalgia

Table 13-2. (*Continued*)

Chronic pain syndromes associated with cancer therapy (*cont.*)
  Chronic postradiation pain syndromes
    Plexopathies
    Chronic radiation myelopathy
    Chronic radiation enteritis and proctitis
    Burning perineum syndrome
    Osteoradionecrosis

[a]Adapted from N.I. Cherny and R.K. Portenoy, (1994). Cancer pain: Principles of assessment and syndromes. In P.D.Wall & R. Melzack (Eds.), *Textbook of Pain* (3rd ed.). New York: Churchill Livingstone, pp. 787–823.

pains can be described in terms of the pain characteristics (continuous or lancinating) or the site of injury (for example, neuronopathy or plexopathy), it is useful to distinguish these syndromes according to the presumed site of the aberrant neural activity (generator) that sustains the pain (Portenoy, 1991). Peripheral neuropathic pain is caused by injury to a peripheral nerve or nerve root and is presumably sustained by aberrant processes originating in the nerve root, plexus, or nerve. Neuropathic pains believed to be sustained by a central generator include sympathetically maintained pain (also known as *reflex sympathetic dystrophy* or *causalgia*) and a group of syndromes traditionally known as the *deafferentation pains* (e.g., phantom pain). Sympathetically maintained pain may occur following injury to soft tissue, peripheral nerve, viscera, or central nervous system and is characterized by focal autonomic dysregulation in a painful region (e.g., vasomotor or pilomotor changes, swelling, or sweating abnormalities) or trophic changes (Janig et al., 1991). The response of neuropathic pains to opioid drugs is less predictable and generally less dramatic than the response of nociceptive pains (Arner & Meyerson, 1988; Cherny et al., 1994; Dubner, 1991; Portenoy, Foley, & Inturrisi, 1990). Optimal treatment may depend on the use of so-called adjuvant analgesics (Portenoy, 1993a) or other specific approaches, such as sympathetic nerve block.

Table 13-3. Common Patterns of Pain Referral

Pain mechanism	Site of lesion	Referral site
Visceral	Diaphragmatic irritation	Shoulder and root of neck
	Urothelial tract	Ilioinguinal region and genitalia
Somatic	C7–T1 vertebrae	Interscapular
	L1–2	Sacroiliac joint and hip
	Hip joint	Knee
	Pharynx	Ipsilateral ear
Neuropathic	Nerve or plexus	Anywhere in the distribution of a peripheral nerve
	Nerve root	Anywhere in the corresponding dermatome
	Central nervous system	Anywhere in the region of the body innervated by the damaged structure

Idiopathic pains are pains for which no underlying organic pathology can be identified as well as pains which are perceived to be excessive for the extent of identifiable organic pathology. Cancer patients in the latter category should not be given a specific psychiatric diagnosis (somatoform disorder) unless the patient presents with affective and behavioral disturbances that are severe enough to imply a predominating psychological pathogenesis (American Psychiatric Association, 1987). When this inference cannot be made, the label *idiopathic* should be retained, and assessments should be repeated at appropriate intervals. Idiopathic pain, in general, and pain related to a psychiatric disorder, specifically, are uncommon in the cancer population, notwithstanding the importance of psychological factors in quality of life.

An Assessment Strategy

Cancer pain assessment has two major objectives: (1) the accurate characterization of the pain, including the pain syndrome and inferred pathophysiology, and (2) the evaluation of the impact of the pain and its role in the overall suffering of the patient. This assessment is predicated on the establishment of a trusting relationship with the patient. Even with such a relationship, however, the clinician should not be cavalier about the potential for symptom underreporting. Symptoms are frequently described as complaints, and there is a common perception that the "good patient" refrains from complaining (Cleeland, 1989). The clinician must maintain a clinical posture that affirms relief of pain and suffering as central goals of therapy, and that encourages open and effective communication about symptoms. If the patient is either unable or unwilling to describe the pain, a family member may need to be questioned to assess the distress or disability of the patient. The prevalence of pain is so high that an open-ended question about the presence of pain should be included at each patient visit in routine oncological practice.

Data Collection. The complete history is perhaps the most useful tool available to the clinician attempting to define the nature of a pain complaint. Because pain is a subjective experience and because there are complex interactions between the perception of pain, the psyche, and a variety of sociocultural factors, one must begin a pain assessment respecting the patient's complaint of pain. This also holds true for frail and cognitively impaired elderly patients (Parmelee, Smith, & Katz, 1993).

The pain-related history must elucidate the relevant pain characteristics, as well as the responses of the patient to previous disease-modifying and analgesic therapies. The presence of multiple pain problems is common, and if more than one is reported, each must be assessed independently. Validated pain assessment instruments can provide a format for communication between the patient and health care professionals and can also be used to monitor the adequacy of therapy (Daut & Cleeland, 1982; Fishman et al., 1987; Foley, 1989a; Herr & Mobily, 1993; Melzack, 1975).

The consequences of the pain must also be assessed. An appreciation of the effect of the pain on the patient's functional status, including activities of daily living, and social interactions is crucial. Cultural, environmental, and psychological factors must be assessed in directing appropriate diagnostic and therapeutic approaches. The patient's current level of anxiety and depression, presence of suicidal ideation, and degree of functional incapacity should all be assessed in a structured interview. Information about prior medical and psychiatric illnesses, and about how the patient has coped with them is also highly valuable. Patients who are at high risk for decompensating psychologically in the setting of a painful illness can then be targeted for earlier intervention by appropriate members of the multidisciplinary team. It is important to assess the patient–family interactions, to note both the kind and frequency of pain behaviors and the nature of the family response.

Most patients with cancer pain have multiple other symptoms (Coyle et al., 1990; Reuben et al., 1988; Ventafridda et al., 1990b). The clinician must evaluate the severity and distress caused by each of these symptoms. Symptom checklists and quality-of-life measures may contribute to this comprehensive evaluation (Moinpour et al., 1989; Moinpour, Hayden, Thompson, Feigl, & Metch, 1991).

A physical examination, including a neurological evaluation, is a necessary part of the initial pain assessment. A thorough neurological assessment is justified by the high prevalence of painful neurological conditions in this population (Clouston, De Angelis, & Posner, 1992; Gonzales, Elliot, Portenoy, & Foley, 1991). The physical examination should attempt to identify the underlying etiology of the pain problem, clarify the extent of the underlying disease, and discern the relationship of the pain complaint to the disease. The patient with a normal exam should not be dismissed, but should have further assessment directed by the clinical history alone.

Careful review of previous laboratory and imaging studies can provide important information about the cause of the pain and the extent of the underlying disease.

Provisional Assessment. The information derived from these data provides the basis for a provisional pain diagnosis, an understanding of the disease status, and the identification of other concurrent concerns. This provisional diagnosis includes inferences about the pathophysiology of the pain and an assessment of the pain syndrome. An understanding of disease status requires an evaluation of the extent of the disease, prognosis, and the anticipated goals of therapy (Haines, Zalcberg, & Buchanan, 1990). Evaluation of concurrent concerns includes other symptoms and related psychosocial problems.

Diagnostic Investigations. Additional investigations are often required to clarify areas of uncertainty in the provisional assessment (Gonzales et al., 1991). The extent of diagnostic investigation must be appropriate to the patient's general status and the overall goals of care. For some patients, comprehensive evaluation may require numerous investigations, some targeted at the specific pain problem and others needed to clarify extent of disease or concurrent symptoms.

The lack of a definitive finding on an investigation should not be used to override a compelling clinical diagnosis. For example, in the assessment of bone pain, plain radiographs provide only crude assessment of bony lesions, and further investigation with bone scintigrams, computerized tomography (CT), or magnetic resonance imaging (MRI) may be required to define a specific diagnosis. To minimize the risk of error, the physician ordering the diagnostic procedures should personally review them with the radiologist to correlate pathological changes with the clinical findings.

The comprehensive assessment may also require additional evaluation of other physical or psychosocial problems identified during the initial assessment. Expert assistance from other physicians, nurses, social workers, or others may be essential.

Formulation and Therapeutic Planning. Whenever possible, the findings of this evaluation should be reviewed with the patient. Through candid discussion, current problems can be prioritized to reflect their importance to the patient. The evaluation may also identify potential outcomes that would benefit from contingency planning. Examples include evaluation of resources for home care, prebereavement interventions with the family, and the provision of assistive devices in anticipation of compromised ambulation.

Early treatment of pain while pursuing the diagnostic evaluation improves the patient's ability to participate in the necessary diagnostic procedures, curtails the physical and psychological debilitation which occur in the face of persistent pain, and conveys the message that the physician takes the pain problem seriously and is committed to alleviating it. There is no evidence to support the practice of withholding analgesics while the nature of the pain is being established.

AN INTEGRATED APPROACH TO CHRONIC CANCER PAIN

Most cancer patients can attain satisfactory relief of pain through an approach that incorporates primary treatments, oral or parenteral analgesic therapy, and, at times, other noninvasive psychological or rehabilitative interventions. Occasional patients benefit

Table 13-4. The Roles of the Primary Therapies in the Management of Cancer Pain

Primary therapy	Major pain indications
Radiotherapy	Painful bony metastases
	Epidural spinal cord compression
	Cerebral metastases
	Tumor-related compression or infiltration or peripheral neural structures
Chemotherapy	Nociceptive or neuropathic pain syndromes caused by tumors likely to respond to chemotherapy, i.e., lymphoma, testicular cancer, ovarian, small cell lung cancer, and breast cancer
Sugery	Stabilization of pathological fractures
	Spinal cord decompression
	Relief of remediable bowel obstructions
	Drainage of symptomatic ascites
Antibiotic therapy	Overt infections (e.g., pelvic abscess or pyonephrosis)
	Occult infections (e.g., in head and neck tumors or ulcerating tumors)

from invasive therapies. Continuity of care is essential and requires ongoing assessment and the capacity to respond flexibly to the patient's changing needs.

Primary Therapy

The assessment may reveal a cause for the pain that is amenable to primary therapy aimed at the underlying cause of the pain. Primary therapies for cancer pain syndromes include surgical resection of tumor, cytotoxic chemotherapy, immunotherapy, hormonal therapy, radiation therapy, and antibiotics (Table 13-4). When possible, these treatment should be attempted, but their use should not delay appropriate adjunctive analgesic pharmacotherapy. Responders to primary therapy should then have their analgesic regimen tapered commensurate with the reduction in their pain.

The Analgesic Ladder Approach to Systemic Pharmacotherapy

Analgesics can be classified according to their chemical receptor and pharmacological properties, their sites and mechanisms of analgesia, and the intensity of pain for which they are generally used. Drugs can be separated in to (1) nonopioid analgesics, including aspirin, acetaminophen, and the nonsteroidal anti-inflammatory drugs; (2) opioid analgesics, including propoxyphene, codeine, oxycodone, morphine, hydromorphone, fentanyl, levorphanol, and methadone; and (3) the adjuvant analgesics, including those drugs such as anticonvulsants and antidepressants which enhance the analgesic effects of the opioids and which have intrinsic analgesic activity in certain settings.

Drug therapy with nonopioid, opioid, and adjuvant analgesics, based on the World Health Organization (WHO) analgesic ladder, is the mainstay of cancer pain therapy and should be within the therapeutic repertoire of the general physician (Figure 13-2) (Agency for Health Care Policy and Research: Cancer Pain Management Panel, 1994; American Pain Society, 1992). The three-step analgesic ladder has been validated in a variety of practice settings and can provide adequate pain relief in 70%–90% of patients with advanced cancer (Ventafridda, Tamburini, Caraceni, DeConno, & Naldi, 1987):

1. Patients with mild to moderate cancer-related pain should have treatment initiated with a nonopioid analgesic, which should be combined with adjuvant drugs if a specific indication for one exists.
2. Patients who are relatively nontolerant and present with moderate to severe pain, or who fail to achieve adequate relief after a trial of a nonopioid analgesic, should be treated with an opioid conventionally used for moderate pain (previously termed *weak opioids*); in the United States, these drugs include codeine, hydrocodone, dihydrocodeine, oxycodone, and propoxyphene. This drug is typically combined with a nonopioid and may be coadminstered with an adjuvant analgesic.
3. Patients who present with severe pain, or who fail to achieve adequate relief for less severe pain despite appropriate administration of drugs on the second step

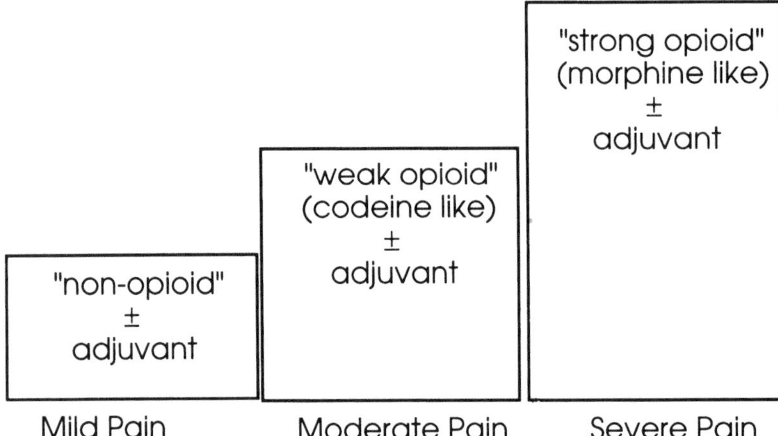

Figure 13-2. The three-step analgesic ladder proposed by an expert committee of the Cancer Unit of the World Health Organization.

of the analgesic ladder, should receive an opioid conventionally used for severe pain (previously termed *strong opioids*). In the United States, these drugs include morphine, oxycodone, hydromorphone, methadone, levorphanol, and fentanyl. These drugs may also be combined with a nonopioid analgesic or an adjuvant drug.

Pharmacokinetic and Pharmacodynamic Considerations in the Geriatric Patient

It appears that all phases of pharmacokinetics are affected by the aging process (Morgan & Furst, 1986). Absorption may be influenced by decreases in gastric acid, intestinal blood flow, mucosal cell mass, and intestinal motility (Geokas & Haverbck, 1969). Concurrently administered medications and medical diseases may also contribute to diminished absorption (Goldberg & Roberts, 1983). Drug distribution can result from reductions in total body water, lean body mass, and serum protein levels, as well as an increase in body fat (Bender, 1965). Lipid solubility and the degree of protein binding of the specific drug determine the effect to which its distribution is affected by these physiological changes of aging. Drugs which are metabolized by the liver show the greatest effect of changes in hepatic mass, hepatic blood flow, and a reduction in enzyme activity. For example, elderly patients have a diminished ability to bind nonsteroidal anti-inflammatory drugs (NSAIDs), which are highly protein-bound in younger patients, resulting in rapidly increasing free drug concentrations after dosing has begun. Finally, drug excretion can be influenced by age-related impairment of renal function. In a single dose study, Kaiko demonstrated higher plasma morphine levels and slower rates of decline of drug levels, suggesting decreased clearance (Kaiko, 1980), and a study comparing the morphine kinetics of middle-aged and old patients found significantly diminished clearance in older patients (Sear, Hand, & Moore, 1989). Similar results have been found with other narcotics (Helmers, Van Peer, Woestenborghs, Noorduin, & Heykants, 1984; Helmers, van Leeuwen, & Zuurmond, 1994; Jaillon et al., 1989; Singleton, Rosen, & Fisher, 1988).

Pharmacodynamic responses may also be altered in older patients. Increased receptor sensitivity and concurrent alterations in mental status may account in part for the increased response elderly patients have to opioid and nonopioid analgesics.

In addition to these pharmacokinetic and pharmacodynamic considerations, several caveats must be emphasized. Excessive use of medications should be discouraged, and the use of each drug should have a specific rationale (Ferrell & Ferrell, 1991). Medications with short half-lives are often preferred in the elderly patient, as their use diminishes the adverse effects associated with drug accumulation. Detailed instructions to the patients with appropriate pill boxes and calendars or diaries can facilitate the proper dispensing of drugs. Finally, as previously mentioned, effective pain management requires continuous reassessment of beneficial and adverse effects and dose titration to provide analgesia which is acceptable to the patient.

SYSTEMIC ANALGESIC PHARMACOTHERAPY

Nonopioid Analgesics

The nonopioid analgesics are available for oral administration. They are useful alone for mild to moderate pain (Step 1 of the analgesic ladder) and provide additive analgesia when combined with opioid drugs in the treatment of more severe pain. The nonopioid analgesics comprise numerous subclasses (Table 13-5). Aspirin and other nonsteroidal anti-inflammatory drugs (NSAIDs) inhibit the enzyme cyclo-oxygenase and consequently block the biosynthesis of prostaglandins, inflammatory mediators known to sensitize peripheral nociceptors (Vane, 1971). A central mechanism of action is also likely to contribute (Malmberg & Yaksh, 1992; Willer, DeBroucker, Bussel, Robi-Brami, & Harrewyn, 1989) and presumably predominates in acetaminophen analgesia (Piletta, Porchet, & Dayer, 1991).

Unlike opioid analgesics, the nonopioid analgesics have a "ceiling" effect for analgesia and produce neither tolerance nor physical dependence. To reduce the risk of therapy, it is reasonable to begin treatment with a relatively low dose and then explore the dose–response relationship through gradual dose escalation.

The safe administration of the nonopioid analgesics also requires familiarity with their potential adverse effects. Aspirin and the other NSAIDs have a broad spectrum of potential toxicity, and caution is required in the administration of these agents to patients at increased risk. These include patients with coagulopathies, ulcer diathesis, and impaired renal function and those receiving concurrent corticosteroid therapy (Brooks & Wood, 1991). In one retrospective study of gastrointestinal bleeding among the elderly, anti-inflammatory analgesics accounted for one-third of acute bleeding episodes necessitating admission for 93 inpatients (Alexander, Veitch, & Wood, 1985).

Table 13-5. Nonopioid Analgesics

Chemical class	Generic name	Half-life (hrs)	Starting dose (mg)	Maximum recommended dose (mg/day)
Nonacidic				
p-Aminophenol derivatives	Acetaminophen	3–4	750 q4hr	4,000
Naphthylalkanones	Nabumetone	22–30	500 q12hr	2,000
Acidic				
Salicylates	Aspirin	3–12	650 q4–6hr	6,000
	Diflunisal	8–12	500 q12hr	1,500
	Choline magnesium Trisalicylate	8–12	1,000 q12hr	4,000
	Salsalate	8–12	1,000 q12hr	4,000
Proprionic acids	Ibuprofen	3–4	400 q6hr	4,200
	Naproxen	1–3	250 q12hr	1,000
	Fenoprofen	2–3	200 q6hr	3,200
	Ketoprofen	2–3	25 q8hr	200
	Flurbiprofen	5–6	100 q12hr	300
Acetic acids	Indomethacin	4–5	25 q12hr	200
	Sulindac	14	150 q12hr	400
	Diclofenac	2	25 q8hr	200
	Ketorolac	4–7	30 q6hr	240
	Tolmetin	1	200 q8hr	2,000
	Suprofen	2–4	150 q6	800
Oxicams	Piroxicam	45	20 q24hr	40
Fenamates	Mefenamic acid	2	250 q6hr	1,000
Pyranocarboxylic acids	Etodolac	7	1,000 q24	2,000

Risk of bleeding can be influenced by drug selection and peptic cytoprotection. The nonacetylated salicylates, such as choline magnesium trisalicylate and salsalate, have less effect on platelet aggregation and no effect on bleeding time at usual clinical doses (Insel, 1990); these drugs are preferred in patients who have a bleeding diathesis and a strong indication for an antiinflammatory drug. H2 antagonists prevent NSAID-related duodenal ulcers but are not effective for prevention of gastric ulcers. Misoprostol is the only agent proven to decrease the risk of gastric ulcers in patients receiving NSAIDs (Ballinger, 1994; Zfass, McHenry, & Sanyal, 1993).

Acetaminophen has fewer adverse effects than the NSAIDs. Acetaminophen-induced hepatic toxicity is a rare occurrence if a ceiling dose of 4,000 mg is observed (Whitcomb & Block, 1994).

Opioid Analgesics

Based on their interactions with the various receptor subtypes, the opioid analgesics can be divided into agonist and agonist–antagonist classes. The mixed agonist–

antagonist opioids (pentazocine, nalbuphine, and butorphanol) and the partial agonist opioids (buprenorphine and probably dezocine) have limited utility in this setting because of a ceiling effect for analgesia, precipitation of withdrawal reactions in patients physically dependent on opioid agonists, and a high prevalence of dose–dependent psychotomimetic side effects (pentazocine and butorphanol) (Houde, 1979).

The pure agonist drugs (Table 13-6) are most commonly used in cancer pain management. They have no clinically relevant ceiling effect to analgesia. As the dose is raised, analgesic effects increases in a log–linear function, until either analgesia is achieved or somnolence occurs. In practice, the efficacy of any particular drug in a specific patient will be determined by the degree of analgesia produced following dose escalation through a range limited by the development of adverse effects.

Relative analgesic potency is the ratio of the dose of two analgesics required to produce the same analgesic effect. By convention, relative potency is expressed in comparison to 10 mg of parenteral morphine. Equianalgesic dose information provides a useful guide for dose selection when the drug or route of administration is changed (see below).

Indications. A trial of opioid therapy should be administered to all patients with pain of moderate or greater severity, irrespective of the pathophysiological mechanism underlying the pain (Cherny, Thaler, Friedlander-Klar, Lapin, & Portenoy, 1992; Jadad, Carroll, Glynn, Moore, & McQuay, 1992; McQuay et al., 1992; Portenoy et al., 1990). Patients who present with severe pain are usually treated with an opioid customarily used

Table 13-6. Opioid Agonist Drugs

Drug	Dose (mg) equianalgesic to 10mg IM morphine		Half-life (hrs)	Duration of action (hrs)
	IM	PO		
Opioid agonist drugs customarily used to treat moderate pain (formerly called *weak opioids*)				
Codeine	130	200	2–3	2–4
Oxycodone[a]	15	30	2–3	2–4
Propoxyphene	100	50	2–3	2–4
Opioid agonist drugs customarily used to treat severe pain (formerly called *strong opioids*)				
Morphine	10.0	30.0	2–3	3–4
Oxycodone	15.0	30.0	2–3	2–4
Hydromorphone	1.5	7.5	2–3	2–4
Methadone	10.0	20.0	15–190	4–8
Meperidine	75.0	300.0	2–3	2–4
Oxymorphone	1.0	10.0 (PR)	2–3	3–4
Levorphanol	2.0	4.0	12–15	4–8
Fentanyl transdermal system	[b]			48–72

[a]When combined with a nonopioid.
[b]Transdermal fentanyl 100 μg/hr. ≃ Morphine 4 mg/hr.

in Step 3 of the analgesic ladder. Patients with moderate pain are commonly treated with a combination product containing acetaminophen or aspirin plus a conventional Step 2 opioid (codeine, dihydrocodeine, hydrocodone, oxycodone, and propoxyphene) (World Health Organization, 1986, 1990). The doses of these combination products can be increased until the maximum dose of the nonopioid coanalgesic is attained (e.g., 4,000–6,000 mg acetaminophen).

Selecting an Opioid. For the patient without major organ failure who is opioid-naive, any of the available agonist opioids can be selected. Short half-life opioid agonists (morphine, hydromorphone, fentanyl, oxycodone, or oxymorphone) are generally favored because they are easier to titrate than the long half-life drugs, which require a longer period to approach steady-state plasma concentrations. For ambulatory patients who are able to tolerate oral opioids, morphine sulphate is often preferred since it has a short half-life and is easy to titrate in its immediate release form and is also available as a controlled-release preparation that allows a 8 to 12 hour dosing interval. The long half-life drugs, methadone and levorphanol, are not usually considered first-line therapy because they can be difficult to titrate.

The use of meperidine for the management of cancer pain is discouraged. Meperidine is N-demethylated to normeperidine, which is twice as potent as a convulsant and one-half as potent as an analgesic than its parent compound. Accumulation of normeperidine after repetitive meperidine administration often results in central nervous system excitability characterized by subtle mood effects, tremors, multifocal myoclonus, and occasionally seizures (Eisendrath, Goldman, Douglas, Dimatteo, & Van, 1987; Hagmeyer, Mauro, & Mauro, 1993; Kaiko et al., 1983; Szeto et al., 1977).

It is always important to review the response to previous trials of opioid therapy. If the current opioid is well tolerated, it is usually continued unless difficulties in dose titration occur or the required dose cannot be administered conveniently. If dose-limiting side effects develop, a trial of an alternative opioid should be considered (Crews, Sweeney, & Denson, 1993; de Stoutz, Bruera, & Suarez-Almazor, 1993; Galer, Coyle, Pasternak, & Portenoy, 1992; MacDonald, Der, Allan, & Champion, 1993). To safely implement the technique of sequential opioid trials, the clinician must be familiar with at least three opioid drugs used in the management of severe pain and have the ability to calculate appropriate starting doses using equianalgesic dosing data.

Patients with renal impairment may accumulate the active metabolites of propoxyphene (norpropoxyphene), meperidine (normeperidine), and morphine (morphine-6-glucuronide). Particular vigilance is required in the administration of these drugs to such patients (Chan & Matzke, 1987; Hagen, Foley, Cerbones, Portenoy, & Inturrisi, 1991; McQuay et al., 1990; Osborne, Joel, & Slevin, 1986; Portenoy et al., 1991; Sawe, Svensson, & Odar-Cederlof, 1985).

Selecting an Appropriate Route. Opioids should be administered by the least invasive and most convenient route capable of providing adequate analgesia for the patient. In routine practice, the oral route is usually the most appropriate. Alternative noninvasive routes, including the rectal, sublingual, and transdermal, are sometimes feasible for patients who have impaired swallowing or gastrointestinal obstruction. In the

United States, rectal suppositories containing morphine, hydromorphone, and oxymorphone are available, and controlled-release morphine tablets can also be administered rectally (Wilkinson et al., 1992). The potency of opioids administered rectally approximate that achieved with oral dosing (Beaver & Feise, 1977; Hanning, 1990).

A sublingual preparation of buprenorphine is available in some countries, but not in the United States (De Conno, Ripamonti, Sbanotto, & Barletta, 1993). Nonetheless, all opioids are absorbed sublingually to some extent. In contrast to morphine, which is poorly absorbed by this route, fentanyl and methadone are relatively well absorbed (Weinberg et al., 1988). Sublingual administration of an injectable formulation may be a useful approach in some patients who transiently lose the option of oral dosing.

A transdermal formulation of fentanyl that delivers 25, 50, 75 or 100 μg per hour is now commercially available. The dosing interval for each system is usually 72 hours, but interindividual pharmacokinetic variability is large (Gourlay et al., 1990; Holley & Van-Steennis, 1988; Portenoy et al., 1993), and some patients require a dosing interval of 48 hours. Fentanyl clearance is often impaired in elderly patients, and clinicians must be alert to the possibility of early or delayed toxicity due to drug accumulation (Holdsworth et al., 1994; Singleton et al., 1988).

Parenteral routes of administration should be considered for patients who have impaired swallowing or gastrointestinal obstruction, those who require the rapid onset of analgesia, and highly tolerant patients who require doses that cannot otherwise be conveniently administered. Repeated parenteral bolus injections, which can be delivered by the intravenous (IV), intramuscular (IM), or subcutaneous (SC) routes, are often complicated by the occurrence of untoward "bolus" effects (toxicity at peak concentration and/or pain breakthrough at the trough). Although repetitive IM injections are commonly prescribed, they are painful and offer no pharmacokinetic advantage, and their use is not recommended. Repeated bolus doses, if required, can be accomplished without frequent skin punctures through the use of an indwelling IV or SC infusion device. To deliver repeated SC injections, a 27-gauge infusion device (a "butterfly") can be left under the skin for up to a week (Coyle, Cherny, & Portenoy, 1994b).

Continuous infusions prevent the problems associated with the "bolus" effect and may be administered IV or SC (Bruera et al., 1988a; Coyle et al., 1994b; Coyle, Mauskop, & Maggard, 1986; Portenoy, 1987; Storey, Hill, St. Louis, & Tarver, 1990; Swanson, Smith, Bulich, New, & Shiffman, 1989). Ambulatory infusion devices vary in complexity, cost, and ability to provide patient-controlled "rescue doses" as an adjunct to a continuous basal infusion (see below). Opioids suitable for continuous SC infusion must be soluble, well absorbed, and nonirritant. Extensive experience has been reported with hydromorphone, oxymorphone, and morphine (Bruera et al., 1988b; Bruera, Macmillan, Selmser, & MacDonald, 1990; Coyle et al., 1986; Moulin et al., 1992; Moulin, Kreeft, Murray, & Bouquillon, 1991; Storey et al., 1990; Swanson et al., 1989). Methadone is irritating and is not preferred for SC infusion (Bruera et al., 1991). Studies suggest that dosing with SC administration can proceed in a manner identical to continuous IV infusion (Moulin et al., 1991; Waldmann, Eason, Rambohu, & Hanson, 1984). To maintain the comfort of an infusion site, the SC infusion rate should not exceed 5 cc/hr. Patients who require high doses may benefit from the use of concentrated solutions, which, in selected cases, can be compounded specifically for continuous SC infusion.

Continuous IV infusion may be the most appropriate way of delivering an opioid when there is a need for infusion of a large volume of solution, or when using methadone. If continuous IV infusion must be continued on a long-term basis, a permanent central venous port is recommended.

Continuous infusions of drug combinations may be indicated when pain is accompanied by nausea, anxiety, or agitation. In such cases, an antiemetic, neuroleptic, or anxiolytic may be combined with an opioid, provided it is nonirritant, miscible, and stable in combined solution. Experience has been reported with infusions of an opioid combined with metoclopromide, haloperidol, scopolamine, cyclizine, methotrimeprazine, chlorpromazine, and midazolam (Amesbury, 1989; Dover, 1987; Oliver, 1988; Storey et al., 1990; Trissel, Xu, Martinez, & Fox, 1994).

Switching Routes. During long-term treatment, it is often necessary to switch routes of administration. All such changes require careful attention to relative potency (Table 13-6).

Selecting a Dosing Schedule. Patients with continuous or frequently recurring pain generally benefit from scheduled "around the clock" dosing. Clinical vigilance is required, particularly, in patients with no previous opioid exposure and those administered drugs with long half-lives. With long half-life drugs, such as methadone, delayed toxicity may develop as plasma concentration rises slowly toward steady state levels (Fainsinger, Schoeller, & Bruera, 1993).

A "rescue dose" should be prescribed for all patients who receive an "around-the-clock" opioid regimen as a supplemental dose to treat pain that breaks through the regular schedule. This approach provides a method for safe and rational stepwise dose escalation and is applicable to all routes of opioid administration (Table 13-7). The rescue drug is typically the same as that administered on a continuous basis, with the exception of transdermal fentanyl (for which there is no immediate release formulation currently approved). The frequency with which the rescue dose can be offered depends on the time to peak effect for the drug and the route of administration. Oral rescue doses can be offered up to every 1–2 hours, and parenteral rescue doses can be offered up to every 15–30 minutes. The size of the rescue dose should be equivalent to approximately 5%–15% of the 24-hour baseline dose.

Controlled release formulations can lessen the inconvenience associated with around-the-clock drug administration (Arkinstall, Goughnour, White, & Stewart, 1989). Controlled-release oral morphine sulphate and transdermal fentanyl are now widely used, and new controlled-release formulations of codeine, dihydrocodeine, oxycodone, and hydromorphone are under development (Hayes et al., 1994). Controlled-release preparations of morphine sulphate typically achieve peak plasma levels 3–5 hours after a dose and have a duration of effect of 8–12 hours (Shepherd, 1990). An immediate-release formulation of a short half-life opioid (usually the same drug) is generally used as the rescue medication (Table 13-7).

An approach using "as-needed" dosing alone is useful during the initiation of opioid therapy in the opioid-naive patient, particularly when rapid dose escalation is

Table 13-7. Examples of Stepwise Dose Escalation of Morphine Sulphate Administered as Oral Immediate-Release Preparation and Oral Controlled Release and Continuous Infusion

	Oral immediate release		Oral controlled release (with immediate release rescue dosing)		SC infusion with SC rescue doses	
Step[b]	"Around-the-clock" dose (mg q4hr)	Rescue dose (mg q1r prn)	"Around-the-clock" dose (mg)	Rescue dose (mg q1hr prn)	"Around-the-clock" infusion (mg/hr)	Rescue dose (mg q20 min prn)
1	10	5	30 q12hr	7.5	3	2.0
2	15	7.5	30 q8hr	15.0	5	2.5
3	30	15.0	60 q12hr	15.0	7	3.5
4	45	22.5	100 q12hr	30.0	10	5.0
5	60	30.0	100 q8hr	30.0	15	7.5
6	90	45.0	200 q12hr	45.0	20	10.0
7	120	60.0	200 q8hr	60.0	30	15.0
Etc.						

[a]Adapted, with permission, from N.I. Cherny and R.K. Portenoy (1993). Cancer pain management: Current strategy. *Cancer* (supplement), *72*:3393–3415.
[b]Indications for progression from one step to the next: (1) requirement of > 2 rescue doses in any 4-hr interval; (2) requirement of > 6 rescue doses in 24 hours. Min = minute; hr = hour; prn = as needed.

needed or a long half-life drug is administered. This technique is strongly recommended when starting methadone therapy (Sawe et al., 1981).

Patient-controlled analgesia (PCA) is a technique of parenteral drug administration in which the patient controls the administration of bolus doses of an analgesic within the parameters set by the prescribing physician, utilizing a pump designed for this purpose. Use of a PCA device allows the patient to carefully titrate the opioid dose to his or her individual analgesic needs. The parameters typically include dose magnitude and the maximal frequency with which the boluses can be administered. A "lockout interval" is programmed so that after a dose is administered, patient attempts to trigger a dose will not yield a response until the lockout interval has elapsed (Coyle et al., 1994b). The option for bolus dosing is typically administered in conjunction with a continuous opioid infusion (Citron et al., 1993; Swanson et al., 1989). Long-term PCA in cancer patients is accomplished via the subcutaneous or intravenous route using an ambulatory infusion device. In a randomized, controlled trial, elderly patients with postoperative pain who received patient-controlled analgesia had significantly improved analgesia and increased satisfaction compared with those who received intramuscular injections (Egbert, Parks, Short, & Burnett, 1990).

Initial Dose Selection. Patients in severe pain who are opioid-naive should generally begin one of the opioids conventionally used for severe pain at a dose equivalent to 5–10 mg IM morphine every 3–4 hours. If a switch from one opioid drug to another is required, the equianalgesic dose table (Table 13-6) is used as a guide to the starting dose. For patients with good pain control but unacceptable side effects, the starting dose of the new drug should be reduced to 50%–75% of the calculated equianalgesic dose to account for incomplete cross-tolerance among opioids. For patients with poor pain control and unacceptable side effects, the starting dose of the new drug can usually be 75%–100% of the equianalgesic dose. Clinical experience suggests that additional caution is needed when the change is to methadone; a reduction to 24%–35% of the equianalgesic dose is prudent. The need for subsequent dose adjustments is to be expected, and a provision should be made for follow-up during the interval from dose change to reestablishment of steady-state plasma levels, either in person or by phone.

Dose Titration. The persistence of inadequate pain relief should be addressed through a stepwise escalation of the opioid dose until adequate analgesia is reported or unacceptable side effects supervene. A dose increment of 30%–50% is safe and large enough to observe a meaningful change in effects. In most cases, gradual dose escalation identifies a favorable balance between analgesia and side effects that remains stable for a prolonged period (Brescia, Portenoy, Ryan, Krasnoff, & Gray, 1992; Kanner & Foley, 1981). While doses can become extremely large during this process, the absolute dose is immaterial as long as the balance between analgesia and side effects remains favorable. Patients who develop dose-limiting side effects during dose titration require the use of another analgesic approach or a technique to reduce opioid toxicity (see below).

The severity of the pain should determine the rate of dose titration. Patients with very severe pain can be managed by repeated parenteral dosing every 15–30 minutes until pain is partially relieved (Lichter, 1994). Guidelines have been proposed for the calculation of hourly maintenance dosing after parenteral loading with a short half-life opioid (Edwards & Breed, 1990). These guidelines recommend that the starting hourly maintenance dose be approximated by dividing the total loading dose by twice the elimination half-life of the drug. For example, the starting maintenance dose for a patient who has required an intravenous loading dose of morphine sulphate 30 mg (half-life approximately 3 hours) would be 5 mg per hour. Patients with less severe pain can undergo more gradual dose escalation.

It is important to recognize that analgesic tolerance is seldom the dominant factor in the need for opioid dose escalation. Rather, most patients who require an escalation in dose to manage increasing pain have demonstrable progression of disease (Coyle, Adelhardt, & Foley, 1988; Kanner & Foley, 1981). Consequently, concerns about tolerance should not impede the use of opioids early in the course of the disease, and worsening pain in a patient receiving a stable dose of opioids should generally be assessed as presumptive evidence of disease progression or, rarely, increasing psychological distress or delirium (Coyle, Breitbart, Weaver, & Portenoy, 1994a).

Adverse Effects of Opioids and Their Management. A detailed understanding of the strategies used to prevent or manage common opioid toxicities is needed to optimize the balance between analgesia and side effects. The most common adverse effects are constipation, nausea and vomiting, and somnolence or cognitive impairment. Other important dose-limiting adverse effects include dysphoria, myoclonus, and respiratory depression.

The likelihood of opioid-induced constipation is so great that laxative medications should be prescribed prophylactically to most patients, particularly those who are elderly or have coexisting gastrointestinal pathology. Recommendations for laxative therapy are empirical (Sykes, 1993). A combination of a softening agent (docusate) and a cathartic (e.g., senna, bisacodyl, or phenolphthalein) is frequently used. The doses of these drugs should be increased as necessary, and an osmotic laxative (e.g., lactulose or a magnesium-containing product) can be added if needed. Occasional patients are managed with intermittent colonic lavage using an oral bowel preparation such as Golytely®. Rare patients who are refractory to laxative therapy can undergo a trial of oral naloxone, which has a bioavailability less than 3% and presumably acts selectively on opioid receptors in the gut (Culpepper-Morgan et al., 1992; Sykes, 1991). Since there is a small risk of systemic withdrawal from oral naloxone (Culpepper-Morgan et al., 1992), the initial dose should be conservative (0.8–1.2 mg once or twice daily); this dose can be escalated slowly until either favorable effects occur or the patient develops abdominal cramps, diarrhea, or any other adverse effect. Naloxone should not be used in any patient with bowel obstruction.

The incidence of opioid-induced nausea has been estimated to be 10%–40% (Campora et al., 1991). Tolerance to these effects often develops rapidly, and routine prophylactic administration of an antiemetic is not usually indicated except in patients with a history of severe opioid-induced nausea. Three putative mechanisms may produce nausea and vomiting: a direct effect on the chemoreceptor trigger zone, enhanced vestibular sensitivity, and delayed gastric emptying. If nausea is associated with early satiety, bloating, or postprandial vomiting, all of which are features of delayed gastric emptying, metoclopramide is the most reasonable initial treatment. Patients with vertigo, or prominent movement-induced nausea, may benefit from the use of an antivertigenous drug, such as scopolamine or meclizine. If signs of neither gastroparesis nor vestibular dysfunction are prominent, treatment is usually began with a neuroleptic, such as prochlorperazine or metoclopramide. If these drugs are ineffective at relatively high doses, other options include a trial of an alternative opioid or treatment with an antihistamine (e.g., diphenhydramine or hydroxyzine), neuroleptic (e.g., haloperidol, chlorpromazine, or droperidol), benzodiazepine (e.g., lorazepam), steroid (e.g., dexamethasone), or serotonin antagonist (e.g., ondansetron).

The initiation of opioid therapy or significant dose escalation is often associated with a self-limiting problem of somnolence or cognitive impairment that resolves within two weeks (Bruera, Macmillan, Hanson, & MacDonald, 1989). Since opioid-induced somnolence or cognitive impairment increases the risk of falls and fractures (Ryynanen, Kivela, Honkanen, Laippala, & Saano, 1993; Shorr, Griffin, Daugherty, & Ray, 1992), close observation is required particularly in the titration phase. Although tolerance usually develops, some patients continue to have intolerable side effects, particularly if other contributing factors exist.

When somnolence or cognitive impairment occurs, a stepwise management strategy is useful: (1) eliminate nonessential central nervous system depressant medications and evaluate the patient for concurrent causes, including sepsis, metabolic derangement, or intracerebral or leptomeningeal metastases; (2) if analgesia is satisfactory, reduce the opioid dose by 25%; (3) if analgesia is unsatisfactory and the patient is somnolent, consider the addition of a psychostimulant, such as methylphenidate (starting dose 5–10 mg twice daily), dextroamphetamine (starting dose 5–10 mg twice daily), or pemoline (starting dose 18.75–35.5 mg twice daily); (4) if the patient is hallucinating or delirious, consider a trial of haloperidol (starting dose 0.5 mg three times daily); and (5) if these problems persist, consider the addition of a nonopioid or adjuvant analgesic (which may allow reduction in opioid dose), a switch to a different opioid drug, or an anesthetic or neurolytic technique.

Myoclonus is a common dose-related adverse effect of opioids, which, like somnolence and cognitive impairment, is often determined by multiple factors other than the opioid. If the myoclonus is symptomatic and distressing, it can be treated empirically with a benzodiazepine (specifically clonazepam; Eisele, Grigsby, & Dea, 1992), a barbiturate, or valproate.

Among cancer patients whose opioid dose is carefully titrated, respiratory depression is rare. Controlled studies suggest that age does not enhance sensitivity to this effect (Daykin, Bowen, Saunders, & Norman, 1986). Although tolerance may develop rapidly to this effect (Foley, 1991), the observation that some patients on stable opioid therapy develop sedation or respiratory depression after anesthetic or neurodestructive procedures suggests that other pain-related factors may also play a role in the ability to tolerate high-dose opioid therapy (Foley, 1991). Indeed, reduction of the opioid dose is usually necessary after anesthetic or neurolytic techniques (Hanks, Twycross, & Lloyd, 1981).

Clinically significant respiratory depression is always accompanied by other signs of central nervous system depression, including somnolence and mental clouding. Respiratory distress associated with tachypnea and anxiety is never a primary opioid event, and alternative explanations (e.g., pneumonia or pulmonary embolism) should be sought. Due to the risk of systemic withdrawal and the return of pain, naloxone should be administered only for symptomatic respiratory depression. If the patient is arousable and the peak plasma levels of the opioid have already been reached, naloxone should not be administered; the opioid dose should be withheld and the patient monitored until improved. If the patient is becoming progressively obtunded, is unarousable, or has severe respiratory depression, naloxone should be administered using 1-cc bolus injections of dilute solution (0.4 mg in 10 cc saline) every 10–15 seconds until respiratory rate stabilizes (Bradberry & Reabel, 1981; Goldfrank, Weisman, Errick, & Lo, 1986). Partial reversal of respiratory depression with naloxone does not prove that the opioid was the primary cause of the event. An intercurrent cardiac or pulmonary process can precipitate respiratory depression in patients on chronic opioid therapy that partially remits with naloxone. Hence, a naloxone response does not obviate the need for a careful patient evaluation for a cardiopulmonary process. Since naloxone has a short half-life, patients receiving slow-release morphine, transdermal fentanyl, or methadone may require repeated doses or a naloxone infusion to prevent recurrence of respiratory depression.

Physical and Psychological Dependence. Confusion about physical dependence and addiction augments the fear of opioid drugs and contributes to physician reluctance to prescribe opioids and patient reluctance to use them (Cleeland, 1989; Foley, 1989b; Schuster, 1989). This confusion derives, in part, from misunderstanding of the nomenclature used to describe drug use.

Physical dependence is a pharmacological property of opioid drugs that is defined by the development of an abstinence (withdrawal) syndrome following either abrupt dose reduction or administration of an antagonist. Physical dependence is not a clinical problem if patients are warned to avoid abrupt discontinuation of the drug, a tapering schedule is used if treatment cessation is indicated, and opioid antagonist drugs (including agonist–antagonist analgesics) are avoided. In the elderly, unrecognized withdrawal reactions can produce nonspecific symptoms, including transient fevers, arrhythmias, and changes in mental status (Miller, Whitcup, Sacks, & Lynch, 1985).

Addiction refers to a psychological and behavioral syndrome characterized by loss of control over drug use, compulsive use, and continued use despite harm to self or others. Addicts crave the opioid to achieve a psychic effect and manifest aberrant drug-related behaviors, such as unsanctioned dose escalation, acquisition of the drug from multiple providers, or use of illicit drugs. The medical use of opioids is very rarely associated with the development of addiction (Chapman & Hill, 1989; Porter & Jick, 1980; Schuster, 1989). In the largest prospective study, only 4 cases of iatrogenic addiction could be identified among 11,882 patients with no prior history of addiction who received at least one opioid dose in the hospital setting (Porter & Jick, 1980). Extensive clinical experience in the use of opioids for patients with chronic cancer pain affirms that the risk of addiction in this population is extremely low (American College of Physicians Health and Public Policy Committee, 1983; American Pain Society, 1992; Chapman & Hill, 1989; World Health Organization, 1986, 1990).

Some cancer patients who continue to experience unrelieved pain manifest drug-seeking behaviors that are reminiscent of addiction but cease once pain is relieved, often through opioid dose escalation. These behaviors have been termed *pseudoaddiction* (Weissman & Haddox, 1989). Misunderstanding of this phenomenon may lead the clinician to inappropriately stigmatize the patient with the label *addict*, which may compromise care and erode the doctor–patient relationship. In the setting of unrelieved pain, the request for increases in drug dose requires careful assessment, renewed efforts to manage pain, and avoidance of stigmatizing labels.

Adjunctive Techniques: Noninvasive Interventions

Even with optimal management of adverse effects, some patients do not attain an acceptable balance between pain relief and side effects. Several types of noninvasive interventions should be considered for their potential to improve this balance by reducing the opioid requirement. These include the concurrent use of an appropriate primary therapy, alternative pharmacological approaches (nonopioid analgesics, adjuvant analgesics, or a switch to another opioid), and the use of psychological, physiatric, or noninvasive neurostimulatory techniques.

Adjuvant Analgesics. Polypharmacy is undesirable, but it is often a necessary part of pharmacological pain management in the cancer patient population. Balancing the risks and benefits of each additional drug is a particular challenge in the elderly patient. In a patient on an oral narcotic, the use of adjuvant analgesics or medications to control side effects can prevent the need to move to a more invasive route of administration. Adjuvant analgesics can be broadly divided into general-purpose analgesics and those with specific utility for neuropathic, bone, or visceral pain.

Corticosteroids. Corticosteroids are the most widely used general-purpose adjuvant analgesics (Ettinger & Portenoy, 1988). These drugs may ameliorate pain and produce beneficial effects on appetite, nausea, mood, and malaise (Bruera, Roca, Cedaro, Carraro, & Chacon, 1985; Della Cuna, Pellegrini, & Piazzi, 1989; Moertel et al., 1974; Popiela, Lucchi, & Giongo, 1989; Tannock et al., 1989; Wilcox, Corr, Shaw, Richardson, & Calman, 1984). The painful conditions that commonly respond to corticosteroids include raised intracranial pressure, acute spinal cord compression, superior vena cava syndrome, metastatic bone pain, neuropathic pain due to infiltration or compression by tumor, symptomatic lymphedema, and hepatic capsular distention. Patients with advanced cancer who experience pain and other symptoms that may respond to steroids are usually given relatively small doses (e.g., dexamethasone 1–2 mg twice daily). A very short course of relatively high doses (e.g., dexamethasone 100 mg IV followed initially by 96 mg per day in divided doses) can be used to manage an acute episode of very severe pain that is related to a neuropathic lesion (e.g., plexopathy or epidural spinal cord compression) or bony metastasis and cannot be promptly reduced with opioids. In all cases, the dose should be gradually lowered following pain reduction to the minimum needed to sustain relief.

Topical Local Anesthetics. Topical local anesthetics can be used in the management of painful cutaneous and mucosal lesions, and as a premedication prior to skin puncture. Controlled studies have demonstrated the effectiveness of a eutectic mixture of 2.5% lidocaine and 2.5% prilocaine (EMLA) in reducing pain associated with venipuncture (Cooper, Gerrish, Hardwick, & Kay, 1987; Halperin et al., 1989; Maunuksela & Korpela, 1986; Soliman, Broadman, Hannallah, & McGill, 1988; Wig & Johl, 1990), lumbar puncture (Halperin et al., 1989; Kapelushnik, Koren, Solh, Greenberg, & De Veber, 1990) and arterial puncture (Nilsson, Danielson, Engberg, & Henneberg, 1990). Viscous lidocaine is frequently used in the management of oropharyngeal ulceration (Carnel, Blakeslee, Oswald, & Barnes, 1990; Shortsleeve & Levine, 1992; Watts, Alexander, Fawcett, Check, & Abnrashed, 1986; Welling & Watson, 1990).

Adjuvants for Neuropathic Pain. Neuropathic pain such as painful brachial or lumbosacral plexopathy can present a major therapeutic challenge. The use of adjuvant analgesics can contribute substantially to the successful management of these problems. For the purpose of drug selection, it is useful to distinguish between continuous, lancinating, and sympathetically maintained neuropathic pain (Table 13-8) (Portenoy, 1993a). Given the great interpatient and intrapatient variability in the response to adjuvants in this setting (including those within the same class), sequential trials are frequently required.

Adjuvants for Bone Pain. The management of bone pain frequently requires the integration of opioid therapy with multiple ancillary approaches. Although a meta-

Table 13-8. A Guide to the Selection of Adjuvant Analgesics for Neuropathic Pain Based on Clinical Characteristics

Continuous pain	Lancinating pain	Sympathetically-maintained pain
Antidepressants	Anticonvulsant drugs	Phenoxybenzamine
Amitriptyline	Carbamazepine	Prazosin
Doxepin	Phenytoin	Corticosteroid
Imipramine	Clonazepam	Nifedipine
Despiramine	Valproate	Propranolol
Nortriptyline	Baclofen	Calcitonin
Trazodone	Oral local anesthetics	
Maprotiline	Pimozide	
	Ketamine	
Oral local anesthetics		
Mexiletine		
Clonidine		
Capsaicin		

analysis of NSAID therapy in cancer pain that reviewed data from 1,615 patients in 21 trials found no specific efficacy in bone pain and analgesic effects equivalent only to "weak" opioids (Eisenberg, Berkey, Carr, Mosteller, & Chalmers, 1994), some patients appear to benefit greatly from the addition of such a drug.

The radiopharmaceutical strontium-89 (Dearnaley et al., 1992; Fossa, Paus, Lochoff, Backe, & Aas, 1992; Laing et al., 1991; Lewington et al., 1991; Porter et al., 1993; Robinson, Preston, Spicer, & Baxter, 1992) has recently been approved for the treatment of bone pain caused by metastatic disease. Strontium-89 is absorbed into areas of high bone turnover and can reduce pain, generally without causing significant bone marrow depression (Bayouth, Macey, Kasi, & Fossella, 1994). Other radiopharmaceuticals currently under investigation include samarium-153-ethylenediaminetetramethylene phosphonic acid (Turner, Claringbold, Heatherington, Sorby, & Martindal, 1989; Turner & Claringbold, 1991) and rhenium-186-hydroxyethylidene diphosphonate (Maxon et al., 1988, 1992).

The bisphosphonates drugs, pamidronate and clodronate, inhibit osteoclast activity and have also been demonstrated to relieve malignant bone pain (Clemens, Fessele, & Heim, 1993; Coleman, Woll, Miles, Scrivener, & Rubens, 1988; Ernst et al., 1992; Morton et al., 1988; Thiebaud et al., 1991; van Holten-Verzantvoort et al., 1991, 1993). Parenteral administration of pamidronate every two weeks is generally well tolerated, and the risk of symptomatic hypocalcemia is low. Other agents worthy of consideration include corticosteroids, calcitonin (Roth & Kolaric, 1986), and gallium nitrate (Warrell, Lovett, Dilmanian, Schnieder, & Heelan, 1993).

Adjuvants for Visceral Pain. There are limited data that support of the potential efficacy of a range of adjuvant agents for the management of bladder spasm, tenesmoid pain, and colicky intestinal pain. Based on limited clinical experience and in vitro evidence that prostaglandins play a role in bladder smooth-muscle contraction, a trial of

NSAIDs may be justified for patients with painful bladder spasms (Abrams & Fenely, 1976; Cardozo & Stanton, 1981; Hanks, Portenoy, MacDonald, & O'Niel, 1993). Although there is no well established pharmacotherapy for painful rectal spasms, diltiazem, a calcium channel blocker that reduces smooth-muscle contraction, has been effective in the management of proctalgia fugax (Boquet, Moore, Lhuintre, & Boismare, 1986; Castell, 1986), and chlorpromazine (Twycross & Lack, 1990) and benzodiazepines (Hanks, 1984) have been used anecdotally. Pain due to inoperable bowel obstruction has been treated empirically with intravenous scopolamine (hyoscine) butylbromide (Baines, 1993; De Conno, Carraceni, Zecca, Spoldi, & Ventafridda, 1991; Ventafridda et al., 1990a), sublingual scopolamine (hyoscine) hydrobromide (Baines, 1990), and, most recently, the somatostatin analogue, octreotide. Despite the theoretical advantages of antimuscarinic drugs in these conditions, and some limited support for the use of emepronium bromide (Syversen, Mollestad, & Semb, 1976), dicyclomine, and flavoxate (Bradley & Cazort, 1970), anticholinergic adverse effects are frequent, and benefit is rarely observed (Hanks et al., 1993).

In the management of pain due to pancreas cancer, there is limited evidence supporting the effectiveness of octreotide (Canobbio, Boccardo, Cannata, Gallotti, & Epis, 1992), as well as the oral administration of trypsin (Ihse & Permerth, 1990). It is speculated that these effects are mediated by reduction in pancreatic exocrine secretion.

Other Noninvasive Techniques

Psychological Therapies. All cancer patients benefit from psychological assessment and support. Some also benefit from specific psychological interventions used in the management of pain. Cognitive-behavioral interventions can help reduce pain-related distress through the development of coping skills and the modification of thoughts, feelings, and behaviors (Ferrell et al., 1994). Some patients may be able to use relaxation techniques to reduce muscular tension and emotional arousal, or to enhance pain tolerance (Linton & Melin, 1983). Other approaches reduce anticipatory anxiety that may lead to avoidant behaviors. Successful application of these therapies requires a cognitively intact patient and a dedicated, well-trained clinician (Ferrell et al., 1994). In a controlled study, a structured nondrug program in which elderly patients were educated in the use of various strategies, including heat, cold, massage-vibration, distraction, and relaxation was shown to diminish pain and enhance patient satisfaction (Rhiner, Ferrell, Ferrell, & Grant, 1993).

Physiatric Techniques. Physiatric techniques can be used to enhance analgesia and optimize the function of the patient with chronic cancer pain. Therapeutic modalities, such as electrical stimulation (including transcutaneous electrical neurostimulation), heat, or cryotherapy, can be useful adjuncts to standard analgesic therapy. The treatment of lymphedema by use of wraps, pressure stockings, or pneumatic pump devices may both improve function and relieve pain and heaviness (Brennan, 1992). Orthotic devices can immobilize and support painful or weakened structures, and assistive devices can enhance comfort for patients with pain precipitated by weight bearing or ambulation.

Adjunctive Techniques: Invasive Interventions

Patients who are unable to achieve a satisfactory balance between analgesia and side effects from systemic analgesic therapies may be candidates for the use of invasive anesthetic and neurosurgical techniques. These approaches may reduce the requirement of systemically administered opioids. Techniques such as intraspinal opioid and local anesthetic administration can achieve this end without compromising neurological integrity. The use of neurodestructive procedures should be based on an evaluation of the likelihood and duration of analgesic benefit, the immediate and long-term risks, the likely duration of survival, and the anticipated length of hospitalization.

Intraspinal (Epidural and Intrathecal) Opioids. The delivery of low opioid doses near the sites of action in the spinal cord may decrease supraspinally mediated adverse effects. In the absence of randomized trials that compare the various intraspinal techniques with other analgesic approaches, the indications for the spinal route remain empirical (Plummer et al., 1991). A recent survey reported that only 16 of 1,205 cancer patients with pain required intraspinal therapy (Hogan et al., 1991). Compared to neuroablative therapies, spinal opioids have the advantage of preserving sensation, strength, and sympathetic function. Contraindications include bleeding diathesis, profound leukopenia, and sepsis. A temporary trial of spinal opioid therapy should be performed to assess the potential benefits of this approach before implantation of a permanent catheter. The addition of a low concentration of a local anesthetic, such as 0.125%–0.25% bupivacaine, to an epidural opioid has been demonstrated to increase analgesic effect without increasing toxicity (Du Pen & Ramsey, 1988; Hogan et al., 1991; Nitescu et al., 1990; Sjoberg et al., 1991). The potential morbidity for these procedures indicates the need for a well-trained clinician and long-term monitoring.

Intraventricular Opioids. Limited experience suggests that the administration of an opioid into the cerebral ventricles can provide long-term analgesia in selected patients (Crammond & Stuart, 1993; Dennis & DeWitty, 1990; Leavens, Hill, Cech, Weyland, & Weston, 1982; Lee, Kumar, & Baratham, 1990; Lobato et al., 1987; Nurchi, 1984; Obbens, Hill, Leavens, Ruthenbeck, & Otis, 1987; Roquefeil et al., 1984). This technique has been used for patients with upper body or head pain, or severe with diffuse pain. Schedules have included both intermittent injection via an Ommaya reservoir (Crammond & Stuart, 1993; Lobato et al., 1987; Obbens et al., 1987) and continual infusion using an implanted pump (Dennis & DeWitty, 1990).

Intrapleural local anesthetic. Several authors have described the use of intrapleural local anesthetics in the management of chronic postthoracotomy pain (Fineman, 1989) and cancer-related pains involving the head, neck, chest, arms, and upper abdominal viscera (Lema, Myers, De, & Penetrante, 1992; Myers, Lema, de Leon-Casasola, & Bacon, 1993; Waldman, Allen, & Cronen, 1989).

Celiac Plexus Block. Neurolytic celiac plexus blockade can be considered in the management of pain caused by neoplastic infiltration of the upper abdominal viscera, including the pancreas, upper retroperitoneum, liver, gall bladder, and proximal small bowel (Bonica, Buckley, Moricca, & Murphey, 1990a; Brown, Bulley, & Quiel, 1987; Cousins, Dwyer, & Gibb, 1988; Lillemoe et al., 1993; Mercadante, 1993). Reported analgesic response rates in patients with pancreatic cancer are 50%–90%, and the reported duration of effect is generally 1–12 months (Bonica et al., 1990a; Brown et al., 1987; Cousins et al., 1988; Mercadante, 1993). Common transient complications include postural hypotension and diarrhea (Bonica et al., 1990a; Brown et al., 1987; Cousins et al., 1988). Posterior spread of neurolytic solution occasionally leads to involvement of lower thoracic and lumbar somatic nerves, which may result in a neuropathic pain syndrome. Other uncommon complications include pneumothorax, retroperitoneal hematoma, and paraparesis.

Sympathetic Blockade of Somatic Structures. Sympathetically maintained pain syndromes may be relieved by interruption of sympathetic outflow to the affected region of the body. Lumbar sympathetic blockade should be considered for sympathetically maintained pain involving the legs, and stellate ganglion blockade may be useful for sympathetically maintained pain involving the face or arms.

Rhizotomy. Chemical rhizotomy, which may be produced by the instillation of a neurolytic solution into either the epidural or the intrathecal space, can be an effective method of pain control for patients with otherwise refractory localized pain syndromes (Hellendoorn & Overweg van Kints, 1988; Ischia, Luzzani, Ischia, Magon, & Toscano, 1984). The technique is most commonly used in the management of chest wall pain due to tumor invasion of somatic and neural structures. Other indications include refractory upper limb, lower limb, pelvic, or perineal pain. Satisfactory analgesia is achieved in about 50% of patients (Cousins et al., 1988). Adverse effects can be related to the injection technique (e.g., spinal headache, infection, and arachnoiditis) or to the destruction of nonnociceptive nerve fibers. Specific complications of the procedure depend on the site of neurolysis. Complications of lumbosacral neurolysis include paresis (5%–20%), sphincter dysfunction (5%–60%), impairment of touch and proprioception, and dysesthesias. Although neurological deficits are usually transient, the risk of increased disability through weakness, sphincter incompetence, and loss of positional sense suggests that these techniques should be reversed for patients with limited function and preexistent urinary diversion. Patient counseling regarding the risks involved is essential.

Rhizotomy can be also be achieved surgically using either open or percutaneous techniques (Sindou, Fisher, & Mansuy, 1976). Patients with refractory unilateral head and neck pain, for example, may be candidates for an open cranial rhizotomy which incorporates transection of the trigeminal and glossopharyngeal nerves and the dorsal roots of C2 and C3.

Neurolysis of Primary Afferent Nerves or Their Ganglia. Neurolysis of primary afferent nerves may also provide significant relief for selected patients with localized pain. Refractory unilateral facial or pharyngeal pain may be amenable to trigeminal neurolysis, gasserian gangliolysis, or glossopharyngeal neurolysis. Intercostal or paravertebral neurolysis is an alternative to rhizotomy for patients with chest wall pain. Severe pain limited to the perineum may be treated by neurolysis of the S4 nerve root via the ipsilateral posterior sacral foramen, a procedure that carries a minimal risk of motor or sphincter impairment (Robertson, 1983).

Cordotomy. In cordotomy, the anterolateral spinothalamic tract is interrupted to produce contralateral loss of pain and temperature sensibility (Arbit, 1990; Rosomoff, Carroll, & Brown, 1965). Significant pain relief is achieved in more than 90% of patients during the period immediately following cordotomy (Arbit, 1990; Ischia et al., 1984; Rosomoff et al., 1965; Stuart & Cramond, 1993; Tasker, Tsuda, & Howrylyshn, 1988). Fifty percent of surviving patients have recurrent pain after one year, and repeat cordotomy is sometimes effective. Patients with severe unilateral pain arising in the torso or a lower extremity are most likely to benefit from this procedure (Ischia et al., 1984). Impressive results have also been observed in patients with chest wall pain (Stuart & Cramond, 1993). The percutaneous technique is generally preferred (Arbit, 1990); open cordotomy is usually reserved for patients who are unable to lie in the supine position or are not cooperative enough to undergo a percutaneous procedure (Arbit, 1990). The neurological complications of the procedure include paresis, ataxia, and bladder dysfunction (Tasker et al., 1988). The most serious potential complication is respiratory dysfunction, which manifests as phrenic nerve paralysis or sleep-induced apnea (in patients who undergo bilateral high cordotomy) (Polatty & Cooper, 1986). The potential for this complication relatively contraindicates bilateral high cervical cordotomies or a unilateral cervical cordotomy ipsilateral to the site of the only functioning lung.

Other Techniques. Pituitary ablation by chemical or surgical hypophysectomy has been reported to relieve diffuse and multifocal pain syndromes that have been refractory to opioid therapy and are unsuitable for any regional neuroablative procedure (Bonica et al., 1990a; Levin & Ramirez, 1984). Pain relief has been observed in patients with hormone-dependent and hormone-independent tumors (Bonica et al., 1990a; Levin & Ramirez, 1984).

Anecdotal reports also support the efficacy of cingulotomy in the management of diffuse pain syndromes that have been refractory to opioid therapy (Hassenbusch, Pillay, & Barnett, 1990). The mode of action is unknown, and the procedure is rarely considered.

Patients with Refractory Pain: The Role of Sedation

For some patients with advanced disease, adequate relief of physical symptoms may be achieved only at the cost of profound sedation (Cherny & Portenoy, 1994; Enck, 1991; Greene & Davis, 1991; Truog, Berde, Mitchell, & Greir, 1992; Ventafridda et al.,

1990b). Sedation is an option in the management of intractable pain and suffering at the end of life in patients who fail to benefit from optimal palliative therapy (Cherny & Portenoy, 1994; Greene & Davis, 1991; Truog et al., 1992). Sedation can be accomplished through the use of a systemic opioid, benzodiazepine (e.g., lorazepam, midazolam, or flunitrazepam) (Burke, Diamond, Hulbert, Yeatman, & Farr, 1991; Smales, Smales, & Sanders, 1993), neuroleptic (e.g., chlorpromazine or methotrimeprazine) or barbiturate (e.g., thiopental) (Greene & Davis, 1991; Truog et al., 1992). In one study, 52% of terminally ill patients developed otherwise unendurable symptoms that required deep sedation for adequate relief; in just under half of these patients, pain was the predominant symptom (Ventafridda et al., 1990b).

The use of a short half-life drug facilitates dose titration during controlled sedation. If desired, doses can be titrated down to reestablish lucidity after an agreed-on interval or at the time of preplanned family interactions (Greene & Davis, 1991; Truog et al., 1992). Such changes produce a potentially unstable situation, however, and the possibility that lucidity may not be promptly restored, or that death may ensue, should be explained to both the patient and the family. Patients with persisting distress and those who are imminently dying may elect to be deeply sedated until death ensues. It is the responsibility of the physician to ensure that the patient, family, and staff have a comprehensive understanding of this intervention.

The ethical acceptability of sedation at the end of life is predicated on informed consent and on acknowledgment of the "principle of double effect," which distinguishes between the compelling primary therapeutic intent (to relieve suffering) and unavoidable untoward consequences (the potential for accelerating death) (Latimer, 1991). This approach recognizes the right of dying patients to adequate relief of pain, and the right of all patients to choose between appropriate therapeutic options (Edwards, 1989; Martin, 1989; Wanzer et al., 1989). No patient should have to ask to be killed because of persistently unrelieved pain, and contrariwise, no patient should be sedated without appropriate informed consent of the patient or a proxy. The process of informed decision making requires candid discussion that clarifies the prevailing clinical predicament and presents the alternative analgesic options (including sedation). Other relevant considerations, including existential, ethical, religious, and familial concerns, may benefit from the participation of a religious counselor, social worker, or clinical ethics specialist.

CONCLUSION

The elderly represent the most rapidly growing age group afflicted by cancer, and effective pain control is essential for the preservation of the quality of life in this population. The individual practitioner can effectively treat the majority of pain problems by attending to careful pain assessment and implementing analgesic therapy. Successful long-term management requires continuity of care that provides an appropriate level of monitoring and responds quickly, flexibly, and expertly to the changing needs of the patient. Familiarity with the principles of analgesic pharmacology as it relates to the elderly is critical to this process.

REFERENCES

Abrams, P., & Fenely, R. (1976). The action of prostaglandins on smooth muscle of the human urinary tract in vitro. *British Journal of Urology, 47*, 909–915.

Agency for Health Care Policy and Research: Cancer Pain Management Panel. (1994). *Management of cancer pain*. Washington, DC, U.S. Department of Health and Human Services.

Alexander, A. M., Veitch, G. B., & Wood, J. B. (1985). Anti-rheumatic and analgesic drug usage and acute gastro-intestinal bleeding in elderly patients. *Journal of Clinical Hospital Pharmacology, 10*(1), 89–93.

American College of Physicians Health and Public Policy Committee (1983). Drug therapy for severe chronic pain in terminal illness. *Annals of Internal Medicine, 99*, 870–880.

American Pain Society. (1992). *Principles of analgesic use in the treatment of acute pain and chronic cancer pain. A concise guide to medical practice* (3rd ed.). Skokie, IL: American Pain Society.

American Psychiatric Association. (1987). Somatoform disorders. In *Diagnostic and statistical manual of mental disorders* (pp. 255–267). Washington, DC: American Psychiatric Association.

Amesbury, B. D. W. (1989). Use of SC midazolam in the home care setting. *Palliative Medicine, 3*, 299–301.

Arbit, E. (1990). Neurosurgical management of cancer pain. In K. M. Foley, J. J. Bonica, & V. Ventafridda (Eds.), *Second International Congress on Cancer Pain* (pp. 289–300). New York: Raven Press.

Arkinstall, W. W., Goughnour, B. R., White, J. A., & Stewart, J. H. (1989). Control of severe pain with sustained-release morphine tablets v. oral morphine solution. *Canadian Medical Association Journal, 140* (6), 653–657.

Arner, S., & Meyerson, B. A. (1988). Lack of analgesic effect of opioids on neuropathic and idiopathic forms of pain. *Pain, 33* (1), 11–23.

Baines, M. (1993). The pathophysiology and management of malignant intestinal obstruction. In D. Doyle, G. W. Hanks, & N. MacDonald (Eds.), *Oxford textbook of palliative medicine* (pp. 311–316). Oxford: Oxford University Press.

Baines, M. J. (1990). Management of malignant intestinal obstruction in patients with advanced cancer. In K. M. Foley, J. J. Bonica, & V. Ventafridda (Eds.), *Second International Congress on Cancer Pain* (pp. 327–336). New York: Raven Press.

Ballinger, A. (1994). Cytoprotection with misoprostol: Use in the treatment and prevention of ulcers. *Digestive Diseases, 12*(1), 37–45.

Banning, A., Sjogren, P., & Henriksen, H. (1991). Pain causes in 200 patients referred to a multidisciplinary cancer pain clinic. *Pain, 45* (1), 45–48.

Bayouth, J. E., Macey, D. J., Kasi, L. P., & Fossella, F. V. (1994). Dosimetry and toxicity of samarium-153-EDTMP administered for bone pain due to skeletal metastases. *Journal of Nuclear Medicine, 35* (1), 63–69.

Beaver, W. T., & Feise, G. (1977). Comparison of the analgesic effect oxymorphone by rectal suppository and intramuscular injection in patients with postoperative pain. *Journal of Clinical Pharmacology, 17*, 276.

Bender, A. D. (1965). The effect of increased age on the distribution of pheripheral blood flow in man. *Journal of the American Geriatric Society, 13*, 192–196.

Bonica, J. J., Buckley, F. P., Moricca, G., & Murphey, T. M. (1990a). Neurolytic blockade and hypohysectomy. In J. J. Bonica (Ed.), *The management of pain* (pp. 1980–2039). Philadelphia: Lea & Febiger.

Bonica, J. J., Ventafridda, V., & Twycross, R. G. (1990b). Cancer pain. In J. J. Bonica (Ed.), *The management of pain* (pp. 400–460). Philadelphia: Lea & Febiger.

Boquet, J., Moore, N., Lhuintre, J. P., & Boismare, F. (1986). Diltiazem for proctalgia fugax [letter]. *The Lancet, 1* (8496), 1493.

Bradberry, J. C., & Reabel, M. A. (1981). Continuous infusion of naloxone in the treatment of narcotic overdose. *Drug Intelligence and Clinical Pharmacy, 15*, 85–90.

Bradley, D. V., & Cazort, R. J. (1970). Relief of bladder spasm by flavoxate. A comparative study. *Journal of Clinical Pharmacology, 10* (1), 65–68.

Brennan, M. J. (1992). Management of lymphedema: review of pathophysiology and treatment. *Journal of Pain and Symptom Management, 7*, 110–116.

Brescia, F. J., Adler, D., Gray, G., Ryan, M. A., Climino, J., & Mamtani, R. (1990). Hospitalized advanced cancer patients: a profile. *Journal of Pain Symptom Management, 5* (4), 221–227.

Brescia, F. J., Portenoy, R. K., Ryan, M., Krasnoff, L., & Gray, G. (1992). Pain, opioid use, and survival in hospitalized patients with advanced cancer. *Journal of Clinical Oncology, 10* (1), 149–155.

Brooks, P. M., & Wood, A. J. J. (1991). Nonsteroidal antiinflammatory drugs-differences and similarities. *New England Journal of Medicine, 324*, 1716–1725.

Brown, D. L., Bulley, C. K., & Quiel, E. C. (1987). Neurolytic celiac plexus blockade for pancreatic cancer pain. *Anesthesia and Analgesia, 66*, 869–873.

Bruera, E., Brenneis, C., Michaud, M., Bacovsky, R., Chadwick, S., Emeno, A., & MacDonald, N. (1988a). Use of the subcutaneous route for the administration of narcotics in patients with cancer pain. *Cancer, 62* (2), 407–411.

Bruera, E., Brenneis, C., Michaud, M., MacMillan, K., Hanson, J., & MacDonald, R. N. (1988b). Patient-controlled subcutaneous hydromorphone versus continuous subcutaneous infusion for the treatment of cancer pain. *Journal of the National Cancer Institute, 80* (14), 1152–1154.

Bruera, E., Fainsinger, R., Moore, M., Thibault, R., Spoldi, E., & Ventafridda, V. (1991). Local toxicity with subcutaneous methadone: Experience of two centers. *Pain, 45*, 141–145.

Bruera, E., Macmillan, K., Hanson, J., & MacDonald, R. N. (1989). The cognitive effects of the administration of narcotic analgesics in patients with cancer pain. *Pain, 39* (1), 13–16.

Bruera, E., Macmillan, K., Selmser, P., & MacDonald, R. N. (1990). Decreased local toxicity with subcutaneous diamorphine (heroin): A preliminary report. *Pain, 43* (1), 91–94.

Bruera, E., Roca, E., Cedaro, L., Carraro, S., & Chacon, R. (1985). Action of oral methylprednisolone in terminal cancer patients: A prospective randomized double-blind study. *Cancer Treatment Report, 69*, 751–754.

Burke, A. L., Diamond, P. L., Hulbert, J., Yeatman, J., & Farr, E. A. (1991). Terminal restlessness—Its management and the role of midazolam. *Medical Journal of Australia, 155* (7), 485–487.

Campora, E., Merlini, L., Pace, M., Bruzzone, M., Luzzani, M., Gottleib, A., & Rosso, R. (1991). The incidence of narcotic induced emesis. *Journal of Pain and Symptom Management, 6* (7), 428–430.

Canobbio, L., Boccardo, F., Cannata, D., Gallotti, P., & Epis, R. (1992). Treatment of advanced pancreatic carcinoma with the somatostatin analogue BIM 23014: Preliminary results of a pilot study. *Cancer, 69* (3), 648–650.

Cardozo, L. D., & Stanton, S. L. (1981). A comparison between bromocriptine and indomethacin in the treatment of detrusor instability. *Journal of Urology, 73*, 236–239.

Carnel, S. B., Blakeslee, D. B., Oswald, S. G., & Barnes, M. (1990). Treatment of radiation- and chemotherapy-induced stomatitis. *Otolaryngology—Head and Neck Surgery, 102* (4), 326–330.

Castell, D. O. (1986). Calcium blocking agents for gastrointestinal disorders. *American Journal of Cardiology, 55*, 210B–215B.

Chan, G. L., & Matzke, G. R. (1987). Effects of renal insufficiency on the pharmacokinetics and pharmacodynamics of opioid analgesics. *Drug Intelligence and Clinical Pharmacology, 21* (10), 773–783.

Chapman, C. R., & Hill, H. F. (1989). Prolonged morphine self-administration and addiction liability. *Cancer, 63*, 1636–1644.

Cherny, N. I., & Portenoy, R. K. (1994). Sedation in the treatment of refractory symptoms: guidelines for evaluation and treatment. *Journal of Palliative Care, 10* (2), 31–38.

Cherny, N. I., Thaler, H. T., Friedlander-Klar, H., Lapin, J., Foley, K. M., Houde, R., & Portenoy, R. K. (1994). Opioid responsiveness of cancer pain syndromes caused by neuropathic or nociceptive mechanisms: A combined analysis of controlled single dose studies. *Neurology, 44*, 857–861.

Cherny, N. I., Thaler, H. T., Friedlander-Klar, H., Lapin, J., & Portenoy, R. K. (1992). Opioid responsiveness of neuropathic cancer pain: Combined analysis of single-dose analgesic trials. *Proceedings of the American Society of Clinical Oncology, 11*, Abstract 1330.

Citron, M., Conaway, M., Zhukovsky, D., Kornblith, A. B., Berkowitz, I., Pascall, V., Smith, W., & Vinciguerra, V. (1993). Efficacy of patient-controlled analgesia (PCA) vs continuous iv morphine (CIVM) for the treatment of severe cancer pain: CALGB 8872 (meeting abstract). *Proceedings of the Annual Meeting of the American Society of Clinical Oncologists.*

Cleeland, C. (1991). Research in cancer pain: What we know and what we need to know. *Cancer, 3* (1), 823–827.

Cleeland, C. S. (1984). The impact of pain on the patient with cancer. *Cancer, 54*, 2635–2641.

Cleeland, C. S. (1988). Clinical cancer: 31. Barriers to the management of cancer pain: the roles of patient and family. *Wisconsin Medical Journal, 87* (11), 13–15.

Cleeland, C. S. (1989). Pain control: public and physician's attitudes. In C. S. Hill & W. S. Fields (Eds.), *Drug treatment of cancer pain in a drug-oriented society* (pp. 81–89). New York: Raven Press.

Cleeland, C. S., Cleeland, L. M., Dar, R., & Rinehardt, L. C. (1986). Factors influencing physician management of cancer pain. *Cancer, 58* (3), 796–800.

Clemens, M. R., Fessele, K., & Heim, M. E. (1993). Multiple myeloma: effect of daily dichloromethylene bisphosphonate on skeletal complications. *Annals of Hematology, 66* (3), 141–146.

Closs, S. J. (1994). Pain in elderly patients: A neglected phenomenon? *Journal of Advanced Nursing, 19* (6), 1072–1081.

Clouston, P., De Angelis, L., & Posner, J. B. (1992). The spectrum of neurologic disease in patients with systemic cancer. *Annals of Neurology, 31*, 268–273.

Coleman, R. E., Woll, P. J., Miles, M., Scrivener, W., & Rubens, R. D. (1988). Treatment of bone metastases with (3 amino-1-hydroxyprpylidene)-1, 1-bisphosphonate (APD). *British Journal of Cancer, 58*, 621–625.

Cooper, C. M., Gerrish, S. P., Hardwick, M., & Kay, R. (1987). EMLA cream reduces the pain of venipuncture in children. *European Journal of Anaesthesiology, 4* (6), 441–448.

Cousins, M. J., Dwyer, B., & Gibb, D. (1988). Chronic pain and neurolytic blockade. In M. J. Cousins & P. O. Bridenbaugh (Eds.), *Neural blockade in clinical anesthesia and management of pain* (pp. 1053–1084). Philadelphia: Lippincott.

Coyle, N., Adelhardt, J., & Foley, K. M. (1988). Disease progression and tolerance in the cancer pain patient. 2nd International Congress on Cancer Pain. *Journal of Pain and Symptom Management, 3*, S25.

Coyle, N., Adelhardt, J., Foley, K. M., & Portenoy, R. K. (1990). Character of terminal illness in the advanced cancer patient: Pain and other symptoms during last four weeks of life. *Journal of Pain and Symptom Management, 5*, 83–89.

Coyle, N., Breitbart, W., Weaver, S., & Portenoy, R. K. (1994a). Delerium as a contributing factor to "crecendo" pain: Three case reports. *Journal of Pain and Symptom Management, 9* (1), 44–47.

Coyle, N., Cherny, N. I., & Portenoy, R. K. (1994b). Subcutaneous opioid infusions in the home. *Oncology, 8* (4), 21–27.

Coyle, N., Mauskop, A., & Maggard, J. (1986). Continuous subcutaneous infusions of opiates in cancer patients with pain. *Oncology Nursing Forum, 13*, 53–57.

Crammond, T., & Stuart, G. (1993). Intraventricular morphine for intractable pain of advanced cancer. *Journal of Pain and Symptom Management, 8* (7), 465–473.

Crawford, J., & Cohen, H. J. (1987). Relàtionship of cancer and aging. *Clinical Geriatric Medicine, 3* (3), 419–432.

Crews, J. C., Sweeney, N. J., & Denson, D. D. (1993). Clinical efficacy of methadone in patients refractory to other mu-opioid receptor agonist analgesics for management of terminal cancer pain: Case presentations and discussion of incomplete cross-tolerance among opioid agonist analgesics. *Cancer, 72* (7), 2266–2272.

Culpepper-Morgan, J. A., Inturrisi, C. E., Portenoy, R. K., Foley, K. M., Houde, R. W., Marsh, F., & Kreek, M. J. (1992). Treatment of opioid induced constipation with oral naloxone: A pilot study. *Clinical Pharmacology and Therapeutics, 52*, 90–95.

Daut, R. L., & Cleeland, C. S. (1982).The prevalence and severity of pain in cancer. *Cancer, 50*, 1913–1918.

Daykin, A. P., Bowen, D. J., Saunders, D. A., & Norman, J. (1986). Respiratory depression after morphine in the elderly: A comparison with younger subjects. *Anaesthesia, 41* (9), 910–914.

Dearnaley, D. P., Bayly, R. J., A'Hern, R. P., Gadd, J., Zivanovic, M. M, & Lewington, V. J. (1992). Palliation of bone metastases in prostate cancer. Hemibody irradiation or strontium-89? *Clinical Oncology (Royal College of Radiologists), 4* (2), 101–107.

De Conno, F., Carraceni, A., Zecca, E., Spoldi, E., & Ventafridda, V. (1991). The continuous subcutaneous infusion of hyoscine butyl bromide reduces secretions in patients with gastrointestinal obstruction. *Journal of Pain and Symptom Management, 6*, 484–486.

De Conno, F., Ripamonti, C., Sbanotto, A., & Barletta, L. (1993). A clinical note on sublingual buprenorphine. *Journal of Palliative Care, 9* (3), 44–46.

Della Cuna, G. R., Pellegrini, A., & Piazzi, M. (1989). Effect of methylprednisolone sodium succinate on quality of life in preterminal cancer patients: A placebo-control multicenter study. *European Journal of Cancer and Clinical Oncology, 29*, 1817–1821.

Dennis, G. C., & DeWitty, R. L. (1990). Long-term intraventricular infusion of morphine for intractable pain in cancer of the head and neck. *Neurosurgery, 26*, 404–407.

de Stoutz, N. D., Bruera, E., & Suarez-Almazor, M. (1993). Opiate rotation (OR) for toxicity reduction in terminal cancer patients. In *7th World Congress on Pain: Congress Abstracts* (abstract 894). Seattle: IASP Publications.

Devor, M., Basbaum, A. I., Bennett, G. J., Blumberg, H., Campbell, J. N., Dembowsky, K. P., Guillbaud, G., Janig, W., Koltzberg, M., Levine, J. D., Otten, U. H., & Portenoy, R. K. (1991). Group report: Mechanisms of neuropathic pain following peripheral injury. In A. Basbaum & J.-M. Besson (Eds.), *Towards a new pharmacotherapy of pain* (pp. 417–440). New York: Wiley.

Dover, S. B. (1987). Syringe driver in terminal care. *British Medical Journal, 294*, 553–555.

Dubner, R. (1991). A call for more science, not more rhetoric, regarding opioids and neuropathic pain. *Pain, 47* (1), 1–2.

Du Pen, S. L., & Ramsey, D. H. (1988). Compounding local anaesthetics and narcotics for epidural analgesia in cancer out patients. *Anaesthesiology, 69* (3A), A404.

Edwards, R. B. (1989). Pain management and the values of health care providers. In C. S. Hill & W. S. Fields (Eds.), *Drug treatment of cancer pain in a drug oriented society* (pp. 101–112). New York: Raven Press.

Edwards, W. T., & Breed, R. J. (1990). Treatment of postoperative pain in the post anesthesia care unit. *Anesthesiology Clinics of North America, 8*, 235–265.

Egbert, A. M., Parks, L. H., Short, L. M., & Burnett, M. L. (1990). Randomized trial of postoperative patient-controlled analgesia vs intramuscular narcotics in frail elderly men. *Archives of Internal Medicine, 150* (9), 1897–1903.

Eisele, J. H., Grigsby, E. J., & Dea, G. (1992). Clonazepam treatment of myoclonic contractions associated with high dose opioids: a case report. *Pain, 49* (2), 231–232.

Eisenberg, E., Berkey, C. S., Carr, D. B., Mosteller, F., & Chalmers, T. C. (1994). Efficacy and safety of nonsteroidal antiinflammatory drugs for cancer pain: a meta-analysis. *Journal of Clinical Oncology, 12* (12), 2756–2765.

Eisendrath, S. J., Goldman, B., Douglas, J., Dimatteo, L., & Van, D. C. (1987). Meperidine-induced delirium. *American Journal of Psychiatry, 144* (8), 1062–1065.

Enck, R. E. (1991). Drug-induced terminal sedation for symptom control. *American Journal of Hospice and Palliative Care, 8* (5), 3–5.

Ernst, D. S., MacDonald, R. N., Paterson, A. H. G., Jensen, J., Brasher, P., & Bruera, E. (1992). A double blind, crossover trial of I.V. clodronate in metastatic bone pain. *Journal of Pain and Symptom Management, 7*, 4–11.

Ettinger, A. B., & Portenoy, R. K. (1988). The use of corticosteroids in the treatment of symptoms associated with cancer. *Journal of Pain and Symptom Management, 3*, 99–103.

Fainsinger, R., Schoeller, T., & Bruera, E. (1993). Methadone in the management of cancer pain: A review. *Pain, 52* (2), 137–147.

Ferrell, B. A., & Ferrell, B. R. (1991). Principles of pain management in older people. *Comprehensive Therapy, 17* (8), 53–58.

Ferrell, B. R., Ferrell, B. A., Ahn, C., & Tran, K. (1994). Pain management for elderly patients with cancer at home. *Cancer, 74* (suppl.), 2139–2146.

Fineman, S. P. (1989). Long-term post-thoracotomy cancer pain management with interpleural bupivacaine. *Anesthesia and Analgesia, 68* (5), 694–697.

Fishman, B., Pasternak, S., Wallenstein, S. L., Houde, R. W., Holland, J. C., & Foley, K. M. (1987). The Memorial Pain Assessment Card: A valid instrument for the evaluation of cancer pain. *Cancer, 60*, 1151–1158.

Foley, K. M. (1982). Clinical assessment of pain. *Acta Anaesthica Scandinavica, 74* (suppl.), 91–96.

Foley, K. M. (1985). The treatment of cancer pain. *New England Journal of Medicine, 313*, 84–95.

Foley, K. M. (1989a). Controversies in cancer pain: Medical perspective. *Cancer, 63*, 2257–2265.

Foley, K. M. (1989b). The decriminalization of cancer pain. In C. S. Hill & H. Field (Eds.), *Drug treatment of cancer pain in a drug-oriented society* (pp. 5–18). New York: Raven Press.

Foley, K. M. (1991). Clinical tolerance to opioids. In A. I. Basbaum & J. M. Bessom (Eds.), *Towards a new pharmacotherapy of pain, Dahlem Konfrenzen* (pp. 181–204). Chichester: Wiley.

Fossa, S. D., Paus, E., Lochoff, M., Backe, S. M., & Aas, M. (1992). Strontium-89 in bone metastases from hormone resistant prostate cancer: Palliation effect and biochemical changes. *British Journal of Cancer, 66* (1), 177–180.

Galer, B. S., Coyle, N., Pasternak, G. W., & Portenoy, R. K. (1992). Individual variability in the response to different opioids: Report of five cases. *Pain, 49* (1), 87–91.

Geokas, M. C., & Haverbck, B. J. (1969). The aging gastrointestinal tact. *American Journal of Surgery, 117,* 881–887.

Goldberg, P. B., & Roberts, J. (1983). Pharmacologic basis for developing rational drug regimens for elderly patients. *Medical Clinics of North America, 67,* 315.

Goldfrank, L., Weisman, R. S., Errick, J. K., & Lo, M. W. (1986). A dosing nomogram for continuous infusion of intravenous naloxone. *Annals of Emergency Medicine, 15* (5), 91–95.

Gonzales, G. R., Elliot, K. J., Portenoy, R. K., & Foley, K. M. (1991). The impact of a comprehensive evaluation in the management of cancer pain. *Pain, 47,* 141–144.

Gourlay, G. K., Kowalski, S. R., Plummer, J. L., Cherry, D. A., Szekely, S. M., Mather, L. E., Owen, H., & Cousins, M. J. (1990). The efficacy of transdermal fentanyl in the treatment of postoperative pain; a double blind comparison of fentanyl and placebo systems. *Pain, 40,* 21–28.

Greene, W. R., & Davis, W. H. (1991). Titrated intravenous barbiturates in the control of symptoms in patients with terminal cancer, *Southern Medical Journal, 84* (3), 332–337.

Grossman, S. A., Sheidler, V. R., Swedeen, K., Mucenski, J., & Piantadosi, S. (1991). Correlation of patient and caregiver ratings of cancer pain. *Journal of Pain and Symptom Management, 6* (2), 53–57.

Hagen, N., Foley, K. M., Cerbones, D. J., Portenoy, R. K., & Inturrisi, C. E. (1991). Chronic nausea and morphine-6-glucuronide. *Journal of Pain and Symptom Management, 6,* 125–128.

Hagmeyer, K. O., Mauro, L. S., & Mauro, V. F. (1993). Meperidine-related seizures associated with patient-controlled analgesia pumps. *Annals of Pharmacotherapy, 27* (1), 29–32.

Haines, I. E., Zalcberg, J., & Buchanan, J. D. (1990). Not-for-recussitation orders in cancer patients: Principles of decision making. *Medical Journal of Australia, 153* (7), 225–229.

Halperin, D. L., Koren, G., Attias, D., Pellegrini, E., Greenberg, M. L., & Wyss, M. (1989). Topical skin anesthesia for venous, subcutaneous drug reservoir and lumbar punctures in children. *Pediatrics, 84* (2), 281–284.

Hanks, G. W. (1984). Psycchotropic drugs. *Clinics in Oncology, 3,* 135–151.

Hanks, G. W., Twycross, R. G., & Lloyd, J. W. (1981). Unexpected complication of successful nerve block: Morphine induced respiratory depression precipitated by removal of severe pain. *Anaesthesia, 36* (1), 37–39.

Hanks, G. W. C., Portenoy, R. K., MacDonald, N., & O'Niel, W. M. (1993). Difficult pain problems. In D. Doyle, G. W. Hanks, & N. MacDonald (Eds.), *Oxford textbook of palliative medicine* (pp. 257–274). Oxford: Oxford University Press.

Hanning, C. D. (1990). The rectal absorption of opioids. In C. Benedetti, C. R. Chapman, & G. Giron (Eds.), *Opioid Analgesia* (pp. 259–269). New York: Raven Press.

Hassenbusch, S. J., Pillay, P. K., & Barnett, G. M. (1990). Radiofrequency cingulotomy for intractable cancer pain using stereotaxis guided by magnetic resonance imaging. *Neurosurgery, 27* (2), 220–223.

Hays, H., Hagen, N., Thirlwell, M., Dhaliwal, H., Babul, N., Harsanyi, Z., & Darke, A. C. (1994). Comparative clinical efficacy and safety of immediate release and controlled release hydromorphone for chronic severe cancer pain. *Cancer, 74* (6), 1808–1816.

Hellendoorn, S. M., & Overweg van Kints, J. (1988). Perineal pain: A case report. *European Journal of Surgical Oncology, 14* (2), 197–198.

Helmers, H., Van Peer, A., Woestenborghs, R., Noorduin, H., & Heykants, J. (1984). Alfentanil kinetics in the elderly. *Clinical Pharmacology and Therapeutics, 36* (2), 239–243.

Helmers, J. H., van Leeuwen, L., & Zuurmond, W. W. (1994). Sufentanil pharmacokinetics in young adult and elderly surgical patients. *European Journal of Anaesthesiology, 11* (3), 181–185.

Herr, K. A., & Mobily, P. R. (1993). Comparison of selected pain assessment tools for use with the elderly. *Applied Nursing Research, 6* (1), 39–46.

Hogan, Q., Haddox, J. D., Abram, S., Weissman, D., Taylor, M. L., & Janjan, N. (1991). Epidural opiates and local anesthetics for the management of cancer pain. *Pain, 46* (3), 271–279.

Holdsworth, M. T., Forman, W. B., Killilea, T. A., Nystrom, K. M., Paul, R., Brand, S. C., & Reynolds, R. (1994). Transdermal fentanyl disposition in elderly subjects. *Gerontology, 40* (1), 32–37.

Holley, F. O., & Van-Steennis, C. (1988). Postoperative analgesia with fentanyl: pharmacokinetics and pharmacodynamics of constant-rate I.V. and transdermal delivery. *British Journal of Anaesthesia, 60,* 608–613.

Houde, R. W. (1979). Analgesic effectiveness of narcotic agonist-antagonists. *British Journal of Clinical Pharmacology, 7,* 297–308.

Ihse, I., & Permerth, J. (1990). Enzyme therapy and pancreatic pain. *Acta Churgica Scandinavica, 156,* 281–283.

Insel, P. A. (1990). Analgesic-antipyretics and antiinflammatory agents: drugs employed in the treatment of rheumatoid arthritis and gout. In A. G. Gilman, T. W. Rall, A. S. Nies, & P. Teylor (Eds.), *The pharmacological basis of therapeutics* (pp. 638–681). New York: Permagon Press.

Ischia, S., Luzzani, A., Ischia, A., Magon, F., & Toscano, D. (1984). Subarachnoid neurolytic block (L5-S1) and unilateral percutaneous cervical cordotomy in the treatment of pain secondary to pelvic malignant disease. *Pain, 20* (2), 139–149.

Jadad, A. R., Carroll, D., Glynn, C. J., Moore, R. A., & McQuay, H. J. (1992). Morphine responsiveness of chronic pain: double blind randomised crossover study with patient controlled analgesia. *The Lancet, 339,* 1367–1371.

Jaillon, P., Gardin, M. E., Lecocq, B., Richard, M. O., Meignan, S., Blondel, Y., Grippat, J. C., Bergnieres, J., & Vergnoux, O. (1989). Pharmacokinetics of nalbuphine in infants, young healthy volunteers, and elderly patients. *Clinical Pharmacology and Therapeutics, 46* (2), 226–233.

Janig, W., Blumberg, H., Boas, R. A., & Campbell, J. N. (1991). The reflex sympathetic dystrophy syndrome: Consensus statement and general recommendations for diagnosis and clinical research. In M. R. Bond, J. E. Charlton, & C. J. Woolf (Eds.), *Proceedings of the VIth World Congress on Pain* (pp. 373–382). Amsterdam: Elsevier.

Kaiko, R. F. (1980). Age and morphine analgesia in cancer patients with postoperative pain. *Clinical Pharmacology and Therapeutics, 28,* 823–826.

Kaiko, R. F., Foley, K. M., Grabinski, P. V., Heidrich, G., Rogers, A. G., Inturrisi, C. E., & Reidenberg, M. M. (1983). Central nervous system excitatory effects of meperidine in cancer patients. *Annals of Neurology, 13,* 180–185.

Kanner, R. M., & Foley, K. M. (1981). Patterns of narcotic drug use in a cancer pain clinic. *Annals of the New York Academy of Science, 362,* 161–172.

Kapelushnik, J., Koren, G., Solh, H., Greenberg, M., & De Veber, L. (1990). Evaluating the efficacy of EMLA in alleviating pain associated with lumbar puncture; comparison of open and double-blinded protocols in children. *Pain, 42* (1), 31–34.

Kellgren, J. G. (1939). On distribution of pain arising from deep somatic structures with charts of segmental pain areas. *Clinical Science, 4,* 35–46.

Laing, A. H., Ackery, D. M., Bayly, R. J., Buchanan, R. B., Lewington, V. J., McEwan, A. J., Macleod, P. M., & Zivanovic, M. A. (1991). Strontium-89 chloride for pain palliation in prostatic skeletal malignancy. *British Journal of Radiology, 64* (765), 816–822.

Latimer, E. J. (1991). Ethical decision-making in the care of the dying and its applications to clinical practice. *Journal of Pain and Symptom Management, 6,* 329–336.

Leavens, E. S., Hill, C. S., Cech, D. A., Weyland, J. B., & Weston, J. S. (1982). Intrathecal and intraventricular morphine for pain in cancer patients. *Journal of Neurosurgery, 56,* 241–245.

Lee, T. L., Kumar, A., & Baratham, G. (1990). Intraventricular morphine for intractable craniofacial pain. *Singapore Medical Journal, 31* (3), 273–276.

Lema, M. J., Myers, D. P., De, L. C. O., & Penetrante, R. (1992). Pleural phenol therapy for the treatment of chronic esophageal cancer pain. *Regional Anesthesia, 17* (3), 166–170.

Levin, A. B., & Ramirez, L. L. (1984). Treatment of cancer pain with hypophysectomy: Surgical and chemical. In C. Benedetti, C. R. Chapman, & G. Moricca (Eds.), *Recent advances in the management of pain* (pp. 631–645). New York: Raven Press.

Lewington, V. J., McEwan, A. J., Ackery, D. M., Bayly, R. J., Keeling, D. H., Macleod, P. M., Porter, A. T., & Zivanovic, M. A. (1991). A prospective, randomised double-blind crossover study to examine the efficacy of strontium-89 in pain palliation in patients with advanced prostate cancer metastatic to bone. *European Journal of Cancer, 27* (8), 954–958.

Lichter, I. (1994). Accelerated titration of morphine for rapid relief of cancer pain. *New Zealand Medical Journal, 107* (990), 488–490.

Lillemoe, K. D., Cameron, J. L., Kaufman, H. S., Yeo, C. J., Pitt, H. A., & Sauter, P. K. (1993). Chemical splanchnicectomy in patients with unresectable pancreatic cancer. A prospective randomized trial. *Annals of Surgery, 217* (5), 447–455.

Linton, S. L., & Melin, L. (1983). Applied relaxation in the management of cancer pain. *Behavioral Psychotherapy, 11*, 337–350.

Lobato, R. D., Madrid, J. L., Fatela, L. V., Sarabia, R., Rivas, J. J., & Gozalo, A. (1987). Intraventricular morphine for intractable cancer pain: rationale, methods, clinical results. *Acta Anaesthesiology Scandinavica, Supplementum, 31*, 68–74.

MacDonald, N., Der, L., Allan, S., & Champion, P. (1993). Opioid hyperexcitability: The application of alternate opioid therapy. *Pain, 53* (3), 353–355.

Malmberg, A. B., & Yaksh, T. L. (1992). Hyperalgesia mediated by spinal glutamate and substance P receptors blocked by spinal cyclooxygenase inhibition. *Science, 92*, 1276–1279.

Martin, R. S. (1989). Mortal values: healing, pain and suffering. In C. S. Hill & W. S. Fields (Eds.), *Drug treatment of cancer pain in a drug oriented society* (pp. 19–26). New York: Raven Press.

Maunuksela, E. L., & Korpela, R. (1986). Double-blind evaluation of a lignocaine-prilocaine cream (EMLA) in children: Effect on the pain associated with venous cannulation. *British Journal of Anaesthesiology, 58* (11), 1242–1245.

Maxon, H., Thomas, S. R., Hertzberg, V. S., Schroder, L. E., Englaro, E. E., Samaratunga, R., Scher, H. I., Moulton, J. S., Deutsch, E. A., & Deutsch, K. F., (1992). Rhenium-186 hydroxyethylidene diphosphonate for the treatment of painful osseous metastases. *Seminars in Nuclear Medicine, 22* (1), 33–40.

Maxon, H. R., Deutsch, E. A., Thomas, S. R., Libson, K., Lukes, S. J., Williams, C. C., & Ali, S. (1988). Initial experience with 186-Re(Sn)-HEDP in the treatment of painful skeletal metastases. *Journal of Nuclear Medicine, 29*, 776.

McCaffery, M., & Thorpe, D. M. (1989). Differences in perception of pain and the development of adversarial relationships among health care providers. In C. S. Hill & W. S. Fields (Eds.), *Drug treatment of cancer pain in a drug oriented society* (pp. 19–26). New York: Raven Press.

McQuay, H. J., Carroll, D., Faura, C. C., Gavaghan, D. J., Hand, C. W., & Moore, R. A. (1990). Oral morphine in cancer pain: Influences on morphine and metabolite concentration. *Clinical Pharmacology and Therapeutics, 48* (3), 236–244.

McQuay, H. J., Jadad, A. R., Carroll, D., Faura, C., Glynn, C. J., Moore, R. A., & Liu, Y. (1992). Opioid sensitivity of chronic pain: A patient controlled analgesia method. *Anaesthesia, 47*, 757–767.

Melzack, R. (1975). The McGill pain questionnaire: Major properties and scoring methods. *Pain, 1*, 277–299.

Mercadante, S. (1993). Celiac plexus block versus analgesics in pancreatic cancer pain. *Pain, 52* (2), 187–192.

Miller, F., Whitcup, S., Sacks, M., & Lynch, P. E. (1985). Unrecognized drug dependence and withdrawal in the elderly. *Drug Alcohol Depend, 15* (1–2), 177–179.

Moertel, C. G., Shutte, A., & Reitemeier, R., (1974). Corticosteroid therapy of preterminal gastrointestinal cancer. *Cancer, 33*, 1607–1609.

Moinpour, C. M., Feigl, P., Metch, B., Hayden, K. A., Meyskens, F. J., & Crowley, J. (1989). Quality of life endpoints in cancer clinical trials: review and recommendations. *Journal of the National Cancer Institute, 81*, 485–495.

Moinpour, C. M., Hayden, K. A., Thomson, I. M., Feigl, P., & Metch, B. (1991). Quality of life assessment in Southwest Oncology Group trials. In N. S. Tchekmedyian & D. Cella (Eds.), *Quality of life in oncology practice and research* (pp. 43–50). Williston Park: Dominus.

Morgan, J., & Furst, D. E. (1986). Implications of drug therapy in the elderly. *Clinics in Rheumatic Disease, 12*, 244–251.

Morton, A. R., Cantrill, J. A., Pillai, G. V., McMahon, A., Anderson, D. C., & Howell, A. (1988). Sclerosis of lytic bony metastases after aminohydroxyprpylidene bisphosphonate (APD) in patients with breast cancer. *British Journal of Medicine, 297* 772–773.

Moulin, D. E., Johnson, N. G., Murray, P. N., Geoghegan, M. F., Goodwin, V. A., & Chester, M. A. (1992). Subcutaneous narcotic infusions for cancer pain: treatment outcome and guidelines for use. *Canadian Medical Association Journal, 146* (6), 891–897.

Moulin, D. E., Kreeft, J. H., Murray, P. N., & Bouquillon, A. I. (1991). Comparison of continuous subcutaneous and intravenous hydromorphone infusions for management of cancer pain. *Lancet, 337*, 465–468.

Myers, D. P., Lema, M. J., de Leon-Casasola, O. A., & Bacon, D. R. (1993). Intrapleural analgesia for the treatment of severe cancer pain in terminally ill patients. *Journal of Pain and Symptom Management, 8* (7), 505–510.

Ness, T. J., & Gebhart, G. E. (1990). Visceral pain: A review of experimental studies. *Pain, 41*, 167–234.

Nilsson, A., Danielson, K., Engberg, G., & Henneberg, S. (1990). EMLA for pain relief during arterial cannulation: A double-blind, placebo-controlled study of a lidocaine-prilocaine cream, *Upsala Journal of Medical Sciences*, *95* (1), 87–94.

Nitescu, P., Appelgren, L., Linder, L. E., Sjoberg, M., Hultman, E., & Curelaru, I. (1990). Epidural versus intrathecal morphine-bupivicaine: Assessment of consecutive treatment is advanced cancer pain. *Journal of Pain and Symptom Management*, *5*, 18–26.

Nurchi, G. (1984). Use of intraventricular and intrathecal morphine in intractable pain associated with cancer. *Neurosurgery*, *15* (6), 801–804.

Obbens, E. A. M. T., Hill, C. S., Leavens, M. E., Ruthenbeck, S. S., & Otis, F. (1987). Intraventricular morphine administration for control of chronic cancer pain. *Pain*, *28*, 61–68.

Oliver, D. J. (1988). Syringe drivers in palliative care: A review. *Palliative Medicine*, *2*, 21–26.

Osborne, R. J., Joel, S. P., & Slevin, M. L. (1986). Morphine intoxication in renal failure: the role of morphine-6-glucuronide. *British Journal of Medicine*, *292*, 1548–1549.

Parmelee, P. A., Smith, B., & Katz, I. R. (1993). Pain complaints and cognitive status among elderly institution residents. *Journal of the American Geriatric Society*, *41* (5), 517–522.

Piletta, P., Porchet, H. C., & Dayer, P. (1991). Central analgesic effect of acetaminophen but not of aspirin. *Clinical Pharmacology and Therapeutics*, *49*, 350–354.

Plummer, J. L., Cherry, D. A., Cousins, M. J., Gourlay, G. K., Onley, M., & Evans, K. H. A. (1991). Long term spinal administration of morphine in cancer and non-cancer pain: a retrospective study. *Pain*, *44*, 212–220.

Polatty, R. C., & Cooper, K. R. (1986). Respiratory failure after percutaneous cordotomy. *Southern Medical Journal*, *79*, 367–379.

Polednak, A. P. (1994). Projected numbers of cancers diagnosed in the US elderly population, 1990 through 2030. *American Journal of Public Health*, *84* (8), 1313–1316.

Popiela, T., Lucchi, R., & Giongo, F. (1989). Methylprednisolone as palliative therapy for female terminal cancer patients: The Methylprednisolone Female Preterminal Cancer Study Group. *European Journal of Cancer and Clinical Oncology*, *25* (12), 1823–1829.

Portenoy, P. K., Southam, M., Gupta, S. K., Lapin, J., Layman, M., Inturrisi, C. E., & Foley, K. M. (1993). Transdermal fentanyl for cancer pain repeated dose pharmacokinetics. *Anesthesiology*, *78*, 36–43.

Portenoy, R. K. (1987). Continuous intravenous infusions of opioid drugs. *Medical Clinics of North America*, *71*, 233–241.

Portenoy, R. K. (1991). Issues in the management of neuropathic pain. In A. Basbaum & J.-M. Besson (Eds.), *Towards a new pharmacotherapy of pain* (pp. 393–416). New York: Wiley.

Portenoy, R. K. (1993a). Adjuvant analgesics in pain management. In D. Doyle, G. W. Hanks, & N. MacDonald (Eds.), *Oxford textbook of palliative medicine* (pp. 187–203). Oxford: Oxford University Press.

Portenoy, R. K. (1993b). Inadequate outcome of opioid therapy for cancer pain. In R. B. Patt (Ed.), *Cancer pain* (pp. 119–128). Philadelphia: Lippincott.

Portenoy, R. K., Foley, K. M., & Inturrisi, C. E. (1990). The nature of opioid responsiveness and its implications for neuropathic pain: New hypotheses derived from studies of opioid infusions. *Pain*, *43* (3), 273–286.

Portenoy, R. K., Foley, K. M., Stulman, J., Khan, E., Adelhardt, J., Layman, M., Cerbone, D. J., & Inturrisi, C. E. (1991). Plasma morphine and morphine-6-glucuronide during chronic morphine therapy for cancer pain: Plasma profiles, steady state concentrations and the consequences of renal failure. *Pain*, *47*, 13–19.

Portenoy, R. K., & Hagen, N. A. (1990). Breakthrough pain: Definition, prevalence and characteristics. *Pain*, *41* (3), 273–281.

Portenoy, R. K., Miransky, J., Thaler, H. T., Hornung, J., Bianchi, C., Cibas-Kong, I., Feldhamer, E., Lewis, M., Matamoros, I., Sugar, M. Z., Olivieri, A., & Foley, K. M. (1992). Pain in ambulatory patients with lung or colon cancer: Prevalence, characteristics and impact. *Cancer*, *70*, 1616–1624.

Porter, A. T., McEwan, A. J., Powe, J. E., Reid, R., McGowan, D. G., Lukka, H., Sathyanarayana, J. R., Yakemchuk, V. N., Thomas, G. M., & Erlich, L. E., (1993). Results of a randomized Phase-III trial to evaluate the efficacy of strontium-89 adjuvant to local field external beam irradiation in the management of endocrine resistant metastatic prostate cancer. *International Journal of Radiation Oncology, Biology, Physics*, *25* (5), 805–813.

Porter, J., & Jick, H. (1980). Addiction rare in patients treated with narcotics (letter). *New England Journal of Medicine*, *302*, 123.

Reuben, D. B., Mor, V., & Hiris, J. (1988). Clinical symptoms and length of survival in patients with terminal cancer. *Archives of Internal Medicine, 148* (7), 1586–1591.

Rhiner, M., Ferrell, B. R., Ferrell, B. A., & Grant, M. M. (1993). A structured nondrug intervention program for cancer pain. *Cancer Pract, 1* (2), 137–143.

Robertson, D. H. (1983). Transsacral neurolytic nerve block: An alternative approach to intractable perineal pain. *British Journal of Anaesthesiology, 55* (9), 873–875.

Robinson, R. G., Preston, D. F., Spicer, J. A., & Baxter, K. G. (1992). Radionuclide therapy of intractable bone pain: Emphasis on strontium-89. *Seminars in Nuclear Medicine, 22* (1), 28–32.

Roquefeil, B., Benezich, J., Blanchet, P., Baiter, C., Frerebeau, P., & Gros, C. (1984). Intraventricular administration of morphine in patients with neoplastic intractable pain. *Surgical Neurology, 21*, 155–158.

Rosomoff, H. L., Carroll, F., & Brown, J. (1965). Percutaneous radiofrequency cervical cordotomy: Technique. *Journal of Neurosurgery, 23*, 639–644.

Roth, A., & Kolaric, K. (1986). Analgesic activity of calcitonin in patients with painful osteolytic metastases of breast cancer. *Oncology, 43*, 283–287.

Ryynanen, O. P., Kivela, S. L., Honkanen, R., Laippala, P., & Saano, V. (1993). Medications and chronic diseases as risk factors for falling injuries in the elderly. *Scandinavian Journal of Social Medicine, 21* (4), 264–271.

Sawe, J., Hansen, J., Ginman, C., Hartvig, P., Jakobsson, P. A., Nilsson, M. I., Rane, A., & Anggard, E. (1981). Patient-controlled dose regimen of methadone for chronic cancer pain. *British Medical Journal (Clinical Research Ed.), 282* (6266), 771–773.

Sawe, J., Svensson, J. O., & Odar-Cederlof, I. (1985). Kinetics of morphine in patients with renal failure (letter). *The Lancet, 2*, 211.

Scapa, E., Horowitz, M., Avtalion, J., Waron, M., & Eschar, J. (1992). Appreciation of pain in the elderly. *Israel Journal of Medical Science, 28* (2), 94–96.

Schuster, C. R. (1989). Does treatment of cancer pain with narcotics produce junkies? In C. S. Hill & W. S. Fields (Eds.), *Drug treatment of cancer pain in a drug oriented society* (pp. 1–3). New York: Raven Press.

Sear, J. W., Hand, C. W., & Moore, R. A. (1989). Studies on morphine disposition: Plasma concentrations of morphine and its metabolites in anesthetized middle-aged and elderly surgical patients. *Journal of Clinical Anesthesia, 1* (3), 164–169.

Shepherd, K. (1990). Review of a controlled-release morphine preparation. In K. M. Foley, J. J. Bonica, & V. Ventafridda (Eds.), *Second International Congress on Cancer Pain* (pp. 191–202). New York: Raven Press.

Shorr, R. I., Griffin, M. R., Daugherty, J. R., & Ray, W. A. (1992). Opioid analgesics and the risk of hip fracture in the elderly: Codeine and propoxyphene. *Journal of Gerontology, 47* (4), 111–115.

Shortsleeve, M. J., & Levine, M. S. (1992). Herpes esophagitis in otherwise healthy patients: Clinical and radiographic findings. *Radiology, 182* (3), 859–861.

Sindou, M., Fisher, G., & Mansuy, L. (1976). Posterior spinal rhizotomy and selective posterior rhizidiotomy. *Progress in Neurosurgical Surgery, 7*, 201–250.

Singleton, M. A., Rosen, J. I., & Fisher, D. M. (1988). Pharmacokinetics of fentanyl in the elderly. *British Journal of Anaesthesiology, 60* (6), 619–622.

Sjoberg, M., Appelgren, L., Einarsson, S., Hultman, E., Linder, L. E., Nitescu, P., & Curelaru, I. (1991). Long-term intrathecal morphine and bupivacaine in "refractory" cancer pain: Results from the first series of 52 patients. *Acta Anaesthesiologica Scandinavica, 35* (1), 30–43.

Smales, O. R., Smales, E. A., & Sanders, H. G. (1993). Flunitrazepam in terminal care. *Journal of Paediatrics and Child Health, 29* (1), 68–69.

Soliman, I. E., Broadman, L. M., Hannallah, R. S., & McGill, W. A. (1988). Comparison of the analgesic effects of EMLA (eutectic mixture of local anesthetics) to intradermal lidocaine infiltration prior to venous cannulation in unpremedicated children. *Anesthesiology, 68* (5), 804–806.

Storey, P., Hill, H. H., St. Louis, R., & Tarver, E. E. (1990). Subcutaneous infusions for control of cancer symptoms. *Journal of Pain and Symptom Management, 5*, 33–41.

Stuart, G., & Cramond, T. (1993). Role of percutaneous cervical cordotomy for pain of malignant origin. *Medical Journal of Australia, 158* (10), 667–670.

Swanson, G., Smith, J., Bulich, R., New, P., & Shiffman, R. (1989). Patient-controlled analgesia for chronic cancer pain in the ambulatory setting: A report of 117 patients. *Journal of Clinical Oncology, 7* (12), 1903–1908.

Sykes, N. P. (1991). Oral naloxone in opioid associated constipation. *Lancet, 337*, 1475.

Sykes, N. P. (1993). Constipation and diarrhoea. In D. Doyle, G. W. Hanks, & N. MacDonald (Eds.), *Oxford textbook of palliative medicine* (pp. 299–310). Oxford: Oxford University Press.

Syversen, J. H., Mollestad, E., & Semb, L. S. (1976). Emepronium bromide (Cetiprin) as a postoperative spasmolytic agent in transvesical prostatectomy. *Scandinavian Journal of Urology and Nephrology, 10* (3), 201–203.

Szeto, H. H., Inturrisi, C. E., Houde, R., Saal, R., Cheigh, J., & Reidengerg, M. M. (1977). Accumulation of normeperidine an active metabolite of meperidine, in patients with renal failure or cancer. *Annals of Internal Medicine, 86* (6), 738–741.

Tannock, I. Gospodarowicz, M., Meakin, W., Panzarella, T., Stewart, L., & Rider, W. (1989). Treatment of metastatic prostatic cancer with low-dose prednisone: evaluation of pain and quality of life as pragmatic indices of response. *Journal of Clinical Oncology, 7*, 590–597.

Tasker, R. R., Tsuda, T., & Howrylyshn, P. (1988). Percutaneous cordotomy—The lateral high cervical technique. In H. H. Schmidek & W. H. Sweet (Eds.), *Operative neurosurgical technique indications, methods and results* (pp. 1191–1205). New York: Grune & Stratton.

Thiebaud, D., Leyvraz, S., von Fliedner, V., Perey, L., Cornu, P., Thiebaud, S., & Burckhardt, P. (1991). Treatment of bone metastases from breast cancer and myeloma with pamidronate. *European Journal of Cancer, 27* (1), 37–41.

Torebjork, H. E., Ochoa, J. L., & Schady, W. (1984). Referred pain from intraneural stimulation of muscle fascicles in the median nerve. *Pain, 18*, 145–156.

Trissel, L. A., Xu, Q., Martinez, J. F., & Fox, J. L. (1994). Compatibility and stability of ondansetron hydrochloride with morphine sulfate and with hydromorphone hydrochloride in 0.9% sodium chloride injection at 4, 22, and 32 degrees C. *American Journal of Hospital Pharmacy, 51* (17), 2138–2142.

Truog, R. D., Berde, C. B., Mitchell, C., & Greir, H. E. (1992). Barbiturates in the care of the terminally ill. *New England Journal of Medicine, 327* (23), 1678–1682.

Turner, J. H., & Claringbold, P. G. (1991). A phase II study of treatment of painful multifocal skeletal metastases with single and repeated dose samarium-153 ethylenediaminetetramethylene phosphonate. *European Journal of Cancer, 27* (9), 1084–1086.

Turner, J. H., Claringbold, B. G., Heatherington, E. L., Sorby, P., & Martindal, A. A. (1989). A phase I study of samarium-153 ethylenedi-amenetetramethylene phosphonate therapy for disseminated skeletal metastases. *Journal of Clinical Oncology, 7*, 1926–1931.

Twycross, R. G., & Fairfield, S. (1982). Pain in far-advanced cancer. *Pain, 14*, 303–310.

Twycross, R. G., & Lack, S. A. (1984). *Symptom control in far-advanced cancer: Pain relief.* London: Pitman.

Twycross, R. G., & Lack, S. A. (1990). *Therapeutics in terminal cancer* (2nd ed.). Edinburgh: Churchill Livingston.

Vane, J. R. (1971). Inhibition of prostaglandin synthesis as a mechanism of action for aspirin-like drugs. *Nature New Biology, 234*, 231–238.

van Holten-Verzantvoort, A. T. M., Zwinderman, A. H., Aaronson, N. K., Hermans, J., van Emmerik, B., van Dam, F., van den Bos, B., Bijvoet, O. L., & Cleton, F. J. (1991). The effect of supportive pamidronate treatment on aspects of quality of life of patients with advanced breast cancer. *European Journal of Cancer, 27* (5), 544–549.

van Holten-Verzantvoort, A. T., Kroon, H. M., Bijvoet, O. L., Cleton, F. J., Beex, L. V., Blijham, G., Hermans, J., Neijt, J. P., Papapoulos, S. E., & Sleeboom, H. P., (1993). Palliative pamidronate treatment in patients with bone metastases from breast cancer. *Journal of Clinical Oncology, 11* (3), 491–498.

Ventafridda, V., Ripamonti, C., Caraceni, A., Spoldi, E., Messina, L., & De Conno, F. (1990a). The management of inoperable gastrointestinal obstruction in terminal cancer patients. *Tumori, 76*, 389–393.

Ventafridda, V., Ripamonti, C., De Conno, F., Tamburini, M., & Cassileth, B. R. (1990b). Symptom prevalence and control during cancer patients' last days of life. *Journal of Palliative Care, 6* (3), 7–11.

Ventafridda, V., Tamburini, M., Caraceni, A., DeConno, F., & Naldi, F. (1987). A validation study of the WHO method for cancer pain relief. *Cancer, 59*, 851–856.

Von Roenn, J. H., Cleeland, C. S., Gonin, R., Hatfield, A., & Pandya, K. J. (1993). Physician's attitudes and practice in cancer pain management: A survey from the Eastern Cooperative Oncology Group. *Annals of Internal Medicine, 119* (2), 121–126.

Waldman, S. D., Allen, M. L., & Cronen, M. C. (1989). Subcutaneous tunneled intrapleural catheters in the long-term relief of right upper quadrant pain of malignant origin. *Journal of Pain and Symptom Management*, *4*, 86–89.

Waldmann, C. S., Eason, J. R., Rambohu, I. E., & Hanson, G. C. (1984). Serum morphine levels. A comparison between continuous subcutaneous infusions and intravenous infusions in postoperative patients. *Anesthesia*, *39* (8), 768–771.

Wanzer, S. H., Federman, D. D., Adelstein, S. J., Cassel, C. K., Cassem, E. H., Cranford, R. E., Hook, E. W., Lo, B., Moertel, C. G., & Safar, P., (1989). The physicians responsibility toward hopelessly ill patients—a second look. *New England Journal of Medicine*, *120*, 844–849.

Ward, S. E., Goldberg, N., Miller-McCauley, V., Mueller, C., Nolan, A., Pawlik-Plank, D., Robbins, A., Stormoen, D., & Weissman, D. E. (1993). Patient related barriers to management of cancer pain. *Pain*, *52*, 319–324.

Warrell, R. P., Lovett, D., Dilmanian, F. A., Schnieder, R., & Heelan, R. T. (1993). Low-dose gallium nitrate for prevention of osteolysis in myeloma: results of a pilot randomized study. *Journal of Clinical Oncology*, *11* (12), 2443–2450.

Watts, S. J., Alexander, L. C., Fawcett, K., Check, F. J., & Abnrashed, A. (1986). Herpes simplex esophagitis in a renal transplant patient treated with cyclosporine A: A case report. *American Journal of Gastroenterology*, *81* (3), 185–188.

Weinberg, D. S., Inturrisi, C. E., Reidenberg, B., Moulin, D., Nip, T. J., Wallenstein, S. L., Houde, R. W., & Foley, K. M. (1988). Sublingual absorption of selected opioid analgesics. *Clinical Pharmacology and Therapeutics*, *44*, 335–342.

Weissman, D. E., Gutmann, M., & Dahl, J. L. (1991). Physician cancer pain education: A report from the Wisconsin Cancer Pain Initiative. *Journal of Pain Symptom Management*, *6* (7), 445–448.

Weissman, D. E., & Haddox, J. D. (1989). Opioid pseudoaddiction—an iatrogenic syndrome. *Pain*, *36*, 363–366.

Welling, L. R., & Watson, W. A. (1990). The emergency department treatment of dyspepsia with antacids and oral lidocaine. *Annals of Emergency Medicine*, *19* (7), 785–788.

Whitcomb, D. C., & Block, G. D. (1994). Association of acetaminophen hepatotoxicity with fasting and ethanol use. *Journal of the American Medical Association*, *272* (23), 1845–1850.

Wig, J., & Johl, K. S. (1990). Our experience with EMLA cream (for painless venous cannulation in children). *Indian Journal of Physiology and Pharmacology*, *34* (2), 130–132.

Wilcox, J. C., Corr, J., Shaw, J., Richardson, M., & Calman, K. C. (1984). Prednisolone as appetite stimulant in patients with cancer. *British Medical Journal*, *288*, 27.

Wilkinson, T. J., Robinson, B. A., Begg, E. J., Duffull, S. B., Ravenscroft, P. J., & Schneider, J. J. (1992). Pharmacokinetics and efficacy of rectal versus oral sustained-release morphine in cancer patients. *Cancer Chemotherapy and Pharmacology*, *31* (3), 251–254.

Willer, J., DeBroucker, T., Bussel, B., Robi-Brami, A., & Harrewyn, J. (1989). Central analgesic effect of ketoprofen in humans: Electrophysiologic evidence for a supraspinal mechanism in a double-blind and cross-over study. *Pain*, *38*, 1–8.

World Health Organization. (1986). *Cancer pain relief*. Geneva: World Health Organization.

World Health Organization. (1990). *Cancer pain relief and palliative care*. Geneva: World Health Organization.

Zfass, A. M., McHenry, L. J., & Sanyal, A. J. (1993). Nonsteroidal antiinflammatory drug-induced gastroduodenal lesions: prophylaxis and treatment. *Gastroenterologist*, *1* (2), 165–169.

CHAPTER 14

Pain in Osteoporosis and Paget's Disease in the Elderly

JACOB MENCZEL

Osteoporosis is a major public health problem affecting a large proportion of the population. Osteoporosis can be defined as a loss of bone mass which is larger than that expected in the aging process.

Peak bone mass of the skeleton is achieved by the age of 20, and bone loss starts around the age of 35. Bone loss related to aging should be considered a physiological process, and when the loss is larger than that expected due to aging, osteoporosis appears. The reduction of bone mass starts in women earlier than in men. Bone formation is larger than bone resorption until the age of 35; after that, bone mass starts to decline.

The loss of bone mass is about 1% per year in women in the perimenopausal period, and during the menopausal years, it can achieve 2% per year, due to the hormonal changes, especially the reduction of estrogen production. Primary osteoporosis due to aging should be differentiated from secondary osteoporosis induced by different causes, such as hyperparathyroidism, immobilization, and corticosteroids (Table 14-1).

Table 14-1 summarizes some of the common forms of osteoporosis, and they can be classified as primary and secondary.

Postmenopausal osteoporosis is the primary form of the disease. The other ones are secondary and are due to different causes, such as immobilization, corticosteroid drugs, or other diseases.

The most common form is postmenopausal osteoporosis, which is six times more prevalent in women than in men. In men, osteoporosis appears later than in women due to the larger bone mass found in men, due to genetic factors. Afro-Americans also have a larger bone mass. Research performed in the last few years shows an important role of genetic factors in the appearance of osteoporosis. Lack of physical activity or immobil-

JACOB MENCZEL • Department of Geriatrics, Sarah Herzog Memorial Hospital, Jerusalem, Israel 91351.

Handbook of Pain and Aging, edited by David I. Mostofsky and Jacob Lomranz. Plenum Press, New York, 1997.

Table 14-1. Types of Osteoporosis

Postmenopausal
Immobilization
Corticosteroid-induced
Hyperparathyroidism
Hyperthyroidism
Multiple myeloma
Malabsorption—pancreatic or gastrointestinal diseases
Gastrectomy

ization of any kind increases bone resorption. Calcium and other minerals, as well as proteins, are lost from the bone tissue in the osteoporosis of disuse.

Increased hormonal secretion of corticosteroids due to disease or when given in the form of medication decreases intestinal calcium absorption, and increases bone turnover. As a result, there is a loss of bone mass, and osteoporosis appears.

In hyperparathyroidism, a higher secretion of parathyroid hormone (PTH) is present, mainly induced by an adenoma of one of the parathyroid glands. PTH increases bone resorption and results in a loss of bone from the skeleton.

Thyroxine, one of the thyroid hormones, decreases calcium absorption and affects bone turnover. Bone is lost, and osteoporosis can appear in thyrotoxicosis. Thyroxine, used in the treatment of hypothyroidism, has the same effect, and persons receiving the medication should be checked for osteoporosis.

Idiopathic osteoporosis is found in men of younger age groups, and the etiology is not completely clear. Lack of calcium intake, and vitamin D deficiency could play a role, as well as intake of alcohol in large amounts. Alcohol affects the intestinal mucosa and decreases calcium absorption.

An increased number of people suffer from osteoporosis, and the condition has reached epidemic proportions. The percentage of osteoporosis and its complications has increased even more than the increase of the elderly in the population due to aging.

The symptoms of osteoporosis are low back pain, pain along the vertebral column, and general skeletal pain. Kyphosis results from loss of bone from the vertebrae; compressed vertebrae are a sign of advanced osteoporosis and can be very painful. Kyphosis appears due to wedging and compression of vertebrae and is a typical finding in osteoporosis.

The complication of osteoporosis is fractures, the common ones being fracture of the wrist (Colles' fracture, appearing around the age of 50–60); fractures of the spines (compressed fractures appearing around the age of 60–70); and fracture of the hip, which is most common after age 70. Hip fracture due to fracture of the neck of the femur is a serious complication and requires surgical-orthopedic intervention.

Compressed fracture of the spine and fracture of the neck of the femur are painful and have to be treated accordingly. In addition to osteoporosis, a main cause of fractures of the neck of the femur is falls.

A definite diagnosis of osteoporosis cannot be made from only clinical signs.

Therefore, densitometric and biochemical tests have to be performed. The best way to determine osteoporosis and/or loss of bone is densitometric measurements and X-ray examinations.

The dual-energy X-ray absorpiometer (DEXA) has proved to be an excellent method of determining bone mass. The bone density and mass can be determined at different points of the skeleton, most commonly the lumbar vertebrae (L2–L4) and the head and neck of the femur. Total body bone content can also be measured. The DEXA determines the bone mass, and the results are compared to those of healthy individuals of the same age and are expressed in percentages of bone content. As to be expected, there is a decrease of bone mass with age. X-ray of the dorsal and lumber spine detects osteoporosis. Usually, radiological signs of osteoporosis appear when 30% of bone mass has been lost from the skeleton. Changes in the vertebrae, such as biconcavity, wedging, and compression, can be observed. Compressed fractures of the spines are typical signs of osteoporosis. Densitometric measurements detect early loss of bone mass and evaluate the amount lost. X-ray examination detects changes in the vertebrae, important findings to determine the severity of the condition and the cause of back pain. X-ray of the spine detects additional changes which can induce pain such as spondylarthrosis, narrowing of the intervertebral space, herniated disks, and scoliosis. An additional cause of back pain in the elderly is spinal stenosis, a narrowing of the spinal canal due to bone changes. In order to detect spinal stenosis, a CT (computed tomography) of the vertebral column has to be performed.

Spinal stenosis induces severe back pain and is a result of pressure of the spinal cord due to calcifications in the vertebrae. Symptomatic treatment of pain has a limited effect, and surgical intervention is often needed.

In the last few years, ultrasound methods have been developed for the determination of bone loss in osteoporosis, and recently, further progress in this field has been achieved.

BONE BIOMARKERS

In recent years, a large number of biomarkers have been made available to measure bone remodeling. Biomarkers can be determined in blood as well as in urine. Further development of these biomarkers and their increase or decrease in serum and urine will make it easier to determine early bone mass changes occurring with age, as well as to study the effect of hormonal changes on the skeleton. Determination of biomarkers makes possible an evaluation of the effect of calcium intake, exercise, and treatment of osteoporosis and bone mass.

Alkaphase-B levels, the bone-specific isoform of alkaline phosphatase (BAP), is an osteoblast membrane-bound protein, thought to be involved in bone formation and skeletal mineralization.

Osteocalcin (bone gla protein, or BGP) comprises 10%–25% of noncollagenous protein in bone and is a biochemical marker of bone formation. In osteoporosis and Paget's disease, osteocalcin is an important marker reflecting the activity of the disease and measures the effects of different treatments.

Pyridinoline (Pyd) and deoxypyridinoline (Dpd), found in urine, are reliable indicators of bone-specific collagen breakdown and bone resorption. The determination of these biomarkers gives an indication of the state of the skeleton and the activity of the bone loss.

RISK FACTORS

Certain people have a higher predisposition to develop osteoporosis and should be examined for loss of bone mass; density measurements should be performed.

Osteoporosis has a higher incidence in women and appears in them earlier than in men. The prevalence of osteoporosis is six times higher in women than in men.

A familial history of osteoporosis has been found to be a risk factor; a higher incidence of bone loss was reported in daughters of mothers with bone loss. Genetic factors have also been recently reported.

A higher correlation of measurements of bone mineral density (BMD) was reported in identical twins than in nonidentical twins, suggesting that BMD is genetically regulated (Pocock et al., 1987; Smith, Nance, Won Kan, Christian & Johnston, 1973; Spector et al., 1995). It was found that genetic factors such as the vitamin D receptor play a role in bone formation and resorption (Farrow, 1994; Kelly et al., 1991; Morrison et al., 1994; Tokita et al., 1994). An association between different vitamin D receptor genotypes and BMD of lumbar spine, hip, and whole-body bone mass was reported in post-menopausal twins (Spector et al., 1995).

Oophorectomy (removal of the ovaries) induces a decrease of hormonal secretion of estrogen and progesterone, as well as an increase in the secretion of follicle-stimulating hormone (FSH) and luteinizing hormone (LH). Loss of bone increases during the peri- and postmenopausal periods.

A dietary history of low calcium intake is an important and predisposing factor. A negative calcium balance induces loss of bone and is one of the causes of osteopenia. With age, calcium absorption is reduced, and when the calcium lost in the urine, stool, and sweat is not replaced, it is permanently lost from the skeleton. The daily recommended intake of calcium is between 1,000 and 1,200 mg. Diary products contain a relatively large amount of calcium, but only the ones low in fat content should be eaten. Table 14-2 gives the calcium content of different foods.

Persons who suffer from lactose deficiency and who do not eat dairy products have a predisposition for osteoporosis.

Limited exposure to sun and low dietary intake of vitamin D decrease calcium absorption and are one of the risk factors in bone loss.

Smoking decreases estrogen secretion and has been found to be a predisposing factor for osteoporosis.

Lack of or reduced physical activity is an important predisposing factor, and immobilization due to various causes induces osteoporosis.

Certain medications, such as corticosteroids, several diuretic drugs, heparin, and barbiturates, affect bone metabolism and induce bone loss. Preventive measures should be taken, or if possible, drugs which do not affect calcium and vitamin D metabolism should be prescribed.

Table 14-2. Calcium Content of Various Foods

Food	Mg calcium/100g	Food	Mg calcium/100g
Milk and dairy products		Vegetables	
Milk (3.5% fat)	120	Broccoli, cooked	75
Dried milk—whole	909	Beans, kidney	100
—nonfat	1,300	Beans, green	60
Skimmed milk	130	Chervil	400
Cottage cheese (5% fat)	105	Dill	230
Yogurt (low-fat)	120	Endive	104
Egg (without shell)	40	Fennel	100
Ice cream	75	Leek	92
Fish		Lettuce	100
Sardines	354	Soybeans, dried	226
Salmon (fresh)	20	Spinach, fresh	130
Shrimp (cooked)	110	Fruits	
Sole (fresh)	70	Dates, dried	59
Bread, nuts, and grain		Olives, green	61
Almonds	254		
Brazil nuts	127		
Cashew nuts	38		
Peanuts	74		
Pecans	73		
Bread, white (no addition)	50		
Bread, whole wheat	70		
Bread, black	100		
Rolls	50		

Skeletal pain is one of the main symptoms of osteoporosis and is induced by microfractures, compressed fractures of the vertebrae, and the other typical fractures of osteoporosis.

The treatment should be directed toward preventing further bone loss, as well as toward reducing pain.

Analgesics and anti-inflammatory nonsteroidal drugs can be used for the relief of pain. Calcitonin, which is used for the treatment of osteoporosis, also has a specific analgesic effect.

PREVENTION OF OSTEOPOROSIS

Prevention of osteoporosis and of fractures is possible by measures which diminish bone loss and induce an improvement in bone mass. In the younger age groups, the aim is to improve peak bone mass.

Peak bone mass is dependent on genetic and environmental factors and can be improved by an adequate dietary calcium intake, with exercise, as well as by avoiding smoking and alcohol. Achieving a higher bone mass at skeletal maturity prepares us for the loss induced by aging.

Table 14-3. Prevention of Osteoporosis

Physical exercise
Dietary calcium intake of 1,000–1,200 mg/day
Calcium supplementation
Hormonal replacement treatment

Prevention of osteoporosis has to start as early as possible. The ways to achieve this are summarized in Table 14-3. Gymnastics, especially weight-bearing exercises, walking, and other physical activity are recommended.

A high calcium intake with a low saturated fat diet is recommended, and foods should be chosen accordingly (Table 14-2). The recommended daily intake of calcium is between 1,000 and 1,200 mg. Calcium absorption decreases with age. Therefore, in older people, a daily intake of 1,200 mg is recommended. The same amount of calcium in the diet is recommended during pregnancy.

Dairy products, fish, and nuts contain the highest amount of calcium. When an optimal dietary intake of calcium cannot be achieved, calcium supplementation should be considered.

A high calcium intake has to be avoided in persons suffering from kidney stones and those who have a high secretion of calcium in urine (hypercalciuria).

Persons who are not able to have an adequate intake of calcium should take it in the form of tablets. Calcium carbonate, phosphate, and gluconate tablets are available.

Hormonal replacement treatment (HRT) with estrogen and progesterone is often recommended at the start of menopause. Estrogen prevents bone loss and increases bone mass, and it must be continued for some time. Estrogen is used in combination with progesterone to prevent endometrial cancer of the uterus.

TREATMENT OF OSTEOPOROSIS

The aim of the treatment of osteoporosis is to improve bone mass, to reduce pain and other complaints connected with the condition, and to reduce the risk of bone fracture. Table 14-4 summarizes the different therapies available.

Physical exercise is an important factor in the prevention and treatment of osteoporosis. Immobilization due to any circumstances (e.g., resulting from other diseases

Table 14-4. Treatment of Osteoporosis

Exercise and mobilization	Estrogen with progesterone
Calcium supplementation	Androgens
Sodium fluoride	Calcitonin
Vitamin D or vitamin D metabolites	Bisphosphonates
Estrogen	1-34 PTH

such as rheumatoid arthritis, stroke, paresis, and depression) will induce a rapid bone loss and decrease of bone mass.

Bone is affected by mechanical forces, and exercise increases bone mass and reduces bone loss. (Smith & Gillighan, 1990). Weight-bearing exercises and physical activity will reduce bone loss in all ages as well as in pre- and postmenopausal women.

Patients suffering from pain due to osteoporosis and preferring bed rest should be encouraged to be active and to avoid lying in bed. An intervention program with physical exercises should start only a few weeks after calcium supplementation and specific drug therapy.

Calcium (500–1,000 mg daily) in the form of tablets should be given daily to osteoporotic patients. Calcium supplementation will maintain bone density and may even reduce fracture rates in the elderly. An inadequate calcium intake induces loss of calcium from the skeleton and a further reduction of bone mass.

Sodium fluoride used in the prevention of dental caries has been shown to have an anabolic effect on bone. Fluoride is well absorbed from the gut and is well taken up by bone. Combined with calcium supplementation, fluoride increases bone mass. Fluoride is given in the form of sodium fluoride or as a monophosphate. The use of fluoride to prevent fracture is controversial and was recently approved in the United States.

Vitamin D and its metabolites are used in the treatment of postmenopausal and corticosteroid-induced osteoporosis. Vitamin D increases calcium absorption, which is impaired in the elderly and stimulates osteoblastic formation. Vitamin D metabolites can be used alone, or in combination with calcium and/or fluoride.

Vitamin D levels decrease with age as a result of limited exposure to sunlight, lower production of vitamin D by the skin, and a reduced dietary intake. Vitamin D serum levels are lower in winter than in summer, and they are found to be higher in persons working outside.

Low levels of the vitamin D metabolite 25(OH)D will induce an increased secretion of parathyroid hormone (PTH) and, therefore, bone resorption increases and osteoporosis appears.

Van Der Wielen et al. (1995) studied serum levels of 25 hydroxyvitamin D—25(OH)D—in elderly people in 11 European countries and found that the levels were lower in those who were not exposed enough to sun, who had lower activities of daily living (ADLs), and who consumed a smaller amount of fish.

Estrogen is used widely in the treatment of osteoporosis to stop loss of bone mass. An increase in bone mass of more than 1% per year can be observed.

In hormonal replacement treatment (HRT), estrogen is given in combination with progesterone and is usually started at the beginning of the menopause. HRT is often used preventively. Estrogen is used together with progesterone to prevent endometrial cancer, and estrogen alone is given only to women after hysterectomy. Kohrt and Birge (1995) reported an increase of bone mass of the lumbar spine and of the proximal femur in osteopenic late postmenopausal women after one year of HRT. In women 10 years after menopause, an increase of BMD of 1.4% of total body bone mass was found. The increase in the lumbar spine was 5.0%, and it was 3.2% in the neck of the femur.

Endogenous gonadal hormones play a role in breast cancer; early menarche and late menopause were reported to increase the risk of breast cancer. Colditz et al. (1995),

Feinleib (1968), Lilienfeld (1956), and others have investigated the effect of the addition of progesterone to estrogen therapy in postmenopausal women and found that progesterone did not reduce the risk of breast cancer. In a questionnaire study of registered nurses, an elevation in the risk of breast cancer was found in women using estrogen alone or in combination with progesterone. The risk was higher in women over the age of 55 and was limited to those who had received HRT for five or more years. Annual breast examination and the performing of a mammogram are recommended in women receiving HRT. A history of breast cancer or a family history of breast cancer is considered a contraindication of estrogen treatment.

Calcitonin, a hormone secreted by the perifollicular C cells of the thyroid gland, inhibits bone resorption by a direct action on bone cells. Calcitonin has been isolated from human thyroid as well as from many animal species. Perifollicular C cells are found in the thyroid gland of mammals and in the ultimobranchial body in fish.

Calcium serum levels are strongly regulated by different hormones. Parathyroid hormone, calcitonin, and vitamin D metabolites play an important role in calcium regulation. Calcitonin lowers serum calcium levels.

Salmon and human calcitonins are mostly used in a synthesized form. Calcitonins cannot be administered orally because they are degraded in the gastrointestinal tract. Therefore, they are given by injection or nasal spray or in the form of rectal suppositories.

In addition to their antiresorptive activity on bone, calcitonins have a direct analgesic effect and are widely used in patients with osteoporosis and compressed fracture of the vertebrae, who are suffering from pain.

Bisphosphonates are used in the treatment of Paget's disease and osteoporosis. They are effective inhibitors of bone resorption and improve both these conditions. Fleisch (1993) has found that plasma and urine contain compounds with inhibit calcium phosphate precipitation due to inorganic pyrophosphate. These compounds inhibit the formation and delay the aggregation and dissolution of calcium phosphate crystals.

Several bisphosphonates are available and have been in use for many years. Others have been introduced recently. The bisphosphonates in use are etidronate (Didronel), pamidronate, clodronate, and alendronate.

Alendronate was recently introduced and is looking promising in the treatment of osteoporosis and Paget's disease. Due to their effect on the bone changes induced by osteoporosis and Paget's disease, they induce a relief of skeletal pain.

BONE PAIN IN OSTEOPOROSIS

A common symptom in osteoporosis and other bone diseases such as Paget's disease and bone metastasis is bone pain due to enhanced bone resorption. The pain in osteoporosis is often induced by microfractures or fractures of bone.

Back pain in osteoporosis can be acute due to the onset of a vertebral collapse. Prolonged and disabling pain can be observed in patients with collapsed vertebrae. The diagnosis of collapsed vertebrae is made by X-ray examination or CT scanning.

SPECT (single-photon emission computed tomography) is a new technique used for the detection of skeletal changes.

Ryan, Evans, Gibson, and Fogelman (1992) investigated 26 patients with spinal osteoporosis and back pain and found that 65% of them had collapsed vertebral bodies, 19% had degenerative disk disease, and 81% had facetal joint disease.

Diminished bone mass at various skeletal sites has been identified as a risk factor for osteoporotic fracture of the spine, the hip, and other skeletal sites. Prevalent fracture of the spine is a predictor of a new spine fracture.

The main causes of bone and back pain are summarized in Table 14-5.

Diagnosis of the etiological cause of the pain is important, and specific treatment can relieve pain.

Specific treatment in osteoporosis should be started as soon as the diagnosis is made, and relief of pain occurs only after a few weeks or months. Therefore, analgesics or NSAIDs (nonsteroidal anti-inflammatory drugs) should be used for relief of the acute pain of osteoporosis.

Orally prescribed analgesics are the cornerstone of pain treatment of osteoporosis and can be used until the specific treatment shows its effect. NSAIDs are effective in the treatment of bone and low back pain due to osteoporosis. Their effect on the gastrointestinal tract should be taken in consideration, especially in elderly people.

PAGET'S DISEASE OF BONE

Paget's disease of bone is one of the most common bone disorders in older age groups and rarely appears before the age of 40. Paget's disease can be relatively easily diagnosed, and the therapies available today can arrest the progress of the disease and induce a relief of the symptoms, especially pain. Paget's disease is a focal disorder affecting sometimes only one bone, or it can appear in a more generalized form, involving several bones. The bones most frequently affected are the vertebrae, especially the lumbar ones, the sacrum and other pelvic bones, the skull, and the weight-bearing bones, the tibia and the femur. The entire skeleton is never involved.

Bone resorption is increased, and a compensatory rise in bone formation occurs, resulting in an architecturally abnormal bone.

The etiology of Paget's disease is not clear, and several causes have been taken into consideration. Genetic and geographic factors have been found to play a role in the etiology of the disease, as well as a slow viral infection, which is considered due to the presence of inclusion bodies in pagetic bone (Hamdy, 1994).

Table 14-5. Main Causes of Bone Pain

Osteoporosis	Scoliosis
Paget's disease	Disk degeneration
Bone metastasis	Spondylolisthesis
Spondylarthrosis	Multiple myeloma
Spinal stenosis	

Most of the patients with Paget's disease are asymptomatic, but some of them suffer from skeletal pain, an enlargement of the skull, and bone deformity of the affected bone. The pain can be severe and more pronounced when increased bone turnover is present.

The diagnosis is made by the typical radiological findings as well as by the laboratory determination of serum alkaline phosphatase and urinary hydroxyproline or pyridinoline cross-links. Elevated serum alkaline phosphatase levels are found due to the increased bone formation, and higher levels of urinary hydroxyproline, a product of collagen breakdown, are detected due to the increased bone resorption.

Specific treatment in Paget's disease will induce a decrease of bone resorption and relief of pain, as well as a reduction of the elevated levels of serum alkaline phosphatase and urinary hydroxyproline. Hamdy (1994) even recommends treatment of asymptomatic active Paget's disease of the skull or the vertebrae, as there is evidence of an improvement of the histological and radiological bone changes, due to the specific therapy.

The two agents now used and recommended in the treatment of Paget's disease are bisphosphonates and calcitonin. Both of them reduce bone resorption and turnover, and as a result, there is relief of pain as well as the excessive warmth found over the involved bone.

Bisphosphonates are administered orally, and several forms such as etidronate, pamidronate, alendronate, risedronate, and tiludronate are available. Etidronate disodium, the first bisphosphate used in Paget's disease, is given orally for six months and is then interrupted for the same period of time. Bone demineralization can be caused by etidronate; therefore, it is used in a cyclical form. The newer generations of bisphosphonates do not induce demineralization and can be given for longer periods of time, when needed. Short-term intravenous treatment with pamidronate in Paget's was reported.

The second drug of choice in the treatment of Paget's disease is calcitonin. Calcitonin inhibits bone resorption, eliciting a sharp decrease of urinary hydroxyproline. Bone turnover is reduced, and as a result, serum alkaline phosphatase levels diminished. Relief of bone pain occurs due to the decreased bone resorption as well as to the direct analgesic effect of calcitonin. The analgesic effect of calcitonin is mediated through its direct action on the central nervous systems.

Calcitonin—salmon and human—is available in synthetic formulation for parenteral administration. As calcitonin cannot be used orally, nasal spray and suppositories were developed and are used in several countries.

Bisphosphonates and calcitonin have been in use for several years and have proved to be very effective in the treatment of Paget's disease—especially in the relief of pain. The availability of potent inhibitors of bone resorption has changed and improved the treatment of Paget's disease.

Analgesics and NSAIDS can be tried for relief of pain, in addition to the specific treatment with bisphosphonates or calcitonin.

REFERENCES

Colditz, G. A., Hankinson, S. E., Hunter, D. J., Willet, W. C., Manson, J. E., Stampfer, M. J., Hennekens, C., Rosner, B, & Speizer, F. E. (1995). The use of estrogens and progestins and the risk of breast cancer in postmenopausal women. *New England Journal of Medicine, 332*, 1589–1593.

Farrow, S. (1994). Allelic variation and the vitamin D receptor. *The Lancet, 343*, 1242.
Feinleib, M. (1968). Breast cancer and artificial menopause: a cohort study. *Journal of the National Cancer Institute, 41*, 315–329.
Fleisch, H. (1993). *Bisphosphonates in bone disease*. Berne: Stampfli-Co.
Hamdy, R. C. (1994). Paget's disease of the bone. In H. M. Perry III (Ed.), *Clinics in geriatric medicine: The aging skeleton* (pp. 719–736). Philadelphia, London, Toronto: W. B. Saunders.
Kelly, P. J., Hopper, J. L., Macaskill, G. T., Pocock, N. A., Sambrook, P. N., & Eisman, J. A. (1991). Genetic factors in bone turnover. *Journal of Clinical Endocrinology and Metabolism, 72*, 808–813.
Kohrt, W. M., & Birge, S. J., Jr. (1995). Differential effects of estrogen treatment on bone mineral density of the spine, hip, wrist and total body in late postmenopausal women. *Osteoporosis International, 5*, 150–155.
Lilienfeld, A. M. (1956). The relationship of cancer of the female breast to artificial menopause and martial status. *Cancer, 9*, 927–934.
Morrison, N. A., Qi, J. C., Tokita, A., Kelly, P. J., Crofts, L., Nguyen, T. V., Sambrook, P. N., & Eisman, J. A. (1994). Prediction of bone density from vitamin D receptor alleles. *Nature, 367*, 284–287.
Pocock, N. A., Eisman, J. A., Hopper, J. L., Yeates, M. G., Sambrook, P. N., & Eberl, S. (1987). Genetic determinants of bone mass in adults: a twin study. *Journal of Clinical Investigation, 80*, 706–710.
Ryan, P. J., Evans, P., Gibson, T., & Fogelman, I. (1992). Osteoporosis and chronic bank pain: A study with single-photon emission computed tomography bone scintigraphy. *Journal of Bones and Mineral Research, 7*, 1455–1460.
Smith, D. A., Nance, W. E., Won Kan, K., Christian J. C., & Johnston, C. C., Jr. (1973). Genetic factors in determinating bone mass. *Journal of Clinical Investigation, 52*, 2800–2808.
Smith, E. L., & Gillighan, C. (1990). Exercise and bone mass. In H. H. Luca & R. Mazess (Eds.) *Osteoporosis, physiological basis, assessment, and treatment* (pp. 285–294). New York, Amsterdam, London: Elsevier.
Spector, T. D., Keen, R. W., Arden, N. K., Morrison, N. A., Major, P. J., Nguyen, T. V., Kelly, P. J., Baker, J. R., Sambrook, P. N., Lanchbury, J. S., & Eisman, J. A. (1995). Influence of vitamin D receptor genotype on bone mineral density in postmenopausal women: A twin study in Britain. *British Medical Journal, 310*, 1357–1360.
Tokita, A., Kelly, P. J., Nguyen, T. V., Leslie, A. L., Morrison, N. A., Risteli, L., Sambrook, P. N., & Eisman, J. A. (1994). Genetic influences on type I collagen synthesis and degradation: Further evidence for genetic regulation of bone turnover. *Journal of Clinical Endocrinology and Metabolism, 78*, 1461–1466.
Van Der Wielen, R. P. J., Lowik, M. R. H., Van Den Berg, H., De Groot, L. C. P. G. M., Haller, J., Moreiras, O., & Van Staveren, W. A. (1995). Serum vitamin D concentrations among elderly people in Europe. *The Lancet, 346*, 207–210.

CHAPTER 15

Oral Facial Pain in the Elderly

JONATHAN A. SHIP, MARC W. HEFT, AND STEPHEN W. HARKINS

INTRODUCTION

With the rapidly expanding proportion of the population older than 65 years of age, clinical problems affecting older adults have received increasing attention. Greater emphasis has been placed on quality-of-life issues, rather than simply living longer. One major issue that has a dramatic influence on the quality of people's lives is pain. Pain in the oral-facial region can be caused by a multitude of factors. Oral diseases; systemic conditions; neurological, immunological, arthritic, and infectious diseases of the maxillofacial region; medications; chemotherapy; and radiotherapy, as well as psychiatric and behavioral disorders, can cause or contribute to oral-facial pain. While the elderly may be less likely to complain about some of these disorders, they are probably at greater risk of experiencing oral-facial pain due to exposure to these etiological factors over time.

An important distinction in geriatrics is between age-related changes in biological phenomena and changes due to diseases and their treatment. Likewise, the presence of oral-facial pain in an older person should not be attributed solely to the aging process. Oral, systemic, and psychological or behavioral problems are more likely to be major contributors to oral-facial pain and require a multidisciplinary approach to the appropriate diagnosis and treatment.

Much of the literature on oral-facial pain has been dedicated to young individuals, with particular attention to temporomandibular joint disorders. However, epidemiological surveys suggest that both acute and chronic oral-facial pain is a significant problem

---

JONATHAN A. SHIP • University of Michigan School of Dentistry, Ann Arbor, Michigan 48109-1078. MARC W. HEFT • Claude Denson Pepper Center and Department of Oral and Maxillofacial Surgery, University of Florida, Gainesville, Florida 32610. STEPHEN W. HARKINS • Department of Gerontology, Medical College of Virginia/Virginia Commonwealth University, Richmond, Virginia 23298-0228.

Handbook of Pain and Aging, edited by David I. Mostofsky and Jacob Lomranz. Plenum Press, New York, 1997.

among the elderly and requires greater recognition and management. Traditionally, it was accepted that there is a decrease in sensitivity to painful stimulation as individuals age. More recently, however, it has been suggested that pain perception is not reduced with advancing age, but that differences in the clinical presentation of disease may account for altered pain association.

The evaluation and management of oral-facial pain in the elderly requires an understanding of the influence of aging on pain perception and how older individuals cope with pain. An examination must include a thorough review of the pain symptoms, medical history, and previous treatments for systemic diseases. A careful inspection of the mouth, face, head, and neck regions is mandatory. Finally, communication with multiple health care providers may be necessary in order to arrive at a diagnosis and a treatment plan. Management strategies depend on the clinical diagnosis and may range from invasive procedures (e.g., tooth extraction, repair of an ill-fitting denture), to pharmacological strategies (e.g., antiseizure drugs for trigeminal neuralgia, tricyclic antidepressants for burning-mouth syndrome).

The purpose of this chapter is to provide an overview of the epidemiology, pathophysiology, clinical signs and symptoms, and treatment of oral-facial in the elderly. The aging process has an influence on pain perception, and some of the recent research findings in this area will be described. Hopefully, health care providers, administrators, politicians, and patients will recognize that oral-facial pain is prevalent among the elderly and requires a multidisciplinary approach to its successful diagnosis and management.

EPIDEMIOLOGY OF ORAL-FACIAL PAIN IN THE ELDERLY

In general, recent epidemiological evidence suggests that a significant proportion of the elderly suffer and have recently suffered from some form of oral-facial pain. Unfortunately, there are some weaknesses in the epidemiological literature: patient populations rather than randomized population surveys have been used, pain has been identified by self-report questionnaires instead of direct examinations, and the use of "older" subjects has been poorly defined. Despite these weaknesses, certain studies do suggest that oral-facial pain does not disappear with aging, and that older adults seek medical and dental care for pain affecting the mouth and face.

In 1993, Lipton, Ship, and Larach-Robinson presented the first nationwide estimates of the prevalence and distribution of several types of mouth and face pains in the U.S. population. As part of the 1989 National Health Interview Survey (NHIS), 42,370 adults (age 18 years and older) were asked about their experience within the past six months of toothache, oral sores, jaw joint pain, face and cheek pain, and burning-mouth pain. Overall, the estimated occurrence of toothache pains was 22 million individuals (12.2% of the U.S. adult population), 15 million with oral sores (8.4%), 9.5 million with jaw joint pain (5.3%), 2.5 million with face and cheek pain (1.4%), and 1.3 million with burning-mouth pain (0.7%). With increased age, the estimated prevalence rates for toothaches, oral sores, and jaw joint pain decreased. Face pain remained essentially stable with increased age, and burning-mouth pain increased with age. The estimated prevalence rates (per 100,000) for individuals aged 75+ years was 3,372 for toothache, 6,209 for oral sores, 3,873 for jaw joint pain, 1,580 for face pain, and 1,184 for burning-mouth pain.

The estimated prevalence rates among women were consistently higher than among men for all reported types of oral-facial pain. Women had nearly twice the rate of jaw joint pain as men, and more than twice the rate of face pain. Interestingly, the prevalence of burning-mouth pain, traditionally described primarily in women, was similar between men and women (804/100,000 in women, 601/100,000 in men). Regarding the influence of race and ethnicity on oral-facial pain, the NHIS data suggest several trends. Whites were found to have the greatest estimated prevalence rate for face pain and jaw joint pain and had rates for oral sores similar to those of the group called "other" (Asian American, American Indians). African-Americans and Hispanics showed the greatest rates for toothache, and the group "other" had the highest rate for burning-mouth pain, more than twice that of Hispanics, the next highest group.

Locker and Grushka (1987b) conducted a randomized study of 594 non-treatment-seeking persons in Toronto, Canada, and collected information on current and recent past experiences with oral and facial pain with the use of a questionnaire. Pain items assessed were toothache, burning sensation in the mouth, pain in the temporomandibular joint (TMJ), and facial pain. Other factors included in the assessment were gender, age, social and psychological impact of the pain, and treatment sought for the pain. There was a significantly greater number of individuals aged 18–24 years who reported pain (62.5%), than persons aged 65 years and older (22.6%; $p < .00001$). However, older respondents were more likely than younger respondents to report an adverse behavioral impact of the pain. Furthermore, the elderly were more likely to seek medical attention concerning the pain. More than one-half of those aged 45 years and older had consulted a physician or dentist because of the pain, compared with only one-third of those aged 45 years or younger ($p < .05$). Regarding gender, there were no significant differences between males and females in the prevalence of reported pain. It was concluded that dental and facial pain imposes a significant burden on the community.

Chronic pain conditions have been reported to be among the leading reasons for ambulatory health care visits (Koch, 1986). In 1986, an age-stratified probability sample of 1,016 adult HMO enrollees (age 18–75 years) in the Seattle region and 242 HMO enrollees seeking treatment for temporomandibular joint pain completed a screening pain questionnaire (Von Korff, Dworkin, LeResche, & Kruger, 1988a,b, 1991; Dworkin et al., 1990). Persons were asked to report only pain problems that had lasted a whole day or more, or that had occurred several times in a year. The use of health care was assessed in persons experiencing pain in both population samples. The screening questionnaire inquired about head and TMJ region pain occurring within the six months prior to interview, and the total volume of use of ambulatory health care for a painful oral-facial condition was reported. Pain severity and persistence, psychological distress, and self-rated health status were also assessed. The results indicated that pain persistence and severity were consistently associated with the likelihood of use of health care for pain. Facial, TMJ, and headache pain prevalence decreased with advancing age, yet the strongest independent association of pain was psychological distress and somatic symptoms (Von Korff et al., 1988a,b). There was a greater percentage of adults older than 45 years who reported use of health care services for headaches and temporomandibular joint disorder (TMJD) pain, compared to persons younger than age 45 (Von Korff, Wagner, Dworkin, & Saunders, 1991). Persons who rated their health as being fair to poor were more likely to use health care services for headaches but not TMJD than subjects who rated their health as excellent to good. After controlling for age, sex, and other variables, chronic pain status and self-rated health status showed a significant association with ambulatory utilization rates. Based on the respondents' self-reported lifetime history of each pain condition and the initial age of onset, the probability was estimated of the occurrence of each pain condition by a given age (Van Korff et al., 1988a). Among persons surviving to age 70 years, the percentage of subjects who would have experienced an episode of facial pain at some during their lifetime was 33.8%, and 43.8% for headache.

In a follow-up study, Dworkin et al. (1990) conducted a field examination following the screening questionnaire, which assessed signs and symptoms of TMJD in two community-dwelling groups (210 subjects who did not report TMJD pain, and 121 subjects who did report TMJD but did not seek treatment), and a group of subjects seeking treatment for TMJD. The age-stratified results indicated that there were no significant differences in the distribution of clinical findings of TMJD by age group, within any of the three population groups. On average, range of mandibular motion did not change with age, nor did the prevalence of joint sounds or muscle palpation tenderness. Dworkin et al. (1990) concluded that common TMJD signs did not represent age-related disease progression.

In 1985, a randomized telephone survey of 1,254 people 18 years of age and older in the United States was conducted to provide quantitative data on the prevalence and severity of different kinds of pain, including headaches and dental pain (Taylor & Curran, 1985). This *Nuprin Pain Report* also examined the impact of pain on work and other activities, the relationship between pain and measures of stress, the use of health care providers for pain treatment, and the effectiveness of treatment. The total percentage of individuals who had experienced pain for 1 or more days within the previous 12 months was 73% for headaches and 27% for dental pains (Sternbach, 1986b). Lost work days projected to the total U.S. adult population attributed to headaches were 637 million and 70 million for dental pains. Regarding age, the younger the adults, the more likely they were to have dental pain. For example, 36% of younger adults (age 18–24 years) complained of dental pains, compared to 14% of older adults (age 65+ years). The relationship between dental pain and self-reported stress and strains of daily living (hassles) was published (Sternbach, 1986a). Individuals who indicated greater stress and hassles were more likely to experience dental pain, and the pain occurred more frequently than in subjects who reported lower stress and hassles. Older retired persons generally reported less stress and fewer hassles, which corresponded to fewer complaints of pain (except joint pains). Sternbach (1986a) also demonstrated that there was a tendency, as pain severity increased, toward less exercise, more smoking, and less frequent but more excessive drinking.

Burning-mouth syndrome is a poorly understood chronic pain condition affecting the oral cavity of predominantly older females (Gruskha & Sessle, 1991; Ship et al., 1995a), and several studies have attempted to assess its prevalence in the general population. Lipton et al. (1993) estimated that 1.3 million individuals in the United States experienced burning-mouth pain more than once in the 6 months before the interview and estimated that the prevalence rate in individuals older than age 75 years was 1,184/100,000 individuals. Burning-mouth pain was combined with "private parts" pain in a sample of community-dwelling nonpatients from Christchurch, New Zealand (James, Large, Bushnell, & Wells, 1991), and the prevalence among individuals between the ages of 45 and 64 was 6.6%. The report of burning-mouth pain was found to be 15.7% in female respondents aged 40–49 years in a general dental survey in England (Basker, Sturdee, & Davenport, 1978), whereas the overall prevalence of burning mouth in English dental patients (Basker et al., 1978) and a random sample of 1,000 individuals from Canada (Locker & Grushka, 1987b) was reported to be 5.1% and 4.5%, respectively.

Significant epidemiological attention has been directed toward understanding the role of aging in oral diseases; however, limited information is available regarding the prevalence of oral-facial pain caused by tooth, periodontal, oral mucosal, and salivary gland disorders in the elderly. Coronal caries remain a significant clinical problem in the elderly, while the prevalence of cervical caries increases substantially (Miller et al., 1987). While it appears that aging per se does not adversely affect the periodontal tissues (Burt, 1994), the exposure to oral and systemic diseases and their treatment over time can significantly impact on periodontal health (Ship & Crow, 1994). While salivary gland function appears to be age-stable in healthy persons (e.g., Ship & Baum, 1990; Wu et al., 1993; Ship et al., 1995b), numerous older persons suffer from salivary gland hypofunction and complaints of a dry mouth (xerostomia) due to medical disorders, medications, and head and neck irradiation (Atkinson & Fox, 1992). Finally, there are numerous oral mucosal diseases which can cause acute or chronic pain in the elderly, including oral vesiculobullous diseases (e.g., lichen planus, pemphigus, and pemphigoid), yeast (candidiasis) and viral (recurrent herpes) infections, and irritations from ill-fitting removable prostheses. All of the above-mentioned disorders occur in older populations (Kleinman, Swango, & Niessen, 1991). Hand and Whitehill (1986) used a random sample of noninstitutionalized persons aged 65+ years from two rural Iowa counties and estimated that the prevalence of all oral mucosal lesions was 23.1%, with a greater prevalence of denture-related lesions (27.0%) than of non-denture-related lesions (8.3%).

PATHOPHYSIOLOGY OF ORAL-FACIAL PAIN IN THE ELDERLY

Pain in the orofacial complex is usually the result of dental and oral diseases afflicting the hard or soft tissues or injury of these tissues. However, in older persons, there may be additional considerations in evaluating causes of the pain. This section will summarize sources and causes of pain in the oral-facial complex in older adults, discuss problems in localization of the etiology of certain types of oral-facial pain, and then review specific problems that are more likely to arise in the older patient.

The oral-facial complex is richly innervated by a broad range of both nociceptive (pain) and nonnociceptive (nonpain) afferents (Cooper & Sessle, 1992; Mumford, 1982). The primary afferents include both free nerve endings and more complex specialized corpuscular or encapsulated endings. The free nerve endings include fast-conducting A delta myelinated fibers (2.5–35 m/sec) and slow-conducting C fibers (0.7–1.5 m/sec), while the specialized encapsulated endings (such as Ruffini-type and Meissner corpuscles) include faster-conducting primary afferents. The different fiber types signal information about touch, temperature, and pain in the oral-facial complex.

Many of the free endings and encapsulated mechanoreceptor fibers provide information about spatial deformation of the skin or oral mucosa and are touch fibers. Some fibers fire continuously in response to a maintained mechanical stimulus and are referred to as *slow-adapting fibers* or *position detectors*. Others are responsive to changes in deformation of tissue and are referred to as *rapid-adapting fibers* or *velocity detectors*. Thus, these fiber types provide information to the central nervous system about the sensory attributes of stimuli, including intensity, localization, duration, quality, and rate of change of a stimulus applied to the oral-facial complex. This capacity is most important in the oral-facial complex because of the prime importance of this region for a broad range of activities, including (but not limited to) eating, speech, and emotion. Further, in the case of specialized tissues such as the periodontal and hair mechanoreceptors, information is also encoded about the stimulus direction. Thermal information is provided by the slow-adapting mechanoreceptors as well as the small-diameter myelinated (A delta) and unmyelinated (C fiber) afferents.

There are three groups of A delta and C fibers which are especially important with regard to nociceptive pain (Cooper, Ahlquist, Friedman, Loughner, & Heft, 1992; Cooper & Sessle, 1992; Dubner, 1985; Dubner & Bennett, 1983; Hu & Sessle, 1988). The first group of primarily A delta afferent fibers (high-threshold mechanoreceptors) are activated only by intense mechanical stimuli such as a pinch. The second group of A (mechanothermal) delta afferent fibers respond to both intense heat (> 40°C, responding maximally at approximately 50°C) and intense mechanical stimuli. These fibers appear to be responsible for the heat-induced intense, well-localized, pricking "first pain." The third group of the C polymodal (nociceptive) afferents respond to intense thermal, mechanical, and chemical stimuli. These fibers appear to be responsible for "second pain," which is dull, poorly localized, aching, and diffuse and is often referred to a site removed from the area of injury.

The most prevalent pains of the oral-facial complex among adults involve the teeth or the supporting structures of the teeth (periodontium). These pains are considered nociceptive pains in that they are related to ongoing activity of the nociceptive pathways described above. Further, most of these nociceptive pains are inflammatory, involving tissue destruction. As the inflammatory process proceeds with the phagocytosis of debris by the polymorphonuclear leukocytes and the release of degradative enzymes, several of the products of breakdown of proteins and lipids as well as other substances released from local tissues maintain and enhance the inflammatory process. Several of the inflammatory products contribute to inflammatory pain (hyperalgesia), most notably serotonin, histamine, substance P, kinins, and products of arachidonic acid degradation (leukotrienes and prostaglandins; Hargreaves et al., 1995). Dental caries and periodontal disease are the most prevalent oral diseases across the life span. While these disease processes may ultimately result in loss of teeth, pain often signals the progression of the disease.

A second type of oral-facial pain which has clinical importance in older adults is neuropathic (nonnociceptive) pain. Neuropathic pain, which is a sequela of nerve injury, is marked clinically by the elicitation of pain by nonnoxious (e.g., touch) stimulation. One example of such an affliction is trigeminal neuralgia, in which light touch such as movement of the hair of an eyebrow can trigger a painful episode (Dubner, Sharav, Gracely, & Price, 1987).

CLINICAL SIGNS AND SYMPTOMS OF ORAL-FACIAL PAIN IN THE ELDERLY

Intraoral Pain (Table 15-1)

Teeth. Pain arising from the tooth is either dentinal or pulpal in origin. The most common cause of tooth pain is dental caries. However, in older adults with a history of periodontal disease and the resultant gingival recession, pain may result from the exposure of the poorly insulated roots of the teeth to thermal stimuli such as hot or cold drinks. This thermal sensitivity is a secondary effect of bone loss and gingival recession from periodontal disease rather than a primary disease of the teeth. Initially, dental caries afflict the dentin (dental radiographs will confirm this) which renders the tooth sensitive to thermal stimuli and sweet or sour substances. With progression of the carious lesion, the level of stimulus-induced sensitivity intensifies in magnitude, duration, and also identified spatial distribution (Sharav, Leviner, Tzukert, & McGrath, 1984). Eventually, if left untreated, the carious lesion will progress into the tooth pulp, resulting in pulpitis, an inflammation of the tooth pulp. At this stage, pain may be stimulus-induced or spontaneous, and typically, the pain will persist beyond the duration of the applied stimulus. The pain will not usually be specifically localized to the afflicted tooth and will often be referred to other facial locations as well. The referred (or "mislocalized") pain is commonly observed with pain from muscles and viscera, and it is related to the convergence of sensory information from skin, mucosa, gingiva, temporomandibular joint, bone, jaw and tongue muscle, and tooth pulp (Cooper & Sessle, 1992). Ultimately, if the microorganisms and products of tissue degradation extend from the tooth pulp to the area around the apex of the tooth, the ensuing abscess will produce continuous, deep, boring pain, which may be exacerbated by chewing or percussion. Dental radiographs will show an area of radiolucency beyond the apex of the tooth. Further, the tooth is no longer sensitive to cold stimuli; however, there may be profound sensitivity to warm or hot stimuli such as hot coffee or tea. On clinical examination, a large carious lesion or missing dental restoration may be noted, especially in the latter stages.

In instances of root sensitivity which is related to gingival recession, the presenting symptoms will be similar to carious progression in dentin. The patient typically complains of sensitivity to cold and hot temperatures, with the sensitivity usually not

Table 15-1. Characteristics of Intraoral Pain

	Tooth (dental)				
	Dentinal	Pulpal	Gingival	Periodontal	Mucosal
Localization	Poor	Poor	Good	Good	Good
Location	Teeth, jaws, cheeks, face	Teeth, jaws, cheeks, face	Gingiva	Tooth (periodontal ligament)	Mucosa
Evoking stimulus	Thermal, sweet, sour	Thermal, chewing (abscess)	Food impaction, tooth brushing	Chewing	Thermal, sour
Findings	Dental caries, exposed dentin, tooth fracture	Dental caries, extensive restorations	Gingival inflammation, chemical burn (aspirin), abrasion (trauma)	Periodontal swelling, tooth mobility	Erosion or ulcer, redness
Treatment	Dental restorations, endodontics	Endodontics, extraction	Dental restorations, palliative	Drainage, debridement	Depending on cause

outlasting the stimulus. On clinical examination, areas of gingival recession will be noted. Recession is quite common in the mandibular anterior region, affecting the incisor and cuspid teeth; however, in individuals with an extensive history of periodontal disease, the recession can be more widespread. The pain can usually be evoked by applying a cold stimulus such as ice or ethyl chloride spray applied to a cotton pellet to the exposed root surface. Fortunately, this annoying symptom does not usually signal a progressive process within the afflicted teeth.

Periodontium. *Periodontium* refers to the supporting structures of the tooth, including the alveolar supporting bone, the periodontal ligament which attaches the tooth to the alveolar bone, and the overlying keratinized gingival tissues. The innervation of periodontium with specialized receptors allows for excellent localization of pain.

Gingival pain most often results from mechanical irritation, but it is less often noted as a concomitant of acute gingival infection such as gingivitis or pericoronitis. These latter problems are more often seen in a young patient. The source of mechanical irritation is usually food impaction between two teeth when an inadequate contact (due to either dental caries or a defective dental restoration or drifting of the teeth) between adjacent teeth allows food to become lodged. Debridement of the inflamed tissues and placement of a dental restoration or replacement of the existing restoration will usually eliminate the problem. In the older patient with removable dentures, the pain may be denture-related trauma.

In general, periodontal pain results from an acute inflammatory process involving the gingiva, periodontal ligament, and supporting alveolar bone, and the pain is quite well localized by the patient. The pain results either from the sequelae of a chronic infection of the tooth pulp which spreads to the periapical tissues (abscess), or from a periodontal infection and pocket formation which involves the lateral periodontal tissues (periodontal abscess). The pain is well localized and is elicited by percussion or chewing. Localized swelling may be noted, and the patient may be febrile. Immediate management of the pain will include debridement and occasional antibiotic administration. In general, periodontal pain does not arise from chronic periodontitis, the most prevalent periodontal disease, but rather from acute periodontal inflammation.

Periodontal pain may also arise from an "overstressing" of teeth. The affected teeth will be sensitive to chewing and percussion. Examples include occlusal overload that may be related to bruxism (abnormal parafunctional clenching and grinding of teeth) or trauma to teeth under normal function due to inadequate support of the occlusion. This is due to the loss of multiple teeth, a problem which is seen in many older adults, especially those without tooth replacement with partial dentures or fixed bridges. The periodontal pain related to bruxism can usually be alleviated quite effectively by providing an acrylic splint ("night guard"), which effectively distributes the grinding forces more evenly among the remaining teeth, and grinding away occlusal high spots (occlusal adjustment). The latter treatment is usually a consideration only if a dental restoration has been recently placed. Replacement of missing teeth with bridges or dentures will often alleviate the latter symptoms.

In addition, it is important to consider that the source of pain may be located at a site removed from the pain. It is common that craniofacial muscles, especially the masticatory muscles, may refer pain to the teeth and supporting structures. Similarly, pain may be experienced in the head or at a site remote from the periodontal sites.

Mucosa. Mucosal pain in older adults is most likely related to trauma but may also be caused by viral, bacterial, or fungal infections; allergy; nutritional deficiency; and neoplasia. Individuals who experience salivary gland dysfunction and xerostomia from systemic disease (e.g., Sjögren's syndrome), medication usage (e.g., tricyclic antidepressants), and other medical treatments (e.g., head and neck irradiation for cancer) are more susceptible to mucosal trauma because of a decrease of the protective salivary lubricating and coating proteins. Mucosal injury and pain are quite prevalent in individuals with removable partial dentures, which replace missing teeth. The painful mucosal tissues underlying the dentures may be erythematous or ulcerative. Symptoms may be relieved by relining, rebasing, or refabricating the dentures.

"Burning-mouth syndrome" or "burning tongue" (glossodynia) is a painful intraoral disorder that is typically unaccompanied by clinical signs (Grushka, 1987; Ship et al., 1995a). This disorder is marked by complaints of burning and pain of the tongue and lips, mouth dryness, and altered taste. The symptom reports of dryness and altered taste are not necessarily corroborated by clinical examination of the oral cavity for dryness or psychophysical taste testing, respectively. Symptoms may increase in response to certain foods, especially spicy and hot foods, and when chewing. Patients are typically postmenopausal females, which has led investigators to seek a hormonal etiology for this disorder (Forabosco et al., 1992), although this linkage has not been established. Other suggested etiologies include xerostomia, oral candidiasis, nutritional deficiencies, denture trauma, and psychological factors, yet none have been definitively linked to burning-mouth syndrome. Management is often palliative but may include anxiolytic and antidepressant medications (Ship et al., 1995a).

Other potential causes of mucosal pain and soreness are nutritional deficiencies, blood dyscrasias, diabetes, pemphigus, and recurrent aphthous stomatitis. Numerous vitamin deficiencies can cause oral pain, especially niacin and folic acid (Lamey & Lamb, 1988). Typically with niacin deficiency, the tongue and oral mucosa are red, inflamed, and painful. Folic acid deficiency is marked by swelling and redness of the tip and lateral borders of the tongue, and with further progression, depapillation of the tongue occurs which renders it smooth and shiny.

Bone. The most common osseous sources of pain are the alveolar bone and the temporomandibular joint (the latter to be discussed in the next section). Osseous oral-facial pain results from trauma (fractures) and infection, as a complication of systemic conditions such as Paget's disease, or, more commonly, as an untoward sequela of tooth extraction (dry socket). This latter condition, which is the most prevalent oral-facial pain of osseous origin, develops one day or more after a tooth extraction, and it is characterized by intense, well-localized pain at the extraction sites; however, referred pain is also noted at distal sites on the face and head, and muscle splinting (tightness and soreness) may be present. Clinically, the blood clot overlying the extraction site (or socket) has been lost, and the denuded bone is exposed to the oral environment. The pain typically subsides over the next one to two weeks as the exposed bone becomes covered with granulation tissue.

Extraoral Facial Pain Exclusive of Headache (Table 15-2)

Temporomandibular Disorders. The term *temporomandibular disorders* refers to a class of painful disturbances of the masticatory system marked by the symptoms of temporomandibular joint pain on function or pain in the face (including the preauricular area), as well as the presence of one or more of the following signs: (1) limitation in the range of motion of the mandible on function; (2) deviation of the mandible on function; (3) pain or tenderness in the muscles of mastication; or (4) noises in the temporomandibular joint (Heft, 1984; Laskin & Greene, 1990). Patients seeking care for these disorders are typically females between the ages of 20 and 40. Two putative risk factors that were thought to support the potential increase in prevalence of these disorders with age are increased rates of tooth loss (and edentulousness) and the increased prevalence of arthritis in older adults. With loss of teeth, especially the posterior teeth, there is increased loading in the temporomandibular joint, rendering it more likely to arthritic changes. However, epidemiological studies of these disorders do not support an age-related increase (see above).

A major concern is that the term *temporomandibular disorders* is misleading, and that, in fact, it includes both conditions of the temporomandibular joint and conditions of the muscles of mastication (Dolwick & Saunders, 1985; Laskin & Greene, 1990). Temporomandibular joint conditions include developmental problems, neoplasms, trauma, arthritis, dislocation, ankylosis, internal derangement, and arthrosis (noninflammatory degenerative changes). These conditions may have symptoms in common, most notably facial pain and pain in the mandible on function, yet the underlying problems and their correct treatment are distinctly different. For the majority of patients, symptoms can be managed quite effectively with nonsteroidal anti-inflammatory medications and physical therapy (Clark, Choi, & Browne, 1995). When bruxism is suspected, acrylic bite splints are effective in managing symptoms because they limit the loading forces delivered to the temporomandibular joint and are effective in managing symptoms (Clark et al., 1995).

Trigeminal Neuralgia (Tic Douloureux). Trigeminal neuralgia is a painful condition of the face which is marked by sharp, stabbing, electric-shock-like pain which is elicited by innocuous stimulation (e.g., light touch) to trigger points on the face (Fromm, 1989). Typically, the pain is unilateral and afflicts one or more divisions of the trigeminal nerve. The condition is marked by refractory periods when the patient is pain-free; however, episodes may then begin and terminate abruptly. The trigger points are most often centrally located on the face around the nose and lips (Kugelberg & Lindblom, 1959), yet trigger points have been reported in the periodontium, alveolar ridge, and hairs of the eyebrow as well. A further noteworthy characteristic of the pain is that it radiates outside the area and nerve division that is stimulated. A similar condition with lower

Table 15-2. Characteristics of Extraoral Facial Pain Exclusive of Headache

	Temporomandibular disorders	Trigeminal neuralgia	Postherpetic neuralgia	Atypical facial pain
Localization	Fair-poor	Good	Good	Poor
Location	Usually unilateral	Unilateral	Unilateral	Unilateral or bilateral
Evoking stimulus	Chewing	Ipsilateral, nonpainful stimulus	Ipsilateral nonpainful stimulus	None
Findings	Limited opening, TMJ clicking, popping, or crepitation; palpable tenderness of TMJ or masticatory muscles	None	Scarring, history of herpes zoster (varicella)	None
Treatment	NSAIDs, tranquilizers, physiotherapy, behavioral therapy, TMJ surgery	Carbamazepine, phenytoin, baclofen, nerve block, neurosurgery	Tricyclic antidepressants and neuroleptics, topical capsaicin	Tricyclic antidepressants, behavioral therapy

prevalence afflicts the glossopharyngeal nerve (posterior tongue, tonsilar fossa or larynx), the nervus intermedius (ear or posterior pharynx) or both.

Trigeminal neuralgia usually begins in the fifth to sixth decade of life, with females affected slightly more often than males. The majority of patients are between 50 and 70 years of age (Fromm, 1989). It is marked by periods of exacerbation and remission, and the clinical presentation may differ from one episode to another. A condition called *pretrigeminal neuralgia* (Fromm, Graff-Radford, & Terrence, 1988) has been described, in which patients may experience a toothache or sinusitis-like pain lasting for several hours which may be triggered by jaw movement or thermal stimuli. Classic trigeminal neuralgia may then develop days to years later in the same division of the trigeminal nerve. A modest association has been reported between multiple sclerosis and trigeminal neuralgia (1–8%) (Brisman, 1987).

The presentation of trigeminal neuralgia is so characteristic that the diagnosis is readily established. Severe pain is elicited by stimulation of a trigger point in the absence of neurological deficits in an older adult. Other painful conditions to consider in the differential diagnosis include atypical facial pain, postherpetic neuralgia, cluster headache, and temporomandibular joint disorder. However, these conditions are not precipitated by tactile triggering of painful episodes.

The two theories of the pathogenesis of trigeminal neuralgia have considered either a peripheral or a central mechanism for the disorder (e.g., Fromm, 1989). The peripheral model suggests that the cause of trigeminal neuralgia is compression or stretching of the trigeminal roots by aberrant arteries, vascular malformations, or slow-growing tumors. The central mechanism theory is supported by the clinical presentation, including (1) measurable latency between triggering event and pain; (2) attacks which are self-sustained after being provoked and are followed by a refractory period of no pain; (3) attacks which are stimulated by low-threshold tactile stimulation; and (4) pain which radiates to another nerve division from that which triggered the attack. Pharmacological treatment has included anticonvulsant drugs (e.g., phenytoin, carbamazepine), clonazepam, and baclofen (Zakrzewska & Patsalos, 1992). Patients who have become refractory to medications may be candidates for neurosurgical intervention, such as microvascular decompression and radiofrequency or glycerol gangliolysis, and rhizotomy (Heft, 1992). The former procedure is geared toward attacking the presumed etiology of the condition. The latter procedures avoid the risks of the craniotomy.

Postherpetic Neuralgia. Postherpetic neuralgia is a neuropathic pain sequela of a herpes zoster infection that is caused by the reactivation of the varicella zoster virus of chicken pox. This painful condition usually afflicts either the thoracic or the trigeminal dermatomes, although other sites are also at risk (Loeser, 1986; Watson, 1990). For example, infection of the motor division of the facial nerve may result in Bell's palsy. During the course of the varicella infection, the virus is thought to enter the sensory axons and to be transported to trigeminal, geniculate, and dorsal root ganglia, where it remains after the infection has subsided. The virus then lies inactive and reerupts at a later time, usually within a distinct segmental distribution. The herpes zoster eruption may be quite painful, beginning with pain and dysesthesia within the afflicted dermatome several days before the acute vesicular eruption. Normally the vesicles will begin to heal within a week, and the pain and dysesthesia will resolve within a month. Residual pain and dysesthesia are referred to as *postherpetic neuralgia.*

Two distinct populations of patients are identified as being at risk: older adults and immunosuppressed patients. The relationship between age-related changes in immune function and reemergence of the herpes zoster has not been established; it is believed that the reeruption of the dormant virus is related to changes in immune competence (Berger, Florent, & Just, 1981; Burke et al., 1982). There is a broad range in incidence of postherpetic neuralgia following herpes zoster infection (from 9% to 34%), and it is related to age differences in patient pools, and to whether patients were identified at primary-care or referral sites (Watson et al., 1991).

Facial postherpetic neuralgia most often afflicts the ophthalmic division of the trigeminal nerve. The pain is unilateral, and it is usually described as burning or aching. Pain is almost always constant, and it may be intensified by noxious or nonnoxious (light touch) stimulation. After healing of the acute phase, pigmental changes and scarring are noted within the afflicted area. Sensory testing within this area reveals diminished sensitivity to touch and pinprick (Fromm, 1993; Bowsher, 1993). The diagnosis of postherpetic neuralgia is firmly established by a history of herpes zoster infection, unilateral burning pain, pigmental changes, and sensory blunting in the afflicted region.

Reported effective pharmacological treatments have included the use of analgesics, tricyclic antidepressants in low dosages (Watson et al., 1982), tricyclic antidepressants with phenothiazines (Taub, 1973), and, more recently, topical agents such as capsaicin (Bernstein et al., 1989; Watson, Evans, & Watt, 1988).

Atypical Facial Pain. *Atypical facial pain* refers to a painful condition of the oral-facial complex marked by either unilateral or bilateral presentation of pain characterized as throbbing, boring, aching, pulling, or burning (Blasberg, Remick, Conklin, & Keller, 1984). The pain is usually not elicited or modified by peripheral stimulation. *Atypical facial pain* describes a clinical condition of pain complaints in the absence of objective signs or diagnostic tests. The term was discarded by the International Association for the Study of Pain Subcommittee on Taxonomy (Merskey, 1986) because it did not describe a definite syndrome but was used by many writers to describe a variety of oral and oral-facial painful conditions, including atypical facial neuralgia (Frazier & Russell, 1924), phantom tooth pain (Marbach, Hubrock, Holn, & Segal, 1982), syndrome of oral complaints (Lowenthal & Pisanti, 1978), and atypical odontalgia (Brooke, 1980; Rees & Harris, 1979). The patient population is predominantly female, and the reported age range is very broad: 20–80 years. The mean ages of the patients' categories varies from the fourth to the fifth decades.

In the absence of objective diagnostic findings, several reports have considered atypical facial pain a psychiatric disorder (Blasberg et al., 1984; Sharav, 1989), most likely related to depression. Other reports have suggested a vascular etiology (Rees & Harris, 1979) and serum iron deficiency (Brooke & Seganski, 1977).

Age Differences in Pain Perception

It is often asserted that elderly persons have less pain acuity than younger adults. This was described by Chritchley (1931), who noted that the elderly may tolerate minor surgical procedures and even dental extractions with little or no discomfort. More recently, it has been observed that older adults can endure skin biopsy (shave biopsy) with virtually no pain (Klingman & Balin, 1989). These findings are consistent with clinical observations of reduced and atypical presentation of pain as a symptom in the older adult. For example, silent (painless) acute myocardial infarctions occur more frequently in older adults, and decreased pain perception is implicated in why burns tend to be more frequent and worse in older than in younger adults (Linn, 1980). A problem, however, is that the literature on age differences in pain perception is not clear as to whether sensitivity to painful stimuli differs in younger versus older, healthy adults.

Experimental pain studies conducted in the controlled environment of the laboratory provide evidence for a decrease in pain sensitivity, an increase in pain sensitivity, and no differences in pain sensitivity in older compared to younger adults. Thus, there is literature to support any point of view. All pains are not equivalent, and aging may influence them differently. Different types of experimental pain, acute pain from procedures or surgery, and chronic pain vary considerably in both quantity and quality. The importance of this does not always appear to be recognized.

Age Differences in Experimental Pain. Tables 15-3 to 15-5 summarize much of the literature on age differences in experimental pain. It has been suggested that the differences in outcome among these studies are due, in large part, to methodological differences between the studies (Harkins & Warner, 1980; Harkins, 1988; Harkins & Price, 1992; Harkins, Kwentus, & Price, 1990). For example, the studies employing radiant heat pain that do not show age effects appear to involve specific instructions to report the "pricking" pain threshold that is characteristic of A-delta-mediated nociceptive sensations. Those studies which show the elderly to have a higher threshold to radiant heat stimulation of the skin seem to instruct the subject to simply report "pain." The difference in instructions between these two conditions, combined with current knowledge of A-delta- and C-fiber-mediated nociceptive sensations from skin suggests that future studies can more precisely define the source of the differences in investigational outcomes. Which effects, if any, are due to peripheral changes in skin, receptor, and transduction mechanisms and which are due to instruction, cohort, or secular differences in definition of "pain" are answerable questions.

Acute Pain. The most commonly studied example of acute pain outside the laboratory is pain that accompanies clinical procedures (e.g., pain from injection and drawing blood and pain from minor surgical procedures). These have been extensively studied in neonates, infants, children, and adolescents and include various age-appropriate dependent measures of pain associated with procedures such as heel prick in infants, allergy shots in children, and third-molar extractions in young adults (Bush & Harkins, 1992). To our knowledge, there has been no systematic research involving age differences in sensitivity to procedural pain in younger versus older adults.

There is evidence that there is a reduction in usage of analgesics for acute postsurgical pain in older compared to younger adults (Melzack, Abbott, Zackon, Mulder, & Davis, 1987). These studies, however, appear to confound expectations concerning age differences in pain sensitivity (i.e., less sensitivity in the older patient) and concerns about age differences in pharmacokinetics and pharmacodynamics. One study, for example, reports reduced use of analgesics in the older postsurgical patient but suggests

Table 15-3. Laboratory Studies of the Effect of Age on Psychophysical Indices of Pain Sensitivity: Thermal Stimuli[a]

Source	Psychophysical end points and findings
	Radiant heat
Schumaker et al., 1940	Sensory—thresholds No age effects
Hardy et al., 1943	Sensory—thresholds No age effects
Chapman and Jones, 1944	Sensory—thresholds higher in elderly Reaction—thresholds higher in elderly
Chapman and Jones, 1944	Sensory—thresholds higher in elderly Reaction—thresholds higher in elderly
Birren et al., 1950	Pain sensory—thresholds No age effects Pain reaction—thresholds No age effects
Sherman and Robillard, 1964a,b	Sensory—thresholds higher in elderly Reaction—thresholds higher in elderly
Procacci et al., 1970	Sensory—thresholds higher in elderly
Clark and Mehl, 1971	Sensory—thresholds higher in 55-year-olds compared to younger adults
	Contact heat
Kenshalo, 1986	Sensory—thresholds No age effects
Harkins et al., 1986	Magnitude matching Slight age effects
	Cold pressor
Walsh et al., 1989	Tolerance (time) Males: Lower with increasing age Females: Minimal increase with increasing age

[a]From Harkins et al. (1992), as modified from Harkins and Warner (1980).

this is due to expectations on the part of staff that the elderly feel less pain than younger patients (Melzack et al., 1987). Such a finding suggests a need for systematic attention to actual age-related differences in pain sensitivity versus expectations on the part of both clinical staff and patients.

Another manifestation of acute patient is referred pain. While referred pain is poorly understood, in the review below there is substantial evidence that a significant percentage of the population may be relatively insensitive to some forms of acute referred pain.

Acute Pain as a Symptom. Acute pain is frequently defined in terms of its warning value: it warns of impending or actual tissue damage. Therefore, acute pain has survival value and calls attention to potential or actual threats to bodily integrity. Failures in the signaling capacity of pain in its acute form, or changes in how acute pain presents as a symptom in the older adult, may lead to errors in diagnosis, lack of motivation to seek treatment, or delays in diagnosis.

Table 15-4. Laboratory Studies of the Effect of Age on Psychophysical Indices of Pain Sensitivity: Electrical Shock[a]

Source	Psychophysical end points and findings
	Cutaneous
Collins and Stone, 1966	Sensory—thresholds lower in elderly
	Tolerance—lower in elderly
Tucker et al., 1989	Sensory—thresholds higher in elderly
Evans et al., 1992	Sensory—thresholds
	No age effect in nondiabetics; old diabetics higher thresholds than younger diabetics
	Tooth
Mumford, 1965	Sensory—thresholds
	No age effects
Mumford, 1968	Sensory—thresholds
	No age effects
Harkins and Chapman, 1976	Sensory—thresholds
	No age effects
	Discrimination accuracy—lower in elderly
	Response bias (criteria)
	Age effects: Variable
Harkins and Chapman, 1977	Sensory—thresholds
	No age effects
	Discrmination accuracy—lower in elderly
	Response bias (criteria)
	Age effects: Variable

[a]From Harkins et al (1992), as modified from Harkins and Warner (1980).

The elderly, particularly the oldest-old, are at risk for atypical pain presentation as a symptom of acute disease. This occurs, for example, in silent myocardial infarctions (Applegate, Graves, Collins, Zwaag, & Akins, 1984; MacDonald, Baillie, Williams, & Ballantyne, 1983; Miller et al., 1990; Pathy, 1967) and absence of pain with peptic ulcer (Clinch, Banerjee, & Ostick, 1984; Coleman & Denham, 1980). Silent myocardial infarct (MI) occurs more frequently in elderly (30%) than in younger patients (23%) (MacDonald et al., 1983; Montague et al., 1990). Severe acute pain consequent to MI develops

Table 15.5 Laboratory Studies of the Effect of Age on Psychophysical Indices of Pain Sensitivity: Pressure[a]

Source	Psychophysical end points and findings
Woodrow et al., 1972	Tolerance—lower in elderly
Jensen et al., 1992	Muscle tenderness and pressure pain to age 65.
	Sensory—thresholds higher in elderly

[a]From Harkins et al. (1992), as modified from Harkins and Warner (1980).

when sufficient levels of afferent impulses are reached and when an appropriate activation of central ascending pathways has been established (Hammermeister & Bonica, 1990; Harkins et al., 1990). In patients with silent MI, such levels are apparently not reached, perhaps because of insufficient stimulation by the myocardium or decreased capacity for cephalad transmission, or for other unknown pathophysiological reasons (Harkins et al., 1990). These age differences in presentation of pain as a symptom have been cited as evidence of the decline in pain sensitivity in the elderly. Nevertheless, the relative increase in incidence and prevalence of angina in older adults (Harkins et al., 1990; Harkins & Price, 1992) suggests that a large number of old individuals maintain physiological processes subserving referred-pain associated with ischemia of the myocardium.

Cardiovascular stress testing suggests that suppression of the S-T segment, without pain, occurs relatively frequently in young adults (Glazier, Vrolix, Kesteloot, & Piessens, 1991). Thus, frequency of silent MI in different age groups, particularly when the elderly are from a "special" population (e.g., nursing-home residents), is not compelling evidence for age changes in pain perception *per se*.

It is probably unwise to consider age-related increases in silent MIs or exertional ischemia as functional losses resulting from the aging process. Rather, until further evidence indicates otherwise, atypical presentation of pain in the elderly should be considered a reflection of manifest or latent chronic disease. The critical issues with regard to age differences in acute deep or referred pain have been articulated by Ambepitiya, Iyengar, and Roberts (1993): (1) How can anginal pain (and deep or referred pains) be measured? (2) What are the clinical implications of impaired perception of such pains? (3) What are the mechanisms involved?

It is likely that atypical disease presentation such as silent MIs and exertional ischemia do not reflect a generalized age-dependent hyposensitivity to pain. As yet, no studies have systematically evaluated atypical pain as a symptom in relation to superficial pain (particularly experimental pain; see Tables 15-3 to 15-5). Such studies are needed before concluding that increased age results in a generalized hyposensitivity to pain.

Chronic Pain. Studies to date that have evaluated chronic pain in younger and older individuals find more similarities than differences (Tait, Chibnall, & Margilis, 1990; Sorkin, Rudy, Hanlon, Turk, & Stieg, 1990; Middaugh et al., 1991). Sorkin et al. (1990) conclude that there is no support from their studies to suggest "that older age should be viewed as a contraindication of multidisciplinary pain management despite negative [age] stereotypes and greater physical pathology" in older compared to young pain patients (p. 67).

Middaugh et al. (1991) present evidence that older and younger chronic pain patients are indeed quite similar. Patients' responses to a multidisciplinary chronic pain rehabilitation program were evaluated. At baseline, multiple indices related to pain were assessed, including ratings of pain intensity, health care utilization, activity tolerance, medication usage, somatization, depression, and anxiety. At post-treatment follow-up (approximately one year), the older group had benefitted as much as or more than the younger group on most of the responses assessed at entry into the study. Similar positive treatment results based on cognitive-behavioral intervention in older chronic pain patients have been reported (Puder, 1988).

Psychophysical studies indicate that the sensory and immediate unpleasantness of chronic pain were quite similar in younger and older adults attending a chronic pain diagnostic and treatment center (Harkins & Price, 1992). Nevertheless, the elderly are grossly underrepresented at these clinics, particularly the oldest-old and the frailest (Harkins & Price, 1992).

Helme, Katz, Neufeld, Lachal, and Carron (1989) described a multidisciplinary pain management clinic specifically directed to the geriatric population that was established in 1986 in Melbourne, Australia. Based on a review of their first 100 cases, they reported a 50% improvement in their elderly pain patients. Helme et al. (1989) concluded:

> The recognition of multiple pathology influences, difficult management decisions, the particular limitations and side-effects of drugs used in this age group, and the need to consider the contribution of home, social and family factors in the management plan make the pain clinic for the elderly a particularly useful recourse for the practicing physician. (p. 30)

It is clear that there is a great need worldwide for the establishment of geriatric pain clinics.

The oldest segments of the population are increasing the most, and they have the greatest risk of chronic health problems associated with significant pain and suffering. The notable absence of oldest adults in the clinics best equipped to reduce unnecessary pain and suffering reflects a number of prejudices and myths. These include acceptance of pain by the older individual. The myth that pain is a normal consequence of growing older is a powerful force. The health care delivery system suffers from varying degrees of frank ageism and ignorance resulting in a referral bias against the older adult. In fact, there is no convincing evidence that age *per se* is a factor in treatment outcome for the oldest of patients with pain (e.g., Sorkin et al., 1990).

TREATMENT OF ORAL-FACIAL PAIN IN THE ELDERLY

The principles for treatment of oral-facial pain in the elderly do not differ from those established for younger persons. The approach to management is more complicated in older persons due to the presence of multiple medical conditions, the treatment of oral and systemic diseases, and numerous psychosocial, behavioral, and financial limitations. The correct treatment for oral-facial pain depends on the accurate establishment of a diagnosis in any person, regardless of age. It is beyond the scope of this chapter to detail the comprehensive treatment of oral-facial pain in the elderly. Instead, a brief overview is provided, from intraoral to facial to systemic sources of pain, and several papers are referenced which can further assist the clinician.

The range of diagnostic and therapeutic options available to the clinician for oral problems is the same regardless of patient age, but the therapeutic approach and the actual procedures employed in delivering the care vary according to patient characteristics (Berkey & Shay, 1992; Berkey & Ettinger, 1991). Intraoral pain in the elderly can arise from the teeth, periodontium, oral mucosa, and bone (see above). Dental caries should be restored with permanent filling materials, unless the tooth is deemed nonrestorable and should be extracted. If the caries has extended into the nerve chamber, then endodontic therapy should be initiated or the tooth extracted. As with other dental procedures, the medical status of the patient must be considered prior to performing dental-alveolar surgery (Gilbert & Dolwick, 1992). Root sensitivity due to gingival recession responds to toothpastes with desensitization formulations, as well as fluoride treatments provided by the dentist.

Periodontal pain usually arises from an acute inflammatory process involving the gingiva, periodontal ligament, and supporting alveolar bone, and acute problems need to be addressed to prevent the development of a septicemia, bacteremia, or cellulitis. Periodontal abscesses should be curetted and/or incised and drained, in order to remove the source of the infection. If available, culture and sensitivity tests should be performed to assist in the diagnosis and treatment. Anaerobic bacteria, such as *Porphyromonas*, *Prevotella*, and *Treponema* (e.g., Ellen 1992), have frequently been implicated in periodontal infections, and therefore, appropriate antibiotic therapy (e.g., tetracycline, metronidazole, clindamycin) and/or oral rinses can be initiated in addition to local surgical measures (Ship & Crow, 1994). Antibiotics should always be considered for acute periodontal as well as caries-related abscesses in patients with multiple medical problems and in immunocompromised adults.

Oral mucosal pain may be due to oral problems (e.g., trauma, recurrent aphthous ulcer, denture sore, contact allergen), an oral manifestation of a vesiculobullous disorder (e.g., lichen planus, pemphigus vulgaris), salivary gland hypofunction, a systemic disease (e.g., blood dyscrasia, diabetes, or nutritional deficiency), or idiopathic burning-mouth syndrome. Candidiasis is a frequent cause of intraoral mucosal pain in the elderly and responds well to oral as well as systemic antifungal drugs (Peterson, 1992). If the patient is wearing a denture, which is a source of *Candida*, it should be removed and soaked daily in an antifungal or 0.12% chlorhexidine solution. Contact allergens from denture materials, foods, and dental restorative materials can cause mucosal changes and pain. Treatment can be directed toward removing the allergen; if not successful, the patient can be referred to an allergist for specific allergy testing. Oral mucosal problems that do not have an obvious etiology and do not resolve spontaneously should be re-examined within two to three weeks. If there has been no healing, and a diagnosis has not been made, an incisional or excisional biopsy is recommended to rule out the possibility of a vesiculobullous disease (Beck & Watkins, 1992) or a precancerous or cancerous lesion (Silverman, 1992).

Bone pain may arise from infections (dental-periodontal or intraosseous), trauma, pathological conditions, or excessive bone resorption (Gilbert & Dolwick, 1992). The source of infections must be identified and immediately treated, especially in immunocompromised patients, and in individuals who have received head and neck irradiation. Osseous lesions must be closely observed and biopsied, if necessary, to provide a diagnosis. Dentate and edentate adults who have received head and neck irradiation for the treatment of cancer are particularly prone to developing osteoradionecrosis (Peterson & D'Ambrosio, 1994) and therefore must be followed closely for many years.

The treatment of burning-mouth syndrome is based on the etiology of the burning and painful sensations. Since there are multiple etiological factors of the disease (see above), careful attention needs to be directed first to the diagnostic work-up before instituting therapy. If local factors are the cause (e.g., candidiasis infection, periodontal disease, denture trauma, salivary gland hypofunction, contact allergy), then appropriate treatment should be instituted.

Systemic disorders (e.g., iron, zinc, folic acid, vitamin B complex deficiencies; diabetes) can cause intraoral pain and burning-mouth syndrome and should be treated with replacement therapy, or patients should be referred to a physician for necessary treatment. Menopause has been implicated as a potential cause of burning-mouth pains, yet clinical evidence does not favor a direct hormonal effect on the oral mucosa (Tourne & Fricton, 1992). While hormone replacement therapy has been suggested for postmenopausal females with burning-mouth pains, it is efficacious only in some women and should be used judiciously (Forabosco et al., 1992). Psychogenic factors can be associated with burning-mouth syndrome. Anxiety and depression are associated with the condition (Lamey & Lamb, 1989), and therefore, consideration should be given to interventional treatment for these factors. The use of tricyclic antidepressants and anxiolytics has been suggested to treat burning-mouth syndrome when no etiology can be identified, and symptom improvement has been observed (Grushka & Sessle, 1991; Ship et al., 1995a).

Salivary gland hypofunction may be due to multiple medications (Sreebny & Schwartz, 1986), numerous medical problems, head and neck irradiation, and certain autoimmune exocrinopathies such as Sjögren's syndrome (Atkinson & Fox, 1992). If dry mouth symptoms are accompanied by dry eyes and/or a systemic autoimmune condition (e.g., rheumatoid arthritis, lupus, thyroiditis, Raynaud's disease), then the diagnosis of Sjögren's syndrome should be contemplated. The treatment of salivary gland hypofunction depends on the etiology. In general, nonsugared mints, gums, and lozenges increase salivary output, as well as drugs (pilocarpine) and salivary substitutes.

Temporomandibular joint disorders and masticatory myalgia are best treated initially with conservative therapies, which include bite splints, physical therapy, nonsteroidal anti-inflammatory drugs and skeletal muscle relaxers, and behavior modification (Clark et al., 1995). Consultation with numerous health care providers is frequently warranted to effectively treat this multifactorial disease. As with other oral and nonoral pain conditions, treatment success depends on a methodical diagnostic approach.

Several painful facial conditions are caused by neurological diseases, including trigeminal neuralgia (tic douloureux) and postherpetic neuralgia. The severe pain in trigeminal neuralgia is elicited by stimulation of a trigger point in the absence of neurological deficits and responds to anticonvulsant medications (phenytoin, carbamazepine, baclofen, clonazepam) (Zakrzewska & Patsalos, 1992). Patients who become refractory to medications may be candidates for neurosurgical intervention, including microvascular decompression and radiofrequency or glycerol gangliolysis and rhizotomy (Heft, 1992). For postherpetic neuralgia, several pharmacological approaches have been recommended: analgesics, tricyclic antidepressants in low dosages, tricyclic antidepressants with phenothiazines, and topical agents such as capsaicin (Bernstein et al., 1989; Watson et al., 1988).

Finally, there are situations where the cause of oral-facial pain in an older person cannot be identified, despite numerous evaluations by many health care specialists. In this event, successful coping strategies may be the only way to help the patient live with his or her pain. Patients who believe that they can control their pain, who avoid catastrophizing about their condition, and who believe they are not severely disabled appear to function better than those who do not (Jensen, Turner, Romeno, & Karoly, 1991). Multidisciplinary care involving primary health care providers, psychiatrists and psychologists, behavior specialists, and counselors may be necessary to help these individuals cope with their potentially disabling pain.

REFERENCES

Ambepitiya, G. B., Iyengar, E. N., & Roberts, M. E. (1993). Review: Silent exertional myocardial ischaemia and perception of angina in elderly people. *Age and Aging*, *22*, 302–307.

Applegate, W. B., Graves, S., Collins, T., Zwaag, R. V., & Akins, D. (1984). Acute myocardial infarction in elderly patients. *Southern Medical Journal*, *77*, 1127–1129.

Atkinson, J. C., & Fox, P. C. (1992). Salivary gland dysfunction. *Clinics in Geriatric Medicine*, *8*, 499–512.

Basker, R. M., Sturdee, D. W., & Davenport, J. C. (1978). Patients with burning mouths. A clinical investigation of causative factors, including the climacteric and diabetes. *British Dental Journal*, *145*, 9–16.

Beck, J. D., & Watkins, C. (1992). Epidemiology of nondental oral disease in the elderly. *Clinics in Geriatric Medicine*, *8*, 461–482.

Berger, R., Florent, G., & Just, M. (1981). Decrease of the lympho-proliferative response to varicella-zoster virus antigen in the aged. *Infections and Immunology*, *32*, 24–27.

Berkey, D. B., & Ettinger, R. L. (1991). Oral assessment of the older adult. In A. Papas, L. Niessen, & H. Chauncey (Eds.), *Geriatric dentistry: Aging and oral health* (pp. 105–125). St. Louis: Mosby.

Berkey, D. B., & Shay, K. (1992). General dental care for the elderly. *Clinics in Geriatric Medicine*, *8*, 579–597.

Bernstein, J. E., Korman, N. J., Bickers, D. R., Dahl, M. V., & Millikan, L. E. (1989). Topical capsaicin in chronic postherpetic neuralgia. *Journal of the American Academy of Dermatology*, *21*, 265–270.

Birren, J. E., Shapiro, H. B., & Miller, J. H. (1950). The effect of salicylate upon pain sensitivity. *Journal of Pharmacology and Experimental Therapeutics*, *100*, 67–71.

Blasberg, B., Remick, R. A., Conklin, R., & Keller, F. D. (1984). Atypical facial pain in the elderly. *Gerodontology*, *3*, 77.

Bowsher, D. (1993). Sensory change in postherpetic neuralgia. In C. P. N. Watson (Ed.), *Herpes zoster and postherpetic neuralgia* (pp. 97–107). Amsterdam: Elsevier.

Brisman, R. (1987). Trigeminal neuralgia and multiple sclerosis. *Archives of Neurology*, *44*, 379–381.

Brooke, R. I. (1980). Atypical odontalgia. *Oral Surgery*, *49*, 196–199.

Brooke, R. I., & Seganski, D. P. (1977). Aetiology and investigation of the sore mouth. *Journal of the Canadian Dental Association*, *10*, 504–506.

Burke, B. L., Steele, R. W., Beard, O. W., Wood, J. S., Cain, T. D., & Marmer, D. J. (1982). Immune responses to varicella-zoster in the aged. *Archives of Internal Medicine*, *142*, 291–293.

Burt, B. A. (1994). Periodontitis and aging: Reviewing recent evidence. *Journal of the American Dental Association*, *125*, 273–279.

Bush, J. P., & Harkins, S. W. (1992). *Children in pain: Clinical and research issues from a developmental perspective*. New York: Springer-Verlag.

Chapman, W. P., & Jones, C. M. (1944). Variations in cutaneous and visceral pain sensitivity in normal subjects. *Journal of Clinical Investigations*, *23*, 81–91.

Clark, G. T., Choi, J.-K., & Browne, P. A. (1995). The efficacy of physical medicine treatment, including occlusal appliances, for a population with temporomandibular disorders. In B. J. Sessle, P. S. Bryant, & R. A. Dionne (Eds.), *Temporomandibular disorders and related pain conditions* (pp. 375–397). Seattle: IASP Press.

Clark, W. C., & Mehl, L. (1971). Thermal pain: A sensory decision theory analysis of the effect of age and sex on d′, various response criteria, and 50 percent pain threshold. *Journal of Abnormal Psychology*, *78*, 202–212.

Clinch, D., Banerjee, A. K., & Ostick, G. (1984). Absence of abdominal pain in elderly patients with peptic ulcer. *Age and Aging, 13*, 120–123.

Coleman, J. A., & Denham, M. J. (1980). Perforation of peptic ulceration in the elderly. *Age and Aging, 9*, 257–261.

Collins, G., & Stone, L. A. (1966). Pain sensitivity, age and activity level in chronic schizophrenics and in normals. *British Journal of Psychiatry, 112*, 33–35.

Cooper, B., Ahlquist, M., Friedman, R. M., Loughner, B., & Heft, M. (1992). Properties of high threshold mechanoreceptors in the gingival mucosa: I. Responses to dynamic and static pressure. *Journal of Neurophysiology, 66*, 1273–1279.

Cooper, B. Y., & Sessle, B. J. (1992). Anatomy, physiology and pathophysiology of the trigeminal system and its relationship to the development and maintenance of paresthesias, dysesthesias and chronic pain. In J. Gregg & J. LaBanc (Eds.), Trigeminal nerve injury: Diagnosis and management. *Oral and Maxillofacial Surgery Clinics of North America, 4*, 297–322.

Critchley, M. (1931). The neurology of old age. *The Lancet, 1*(225), 1221–1230.

Dolwick, M. F., & Saunders, B. (1985). *TMJ internal derangement and arthrosis*. St. Louis: Mosby.

Dubner, R. (1985). Recent advances in our understanding of pain. In I. Klineberg & B. Sessle (Eds.), *Orofacial pain and neuromuscular dysfunction: Mechanisms and clinical correlates* (pp. 3–19). Oxford: Pergamon.

Dubner, R., & Bennett, G. J. (1983). Spinal and trigeminal mechanisms of nociception. *Annual Review of Neuroscience, 6*, 381–418.

Dubner, R., Sharav, Y., Gracely, R. H., & Price, D. D. (1987). Idiopathic trigeminal neuralgia: Sensory features and pain mechanisms. *Pain, 31*, 23–33.

Dworkin, S. F., Huggins, K. H., LeResche, L., Von Korff, M., Howard, J., Truelove, D., & Sommers, E. (1990). Epidemiology of signs and symptoms in temporomandibular disorders: Clinical signs in cases and controls. *Journal of the American Dental Association, 120*, 273–281.

Ellen, R. P. (1992). Considerations for physicians caring for older adults with periodontal disease. *Clinics in Geriatric Medicine, 8*, 599–616.

Evans, E. R., Rendall, M. S., Bartek, J. P., Bamisedun, O., & Giiter, M. (1992). Current perception threshold in ageing. *Age and Aging, 21*, 273–279.

Forabosco, A., Criscuolo, M., Coukos, G., Uccelli, E., Weinstein, R., Spinato, S., Botticelli, A., & Volpe, A. (1992). Efficacy of hormone replacement therapy in postmenopausal women with oral discomfort. *Oral Surgery, Oral Medicine, and Oral Pathology, 73*, 570–574.

Frazier, C. H., & Russell, E. C. (1924). Neuralgia of the face: An analysis of seven hundred and fifty-four cases with relation to pain and other sensory phenomena before and after operation. *Archives of Neurology and Psychiatry, 11*, 557–563.

Fromm, G. H. (1989). Trigeminal neuralgia and related disorders. *Neurologic Clinics, 7*, 305–319.

Fromm, G. H. (1993). Physiological rationale for the treatment of neuropathic pain. *APS Journal, 2*, 1–7.

Fromm, G. H., Graff-Radford, S., & Terrence, C. F. (1988). Does trigeminal neuralgia have a prodrome? *Neurology, 38* (Suppl. 1), 112.

Gilbert, G. H., & Dolwick, M. F. (1992). Oral and maxillofacial surgical therapy for the older adult. *Clinics in Geriatric Medicine, 8*, 617–641.

Glazier, J. J., Vrolix, M., Kesteloot, H., & Piessens, J. (1991). Silent ischemia: An update on current concepts. *Acta Cardiology, 46*, 461–469.

Grushka, M. (1987). Clinical features of burning mouth syndrome. *Oral Surgery, Oral Medicine, and Oral Pathology, 63*, 30–36.

Grushka, M., & Sessle, B. J. (1991). Burning mouth syndrome. *Dental Clinics of North America, 35*, 171–184.

Hammermeister, K. E., & Bonica, J. J. (1990). Cardiac and aortic pain. In J. J. Bonica (Ed.), *The management of pain* (2nd ed., pp. 552–559). Philadelphia: Lea & Febiger.

Hand, J. S., & Whitehill, J. M. (1986). The prevalence of oral mucosal lesions in an elderly population. *Journal of the American Dental Association, 112*, 73–76.

Hardy, J. D., Wolff, H. G., & Goodell, H. (1943). The pain threshold in man. *American Journal of Psychiatry, 99*, 744–751.

Hargreaves, K. M., Roszkowski, M. T., Jackson, D. L., Bowles, W., Richardson, J. D., & Swift, J. Q. (1995). Neuroendocrine and immune responses to injury, degeneration, and repair. In B. J. Sessle, P. S. Bryant,

& R. A. Dionne (Eds.), *Temporomandibular disorders and related pain conditions* (pp. 273–292). Seattle: IASP Press.

Harkins, S. W. (1988). Pain in the elderly. In R. Dubner, F. G. Gebhart, & M. R. Bond (Eds.), *Proceedings of the Vth World Congress on Pain* (pp. 355–357). New York: Elsevier (Biomedical Division).

Harkins, S. W., & Chapman, C. R. (1977). The perception of induced dental pain in young and elderly women. *Journal of Gerontology, 32*, 428–435.

Harkins, S. W., & Chapman, C. R. (1976). Detection and decision factors in pain perception in young and elderly men. *Pain, 2*, 253–264.

Harkins, S. W., & Price, D. D. (1992). Assessment of pain in the elderly. In D. C. Turk & R. Melzack (Eds.), *Handbook of pain assessment* (pp. 315–331). New York: Guilford Press.

Harkins, S. W., Kwentus, J., & Price, D. D. (1990). Pain and suffering in the elderly. In J. J. Bonica (Ed.), *Management of Pain* (2nd ed., pp. 552–559). Philadelphia: Lea & Febiger.

Harkins, S. W., Price, D. D., & Martelli, M. (1986). Effects of age on pain perception: Thermonociception. *Journal of Gerontology, 41*, 58–63.

Heft, M. W. (1984). Prevalence of TMJ signs and symptoms in the elderly. *Gerodontology, 3*, 125–130.

Heft, M. W. (1992). Orofacial pain. *Clinics in Geriatric Medicine, 8*, 557–568.

Helme, R. D., Katz, B., Neufeld, S., Lachal, J., & Carron, H. T. (1989). The establishment of a geriatric pain clinic: A preliminary report of the first 100 patients. *Australian Journal of Aging, 8*, 27–30.

Hu, J. W., & Sessle, B. J. (1988). Properties of functionally identified nociceptive facial primary afferents and presynaptic excitability changes induced in their brainstem endings by raphe and orofacial stimuli in cats. *Experimental Neurology, 101*, 385–399.

James, F. R., Large, R. G., Bushnell, J. A., & Wells, J. E. (1991). Epidemiology of pain in New Zealand. *Pain, 44*, 279–283.

Jensen, M. P., Turner, J. A., Romano, J. M., & Karoly, P. (1991). Coping with chronic pain: A critical review of the literature. *Pain, 47*, 249–283.

Jensen, R., Rasmussen, B. K., Pedersen, B., Lous, I., & Olesen, J. (1992). Cephalic muscle tenderness and pressure pain threshold in a general population. *Pain, 48*, 197–203.

Kenshalo, D. R., Sr. (1986). Somesthetic sensitivity in young and elderly humans. *Journal of Gerontology, 41*, 732–742.

Kleinman, D. V., Swango, P. A., & Niessen, L. C. (1991). Epidemiologic studies of oral mucosal conditions—methodological issues. *Community Dentistry Oral Epidemiology, 19*, 129–140.

Klingman, A. M., & Balin, A. K. (1989). Aging of human skin. In A. K. Balin & A. M. Klingman (Eds.), *Aging and the skin* (pp. 1–42). New York: Raven Press.

Koch, H. (1986). The management of chronic pain in office-based ambulatory care. National Ambulatory Medical Care Survey. *Advance Data for Vital and Health Statistics*, No. 123, DHHS Publication No. (PHS) 86-1250, Public Health Service, Hyattsville, MD.

Kugelberg, E., & Lindblom, U. (1959). The mechanism of pain in trigeminal neuralgia. *Journal of Neurology, Neurosurgery and Psychiatry, 22*, 36–43.

Lamey, P. J., & Lamb, A. B. (1988). Prospective study of aetiological factors in burning mouth syndrome. *British Medical Journal, 296*, 1243–1246.

Lamey, P. J., & Lamb, A. B. (1989). The usefulness of the HAD scale in assessing anxiety and depression in patients with burning mouth syndrome. Oral Surgery, Oral Medicine, and Oral Pathology, *67*, 390–392.

Laskin, D. M., & Greene, C. S. (1990). Diagnostic methods for temporomandibular disorders: What we have learned in two decades. *Anesthesia Progress, 37*, 66–71.

Linn, B. S. (1980). Age differences in the severity and outcome of burns. *Journal of the American Geriatric Society, 28*, 118–130.

Lipton, J. A., Ship, J. A., & Larach-Robinson, D. (1993). Estimated prevalence and distribution of reported orofacial pain in the United States. *Journal of the American Dental Association, 124*, 115–121.

Locker, D., & Grushka, M. (1987a). The impact of dental and facial pain. *Journal of Dental Research, 66*, 1414–1417.

Locker, D., & Grushka, M. (1987b). The prevalence of oral and facial pain and discomfort: Preliminary results of a mail survey. *Community Dentistry Oral Epidemiology, 15*, 169–172.

Loeser, J. D. (1986). Herpes zoster and postherpetic neuralgia. *Pain, 25*, 149–164.

Lowenthal, U., & Pisanti, S. (1978). The syndrome of oral complaints: Etiology and therapy. *Oral Surgery, 46*, 2–6.

MacDonald, J. B., Baillie, J., Williams, B. O., & Ballantyne, D. (1983). Coronary care in the elderly. *Age and Aging, 12*, 17–20.
Marbach, J. J., Hubrock, J., Hohn, C., & Segal, A. G. (1982). Incidence of phantom tooth pain: An atypical facial neuralgia. *Oral Surgery, 53*, 190–193.
Melzack, R., Abbott, F. V., Zackon, W., Mulder, D. S., & Davis, M. W. L. (1987). Pain on a surgical ward: A survey of the duration on intensity of pain and the effectiveness of medication. *Pain, 29*, 67–72.
Merskey, H. (Ed.) (1986). Classification of chronic pain: Descriptions of chronic pain syndromes and definitions of pain terms. *Pain* (Suppl. 3), pp. S1–S226.
Middaugh, S. J., Woods, S. E., Kee, W. G., Harden, N., & Peters, J. R. (1991). Biofeedback-assisted relaxation training for the aging chronic pain patient. *Biofeedback and Self-Regulation, 16*, 361–377.
Miller, A. J., Brunelle, J. A., Carlos, J. P., Brown, L. J., & Loe, H. (1987). *Oral health of United States adults: 1985–1986*. NIH Publication No. 87-2868. National Institutes of Health, Public Health Service, Department of Health and Human Services.
Miller, P. F., Sheps, D. S., Bragdon, E. E., Herbst, M. C., Dalton, J. L., Hinderliter, A. L., Hoch, G. G., Maizner, W., & Eketund, L. G. (1990). Aging and pain perception in ischemic heart disease. *American Heart Journal, 120*, 22–30.
Montague, T., Wong, R., Crowell, R., Bay, K., Marshall, D., Tymchak, W., Teo, K., & Davies, N. (1990). Acute myocardial infarction: Contemporary risk and management in older versus younger patients. *Canadian Journal of Cardiology, 6*, 241–246.
Mumford, J. M. (1965). Pain perception threshold and adaptation of normal human teeth. *Archives of Oral Biology, 10*, 957–968.
Mumford, J. M. (1968). Pain perception in man on electrically stimulating the teeth. In A. Soulairac, J. Cahn, & J. Charpentier (Eds.), *Pain* (pp. 224–229). London: Academic Press.
Mumford, J. M. (1982). *Orofacial pain: Aetiology, diagnosis and treatment*. New York: Churchill Livingstone.
Pathy, M. S. (1967). Clinical presentation of myocardial infarction in the elderly. *British Heart Journal, 29*, 190–199.
Peterson, D. E. (1992). Oral candidiasis. *Clinics in Geriatric Medicine, 8*, 513–528.
Peterson, D. E., & D'Ambrosio, J. A. (1994). Nonsurgical management of head and neck cancer patients. *Dental Clinics of North America, 38*, 425–446.
Procacci, P., Bozza, G., Buzzelli, G., & Della Corte, M. (1970). The cutaneous pricking pain threshold in old age. *Gerontology Clinics, 12*, 213–218.
Puder, R. S. (1988). Age analysis of cognitive-behavioral group therapy for chronic pain outpatients. *Psychology and Aging, 3*, 204–207.
Rees, R. T., & Harris, M. (1979). Atypical odontalgia. *British Journal of Oral Surgery, 16*, 212–218.
Schumacher, G. A., Goodell, H., Hardy, J. D., & Wolff, H. G. (1940). Uniformity of the pain threshold in man. *Science, 92*, 110–112.
Sharav, Y. (1989). Orofacial pain. In P. D. Wall & R. Melzack (Eds.), *Textbook of pain* (pp. 441–454). New York: Churchill Livingstone.
Sharav, Y., Leviner, E., Tzukert, A., & McGrath, P. A. (1984). The spatial distribution, intensity and unpleasantness of acute dental pain. *Pain, 20*, 363–370.
Sherman, E. D., & Robillard, E. (1964a). Sensitivity to pain in relationship to age. In P. F. Hansen (Ed.), *Age with a future: Proceedings of the Sixth International Congress of Gerontology, Copenhagen, 1963* (pp. 325–333). Philadelphia: F. A. Davis.
Sherman, E. D., & Robillard, E. (1964b). Sensitivity to pain in relationship to age. *Journal of the American Geriatrics Society, 12*, 1037–1044.
Ship, J. A., & Baum, B. J. (1990). Is reduced salivary flow normal in old people? *The Lancet, 336*, 1507.
Ship, J. A., & Crow, H. C. (1994). Diseases of periodontal tissues in the elderly: Description, epidemiology, aetiology and drug therapy. *Drugs and Aging, 5*, 346–357.
Ship, J. A., Grushka, M., Lipton, J., Mott, A., Sessle, B., & Dionne, R. (1995a). An update on burning mouth syndrome. *Journal of the American Dental Association, 126*, 842–853.
Ship, J. A., Nolan, N., & Puckett, S. (1995b). Longitudinal analysis of parotid and submandibular salivary flow rates in healthy, different aged adults. *Journals of Gerontology: Medical Science, 50A*, M235–M289.
Silverman, S., Jr. (1992). Precancerous lesions and oral cancer in the elderly. *Clinics in Geriatric Medicine, 8*, 529–542.

Sorkin, B. A., Rudy, T. E., Hanlon, R. B., Turk, D. C., & Stieg, R. L. (1990). Chronic pain in old and young patients: Differences appear less important than similarities. *Journal of Gerontology*, *45*, 64–68.

Sreebny, L. M., & Schwartz, S. S. (1986). A reference guide to drugs and dry mouth. *Gerodontology*, *5*, 75–99.

Sternbach, R. A. (1986a). Pain and "hassles" in the United States: Findings of the Nuprin Pain Report. *Pain*, *27*, 69–80.

Sternbach, R. A. (1986b). Survey of pain in the United States: The Nuprin Pain Report. *Clinical Journal of Pain*, *2*, 49–53.

Tait, R. C., Chibnall, J. T., & Margilis, R. B. (1990). Pain extent: Relations with psychological state, pain severity, pain history and disability. *Pain*, *41*, 295–301.

Taub, A. (1973). Relief of postherpetic neuralgia with psychotropic drugs. *Journal of Neurosurgery*, *39*, 235–239.

Taylor, H., & Curran, N. M. (1985). *The Nuprin Pain Report*. New York: Louis Harris.

Tourne, L. P. M., & Fricton, J. R. (1992). Burning mouth syndrome: Critical review and proposed clinical management. *Oral Surgery, Oral Medicine, and Oral Pathology*, *74*, 158–167.

Tucker, M. A., Andrew, M. F., Ogle, S. J., & Davison, J. G. (1989). Age associated change in pain threshold measured by transcutaneous neuronal electrical stimulation. *Age and Aging*, *18*, 241–246.

Von Korff, M., Dworkin, S. F., LeResche, L., & Kruger, A. (1988a). An epidemiologic comparison of pain complaints. *Pain*, *32*, 173–183.

Von Korff, M., Dworkin, S. F., LeResche, L., & Kruger, A. (1988b). Epidemiology of temporomandibular disorders: 2. TMD pain compared to other common pain sites. In R. Dubner, G. F. Gebhart, & M. R. Bond (Eds.), *Proceedings of the Vth World Congress on Pain* (pp. 506–511). New York: Elsevier.

Von Korff, M., Wagner, E. H., Dworkin, S. F., & Saunders, K. W. (1991). Chronic pain and use of ambulatory health care. *Psychosomatic Medicine*, *53*, 61–79.

Walsh, N. E., Schoenfeld, L., Ramamurthy, S., & Hoffman, J. (1989). Normative model for cold pressor test. *American Journal of Physical and Medical Rehabilitation*, *68*, 6–11.

Watson, C. P. N. (1990). Postherpetic neuralgia: Clinical features and treatment. In H. L. Fields (Ed.), *Pain syndromes in neurology* (pp. 223–228). London: Butterworths.

Watson, C. P. N., Evans, R. J., Reed, K., Merskey, H., Goldsmith, L., & Warsh, J. (1982). Amitriptyline versus placebo in postherpetic neuralgia. *Neurology*, *32*, 671–673.

Watson, C. P. N., Evans, R. J., & Watt, V. R. (1988). Postherpetic neuralgia and topical capsaicin. *Pain*, *33*, 333–340.

Watson, C. P. N., Watt, V. R., Chipman, M., Birkett, N., & Evans, R. J. (1991). The prognosis with postherpetic neuralgia. *Pain*, *46*, 195–199.

Woodrow, K. M., Friedman, G. D., Siegelaub, A. B., & Collen, M. F. (1972). Pain tolerance: Differences according to age, sex, and race. *Psychosomatic Medicine*, *34*, 548–556.

Wu, A. J., Atkinson, J. C., Fox, P. C., Baum, B. J., & Ship, J. A. (1993). Cross-sectional and longitudinal analyses of stimulated parotid salivary constituents in healthy, different-aged subjects. *Journals of Gerontology: Medical Sciences*, *48*, M219–M224.

Zakrzewska, J. M., & Patsalos, P. N. (1992). Drugs used in the management of trigeminal neuralgia. *Oral Surgery, Oral Medicine, and Oral Pathology*, *74*, 439–450.

CHAPTER 16

Exercise in Aging and Pain Control

C. ZVI FUCHS AND LEONARD D. ZAICHKOWSKY

The purpose of this chapter is to describe the use of exercise to control pain, in the prevention of disease, maintenance of good health, and the process of rehabilitation in the elderly. For purposes of this paper, elderly will be defined as 65 years and older. The research concerning the physical, psychological, and social diseases and problems in the elderly that are particularly susceptible to pain is reviewed and criticized in the context of the use of exercise as an intervention and therapeutic mode. It is important to note that people seek medical care primarily because they feel ill and are in pain, not for treatment of a specific disease. As a result, a substantial part of most treatments is to try and alleviate the pain symptoms associated with the disease. We will conclude the chapter with recommendations for implementing exercise programs for the elderly in order to promote health and reduce pain that is associate with the aging process.

BENEFITS OF EXERCISE IN THE ELDERLY

Although exercise has the potential to be the most potent method for preventing pain, and treating pain, as well as promoting overall health and fitness, to date very few authors of chapters or books on "pain" have discussed the role of exercise in pain management. A content analysis of the pain publications showed that only a few authors have mentioned the role of exercise in preventing or treating pain, and when they have, the discussions have been brief and generally devoid of research support (cf. Linchitz, 1987; Saxon, 1991).

C. ZVI FUCHS • Behavioral Medicine Program, Cambridge Hospital, Department of Psychiatry, School of Medicine, Harvard University, Cambridge, Massachusetts 02139. LEONARD D. ZAICHKOWSKY • Department of Developmental Studies and Counseling, School of Education, Boston University, Boston, Massachusetts 02215.

Handbook of Pain and Aging, edited by David I. Mostofsky and Jacob Lomranz. Plenum Press, New York, 1997.

Over the years, it has been widely accepted that, with increased age, there is a progression of deterioration of soft tissue flexibility, muscle strength, and cardiovascular conditioning, as well as an increase in postural imbalance, chronic fatigue, and mood changes (Perry, Morley & Coe, 1993; Saxon & Etten, 1978). This results in reduced motor function and often an increase in pain. Recent research suggests, however, that a great deal of this deterioration results from lack of exercise and proper diet rather than simply the passing of time (Biegel, 1984; Harris, Harris, & Harris, 1992; Perry, et al., 1993; Province et al. 1995; Saxon & Etten, 1978; Saxon & Etten, 1984; Shephard, 1987, 1993).

The recent research on aerobic strength training echoes the benefits demonstrated with aerobic training (Rogers & Evans, 1993). Muscle mass is not only vital for facilitating locomotion, it is critical for good metabolism. Having good metabolism helps the elderly deal with the common disease of diabetes. It is believed today that the inability to process sugar optimally is caused not by age but by increased fatness brought about by redistribution of body fat and physical inactivity.

In addition to research that has demonstrated unequivocally the value of exercise in slowing down the aging process, disease, and accompanying pain, there is research that shows fitness to be correlated with reduced back pain. In a prospective study by Cady, Bischoff, O'Connell, Thomas, and Allan (1979), 1,652 California fire fighters were tested for flexibility, strength, and cardiovascular endurance and the occurrence of back injuries. The results indicated that high overall fitness produced a "protective effect" against back injuries—a major health issue in all segments of the adult population. This study was not done on an elderly population; however, it seems reasonable to believe that a comprehensive exercise program will help prevent back pain in this population as well.

Although exercise, particularly the marketing of exercise and fitness, has increased in North America, the majority of the population has little to do with exercise. According to Linchitz (1987), only about 4% of adult Americans exercise sufficiently to have a positive influence on chronic pain. The elderly population (65 and over) have an even lower rate of exercise participation.

Ironically, most people associate the beginning of an exercise program with the induction, rather than elimination, of pain. However, Kilbom, Gamberale, Persson, and Annwell (1983) showed that, even though there is a close relationship between the two, pain does not reach maximal levels with total exercise exhaustion. The reasons may be several. Pain is usually measured indirectly through self-report, whereas exercise load can be measured objectively. This subjectiveness also does not enable comparisons between different individuals who might have different thresholds for pain. Some researchers (Ben-Sira, 1986) speculate that the elderly may perceive exercise-induced pain differently from younger people by delaying their pain response (Ambepitiya, Roberts, Ranjadayalan, & Tallis, 1994) or accentuating the intensity of their pain complaints (Parmelee, Katz, & Lawton, 1991).

As a matter of fact, at any age, even healthy nonexercisers who start an exercise program may experience an acute short-term pain, due to accumulation of lactic acid in the blood and the exercised muscles. A more prolonged common pain, which usually lasts 24–72 hours after exercising, is termed *delayed muscle soreness* and is associated with eccentric contractions and lack of stretching (Fox, 1979). These "pains and aches" are considered normal and should dissipate with the continuation of a supervised, graded exercise program. In cases where the pain continues, medical advice is essential, since the pain may indicate the existence of a previously undetected condition, such as inflammatory myopathies, metabolic irregularities, or ischemic diseases (Bove, 1983).

As indicated earlier, this chapter will mainly review exercise as a therapy for the most common diseases in the elderly. These diseases and conditions are almost always associated with pain, and participation in an exercise program is recommended as an adjunct therapy for the disease and/or for the alleviation of the pain only. These different exercise regimen prescriptions for the elderly are beyond the scope of this chapter. They can be found in a variety of readily available sources that match exercise regimens with certain diseases and conditions (e.g., Bender, 1992; Biegel, 1984; Herning, 1993; Kerlan, 1991; Lehr & Swanson, 1990; Saxon & Etten, 1984).

Finally, it is important to emphasize that at the beginning of an exercise program, elderly people may have different starting points from younger ones. It is essential that special measures be taken to decrease the risk of injury and pain and to optimize the benefits of the exercise program. Major factors that should be considered in order to achieve these goals include:

1. Medical examination before starting an exercise program and a follow-up routine.
2. Any exercise program should bring into consideration clumsiness and deterioration of balance, which are usually part of the aging process.
3. Shortness of tendons, decrease in strength and endurance, joint and flexibility limitations, associated with many years of inactivity.
4. Avoiding rapid progression and exercise that is too difficult, complex, or risky.
5. Making sure that adequate and comfortable exercise clothing and, especially, footwear are used.
6. Training and rehearsing procedures for emergency situations (Shephard, 1987).

EXERCISE AND PAIN CONTROL IN PHYSICAL CONDITIONS

Most of the research literature is devoted to control of pain through exercise in diseases and conditions that have clear physical manifestations, such as ischemic pain, chronic back pain, arthritic pain, and osteoporosis and hip fracture pain. However, in most studies, the sample consists of a mixed bag of young and older patients. These studies will be reviewed in a very limited way. The more direct studies, which deal specifically with the elderly (defined here as 65 years and older), will be reviewed more extensively and will be our major source for drawing conclusions and making recommendations.

Cardiovascular Diseases

Treadmill or bicycle ergometer testing in the diagnosis of cardiovascular disease is a common modality to obtain myocardial or peripheral ischemic pain threshold information. This form of stress testing provides information about the patient's current status, effect of medications, and exercise tolerance as a means for therapeutic exercise, surgery selection, and medication prescription in younger as well as in older populations (deVries et al., 1994; McCully, Halber, & Posner, 1994; Thompson, Crist, & Atterbom, 1990). It is also known that regular participation in an aerobic exercise program, in addition to lifestyle changes (e.g., diet, relaxation), can increase the aerobic power of the elderly by at least 20% over sedentary seniors (Shephard, 1993), may decrease the susceptibility to primary cardiovascular diseases in highly symptomatic patients (Ornish et al., 1990), improves rehabilitation efforts after a myocardial infarction (MI) (Dixhoorn, Duivenvoorden, Pool, & Verhage, 1990), and leads to reports of less chest pain 6–12 months after the MI (Fridlund, Hogstedt, Lidell, & Larson, 1991).

The mechanisms involved seem to incorporate the regression of atherosclerosis and myocardial stenosis and enhanced myocardial oxygen supply. Surprisingly enough, up to now, these data were primarily obtained with mixed samples, where most of the subjects were middle-aged adults. Until recently, the specific effects on the elderly (65 years and older) has been mostly speculative, since only a few studies have involved elderly subjects. One of these studies that involved elderly subjects (ages 68–77) showed improved aerobic capacity and physical performance mainly through peripheral mechanisms (Marchini, Perretti, Passeri, & Cucinotta, 1992). In addition, these researchers documented a noticeable reduction in pain complaints when comparing pre- to posttraining exercise tests. This pain reduction may also be one of the reasons for the impressive compliance in this study.

Other studies that used mixed age populations found similar results. Stern, Gorman, and Kaslow (1983) found that exercise increased work capacity, decreased fatigue, and improved psychosocial skills in 30- to 69-year-old postmyocardial infarction (MI) patients. These results were the same as those of the control group, who received counseling, except that the exercise group had less anginal pain in the 6- to 12-month follow-up.

In one of the few studies using "elderly" subjects, Kohrt et al. (1991) reported that relatively healthy subjects aged 60–71 were able to significantly increase their maximum aerobic power ($\dot{V}o_2$ max). This is important, since increased aerobic power may be a preventive factor in the control of cardiovascular pain and disease. The most interesting finding in this study is that dividing subjects by age groups (60–62, 63–66, and 67–71 years) showed no significant differences among the groups in the relative increases in their $\dot{V}o_2$ max. Kohrt and co-workers' finding indicates clearly that at least relatively healthy elderly male and female subjects respond similarly to younger adults when exercised aerobically.

It seems that the major problem in prescribing exercise to cardiac patients lies in the reluctance of their physicians to recommend exercise programs. Since about half of the hospitalized patients in the cardiac units in the United States for MI and bypass operations are in their 60s and older (Ades, Waldmann, McCann, & Weaver, 1992), it is surprising that less than half (21%) of post-MI and bypass patients, ages 62–92 years, are referred for exercise rehabilitation. These findings are alarming because the Ades et al. (1992) study demonstrates a bias that may prevent older individuals from rehabilitating themselves. Also, the reluctance to refer elderly patients to an exercise program in this study was based on psychosocial-educational factors, rather than on the primary medical condition. This finding is especially disturbing when it becomes more and more clear that the physical, as well as the psychosocial, rehabilitation of elderly cardiac patients is as significant as it is for younger populations. This issue is discussed further in our section on "Exercise and Pain Control in Psychosocial Conditions."

Rheumatoid and Osteoarthritis

Loss of muscle and bone mass affects joint function in the elderly, even in the absence of a specific disease process. *Arthritis* literally means "joint inflammation." However, the term became an umbrella for diverse joint and secondary muscular disease, the most prevalent being osteoarthritis and rheumatoid arthritis. These arthritic changes may affect the weight-bearing joints of the lower extremities, the small joints of the hands, may cause degenerative changes in the articulations of the spine, and normal vertebral disk function. These changes often lead to chronic pain, deformity, loss of function, and in some cases, mood changes, especially depression (Flynn & Wigley, 1995; Lewis, 1984; Smith, Christensen, Peck, & Ward, 1994).

Exercise programs can be designed for the reduction of joint stress, and the maintenance of strength, stability, and mobility and, therefore, may reduce pain (Flynn & Wigley, 1995). A significant number of studies have shown that patients with arthritic diseases can improve their aerobic capacity, strengthen their muscles and bones, maintain mobility and stability, reduce joint pain and alleviate depression (Fisher, Gresham, & Pendergast, 1993; Lindroth, Bauman, Barnes & McCredie, 1989; Miller & LeLieuvre, 1982; Minor & Brown, 1993; Perlman, Connell, Clark, & Robinson, 1990). The exercise programs range from aquatics, which add resistance to motion while providing general buoyancy in a warm environment, to isometric or dynamic exercise, executed in a minimal weight-bearing position.

A shortcoming of these studies is that they used mixed age samples (the range of the subjects' ages was 21–89 years), combined therapy modalities (e.g., cognitive therapy, pain management) in a variety of exercise modalities and regimens, and different measurement instruments. It might be the case that the younger subjects and specific interventions skewed the favorable results, therefore not revealing the true effect of exercise on the elderly. In fact, Minor and Stanford (1993), in a review of this literature, concluded that interventions that combined physical agents and exercise were more successful in attenuating pain and decreasing impairment than physical agents used alone. Indeed, when evaluating the findings according to age, Davis, Cortez, and Rubin (1990) showed clearly that arthritic elderly patients (ages 65–82) are different from younger ones (ages 25–63) in their ability to utilize and benefit from combined treatment approaches. It should not be surprising that, in a mixed aged group, the younger group used more therapeutic modalities, rated relaxation techniques as most beneficial, and were more positive about the program outcome.

Meyer and Hawley (1994) showed that elderly subjects (mean age 68 years) with rheumatic disease who participated in a water exercise program decreased pain and increased strength when compared to a control group that received standard care in a rheumatic clinic. However, the researchers noted that severely affected patients were underrepresented in similar water exercise programs. This observation should not be surprising, since adherence to home exercise and self-management of pain in the elderly appears to be quite low (Bradley, 1989), and only about 50% of the treating physicians advise exercise as a treatment for elderly chronic rheumatic and osteoarthritic pain. In fact, Dexter (1992) found that only 10% of the patients, who received exercise advice and instructions were actually exercising at a level that was therapeutically beneficial.

Other recent studies address the relationship between short-term exercise and pain in elderly patients with a history of arthritis. Coleman, Buchner, Cress, Chan, and de Lateur (1996) found that older men and women (ages 68 to 85) showed neither improvement nor deterioration in pain as a result of various exercise programs. In contradiction, Schilke, Johnson, Hough, and O'Dell (1996) found a significant decrease in pain and stiffness with short-term strength training in elderly subjects (mean age, 64.5; range, 59 to 74) with osteoarthritis of the knee joint.

In conclusion, based on the findings of Ettinger and Afable (1994), who reviewed a series of short-term studies with small samples of aged patients with arthritis, we agree that exercise programs seem not only to improve physical parameters, but also to decrease pain and disability. However, the lack of rigorous methodological research on exercise and pain in the elderly who suffer from rheumatic disease point out the shortcomings of this body of research. These flaws can be attributed to the absence of exercise prescription and lack of patients' adherence. While the absence of medical advice and care is surprising considering the convincing beneficial effects of exercise in various populations, the compliance problem can be expected in an elderly population where memory, perseverance, and motivation are usually less than desired. It is also worthwhile to mention that reliable data on the long-term effects of exercise intervention in arthritic diseases are completely absent (Stenstrom & Christina, 1994). Despite the positive short-term aspects of exercise, there is a remote possibility that exercise actually accelerates the underlying long-term progress of the disease (Ettinger & Afable, 1994). However, recent findings seem to refute this hypothesis. In an excellent 6-year longitudinal study, Fries, Singh, Morfeld, O'Driscoll, and Hubert (1966) showed that vigorous runners aged 53 to 75 actually decreased pain, stiffness, and cartilage degeneration, but the pain decreases were only statistically significant for women. These results are impressive and call for future replication.

Chronic Back, Hip and Knee Pain

Back pain is probably the most common complaint in the general population. It is less likely that the elderly will suffer from acute back strain. However, chronic pain associated with degenerative disk disease, localized in the cervical and/or lumbar area, and spinal stenosis, which may radiate pain to the hip, buttocks, and legs, is common in the elderly (Dougherty, 1992; Flynn & Wigley, 1995). It is also important to keep in mind that the prevalence of major depression in chronic-low-back-pain patients is about three to four times greater than in the general population (Sullivan, Reesor, Mikail, & Fisher, 1992), probably because chronic low back pain may be considered more socially acceptable than complaints of depression. Indeed, tricyclic antidepressants are widely used for the treatment of chronic pain when depression is evident (Goodkin & Gullion, 1989; Sullivan et al., 1992).

A review of the research literature on back pain and exercise showed that all studies involved mixed age groups. In a comparison of treatment for low back pain in 20- to 65-year-old patients, Turner, Clancy, McQuade, and Cardenas, (1990) found, in a follow-up study, that patients significantly improved regardless of the treatment group (aerobic exercise, behavioral therapy, or a combination of both). However, only the combined-treatment group demonstrated a decrease in pain using self-report and observer ratings. Manniche, Lundberg, Christensen, and Bentzen, (1991) found that only intensive dynamic exercise of the back extensors had significantly reduced the pain complaints of patients in a one-year follow-up study. Their patients' ages ranged from 20 to 70. Similar findings of the superiority of exercise to improve muscle strength, endurance, and mobility in a sample of patients 18–63 years old, were found by Altmaier, Lehmann, Russell, and Weinstein, (1992). Altmaier's group found a significant decrease in pain at discharge and follow-up visits using the McGill Pain Questionnaire (MFQ) and the mode and interference subscales of the West Haven-Yale Multidimensional Pain Inventory (WHYMPI). Recently, similar significant results of a decrease in reported pain and increased strength, with a mixed group of chronic-low-back-pain patients, was reported by Risch et al. (1993).

A single case study of a 75-year-old man with bilateral total knee replacement showed that exercise in combination with electromyographic (EMG) biofeedback decreased pain and improved the overall levels of health distress at posttreatment (Beckham, Keefe, Caldwell, & Brown, 1991). This last single case study demonstrated clearly that exercise prescription is age-dependent, where younger pain patients (average age 40) are favored because of the general belief that their prognosis is better and the possible complications of exercise (e.g., falls) are less. It also indicates that health care professionals conveniently prefer cautious passive exercises (e.g., heat and cold applications, massages, and electrotherapy) over more active and dynamic exercises in treating pain in the elderly. We hope that highly publicized studies, such as that by Fiatarone et al. (1990) on the benefits of high-intensity strength training in the frail elderly (nonagenarians), where only 1 subject out of 10 stopped training because of pain, will change this prevailing attitude.

Osteoporosis and Female Pain Issues

The 19th-century medical approach to female exercise reflected Victorian ideology. If the elderly female were to be allowed any exercise, it should include only slow, steady movements in order to preserve energy (Vertinsky, 1990). It is clear today that the elderly female exercise needs were dictated solely by cultural assumptions, social order, and power relationships. However, this attitude seems to prevail even today, when mounting scientific evidence support active and vigorous exercise for females in general and especially postmenopausal women. Osteoporosis seems to be the vehicle that rules the justification for regular exercise, combined with proper nutrition, in order to alleviate the pain, deformation, and fractures associated with this condition, which is common in middle-aged and especially older females.

In a preliminary study of its kind, Steege and Blumenthal (1993) showed that the painful symptoms associated with the premenstrual period, in middle-aged women, can be eased by participation in an exercise program. Their aerobic and the nonaerobic groups showed general improvement; however, the aerobically exercised group improved on more symptoms, especially depression. This study appears to be of great importance, since these women who experienced relief in symptoms may have been more likely to continue exercising and to prevent or delay the maladies of full-blown osteoporosis.

Limburg, Sinaki, Rogers, Caskey, and Pierskalla (1991) reported a measurement and an exercise instrument (BID-2000) as a therapeutic measure for chronic low back pain and osteoporosis. The BID-2000 was tested on females, 30–79 years old, and proved to be safe, valid, and reliable. This study is a good example of catering to the increased exercise needs of the growing elderly female population. Exercise such as weight training, swimming, and walking, in combination with other therapies, is recommended to prevent, slow down, and restore muscle and bone mass in this growing older population (Sardana & Mikhail, 1992). Lyles et al. (1993) showed that older women (mean age = 81.9 years) who had suffered vertebrae compression fractures due to osteoporosis were functionally more impaired in their performance and suffered from increased pain compared to controls.

The devastating effects of osteoporosis are well documented (Horowitz, Need, Morris, & Nordin, 1993; Shephard, 1987; Sykes, 1992). Preventive treatment approaches are, however, conspicuous by their absence. Theoretically, osteoporosis can be prevented, either by slowing down or by preventing the bone loss that occurs with age and eventually by preventing fractures (Block, 1992). Although there is research evidence that documents the positive role of exercise and nutrition in osteoporosis prevention and treatment, there is an absence of long-term controlled clinical trials in the elderly (Kohrt & Snead, 1993; Yarasheski, 1993). Recently, Lohman (1995) published an excellent review of the effects of exercise on bone mineral density and osteoporosis.

The usual outcome of exercise in the aged is decreased levels of physical activity. This reduced activity starts a chain of events, where muscle and bone composition changes. As a percentage of body weight, fat tissue increases, whereas lean tissue decreases, glucose tolerance decreases, circulating levels of anabolic hormones decrease, and bone mineral density decreases. These changes cause muscle atrophy and muscle and bone weakness, making the elderly more susceptible to falls, injuries, fractures, and pain (Yarasheski, 1993). As a matter of fact, in a recent editorial, Buckwalter (1995) states that, regardless of age, when treating bone, soft tissue, and joint injuries, "orthopedists can conclude that, although temporary rest may be necessary to avoid further tissue injury and, in some instances, to allow formation of repair tissue, the optimal treatment of most musculoskeletal injuries includes early controlled activity" (p. 155).

A series of recent studies report that exercise may in fact slow down the aging process. Increases in muscle size (hypertrophy) and strength were obtained in elderly subjects who were subjected to heavy resistance training. The exercises were done 3 to 4 days a week for 8–12 weeks, with gradual progression in resistance intensity to 80%–90% of the maximum subject's strength. Such studies include training of 60- to 72-year-old males (Frontera, Meredith, O'Reilly, Knutgen, & Evans, 1988), 86- to 96-year-old males and females (Fiatarone et al., 1990), 60- to 70-year-old males (Brown, McCartney, & Sale, 1990), and 64- to 86 (average = 69.9) year-old females (Charette et al., 1991). The effects of aging on skeletal muscles and the possible reversal via exercise training are summarized in an excellent review chapter by Rogers and Evans (1993).

There is also some evidence that skeletal adaptation occurs after a longer period of exercise time of similar high intensity. For example, Dalsky, et al. (1988) showed that exercise in combination with daily 1500-mg calcium supplements significantly increased bone mineral content in 55- to 70-year-old sedentary postmenopausal women. Similar results were indicated in a earlier study by Krolner, Toft, Nielsen, and Tondevold (1983) in postmenopausal women aged 50–75, where lumbar vertebrae bone loss was stopped in exercising subjects. Later, it was also shown that elderly active athletic women (55–75 years old) had the same bone density, in several sites, as younger women and that, in comparison to an age-matched group, their bone loss had been arrested (Jacobson, Beaver, Grubb, Taft & Talmage, 1984). This last study used the most rigorous methodology; however, even in this study, the elderly (> 65) subgroup was too small to allow one to draw significant conclusions.

After reviewing the literature on exercise and bone density, Lohman (1995) came to the following conclusions:

> Exercise effects on bone mineral density is [*sic*] between 1% and 2% for training programs, between 5 months and one year. Long term effects of exercise, especially in the post-menopausal population, have not been studied. In post-menopausal estrogen-replete women, the exercise response appears to be greater; however, only a few studies with limited sample size have been carried out in this population (p. 359).

Lohman (1995) further concluded that the relationship between exercise and bone fracture risk is an area in need of further study as a subspecialty of exercise and the prevention of osteoporosis. Like us, Lohman argues for more prospective studies to better establish the relationship between exercise, bone density, and fracture risk.

EXERCISE AND PAIN CONTROL IN PSYCHOSOCIAL CONDITIONS

It seems that the elderly are more susceptible to psychosocial pain than younger people. In addition to physical aches and pains that come with chronic diseases that are characteristic of old age, the elderly may experience painful negative emotional states such as anxiety, depression, and anger, as well as the pain of loneliness and social isolation associated with the loss of a spouse, friends, and the reduction in the social network (Helme & Katz, 1993; Shephard, 1987; Willis & Campbell, 1992). Furthermore, when depression and chronic medical conditions occur together, the adverse effects on functioning are additive (Wells et al., 1989). While the psychological benefits of exercise in young and middle-aged healthy and patient populations has been well documented in recent years, the few studies that involve the elderly have been plagued with methodological problems and inadequacies (Emery, Pinder, & Blumenthal, 1989). The following section will review and critique selected studies that have investigated the psychosocial benefits of exercise in the elderly.

Depression, Anxiety and Exercise

Depression, stress, and anxiety are by far the most studied psychological conditions in relation to exercise. In mixed samples that consist mainly of healthy younger populations, it seems clear that prolonged regular exercise can be used to induce changes in pain perception by increasing the pain threshold (Janal, Colt, Clark, & Glusman, 1984; Olausson et al., 1986). The increased threshold can be attributed to the activation of the central opioid systems by triggering increased discharge of beta endorphin to afferent nerve fibers (Group III or A delta) in the rhythmically contracting skeletal muscles (Thoren, Floras, Hoffmann, & Seals, 1990). Exercise appears to be as effective as medications and/or psychotherapy in treating selected types of stress, anxiety, depression, and other mood disorders (Gleser & Mendelberg, 1990; Brown, 1991). The previously mentioned practice of prescribing antidepressants, such as tricyclics, rather than narcotics, to pain patients (Avent, 1987; Goodkin & Gullion, 1989; Sullivan, Reesor, Mikail, & Fisher, 1992) strongly supports this suggestive connection.

Indeed, as most clinicians have noticed in their practice, a substantial number of acute pain patients are in an anxiety state, whereas the chronic pain patients seem to have a depressed affect, usually accompanied by some anxiety. Psychosocial stress tends only to aggravate these situations. As clinicians, we should also suspect that complaints of diffused, nonspecific pain in the elderly may be an indication of masked depression and anxiety, because complaints of chronic pain are socially more accepted (Willis & Campbell, 1992).

Some reports have shown a decrease in state, but not trait, anxiety in postmyocardial-infarction (MI) exercising patients (Shephard, 1987). In acute exercise that induced ischemia during testing, Light, Herbst, Bragdon, Hinderliter, and Alan (1991) reported that those subjects (ages 46–79) who developed anginal pain also showed less increase of plasma beta-endorphin levels and higher scores on the MMPI depression subscale. In addition, post-MI exercising patients who used a regimen of high-intensity aerobic exercise seemed to reduce depression scores on the same (MMPI) depression subscale (Kavanagh, Shepard, Chisholm, Qureshi, & Kennedy, 1977). Similar results of reduction in anxiety and depression, as well as other psychosocial benefits, were also reported by Lewin, Robertson, Cay, Irving, and Campbell (1992) in a home-based exercise program for people 55 ($\pm$ 10.7) years old. Stern, et al. (1983) also reported reduced anxiety and depression, but their sample (30–69 years old) was strongly biased toward a younger population. Earlier research found no change in depression scores in groups of older subjects (Blumenthal, Williams, Wallace, Williams, & Needles, 1982; Molloy, Beerschoten, Borrie, Crilly, & Cope, 1988) and post-MI patients (Mayou, 1983).

The conflicting results may be attributed to different sample ages, conditions, and exercise programs, especially the type and length of the exercise involved. In addition, most elderly also take medication which may influence their mood (Helme & Katz,

1993). It seems that, at the present time, no definite conclusion can be made regarding the specific role of exercise in the control of emotional pain in the elderly. Research suggests that elderly institutionalized subjects (ages 61–99) who showed more depressive symptoms also had significantly more pain complaints (Parmelee et al., 1991), and that emotional pain can be alleviated in some elderly via participation in an exercise program (e.g., Lewin et al. 1992).

Self-Esteem

In an attempt to investigate the effects of exercise on psychological well-being, Schultz and Gavron (1992) surveyed 85 residents (65 years and older) from 12 nursing homes in northwest Ohio who were involved in a regular exercise program. Their results showed that the elderly people gained in positive self-esteem. They attributed this change to the physical, emotional, and social benefits of the exercise programs.

Similar results of improved feelings of well-being, a sense of accomplishment, and more pain-free range of motion were demonstrated in a seven-week aerobic dance program with 60- to 90-year-old residents of a nursing home (Atterbury, Sorg, & Larson, 1983). Ebrahim and Williams (1992), in a controlled study with Afro-Caribbean elderly (58–87 years old), and McMurdo and Burnett (1992), in another randomized and controlled study (60–81 years old), also found substantial improvement in perceived health and life satisfaction in the exercise group. Their program was composed of mild exercise over a longer period of time. A recent study that also used low-level exercises with a weighted vest in older subjects (58–80 years old) showed a significant reduction in body pain, improved physical function, and increased internal locus of control (Greendale, Hirsch, & Hahn, 1993).

From the few studies that have investigated the effects of exercise on self-esteem, it appears that, with improved physical status, the elderly feel less pain, physically and emotionally, which consequently improves their self-esteem.

Social Isolation

There is an increased awareness that the emotional pain of isolation in the elderly does affect their physical well-being. In 1984, Rubernan et al., in a large sample of 2,520 males of various ages who had survived an acute MI, showed that being socially isolated and having a high degree of stress in life makes people four times more likely to risk subsequent death than men with a good social network and low stress. Other studies have confirmed these findings when isolation was the main factor (Unden, Orth-Gomer & Elofsson, 1991; Orth-Gomer, Unden, & Edwards, 1988). These results seem to be particularly true in Western society, where the elderly are especially prone to social isolation.

All of the studies reviewed in this chapter neglected the investigation of social support as an independent variable. It is possible that social support is confounded with treatment conditions such as exercise. Social-group situations do have an effect on outcomes (e.g., Atterbury et al., 1983; Saxon & Etten, 1978; Stern, et al., 1983). It seems that research on the effect of exercise on social isolation in the exercising elderly is urgently needed, especially in rehabilitation exercises for post-MI elderly.

EXERCISE AS PART OF A NATURAL LIFESTYLE FOR THE ELDERLY

We should recognize that the importance and benefits of exercise in preserving health, preventing disease, and assisting in rehabilitation are too valuable to be limited to the young alone. Exercise must be extended to the healthy elderly as well as to the frail elderly. Exercise is not only an integral part of a healthy lifestyle through the life span of an individual but also a means to combat primary or secondary pain in the growing elderly population.

Some of the evidence regarding exercise and pain is solid and established; other questions are in need of further research. However, it is clear today that elderly people who exercise regularly can improve their physical, mental, and social situation as well as prevent and/or alleviate pain and suffering. The positive outcomes of exercise in the elderly include some of the conditions reviewed in this chapter and others as well. In summary, the benefits may include:

Physical:
- Increased muscle tone, strength, and endurance.
- Improved flexibility of joints.
- Improved circulation and respiration, especially as related to the pulmonary and cardiovascular systems.
- Increased bone density and strength.
- Improved kinesthetic awareness and balance.

Psychological:
- Help in releasing tension and promoting relaxation.
- Decreased mild to moderate symptoms of depression and anxiety.
- Contribution to greater emotional stability.
- Improved self-confidence and self-esteem.

Social:
- Increased social interaction.
- Help in diminishing loneliness and isolation.
- Improved interpersonal relationships.
- Facilitation of play, fun, and creativity (Buchner, Beresford, Larson, LaCroix, & Wagner, 1992; Campbell, Barrie, & Spears, 1989; Holmes, 1993; Saxon & Etten, 1984).

The very current debate, concerning the modes and intensity of exercise programs to achieve these goals was purposely eliminated in order to prevent confusion and impossible comparisons. The conflicting recommendations concerning exercise intensity on the pages of JAMA (Lee, Hsieh, & Paffenbarger, 1995; Pate et al., 1995) pertain mainly to longevity and pain control is not considered a factor. However, we accept and recommend the conclusions of the Centers for Disease Control and Prevention, the American College of Sports Medicine (Pate et al., 1995), and the American Heart Association (1989) that "Every U.S. adult should accumulate 30 minutes or more of moderate intensity physical activity on most, preferably all, days of the week" (Pate et al., 1995, p. 402). This activity can be any sport, fitness, or recreational activity that resembles the intensity of walking two miles briskly per day. The activity can be continuous or intermittent and supervised if needed. Such activity should enable the elderly to reduce their risk of chronic disease, to control pain, and to enhance their quality of life.

The most common excuses for not exercising are time constraints and "exercise-induced pain." The recommended time frame, especially in the elderly, who usually do not hold a job, seems to be reasonable. It may also take care of possible pain by enabling gradual and intermittent execution of a program. The elderly can start the program for 5–10 minutes; and if pain starts, they can stop, rest, and continue again until the quota of an accumulated 30 minutes is reached. The moderate intensity should also not be a problem with most of the elderly, especially when the program is done under the supervision of health care professionals (Saxon, 1991). It is ironic that most people associate exercise with pain. Indeed, exercising vigorously and sporadically may result in pain and injury. On the other hand, making regular, supervised exercise a part of a natural lifestyle in the elderly is not only associated with psychophysiological benefits but may also become an antidote to various forms of primary or secondary pain.

Finally, our review highlighted some serious research flaws in the methodology of most of the studies presented. It is especially bothersome that a substantial portion of our conclusions are implied from mixed samples and not from samples that involve only subjects 65 years or older. However, all of our conclusions and recommendations are based on conclusive findings and/or highly suggestive findings. We feel that these conclusions can be adopted for the elderly with the most professional confidence and integrity.

REFERENCES

Ades, P. A., Waldmann, M. L., McCann, W. J., & Weaver, S. O. (1992). Predictors of cardiac rehabilitation participation in older coronary patients. *Archives of Internal Medicine, 152* (5), 1033–1035.

Altmaier, E. M., Lehmann, T. R., Russell, D. W., & Weinstein, J. N. (1992). The effectiveness of psychological interventions for the rehabilitation of low back pain: A randomized controlled trial evaluation. *Pain, 49* (3), 329–335.

Ambepitiya, G., Roberts, M., Ranjadayalan, K., & Tallis, R. (1994). Silent exertional myocardial ischemia in the elderly: A quantitative analysis of anginal perceptual threshold and the influence of autonomic function. *Journal of the American Geriatric Society, 42* (7), 732–737.

American Heart Association. (1989). *E. is for exercise.* National Center, 7272 Greenville Ave., Dallas, TX 75231-4596. Publication #51-1039 (CP), 6-92, 89, 10, 18B.

Atterbury, C., Sorg, J., & Larson, M. A. (1983). Aerobic dancing in a long-term care facility. *Physical and Occupational Therapy in Geriatrics, 2* (3), 71–73.

Avent, R. (1987). Diagnosis and treatment of depression. Symposium: Fulfilling the promise. *Psychophysiology, 20,* (Suppl. 1), 13–19.

Beckham, J. C., Keefe, F. J., Caldwell, D. S., & Brown, C. J. (1991). Biofeedback as a means to alter electromyographic activity in a total knee replacement patient. *Biofeedback and Self Regulation, 16*, (1), 23–35.

Bender, R. (1992). Yoga exercises and gentle movements for the elderly. In S. Harris, R. Harris, & W. S. Harris (Eds.), *Physical activity and sports: Practice, program and policy* (Vol. 2, pp. 344–371). Albany, NY: Center for the Study of Aging.

Ben-Sira, D. (1986). The perception of effort during physical exercise. In L. D. Zaichkowsky, & C. Z. Fuchs (Eds.), *The psychology of motor behavior: Development control, learning and performance* (pp. 175–190). Ithaca, NY: Mouvement Publications.

Biegel, L. (1984). *Physical fitness and the older person: A guide to exercise for health care professionals.* Rockville, MD: Aspen.

Block, J. E. (1992). Osteoporosis prevention: Theory and practice. In S. Harris, R. Harris, & W. S. Harris (Eds.). *Physical activity and sports: Practice, program and policy* (Vol. 2, pp. 83–89). Albany, NY: Center for the Study of Aging.

Blumenthal, J. A., Williams, R. S., Wallace, A. G., Williams, R. B., & Needles, T. L. (1982). Physiological and psychological variables predict compliance to prescribed exercise therapy in patients recovering from myocardial infraction. *Psychosomatic Medicine, 44* (6), 519–527.

Bove, A. A. (1983). Exercise in the elderly. In A. A. Bove, & D. T. Lowenthal (Eds.), *Exercise medicine: Physiological principles and clinical applications.* (pp.173–181). Orlando, FL: Academic Press.

Bradley, L. A. (1989). Adherence with treatment regiments among adult rheumatoid arthritis patients: Current status and future directions. *Arthritis Care and Research, 2* (3), S33–S39.

Brown, B. A., McCartney, N., & Sale, D. G. (1990). Positive adaptations to weight lifting training in the elderly. *Journal of Applied Physiology, 69* (5), 1725–1733.

Brown, J. D. (1991). Staying fit and staying well: Physical fitness as a moderator of life stress. *Journal of Personality and Social Psychology, 60* (4), 555–561.

Buchner, D. M., Beresford, S. A., Larson, E. B., LaCroix, A. Z., & Wagner, E. H. (1992). Effects of physical activity on health status in older adults, 2: intervention study. *Annual Review of Public Health, 13*, 469–488.

Buckwalter, J. A. (1995). Should bone, soft tissue and joint injuries be treated with rest or activity? *Journal of Orthopedic Research, 13*, 155–156.

Cady, C. D., Bischoff, D. P., O'Connell, E. R., Thomas, P. C., & Allan, J. H. (1979). Strength and fitness and subsequent back injuries in fire fighters. *Journal of Occupational Medicine, 21*, 269–272.

Campbell, A. J., Borrie, M. J., & Spears, G. F. (1989). Risk factors for falls in a community-based prospective study of people 70 years and older. *Journal of Gerontology: Medical Sciences, 44* (4), M112–M117.

Charette, S. L., McEvoy, L., Pyka, G., Show-Harter, C., Guido, D., Wiswell, R. A., & Marcus, R. (1991). Muscle hypertrophy response to resistance training in older women. *Journal of Applied Physiology, 70* (5), 1912–1916.

Coleman, E. A., Buchner, D. M., Cress, M. E., Chan, B. K. S., & de Lateur, B. J. (1996). The relationship of joint symptoms with exercise performance in older adults. *Journal of the American Geriatric Society, 44*(1), 14–21.

Dalsky, G. P., Stocke, K. S., Ehsani, A. A., Slatopolsky, E., Lee, W. C., & Birge, S. J., Jr., (1988). Weight bearing exercise training and lumbar bone mineral content in post menopausal women. *Annals of Internal Medicine, 108* (6), 824–828.

Davis, G. C., Cortez, C., & Rubin, B. R. (1990). Pain management in the older adult with rheumatoid arthritis or osteoarthritis. *Arthritis Care and Research, 3* (3), 127–131.

de-Vries, R. J., Dunselman, P. H., Van-Veldhuisen, D. J., van-den-Heuvel, A. F, Wielenoa, R. P., & Lie, K. I. (1994). Comparison between felodipine and isosorbide mononitrate as adjunct to beta blockage in patients > 65 years of age with angina pectoris. *American Journal of Cardiology, 74* (12), 1201–1206.

Dexter, P. A. (1992). Joint exercises in elderly persons with symptomatic osteoarthritis of the hip or knee: Performance patterns, medical support patterns and the relationship between exercising and medical care. *Arthritis Care and Research, 5* (1) 36–41.

Dixhoorn, J. V., Duivenvoorden, H. J., Pool, J., & Verhage, F. (1990). Psychic effects of physical training and relaxation therapy after myocardial infarction. *Journal of Psychosomatic Research, 34* (3), 327–337.

Dougherty, J. (1992). Back pain in an aging population. In S. Harris, R. Harris, and W. S. Harris (Eds.), *Physical activity and sports: Practice, program and policy*, (Vol. 2, pp. 311–316). Albany, NY: Center for the Study of Aging.

Ebrahim, S., & Williams, J. (1992). Assessing the effects of a health promotion program for elderly people. *Journal of Public Health Medicine, 14* (2), 199–205.

Emery, C. F., Pinder, S. L., & Blumenthal, J. A. (1989). Psychological effects of exercise among elderly cardiac patients. *Journal of Cardiopulmonary Rehabilitation, 9* (1), 46–53.

Ettinger, W. H., Jr., & Afable, R. F. (1994). Physical disability from knee osteoarthritis: The role of exercise as an intervention. *Medicine and Science in Sports and Exercise, 26* (12), 1435–1440.

Fiatarone, M. A., Marks, E. C., Ryan, N. D., Meredith, C. N., Lipsitz, L. A., & Evans, W. J. (1990). High-intensity strength training in nonagenarians: Effects on skeletal muscle. *Journal of the American Medical Association, 263,* 13 (22), 3029–3034.

Fisher, N. M., Gresham, G., & Pendergast, D. R. (1993). Effects of quantitative progressive rehabilitation program applied unilaterally to the osteoarthritic knee. *Archives of Physical Medicine and Rehabilitation, 74* (12), 1319–1326.

Flatten, K., Wilhite, B., & Reyes-Watson, E. (1988). *Exercise activities for the elderly.* New York: Springer.

Flynn, J. A., & Wigley, F. M. (1995). Musculoskeletal and rheumatic diseases common in the elderly. In W. Reichel, J. J. Gallo, J. Busby-Whitehead, J. R. Delfs, & J. B. Murphy (Eds.), *Care of the elderly: Clinical aspects of aging* (4th ed., pp. 308–325). Baltimore: Williams, & Wilkins.

Fox, E. L. (1979). *Sports physiology.* Philadelphia: Saunders.

Fridlund, B., Hogstedt, B., Lidell, E., & Larson, Par-A. (1991). Recovery after myocardial infraction: Effects of a caring rehabilitation program. *Scandinavian Journal of Caring Sciences, 5* (1), 23–32.

Fries, J. F., Singh, G., Morfeld, D., O'Driscoll, P., & Hubert, H. (1966). Relationship of running to musculoskeletal pain with age. *Arthritis and Rheumatism, 39*(1), 64–72.

Frontera, W. R., Meredith, C. N., O'Reilly, K. P., Knutgen, H. G., & Evans, W. J. (1988). Strength conditioning in men: Skeletal muscle hypertrophy and improved function. *Journal of Applied Physiology, 64* (3), 1038–1044.

Gleser, J., & Mendelberg, H. (1990). Exercise and sport in mental health: A review of the literature. *Israel Journal of Psychiatry and Related Sciences, 27* (2), 92–112.

Goodkin, K., & Gullion, C. M. (1989). Antidepressants for the relief of chronic pain: Do they work? *Annals of Behavioral Medicine, 11* (3), 83–101.

Greendale, G. A., Hirsch, S. H., & Hahn, T. J. (1993). The effect of weighted vest on perceived health status and bone density in older persons. *Quality of Life Research: An International Journal of Quality of Life Aspects of Treatment, Care and Rehabilitation, 2* (2), 141–152.

Harris, S., Harris, R., & Harris, W. S. (Eds.) (1992). *Physical activity and sports: Practice, program and policy* (Vol. 2). Albany, NY: Center for the Study of Aging.

Helme, R. D., & Katz, B. (1993). Management of chronic pain. *Medical Journal of Australia, 158*(7), 478–481.

Herning, M. M. (1993). Posture improvement in the frail elderly. In H. M. Perry, III, J. E., Morley, & R. M. Coe (Eds.), *Aging and musculoskeletal disorders: Concepts, diagnosis and treatment* (pp. 334–353). New York: Springer.

Holmes, D. S. (1993). Aerobic fitness and the response to psychological stress. In P. Seraganian (Ed.), *Exercise psychology: The influence of physical exercise on psychological processes* (pp. 39–62). New York: Wiley.

Horowitz, M., Need, A. G., Morris, H. A., & Nordin, C. (1993). Osteoporosis in post menopausal women. In H. M. Perry, III, J. E. Morley, & R. M. Coe (Eds.), *Aging and musculoskeletal disorders: Concepts, diagnosis and treatment* (pp 78–98). New York: Springer.

Jacobson, P. C., Beaver, W., Grubb, S. A., Taft, T. N., & Talmage, R. V. (1984). Bone density in women: College athletes and older athletic women. *Journal of Orthopedic Research, 2* (4), 328–332.

Janal, M. N., Colt, E. W. D., Clark, W. C., & Glusman, M. (1984). Pain sensitivity, mood and plasma endocrine levels in man following long distance running: Effects of naloxone. *Pain, 19,* 13–25.

Kavanagh, T., Shephard, R. J., Chisholm, A. W, Qureshi, S., & Kennedy, J. (1977). Depression following myocardial infarction: The effects of distance running. *Annals of the New York Academy of Sciences, 301,* 1029–1038.

Kerlan, R. K. (Ed.). (1991). *Clinics in sports medicine, 10* (2). Philadelphia: Saunders.

Kilbom, A., Gamberale, F., Persson, J., & Annwell, G. (1983). Physiological and psychological indices of fatigue during static contractions. *European Journal of Applied Physiology, 50,* 179–193.

Kohrt, W. M., Malley, M. T., Coggan, A. R., Spina, R. J., Ogawa, T., Ehsani, A. A., Bourey, R. E., Martin, W. H., III, & Holloszy, J. O. (1991). Effects of gender, age and fitness level on response of $\dot{V}o_2$ max to training in 60–71 year olds. *Journal of Applied Physiology, 71* (5), 2004–2011.

Kohrt, W. M., & Snead, D. B. (1993). Effect of exercise on bone mass in the elderly. In H. M., Perry III, J. E. Morley, & R. M. Coe (Eds.). *Aging and musculoskeletal disorders: Concepts, diagnosis and treatment* (pp. 214–227). New York: Springer.

Krolner, B., Toft, B., Nielsen, S. P., & Tondevold, E. (1983). Physical exercise as prophylaxis against involutional vertebrae bone loss: A controlled trial. *Clinical Science, 64*, 541–546.

Lee, I. M., Hsieh, C. C., & Paffenbarger R.S., Jr., (1995). Exercise intensity and longevity in man: The Harvard alumni health study. *Journal of the American Medical Association, 273* (15), 1179–1184.

Lehr, J., & Swanson, K. (1990). *Fit, firm & 50.* Chelsea, MI: Lewis.

Lewin, B., Robertson, I. H., Cay, E. L., Irving, J. B., & Campbell, M. (1992). Effects of self-help post myocardial infarction rehabilitation on psychological adjustment and use of health services. *The Lancet, 339*, (8800), 1036–1040.

Lewis, C. (1984). Arthritis and exercise. In L. Biegel (Ed.), *Physical fitness and the older person: A guide to exercise for health care professionals* (pp. 129–149). Rockville, MD: Aspen.

Light, K. C., Herbst, M. C., Bragdon, E. E., Hinderliter, A. L., & Alan, L. (1991). Depression and type A behavior pattern in patients with coronary artery disease: Relationships to painful versus silent myocardial ischemia and b-endorphin responses during exercise. *Psychosomatic Medicine, 53* (6), 669–683.

Limburg, P. J., Sinaki, M., Rogers, J. W., Caskey, P. E., & Pierskalla, B. K. (1991). A useful technique for measure of back strength in osteoporotic and elderly patients. *Mayo Clinic Proceedings, 66* (1), 39–44.

Linchitz, R. M. (1987). Life without pain. Reading, MA: Addison-Wesley.

Lindroth, Y., Bauman, A., Barnes, C., & McCredie, M. (1989). A controlled evaluation on arthritis education. *Advances, 6* (3), 17–19.

Lohman, T. G. (1995). Exercise training and bone mineral density. *Quest, 47*, 354–361.

Lyles, K. W., Gold, D. T., Shipp, K. M., Pieper, C. F., Martinez, S., & Mulhausen, P. L. (1993). Association of osteoporotic vertebrae compression fractures with impaired functional status. *American Journal of Medicine, 94* (6), 595–601.

Manniche, C., Lundberg, E., Christensen, I., & Bentzen, L. (1991). Intensive dynamic back exercises for chronic low back pain: A clinical trial. *Pain, 47* (1), 53–63.

Marchini, L. M., Perretti, P. G., Passeri, M., & Cucinotta, D. (1992). Effects of physical exercise in the elderly: Cycling and calisthenics for over 65 years of age. In S. Harris, R. Harris, & W.S. Harris. *Physical activity and sports: Practice, program and policy* (Vol. 2, pp. 322–327). Albany, NY: Center for the Study of Aging.

Mayou, A. (1993). A controlled trial of early rehabilitation after myocardial infarction. *Journal of Cardiac Rehabilitation, 3* (6), 397–402.

McCully, K. K., Halber, C., & Posner, J. D. (1994). Exercise induced changes in oxygen saturation in the calf muscles of elderly subjects with peripheral vascular disease. *Journal of Gerontology, 49* (3), B128–B134.

McMurdo, M. E., & Burnett, L. (1992). Randomized controlled trial of exercise in the elderly. *Gerontology, 38* (5), 292–298.

Meyer, C. L., & Hawley, D. J. (1994). Characteristics of participants in water exercise programs compared to patients seen in a rheumatic disease clinic. *Arthritis Care and Research, 7* (2), 85–89.

Miller, C., & LeLieuver, R. B. (1982). A method to reduce chronic pain in elderly nursing home residents. *Gerontologist, 22* (3), 314–317.

Minor, M. A., & Brown, J. D. (1993). Exercise maintenance of persons with arthritis after participation in a class experience. Special issue: Arthritis health education. *Health Education Quarterly, 20* (1), 83–95.

Minor, M. A., & Stanford, M. K. (1993). Physical interventions in the management of pain in arthritis: An overview for research and practice. Special issue: The challenges of pain in arthritis. *Arthritis Care and Research, 6* (4), 197–206.

Molloy, D. W., Beerschoten, D. A., Borrie, M. J., Crilly, R. J., & Cope, R. D. T. (1988). Acute effects of exercise on neuropsychological function in elderly subjects. *American Geriatrics Society, 36*, 29–33.

Olausson, B., Eriksson, E., Ellmarker, L., Bydenhag, B., Shyu, C., & Andersson, S.A. (1986). Effects of naloxone on dental pain threshold following muscle exercise and low frequency transcutaneous nerve stimulation: A comparative study in man. *Acta Physiologica Scandinavica, 126*, 299–305.

Ornish, D., Brown, S. E., Scherwitz, L. W., Billings, J. H., Armstrong, T. W., Ports, T. A., McLanahan, S. M., Kirkeeide, R. L., Brand, R. J., Brand, K., & Gould, K. L. (1990). Can lifestyle changes reverse coronary heart disease? *The Lancet, 336*, 129–133.

Orth-Gomer, K., Unden, A. L., & Edwards, M. E. (1988). Social isolation and mortality in ischemic heart disease: A 10-year follow up study of 150 middle-aged men. *Acta Medica Scandinavica, 224*, 205–215.

Parmelee, P. A. Katz, I. R., & Lawton, P. (1991). The relationship of pain to depression among institutionalized aged. *Journal of Gerontology, 46* (1), 15–21.

Pate, R., Pratt, M., Blair, S. N., Haskell, W. L., Macera, C. A., Bouchard, C., Buchner, D., Ettinger, W., Heath, G. W., King, A. C., Kriska, A., Leon, A. S., Marcus, B. H., Morris, J., Paffenbarger, R. S., Jr., Patrick, K., Pollock, M. L., Rippe, J. M., Sallis, J., & Wilmore, J. H. (1995). Physical activity and public health: A recommendation from the centers for disease control and prevention and the American college of sports medicine. *Journal of the American Medical Association, 273* (5), 402–407.

Perlman, S. G., Connell, K. J., Clark A., & Robinson, M. S. (1990). Dance based aerobic exercise for rheumatoid arthritis. *Arthritis Care and Research, 3* (1), 29–35.

Perry, H. M., III, Morley, J. E., & Coe, R. M. (Eds.). (1993). *Aging and musculoskeletal disorders: Concepts. diagnosis and treatment.* New York: Springer.

Province, M. A., Hadley, E. C., Hornbrook, M. C., Lipsitz, L. A., Miller, J. P., Mulrow, C. D., Ory, M. G., Sattin, R. W., Tinetti, M. E., Wolf, S. L., for the FICSIT Group. (1995). The effects of exercise on falls in elderly patients: A preplanned meta-analysis of the FICSIT trials. *Journal of the American Medical Association, 273* (17), 1341–1347.

Risch, S. V., Norrell, N. K., Pollock, M. L. Risch, E. D., Langer, H., Fulton, M., Graves, J. E., & Leggett, S. H. (1993). Lumbar strengthening in chronic low back pain patients: Physiologic and psychological benefits. *Spine, 18*(2), 232–238.

Rogers, M. A., & Evans, W. J. (1993). Changes in skeletal muscles with aging: Effects of exercise training. In J. O. Holloszy (Ed.), *Exercise and sport sciences reviews, 21*, 65–102. Baltimore: Williams & Wilkins.

Sardana, R., & Mikhail, B. (1992). Nutritional management of osteoporosis. *Geriatric Nursing and Home Care, 13* (6), 315–319.

Saxon, S. V. (1991). *Pain management techniques for older adults.* Springfield, IL: Charles C Thomas.

Saxon, S. V., & Etten, M. J., (1978). *Physical change and aging: A Guide for the Helping Professions.* New York: Tiresias Press.

Saxon, S. V., & Etten, M. J., (1984). *Psychosocial rehabilitation programs for older adults.* Springfield, IL: Charles C Thomas.

Schilke, J. M., Johnson, G. O., Hough, T. J., & O'Dell, J. R. (1996). Effects of muscle-strength training on the functional status of patients with osteoarthritis of the knee joint. *Nursing Research, 45* (2), 68–72.

Schultz, S. K., & Gavron, S. J. (1992). Physical fitness attitudes of Northwest Ohioans 65 years of age and older in nursing homes. In S. Harris, R. Harris, & W. S. Harris (Eds.), *Physical activity and sports: Practice. program and policy* (Vol. 2, pp. 174–183). Albany, NY: Center for the Study of Aging.

Shephard, R. J. (1987). *Physical activity and aging* (2nd ed.). Rockville, MD: Aspen.

Shephard, R. J. (1993). Benefits of exercise for the elderly. In H. M. Perry III, J. E. Morley, & R. M. Coe (Eds.), *Aging and musculoskeletal disorders: Concepts. diagnosis and treatment.* (pp. 228–242). New York: Springer.

Smith, T. W., Christensen, A. J., Peck, J. R., & Ward, J. R. (1994). Cognitive distortion, helplessness and depressed mood in rheumatoid arthritis: A four-year longitudinal analysis. *Health Psychology, 13* (3), 213–217.

Steege, J. F., & Blumenthal, J. A. (1993). The effects of aerobic exercise on premenstrual symptoms in middle age women: A preliminary study. *Journal of Psychosomatic Research, 37* (2), 127–133.

Stenstrom, C. H., & Christina, H. (1994). Therapeutic exercise in rheumatoid arthritis. Special Issue: Exercise and Arthritis. *Arthritis Care and Research, 7* (4), 190–197.

Stern, M. J., Gorman, P. A., & Kaslow, L. (1983). The group counselling v. exercise therapy study: A controlled intervention with subjects following myocardial infarction: *Archives of Internal Medicine, 143* 1719–1725.

Sullivan, M. J. L., Reesor, K., Mikail, S., & Fisher, R. (1992). The treatment of depression in chronic low back pain: Review and recommendations. *Pain, 50*, 5–13.

Sykes, J. C. (1992). Practical nutrition for older people. In S. Harris, R. Harris, & W. S. Harris (Eds.), *Physical activity and sports: Practice, program and policy* (Vol. 2, pp. 284–285). Albany, NY: Center for the Study of Aging.

Thompson, R. F., Crist, D. M., & Atterbom, H. A. (1990). Treadmill exercise electrocardiography in the elderly with physical impairments. *Gerontology, 36* (2), 112–118.

Thoren, P., Floras, J. S., Hoffmann, P., & Seals, D. R. (1990). Endorphins and exercise: Physiological mechanisms and clinical applications. *Medicine and Science in Sports and Exercise, 22* (4), 417–428.

Turner, J. A., Clancy, S., McQuade, K. J., & Cardenas, D. D. (1990). Effectiveness of behavioral therapy for chronic low back pain: A component analysis. *Journal of Consulting and Clinical Psychology, 58* (5), 573–579.

Unden, A.L., Orth-Gomer, K., & Elofsson, S. (1991). Cardiovascular effects of social support in the work place: Twenty-four hour ECG monitoring of men and women. *Psychosomatic Medicine, 53*, 50–60.

Vertinsky, P. (1990). *The eternally wounded woman.* Nachester, UK: Manchester University Press.

Wells, K. B., Stewart, A., Hays, R. D., Wells, K. B., Stewart, A., Hays, R. D., Burnam, M. A., Rogers, W., Daniels, M., Berry, S., Greenfield, S., & Ware, J. (1989). The functioning and wellbeing of depressed patients: Results from the medical outcome study. *Journal of the American Medical Association, 262*, 914–918.

Willis, J. D., & Campbell, L. F. (1992). *Exercise psychology.* Champaign, IL: Human Kinetics.

Yarasheski, K. E. (1993). Effect of exercise on muscle mass in the elderly. In H. M. Perry III, J. E. Morley, & R. M. Coe, (Eds.), *Aging and musculoskeletal disorders: Concepts, diagnosis and treatment* (pp. 199–213). New York: Springer.

CHAPTER 17

Behavioral Treatments for Pain Experienced by Older Adults

PATRICIA A. WISOCKI AND CHARLES B. POWERS

In the first part of this chapter, we delineate the characteristics of a behavioral approach to the treatment of pain and then describe four different theoretical perspectives on pain which have been derived from a behavioral model. These perspectives are respondent conditioning, operant conditioning, social learning theory, and cognitive behavior therapy. Examples of treatment methods derived from each perspective are presented, along with available research evidence pertinent to that method or perspective. In the second part of the chapter, we present the research evidence comparing different behavioral treatment modalities with the pain problems of older adult patients.

While there is a large body of research evidence substantiating the use of behavioral methods for the treatment of pain, few studies have been conducted with older adults as patients. There is no reason to believe, however, that findings from studies with younger adult populations will not be relevant to the older adult patient. The reader interested in learning more about behavioral methods of treatment for the problems of the older adult patient is encouraged to explore the general behavioral literature. A recent review of behavioral gerontology is presented by Wisocki (1991).

CHARACTERISTICS OF BEHAVIORAL TREATMENTS FOR PAIN

Early applications of behavioral theory and therapy to the pain experience were reported by Fordyce and his colleagues more than 30 years ago (Fordyce, 1973, 1974;

PATRICIA A. WISOCKI AND CHARLES B. POWERS • Psychology Department, University of Massachusetts, Amherst, Massachusetts 01003.

Handbook of Pain and Aging, edited by David I. Mostofsky and Jacob Lomranz. Plenum Press, New York, 1997.

Fordyce, Fowler, Lehmann, & Delateur, 1968; Fordyce et al., 1973) and are still very much at the core of treatment for chronic pain and illnesses. Behavioral methods are distinguished from other treatment methods in that their primary focus is on *behaviors* related to the experience of pain, including such elements as the physical or verbal expression of pain, methods developed by people to cope with or manage pain (e.g., a certain gait, restricted movement, systematic contact with health care professionals, ways of obtaining various prescriptions, and maintaining a schedule of medications). A behavioral approach to pain includes a broader social and economic context, such as the effects of pain on a person's employment, family relationships, recreational activities, and the ways health care providers analyze and treat pain. In that context, behavioral interventions may be introduced to target collateral problems of the pain experience, such as anxiety, depression, mood disorders, diminished self-concept, sexual inhibitions, sleep or appetite difficulties, and a patient's beliefs and expectancies about the illness or disease causing the pain. In addition, it includes the promotion of good health behaviors, such as self-monitoring, exercise, health-promoting nutritional habits, and others.

In using a behavioral approach in the treatment of pain, one does not deny the physical experience of the pain itself nor the need for direct treatment of the cause(s) of the pain. Behavioral treatment methods are meant to be employed along with other medical and pharmacological management methods for the treatment of pain. A behavioral assessment of pain is not a replacement for a medical assessment of a disease. Using learning theory principles and procedures, a behavioral approach proposes additional and alternative explanations for the pain phenomenon.

RESPONDENT CONDITIONING

Respondent conditioning directs attention to the stimulus nature of the pain experience. Nociception, the neurophysiological process associated with tissue damage that is experienced as pain, serves to trigger a number of observable behaviors that signal pain, such as verbal complaints, medication intake, and favoring a particular body part. These behaviors, which are activated in the presence of nociceptive stimuli, are called *respondent pain behaviors*. They may be reduced by a process of counterstimulation brought about by movement (e.g., rubbing a part of the body) or by exogenous electrical stimulation through the skin, resulting in the inhibition of the transmission of a pain sensation (Fordyce, 1976). Counterstimulation mobilizes central neural mechanisms, which may exercise control or influence over the "gate," a mechanism proposed by Melzack and Wall (1965) to mediate the experience of pain between the spinal cord and various brain centers. This inhibitory process may be conditioned, through a process of association and reinforcement, to the extent that the nociceptive cues may lead to an increase in the movement or action behaviors instead of the pain behaviors (Fordyce, 1976).

Particular intervention techniques have been derived from this theory of respondent pain. In the following section, three different respondent procedures are described, and where available, some clinical and research support is provided.

Biofeedback

Biofeedback procedures are used to teach patients a way of controlling the pain experience by systematically conditioning brain wave activity to moderate or replace the pain experience with a more pleasant subjective state (Melzack & Chapman, 1973). Biofeedback training has been shown to be effective in reducing tension, improving posture, and retraining musculature associated with the pain experience (Dolce & Raczynski, 1985; Wolf, Nacht, & Kelly, 1982).

One clinical example of the application of biofeedback to osteoarthritic pain is provided by Boczkowski (1984). Boczkowski taught an 80-year-old patient to avoid contracting the muscles surrounding her joints in order to maintain a proper blood flow, which, in turn, reduced the experience of pain and stiffness.

A second clinical example is presented by King and Arena (1984), who taught a 69-year-old man with cluster headaches to use biofeedback and self-monitoring. They also taught his wife to avoid reinforcing the headache behavior. The result was a 44% decrease in intensity of headache pain after treatment and an improvement in the couple's relationship.

In a larger study on the effects of electromyographic (EMG) biofeedback training on tension headaches in eight elderly subjects, Arena, Hannah, Bruno, and Meador (1991) found that four of the subjects reduced their headache activity by 50%, while three other subjects reduced it by 35%–45%. There were also significant positive changes in the number of headache-free days, peak headache activity, and pain medication usage. This treatment program had been slightly modified from a standard EMG biofeedback training program to accommodate the elderly sample by giving instructions at a slower rate and having the subjects repeat the session instructions verbally in order to ensure accurate comprehension. The instructions were also simplified as much as possible by omitting technical jargon. Information and instructions from the previous session were reviewed briefly at the beginning of each subsequent session. The therapists were actively encouraged to be as patient as possible with the subjects by scheduling sessions 10 minutes longer than usual and by spending more time listening to the subjects.

Even though biofeedback training produces positive results, some investigators have felt that the costs of using biofeedback do not justify the results, which may be achieved as well with treatment based on relaxation and imagery (Achterberg, Kenner, & Lewis, 1988).

Relaxation Training

Relaxation training is another effective adaptation of respondent learning principles to reduce the pain experience, particularly that brought on by or associated with muscle tension. In relaxation training, sometimes done in conjunction with biofeedback training, the patient learns control over pain and stress through a series of deep-breathing exercises and a graduated rehearsal of tensing and relaxing different muscle groups of the body (Turk & Rennert, 1981).

Three case studies have been published in which relaxation procedures have been clinically effective for elderly pain patients. In the first case, Linoff and West (1982) described the use of taped relaxation instructions, accompanied by soothing background music, in the treatment of an 89-year-old male resident of a nursing home who suffered with headache pain. After 19 sessions of treatment, the patient reported a significant reduction in pain and other somatic problems, and staff reported a significant reduction in requests for pain medication. In the second case, Hamburger (1982) treated an elderly female patient who continued to feel the side effects of her chemotherapy treatments for cancer long after the chemotherapy had ended, stimulated apparently by feelings of anxiety or anger. The patient learned to use relaxation to cope with the emotional stimuli and reported satisfaction with the technique a year later. In the third case, Czirr and Gallagher (1983) treated an elderly man, who suffered from severe rheumatoid arthritis and moderate depression, with relaxation and imagery techniques and encouraged him to become an active participant in pleasant events. After seven weeks of treatment, the patient reported a 50% reduction in pain and a significant decrease in depression. Three months later he continued to report success.

In a prospective study of behavioral treatment for tension headache in an elderly sample, Arena, Hightower, and Chong (1988) evaluated an eight-week program of modified progressive muscle relaxation with 10 subjects. In addition to making sure that subjects did not use full isometric contractions of some muscle groups, the standard procedure was modified to include having the subjects verbalize the instructions for the exercises to be practiced during the next week. Results at three months' posttreatment showed that 7 of the 10 subjects reported significant increases in number of headache-free days and decreases in headache activity, peak headache activity, and medication usage. The authors attributed the positive findings to the rehearsal of instructions.

In an earlier study, De Berry (1981–1982) reported similar results with progressive muscle relaxation to reduce stress and anxiety among older individuals who also had headache symptoms. In this study, 10 anxious older female subjects were randomly assigned to either a 10-week program of progressive muscle relaxation, which included home practice with videotapes, or 10 weeks of a pseudorelaxation group. Relative to the control group, the treatment group showed improvement 1 week following treatment on measures of headaches, anxiety, muscle tension, and sleep. More recently, relaxation training has been shown to be effective in reducing anxiety and other psychological symptoms of elderly clients, even after one year posttreatment (Rickard, Scogin, & Keith, 1994).

Pain Cocktail

Perhaps the best-known adaptation of respondent conditioning principles to the treatment of pain is the "pain cocktail," a strategy developed to reduce a patient's dependency on pain medication by attempting to eliminate the stimulus–response connection between the feeling of pain and the taking of medication. Pain-contingent medicating, Fordyce (1976) believes, increases the demand for and amount of medication, the risk of addiction, and the probability that environmental events, not the tissue damage of the organism, will control the pain behaviors. Berntzen and Gotestam (1987) found that such a schedule is related to higher ratings of subjective pain and poorer moods. With the pain cocktail, the medication schedule is based on fixed intervals of time. All medications needed are incorporated into a single dose, mixed into a taste-masking substance, and taken before the pain begins or before it becomes severe. The amount of the active ingredients in the medication is gradually reduced to levels acceptable to the patient.

OPERANT CONDITIONING

The second method of learning is based on operant conditioning principles, which stress the importance of environmental contingencies which might induce, maintain, or reduce both the pain experience and behaviors necessary to promote good health. As is true of respondent pain behaviors, operant pain behaviors may occur as a direct and automatic response to antecedent stimuli, but they may also occur because they are followed by reinforcing consequences (Fordyce, 1976). The rate of pain behaviors increases when the consequences are positive; the rate decreases when the consequences are negative or when positive reinforcers are withdrawn. The same is true of those behaviors which promote or maintain good health.

This operant explanation of pain is especially appropriate for the occurrence of benign chronic pain problems, which are those that have persisted for at least six months in the absence of physical findings sufficient to explain the severity of the pain (Dolce & Dickerson, 1991). Respondent-based methods, on the other hand, are considered most relevant for acute pain, which is that pain occurring for less than six months, is associated with the stimulation of nociception, and is generally indicative of the need for medical assistance to facilitate healing by discovering and treating the physical pathology antecedent to the respondent pain behaviors. In the operant model, the role of nociception is minimized, while the management of pain, suffering, and disability is emphasized.

In addition to the key principle of operant conditioning (i.e., that behaviors are influenced by the consequences following their occurrence), Fordyce (1976) has delineated three other basic principles necessary to understand the application of operant methodology to the problem of pain. The first principle is that conditioning effects are temporary and will be maintained only if the operant behaviors continue to receive reinforcement. Thus, in order to facilitate effective management of pain, one must consider changing the contingency arrangements in which the pain behaviors were originally maintained. The second principle is that conditioning effects are usually specific to the stimulus conditions which produced them. This means that a behavior acquired in one setting does not necessarily generalize to additional settings without additional training in those settings. In order to broaden the effects of treatment beyond the treatment setting, the behavioral technique of stimulus fading is used. The third principle is that stimuli present when reinforcement or punishment occurs may take on the same reinforcing or punishing properties of the original. Thus, it is possible to expand the number of effective reinforcers for a patient, and conversely, elements present at the time pain occurs (such as people or activities) may take on aversive properties.

It is important to underscore the value of the schedule of reinforcement, both as an explanation for the maintenance of pain behaviors, and as a vital element in treatment programs. Schedules of reinforcement, the connection between the occurrence of a behavior and the timing and frequency of a reinforcer, may be either continuous or intermittent. If a schedule is continuous, a behavior is reinforced each time it occurs. This type of schedule is especially useful if one wants to establish a new behavior or rejuvenate a behavior which has not occurred very often. If a schedule is intermittent, a behavior is reinforced in either a ratio pattern, which is based on either a fixed or a variable number of behavior repetitions, or an interval pattern, which is based on either a fixed or a variable interval of time. Variable ratio schedules produce the highest and most consistent performance levels because they differentially reinforce rapid responding in an unpredictable pattern. Interval schedules tend to produce low rates of behavior, but they also produce more durable behavior. Behavior acquired on an interval schedule will persist longer after reinforcement has been withdrawn.

In the application of reinforcement schedules to the treatment of pain, once a behavior has been established by means of a continuous schedule, a ratio schedule should be used so that reinforcement is given only after certain levels of behavioral output are achieved. The use of interval schedules in the early stages of a treatment program is not recommended because there is no guarantee that behavioral output has occurred during the passage of time between reinforcements. Finally, once the patient has made considerable progress, an intermittent reinforcement schedule may be used. Thus, as Fordyce (1976) points out, reinforcement progresses toward a diminishing schedule, so that, as more of the desired behavior is emitted, it receives less reinforcement.

There are a number of operant procedures typically used in treatment programs for pain. These are now described briefly.

Shaping is a process by which the behavior to be acquired or increased is divided into its constituent parts, each of which is reinforced as it occurs, using a method of successive approximations until the entire behavior is established. In trying to change a person's pain-avoidant posturing, for example, each small increment approximating the end goal is reinforced until the goal is reached.

Fading is a similar process, but it is done in the reverse to shaping. New behavior is brought under the control of complex stimuli or naturally occurring reinforcers by being exposed to increasingly varied and complex settings, which may then serve to maintain the behavior while the stimuli and reinforcers used initially to establish the behavior are gradually eliminated. For example, if one wanted to decrease dependence on a wheelchair and increase walking with a cane, time in the wheelchair would be reduced gradually while time used for walking with a cane would be increased proportionately.

Stimulus generalization is a procedure essential for ensuring that any behavior change is maintained outside the setting in which it was learned and should be a part of every treatment program. It refers to the extent to which behavior occurring in one setting broadens in scope or occurs at other times and in other environments. Stimulus generalization strategies include (1) teaching the patient methods of self-control for his or her own behavior, especially ways to establish and carry out one's own reinforcement program; (2) programming the patient's environment to enhance effective reinforcers which will help maintain the desired behavior; and (3) optimizing the chances for naturally occurring reinforcers to take over the maintenance of the desired behaviors.

All of these procedures are incorporated into one operant program for pain reduction which is at the heart of most pain management programs: exercise. As an activity which is incompatible with pain behavior (Fordyce, 1976), exercise facilitates a decrease in pain behaviors and simultaneously builds a maintenance pattern for health-promoting behaviors after treatment. Fordyce (1976) points out that exercise has the added benefit of eliciting from others "responses or reactions much different from those elicited by displays of pain behaviors" (p. 168). Patients who are exercising or otherwise engaged in activities are not seen as impaired or functionally limited. Other physical benefits of exercise include increasing range of motion, strengthening musculature, improving endurance, and deconditioning activity avoidance (Sturgis, Dolce, & Dickerson, 1987).

Exercise programs are established for each pain patient, following these general guidelines:

1. The selected exercise activity is quantified in measurable amounts (e.g., distance traveled, cycles per minute).
2. A baseline measure is taken of the amount of the exercise the patient is able to perform at tolerable levels before pain, weakness, or fatigue requires him or her to stop.
3. Quotas are established in gradually increasing amounts. These quotas must be possible for the patient to reach successfully, without experiencing undue amounts of pain. The patient is instructed not to exceed the quotas because that may result in working to tolerance and possibly make the exercise pain-contingent.
4. After the exercise activity, the patient is asked to rest or relax, thereby making rest the contingent reinforcement for the behavior one wishes to increase (i.e., exercise). Attention and praise from the therapist or a family member also serve to reinforce the exercise activity and any gains the patient makes.

Exercise programs based on this quota system have been positively evaluated with nonelderly clients experiencing chronic pain (Doleys, Crocker, & Patton, 1982; Fordyce, 1973) and with elderly adults who were not pain patients (e.g., Libb & Clements, 1969; Matteson, 1989; Perkins, Rapp, Carlson, & Wallace, 1986).

In the one study which examined the benefits of an exercise program for elderly pain patients (Miller & LeLieuvre, 1982), results were positive, but not necessarily attributable to the interventions. Using an uncontrolled multiple-baseline design, Miller and LeLieuvre reinforced four elderly osteoarthritic nursing-home residents with attention and praise and used extinction techniques (lack of attention and interaction) to decrease pain behaviors and pain talk. After treatment, the patients reported decreases in the amount of prn pain medication taken, the frequency of pain behaviors, and subjective reports of pain. The patients were not, however, able to increase their exercise quotas beyond the initial levels. Neither did the dependent variables return to pretreatment levels during the second baseline condition, suggesting that other factors may have influenced treatment along with the intervention methods. No follow-up was conducted.

Operant methodology also emphasizes the importance of the family members in the pain management process. With elderly individuals, pain symptoms may be inadvertently reinforced by the attention that spouses, children, and/or care staff provide the patient. Conversely, the family and friends of the chronic pain patient could be taught to promote and reinforce positive behavior and extinguish pain behavior. In evaluating the effects of this contingent model of family support on pain behavior and symptoms on a group of 59 rheumatoid arthritis sufferers (mean age of 54), however, Radojevic, Nicassio, and Weisman (1992) did not find that patients given family support along with a behavioral pain program gained more than the patients given the same pain management program and no family support, although the supported group experienced more immediate gains than the other.

SOCIAL LEARNING THEORY

A third type of behavioral methodology is based on social learning theory or modeling. This theory capitalizes on the fact that humans learn a great deal by observing the behavior of others and, most important, the consequences of others' behavior. If a person observes someone else receiving reinforcement or punishment for some action—a response to pain, for example—he or she is likely to emulate the behavior which was rewarded and avoid the behavior which was punished or extinguished. Fordyce (1976) has noted that a disproportionately large number of "chronic pain patients come from homes in which chronic illness or chronic pain was modeled by parental figures" (p. 49). Likewise, health-promoting behaviors may be modeled effectively by parents to the benefit of the child.

In applying this model of learning to the problems of the elderly pain patient, one must include questions about modeled behavior in the assessment and history-taking process. One must also look into current occasions in which modeling is evident. If, for instance, the peers of an elderly person receive reinforcement for pain behaviors or little reinforcement for engaging in health-promoting behaviors, the treatment program may need to address that facet of a patient's life with strategies to counteract those effects.

There are no published reports of the use of modeling in the treatment of pain experienced by elderly patients, but there is every reason to believe it would be as effective for older adults as it is for younger adults. Modeling techniques, in which patients observe targeted behaviors of peers managing a task effectively, have been used in social skills training with older adults (e.g., Lopez, 1980; Engels & Poser, 1987) and in reducing anxiety (e.g., Downs, Rosenthal, & Lichstein, 1988).

COGNITIVE-BEHAVIORAL THERAPY

Cognitive behavior therapy is the fourth approach to the application of behavioral principles to the treatment of pain. In this theoretical system, the cognitive aspects of chronic pain are the main focus, but the theoretical framework is a behavioral one. With this approach, the patient's thoughts, feelings, and emotions are examined and targeted for treatment, along with the overt behaviors. The way the patient appraises or thinks about painful stimuli, the beliefs he or she holds about pain, and the expectancies regarding treatment are all important elements in the use of a cognitive-behavioral treatment program for pain. These variables affect the way a patient copes with pain (Chapman, 1978; McCaul & Malott, 1984; Tan, 1982; Thorn & Williams, 1989).

Three sets of cognitive factors have been researched in the area of pain management. The first is pain-related, overly negative cognitive distortions made by patients about their own performance. For example, patients experiencing chronic pain may underestimate their activity levels, overgeneralize about their problems, and make catastrophizing statements, all of which enhance the perception of pain and may lead to symptoms of depression (Smith, Follick, & Ahern, 1986).

The second cognitive factor deals with the beliefs about pain held by the patient. For example, patients may believe their pain will not be reduced and thus may not comply with recommended behavioral or medical interventions (Williams & Thorn, 1989). As another example, patients may believe that their pain is the result of something completely alien to medical explanations, may begin a search for a "miracle cure," and may refuse to comply with medical recommendations for treatment.

The third cognitive variable has to do with the use and perceived effectiveness of cognitive pain-coping strategies. For instance, Keefe and his colleagues (1987) found that patients who rate the effectiveness of their coping strategies as high and who avoid irrational catastrophizing cognitions cope more successfully with their pain.

Keefe and Beckham (1994) have described the following basic elements in the application of a cognitive-behavioral approach to the treatment of pain: (1) presenting to the patient a treatment rationale which includes the influence of psychological variables (especially depressive thinking, anxiety, and preoccupation with somatic symptoms) and the value of the patient's own coping efforts in managing pain; (2) changing the activity levels of patients and encouraging them to become more involved in pleasant events; (3) changing maladaptive pain-related cognitions with the use of such techniques as cognitive restructuring, self-instructional training, distraction and imagery, along with other procedures, such as reinterpretation, thought stopping, stress inoculation, and problem solving; and (4) changing psychophysiological responses with the use of relaxation and biofeedback procedures.

It may be worthwhile to elaborate somewhat on the procedures used to change maladaptive cognitions and present some of the research, when available, on the application of these procedures to the pain problems of the elderly.

Cognitive Restructuring

With this strategy, patients are taught to recognize the relationship between thoughts, feelings, behavior, and pain; to identify irrational, maladaptive thoughts; and to replace them with positive, counteractive, coping thoughts and self-statements (Turk, Meichenbaum, & Genest, 1983).

Self-Instructional Training

In self-instructional training, patients are taught to examine painful events within three phases: preparation for intense stimulation before it develops; confrontation of painful stimuli; and the use of designated coping strategies for thoughts, feelings, and self-statements which arise at critical points in time. Patients are also taught, through behavioral rehearsal, to use these coping self-statements whenever they experience pain (Turk et al., 1983).

Distraction Techniques

Of the methods of distraction which may be taught to patients, the common goal is to enable the patient to learn systematic ways of taking his or her mind away from the painful stimuli. Some examples of applying distraction include counting backward, making a mental list of something, or focusing attention on music or on an elaborate task, such as organizing one's desk or decorating a room.

Imagery

There is a wide variety of imagery procedures which may be taught to patients to help them manage their pain. In fact, many of the standard behavioral procedures in the respondent, operant, and social learning methodologies have imagery components. Systematic desensitization, for instance, includes an intensity-graduated presentation of anxiety-inducing elements in the context of imagery. Relaxation training is often accompanied by imagery techniques which are said to enhance the sensation of calm. The rules of applying reinforcement procedures may be followed in an imagery format as well as in an overt behavioral format. The covert conditioning procedures, for example, have been developed within an operant framework and have been applied clinically both to problems of pain management (Cautela, 1986) and to problems experienced by older adults (Wisocki, 1993). Imagery-based modeling procedures have been described by Kazdin (1975). It is beyond the scope of this chapter, however, to describe these techniques in detail.

The imagery techniques used most frequently in pain management are simple ones, generally. Patients are asked to identify pleasant images such as sitting on a beach watching the waves, or taking one's dog for a walk, or being in the company of good friends, for example, and to use these images or scenes to divert their attention from painful stimuli.

Pearson (1987) described an interesting application of imagery procedures in a case study of an 84-year-old woman who experienced severe pain in her foot and ankle. Relying on the patient's devout Catholicism, the nurse asked the patient to visualize the characteristics of the pain and what the inflamed area would be like without the pain. She was told to picture the Holy Spirit entering her body and the painful area to make the pain "escape." Pearson reports that such instruction was effective in reducing the patient's pain.

In a review of the value of distraction and imagery techniques for pain management, McCaul and Malott (1984) reported that these procedures are more effective for the control of low-intensity pain stimuli, as opposed to high-intensity pain.

Reinterpretation

Reinterpretation techniques consist of having the patient relabel the pain sensation with less emotionally laden words, such as *dull*, *cold*, *sharp*, and *warm*. Imagery training is often helpful in this process as well (Rybstein-Blinchik, 1979). In many cases reinterpretation techniques are more helpful in reducing pain than distraction techniques (Keefe & Beckham, 1994).

Thought Stopping

Thought stopping has been described in clinical work with elderly clients by Wisocki (1993), although not in the context of pain management. It consists of having the patient identify persistent, troubling thoughts which enhance the intensity of the targeted experience, shouting "stop" in a loud voice, and thinking of a counteractive, coping thought. This process may or may not be followed by an image of a pleasant activity, which theoretically serves to reinforce the coping statement. For example, if a patient reports that he or she often thinks that the pain is unbearable, he or she might be taught to stop that specific thought and think instead that the pain is bearable one day at a time.

Stress Innoculation

Stress innoculation combines cognitive restructuring with training in verbal self-instruction and behavioral self-management techniques. Clients are encouraged to apply these procedures to a series of increasingly stressful situations.

In a nicely designed study, Puder (1988) examined the value of stress inoculation training for 69 patients experiencing chronic pain. The subjects ranged in age from 27 to 80, with a mean age of 53 years. Twenty-two of the subjects were over age 60. Subjects were divided into two groups: immediate and delayed treatment. After a week of baseline, in which subjects recorded and rated their daily pain experiences, indicated the amount of pain-induced interference in their daily activities, and reported on their abilities to cope with pain and their use of medication and other treatments, the participants were instructed in the procedures. Their progress was reviewed during each session, and problems were discussed. Therapy was conducted once a week for 10 weeks in a group format. The self-report measures continued throughout treatment and a one-month follow-up. At six months the participants collected the same data for 1 week. Results indicated that the treatment was effective in managing the pain experience, but it only slightly affected the perceived intensity of pain.

The author also analyzed the effect of age on treatment outcome. He found that age was not a factor in treatment success and recommended the inclusion of older adults in programs for chronic pain as an alternative to drug therapy, which may be risky for elderly people. Puder pointed out that reliance on self-report data and the lack of an alternative treatment group are limitations of the study.

Problem Solving

Problem-solving techniques are also regarded as one set of principles necessary for cognitive change (Craighead, Craighead, Kazdin, & Mahoney, 1994). Patients are taught to apply a set of rules for dealing with problems as they arise. These rules include developing a general orientation to recognizing a problem; defining the specifics of the problem and determining goals; generating alternative courses of action for resolving the problem and achieving the goals; evaluating the relative benefits and losses of the alternatives; verifying the results of the decision process; and determining if the alternative selected is achieving the goals one wants (D'Zurilla & Goldfried, 1971).

Lorig, Laurin, and Holman (1984) prepared a self-management course in problem solving, relaxation, exercise, and instruction for middle-aged and elderly arthritic sufferers. After the program, the participants demonstrated more knowledge about arthritis and reported a lessening of pain and fewer visits to a physician. Five years later, Lorig and Holman (1989) studied 589 arthritis sufferers who had taken the six-week course. They randomly assigned subjects to a group that received a bimonthly newsletter about arthritis, a group that attended an additional six-week course in reinforcement procedures, and a control group. After 20 months, all participants were queried about their pain experiences, feelings of depression, and visits to their physicians. There were no differences between the groups: all participants decreased pain by 20%, depression by 13%, and visits to physicians by 35%. The authors were confident that these trends would continue over time. They concluded that the additional information provided to patients did not alter the effects of the original self-management course.

Using the same educational program as Lorig et al. (1984), Keefe and his colleagues (1990) compared it with the effects of a cognitive-behavioral pain-coping skills-training program and a standard care control condition for 94 patients with osteoarthritic knee pain. The mean age of the group was 64 years. Pre- and postintervention measures were taken on the behavior of patients as they engaged in a set of standard activities which allowed observers to record pain behaviors. After random assignment to groups, patients in the behavioral treatment group were educated about the complexity of the pain experience, along with cognitive and behavioral coping methods. They were also taught the following strategies: relaxation, imagery, distraction, task management, ways to schedule activity–rest cycles and pleasant activities, and cognitive restructuring. Patients in the control condition continued regular treatment. After 10 weeks, the patients reported on the coping strategies they had used, their health status, and their use of medications. The patients in the cognitive-behavioral training group had significantly lower levels of pain and psychological disability after treatment than the patients in the other two groups. Improvement appeared to be related to the patients' perceptions of the effectiveness of their coping strategies. Keefe et al. found no improvement in physical disability or pain behavior in any group, a condition they related to the age of the subjects in this study.

In another controlled study, behavioral treatment was shown to be effective in reducing the levels of pain associated with rheumatoid arthritis in a sample of two groups of nine older veterans in a matched control design (Appelbaum, Blanchard, Hickling, & Alfonso, 1988). These investigators compared a group trained in progressive muscle relaxation, thermal biofeedback, and cognitive-behavioral techniques with a group asked simply to monitor their symptoms. Immediately following the program, the treatment group demonstrated significant improvement on measures of perception of pain, control of pain sensations, and use of coping techniques. The treatment group also characterized themselves as more functionally active and having less difficulty with daily tasks after treatment than did the control group. Moderate positive changes in measures of range of motion were seen in the treatment group as well. The treatment gains were not maintained, however, at an 18-month follow-up, in which only 10 of the original subjects (6 treated and 4 controls) participated.

AGE EFFECTS IN BEHAVIORAL TREATMENTS FOR PAIN

In several studies in which different age groups have been compared for their response to behavioral treatments for pain problems, investigators have suggested that older patients may not be as responsive to treatment as younger patients. For example, in a retrospective study of 395 headache patients (the oldest of which was 47), Diamond and Montrose (1984) found a significant age effect on improvement rates immediately after treatment, on the reduction in medication usage, and on subjective feelings of controllability of pain. The older the patient, the less positive the results. In a meta-analysis of studies using behavioral methods for treatment of headache, Holroyd and Penzien (1984) found a significant negative relationship between mean improvement rate and age, suggesting that older adults may be the least likely to report pain relief following behavioral interventions.

Blanchard, Andrasik, Evans, and Hillhouse (1985) analyzed data from 11 subjects over 60 years old who had received treatment for headaches from an earlier study of 250 headache patients (Blanchard et al., 1985). Their results were consistent with previous findings, in that only about 18% had shown a 50% reduction in headache activity. The authors suggested that these older adult subjects might have benefitted from a longer treatment regimen due to the apparently slower rate at which older patients learn self-regulatory skills (Arena, Blanchard, Andrasik, & Myers, 1983).

Keefe and Williams (1990) found that age may influence which pain coping strategy patients choose to use. Praying and hoping were strategies preferred by some older adult patients but were used less by younger patients.

On the other hand, some researchers found no difference between age groups in their ability to benefit from behavioral intervention programs. Middaugh, Levin, Kee, Barchiesi, and Roberts (1988) found that both young and older chronic pain patients improved equally on objective measures of pain.

In a follow-up study, Middaugh, Woods, Kee, Harden, and Peters (1991) found that the specific ability of young and old patients to learn biofeedback and relaxation techniques was not different. Both age groups, who were similar on diagnosis (chronic musculoskeletal pain) and duration of pain complaints, were able to reach the same levels of physiological change in the same number of training sessions and reported equal improvements in experienced pain.

Evidence that older individuals with headache pain may benefit from behavioral methods modified to suit their unique characteristics has been supplied by Kabela, Blanchard, Appelbaum, and Nicholson (1989). They found that, at a one-month follow-up, 10 out of 16 elderly subjects who had completed their program showed clinically significant improvement (50% reduction in headache activity and pain medication usage) after an eight-week program of progressive muscle relaxation for all subjects. Twelve subjects received clinic-based sessions and four subjects received home-based training via manuals and audiotapes. All subjects were asked to practice the relaxation techniques twice a day at home using audiotapes. The program began with a muscle tension–release cycle of 16 muscle groups and then decreased to 8 and 4 muscle groups until the subjects were able to relax 4 muscle groups by recall. As the treatment progressed, the subjects were instructed to use imagery, abdominal breathing exercises, and the muscle relaxation techniques to cope with stress and headaches. Eleven of the subjects also were introduced to cognitive coping strategies for dealing with stress which focused on understanding the connections between thoughts, feelings, and behaviors; self-monitoring of these connections during stressful periods; using coping self-statements; and identifying cognitive distortions. Nine subjects also received biofeedback training. Modifications in the treatment protocol included simplification of the cognitive components and an emphasis on reviewing the instructions for all procedures.

Nicholson and Blanchard (1993) studied the benefits of modifying the standard behavioral procedures for seven older patients with chronic headaches by means of a multiple-baseline across-subjects design. Patients were matched on diagnosis and baseline headache activity. One patient in each pair was treated with a 12-session multicomponent program of relaxation, biofeedback, and cognitive-behavioral therapy. The other patient was asked simply to monitor headache activity. The standard treatment approach was modified in the following ways: the sessions were extended by 50% to ensure comprehension of instructions; audiotapes were used by patients at home during the first four weeks of the program to facilitate practice and decrease reliance on memory; therapists remained with the patients at all times during the biofeedback training sessions and provided positive verbal feedback and encouragement; and patients were given supplements for all material learned in the program. For five of the seven patients, treatment was more effective in decreasing headaches than headache monitoring. Only the patients assigned to the active treatment condition showed significant within-group reductions in headache pain at posttreatment. Interestingly, the authors reported that the modifications made in the procedures for this group of older adult patients were not unanimously positively received. Some patients appeared to benefit greatly from the longer time spent in explaining the material, while others were insulted by it.

A recent study by Mosley, Grothues, and Meeks (1995) underscored the benefits of cognitive-behavioral therapy for relieving the headache pain of older adults. These investigators examined the incremental effects of adding cognitive-behavioral therapy to relaxation training for 30 patients who ranged in age from 60 to 78 years. Patients were matched on pretreatment headache index and headache chronicity, with secondary matching on age and gender, and were then randomly assigned to a relaxation-only group, a combined-treatment group of relaxation and cognitive-behavioral therapy, or a monitoring group for a 12-week period of time. The standard treatment protocol was modified for these patients because of their age: the treatment program was lengthened by 3 weeks, audiotapes and extensive written materials were provided to assist in the acquisition of self-regulatory skills, and patients were contacted by phone between clinic visits to answer questions about the previous session, address any problems, and reinforce practice efforts. Of the 23 patients remaining in the study at posttreatment, those in the relaxation-only and the combined-treatment group showed statistically significant reductions in headache activity and in the use of analgesic medications. The patients in the combined group, however, demonstrated greater improvements than those in either of the other groups.

CONCLUSIONS

As we have seen, a behavioral approach to the study of pain management offers a wide variety of effective treatment procedures to a vital aspect of the pain experience. Both behavioral theory and behavioral methodology suggest useful treatment strategies for a wide-ranging area of pain-related problems, including, more specifically, headache, back pain, and arthritis. When these strategies are used in conjunction with medical treatment, the pain patient has access to an extensive and well-balanced blend of beneficial technology.

Although older adults are underrepresented in the research studies of the application of behavioral procedures and principles to the relief of pain, the work which does exist suggests promising directions for treatment of older pain patients. Treatment programs which utilize cognitive-behavioral management strategies, in particular, have a good track record with older adults suffering from various kinds of pain-related ailments.

As additional research is conducted in this area, researchers are encouraged to investigate more fully the value of modifying behavioral pain programs for older adults. While the modifications made in several of the programs described in this chapter seem intuitively warranted, the results are equivocal. Obviously, more systematic work on the question is needed.

REFERENCES

Achterberg, J., Kenner, C., & Lewis, G. (1988). Severe burn injury: A comparison of relaxation, imagery, and biofeedback for pain management. *Journal of Mental Imagery*, *12*, 71–87.

Appelbaum, K. A., Blanchard, E. B., Hickling, E. J., & Alfonso, M. (1988). Cognitive behavioral treatment of a veteran population with moderate to severe rheumatoid arthritis. *Behavior Therapy*, *19*, 489–502.

Arena, J. G., Blanchard, E. B., Andrasik, F., & Myers, P. E. (1983). Psychophysiological responding as a function of age: The importance of matching. *Journal of Behavioral Assessment, 5,* 131–141.

Arena, J. G., Hannah, S. L., Bruno, G. M., & Meador, K. J. (1991). Electromyographic biofeedback training for tension headache in the elderly: A prospective study. *Biofeedback and Self-Regulation, 16*(4), 379–390.

Arena, J. G., Hightower, N. E., & Chong, G. C. (1988). Relaxation therapy for tension headache in the elderly: A prospective study. *Psychology and Aging, 3*(1), 96–98.

Berntzen, D., & Gotestam, G. (1987). Effects of on-demand versus fixed-interval schedules in the treatment of chronic pain with analgesic compounds. *Journal of Consulting and Clinical Psychology, 55,* 213–217.

Blanchard, E., Andrasik, E., Evans, D., & Hillhouse, J. (1985). Biofeedback and relaxation treatments for headache in the elderly: A caution and a challenge. *Biofeedback and Self-Regulation, 10,* 69–73.

Blanchard, E. B., Andrasik, F., Evans, D. D., Neff, D. F., Appelbaum, K. A., & Rodichok, L. D. (1985). Behavioral treatment of 250 chronic headache patients: A clinical replication series. *Behavior Therapy, 16,* 308–327.

Boczkowski, J. (1984). Biofeedback training for the treatment of chronic pain in an elderly arthritic female. *Clinical Gerontology, 2,* 39–46.

Cautela, J. (1986). Covert conditioning and the control of pain. *Behavior Modification, 10,* 205–217.

Chapman, C. (1978). Pain: The perception of noxious events. In R. A. Sternbach (Ed.), *The psychology of pain* (pp. 169–202). New York: Raven Press.

Craighead, L., Craighead, W. E., Kazdin, A., & Mahoney, M. (1994). *Cognitive and behavioral interventions.* Boston: Allyn & Bacon.

Czirr, R., & Gallagher, D. (1983). Case report: Behavioral treatment of depression and somatic complaints in rheumatoid arthritis. *Clinical Gerontology, 2,* 63–66.

De Berry, S. (1981–1982). An evaluation of progressive muscle relaxation on stress related symptoms in a geriatric population. *International Journal of Aging and Human Development, 14,* 255–269.

Diamond, S., & Montrose, D. (1984). The value of biofeedback in the treatment of chronic headache: A four-year retrospective study. *Headache, 24,* 5–18.

Dolce, J., & Dickerson, P. (1991). Pain management. In P. Wisocki (Ed.), *Handbook of clinical behavior therapy with the elderly client* (pp. 383–398). New York: Plenum Press.

Dolce, J., & Raczynski, J. (1985). Neuromuscular activity and electromyography in painful backs: Psychological and biomechanical models in assessment and treatment. *Psychological Bulletin, 97,* 502–520.

Doleys, D., Crocker, M., & Patton, D. (1982). Response of patients with chronic pain to exercise quotas. *Physical Therapy, 62,* 1111–1114.

Downs, A., Rosenthal, T., & Lichstein, K. (1988). Modeling therapies reduce avoidance of bath time by institutionalized elderly. *Behavior Therapy, 19,* 359–368.

D'Zurilla, T., & Goldfried, M. (1971). Problem solving and behavior modification. *Journal of Abnormal Psychology, 78,* 107–126.

Engels, M. L., & Poser, E. (1987). Social skills training with older women. *Clinical Gerontologist, 6,* 70–73.

Fordyce, W. (1973). An operant conditioning method for managing chronic pain. *Postgraduate Medicine, 53,* 123–128.

Fordyce, W. (1974) Treating chronic pain by contingency management. In J. Bonica (Ed.), *Advances in neurology: Vol. 4. International symposium on pain* (pp. 585–587). New York: Raven Press.

Fordyce, W. (1976). *Behavioral methods for chronic pain and illness.* St. Louis: Mosby.

Fordyce, W., Fowler, R., Lehmann, J., & Delateur, B. (1968). Some implications of learning in problems of chronic pain. *Journal of Chronic Diseases, 21,* 179–190.

Fordyce, W., Fowler, R., Lehmann, J., Delateur, B., Sand, P., & Trieschmann, R. (1973). Operant conditioning in the treatment of chronic clinical pain. *Archives of Physical Medicine Rehabilitation, 54,* 399–408.

Hamburger, L. (1982). Reduction of generalized aversive responding in a post-treatment cancer patient: Relaxation as an active coping skill. *Journal of Behavior Therapy and Experimental Psychiatry, 12,* 241–247.

Holroyd, K. A., & Penzien, D. B. (1984). *Client variables and the behavioral treatment of recurrent tension headache: A meta-analytic review.* Paper presented at the 1984 meeting of the Association for the Advancement of Behavior Therapy, Philadelphia.

Kabela, E., Blanchard, E. B., Appelbaum, K. A., & Nicholson, N. (1989). Self-regulatory treatment of headache in the elderly. *Biofeedback and Self-Regulation, 14*(3), 219–228.

Kazdin, A. (1975). Covert modeling, imagery assessment, and assertive behavior. *Journal of Consulting and Clinical Psychology*, *43*, 716–724.

Keefe, F., & Beckham, J. (1994). Behavioral medicine. In L. Craighead, W. E. Craighead, A. Kazdin, & M. Mahoney (Eds.), *Cognitive and behavioral interventions* (pp. 197–213). Boston: Allyn & Bacon.

Keefe, F., Caldwell, D., Williams, D., Gil, K., Mitchell, D., Robertson, C., Martinez, S., Nunley, J., Beckman, J., Crisson, J., & Helms, M. (1990). Pain coping skills training in the management of osteoarthritic knee pain: A comparative study. *Behavior Therapy*, *21*, 49–62.

Keefe, F., Caldwell, D., Queen, K., Gil, K., Martinez, S., Crisson, J., Ogden, W., & Nunley, J. (1987). Osteoarthritic knee pain: A behavioral analysis. *Pain*, *28*, 309–321.

Keefe, F., & Williams, D. A. (1990). A comparison of coping strategies in chronic pain patients of different age groups. *Journal of Gerontology*, *45*(4), 161–165.

King, A. C., & Arena, J. G. (1984). Behavioral treatment of chronic cluster headache in a geriatric patient. *Biofeedback and Self-Regulation*, *9*, 201–208.

Libb, J. W., & Clements, C. B. (1969). Token reinforcement in an exercise program for hospitalized geriatric patients. *Perceptual and Motor Skills*, *28*, 957–958.

Linoff, M., & West, C. (1982). Relaxation training systematically combined with music: Treatment of tension headaches in a geriatric patient. *International Journal of Behavioral Geriatrics*, *1*, 11–16.

Lopez, M. (1980). Social skills training with institutionalized elderly: Effect of pre-counseling structuring and over-learning on skill acquisitions and transfer. *Journal of Counseling Psychology*, *27*, 286–293.

Lorig, K., & Holman, H. (1989). Long term outcomes of an arthritis self-management study: Effects of reinforcement efforts. *Social Science and Medicine*, *29*, 221–224.

Lorig, K., Laurin, J., & Holman, H. (1984). Arthritis self-management: A study of the effectiveness of patient education for the elderly. *The Gerontologist*, *24*, 455–457.

Matteson, M. (1989). Effects of a cognitive-behavioral approach and positive reinforcement on exercise for older adults. *Educational Gerontology*, *15*, 497–513.

McCaul, K., & Malott, J. (1984). Distraction and coping with pain. *Psychological Bulletin*, *95*, 516–533.

Melzack, R., & Chapman, C. (1973). Psychological aspects of pain. *Postgraduate Medicine*, *53*, 69–75.

Melzack, R., & Wall, P. (1965). Pain mechanisms. A new theory. *Science*, *150*, 971–979.

Middaugh, S. J., Levin, R. B., Kee, W. G., Barchiesi, F. D., & Roberts, J. M. (1988). Chronic pain: Its treatment in geriatric and younger patients. *Archives of Physical Medicine and Rehabilitation*, *69*, 1021–1026.

Middaugh, S. J., Woods, E., Kee, W. G., Harden, N., & Peters, J. R. (1991). Biofeedback-assisted relaxation training for the aging chronic pain patient. *Biofeedback and Self-Regulation*, *16*(4), 361–377.

Miller, C., & LeLieuvre, R. B. (1982). A method to reduce chronic pain in elderly nursing home residents. *The Gerontologist*, *22*(3), 314–317.

Mosley, T., Grothues, C., & Meeks, W. M. (1995). Treatment of tension headache in the elderly: A controlled evaluation of relaxation training and relaxation training combined with cognitive behavior therapy. *Journal of Clinical Geropsychology*, *1*, 175–188.

Nicholson, N. L., & Blanchard, E. B. (1993). A controlled evaluation of behavioral treatment of chronic headache in the elderly. *Behavior Therapy*, *24*, 395–408.

Pearson, B. (1987). Pain control: An experiment with imagery. *Geriatric Nursing*, *8*, 28–30.

Perkins, K., Rapp, S., Carlson, C., & Wallace, C. (1986). A behavioral intervention to increase exercise among nursing home residents. *The Gerontologist*, *26*, 479–481.

Puder, R. (1988). Age analysis of cognitive-behavioral group therapy for chronic pain outpatients. *Psychology and Aging*, *3*, 204–207.

Radojevic, V., Nicassio, P. M., & Weisman, M. H. (1992). Behavioral intervention with and without family support for rheumatoid arthritis. *Behavior Therapy*, *23*, 13–30.

Rickard, H. C., Scogin, F., & Keith, S. (1994). A one-year follow-up of relaxation training for elders with subjective anxiety. *The Gerontologist*, *34*(1), 121–122.

Rybstein-Blinchik, E. (1979). Effects of different cognitive strategies in the chronic pain experience. *Journal of Behavioral Medicine*, *2*, 93–102.

Smith, R., Follick, M., & Ahern, D. (1986). Cognitive distortion and disability in chronic low back pain. *Cognitive Therapy and Research*, *10*, 201–210.

Sturgis, E., Dolce, J., & Dickerson, P. (1987). Pain management in the elderly. In L. Carstensen & B. Edelstein (Eds.), *Handbook of clinical gerontology* (pp. 190–203). New York: Pergamon Press.

Tan, S. (1982). Cognitive and cognitive-behavioral methods for pain control: A selective review. *Pain, 12*, 201–228.

Thorn, B., & Williams, G. (1989). Goal specification alters perceived pain intensity and tolerance latency. *Cognitive Therapy and Research, 13*, 171–183.

Turk, D., Meichenbaum, D., & Genest, M. (1983). *Pain and behavioral medicine: A cognitive-behavioral perspective*. New York: Guilford Press.

Turk, D., & Rennert, K. (1981). Pain and the terminally ill cancer patient: A cognitive-social learning perspective. In H. Sobel (Ed.), *Behavior therapy in terminal care: A humanistic approach* (pp. 95–124). Cambridge, MA: Ballinger.

Williams, G., & Thorn, B. (1989). An empirical assessment of pain beliefs. *Pain, 36*, 351–358.

Wisocki, P. (1991). Behavioral gerontology. In P. Wisocki (Ed.), *Handbook of clinical behavior therapy for the elderly client* (pp. 3–51). New York: Plenum Press.

Wisocki, P. (1993). The treatment of an elderly woman with orofacial tardive dyskinesia by relaxation and covert reinforcer sampling. In J. Cautela & A Kearney (Eds.), *Covert conditioning casebook* (pp. 108–116). Pacific Grove, CA: Brooks/Cole.

Wolf, S., Nacht, M., & Kelly, J. (1982). EMG feedback training during dynamic movement for low back pain patients. *Behavior Therapy, 13*, 395–406.

Index

A "*t*" suffix indicates that the subject is mentioned in a table.

ISBN 0-306-45458-0

90000

9 780306 454585